D0909318

CMP

Acknowledgement is made to Z. Létray and P. Bernus for the use of part of Figure 2 on page 81, which appears on the front cover of this book.

Artificial Intelligence in Manufacturing

Proceedings of the fourth International Conference on the Applications of Artificial Intelligence in Engineering, Cambridge, UK, July 1989

Editor:
G. Rzevski

Computational Mechanics Publications
Southampton Boston

Springer-Verlag Berlin Heidelberg
New York London Paris Tokyo

G. Rzevski
Faculty of Technology
The Open University
Walton Hall
Milton Keynes
MK7 6AA
UK

Associate Editor: R.A. Adey
Computational Mechanics Institute
Ashurst Lodge
Ashurst
Southampton
SO4 2AA
UK

British Library Cataloguing in Publication Data

Artificial intelligence in manufacturing
1. Manufacturing. Applications of artificial intelligence
I. Rzevski, G. (George), *1932-*
670'.28'563
1-85312-038-3

Library of Congress Catalog Card Number 89-061419

ISBN 1-85312-038-3 Computational Mechanics Publications Southampton
ISBN 0-945824-22-X Computational Mechanics Publications Boston
ISBN 3-540-51343-4 Springer-Verlag Berlin Heidelberg New York London Paris Tokyo
ISBN 0-387-51343-4 Springer-Verlag New York Heidelberg Berlin London Paris Tokyo
ISBN 1-85312-039-1
ISBN 3-540-51344-2 2 volume set
ISBN 0-387-51344-2

This work is subject to copyright. All rights are reserved, whether the whole or part of the material is concerned, specifically the rights of translation, reprinting, re-use of illustrations, recitation, broadcasting, reproduction on microfilms or in any other way, and storage in data banks. Duplication of this publication or parts thereof is only permitted under the provisions of the German Copyright Law of September 9, 1965, in its version of June 24, 1985, and a copyright fee must always be paid. Violations fall under the prosecution act of the Germany Copyright Law.

© Computational Mechanics Publications 1989
© Springer-Verlag Berlin Heidelberg 1989

Printed in Great Britain by Bookcraft (Bath) Ltd.

The use of registered names, trademarks etc. in this publication does not imply, even in the absence of a specific statement, that such names are exempt from the relevant protective laws and regulations and therefore free for general use.

CONTENTS

SECTION 6: ROBOTICS

SECTION 7: DIAGNOSIS, SAFETY AND RELIABILITY

PREFACE

This volume and its companion on Artificial Intelligence in Design contain papers presented at the fourth International Conference on Applications of Artificial Intelligence in Engineering held in Cambridge, UK in July 1989. The first conference in this series was held in Southampton, UK in 1986, the second in Cambridge, Massachusetts, USA in 1987 and the third in Palo Alto, California, USA in August 1988. The conference series is establishing itself as the unique forum for the presentation of the latest research, development and application of artificial intelligence in all fields of engineering.

Early applications of artificial intelligence were mainly in areas where high-level expertise was required for the solution of diagnostic problems, eg. in medicine. We now have many examples of knowledge systems usefully employed in manufacturing which are based on empirical, domain-specific knowledge considerably less sophisticated than that of a medical consultant. These systems, often neglected by AI researchers as too simple to be of interest, have many useful roles: they add value to manufacturing in their own small way; their development serves as a means of polishing in-house AI skills and thus prepares manufacturing industry for the next important step - the integration of knowledge systems with information systems; above all they help to organise and refine manufacturing knowledge which is, as a rule, incomplete, dispersed throughout the shop floor and various offices, contains mutually contradictory elements and is often, at least in part, out of date.

From a large number of submitted proposals thirty three papers have been selected by members of the Advisory Committee who acted as referees. Two papers are by invited speakers, Professor D. Williams and Professor N.V. Findler. Papers have been grouped under the following headings.

Section 1 - Manufacturing Systems
Section 2 - Production Planning and Scheduling
Section 3 - Simulation
Section 4 - Process Planning
Section 5 - Process Monitoring and Control
Section 6 - Robotics
Section 7 - Diagnosis, Safety and Reliability

My sincere thanks to members of the Advisory Committee and all those who have helped with the difficult task of refereeing, selecting and presenting this valuable selection of papers.

George Rzevski
The Open University, UK

International Advisory Board Members
A. Agogino, R. Allen, A. Bijl, B-C. Björk, D. Brown,
G.Carrara, R.Coyne, B.B. Faltings, W. Fawcett,
J.S. Gero, S. Hardy, P. Haren, T. Holden, K. Ishii,
J. Lansdown, K. MacCallum, M.L. Maher, S. Mittal,
D. Navinchandra, T. Oksala, R. Oxman, M. Rosenman,
G. Rzevski, G. Schmitt, T. Smithers, P. Struss,
T. Takala, T. Tomiyama, B. Topping, E. Tyugu

SECTION 1 - MANUFACTURING SYSTEMS

Manufacturing Intelligence - from Systems to Processes

David J. Williams

Department of Manufacturing Engineering, University of Technology, Loughborough, Leics LE11 3TU, UK

ABSTRACT

The paper begins with a description of the manufacturing context to set the scene for the discussion that follows. The paper then continues with an approach which attempts to structure and review some of the areas that are just beginning to exercise the computationally literate manufacturing research community. These include:

> How can manufacturing process plans best be represented? How can appropriate architectures for the control of complex manufacturing execution environments be decided? How can tools be built that allow the manufacturing process and system, when described in a high-level manner, to be matched to the execution environment and to generate executable code easily for this environment? What is the next programmable process?

These are issues that are sometimes grouped together as areas that require the application of manufacturing intelligence techniques.

INTRODUCTION

This paper describes some of the current issues in manufacturing research. It concentrates on the **programmable automation** of the manufacturing activity and its associated organisation.

The paper begins with a description of the manufacturing context to set the scene for the discussion that follows. The paper then continues to structure and review some of the areas that are just beginning to exercise the computationally literate manufacturing research community. Those addressed include process planning for future execution environments, the appropriate architectures for these environments and the creation of tools that allow programming of these complex environments - these issues are sometimes grouped together as areas that require the application of manufacturing intelligence techniques.

THE MANUFACTURING CONTEXT

Manufacturing can be defined as "the shape or property changing activity that adds value to a component or assembly" (Williams 88). Manufacturing benefits the community by creating the goods it requires and, in this creation, creates, in turn, jobs in our manufacturing communities. Traditionally these jobs have been, in many cases, unpleasant physical tasks carried out in an unsavoury factory environment or deskilled "Taylorist" style tasks more suited for automata. The manufacturing community has therefore always been eager to embrace the technologies that the mechanical and electrical engineers have, with the computer scientists, created for them.

These technologies of programmable automation are, however, a two edged sword - is removing an unpleasant job by replacing a man with a machine uniformly good for society? Such philosophies are a luxury in the present atmosphere of international competition, the manufacturing or industrial engineer has to keep his company and his country competitive so that all may keep their jobs. The key distinction between the application of man or machine, therefore, is made on whether the innovation is financially justified or strategically important.

Let us now turn to examine the complexity of the manufacturing activity. Manufacturing, as carried out at present, usually occurs within a large or medium sized organisation. Such organisations, for example, need to be sufficiently large to be able to afford the investment in capital plant needed, for example, for domestic appliance or automotive product manufacture. These organisations are **complex** groupings of people and their opinions, as well as manufacturing machines and a large volume and variety of manufactured products. The control of such enterprises is therefore a difficult and complex problem. Scheduling alone - the definition of which product visits which machine when in the factory - is recognised as NP hard (Parunak 87), without even considering any of the other manufacturing sub-systems. Such problems, therefore, are not easily solved by concepts borrowed from other disciplines alone. They are also not solved with **small** efforts in computation, software engineering, or artificial intelligence.

As well as being a complex logical or control problem, the factory is also a difficult **mechanical** problem. Consider for a moment CAD/CAM (Computer Aided Design to Computer Aided Manufacture), essentially the semi-automatic generation of NC machine tool part programs from computer aided design descriptions of the workpiece. The reason that CAD/CAM succeeds is that a computer based description of the product shape can be used to drive a predictable manufacturing machine. The predictability of the machine arises from some 130 years of mechanical development of the milling machine (the Universal Milling Machine was patented in 1861 (Science Museum 66)) and nearing 40 years' development of NC (Numerical Control or servo-axis control), the first NC machine being exhibited in the UK in 1956 (Machinery 87). Modern manufacturing is therefore characterised by the application of computer science techniques to problems that have been constrained by mechanical or organisational design such that they have reduced complexity.

MANUFACTURING INTELLIGENCE

As has been implied earlier, the application of computer science and computational solutions to the manufacturing task, where the computing solutions are perhaps more complex than they have been in the past, is becoming known as manufacturing intelligence. Manufacturing intelligence has grown out of mechanical and production engineers' experiments with the application of "AI" techniques and work in advanced robotics. Advanced robotics is, essentially, reasoning about sensor data and using the results of this reasoning to perform a useful task, especially in an unstructured environment (Brady 86 and Egginton 87), in an effort to create systems that are able to adapt to changes in their environment. Manufacturing intelligence within the UK has become the focus of a £3M Department of Trade and Industry initiative.

(Wright and Bourne 88), in their recent book, major on an anthropomorphic definition of intelligent manufacturing, saying that the goal of manufacturing intelligence is to "model the skills and expertise of manufacturing craftsmen so that intelligent machines can make small batches of parts without human intervention" by "integrating research in knowledge engineering, manufacturing software systems, robotic vision and robotic manipulation". A more expansive view would extend this definition to include the application of more intelligent decision making systems throughout the manufacturing organisation.

Intelligent devices for manufacturing usually operate in more structured environments than those expected of advanced robots and must be capable of accepting instructions from an external manual or "automatic" system, such as a management or CAD system. These instructions are usually **complete and detailed**, in contrast to those supplied to the more usual autonomous systems. Examples of such instructions are a design description of a component or a requirement to output a fixed part mix within a given time interval. This is as a result of the need for the systems around the particular sub-system to have predictable behaviour from the sub-system. The designer requires the part to be **exactly** as specified in the discussion between the designer and the manufacturing engineer so that it fulfils its designed function and is interchangeable with all the others of its design. The customer requires the product when he needs it in his inventory, not the day before he has to pay for it and not the day after his customer no longer requires it!

To allow complex computer based techniques to reach the worldwide shopfloor, two enabling technologies are required. The first, cheap and powerful computing, approaches more closely every day with the advent of the inexpensive engineering workstation, at a cost an order of magnitude less than that of any machine tool. The second, reliable and inexpensive sensing technology, is more difficult, as each technology is likely to be situation specific and therefore expensive and time consuming to develop.

MANUFACTURING TECHNOLOGY

It is now appropriate to review briefly the technologies that have reached shopfloors worldwide and describe in summary the problems associated with the wider application of these technologies.

The basic building block of the factory of the near future is the programmable processing machine (metal cutting numerically controlled machine tool, component placement machine, assembly machine, spot welding robot ...) linked with a component transfer device (robot, automated guided vehicle (AGV), rail-car ...) into a cell of closely co-operating machines to create an autonomous production unit. Such cells (or sometimes individual machines of very high functionality, such as machining centres) can then be linked into transfer lines or other forms of manufacturing systems. These systems and sub-systems are controlled by computers and linked by some form of communication network, and take their data from a variety of sensors, including high-level sensors such as machine vision.

Such automated systems have a number of problems associated with them:

(i) The development and speed of installation of such facilities is largely limited by the preparation and restricted application of the integrating system control software and purpose designed mechanical hardware as a consequence of their complexity and need for minimally manned operation.

(ii) Once created, such systems are particularly difficult to reconfigure to manufacture a different range of parts to those envisaged in the original design.

The solutions that are demanded to these linked design and operational problems have to be integrated, real-time, robust and pragmatic; and must not reduce the functionality of the low level devices.

THE REPRESENTATION OF PROCESS PLANS

In the intelligent manufacturing facility of the future it will be necessary for the system to adapt to changes caused by external systems, for example the arrival of a part from another system, or to recover from changes occurring within the system, such as the breakdown of a machine. This is an issue involving planning and execution for manufacturing, and especially the representation of manufacturing process plans. Existing work in process planning (for example Darbyshire 87, Husbands 87, Jared 87, Chang 88) concentrates on the generation of what is usually presently regarded as the process plan, the NC part program (generated from a CAD description), to manufacture the geometry of a part and **in extremis** a description of the sequence of process steps required to make the part.

These approaches generate a completely worked out plan that is then executed. An alternative approach which is of real practical interest is opportunistic scheduling, which exploits the "executional uncertainty" (Fox 87) within real systems. In any system there will be unforeseen or fortuitous events that occur and these can be used to advantage. In opportunistic scheduling, a plan with only partial ordering (events that necessarily follow each other), and which allows a number of options at execution time, is generated. This is pruned by data, the results of the unforeseen events and the balance of the system state description, that arrives during the time the schedule is being executed. B R Fox and Kempf have applied this to the building of a gearbox to show that this approach is more successful than other scheduling approaches in situations of organisational uncertainty where, for example, different parts of the gearbox arrive at different times.

The approach, however, has some severe practical problems in situations of real manufacturing complexity. Consider the case of a prismatic machining cell (explored briefly by Newman 85) where workpieces are put into machining centres by a transport system. Executional uncertainty can be exploited to send the workpieces to any of the machines, as these are functionally equivalent (the system has redundancy). In this way the system can recover from machine breakdowns and other unforeseen events, and perhaps get increased system utilisation. However, associated with this is the practical problem of scheduling the, perhaps manual, tool transport system around the parts transport system. This scheduling problem is of the order of 40 times as complex as the machine scheduling problem because there are about 40 different tools required to manufacture each prismatic workpiece within such systems. This complexity makes the product process plan and the state description of the system very complex and difficult to represent. This state description is needed to build any sort of "intelligent cell controller" capable of making any decision based on knowledge of the cell. The key research issue is to resolve the significant elements needed in the state description for practical cell controllers.

THE MANUFACTURING CONTROL STRUCTURE

Most automated factory control systems are devolved hierarchically to keep the control problem manageable. The most well known model for this with "intelligent" behaviour is that developed at the Advanced Manufacturing Research Facility (AMRF) at the National Bureau of Standards, now the National Institute of Standards and Technology (Albus 81a&b, Jones 86). In this model, high-level goals are successively decomposed by lower level control modules until they form a sequence of co-ordinated primitive actions. These primitive actions are simple machine-level commands which can be understood by, for example, a proprietary robot controller or other shopfloor controller.

Much of the system level work in intelligent manufacturing explores the possibility of controlling manufacturing systems without employing such strict hierarchical control strategies. The thrust of the argument for this is that hierarchical control could be replaced at all levels of a company's operations by autonomous co-operating sub-systems which work together to achieve a corporate goal. This philosophy is based on a "market place" model where autonomous intelligent entities interact to satisfy their needs. There would be no supervisor in such a system; all of the entities would be equal in the negotiation process to obtain services and customers, and would co-operate with each other to obtain mutual satisfaction.

This "co-operative heterarchy" for manufacturing was first proposed by (Hatvany 84) and is being reinforced by the current factory networking emphasis in CIM applications. Perhaps the only experimental work in this area is that of Duffie et al (Duffie and Piper 86, Duffie 86) who have created a cell that has been programmed with a number of styles of controller, ranging from the strictly hierarchical to the co-operative, to show that the software effort to generate the latter is much smaller than that to generate the hierarchical system. Bid scheduling concepts (for example Upton 88) add to the discussion, suggesting that in large systems the devices in the system should bid for their work (having a "cost" associated with the production process on the device) to build a distributed decision making system, rather than have jobs allotted by a host computer.

These concepts are of interest to manufacturing engineers because in large, necessarily distributed systems, the sub-systems know more about their state than a system host and can therefore make more appropriate decisions. They further show promise in robustness to sub-system failure. Also, strict hierarchical control structures (with no peer to peer communication) have been built for large manufacturing systems and have resulted in the system cycle time being decided by the controller complexity rather than the production constraints of the system.

There are, however, some problems for heterarchic structures in manufacturing. A manufacturing system needs goal directness - if the system is to be useful it cannot decide for itself what it is going to make. This **must** be decided by an external system, be it manual or a computer based high-level scheduling system. It seems likely that the system must also be able to take data from "development" systems. These development systems are likely to be CAD in its broadest sense - CAD for NC, robot programming, intelligent and geometric systems for error recovery, and system control program development environments.

Both of these arguments imply hierarchies of control, even if levels of the hierarchy are implemented as co-operating heterarchies and imply that one processor in the system must direct the activities of the others, either as an interface to a higher level computer system or as an operator interface.

There is, further, the multivendoring problem; manufacturing equipment comes from different suppliers and is usually programmed with different languages and machine parameters. This implies that, to interface with the system, each device needs a translator (Duffie 86, Bourne 87, Jones 86). Also, it is not clear that networks are suitable for real-time control of different vendors' equipment, serial lines seem to be almost inevitable for some connections. These practical considerations force us into hierarchical control.

Also, from work in distributed control it becomes clear that, in the future, in manufacturing there will be more and more intelligent manufacturing devices passing more messages to one another. These messages will be passed across a shallow hierarchy of computers, some of these computers being linked as heterarchies in some of the layers of the hierarchy. The real manufacturing computer science problem is **what are the forms of these systems for different applications?**

To decide the shape of future manufacturing architectures, it is necessary to resolve a few searching questions, whatever the final architecture:

> What is real-time, how fast does manufacturing integration need to be? What is a message, how big is it, how far does it need to go (Weston 88, Hodgson 88)? How many layers are there in a manufacturing hierarchy - which of the layers are heterarchies - for a particular style of application? Are these architectural arrangements functionally equivalent? What processing gets done where? How much duplication (modularity) of control/software is there in a co-operating heterarchy? **How is it appropriate to model architectures to aid this decision making?**

These questions must be answered to get efficient (simple, fast, fault tolerant) implementations in manufacturing and to get reduced design times because of the present massive programming overhead.

Many people have informally described the manufacturing control problem that has been outlined above as "the development of the manufacturing operating system", which can be summarised as the method of distributing the processes, processors and data in the computing system. Hence, for example, the borrowing of tools developed for operating system design, like Petri nets (Ravichandran 86), by manufacturing researchers.

PROGRAMMING THE MANUFACTURING SYSTEM

Once the hardware of the control architecture has been decided, it is necessary to tackle the manufacturing system programming problem: **translating a global system goal stated in a "high-level language" into device specific instructions.**

It is becoming clear that there is a continuum of representations for the high-level description of the task in the design of intelligent manufacturing machine control systems. These range from pure "AI" approaches, for example actors or agents, through production rule based systems to state machines, neural network simulations and adaptive control systems. These can be used to describe, in a very high-level way, the manufacturing task in terms of the process plan and high-level interactions between the machines within the system. These can be implemented, with much human effort, for many systems.

To reduce this effort, the key problem to resolve is the "translator" that matches the high-level description to the particular manufacturing computational and mechanical hardware to generate real code executable on commercial manufacturing devices. It is therefore of value to work on the generation of such "translation" systems that take a description of the process and the equipment and, from these two descriptions, compile the real code that will run on the manufacturing devices.

Unfortunately this "matcher" is probably application specific, where application implies the base level computational and mechanical technology. Further, the high-level description of the control rules is doubly application dependent, once on the knowledge within the domain itself and once on the particular implementation.

A route to this would be to extend the interpreters of the CML environment invented by Bourne et al (Bourne 86) to generate a compiler to translate complex system level instructions incorporating particular machine descriptions and process plan descriptions. Such a compiler will operate on the highest level description capable of handling a sub-element of the manufacturing domain and will generate code in a manufacturing language, this manufacturing language running over a set of interpreters that parse messages to the real devices in their own language. This type of compiler is likely to be situation specific. An approach would therefore be to generate, in the manner of the computer scientist, a generic compiler compiler that could be tailored to particular situations.

To generate such tools using the experience of the computer scientists requires the manufacturing community to understand its environment in a suitable form. It must begin to represent manufacturing tasks and transformations in a formal way and develop a compact set of constructions to describe the semantics of the factory (Wu 86, for example, is examining manufacturing grammars). Once this has been achieved, the community will be able to build parsing and pattern matching tools to describe the manufacturing task and the environment in which it is carried out as a step towards the design of generic programming tools.

THE NEXT PROGRAMMABLE MANUFACTURING PROCESS

Many manufacturing engineers have avoided process problems for the past few years, they have been content to follow the path to CAD/CAM, FMS and CIM mapped out by controllable metal cutting machines. In manufacturing industry there are, however, many other processes that need to be controlled to give consistent quality, and integrated into CIM and even intelligent systems. There are difficulties, though, associated with the programmable automation of manufacturing processes and these problems are multidisciplinary; mechanical engineering and materials science extended with computer science. However, with no programmable processes, all this high-level work has no purpose. The next really programmable process is the manufacturing holy grail.

One of the key "mechanical" process problems is shown, for example, in metal cutting - holding the parts in a variety of attitudes, with high stiffness, which is the key to both metal cutting and assembly - but the solution is not that of the Salisbury style anthropomorphic dextrous hand, which has insufficient stiffness. Typical practical manufacturing solutions begin to look like those of (Englert 88), more capable, programmable machine-tool-like fixtures. Mechanical solutions that are appropriate, for the foreseeable future, to manufacturing do not look anthropomorphic - they look like machines which have a little more programmability than they used to have.

Comparison of the different geometries of the Programmable Universal Machine for Assembly, PUMA, and the Selective Compliance Arm for Robot Assembly, SCARA, echoes this. When you have built a machine that can pick things up as fast as people - you are building people - until then you are building machines!

To consider further assembly, work in this area confirms that the new machine geometries are not anthropomorphic. The Sony "Separated Motion Machine" developed to build the Walkman is essentially a number of moveable fixed function devices held over an x-y worktable. AT&T Bell Labs are extending this idea by replacing the x-y table with small "tethered agv's" to allow looping and branching in the assembly and test process for electronic assembly. Vic Scheinman is also building a similar machine. We should all learn from these non-anthropomorphic approaches - a temptation in the manufacturing AI community.

These new machine configurations are hard mechanical problems extended with computing problems, to solve more general non-cutting non-assembly manufacturing processes we have to solve difficult "materials science" problems. Model based process control seems an attractive way forward for this. This work is, however, a largely restricted domain - restricted to the process that has been modelled. The task is further perturbed by the need to develop fast and robust sensor development to allow process state feedback.

CONCLUSIONS

As the reader will have noticed, none of the fashionable topics - geometric reasoning or AI planning - have been mentioned in this paper. There are sufficient problems to resolve in real manufacturing before bringing in research topics from other areas.

The key topics that should be exercising those of us interested in results that are applicable to the manufacturing world are:

How can manufacturing process plans best be represented? How can appropriate architectures (hardware and software) for the control of complex manufacturing execution environments be decided? How can tools be built that allow the manufacturing process and system, when described in a high-level manner, to be matched to the execution environment and to generate executable code easily for this environment? What is the next programmable process?

All this has to be done within the financial restraints associated with manufacturing and with the appropriate use of people.

ACKNOWLEDGEMENTS

A paper such as this is never really the work of a single author, it builds upon many beery conversations with colleagues and half remembered reading of others' work. I acknowledge you all.

REFERENCES

(Albus 81a) J Albus et al. Theory and Practice of Hierarchical Control. Proceedings of the 23rd IEEE Computer Society International Conference, September 1981.

(Albus 81b) J Albus. Brains, Behaviour and Robotics. Byte Books, 1981.

(Bourne 87) D A Bourne. CML, A Meta-Interpreter for Manufacturing. AI Magazine, Fall 1987.

(Brady 86) M Brady. The Advent of Intelligent Robots. An address to the British Computer Society at the Royal Society, 1986.

(Burnett 85) L Burnett. Factory-Level Planning and Control. NSF Workshop on Manufacturing Systems Integration, St Clair, Michigan, 1985.

(Darbyshire 87) I Darbyshire. EXCAP, Application of IKBS Techniques to CAPP. Second UMIST/ACME Workshop on Advanced Research in Computer Aided Manufacturing, UMIST, January 1987.

(Duffie and Piper 86) N A Duffie and Piper. Non-Hierarchical Control of Manufacturing. Journal of Manufacturing Systems, 5, 137-139, 1986.

(Duffie 86) N A Duffie et al. Hierarchical and Non-Hierarchical Cell Control with Dynamic Part-Oriented Scheduling. Proceedings of NAMRC-XIV, Minneapolis, May 1986.

(Egginton 87) Terms of Reference, Advanced Robotics Initiative, DTI, 1987.

(Englert 88) P Englert and P Wright. Principles for Part Set-Up and Workholding in Automated Manufacturing. Journal of Manufacturing Systems, 7, 2, 147-162, 1988.

(Fox 87) B R Fox and K G Kempf. Reasoning About Opportunistic Schedules. IEEE International Conference on Robotics and Automation, Raleigh, 1876-1882, 1987.

(Husbands 87) P Husbands, F G Mill and S W Warrington. Process Planning: Knowledge Representation. Second UMIST/ACME Workshop on Advanced Research in Computer Aided Manufacturing, UMIST, January 1987.

(Hatvany 84) J Hatvany. Intelligence and Co-operation in Hierarchic Manufacturing Systems. Proceedings of CIRP, International Seminar on Manufacturing Systems, Tokyo, 1984.

(Hodgson 88) A Hodgson, R H Weston, C M Sumpter, J D Gascoigne and A Rui. Planning and Control Flow in CIM: Current Research Directions and the Need for Intermediate Solutions. IERE Factory 2000 Conference, Churchill College, Cambridge, September 1988.

(Jared 87) G Jared. Intelligent Data Extraction from Solid Models. Second UMIST/ACME Workshop on Advanced Research in Computer Aided Manufacturing, UMIST, January 1987.

(Jones 86) A Jones and C McClean. A Proposed Hierarchical Control Model for Automated Manufacturing Systems. Journal of Manufacturing Systems, 5, 15-26, 1986.

(Machinery 87) Anon. Special Anniversary Issue, Machinery and Production Engineering, September 1987.

(Naylor and Volz 84) A Naylor and R Volz. Using ADA as a Programming Language for Robot Based Manufacturing Cells. IEEE Trans of Systems, Man and Cybernetics, 14, 6, 863-878, 1984.

(Newman 85) P A Newman and K G Kempf. Opportunistic Scheduling for Robotic Machine Tending. IEEE Conference on AI Applications, Miami, 1985.

(Parunak 87) H V D Parunak. Why Scheduling is Hard (and how to do it anyway). Proceedings of the 1987 Material Handling Focus (Research Forum), Georgia Institute of Technology, September 1987.

(Ravichandran 86) R Ravichandran and A Chakravarty. Decision Support in FMS Using Timed Petri Nets. Journal of Manufacturing Systems, 5, 89-112, 1986.

(Science Museum 66) Catalogue of Machine Tools in the Science Museum Collection, Her Majesty's Stationery Office, 1966.

(Upton 87) D M Upton. The Operation of Large Computer Controlled Manufacturing Systems. Purdue University, PhD Thesis, 1988.

(Weston 88) R H Weston, J D Gascoigne, A Hodgson and C M Sumpter. System Integration in PCB Manufacture. IERE Factory 2000 Conference, Churchill College, Cambridge, September 1988.

(Williams 88) D J Williams. Manufacturing Systems, An Introduction to the Technologies. Halsted Press, 1988.

(Wu 86) H L Wu, R Vengopal and M M Barash. Design of a Cellular Manufacturing System: A Syntactic Pattern Recognition Approach. Journal of Manufacturing Systems, 5, 2, 81-88, 1986.

(Wright and Bourne 88) P K Wright and D A Bourne. Manufacturing Intelligence. Addison Wesley, 1988.

Distributed Knowledge-Based Systems in Manufacturing

Nicholas Findler

Computer Science Department and AI Laboratory, Arizona State University, Tempe, AZ 85287-5406, USA

Institute of Computer Science, University of Zurich, CH-8057 Zurich, Switzerland

ABSTRACT

The paper will first discuss some general issues of Distributed Planning and Problem Solving Systems, such as research objectives, different methodologies, theoretical and application-oriented concerns. One of the important areas of application is aimed at generating a dynamic hierarchical control mechanism for distributed manufacturing operations. The environment consists of a group of dissimilar plants distributed geographically and connected by a transportation and a communication network. Each plant — and its associated computer — is a problem solving node in the network. The plants have to produce cooperatively a certain number and type of products. Each plant is characterized by the skills and equipment it possesses. The skills, in turn, have certain attributes: the number of time units and the cost needed to execute the skill, and its availability on given equipment.

The final product consists of components, each of which comprises subcomponents, and so on up to varying depths. At each level of assembly, the quantity of the relevant subcomponent and the skills needed characterize the process in question. The total cost of producing the final product at a given plant is the sum of production costs of components one level below, the transportation expenses incurred in bringing them to the plant in question, and the cost of processing/assembly at the top level. Similar relations hold for lower level components.

The task of planning is to assign manufacturing/assembly responsibilities to the proper plants so that the required number of products are produced either (i) at a minimum overall cost in a given time period or (ii) at a given cost in a minimum time period. Transportation not only costs time and money but is also restricted in volume. Idle plants and setting-up processes cost money, too.

INTRODUCTION

There are problem-solving tasks whose size and certain other characteristics do not allow them to be processed effectively and efficiently by a single computer system. Such tasks are characterized by one or several of the following properties:

- spatially distributed input/output operations,
- extensive communication over long distances,
- time-stressed demands for solution,
- a large degree of functional specialization,
- a need for reliable computation with incomplete data and knowledge,
- a need for graceful degradation,
- shared and limited resources to work on common objectives, etc.

Advances in computer and communication technology have enabled researchers to study Distributed Artificial Intelligence (DAI). DAI has followed two major paradigms. First, planning for multiple agents is done by one single agent in the network. Second, a group of agents collaborate to generate a plan for distributed problem solving. The decentralized knowledge sources are called 'loosely-coupled' when the node processors perform more computation than communication. Such a feature is desirable since computation, broadly speaking, is usually less expensive, faster and more reliable than communication.

We have followed the distributed problem solving approach, an indispensable part of which is distributed planning. The criteria of efficient operation include the requirements that an agent should not undo the results of others nor should it unnecessarily duplicate any part of the performance of others. The decisions made and the activities taken by the nodes should make sense given the overall network goals. Computation and communication loads should be balanced between all the nodes in the network. No nodes should sit idle while others are swamped with work. Also, limited resources should be shared effectively and conflicts arising here have to be resolved in a satisfactory manner.

The systems studied consist of a group of agents, a network of processors, each cooperating with a selected subset of others to achieve a common set of objectives. We have aimed at optimizing the way the individual processors are interconnected so that their capabilities are fully utilized and their goals can be accomplished effectively. We have been interested in how knowledge is distributed in the network and how incomplete information is handled during the problem solving process without having to report failure. We have wanted to show the relationship between overall system performance and the amount of knowledge and meta-level knowledge an individual node has. (The latter refers to, for example, the knowledge about the past, present and intended future activities of other nodes). It is critical to determine the kind of planning activity the individual agents should engage in. The architecture or the organizational structure the nodes form is important because it will not only influence the processes of communication and control inside the system but will also affect the flow of the relevant information. Furthermore, the system should be able to reconfigure itself in response to a dynamically changing environment.

The main problems that arise in such Centralized Planning systems are about how to limit search in avoiding unnecessary efforts and how to resolve the conflict between interacting subgoals (subproblems). The major methodologies are as follows.

- Hierarchical planning constructs a hierarchy of plan representations, each level being associated with a different degree of abstraction (lower levels have more detail).

• Non-hierarchical planning uses only one level and may get bogged down in less important details.

• Script-based planning relies on stored plans, ranging from very general ones (used at first) to rather specific one (used for the details).

• Opportunistic planning is asynchronous (different specialists make suggestions on the 'blackboard') and opportunistic (planning decisions are made only when the need arises).

• Simulation-based planning is based on look-ahead simulations in an extrapolated world, yielding desirable plan segments at the decision points.

Our approach, Distributed Planning and Problem Solving, offers a methodology in response to the above concerns. The techniques developed involve four major phases:

- problem decomposition,
- subproblem distribution among qualified nodes,
- subproblem solution, and
- answer synthesis.

The major issues one must consider with at each phase are:

• The connection problem is concerned about how the nodes are interconnected for full utilization of resources and effective goal accomplishment (network architecture); that is, how nodes with tasks find nodes best capable of executing them (e.g., negotiation in the 'contract net' in going through the 'announce-bid-award' cycle).

• The limited communication-bandwidth problem affects reliability, cost and delays. Communication schemes used include broadcast at large, group-broadcast and point-to-point broadcast. The overall performance is to be optimized, not the number of messages is minimized.

• The coherence problem references the need for mutually supportive, not mutually interfering actions by agents, which rely on hierarchically distributed knowledge and meta-knowledge. The system must aim at a balanced network load, and use 'network perception' for global coherence. The 'perceive-plan-act' cycle is an effective technique with a low communication overhead.

• The timing problem is solved by ordering task execution according to task urgency and the need of other tasks.

• The problem of node architecture, that is of interconnecting individual processors, may have the following possible solutions:

• master-slaves — forced cooperation with fixed relations.

• same-class-citizens — free cooperation with "friendly" negotiations.

• contractor-workers — cooperation with "best qualification" type negotiation and no fixed relations.

• self-reliant — each processor on its own.

• The problem control architecture is met by dynamically generating a control relationship during the problem-solving process, in response to changing environments. The network can reconfigure itself when necessary — an important facility in conflict and emergency situations. Individual nodes may have multiple roles in the network.

• The problem of learning and sharing the improved skills uses tentative solutions which are arrived at in modifying solutions of 'similar' problems.

• The problem of dynamic plan mending may be solved by employing the least possible change in an existing plan in response to changes in the environment (cf. 'dependency-directed backtracking').

• The problem of coordination necessitates signalling between different planning activities via distributed scratch pads.

• The problem of incorrect and incomplete knowledge (uncertainty) in individual nodes — due to unexpected changes in the environment and inherent noise in communication — means that unforeseen consequences may occur. Continual feedback about the current situation is needed for replanning, using judiciously distributed information of a measured degree of redundancy.

APPLICATIONS

We have developed a flexible testbed with high-level interactive and graphical facilities. In addition to the subject matter of this paper, we have been designing, implementing and studying the following three problem areas, which have significant theoretical and practical interests:

- The Optimum Distributed Resource Allocation System would allocate movable resources to constant and partially unscheduled tasks of changing locations. This paradigm represents a situation in which certain moving entities need to be processed (repaired, intercepted, etc.) by a limited number of processing resources under time-stressed conditions. This work is being done on a contract with the U.S. Coast Guard R&D Center, and is aimed at computerizing the Command, Communication and Control operations as well as optimizing the Resource Acquisition process.

- The Location-Centered, Cooperative Control System for future Air Traffic Control would exert control over the operation of dynamically formed, loosely-coupled clusters of nodes (airborne computers). Coordinators for each group are elected through implicit or explicit agreements. Coworkers are selected by a Coordinator on the basis of their qualifications and availability.

- Distributed Control for Street Traffic Light Operations optimizes traffic flow (minimizes average travel time, or maximum waiting time, or average number of stops), in using both global and local criteria. Direct communication takes place between a processor at an intersection and the processors at the four adjacent intersections. However, 'processed data' (features of the traffic flow) and 'expert advice' (control information) propagate over an indefinite number of intersections.

The above applications of the Distributed Planning paradigm are characterized by very different

- domains,
- reliability concerns,
- quality measures,
- computational and communication requirements,
- timing aspects.

However, they share certain common features, such as

- geographically distributed input and output operations,
- each node cooperates with a selected set of other nodes,
- subgroup formation (partitioning) may change according to task status, current node activity and availability,
- there is a need for reliable and gracefully degrading performance when some operational and/or computational units become disabled,
- some knowledge is universally needed but some is specific to individual nodes.

THE DYNAMIC, HIERARCHICAL CONTROL MECHANISM FOR DISTRIBUTED MANUFACTURING SYSTEMS

We have wanted to establish a system that can control, for example, the operation of a nation-wide distributed manufacturing organization. The characteristic features of the environment are:

- The constituent plants have both spatial specialization (geographical location) and functional specialization (capabilities, skills and cost functions).
- The plants are connected by a transportation network of limited capability.
- Cooperation between plants is crucial both in plan generation and plan execution.
- The information is volatile and incomplete due to dynamically changing conditions and lack of global knowledge.
- There is a critical dependency and asynchronous communication as well as possible conflicts, incompatibility and contest between subsystem controllers.
- The hierarchical network defined by the product and its manufacturing operation corresponds (is homomorphous) to the

problem solving network. It can change any time in responding to new conditions, conflicts and emergencies.

• The cost functions and the availability of manufacturing and transportation resources may change intermittently or regularly. Idle plants and setting-up operations also cost money.

The objective is to produce a required number of products either (i) at a minimum overall cost within a given time period or (ii) at a given cost figure within a minimum period of time. This requires an optimum allocation schedule of processing/assembly operations to individual plants over space and time.

This is a good domain to study the problems of connection, timing, network perception, load balancing, communication minimization, and others. A user-friendly programming environment has been created that enables fast and errorfree problem specification, on-line problem modification, monitoring and evaluation of plan generation and execution, and the utilization of a learning facility that improves system performance on the basis of experience.

We have worked on the solution based on a decentralized, loosely-coupled collection of problem solvers located at the distinct network nodes. These terms mean the following:

• decentralized — both control and data may be distributed;

• loosely-coupled — "less time" spent on communication than on computation;

• network — a collection of semi-autonomous individual problem solving nodes; some of the decisions are internal (made about its own activity) and some are external (made by another node).

The hierarchical network structure enhances multi-agent planning. Nodes at a higher level have more global knowledge of the problem solving environment and make more general plans than those at a lower level. Nodes are said to be semi-autonomous, which means that the mode of decision making is network status-dependent — 'external' decision makers are used when the need for communication and computation is relatively small whereas 'internal' decision making is employed when the urgency of subtasks is not an issue and there is no danger of duplicating certain processes.

Planning can be considered as the (constrained) process of selecting a subset of the Cartesian product of three performance-related sets,

WHAT x WHERE x WHEN

- WHAT denotes the set of manufacturing/assembly responsibilities of all components every element of which must appear in the subset;
- WHERE refers to the set of plant locations some elements of which may not be selected and some may be selected several times;
- WHEN references a set of times.

The constraints refer to the optimization criterion used.

There can be a number of additional difficulties, such as

- some components are common to several products,
- some components can be processed by only a limited number of plants,
- some plants have only a very limited set of skills,
- some components may have to be produced by several plants,
- beginning and/or finishing times of processing may have various restrictions,
- storage space and transportation may be limited in volume and cost, idle plants and setting-up operations cost money, etc.

THE GENERAL PARADIGM

The domain contains a group of dissimilar plants distributed geographically. Each plant has a computer which is connected to a communication network. Messages can be sent from a given plant to a particular plant, to a set of plants selected according to some criteria, or broadcasted at large to all plants.

The plant X_i (i=1, 2,..., k) is characterized by a descriptor, D, specializing its skills, equipment, current inventory, direct transportation to other plants, and available storage space:

$$D(X_i): [S_1(X_i), S_2(X_i),..., S_m(X_i); E_1(X_i), E_2(X_i),..., E_n(X_i);$$

$$I_1(Xi), I_2(Xi),..., I_o(Xi);\ \ T_1(Xi), T_2(Xi),..., T_p(Xi);\ \ V(Xi)]$$

Here $S_s(Xi)$, $E_t(Xi)$ and $I_i(Xi)$ denote the s-th skill (s=1, 2,..., m), t-th equipment (t=1, 2,..., n) and u-th component or raw material (u=1, 2,..., o) the plant X_i has, respectively. $T_v(Xi)$ stands for the direct transportation connection between plants X_i and X_v (v=1, 2,..., k; i≠v). $V(X_i)$ is the storage space available at plant X_i.

Each skill has certain attributes:

$$S_s(X_i):\ \ [N_s(X_i), C_s(X_i), O_i(X_i,t)]$$

Here $N_s(X_i)$ represents the number of time units needed for executing skill $S_s(X_i)$; $C_s(X_i)$ is the cost of doing so per unit time; and $O_s(X_i,t)$ is the availability status of the skill at time t.

Each equipment $E_t(X_i)$ is identified by its name and has the attribute 'availability status' with two values: the total number of units and the currently available number of units.

Each raw material or subcomponent $I_u(X_i)$ has four attributes: the amount available, unit cost, and unit weight or volume (depending on how it is packaged, transported and used).

Each transportation connection $T_v(X_i)$ is characterized by five attributes: the name of the other plant X_i is connected with, the distance between the two plants, unit transportation cost per batch, batch size and batch transportation time.

The final product P_j has components and subcomponents over several levels. It is described as

$$P_j:\quad [P_{j,1}, P_{j,2},...,P_{j,r};\ \ M_{j,1}, M_{j,2},...,M_{j,r};$$

$$S_1(P_j), S_2(P_j),..., S_g(P_j);\ E_1(P_j), E_2(P_j),..., E_h(P_j)]$$

Here $P_{j,c}$ is the c-th first-level component of the final product P_j ($c=1, 2, \ldots r$); $M_{j,d}$ is the amount of $P_{j,d}$ needed for one unit of P_j ($d=1, 2, \ldots, r$); $S_e(P_j)$ and $E_f(P_j)$ are the e-th skill and f-th equipment needed for the processing/assembly of its components.

Each component may have subcomponents and is then described as:

$$P_{j,c}: [P_{j,c,1}, P_{j,c,2}, \ldots, P_{j,c,w}; \ldots]$$

An example is shown in Figure 1 below:

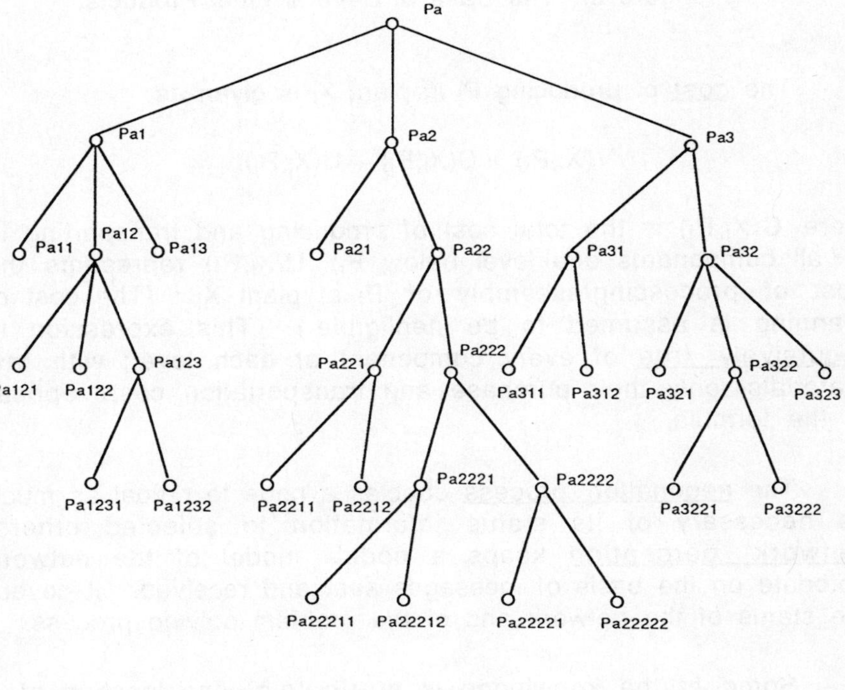

Figure 1. The Hierarchical Structure of Product-A

Multiple final products require a dummy task acting as the root of the hierarchy tree, the parent node of each final product, as shown on Figure 2.

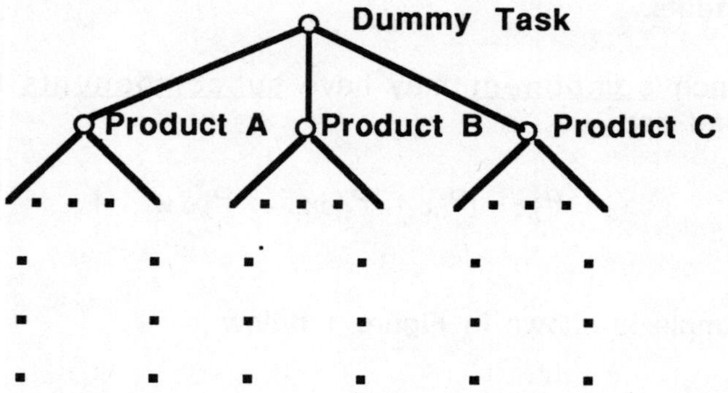

Figure 2. The Case of Several Final Products.

The cost of producing P_j in plant X_i is given as

$$V(X_i,P_j) = C(X_i,P_j) + U(X_i,P_j).$$

Here $C(X_i,P_j)$ is the total cost of producing and transporting to X_i all components one level below P_j; $U(X_i,P_j)$ represents the cost of processing/assembly of P_j at plant X_i. (The cost of planning is assumed to be negligible.) This expression is recursively true of every component at each level; with raw materials, only their purchase and transportation costs appear in the formula.

The negotiation process enables a node to reveal as much as necessary of its status information to selected others. Network perception keeps a node's model of the network uptodate on the basis of messages sent and received. It covers the status of the network and of the problem solving process.

Some of the knowledge is static (e.g., the location of a given plant), some changes infrequently (e.g., the number and type of machines at a given plant), some changes dynamically (e.g., the set of qualified receivers of a given message).

There are two types of strategies possible:

- The top-down strategy starts at the root, generates an abstract overall plan and refines it level-by-level. Its disadvantage is that component costs and timing are unknown within the abstract plan.

- The bottom-up strategy starts with raw materials. Its disadvantage is that there are resource allocation conflicts, possibly only locally optimum resource allocations, and the load distribution is unbalanced. Backtracking is often needed to rectify these problems

We have selected the latter approach. To reduce resource allocation conflicts, 'reservation rules' were added (the capabilities for a task are reserved if less than a predefined number of bidders occur). Also, we have allowed 'over-bidding' by a node for the better utilization of resources — except when a node is the single bidder for a certain task, it no longer bids for other tasks ('self-reservation'). Negotiation is kept as the last resort since it may become costly in time and message interpretation.

We have adopted the architecture based on dynamically generated Contractor-Workers interaction. The nodes are partitioned into need-defined groups. The significant advantage is that negotiation and communication are constrained to smaller regions of the network

The Coordinator receives the problem from the user. A top-level Contractor is first appointed by the Coordinator. At lower levels, Contractors are selected by the Contractor of one level higher. A particular node can have multiple roles over the whole network but, at any single level, it may have only one Contractor role in order to reduce communication problems.

Problem decomposition is usually on the basis of AND-OR trees, as shown on Figure 3.

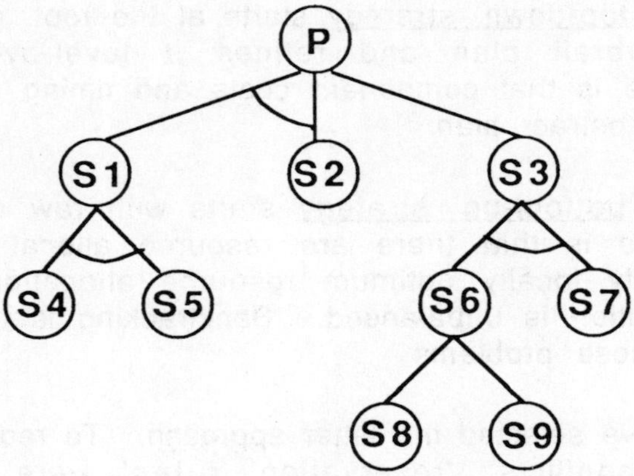

Figure 3. Problem Decomposition with an AND-OR Tree

'Network perception' is useful for acquiring the specific knowledge of what has been done, what is being done and what else needs to be done. Four heuristic rules assist with it in selecting the next task:

Rule 1: Tasks located closest to the bottom of the task hierarchy should be selected first since longer paths are more likely to develop into bottlenecks concerning overall response time.

Rule 2: Out of several ready tasks at the same level, the one with finished sibling tasks should be selected. Once this is accomplished, the parent tasks can be considered.

Rule 3: Out of several ready tasks at the same level, the one whose parent task is not in the current job queue should be selected in order to balance completed levels as much as possible.

Rule 4: Out of several ready tasks at the same level, the one with the shortest time requirement should be selected.

The system design is shown in Figure 4. The individual components have the following responsibilities:

- The Network Planner, being in charge of node cooperation, sends and receives messages via the Communication Unit. It also decides which node should bid for a given task.

• The Local Planner generates the detailed bids using its local status information. The Meta-Level Planner refines the high-level, long-term plans into low-level, short-term ones in considering the current network status (e.g., the needs of other nodes).

• The Perception Unit comprises the Message Record Unit, the Perception Processing Unit and the Perception Model. The first files the messages sent and received. The second identifies those messages that can cause a change in the Perception Model. It updates the Perception Model only when the Meta-Level Planner directs it to do so.

In addition, each node has a Graphics Display Unit, a Knowledge Base Maintaining Unit, and a Plan Execution Monitoring Unit.

Finally, the operational cycle of a node is based on the 'perceive-plan-act' loop mentioned before.

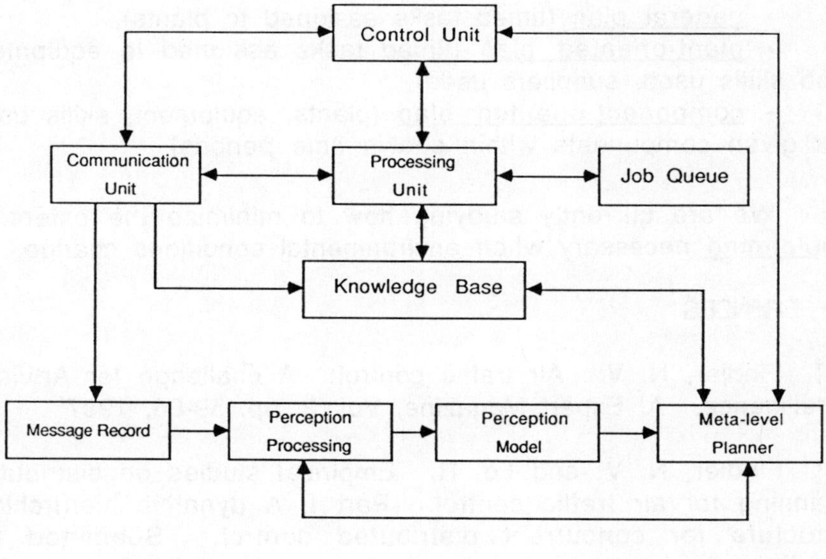

Figure 4. The System Design

The system can be used in any one of four modes:

• In the Creating Mode, the user can specify the whole environment and the products to be produced (the equipment, skills and inventory of plants, transportation routes between plants, costs, product hierarchy, etc.).

• The Modifying Mode enables the user to change any of the above, including those items that are automatically identified by the system as affected by such action.

• The user may wish to see on a graphics display and print out any of the above in the View Mode.

• The Operational Mode receives information from the user about the name and the amount of the products to be produced, desired starting and finishing times, and the manufacturing criterion (time or cost priority). The correctness and the feasibility of these are then checked by the system.

The manufacturing plan generated can be displayed as a

• general plan (timed tasks assigned to plants),
• plant-oriented plan (timed tasks assigned to equipment and skills used, suppliers used),
• component-oriented plan (plants, equipment, skills used for given components within shown time periods).

We are currently studying how to minimize the extent of replanning necessary when environmental conditions change.

REFERENCES

[1] Findler, N. V. Air traffic control: A challenge for Artificial Intelligence. AI Expert Magazine, Vol. 2, pp. 59-66, 1987.

[2] Findler, N. V. and Lo, R. Empirical studies on distributed planning for air traffic control. Part I: A dynamic hierarchical structure for concurrent distributed control. Submitted for publication.

[3] Findler, N. V. and Lo, R. Empirical studies on distributed planning for air traffic control. Part II: The location centered, cooperative planning system. Submitted for publication.

[4] Findler, N. V. and Lo, R. Empirical studies on distributed planning for air traffic control. Part III: Experimental results. Submitted for publication.

[5] Findler, N. V. and Gao, J. Dynamic hierarchical control for distributed problem solving. Data and Knowledge Engineering, Vol. 2, pp. 285-301, 1987.

[6] Findler, N. V. and Ge, Q. Perceiving and planning before acting — an approach to enhance global network coherence. Accepted for publication by International Journal of Intelligent Systems.

Strategic Issues for Knowledge Based Systems in the Design of Manufacturing Systems

J.A. Brandon and G.Q. Huang

Mechanical Engineering Division, School of Engineering, University of Wales College of Cardiff, PO Box 917, Cardiff, CF2 1XH, Wales, UK

ABSTRACT

The paper explains the effects of the difficulties widely experienced in integrating CAPM into overall CIM systems, remarked by Waterlow and Monniot in their 1986 survey. This is illustrated by consideration of Production Flow Analysis.

Production Flow Analysis infers technological relationships between machines and components by retrospective analysis of production routings. The means of incorporation of heuristics into PFA are outlined in the paper.

1 INTRODUCTION

1.1 SCOPE

In considering the strategic issues in Manufacturing Systems design, it is inevitable that there will be a significant element of review, although this is not the primary purpose of the paper. This is the identification of generic properties of existing knowledge based systems for manufacturing systems design, paying particular attention to consistency and compatibility of knowledge representation and processing. This paper is an extension of previous work by the authors (Huang and Brandon[1-4]), which concentrated particularly on technologically oriented problem definition. Whereas in these papers the analysis became progressively closer focussed, the current paper takes a wider view, although the work will be illustrated with specific examples which have not been addressed before.

1.2 BACKGROUND

A very large number of Knowledge Based Systems have been developed, intended for Manufacturing Systems Design. The majority of these systems are Knowledge Based but not Expert, ie although they conform to IKBS structures, in having an Inference Engine and Knowledge Base, there has not been an effort to capture the specialised expertise possessed by domain operatives. This is because the existing formal methodologies have been developed systematically with a priori procedures.

In the authors' earlier papers, significant incompatibilities have been identified between existing knowledge based systems for manufacturing facilities design, even, in the case of Ito, between different systems produced by the same researchers (see for example: Ito and Saito[5], Ito and Shinno[6-8] Ito[9]). A complementary problem is that some systems are generically similar, although this is obscured by domain specific terminology, although their developers have failed to appreciate the structural similarities.

A feature of the incompatibility of differing strategies, when applied to the same problem, is what Efstathiou[10] defines as ontology. The term is used to describe the differing experiential outlook, methodology and paradigms of the various professional groups who may be asked to solve a particular problem.

1.3 APPROACH USED IN THE CURRENT PAPER

The authors have used, as a foundation of their work, the work of Kim[11]. The work of Iwata and Sugimura[12] on Computer Assisted Process Planning, is also of relevance to the current work.

The paper will consider particularly a problem which the authors have not discussed elsewhere, that of Group Technology (see Gallagher and Knight[13]). There have been a number of Knowledge Based systems devised for the technological aspects of Group Technology, but rather fewer for the allied Production Flow Analysis (PFA), which uses techniques from a more general managerial perspective. This is particularly instructive for the authors, who are of a strongly technological ontology, taking into account the widely held view that it is difficult for domain specialists to define and capture the expertise within their own domain. Much of the credit for the development of

Production Flow Analysis (PFA) is attributed to Burbidge (see for example Burbidge[14,15]).

In PFA relationships between production workstations are inferred from the historical production records of the company. In the established methodologies each production operative is regarded as having equal expertise. No effort is made to identify operatives with particularly strong expertise, although it could be established behaviourally, through peer esteem surveys or by statistical identification of consistent process planning, either relatively or against a standard. There is obvious scope for a Knowledge Based approach.

The attractiveness of Production Flow Analysis as a case study owes much to the fact that the inferential mechanisms are explicitly defined, a-priori rather than identifiable a posteriori. Thus many of the techniques of Knowledge Engineering, for example clustering strategies, are integral features of these systems, without however any overt partition into inference engine and knowledge base.

As has been mentioned, the other aspects of group Technology demand the attention of another, ontologically distinct, group, who are technologically trained and orientated. Thus the paper will identify particularly those generic aspects of the systems which are domain independent, and hence the basis of a knowledge based system without strongly domain dependent features.

2 DOMAIN DEFINITION AND ANALYSIS

2.1 ONTOLOGICAL DISTINCTIONS

As has been suggested above, the Domain of Production Management may have strong ontological differences from the other related Domains of Manufacturing Systems. Specifically it is by no means unusual for managers and operatives within the production management function to have little or no formal technological training, in contrast to the numerate and/or technological training background of the other functional groups. Indeed there was a fashion, in the late 1960s and early 1970s, to appoint trainee production managers whose degree qualifications were in the classics. (This was based on the (ontological) argument that the etymological core of the classicist's training was an ideal basis for the taxonomic approach demanded by production management.) Thus operatives and managers may be incapable of defining, let alone solving, problems relating to the materials or processes involved in manufacture. Procedures within this domain tend to be strongly prescriptive, usually devised externally either by technologists or specialist systems analysts.

In contrast, for the majority of other functions within the manufacturing organisation, a general technological training provides the degree of versatility for operatives to specify, as well as solve, the problems within both their own domain and that of interacting functional groups, including, but not restricted to, the production management function. Procedures are typically a mixture of prescriptive and descriptive formulations, often constructed by the users themselves or by external specialists with the same cognate paradigms.

This dichotomy has led to difficulties of definition and integration of Computer Aided Production Management (CAPM) within overall Computer Integrated Manufacturing (CIM) Systems. Consider for example the conclusion of Waterlow and Monniot[16]:

> "Leading edge companies appear to be having difficulty in addressing CAPM within a CIM framework. This may be because CAPM takes a "top-down" business approach to system integration, whereas the majority of other CIM systems are evolving both from the "bottom-up" in business terms."

and further:

> "The reports on the few companies in the sample which had achieved full CAPM integration and some integration of CAPM with other business functions, indicated that the global scale of such systems can be incomprehensible to staff, especially in middle management".

A case study for the systematic "top-down" design of a CAPM system has been given by Thomas et al[17].

2.2 PRODUCTION CONTROL DEFINED

Production Control is often analysed in terms of four distinct phases (see for example the general texts by Wild[15] and Hill[19], the specialised, but rather dated work by Greene[20] and the guide by Corke[21]). Of these, only the first stage, that of process planning, is necessarily technologically based. In this phase the manufacturing options are assessed and the sequence of feasible and preferred production operations determined. In the subsequent three stages, those of scheduling, loading and expediting, the work is primarily clerical.

Process planning entails the analysis of the demands of products on manufacturing systems. It includes choice of process and the matching of product demands to in-house production capability, which would influence, although not necessarily determine make-or-buy decisions. During process planning a number of feasible production routings may be evaluated and stored for later priority evaluation against current capacity forecasts. Process planning, in contrast to the other three phases of production control, is independent of current workload and can therefore be viewed as a static procedure, whereas current demand influences decisions in scheduling, loading and monitoring manufacture and hence these are essentially dynamic processes.

There is a substantial body of research into knowledge based strategies for process planning. As has been suggested above, these will be predominantly knowledge based but not expert. In addition to the research already mentioned the work of Toth and his co-workers (Toth and Vadasz[22] Toth et al[23]), and Milacic[24] are of interest. Jagdev et al[25] produced a useful survey of the relevant properties of commercially available software, although this must now be considered rather dated.

In production scheduling, feasible process routings, prepared in the process planning stage, are evaluated against current and planned manufacturing loads. At this stage it is quite common to make make-or-buy decisions, taking into account perceived capacity limitations. Loading and monitoring are mechanistic activities related to the implementation of the schedule.

The domain boundary relationships are shown in figure 1.

2.3 PRODUCTION FLOW ANALYSIS

Production Flow Analysis is a strategy for rationalisation of production facilities, based solely on the analysis of historical production data. As described by Gallagher and Knight:

> " The technique is concerned principally with existing methods of manufacture but does not

consider other features such as material type and form, to help in the creation of groups. The minimum data essential for each part are an identification number, a record of the sequence which each part follows numerically identified or coded, and a list of all parts and their sequence of operations, coded into a numeric form."

Whereas in process planning the geometry and function of the component determine the choice and sequence of production operations, in PFA abstract relationships between machines are inferred from analysis of component routings, and relationships between components are inferred by considering common requirements of choice and sequence of machines. The central algorithmic procedure used is that of cluster analysis. (This is discussed by Carrie[26] and Standel[27]).

PFA is commonly used as part of a wider Group Technology exercise, which will also include the collation and incorporation of technological data, particularly precedence and exclusivity constraints. For example PFA will relate a die casting machine to a subsequent lathe operation, but will not indicate that it may be necessary to allow for a protracted period to elapse, for complete solidification of the casting. Similarly the system will not perceive that part of a process involves wet machining with finishing undertaken under dry machining conditions. Hence a suggested rationalisation of facilities based solely on PFA may lead to an unnecessary, and perhaps undesirable, linking of two process stations.

A limitation of the effectiveness of PFA is inherent in the method. Because the procedures depend on collation of a substantial database of historical data, the reconfiguration of production facilities may be based on out of date production methods and give undue consideration to the requirements of obsolescent components, and hence fail to anticipate future changes in processes or product ranges. Askew et al[28] discuss methods which are intended to counter this tendency.

3 IDENTIFYING KNOWLEDGE AND EXPERTISE IN PROCESS PLANNING

3.1 IMPLICIT ASSUMPTIONS ABOUT KNOWLEDGE AND EXPERTISE

PFA entails the use of algorithms subject to combinatorial complexity, ie there is a factorial effect in the relationship between problem size and the number of operations (and hence time) for its solution. Consequently the use of knowledge based heuristic techniques to identify the most significant variables in the analysis is of a high priority for expanding the applicability of the methods.

In the form used historically, PFA imbues all production planners with equal degrees of knowledge and expertise. What has not been recognised is that embedded in the process of specification of production routings is a wealth of information which may be either knowledge, in that it is unambiguous and available to all process planners, or expertise, based on particular individual talents of personal judgement (both attitudinal and experiential). Further, as has already been remarked, the method weights all historical data equally, rather than considering recent data to be more reliable.

In practice there are likely to be wide differences in performance between different process planners. For example the best planners will review their practices to reflect new production technology and methods, whereas less able/ motivated staff will continue to route components to workstations which they have used habitually, based on feasibility rather than optimality. In addition, it is by no means uncommon for the installation of new production equipment only to affect feasible routes prepared subsequently.

3.2 NATURE OF KNOWLEDGE AND EXPERTISE

Knowledge about the production system falls into two general classes. Process planners are likely to have, or have access to, codified or official information about:

> specialised jigs and fixtures which may be the only distinguishing factor between otherwise identical machines (particularly when a Group Technology philosophy has been used);
>
> relative performance data, including metrological conformance, of machines with similar specifications;

They are also likely to have (unofficially) data concerning:

> capability of process operatives. (This data may be held officially, in terms of scrap ratios, rework instructions etc, but is unlikely to be available formally to the process planners);

performance data on cells and shops;

The manner in which this knowledge is utilised is indicative of the expertise of the process planner, although there is not necessarily a direct correspondence, since expertise may be obscured by motivational or cultural factors.

3.3 ELICITATION STRATEGIES

In distinguishing expert planners from their peers, it is first necessary to form an assessment of expertise. This could be in terms of subjective, behavioural measures, including, for example, questionnaires to ascertain rankings of mutual esteem. Alternatively, a more objective measure could be achieved by using the concept of "Key Components", (see Askew et al[28]), asking each planner to provide routings for a representative sample of common parts. It would be natural to compare these results in terms of the calculated floor-to-floor time, derived as part of the planning exercise. What might be more advantageous however, would be to process actual components (or batches) through the manufacturing facility, to give door-to-door time, since a central factor in the expertise of the expert process planner could well be the perception of scheduling difficulties due to insufficient capacity on one machine, whilst there is excess capacity on a similar, or only marginally inferior, facility.

The evaluation of the relative capability of the personnel involved in process planning enables the incorporation of knowledge eliciting procedures into the PFA process.

3.4 INCORPORATION OF EXPERTISE INTO PFA PROCEDURES

The identification of expertise in planners enables the adaptation of PFA to identify those aspects of their historical behaviour which can be exploited to improve the capability of the manufacturing systems, rather than emphasis on the capability of individual facilities which is the primary preoccupation in process planning.

There is also some potential in applying the door-to-door evaluation directly, as part of the PFA analysis, based on achieved production performance. This would complement, and reinforce, the information gained from the key component approach used by Askew et al[26].

The effectiveness of the recommended approach could be quantified by adapting the clustering methods commonly used in PFA to incorporated a-priori objective functions based on the flexibility vector proposed by Ito et al[29].

A further improvement in PFA would be derived by the incorporation of time weighting into the data, emphasising particularly production routings devised recently.

4 CONCLUSIONS

PFA is commonly used to devise facility groupings without technological appraisal. Consideration of the problems of combinatorial complexity leads to a conclusion that it will be beneficial to incorporate specialist expertise into the procedure to improve its efficiency.

The paper outlines some of the strategies which are likely to improve the effectiveness of PFA.

5 REFERENCES

1. G Q Huang and J A Brandon, Topological representations for machine tool structures, 27th Machine Tool Design and Research Conference, Manchester, Editor B J Davies, Macmillan, pp173-178, 1988

2. G Q Huang and J A Brandon, An investigation into machine representation models for machine tool design, Conference Factory 2000, Institution of Electronic and Radio Engineers, Churchill College Cambridge, 31 August- 2nd September 1988, pp331-336, 1988

3. G Q Huang and J A Brandon, Machine Tool analysis and synthesis based on the graphical machine representation model, in Advances in Manufacturing Technology Volume 3, Editor B Worthington, Kogan Page, pp100-104, 1988

4. G Q Huang and J A Brandon, Specification and management of the knowledge base for design of machine tools and their integration into manufacturing facilities, in D T Pham (editor), Artificial Intelligence in Design, IFS/Springer Verlag, to be published 1989

5. Y Ito and Y Saito 'Computer-aided draughting system 'ALODS' for machine tool structures' Proceedings of 22nd International Machine Tool Design and Research Conference pp 69-76 1981

6. Y Ito and H Shinno 'structural description and similarity evaluation of the structural configuration in machine tools' Int. J Machine Tool Design and Research Vol 22 No 2 pp 97-110 1982

7. Y Ito and H Shinno 'Generating method for structural configuration of machine tools' Transactions of the Japanese Society of Mechanical Engineers, 50 (449) pp213 1984

8. Y Ito and H Shinno 'A proposed generating method for the structural configuration of machine tools' ASME 84-WA/Prod-22 1984

9. Y Ito, 'Description of machine tools and its applications-CAD system for machine tools structures' Bulletin of the Japan Society of Precision Engineering Vol 18 No 2

10. J Efstathiou, Intelligent Knowledge Based Systems for Factory Management, Conference Factory 2000, Institution of Electronic and Radio Engineers, Churchill College Cambridge, 31 August- 2nd September 1988, pp271-277

11. S H Kim, Mathematical Foundations of Manufacturing Science, PhD Thesis, Massachusetts Institute of Technology, 1985

12. K Iwata and N Sugimura 'An integrated CAD/CAPP system with "know-hows" on machining accuracies of parts', Trans. of the ASME, Journal of Engineering for Industry Vol 109 pp128-133 1987

13. C C Gallagher and W A Knight, Group Technology Production Methods in Manufacture, Ellis Horwood, Chichester, 1986.

14. J L Burbidge, Production Flow Analysis, Proceedings of the Seminar on Group Technology, International Centre for Advanced Technical and Vocational Training, Turin, 1970.

15. J L Burbidge, Group Technology in the Engineering Industry, Mechanical Engineering Publications, 1979.

16. J G Waterlow and J P Monniot, A study of the State

of the Art in Computer Aided Production Management, ACME Directorate, U K Science and Engineering Research Council, 1986

17. C N Thomas, J A Brandon and R P Chapman, Bespoke CAPM- Still an affordable option for the small company?, in Engineering Management: Theory and Applications, Eds Leech et al, M Jackson pp243-251, 1986.

18. R Wild, Production and Operations Management-Principles and Techniques, Holt Rinehart and Winston, 3rd Edn, 1984.

19. T Hill, Production/Operations Management, Prentice Hall, 1983.

20. J H Greene, Production and Inventory Control: Systems and Decisions, Irwin, 1974.

21. D K Corke, A Guide to CAPM, Institution of Production Engineers, 1985.

22. T Toth and D Vadasz, The TAUPROG System Family: Application Experiences and New Results of Development, Report CJA 156, Institute of Technology for Machine Industry, Budapest, Hungary, 1985.

23. T Toth, I Detsky and L Eszes, Optimisation of Discrete Technology Processes using a Method Traced Back to Constrained Travelling Salesman Problem, 27th International Machine Tool Design and Research Conference, Manchester, 1988.

24. V R Milacic, A Contribution to the Development of a Process Planning Method in Industrial Environment, 22nd International Machine Tool Design and Research Conference, UMIST, Manchester, 1981.

25. H Jagdev, J Browne and B J Davies, The Architecture of Production Control Module for Job Shops, 25th International Machine Tool Design and Research Conference, Birmingham, 1985.

26. A S Carrie, Numerical Taxonomy Applied to Group Technology and Plant Layout, International Journal of Production Research, 11, pp337-354, 1973.

27. L E Standel, Machine Clustering for Effective Production, Engineering Costs and Production Economics, 9, pp73-81, 1985.

28. M Askew, M Edkins, R Leonard and B R Kilmartin, Modelling Multi-Product Manufacturing Systems to Identify Key Components for Selecting CNC Machining Centres and to Aid the Design of Flexible Manufacturing Cells, 24th International Machine Tool Design and Research Conference, Manchester, pp449-461, 1983.

29. Y Ito, T Ohmi and Y Shima, An Evaluation Method of Flexible Manufacturing System- A Concept of Flexibility Evaluation Vector and its Application, 25th International Machine Tool Design and Research Conference, Birmingham, pp89-95, 1985.

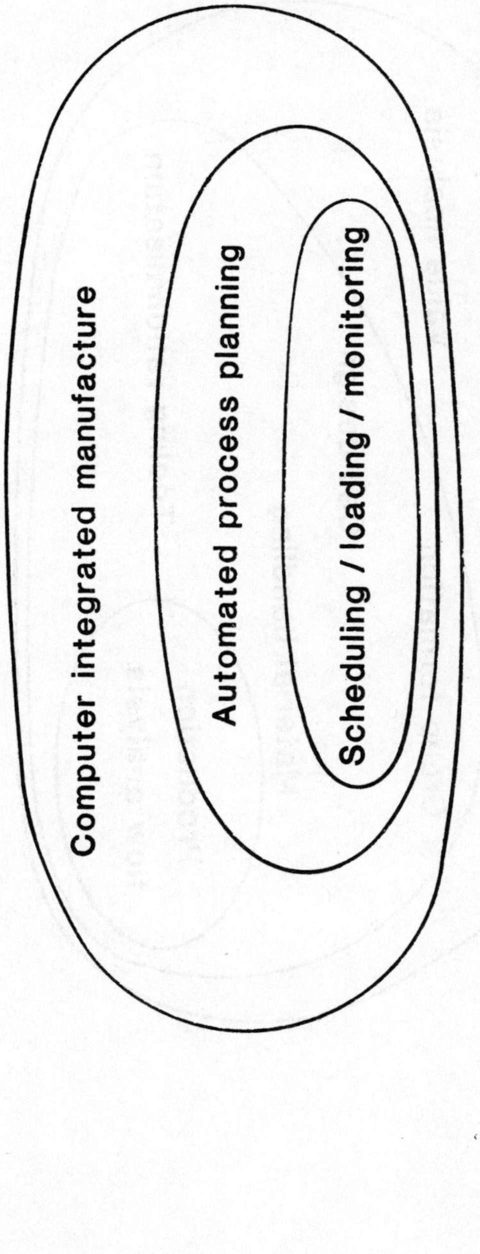

Figure 1 Domain representation describing integration problems of CIM

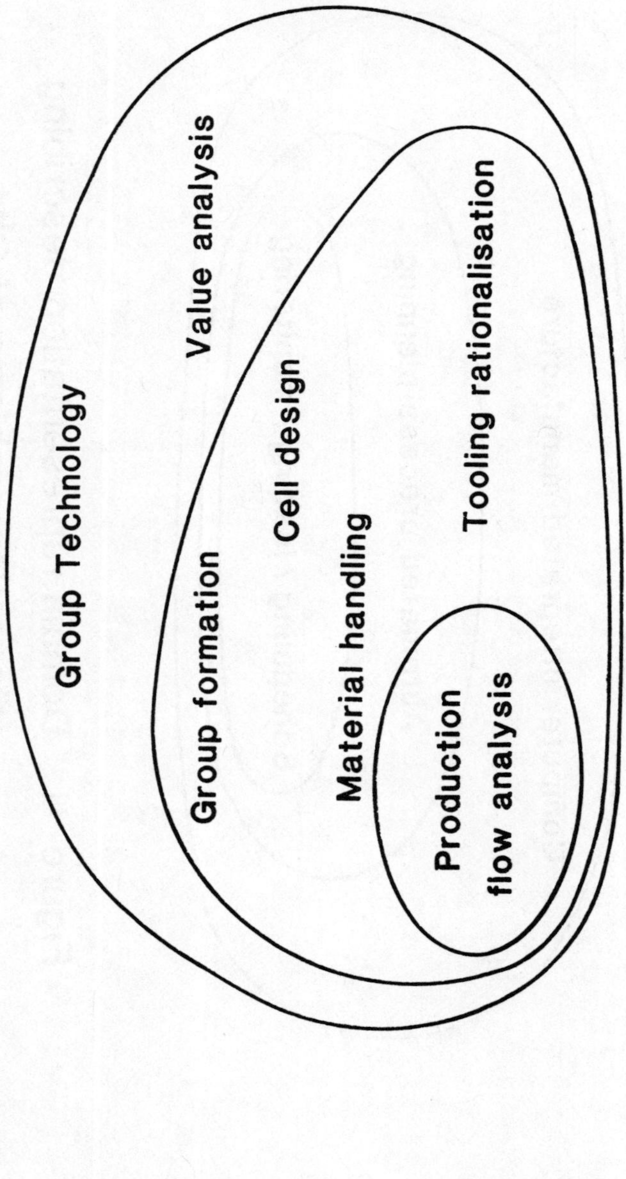

Figure 2 PFA within Group Technology A limitation of the effectiveness of PFA

PROKERN-XPS: A Mixed Architecture Expert System for Industrial Automation System Configuration

B.R. Clarke

Siemens AG, Corporate Research and Development, Dept. ZFE F 2 INF 31, Otto-Hahn-Ring 6, D-8000 Munich 83, FRG

ABSTRACT

One of the earliest and best-known configuration expert systems is R1, used for configuring VAX computers. Due to features of the domain and the configuration problem, R1 could be implemented as a rule system without the need for backtracking. In other domains, such as industrial automation system configuration, a simple R1-like approach is not possible because multiple types of knowledge and complex reasoning processes are employed within the configuration process. Instead, architectures employing a mixture of knowledge representations and inference mechanisms are demanded to tackle these more complex configuration tasks. An expert system for industrial automation system configuration with such a mixed architecture, PROKERN-XPS, is presented.

The first part of this paper argues that configuration is a sub-field of design, and aims to summarise some of the most important requirements for a configuration system for a complex configuration task. The second part describes a mixed architecture expert system to configure industrial automation systems, PROKERN-XPS, which satisfies all of the requirements. The domain of industrial automation system configuration is described, together with the architecture of PROKERN-XPS and the use of the Assumption-based Truth Maintenance System (ATMS) for representing configuration dependencies in PROKERN-XPS.

1 INTRODUCTION

There is a great deal of interest within industry in applying expert system techniques to automate the configuration process, in order to produce more optimal configurations, cheaper, more rapidly, with reduced human error, better documentation and improved repeatability. One of the earliest and best-known configuration systems is R1 (now named XCON) used successfully for configuring DEC VAX computers (McDermott [10]). Since R1, numerous other systems have been developed for different domains (Baginsky et al [1], Cunis et al [3], Marcus et al [9]) resulting in a clearer definition of configuration and its relation to the general field of design.

Due to features of R1's domain and configuration problem, the configuration task could be performed by a rule system without the need for backtracking. However, many configuration expert systems implemented since R1 address more complex configuration problems where multiple types of knowledge and complex reasoning processes are employed. On examining these systems, a number of basic requirements surface which must be satisfied to enable the system to successfully perform its task: *representation of the current (and possibly past) configuration state*; *recording of configuration decisions and the reasons behind them*; *representation of the goal structure*; *representation and usage of configuration constraints*; *the use of generative search*; *control of the configuration process*; and *representation of structure and function*. In order to meet these requirements, an R1-like approach is not possible, instead an architecture integrating different knowledge representations and inference techniques is required which will be referred to as a *mixed architecture* within this paper.

Siemens has long been active in the manufacture and installation of industrial automation systems. As automation technology becomes more powerful and sophisticated, the cost and time in configuring a system increases. In the last few years, the application of expert systems to assist the configuration engineer in industrial automation system configuration has been investigated to enable costs and time to be reduced (Baginsky et al [1]).

Configuration of industrial automation systems is an extremely complex process. The engineer adopts a *construct-and-revise* approach in configuring: on assembling objects from a given product range together to produce the automation system, it is impossible for the engineer to check all technical and functional constraints on a configuration are satisfied, so inconsistencies in the configuration, ie. constraint violations, are allowed to occur which are later resolved. In resolving an inconsistency a change is made to the configuration such that the violated constraint is satisfied. The consequences of this change are then propagated throughout the configuration by the engineer through knowledge of the dependencies between objects comprising the configuration. In assembling objects together a number of complex *configuration steps* corresponding to the breakdown of the objects in the product range may be performed in various sequences according to the strategy adopted by the engineer to meet the goals of a specific automation application. Additionally, in assembling objects a large amount of knowledge concerning the functionality as well as compositional structure of each object to be configured is needed.

Currently, an expert system called PROKERN-XPS, satisfying all of the previously stated requirements via the use of a mixed architecture, is being developed to assist a configuration engineer in his or her task. A blackboard system (Nii [13]) executes a *configuration cycle* emulating the construct-and-revise approach of the engineer. The configuration cycle consists of three phases: construction, consistency-checking; and conflict-resolution, each of which are performed by construction knowledge sources (KSs), a consistency-checking KS and a conflict-resolution KS respectively. *Construction Strategies* can be described which control the scheduling of the construction KSs allowing strategies adopted by the configuration engineer in assembling objects to be emulated. Knowledge describing how objects can be assembled and their individual properties is represented in a semantic net referred to as the *Construction Net*. A configuration is an instantiation of this net represented in a second semantic net referred to as the *Elaboration Net*.

On handling an inconsistency, the configuration engineer makes a change to the configuration and propagates the consequences of the change throughout the configuration through knowledge of dependencies between configuration goals (requirements of the automation system), configuration decisions and configuration components. In order to enable conflict-handling in PROKERN-XPS, dependencies had to be represented. They are represented in a dependency net implemented using the Assumption-based Truth Maintenance System (ATMS) of deKleer (deKleer [4]).

In this paper, firstly, the configuration process is defined and its relation to design clarified. Secondly, the requirements for configuration expert systems for complex configuration tasks are presented. Thirdly, the architecture and operation of PROKERN-XPS with reference to the requirements is described, and finally, representation and manipulation of configuration dependencies is discussed in detail.

2 WHAT IS CONFIGURATION?

Configuration as proposed by Navinchandra et al [12] is the process of assembling an artefact by piecing together generic objects chosen from a given set of objects. Configuration may involve the shaping and resizing of objects to fit the artefact, but does not involve mutations or creations of new forms. However, it must also be noted that the artefact must satisfy the goals of the configuration process, eg. functionality and cost. It is usually straightforward to assemble objects, but much more complex to guarantee that the resultant configuration is consistent, ie. is legal, suits cost requirements, produces the correct functionality, etc.

Examples of configuration can be taken from many different domains: configuration of computers to suit customer requirements from a company's component range, ie. from PCBs, racks, cabinets, power supplies (McDermott [10]); configuring of distributed automation systems to control industrial plants using components selected from a control equipment product range (Baginsky et al [1]); and configuring lift systems to suit customer requirements and building structural properties (Marcus et al [9]).

How does configuration relate to design? Navinchandra et al [12] differentiate between *configuration design*, which is basically the configuration process, and *formation design*, which involves mutating or fundamentally modifying the generic objects, eg. designing a vase involves the mutation of a cylinder object. Most everyday designs involve both of these processes. Configuration problems can be regarded as a narrow subset of design problems which consist of putting together generic objects from a given set of objects, with the restriction that they may be re-shaped or re-sized, but not mutated, to form an artefact that is consistent and fulfils a functional goal.

3 FUNDAMENTAL REQUIREMENTS

Through protocol analysis work with designers and configurers, and the development of expert systems for configuration and design, the configuration process has become better understood. Also resulting from this work is a clearer statement as to what the requirements of expert systems for automating a complex configuration process are:

(1) Representation of the configuration state: At any moment in the configuration process the state of the configuration, ie. the objects selected to make an artefact and how they are combined, must be represented (Mostow [11]). This is for two reasons: firstly, to allow the results of the design process to be communicated; and secondly, as a structure to be reasoned about. In a design office the configuration state is normally contained in engineering drawings or within a CAD system.

Within a configuration expert system, a dynamic structure is required to represent the current configuration state to allow it to be reasoned about. Each state of the configuration can be recorded to give the configuration history, enabling any previous state to be returned to, but can be expensive in storage requirements. This is useful if part of the configuration must be changed to overcome a design inconsistency. The configuration decision which led to the inconsistency can be *chronologically-backtracked* to, amended, and the configuration continued.

(2) Recording of configuration decisions and the reasons behind them: In order to configure an artefact to fulfil a specification, objects must be selected and assembled together. As the configuration evolves, numerous decisions between various options must be made and recorded (Mostow [11]). Regarding configuration as a search problem where the instantiation of a path through the search tree is a configuration, a configuration decision represents a commitment to a branch of the search tree. Configuration decisons range from the high-level, such as selecting a sub-plan to fulfil a goal, to the low-level, such as choosing between two minor components. Configuration decisions are implicitly recorded when the configuration state is recorded. Explicitly recording them in the chronological sequence in which they were made provides a history of the configuration process allowing it to be replayed.

When a configuration decision is made, it is based on some kind of reason or rationale. For example, components are selected because their combination satisfies the specification in some manner. A record of the reasons for a configuration decision enables the configuration route for an artefact to be explained.

The idea of recording design reasons can be extended to encompass all configuration dependencies enabling the provision of *dependency-directed backtracking*. If an inconsistency in the configuration arises, a change to the configuration can be made to overcome the problem and the consequences of the change can be propagated throughout the rest of the configuration (Clarke [2]). This has an advantage over chronological-backtracking where the configuration state at the point before the decision causing the inconsistency must be returned to in order to overcome the inconsistency causing loss of configuration work.

(3) Representation of the goal structure: Goals give a focus in the configuration process, providing a problem description and guiding the process. Objects are assembled to produce an artefact in such a manner that the artefact and the configuration process itself fulfils the goals. The goals that have to be satisfied can be of several types: functional, eg. a specification of the artefact's functionality or performance; cost, eg. cost of part of the final artefact; and configuration process goals, eg. minimising configuration costs or time. They can often be represented in a tree structure (Mostow [11]).

(4) Representing and using configuration constraints: Configuration constraints describe how objects relate to one another and restrictions on their properties. When an artefact is configured, the objects comprising it must obey all the configuration constraints, ie. it must be legal. For instance, a simple constraint between a nut and bolt is that in order for them to fasten together the diameter of the nut's hole equals the diameter of the bolt's shaft. Configuration constraints can be used in two modes:

- To select objects or determine the values of their properties: Configuration constraints are used to construct the artefact by determining the objects comprising the artefact or the values of the objects' properties. Taking the previous example, if the diameter of the bolt's shaft is known, then the diameter of the nut's hole can be determined.

- To check the consistency of a partially or completely configured artefact: Again recalling the previous example, the diameter of the bolt's shaft must equal the diameter of the nut's hole in the partially or completely configured artefact.

When configuring, a balance must be found between both these modes. It can be computationally too expensive to check that every constraint holds when selecting an object or determining the value of an object's property in order to avoid configuration inconsistencies. However, if too many inconsistencies arise, modifying the configuration to overcome them can be prohibitively expensive.

(5) Generative search: Configuration is a form of generative or synthesis search which operates by constructing an item from sub-items and results in a large solution space (Dietterich et al [6]). This is extremely different from the approach of most current expert systems, which only consider a pre-enumerated set of possible solutions (often referred to as "classification" systems).

(6) Control of the configuration process: The simplest form of control is depth or breadth-first search often employed by classification expert sysems. This is not feasible in a configuration expert system, because the design search-space is vast. Therefore, strategies incorporating knowledge of the configuration domain must be adopted to guide and optimise the search process.

(7) Representation of structure and function: An artefact is assembled from objects, therefore, the artefact inherently has a compositional structure. For example, a computer is assembled from processor, memory and I/O boards, power supplies, cables and racks, and in turn the boards are assembled from a printed circuit board, chips, resistors, capacitors, etc.

A formalism for representing structure needs to be provided in a configuration expert system. This is especially so for configuration systems in technical domains such as mechanical, electrical or civil engineering domains (Dietterich et al [6]). This formalism can be extended to describe functionality. Usually, not only is structure of individual objects and artifacts needed, but also the functionality (Struss [15]). Returning to the example, a functional description of each object is required in order to assemble the computer, eg. a memory board is a storage mechanism for X amount of data with an access time of Y microseconds.

4 PROKERN-XPS

In this section, a configuration expert system with a mixed architecture, PROKERN-XPS, that meets the requirements previously stated is described.

4.1 The Domain

A client requests Siemens to provide an automation system which will control their process. The size of the process can vary from small bakeries to large steel rolling mills, and the type of process can vary from continuous or discrete process control to power distribution. The client describes in detail the process, the equipment the automation system is to control, and the high-level functionality of the automation system. It is now the task of one or more configuration engineers to configure an automation system from items in a distributed multi-computer product range to control the process. Fig. 1 shows an extremely simple configuration, nb. it is not unusual to have over a hundred sub-systems in a configuration. Configuration is usually split into two main parts:

Part I - Functional decomposition: The function of the automation system is decomposed into sub-functions so that it can be mapped onto concrete hardware and software in the second part of configuration. The function is decomposed in a top-down manner into four levels: operations; process; group; and component control levels. For example, the top-level function to *control the process* is split into *monitoring*, *diagnosis* and *control* functions, and in turn, *control* is split into functions controlling individual machines, see the top of Fig. 2. This is a technique widely used throughout control engineering.

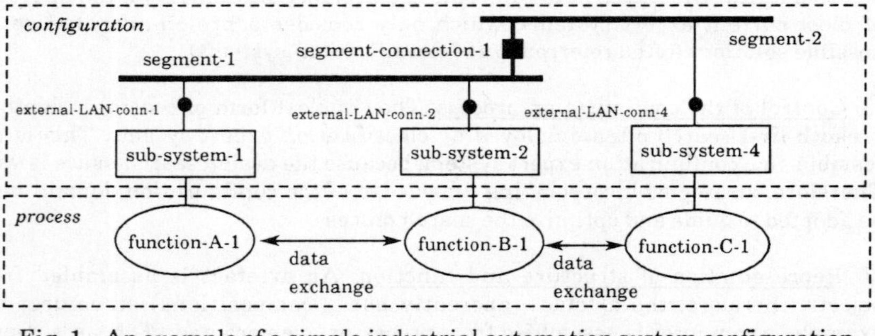

Fig. 1 An example of a simple industrial automation system configuration

Part II - Hardware and software configuration: The results from the first part, functional decomposition, are mapped onto automation system hardware and software. Hardware and software configuration is carried out in parallel. The hardware configuration process is composed of functional and spatial configuration.

Functional configuration is made up of a number of configuration steps: system overview; sub-system configuration; rack configuration; and board parameterisation, see the right side of Fig. 2. In the system overview step, the functions and data flow requirements between the functions (from functional decomposition) are mapped onto sub-systems of various types and Local Area

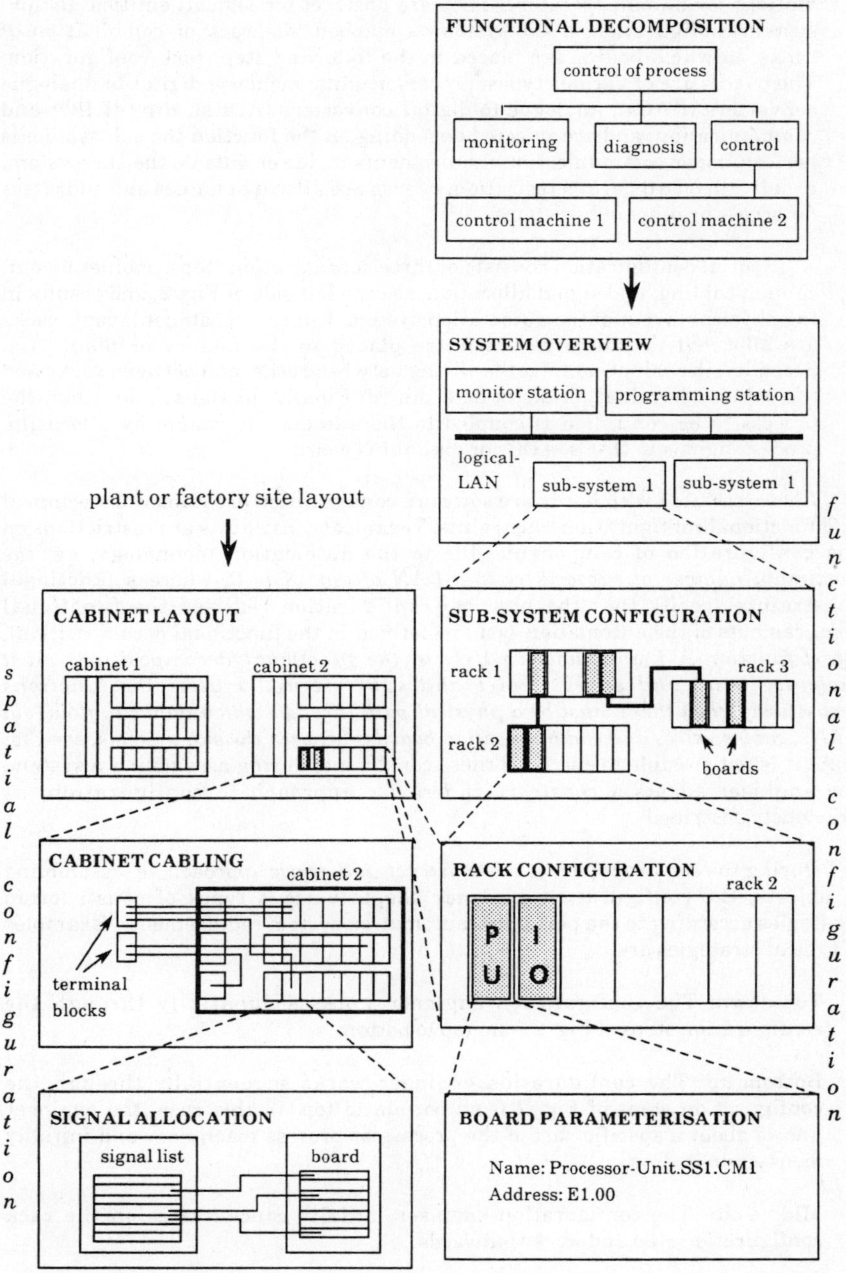

Fig. 2 The configuration process for an industrial automation system

Networks (LANs) or point-to-point connections (cables) respectively. Sub-systems can be units controlling one or more machines in the process, stations for programming the automation system, or process monitoring/supervisory stations for human operators. They are abstract (or logical) entities. In sub-system configuration, a sub-system is mapped to a rack or combination of racks, in which boards are placed in the following step, rack configuration. The boards are of various types: processor units; memory; digital-to-analogue converters (DACs); analogue-to-digital converters (ADCs); digital I/O; and communication, and are selected depending on the function the sub-system is performing or communication requirements inside or outside the sub-system. Finally, in board parameterisation, boards are allocated names and addresses for access by other sub-systems.

Spatial configuration consists of three configuration steps: cabinet layout; cabinet cabling; and signal allocation, see the left side of Fig. 2, and results in the physical layout of the automation system. Firstly, in cabinet layout, racks are allocated to cabinets, which are placed in the factory or plant site. Secondly, in cabinet cabling, the wiring between racks, and between racks and the cabinet terminal blocks is determined. Finally, in signal allocation, the process to be controlled is coupled to the automation system by allocating process signals to DACs, ADCs or digital I/O boards.

Also associated with hardware/software configuration are numerous technical and functional configuration constraints. Technical constraints are restrictions on the configuration of components due to the automation technology, eg. *the maximum number of subscribers to a LAN of type X is 8,* whereas functional constraints specify that the physical configuration realises the functional requirements of the automation system (defined in the functional decomposition), eg. *if function-A-1 and function-B-1 (in the functional decomposition) must exchange data, and sub-system-1 and sub-system-2 realise the functions respectively, then there must be a physical path through which data can flow (via LANs, cables, wires and communication boards) between the sub-systems,* see Fig. 1. As it is not possible to check all these constraints during assembling a system, the engineer adopts a *construct-and-revise* approach to configuration, as previously described.

During the construct part of the *construct-and-revise* approach, ie. assembling of objects, the configuration engineer adopts various types of construction strategies according to the particular automation system requirements. Examples of typical strategies are:

- Top-down: The configuration engineer works sequentially through the configuration steps of Fig. 2 from top to bottom.

- Bottom-up: The configuration engineer works sequentially through the configuration steps of Fig. 2 from bottom to top. In this case, the engineer knows about a specific part of the process or process machinery and initially focusses on it.

- Middle-out: The configuration engineer initially concentrates on the rack configuration step and works outwards.

- Mixed: The engineer does not sequentially work through the steps, but adopts a strategy combining those previously listed, so he or she 'jumps' around from step to step according to the task. This often happens when the engineer concentrates on a specific part of the configuration and wants to fully develop it before continuing with the rest.

4.2 Function

PROKERN-XPS is an expert system for configuring an industrial distributed multi-microcomputer automation systems from a particular range of process control products (Siemens MMC-216). As the domain is so large, the application area of PROKERN-XPS has been limited to only hardware configuration for the three configuration steps: system overview; sub-system configuration; and rack configuration, as shown in Fig. 2.

PROKERN-XPS configures an automation system from a given set of requirements (the desired functionality of the automation system resulting from the functional decomposition) under the control of a configuration engineer, who is also the domain expert. The configuration engineer can invoke automatic configuration (as explained in the following section), choose components when a choice is insufficiently restricted to be made automatically, and configure manually, because the system cannot handle a part of a configuration due to omissions in its knowledge base, or because the configuration engineer is dissatisfied with the system's results.

4.3 The Configuration Cycle: Phases and Modes

It was decided to have a configuration cycle (similar to that described by Cunis et al [3] and Gray [8]) made up of three configuration phases: construction; consistency-checking; and conflict-resolution, because this appeared to be consistent with the phases in the *construct-and-revise* approach adopted by configuration engineers, and also it facilitated the provision of the two modes of operation and switching between these modes in a single consultation, see Fig. 3(a).

In the first configuration phase, construction, the configuration is built up by selecting components, eg. boards, racks, LANs and cables, and assembling them to fulfil the functional requirements of the automation system. In the manual mode this is executed by the configuration engineer using the system in a CAD-like fashion, and in the automatic mode is executed by the system, see Fig. 3(b). However, in both modes a single static knowledge base is accessed for configuration knowledge or data, eg. component types and relations between components, and a single dynamic knowledge base (holding the configuration state) is modified.

During the construction configuration phase, it is possible for either the system or the user to create inconsistent configurations: configurations that are not technically realisable, eg. more than 18 boards allocated to an 18-slot rack; or configurations which do not match the functional specification of the required automation system, eg. a sub-system cannot perform the automation function it is supposed to because it does not have access to the data it requires. Therefore, in the second configuration phase, consistency-checking, the system determines

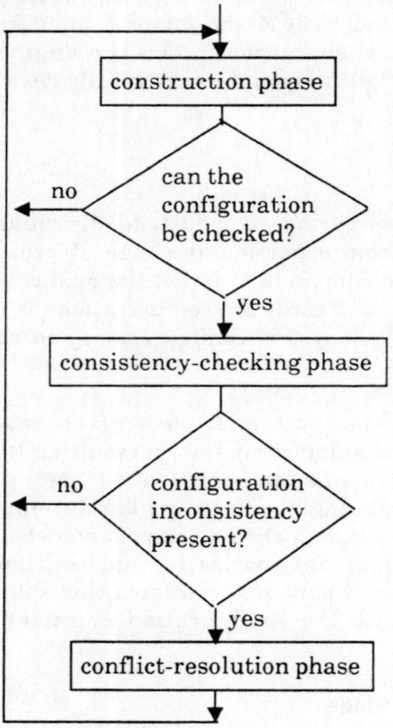

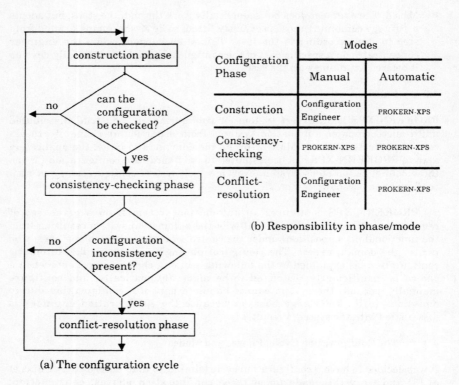

(a) The configuration cycle

Configuration Phase	Modes	
	Manual	Automatic
Construction	Configuration Engineer	PROKERN-XPS
Consistency-checking	PROKERN-XPS	PROKERN-XPS
Conflict-resolution	Configuration Engineer	PROKERN-XPS

(b) Responsibility in phase/mode

Fig.3 The modes and phases of PROKERN-XPS

whether any inconsistencies have arisen in the configuration, if so, the conflict-resolution phase is entered, otherwise, the construction phase is returned to.

In the third configuration phase, conflict-resolution, changes are made to the configuration to overcome an inconsistency and these are propagated throughout the rest of the configuration. In the manual mode, this is carried out by the configuration engineer using the system in a CAD-like fashion, and in the automatic mode it is carried out by the system. In cases where the system cannot resolve a conflict, it indicates its inability and calls upon the configuration engineer to resolve the problem. This facility is required as resolving conflicts is one of the most complex tasks in industrial automation system configuration, and thus sometimes for large configurations the system will not be able to cope. Once an inconsistency has been resolved, the construction phase is re-entered. At the boundaries between phases, an alternative mode can be selected in the following phase.

4.4 Architecture and Operation

4.4.1 Why a *Mixed Architecture*?

During the three configuration phases of PROKERN-XPS, different knowledge types and reasoning processes are adopted, and also manual and automatic modes must coexist within the same system, giving rise to the need for a mixed architecture, as shown in Fig. 4, employing a number of different knowledge representations and a sophisticated inference control mechanism:

- Construction knowledge and the configuration state are represented using semantic nets as this allows the relations between objects and the properties of objects to be efficiently captured.

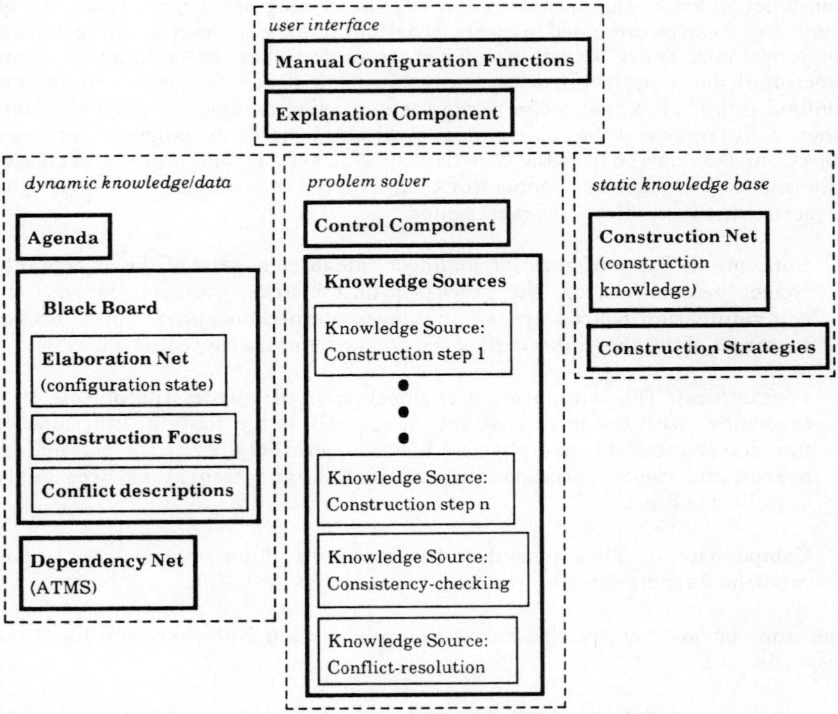

Fig.4 Overview of PROKERN-XPS' architecture

- Construction execution knowledge is represented as a mixture of meta-rules, where default values are used in configuration, and domain rules, where heuristics are used.

- Constraints and conflict handling knowledge is represented as domain rules as these allow heuristics employed by the configuration engineer to be represented easily.

- The overall automatic configuration process is performed by a blackboard architecture. In the construction phase, it is guided by a Construction Strategy described using a simple strategy description language. A blackboard architecture enables multiple types of knowledge to be used in the reasoning process and its control component can be implemented such that construction strategies employed by the configuration engineer can be emulated by the system.

- Configuration dependencies (reasons or rationale) are represented using deKleer's ATMS (deKleer [4]) as this provides an efficient and domain-independent form of representing dependencies. It also allows configuration inconsistencies to be represented so they are not re-encountered.

4.4.2 Construction knowledge (The Construction Net)

Construction knowledge is static knowledge describing how objects relate to one another and can be combined to create a configuration, ie. it describes all potential configurations. These objects can be abstract concepts, eg. a function (from functional decomposition) or physical objects, eg. boards (from sub-system configuration). This knowledge is represented using a semantic net formalism where nodes represent the object classes and links describe the properties between objects, and is referred to as the Construction Net, see Fig. 5(a). The object classes fall into two categories: connections; and non-connections. The following properties between objects are represented:

- Conceptual: The configuration engineer categorises many of the objects into conceptual classes, eg. the processor unit boards, memory boards and communication boards are all instances of the conceptual class, board. Instances of the class inherit all of the properties of the conceptual class.

- Hierarchical: The configuration engineer mentally places the objects in a taxonomy with the most abstract (or logical) at the top, eg. functions or function connections, and physical (or real world) objects at the bottom, eg. boards and racks, corresponding to the configuration steps previously described in Fig. 2.

- Compositional: This describes the make-up of an object, that is the components comprising it.

The links between object classes in the Construction Net representing these properties are:

- *is-a* describes how one object may be a specialisation of another. Consider the relation, *logical-LAN is-a ss-connection,* from Fig. 5(a). This means a logical LAN is a specialisation of a sub-system connection.

- *has-parts* describes the non-connectional sub-objects comprising an object. Consider the relation, *sub-system has-parts 1 central-rack and 0...2 extension-racks,* from Fig. 5(a). This means that the non-connectional part of a sub-system comprises of a central rack only or a central-rack and one or two extension racks.

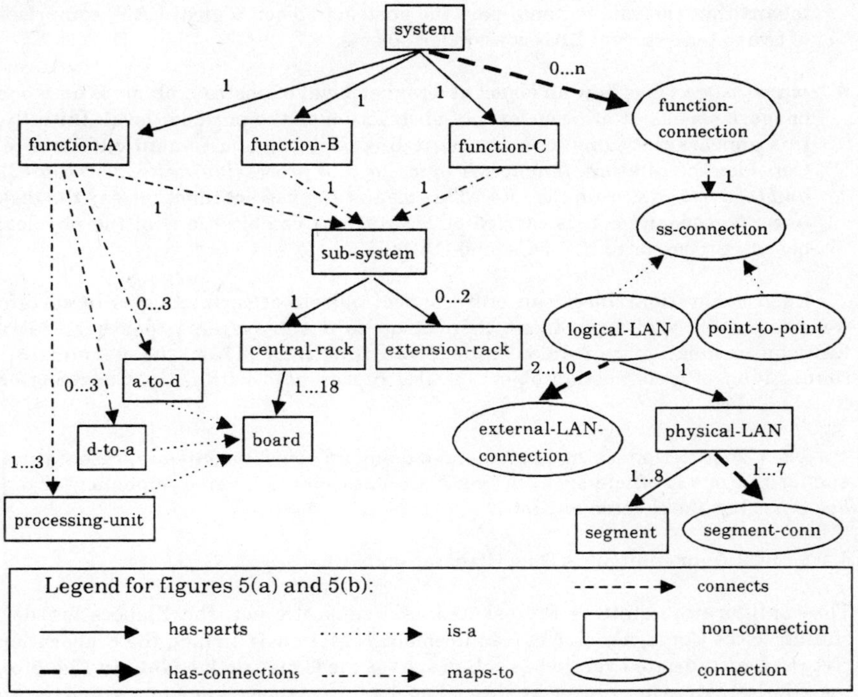

Fig. 5(a) Example of a Construction Net (nb. nodes are object classes)

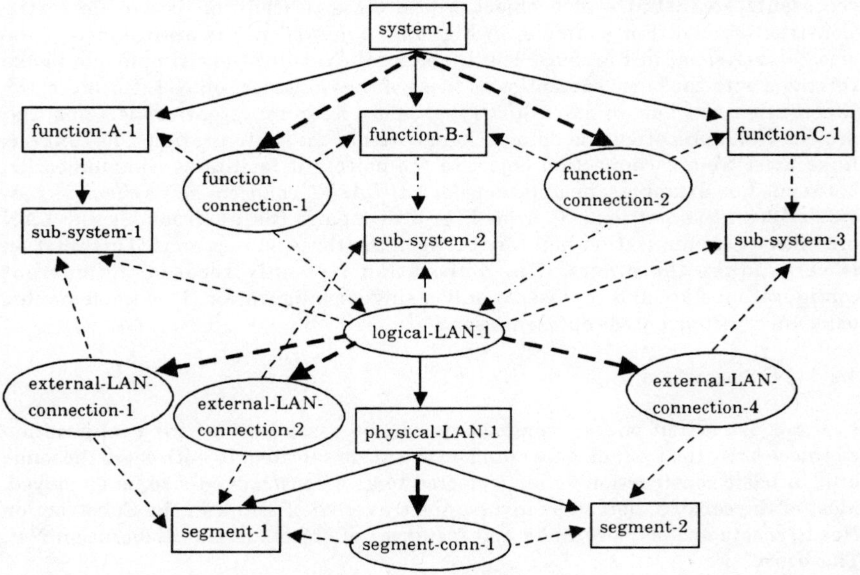

Fig. 5(b) Example of an Elaboration Net (nodes are object instances)

- *has-connections* is similar to the *has-parts* relation, but describes the connection sub-objects comprising an object. For example, the relation, *logical-LAN has-connections 2..10 external-LAN-connections,* from Fig. 5(a), means that the connectional part the abstract object, logical LAN, comprises of two to ten external LAN connection objects.

- *maps-to* describes how an object at a higher level of abstraction maps onto one or more objects at a lower level of abstraction or the physical level. Initially, this appears the same as a *has-parts* link, but it has a semantic difference. Consider the relation, *function-A maps-to 1...3 processing-units, 0...3 a-to-d's and 0...3 d-to-a's*, from Fig. 5(a). This means an abstract function, say the task to control machine 1, is carried out by various combinations of the physical boards: processor unit; ADCs; and DACs.

Each connection object can only connect objects of certain types in certain ways, eg. a LAN of type X can connect up to 8 sub-systems together, but a function-connection can only connect two functions. This, the permissible connectivity of a connection object, is also represented within the Construction Net.

The Construction Net is implemented using an object-oriented representation, and for reasons of efficiency each link has an associated inverse implemented, eg. *has-parts* has the inverse *is-part-of.*

4.4.3 Configuration State (The Elaboration Net)

The configuration state is represented as a semantic net, the Elaboration net, similar to the Construction Net (requirement 1, section 3). In fact, the Elaboration Net is an instantiated version (a sub-graph) of the Construction Net. In Fig. 5(b), the configuration of Fig. 1 is described by an elaboration net, which is an instantiation of the Construction Net shown in Fig. 5(a). An Elaboration Net node represents an instance of a object whose class description is a node in the Construction Net. For example, in Fig. 5(b), *sub-system-1* is an instance of the class, *sub-system*, in Fig. 5(a). The Elaboration Net links are simple one-to-one relations with the same semantics as those of the Construction Net. However, the Elaboration Net has an extra link type, *connects*, to represent connections that provide communication and data exchange within the configuration. The *connects* links exist from a connection object to the objects it facilitates communication between. For example, the relation, *logical-LAN-1 connects sub-system-1, sub-system-2 and sub-system-3,* from Fig. 5(b) means the abstract logical LAN provides a communication highway between the three sub-systems. This relation is very unlike the others. The Elaboration Net only records the current configuration state and represents only a single configuration. It is implemented using an object-oriented representation.

4.4.4 Construction

In the construction phase, components can be assembled by the configuration engineer or by the system, depending on the mode selected. In both cases the same kind of basic construction action, referred to as a *construction step,* is employed. Most of the construction steps involve the traversal of a link in the Construction Net to create one or more links and instances of objects in the Elaboration Net. These are:

- Decomposition-parts: In this step an object instance in the Elaboration Net is decomposed into its non-connectional constituents which are found by traversing the *has-parts* links of the object's class in the Construction Net. Consider decomposing the object instance, *physical-LAN-1*, in Fig. 5(b). Initially the class of the object is found in the Construction Net, *physical-LAN*, and the *has-parts* links are traversed to find a *physical-LAN* can be decomposed into one to eight *segments*, see fig. 5(a). In this case, *physical-LAN-1* is decomposed into two segments, *segment-1* and *segment-2*.

- Aggregation-parts: In this step the *has-parts* link is traversed in the reverse direction. A set of object instances in the Elaboration Net with the same parent is found, and an instance of the parent with *has-parts* links to the child object instances is created in the Elaboration Net.

- Decomposition-connections and Aggregation-connections: These steps are basically the same as decomposition-parts and aggregation-parts, respectively, but use the *has-connections* links.

- Transformation-to: In this step an object instance in the Elaboration Net is transformed into objects at a lower level of abstraction that realise it. These are found by traversing the *maps-to* links from the instance's class in the Construction Net.

- Transformation-from: In this step, the *maps-to* link is traversed in the reverse direction. A group of object instances in the Elaboration Net realising an object at a higher level of abstraction are found, and an instance of the higher level object with *maps-to* links is created in the Elaboration Net.

- Specialisation: In this step an object instance in the Elaboration Net is specialised by traversing in the reverse direction the *is-a* link to the instance's class in the Construction Net. No new links or instances in the Elaboration Net are created, instead the existing object instance is given the properties of the specialised object.

Other construction steps not involving a link traversal are:

- Connection: When two or more object instances in the Elaboration Net can be connected together, an instance of an appropriate connection object with *connects* links from it to the instances requiring to be connected is created in the Elaboration Net.

- Parameterisation: A property of an object instance in the Elaboration Net is given a value, eg. a processing unit board is given an address.

During the construction phase, in both modes, the reasons (dependencies) for a component's existence are recorded within a dependency net based upon deKleer's ATMS. The representation and use of the dependency net is discussed in a later section.

4.4.4.1 Manual Construction

The configuration engineer performs construction (and conflict-resolution) by using the system in a CAD-like fashion to execute construction steps. Manual

Configuration Functions implemented in LISP can be invoked, each of which executes a construction step in an interactive fashion. For example, on the manual configuration function, decomposition-parts, being invoked, the user is asked to select an object to be decomposed. The user 'mouses' on the object and the system displays a pull-down menu listing all the sub-objects the selected object can be decomposed to. The system retrieves this knowledge from the Construction Net by finding the class of the selected object instance in the Construction Net, and traversing the *has-parts* links from it. The user then selects one or more objects, and the system creates instances of these objects with *has-parts* links in the Elaboration Net. In manual construction the configuration engineer is provided with an extra construction step, deletion.

4.4.4.2 Automatic Construction

Blackboard architecture: Automatic construction is performed using a blackboard architecture (Nii [13]), as are consistency-checking and automatic conflict-resolution (described in the following sections). In automatic construction, each construction step is implemented as a Knowledge Source (KS) comprising of two parts: a precondition and an execution component.

A construction KS precondition determines the applicability of the KS by finding object instances in the Elaboration Net that can be processed, ie. object instances to which the construction step is suitable. Also, the KS precondition infers if the construction step the KS performs fits into the Construction Strategy by examining the Construction Focus (this will be clarified in the following sub-section). If the KS is applicable, it generates an agenda entry specifying the construction step, object instances involved in the step and any other relevant information to aid the control component. An example domain-independent rule (in an English-like format) from the decomposition-parts KS precondition is:

if decomposition-parts construction step is permitted by Construction Focus &
Elaboration Net object instance <OI> can be decomposed &
Construction Focus permits the step to be performed on <OI>
then create an agenda entry stating decomposition-parts on object instance <OI> can be executed

When the blackboard control component selects an agenda entry for execution, the KS execution component for the KS specified in the agenda entry carries out the construction step. It modifies the Elaboration Net using knowledge held within the Construction Net. An example domain-independent rule (in an English-like format) from the decomposition-parts KS construction component is:

if object instance <OI> is to be decomposed (from agenda entry)
then find object class <OC> in Construction Net corresponding to <OI> &
for <OC>, find the child object classes <COCs> with default numbers of each <Ns> to which <OC> can be decomposed to by traversing the has-parts links from <OC> &
for each child object class <COCs>, create the default number of instances as specified by <Ns> in the Elaboration Net with has-parts links from the object instance <OI> to the newly created instances (updating the dependency net with justifications)

Each KS has domain-independent rules, as in the previous examples, and domain-dependent rules, where heuristics specific to the product range being configured are encoded. If a new product range is switched to, the domain-dependent rules and Construction Net would be discarded. A new Construction Net would be created using the same representation (links and object classes) and the domain-independent rules would be re-employed.

In order to perform automatic construction, a specification of the automation system is required (requirement 3, section 3). The configuration engineer provides this by entering a functional description of the required automation system (obtained from functional decomposition) using the manual construction functions. This consists of the functions and function-connections, and is used as the goal of automatic construction.

When a configuration engineer performs the construction process, he or she does not do it in a random, ad-hoc fashion for reasons of efficiency and economy. Instead, a construction strategy is employed (consciously or unconsciously). Within PROKERN-XPS we have attempted to model this cognitive strategy to enable PROKERN-XPS to construct systems in a computationally efficient manner (requirement 6, section 3). In order to capture and use strategies within PROKERN-XPS, the control of the basic blackboard architecture has been augmented. There are two points where control can be effected within the basic blackboard system: by limiting and focussing the number of agenda entries generated during KS precondition firing; and by determining which agenda entry is selected for execution. Control is affected at both of these points through the use of the Construction Focus, Construction Strategies and Control Component mechanisms.

Construction Focus: In the automation system configuration domain, configurations can be large (several hundred components) resulting in many construction steps being possible at one instance. Therefore, if agenda generation is left unregulated, it could take a long time to generate the agenda (a KS precondition match per configuration step) and the resulting agenda could contain a vast number of entries. The Construction Focus has thus been introduced to limit and focus agenda entry generation. It consists of dynamic data on the blackboard. Each KS has a precondition that checks the Construction Focus to determine if it is applicable. The Construction Focus consists of a number of Construction Focus Units (CFUs). Within each CFU it is possible to specify a construction step to be executed, construction method (take defaults or use heuristics), object class and object instance. For example, the Construction Focus with the following two CFUs would limit the agenda entries to KSs executing either the decomposition construction step on sub-systems or the parameteristion construction step to board-B1 only.

Construction Focus:

Construction Focus Unit: 1	Construction Focus Unit: 2
Construction step: decomposition	Construction step: parameterisation
Construction method: unspecified	Construction method: unspecified
Object class: sub-system	Object class: unspecified
Object instance: unspecified	Object instance: board-B1

The contents of the Construction Focus are set by the Control Component interpreting the Construction Strategy.

Construction Strategies: A Construction Strategy describes how the automatic construction process should be performed and is interpreted by the Control Component. This interpretation is employed by the Control Component to set up the Construction Focus, which limits the number of KS preconditions triggering, ie. the agenda size, and once the agenda has been generated, to select an agenda entry for execution. Thus, the basic blackboard execution cycle has now been modified to:

1. Setting up of Construction Focus (CFUs) by the Control Component interpreting the Construction Strategy.
2. KS preconditions trigger adding entries to the agenda.
3. Agenda entry selection by the Control Component using the Construction Strategy.
4. Execution of KS execution component corresponding to the agenda entry.

In order to allow the configuration engineer to describe strategies, a simple strategy representation language was required. To determine the language's format, the key features describing a strategy were found:

- Preference: A part of the configuration or construction step is preferred over another (preference A), so it is constructed first. When no more work can be done on it, the next highest preferred part or construction step (preference B) is worked on. If this enables more work to be carried out on a part or construction step of higher preference (preference A), then this is returned to and worked on next.

- Sequence: Parts of the configuration and construction steps are given an order for their development and execution respectively. So, the first configuration part or construction step in the sequence is initially worked on, followed by the second, etc. If a step allows more work to be done in a previous step, the previous step is not re-selected until the complete sequence has been worked on, ie. after the last step.

- Construction method: For each part of the configuration and each construction step, the configuration engineer employs a method for developing the configuration part or executing the construction step: default, where default numbers or values of object properties are taken; and heuristics learnt from experience.

Most of the strategies can be described by a combination of the previous terms. These were adopted as the keywords in a simple language to describe construction strategies. A simple example of a Construction Strategy described using this language is:

```
(sequence (preference   (decomposition-parts default functions)
                        (transformation-to heuristic function-connections))
          (sequence     (decomposition-parts default sub-systems)
                        (transformation-to default functions)
                        (decomposition-parts heuristics logical-LAN))
          (preference   (unspecified default PU-boards)
                        (unspecified heuristics memory-boards)))
```

This strategy consists of three main steps to be procedurally executed. In the first step decomposition of functions using default rules is preferred over transformation of function-connections using heuristics. The second step comprises of three sub-steps: decomposition of any sub-system using default rules; transformation of any function using default rules; and decomposition of any logical-LAN using heuristics. Finally, in the third step, the execution of any construction step on PU boards using defaults is preferred over any construction step on memory boards using heuristics.

4.4.4.3 Swapping Between Manual and Automatic Construction

The configuration process commences in the construction phase in manual mode in which the configuration engineer can construct using the Manual Configuration Functions. At any point during this phase the automatic mode can be selected. On entering the mode the user selects a Construction Strategy and sets the *construction increment* which specifies how much work the system should do before returning to the user: after a rule firing; completion of a knowledge source; or completion of a step in the strategy. PROKERN-XPS then commences automatic construction for one construction increment, and returns to the configuration engineer after its completion.

4.4.5 Consistency-checking

At any point in the manual mode during the construction phase, the configuration engineer can enter the consistency-checking phase. In the consistency-checking phase in both modes, the configuration constraints are used to determine the consistency of a configuration with respect to technical and functional constraints. Constraints are represented as rules within a KS specifically dedicated to consistency-checking, as shown in Fig. 4, which is scheduled on the mode being selected. A consistency-checking rule matches on objects within the Elaboration Net. When a configuration inconsistency is found, the rule's consequent posts an inconsistency description object on the blackboard and marks the inconsistency within the ATMS-based dependency net (described in a later section). The inconsistency description object contains a summary of the inconsistency and data used in handling the inconsistency in the conflict-resolution phase. An example rule to check the fictitious technical constraint, *two or less subscribers (eg. sub-systems) can be connected to a LAN segment is:*

if a LAN segment <LS > in the Elaboration Net exists &
segment <LS> has more than 2 subscribers
then create conflict description object on blackboard (containing "over-subscribed LAN segment" and <LS>) &
mark conflict in dependency net with a justification of the node *FALSE*

It is hoped later to partition the rules within consistency-checking knowledge source into more knowledge sources or rule classes to allow more control over consistency-checking.

4.4.6 Conflict-resolution

When an inconsistency is found the conflict-resolution phase is entered. Initially the configuration engineer selects the mode required: manual; or automatic, and then resolution commences as selected.

4.4.6.1 Manual Conflict-resolution

During the conflict-resolution phase, in the manual mode, configuration inconsistencies are resolved by the configuration engineer. A description of the inconsistency discovered in the previous phase is displayed using data from the inconsistency description object. The configuration engineer then uses manual configuration functions (which implement construction steps such as delete, aggregation, etc.) to overcome the inconsistency.

4.4.6.2 Automatic Conflict-resolution

During the conflict-resolution phase, in the automatic mode, inconsistencies are handled by PROKERN-XPS using a form of *knowledge-based backtracking* as implemented in the lift configuration system VT (Marcus et al [9]). Heuristics employed by configuration engineers to resolve conflicts, referred to as *fixes*, are encoded in the form of domain-dependent rules within a KS dedicated to conflict-resolution. A conflict-resolution rule's antecedent matches on an inconsistency description object on the blackboard to which it is appropriate, and its consequent modifies the configuration to overcome the inconsistency. An example of a conflict-handling rule for overcoming an over-subscribed LAN segment (as detected by the rule in the previous section) is:

if conflict description object with description "over-subscibed LAN segment" for segment <LS>
then disconnect subscriber last added <S> from over-subscribed segment <LS> via switching the current context of the dependency net &
create a new LAN segment <NLS> (updating dependency net with justification) &
connect new segment <NLS> to existing segment <LS> (updating dependency net with justification) &
connect uncoupled subscriber <S> to new segment <NLS> (updating dependency net with justification)

In this rule, an *over-subscribed LAN segment* inconsistency is resolved by disconnecting the last subscriber (a sub-system) connected, joining a second LAN segment to the first and connecting the disconnected sub-system to the second segment. The references to the current context of the dependency net and dependency net updating are explained in the next section. In some cases the system is not able to resolve the conflict, so the system switches to the manual mode and asks the configuration engineer to resolve the conflict.

5 USING THE ATMS TO REPRESENT CONFIGURATION DEPENDENCIES

5.1 Why Represent Dependencies?

From the required operation of PROKERN-XPS, it can be seen that dependencies between requirements, configuration decisions and configuration components need to be recorded in order to:

- inform the configuration engineer of the consequences of changing requirements or configuration decisions, or removing a configuration component during the construction and conflict-resolution phase (in manual mode);

- prevent loss of configuration results when recovering from configuration inconsistencies in the conflict-resolution phase (in either modes). The system must not be forced to backtrack to the point where a decision causing an inconsistency was made in order to retract this decision and recover from the inconsistency during conflict-resolution (requirement 2, section 3);

- facilitate explanation.

5.2 Mapping Configuration Dependencies onto the ATMS

We are using the Assumption-based Truth Maintenance System (ATMS) of deKleer (deKleer [4], deKleer [5], Dressler et al [7] and Reinfrank [14]) to record configuration dependencies. The mapping of configuration dependencies onto the ATMS is such:

- Requirements and configuration decisions map onto ATMS *assumptions*. In Fig. 6, *R:function-A-1* (control function A of process), *R:function-B-1* (control function B of process) and *R:functions A & B comm* (functions A and B exchange data, ie. communicate) are requirements, and *CD:functions A & B comm over segment-1* (sub-systems 1 and 2 communicate over LAN segment 1) is a configuration decision.

- Configuration objects (the existence of) map onto ATMS *nodes*. In Fig. 6, *sub-system-1*, *sub-system-2*, *segment-1*, *external-lan-connections-1* and *external-lan-connection-2* are configuration components.

- Dependencies of configuration components on requirements and configuration decisions map onto ATMS *justifications*. In cases where KS rules are being used to infer configuration components, usually the *justification's antecedent* is the instantiated rule's premise and the *justification's consequent* is the instantiated rule's conclusion. The *informant* of the *justification* records the reason for the configuration component, ie. the rule name. In Fig. 6, *R1* (rule 1) through to *R5* (rule 5) are informants of justifications.

- A configuration maps onto an ATMS *context*. In Fig. 6, the resultant configuration is the context of the set of assumptions, {*R:function-A-1*, *R:function-B-1*, *R:functions A & B comm*, *CD:functions A & B comm over segment-1*}.

5.3 Operation

The operation is demonstrated through the use of the example shown in Fig. 6.

<u>Generating the dependency net</u>: The dependency net is constructed during the construction phase of the configuration cycle, as shown in Fig. 3(a). For example, referring to Fig. 6, in the automatic mode, when the transformation-to KS rule *R1* determines that *sub-system-1* is required, it adds the dependence of the existence of *sub-system-1* on the existence of *function-A-1* in the form of a justification with the rule as the informant. In the manual mode, dependencies are determined and

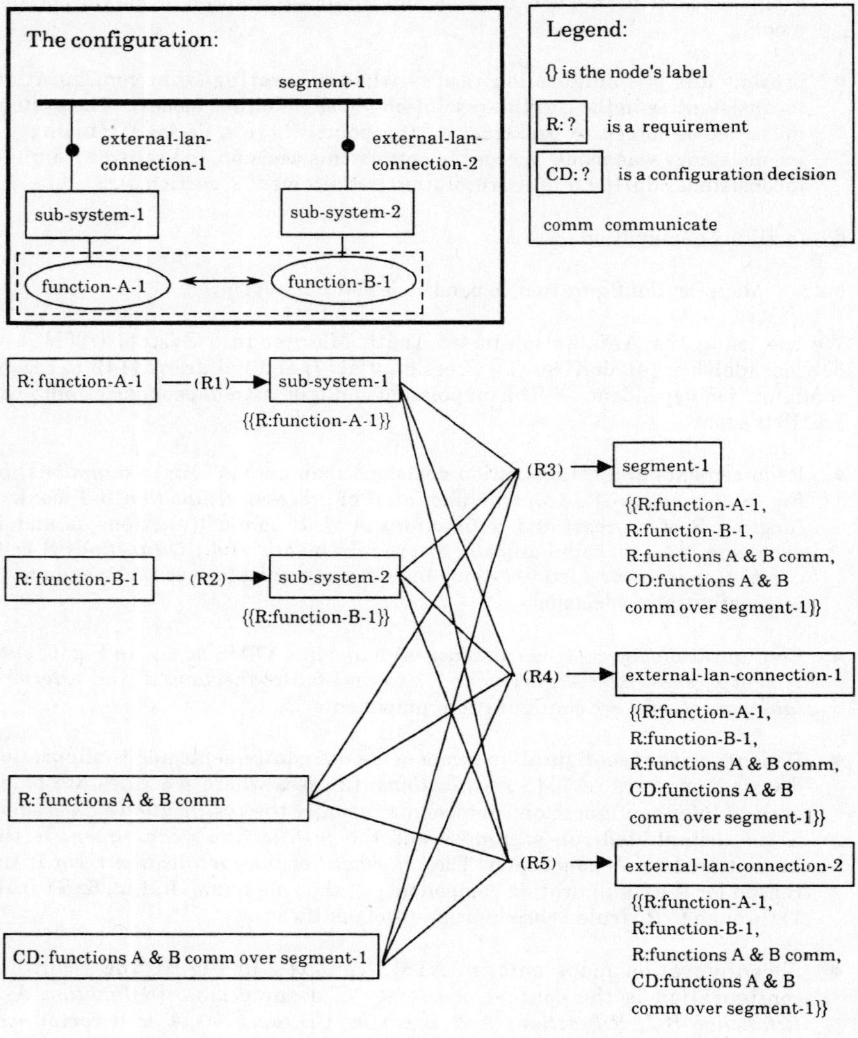

Fig. 6 Example dependency net implemented using the ATMS

created by the invoked Manual Configuration Function. When it cannot, the configuration engineer is asked.

The configuration is given by the context of the set of assumptions {*R:function-A-1*, *R:function-B-1*, *R:functions A & B comm*, *CD:functions A & B comm over segment-1*}. The context of the assumption set giving the current configuration is referred to as the *current context*, ie. the current context is now {*R:function-A-1*, *R:function-B-1*, *R:functions A & B comm*, *CD:functions A & B comm over segment-1*}, see Fig. 6.

Manipulation of the inferred configuration: There are two cases: deletion of a requirement or configuration decision; and deletion of a configuration component. Examples of each are:

- The engineer or PROKERN-XPS decides to delete the requirement for function A of Fig. 6. The new configuration is determined by deleting *R:function-A-1* from the current context, that is, the new configuration is given by the context of {*R:function-B-1*, *R:functions A & B comm*, *CD:functions A & B comm over segment-1*}. Only the nodes that are derivable from this restricted set of assumptions build the new configuration. *Environments* within a node's *label* containing the requirement *R:function-A-1* do not provide support for the node for this new current context, thus, from Fig. 6 it can be seen that the new configuration is *sub-system-2* only.

- The engineer or PROKERN-XPS decides to remove a LAN segment from the configuration of Fig. 6. The label of the node, *segment-1*, can be examined to determine which assumptions (requirements and configuration choices) must be removed in order for the node, *segment-1*, to loose its support. The engineer or PROKERN-XPS can choose one of *R:function-A-1*, *R:function-B-1*, *R:functions A & B comm* or *CD:functions A & B comm over segment-1*. The engineer or PROKERN-XPS may decide there is no requirement for *function-A-1* and *function-B-1* to communicate furthermore. Thus, the assumption, *R:functions A & B comm*, is deleted from the current context, so the new configuration is given by the context of {*R:function-A-1*, *R:function-B-1*, *CD:functions A & B comm* over segment-1} resulting in a configuration containing *sub-system-1* and *sub-system-2* only.

In both cases the unmodified configuration can be re-obtained by adding the deleted nodes to the set of assumptions characterising the current context and determining the context. It is important to note that the dependency net never changes - a new context provides a new view of the net .

Marking constraint violations within the net: After the construction phase, the consistency-checking phase is entered, where the configuration is examined for inconsistencies by the consistency-checking KS. On finding an inconsistency, a justification from the inconsistent nodes (representing the inconsistent configuration objects) to FALSE is added with its informant being the violated constraint rule.

Say, the connection KS develops the configuration of Fig. 6 further by connecting another sub-system to it, *sub-system-3*, resulting in connections, *external-LAN-connection-1*, *external-LAN-connection-2* and *external-LAN-connection-3*, as shown in Fig. 7. The constraint, *constraint-1: two or less subscribers can be connected to a LAN segment*, becomes violated. The violation is marked by the a consistency-checking rule with a justification from the connections to FALSE with an informant being the constraint rule name, CONSTRAINT-1.

Constraint violation recovery: On a constraint being violated, the configuration under consideration given by the current context becomes inconsistent as it contains one or more ATMS *nogoods*. The conflict-resolution phase is now entered, and depending on the mode, the conflict is resolved by the configuration engineer

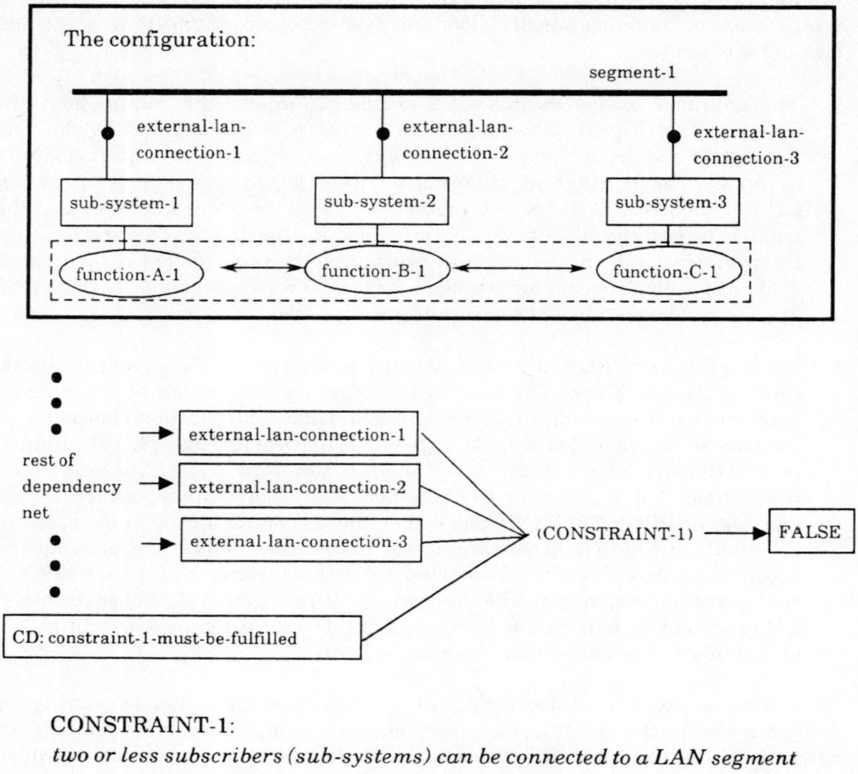

Fig. 7 Representing configuration inconsistencies

using manual configuration functions, or automatically if possible by PROKERN-XPS. As previously stated, PROKERN-XPS employs fixes specific to each constraint stating how to recover from its violation. The fix for this conflict was given in the previous section: the last subscriber, *sub-system-3*, is disconnected by switching out the configuration decision for functions B and C to communicate over *segment-1* from the current context, a second segment, *segment-2*, is created and joined to the existing segment, *segment-1*, with *segment-connection-1*, and the uncoupled subscriber is connected to *segment-2* (updating the dependency net for all operations). The new current context is shown in Fig. 8 (whose configuration is shown in Fig. 1).

In some cases, the engineer may decide that an inconsistency is acceptable. To cope with this case, the assumption stating the constraint must be fulfilled is simply switched out of (or 'removed from') the current context, eg. the assumption, *CD:constraint-1-must-be-fulfilled*, is switched out of the current context.

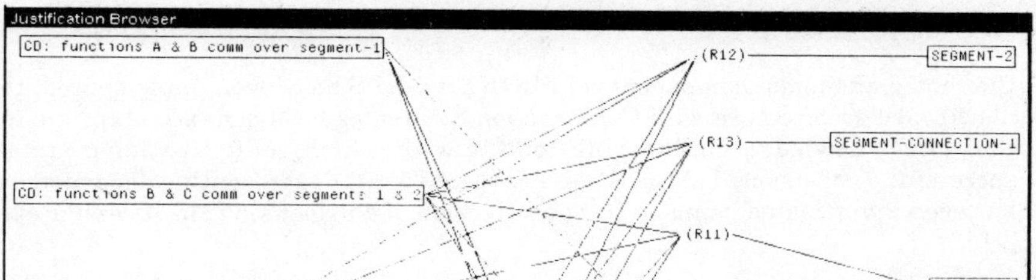

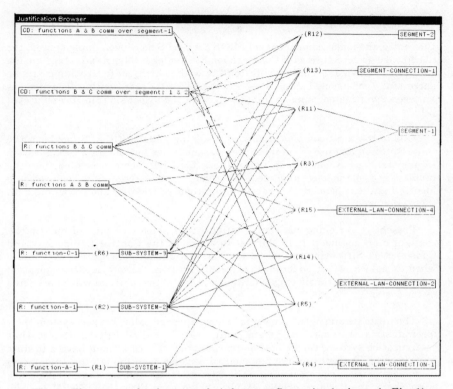

Fig. 8 The context for the example (whose configuration is shown in Fig. 1)

5.4 Breadth-first Verse Depth-first Approach

In the FORLOG system a forward-chaining rule system is combined with the ATMS (Dietterich et al [6]). FORLOG can be used to investigate all design alternatives in parallel. This breadth-first approach enables all designs to be found. This would be extremely useful in configuration, because the optimum design for cost or component count, etc. could be found. However, in this application this would be infeasible, because the configurations typically consist of approximately one to two thousand components. Therefore, the depth-first search approach has been adopted.

5.5 Problem Solver and Dependency Net Separation

In PROKERN-XPS, the problem solving component (the KSs, Construction Net and Elaboration Net) are separate from the dependency net, as presented by deKleer [4]. The rules match on data held within the Construction Net and on the blackboard, eg. the Elaboration Net, and are effectively 'blind' to the dependency net. They can manipulate the dependency net by switching contexts, but not match on it. Therefore, a mapping between ATMS nodes and problem solver data is needed. After a context switch selecting a new current context, the problem solver data corresponding to the ATMS nodes in the current context are marked as *current*. The KS rules only match on *current* data.

6 FUTURE WORK

Currently, the major components of PROKERN-XPS have been implemented: the blackboard architecture with Construction Strategies has been prototyped using the KEE knowledge engineering toolkit with which configurations can be successfully constructed. Also, the use of the ATMS for representing dependencies has been investigated using an in-house version of deKleer's ATMS (Dressler et al [7]).

One of the most complex issues in designing PROKERN-XPS has been the representation and use of configuration dependencies for handling configuration inconsistencies. An approach using the ATMS has been presented, but the problem is by no means completely overcome. Further research is required into identifying the dependencies, representing them efficiently, and reasoning with them effectively.

Presently, switching between configuration phases is carried out by the configuration engineer. It is planned to augment the Control Component and Construction Strategies so that in the automatic mode, the system will 'know' when to make a switch, so for parts of a configuration, the complete configuration cycle (construction, consistency-checking and conflict-resolution) will be executed by the system.

The ultimate aim of the project is to develop a specialised expert system shell for industrial automation system configuration, called PROKERN, so that configuration systems can be built for new product ranges without having to start from nothing. A shell can be implemented because even though the automation technology varies, eg. processing units become faster and LANs can take more subscribers, the basic principles of automation vary little. PROKERN will be extracted from the completed version of PROKERN-XPS by removing knowledge dependent on the product range, Siemens MMC-216, from PROKERN-XPS.

7 SUMMARY

This paper has clarified the definition of configuration and summarised the major requirements for a configuration expert system to perform complex configuration tasks. In order to meet these requirements, a configuration expert system with an architecture integrating multiple knowledge representations and inference mechanisms - a *mixed architecture* - is required. An expert system for configuring industrial automation systems, PROKERN-XPS, with such an architecture meeting all the stated requirements has been presented.

8 ACKNOWLEDGEMENTS

I would like to acknowledge my colleagues in the project, Barbra Schröcksnadl, Werner Zucker, Herman Endres and Günter Geissing. Also, I would also like to thank Oskar Dressler, Robert Frederking, Michael Reinfrank, Peter Suda, Stefan Verplaetse and Kai Zercher for comments on this paper.

9 REFERENCES

1. Baginsky, W., Endres, H., Geissing, G. and Philipp, L. Basic Architectural Features of Configuration Systems for Automation Engineering, in Proceedings of the IEEE Workshop on AI for Industrial Applications, Hitachi City, Japan, 1988. IEEE Computer Society.

2. Clarke, B. Representing Dependencies in an Expert System Shell for Configuring Industrial Automation Systems, in Proceedings of the 2nd Planning and Configuration Workshop (Ed. Hertzberg, J. and Günter, A.), pp. 133-148, Bonn, FRG. 1988. GMD Working Paper 310, Gesellschaft für Mathematik und Datenverarbeitung mbH, FRG.

3. Cunis, R., Günter, A., Syska, I., Peters, H. and Bode, H. PLAKON - An Approach to Domain-independent Construction, BMFT (German Federal Ministry for Research and Technology) TEX-K project. Hamburg University, FRG, 1988.

4. deKleer, J. An Assumption-based TMS, Artificial Intelligence, Vol. 28, pp. 127-162, 1986.

5. deKleer, J. Problem-solving with the ATMS, Artificial Intelligence, Vol. 28, pp. 127-162, 1986.

6. Dietterich, T.G. and Ullman, D.G. FORLOG, in Proceedings of the Expert Systems in Computer-aided Design Working Conference, IFIP WG 5.2, Australia, 1987. North-Holland Publishing Company, Amsterdam, 1987.

7. Dressler, O. and Estenfeld, J. ATMS: Assumption-based Truth Maintenance System, Siemens Report, 1987. Siemens AG, Munich, FRG.

8. Gray, M.A. The Architecture of an Intelligent Design Machine, MCC Technical Report No. ACA-AI-092-88, 1988. Microelectronics and Computer Technology Corporation, Austin, Texas, USA.

9. Marcus, S., Stout, J. and McDermott, J. VT: An Expert Elevator Designer that Uses Knowledge-based Backtracking, AI Magazine, Vol. 8, No. 4, 1987.

10. McDermott, J. R1: A Rule-based Configurer of Computer Systems, Artificial Intelligence, Vol. 19, No. 1, pp. 39-88, 1982.

11. Mostow J. Toward Better Models of the Design Process, AI Magazine, Vol. 6, No. 1, pp. 44-57, 1985.

12. Navinchandra, D. and Marks, D.H. Design Exploration through Constraint Relaxation, in Proceedings of the Expert Systems in Computer-aided Design Working Conference, IFIP WG 5.2, Australia, 1987. North-Holland Publishing Company, Amsterdam, 1987.

13. Nii, H.P. Blackboard Systems: Part 1, AI Magazine, Vol. 7, No. 2, pp. 38-53, 1986.

14. Reinfrank, M. Lecture Notes on Reason Maintenance Systems, Part1: Fundamentals, Siemens Report INF2 ARM-5-88, 1988. Siemens AG, Munich, FRG.

15. Struss, P. Multiple Representation of Structure and Function, in Proceedings of the Expert Systems in Computer-aided Design Working Conference, IFIP WG 5.2, Australia, 1987. North-Holland Publishing Company, Amsterdam, 1987.

Intelligent CAD Environment for Flexible Manufacturing Systems

Z. Létray and P. Bernus
Mechanical Engineering Automation Division, Computer and Automation Institute, Hungarian Academy of Sciences, H-1502 POB 63 Budapest, Hungary

ABSTRACT

This paper outlines some crucial parts of interacting Expert Subsystems within the frame of an Intelligent CAD environment called COOPERATOR. The system will be used to assist in designing Flexible Manufacturing Systems (FMS). Although the system is in the specification phase, we also focus on implementation issues in order to arrive at a practically useful system. A rapid prototype has been implemented applying knowledge engineering methods and tools developed in Hungary.

INTRODUCTION

It has been shown elsewhere [1] that the functional analysis of an evolutionary design process is required to provide an efficient computer support to assist the intellectual activity of the CAD designer.

An important consequence of such a functional analysis is that the design process should involve iterative steps of two main design activities: functional specification and system simulation.

One of the most exciting problems in mechanical engineering design is how to connect the two design steps. Efforts were spent to find links between the functional specification of a system and its physical implementation [2].

Let us suppose that the main functions of a flexible manufacturing system have been specified and decomposed as deeply as is necessary. That means we can allocate the performing mechanisms (operating, physical entities or their simulation models) to all the functional primitives.

The question addressed is: how is it possible to animate the behaviour of the system using a set of "living" objects of a high level simulation environment.

We are going to determine a set of tools to intelligently assist the iterative steps of engineering design, in a narrow domain of FMS.

COOPERATOR - A FRAMEWORK OF INTERACTING EXPERT SUBSYSTEMS

Cooperating expert systems is "the science of breaking up a problem into multiple peer reasoning agents" ([3], page 6). In addition to the possibility of problem decomposition this approach offers techniques to resolve the potentional conflicts in decision making that might occur.

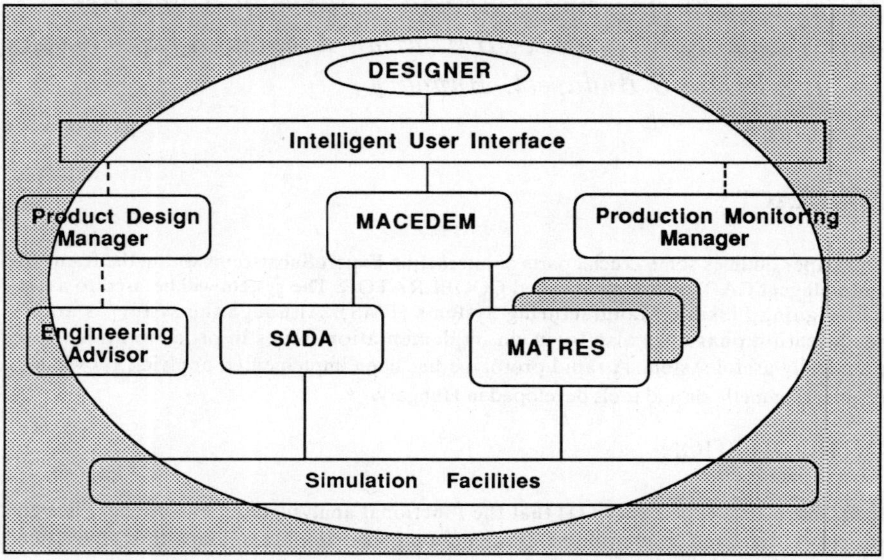

Fig. 1 - COOPERATOR : an Intelligent CAD Environment

This way seems to be more succesful in problem solving than the 'big expert system' with lots of schemas and rules until the problem seems solved and then deployment. Often the end result is an unmanageable and costly-to-maintain blob of capabilities.

There is an important benefit of the cooperating expert system paradigm: breaking up the problem into multiple agents is promising for computationally complex situations. This is a theoretical limit to the 'big expert system' approach in which all of the schemes and all of the rules are contained in the same process.

We discuss cooperating expert subsystems in the context of Flexible Manufacturing Cell (FMC) Design. We consider both the subsystems, and the communication among them.

Within the scope of this paper three subsystems are defined:

- MAnufacturing CEll DEsign Manager (MACEDEM)
- Structured Analysis Design Apprentice (SADA)
- MAterial flow TReating Expert System (MATRES)

In the 'management layer', MACEDEM will be an expert subsystem for the given design domain. Others, such as "Product Design Manager", "Production Monitoring Manager", etc. (Fig.1), might exist to provide a broader environment.

SADA is a general tool used by other manager subsystems in this framework.

MATRES is one of the possible subsystems - in the 'service layer' and may be used in the design session. Service layer subsystems incorporate knowledge of a specific field of the Manufacturing Cell Design.

COOPERATION BETWEEN THE EXPERT SUBSYSTEMS

An intelligent user interface provides the designer with the necessary control and communication facilities. The specification and implementation issues of such an interface have been widely discussed throughout the literature, one solution that might be appropriate for our system has been reported in [4].

MACEDEM incorporates the knowledge about the Manufacturing Cell Design process. Following the steps of the designer in the design state space, MACEDEM activates the cooperating subsystems, and provides communication between such subsystems and the designer.

SADA helps in specifying the functional and physical requirements, offers typical solutions relying on its knowledge base which contains structured analysis and design rules of the field. This subsystem allows the allocation of mechanisms - chosen from a set of requisite simulation models (objects) to the primitive functions and makes it possible to simulate the behaviour of the system. Primitive functions are the result of the functional specification analysis process and can be arrived at by decomposition.

The simulation results are directly used by SADA for further decisions in the functional analysis and for the verification and validation of the specification. Simulation results can also be used by MACEDEM for design mamagement. Functional specification and physical design are two functionally distinct activities in the entire design process but can heavily interact before a complete design results.

In FMC design it is often only simulation models which can be used to determine qualitative and quantitative system properties. Such properties can be fed back to the functional requirements specification and used for refinement or validation. The same results can be used for controlling the design (selection, refinement, validation etc.) of the physical system structure.

This suggests that a crucial part of the COOPERATOR is the set of modules that provide the CAD designer with several forms of simulation facilities at different levels of abstraction, during the design process.

MATRES is a hybrid expert system that includes domain knowledge in the field of material handling in a manufacturing cell [5]. It can make decisions based on rules, heuristics and allows the running of simulation programs, even ones written in traditional programming styles. Some of the most important functions of the system are: selection of the type of material handling system; design of the cell layout; route planning and scheduling of the transportation system.

In specifying the COOPERATOR system we have considered important implementation problems as:

- how to build the subsystems in order to perform intelligently?

- how to represent the knowledge about the design process?

- how to provide the communication between the cooperating agents?

Since MECEDEM is managing the design process it will have generic and specific models of the design situations [16]. Design situation models include

- design rules applicable to the situation, i.e.

  -- possible steps to evolve the design situation towards a specified design goal (this includes the evolution of the designed system and the modification of other parts of the situation description),
  -- rules which guide how to accomodate or apply participant subsystems in the design situation

- 'objects' which participate in the situation, i.e.

  -- participant subsystems and agents (such as MACEDEM, the user/designer, SADA, MATRES, etc.),
  -- other elements, like design object models, files, databases etc. used by the participants, objects are known on this level with their protocol, i.e. their attributes (protocols, functions, capabilities) relevant to the situation,

- relationships between the objects of the situation

  -- predefined relationships of the generic situation,
  -- relationships which result in during the refinement of the situation, generated by the design rules or by the participant subsystems or agents.

MACEDEM interacts with the user on two levels. We imagine a two-paned window, the upper pane for the meta- and the lower pane for the target level interaction. On the meta level we can have a situation editing/selecting facility. Situation presentation can have several forms as graphical (e.g. in form of functional diagrams) or text (e.g. in form of a rule based language). On the target level the given situation evolves. Here one can input new facts (relationships), messages to participants of the situation etc.

We are aware of the fact that several attempts have been made to solve these problems, however none of them seems entirely satisfactory.

In this paper, we try to introduce a possible answer to some elements of the above questions relying on a general purpose Expert System Building Tool.

THE AVAILABLE EXPERT SYSTEM BUILDING TOOL

The CS-PROLOG language and development environment (CS stands for "Communicating Sequential") is an advanced version of the T-PROLOG supporting the modelling of cooperative problem solving and for discrete event simulations based on new principles [6]. It supports concurrent, communicating problem solving provided by several parallel running PROLOG programs. In addition to the traditional implementation approach of process synchronization - using common logical variables -, CS-PROLOG allows message-passing between parallel running processes and makes it possible to dynamically modify the common database. This provides an alternative communication mechanism.

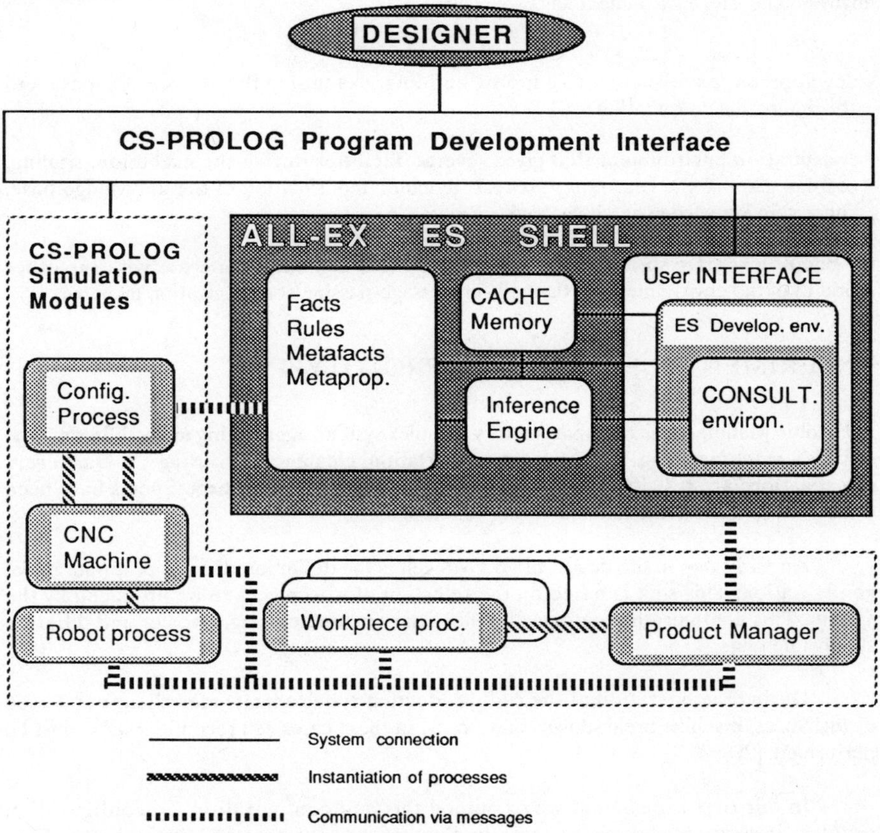

Fig. 2 - ES Shell with simulation facility

In this environment, general simulation models can be defined. The processes are instances of models. The system can change the structure of the original simulation models dynamically, on the basis of logical consequences derived from sophisticated preconditions. In this way the simulation system itself takes over part of the problem-solving effort from the designer.

In CS-PROLOG a process interaction view of simulation is supported. Built-in backtracking in time is based on an abstract concept of time called 'virtual time'. That means: the system-time does not depend on real time nor on the process time required to evaluate the clauses.

The CS-PROLOG development environment makes it possible to build and execute CS-PROLOG programs which can implement both domain specific expert systems and high level interacting simulation models.

ALL-EX is one of the actors in the scene, a CS-PROLOG-based expert system building tool [7] that is used to build and run stand-alone expert systems (Fig. 2). It integrates several results of Knowledge Engineering research and development. This shell allows the building of knowledge bases containing rules, facts, meta-facts in an interactive environment. The environment has two levels:

- development environment to support building, examining the knowledge base and beginning the consultation

- consultation environment that gives several facilities during the execution: tracing, explanation of the reasoning process, dynamic modification of the knowledge base, uncertain knowledge handling, backtracking, etc.

A specific expert system implemented using ALL-EX can cooperate with the other modules of the environment via the built-in message-passing communication facilities.

EXPERIMENTS USING A RAPID PROTOTYPING

A Flexible Manufacturing System is a very complex system, aggregating many different type of cells - manufacturing, warehouse, transportation, cleaning, measuring .... Our recent investigations are restricted to a single manufacturing cell. The experiments have been done so as to assist in the manufacturing cell design [8].

An early step in the design of an FMS cell is the definition of an appropriate initial configuration. This step is based on the selection of workpieces to be produced by the system. This configuration contains the necessary manufacturing, transfer and different supporting units.

During the operation of the cell, production requirements may change and even disturbances, machine break-downs may occur. In these cases cell reconfiguration must be performed. [9]

In our first experiment we examined this cell configuration - reconfiguration problem in order to determine some implementational issues of a central module of COOPERATOR - the "Manufacturing Cell Design Manager". This rapid prototype is also used for gaining experiences with simulation (see Fig. 1).

Within the above constraints and relying on the results achieved investigating the functional of the cell configuration activity, we described a proportion of the available knowledge of human experts in this field using the ALL-EX ES Shell.

In addition to this, we constructed a simulation model in CS-PROLOG that can make use of alternative steps and substitution possibilities in the design process. (That is why we can call our expert system a hybrid one - see Fig. 2).

When an alternative cell-configuration is proposed by the cooperating expert subsystem, the simulation model is activated providing the necessary information about the possible production variation for further decision making.

In this paper, we can focus only on this simulation module.

THE MANUFACTURING CELL SIMULATION MODULE

A typical portion of the life-cycle of a product or part in a manufacturing cell is shown on Fig. 3.

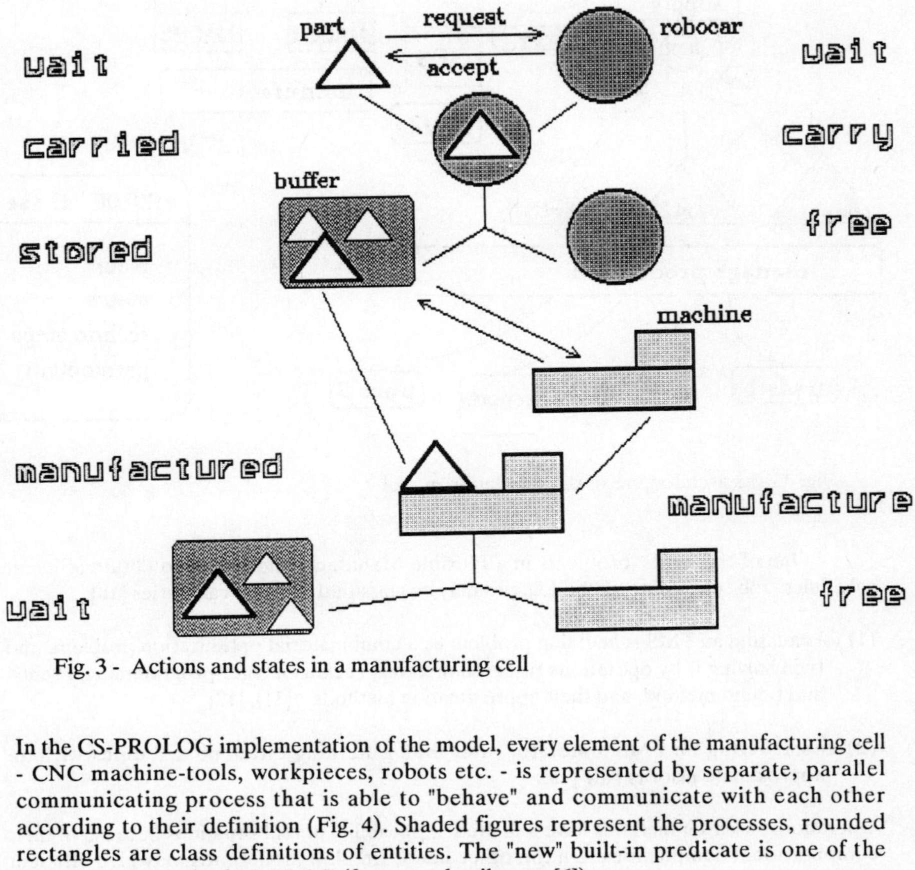

Fig. 3 - Actions and states in a manufacturing cell

In the CS-PROLOG implementation of the model, every element of the manufacturing cell - CNC machine-tools, workpieces, robots etc. - is represented by separate, parallel communicating process that is able to "behave" and communicate with each other according to their definition (Fig. 4). Shaded figures represent the processes, rounded rectangles are class definitions of entities. The "new" built-in predicate is one of the extensions to standard PROLOG (for more details see [6]).

A SOPHISTICATED PROCESS: SCHEDULER EXPERT SYSTEM (SES)

A production process does not have a predetermined schedule. By rule-based strategies and priority-handling provided by the Scheduler Expert System (shown as 'SES' in Fig. 4), the sequences of the technological steps are determined "on line". This can be done, because the processes are "conscious" of their own states and the task list therefore they can "manage" themselves during the simulation process. Conflicts are resolved by the SES using the principles described in the following .

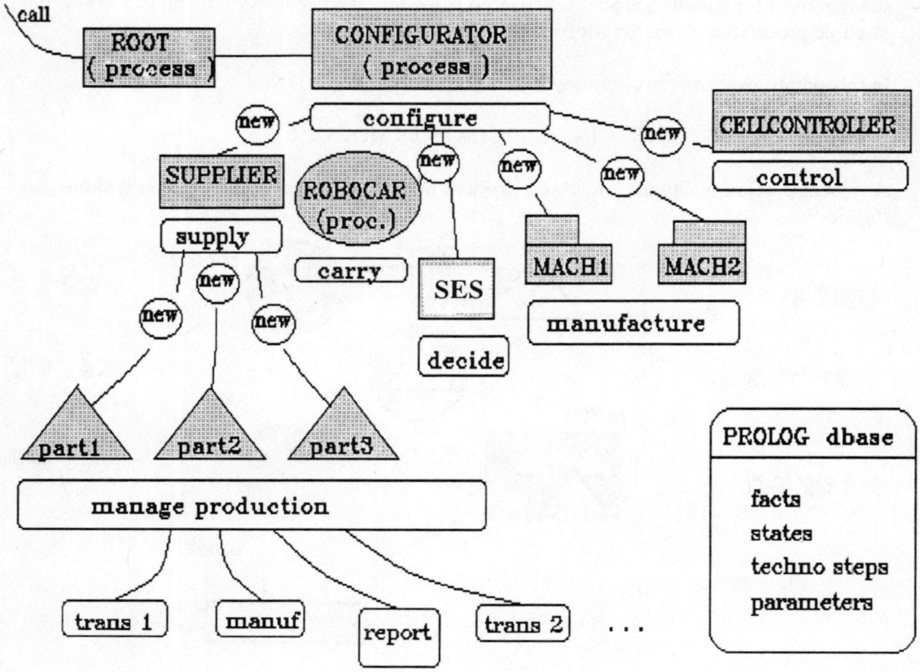

Fig. 4 - the architecture of the simulation model

One of the major problems in a Flexible Manufacturing Cell is to obtain efficient schedules. Job scheduling methodologies may be classified into two categories [10]:

(1) formulating an FMS scheduling problem as a combinatorial optimization problem, and then solving it by operations research methods such as integer programming, branch and bound method, and their approximation methods [11], [12].

(2) constructing an FMS simulator, and then obtaining efficient schedules with an approximate priority rule [13].

Operations research methods have a limited applicability in real situations because of their computational complexities. On the other hand, simulation methods may give efficient schedules in a practical way although they usually cannot give optimal solutions. In simulation methods, however, when several part types can be processed on a machine, a fixed priority rule is applied throughout to select the next part-type to be processed. Therefore a single priority rule may not be a good choice to resolve all possible conflicts among part types.

To cope with difficulties of scheduling problems in FMCs, we apply a knowledge engineering approach, similarly as others do eg. in [14] and [15].

In our model the SES dynamically selects appropriate priority rules at different times and situations in a simulation. This method applies a heuristic meta-rule base to generate priority rules. Meta-rules express how different priority rules perform in achieving given scheduling objectives.

Priority rule selection further depends on timing constraints and on the nature of the conflicting sets. In the following, we briefly introduce a possible rule base which is used dynamically to select appropriate priority rules according to the states of the simulation model.

Scheduling is processed under various scheduling objectives (such as minimizing flow time, completion time, number of tardy jobs, and maximum tardiness time, maximizing production rate, and so forth). SES generates appropriate priority rules which in their turn will be applied to select the most appropriate request in resource management conflicts.

To generate a priority rule, we construct hierarchically structured rules, each of which has the following conventional form:

if Si then Qi.

A condition Si is given by a predicate which describes the states in the CS-PROLOG simulation model such as throughput, remaining number of processes, processing times, and an occupation ratio in each buffer. (A subprocess in SES collects all the state information - arriving in the form of messages - about the states.) Qi is either a priority rule (Ri) or a group of rules for selection (Pij) to be checked next (see. Fig. 5).

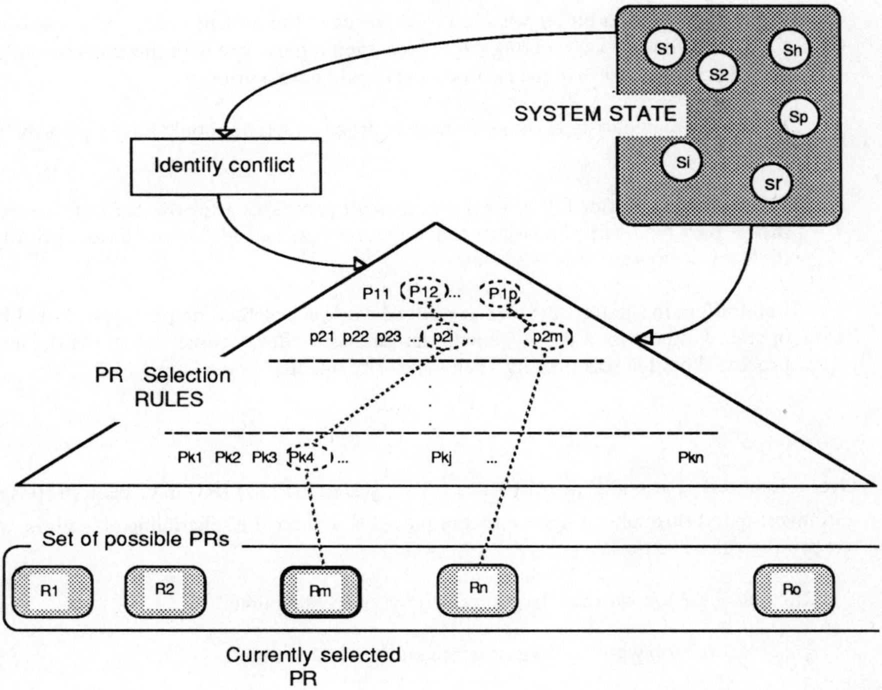

Fig. 5 - Dynamic selection of Priority Rules (PR)

Suppose that a major scheduling objective is to minimize completion time. (Moreover, we might consider another objective; reducing the number of set-ups, so that each machine tends to process the workpieces of the same part type.) Here, we show two predicates as examples which describe the states of a part of the system:

Sk: buffer-i(n,a): true if there exists a buffer in n processes ahead of the current process such that its occupation ratio is greater than or equal to a given %; otherwise false.

Sl: progress(n): true if there exists a part type in the conflicting part types such that its remaining number of processes is less than or equal to n; otherwise false.

Heuristic knowledge to achieve good compliance with the scheduling objectives can be acquired through numerical experiments and by examining the dynamics of simulation models. Here are some heuristic knowledge to be applied to the case where several part-types can be processed on the same machine, and to the case where several part-types can be transported by the same robocar.
(Following demonstrative examples draw much from [10].)

* When all buffers in the current process are full of workpieces,

  (a) if all buffers in the next process are also full of workpieces, then a part-type with the largest processing time should have a prority.

  (b) if there exists a buffer with full workpieces in the next process, and processing times largely vary among part-types, then a part-type with the smallest buffer occupation ratio in the next process should have a priority.

  (c) otherwise, a part-type with the shortest processing time should have a priority.

* If there exists a buffer full of workpieces in all processes after the current process, then a part-type with the largest remaining processing time should have a priority. (Select priority rule 'Rm' -- see later.)

* If all buffers in the next process are full of workpieces, then no part-type should be operated; otherwise a part-type with the smallest buffer occupation ratio in the next process should have a priority. (Select priority rule 'Rp' -- see later.)

Over a hundred of possible priority rules (or suggested actions) (Ri) have been proposed and investigated through simulation techniques [13]. Under the scheduling objectives, we use priority rules like these:

Rm: Select the job with the "largest remaining processing time."

Rn: Select the job with the "largest imminent processing time".

Ro: Select the first job arriving in the operation.

Rp: Select the job with the "smallest occupation ratio in buffer in the next operation."

Rq: Select the job with the "smallest throughput".

Rr: Select the job with the "smallest number of remaining processes."

Rs: Select the job randomly.

The SES rule base was constructed according to the above heuristic knowledge. If there are more part-types selected by a priority rule, then SES must apply other priority rules to select a single part-type.

CONCLUSIONS

Our first experiments in the framework 'COOPERATOR' have demonstrated that the rule based scheduling system proposed in the previous section is usable in a simulation model which is an important part of a hybrid expert system. The evolving structure and the parameters of the final cell configuration model - as the results of the simulation passed back to the rule-based part of the Expert System (via messages and through the common database) - have great importance in further decision making.

In the implemented prototype, graphic representation is added so providing a limited animation of the system behaviour. This makes it easy to follow the operation of the simulation model.

The evaluation of our early experimental results lead us to believe that the approach described is an important first step in the implementation of our envisaged system.

REFERENCES

1. Intelligent CAD Systems 1 -- Theoretical and Methodological Aspects (Eds. P.J.W ten Hagen and T. Tomiyama), Springer-Verlag, Berlin, 1987.

2. Létray, Z. and Bernus, P. The Link between the Functional and the Physical Architecture in Computer Integrated Manufacturing, in Proc. APMS-COMPCONTROL '85., Vol. IV, pp. 954-964, Budapest, Hungary, 1985.

3. Stock, M. AI Theory and Applications in the VAX Environment, McGraw-Hill, New York, N.Y., 1988.

4. Ruttkay, Zs., ten Hagen, Paul J.W. Intelligent User Interface for Intelligent CAD, pp. 421-424, in Proc. of the Second IFIP WG 5.2 Workshhop on Intelligent CAD, 19-22 September 1988., Cambridge, UK, 1988.

5. Mezgár, I. MATRES: an Expert System for Material Flow Analysis and Design, pp. 129-

6. Futó, I. AI and Simulation on PROLOG Basis, Vol. I, pp. 1-6, Int. Symp. on AI, Expert Systems and Languages in Modelling and Simulation, 2-4 June, 1987, Barcelona, Spain, 1987.

7. ALL-EX Expert System Shell - Reference Manual, Applied Logic Laboratory, Budapest, Hungary, 1988.

8. Bertók, P., Haidegger, G., Kovács, Gy., Létray, Z., Mezgár, I. Design Aspects of Reconfigurable Manufacturing Cells as Building Blocks of Flexible Manufacturing Systems, Presented at the IEEE Third International Symposium on Intelligent Control, Aug. 24-26, 1988. Arlington, Virginia, USA, 1988.

9. Heragu, S.S., Kusiak, A. Analysis of Expert Systems in Manufacturing Design, IEEE Trans. on Systems, Man and Cybernetics, Vol. SMC-17, No. 6, pp. 898-912, 1987.

10. Nakamura, Y., Hatono, I., Kohara, Y., Yamagata, K. and Tamura, H. FMS Scheduling using Timed PETRI Net and Rule Base, 2nd US-Japan Symposium on Flexible Automation, Minneapolis, July 18-20, 1988.

11. Conway, R.W., Maxwell, W.L., and Miller, L.W. Theory of Scheduling, Addison-Wesley, 1967.

12. Baker, K.R. Introduction to Sequencing and Scheduling, John Wiley & Sons, New York, 1974.

13. Blackstone, Jr J.H., Phillips, D.T. and Hogg, G.L. A state-of-the-art Survey of Dispatching Rules for Manufacturing Job Shop operations, Int. J. of Production Research, Vol.20, pp. 27-45, 1982.

14. Thensen, A. and Lei, L. An Expert System for Scheduling Robots in a Flexible Electroplating System with Dynamically Changing Workloads, pp. 555-566, in Proceeding of 2nd ORSA/ TIMS Conference on Flexible Manufacturing Systems: Operation Research Models and Applications (Stecke K. E. et al.), Elsevier Science Publishers, Amsterdam, 1986.

15. Kanet, J.J. Expert Systems in Production Scheduling, European Journal of Operational Research, Vol. 29, pp. 51-59, 1987.

16. Bernus, P. and Létray, Z. Intelligent Systems Interconnection: What should come after Open Systems Interconnection?, In. Intelligent CAD Systems I, Theoretical and Methodological Aspects, pp. 44-56. EurographicSeminars Tutorials and perspectives in Computer Graphics, P. J. W. ten Hagen T. Tomiyama (Eds.), Springer-Verlag, 1987.

Computer Intergrated Prototype Development and Toolmaking: an AI Application

Peter Knackfuß

Bremer Institut für Betriebstechnik und angewandte Arbeitswissenschaft an der Universität Bremen, Postfach 330440, D-2800 Bremen 33, West Germany

1. Purpose of this Paper

This paper introduces the problems of computer aided prototype and toolmaking.
The future competitiveness of high-tech countries will depend strongly on their ability to perform rapid prototyping, and increasingly in the area of one-of-a-kind production. The economic success of mass production will surely remain important for insuring future prosperity, but it is plain that developing countries are able to adopt and carry out these manufacturing and production concepts. The ability to produce highly valuable, complex products according to customer specifications is proving to be a more stable competitive advantage, especially for small and medium-sized firms.
Because existing organisational and computational concepts of manufacturing cannot be applied to this area of production, new ways to tackle the problems within this field have to be found.
The paper proposes an alternative organisational and computational concept for the one-of-a-kind workshop.

2. Category, Results and Conclusions of the Work Described

The work described fits into the field of process control and planning. The classical method to gain process planning and control data for a FMS will be discussed. The concept for a one-of-a-kind workshop with special emphasis on human factors based on AI techniques will be described. Application areas of artifical intelligence within each module of the software for a machine tool suitable for this concept will be detailed. Fields for the use of optimisation techniques within the software will be outlined. The necessity of interdisciplinary research making extensive use of AI techniques to succeed with a prototype of such a production environment will be concluded.

3. Summary

The training of skilled workers in the small and very small batch production industries is by tradition more oriented towards practical skill than towards abstraction. The employees of small and large companies producing small batches or prototypes use special equipment and are very experienced in a broad range of manufacturing processes. In such an environment improvisation is an essential part of daily work.
Furthermore the possibilities to transfer prototyping results to medium enterprises and mass production are realized only in a very crude manner in current production systems. To find better solutions it seems good practice to apply advanced information technologies.
A concept tackling the difficulties of transferring prototyping to future mass production and trying to increase the productivity of a prototyping workshop and small batch production should relate to the above mentioned traditionally proven workshop structures.
Therefore a concept for a human-centered CNC workshop using the experience of skilled workers will be described. This concept will take into account the most recent developments in production technology and computer science such as feature-based design and knowledge-based systems. This environment of skilled workers supported by computers will increase productivity in small-batch and one-of-a-kind production.
A machine tool suitable in such an environment for one-of-a-kind and very small batch production might have a self-explaining user interface with a tutorial component capable of guiding inexperienced workers. Input to the machine tool is in the form of features and free-form surfaces. Once a feature or free-form is entered, machining is simulated and necessary production planning steps are proposed to the user. If the worker accepts this, the necessary NC-programme to machine the feature or the free form (delta volumes) is automatically generated. By subsequently entering such volume changes the finished shape of the workpiece is produced.

4. Motivation

The basic thought underlying this concept is that technological developments have made it possible to orient the technological aspects of modern system design more strongly toward existing, proven work organisation and forms, especially in small and medium sized enterprises.
Two development tendencies lay the basis for the project idea:

> The future competitiveness of high-tech countries will depend strongly on their ability, and increasingly in the area of one-of-a-kind production, to offer economical, flexible solutions. The economic success of mass production will surely remain important for insuring future prosperity, but it is plain that emerging industrial countries are able to adapt and carry out these manufacturing and production concepts. The ability to produce highly valuable, complex products according to customer specifications is proving to be a more stable competitive advantage, especially for small and medium-sized firms.

> Experience in computer integrated production has shown that technological innovations in small and medium-sized firms become increasingly effective when their introduction takes into consideration the knowledge and skill of the personnel; in other words, innovation should be imposed on a mature business communication structure and on a base of knowledge gained through experience. In this way technology is introduced in a developed production structure, and oriented toward the existing abilities of the workers.

Until now, introduction of computer-integrated production systems has been preponderantly applied to large and medium enterprises in mass flow-through type work processes. Their economic power and justification consists mainly of the rationalization of repetitive runs and the release of human workers. These concepts are, however, not transferable to one-of-a-kind production, since repetitive runs which are determined in advance are the exception here, and the skilled human worker who deals with unforeseen problems cannot be done without, or regarded as a mere supplement to a high-tech system. Because of these considerations, tools must be developed which will deliver the urgently-needed basis for such system components and interfaces. Due to the importance of one-of-a-kind production, such CIM systems and components must place human labour at the center of the system, thereby creating work places which

- offer assignments with sophisticated content and activities demanding higher qualifications
- demand intervention and control competencies
- make planning flexible

Such a concept for shaping technology which is based on a variety of unique solutions and an understanding of the development of know-how as a collective interaction process of qualified individuals, necessitates new research and development surroundings in which not only the interaction of technical components, but also the productivity of the system interface can be tested and developed with respect to the user.
An essential weakness in existing systems is the prevailing logic orientation and the resulting neglect of operation-oriented system forms. Such generalized solutions often break down in practice because of inflexibility and because new qualifications not always available in the workforce are demanded rather than existing ones being taken advantage of. Operation-oriented forms, however, demand new methods and techniques based on interaction at the workshop level. The use of feature-based design, group technology, and knowledge-based systems form the basis for computer integrated prototype development and tool making.

5. An Alternative Prototyping Concept

5.1. Programming at the Shop Floor Level

In the area of workshop-oriented programming of machine tools today, there is only one means of entering machining operations with the help of an input language which follows ISO 6983. Using this language skilled workers enter simple "go" commands for the machine with the help of an editor and an alphanumeric keyboard.

Because this procedure is very complex, the various producers of machine tools have recently begun offering graphic interfaces for their machine tools which are meant to simplify programming through the graphic input of workpiece geometry. Such interfaces, however, exist almost exclusively for 2 1/2-axis machines. If the skilled worker inputs the workpiece geometry, the "go" commands are generated by compilation. Because of this, modification of the workpiece is impossible, or at most only possible with narrow limits. The programs which are produced are not transferable, since no intermediate language such as APT is generated instead of "go" commands and since the machine control can only work with a subpart of the ISO standardised input language.
The user interfaces are not standardised and, in the most favourable case, support only a small part of the essential functions for the skilled worker listed below:

- suggestions for process planning, e.g. the choice of tools and other resources
- suggestions for the decomposition of a given geometry into its basic elements
- a copier function for repetitive operations sequences
- ability to input reference and chain measures
- calculator functions
- ability to simulate cutting paths
- collision testing with machine parts, workpieces or machine tool storage
- tool libraries which display tools graphically.

Other important functions are not supplied by existing systems at all:

- comprehensive help functions in the user interface
- self-explanatory operation and functionality of the machine tool
- an automated operator's handbook in which key words can be searched for.

A considerable disadvantage is represented by the variety of workshop programming concepts on which existing systems are based. Through the use of new technologies in the field of IT, existing systems can also be improved considerably from the point of view of ergonomics, thereby closing the gap between the convenience of the most modern computers and the state of the art in the operation of workshop machine tools.

5.2. Manufacturing Environments for Mass Production

5.2.1 Todays Flexible Manufacturing Environment

Two main objectives of CIM are the manufacturing of variants and flexible manufacturing. Fig. 1 shows a simplified overview of the production steps in a flexible manufacturing system. Such systems are well suited for the production of small to medium lot sizes, in which the work phases for product engineering, product design, work planning, and NC programming have only an off-line link to the machining process in today's industries.

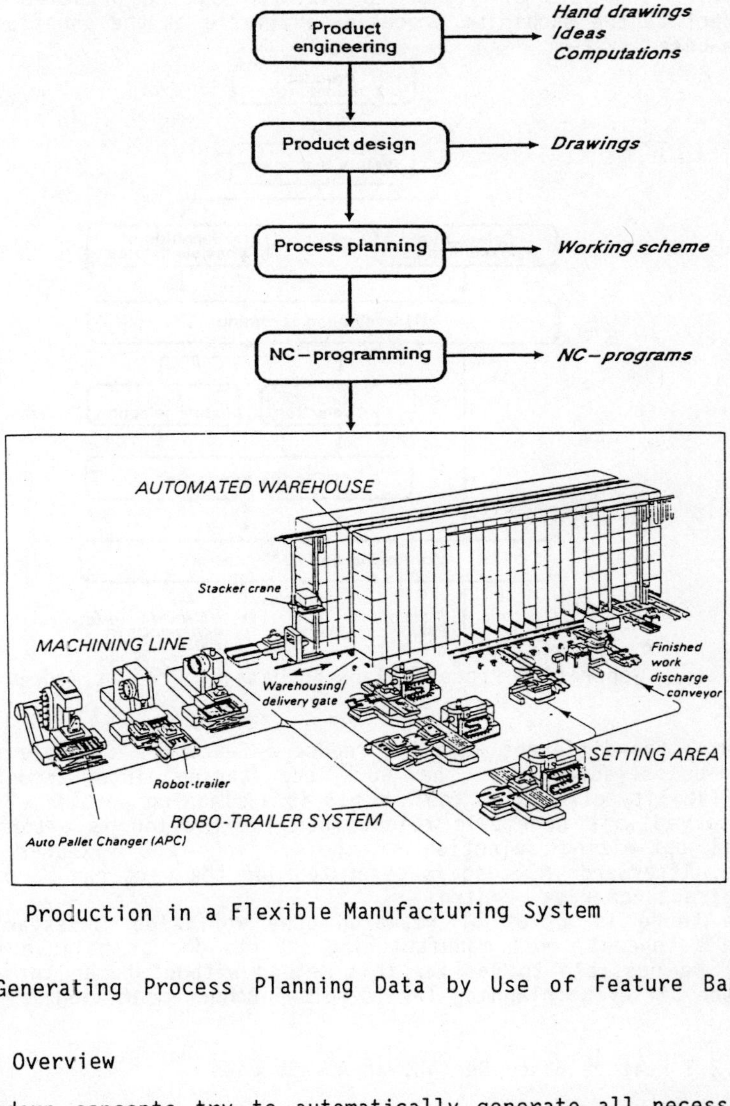

Fig. 1: Production in a Flexible Manufacturing System

5.2.2 Generating Process Planning Data by Use of Feature Based Design

5.2.2.1 Overview

More modern concepts try to automatically generate all necessary data by analysing the output of a so-called "product modeller". A product modeller is a new generation CAD-system. The output of such a CAD system is called product model. It contains a three dimensional representation of the workpiece to be produced and all information relevant for process planning like tolerances and surface roughness.
In order to analyse a product model the first step is to search for machinable units, so called features. This is mostly done in an algorithmic way because of the type of data representation within the modeller. This step is kown as feature recognition. Its output is a sequence of machinable "delta-volumes" often called feature tree. Once the feature-tree is known, suitable cutting tool

families and sets of jiggs and fixtures can be preselected with respect to the machining processes available at the shopfloor by a rule-based system.

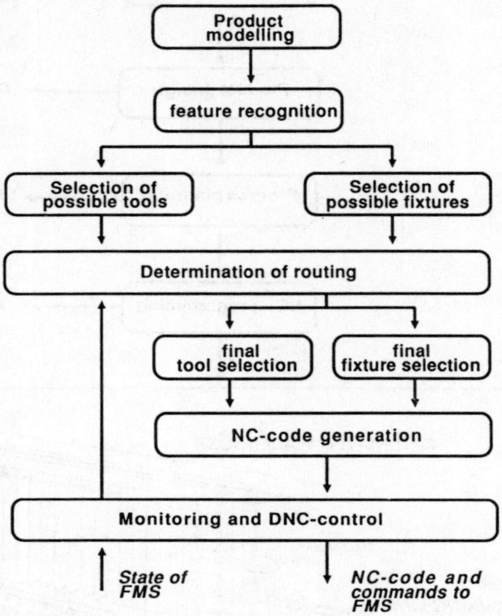

Fig. 2: Generating Process Planning Data by Product Modelling

Knowing the different ways to produce a feature a suitable routing can be selected for the workpiece taking into account the availability of machine tools. This is a planning problem which can be solved with heuristic rules. When the routing is determined a final optimizing selection of tools, jiggs and fixtures can be done. Afterwards NC-code is generated and the part can be produced by direct numerical control.
Even there is a lot of research done worldwide in establishing such a concept, most manufacturing experts do not believe that it will be possible to realize this method without human interaction on the different planning levels below product modelling.

5.2.2.3 Feature Based Design, an AI approach

Many definitions exist for the concept of feature. From the manufacturing engineers' point of view features are a set of operations which can be applied to a raw part. The goal of this approach is to restrict the designer in a way that only such parts can be designed which can be produced later on.
For this reason all kinds of necessary process planning data like shape, different kind of tolerances, and necessary materials have to be specified already in the design phase.
Fig. 5 shows the feature tree of a simple part. This feature tree can be represented with a knowledge representation form found in AI research, e.g. schemata and slots. In this way data recognized on different levels of the tree hierarchy can be inherited to be used

later on. In the example below the material used for a workpiece can be inherited from the raw part. Afterwards, when generating cutting forces and specifying the speed needed for production of the holes, data stored in only one place can easily be accessed. Knowledge about how process planning data is to be generated often does not exist in an algorithmic representation. Because of this reason it seems to be appropriate to make use of heuristic rules.

```
APPLICATION hole
ASSIGNMENT
   minimum-pre-drill-diameter = 0.4 * hole-diameter
   maximum-pre-drill-diameter = 0.6 * hole-diameter
IF   volume-to-be-removed LARGER-THAN 0.
 AND hole-bottom-type      EQUALS      "through-bottom"
 AND drill-available ( minimum-pre-drill-diameter,
                       maximum-pre-drill-diameter )
THEN
   CALL drilling
   hole-diameter = 0.5 * hole-diameter
ENDIF
```

Fig. 3 Example of a process planning rule

The example in Fig. 3 shows a process planning rule [2]. A tool is looked for which is suitable to drilling a hole of type "through-bottom".
A production environment must be tailored to the needs of the company it is used by. Each company, however, has its own procedure for the solution of different problems. One of these problems could be to find a machines turret in sheet metal production. Different company specific methods are used for the solution of this problem. Applying methods of rapid prototyping could lead to company-specific solutions. In the following a set of heuristic rules is described which is used to solve the above mentioned problem using standard turrets avoiding nibbling as far as possible.

Remarks:

- The standard turret is a part of the machine's turret which should not be changed during production of the different sheets.
- A standard tool is a tool belonging to the standard turret.
- The new turret is the turret for processing the new sheet.
- Standard turretplaces are places on the new turret which are reserved for the standard turret.
- Remaining turretplaces are places on the new turret which are not reserved for the standard turret.

1. Goal:
   All elements which can only be produced by one tool or toolset must be selected with highest priority.
1. Action:
   If an element can be produced with only one tool, this tool is added to the new turret on standard turretplaces if belonging to the standard turret, and on remaining turret places otherwise.

Afterwards these elements are marked as checked.

2. Goal:
Usage of as many standard non-nibbling tools as possible.
2. Action:
Scan for all standard non-nibbling tools which can produce remaining elements and add them to the new turret on standard turretplaces.
Afterwards these elements are marked as checked.

3. Goal:
The remaining elements should be produced without nibbling.
3. Action:
Search for the mostly needed non-nibbling tools and add them to the remaining turretplaces in the new turret.
Afterwards these elements are marked as checked.

4. Goal:
The remaining elements should be produced with standard nibbling tools.
4. Action:
Search for standard nibbling tools to produce the remaining elements and assign them to the new turret.
Afterwards these elements are marked as checked.

5. Goal:
Nibble the remaining elements.
5. Action:
Produce the remaining elements with the biggest possible nibbling tool and assign it to the new turret.
Afterwards these elements are marked as checked.

6. Goal:
Notify operator if no turret can be found.
6. Action:
If there are elements which can not be produced with the new turret found, send an error message to the operator.

Many other heuristics exist for finding new turrets which depend strongly on the needs of the company using them.

5.2.3 Human Factors in Prototype Manufacturing

Both methods described above require extensive, highly specialized computer programmes which need qualified personnel - mostly engineers - for their operation and maintenance.
Every time small changes in the workpiece are needed - and this is often the case in prototype manufacturing - the lengthy work preparation process must be repeated entirely. Beside this, the flexibility necessary in a one-of-a-kind production environment cannot be supported by these methods.
For this reason it would be very desirable to revitalize old and proven workshop principles with the help of suitable computer support, in order to make one-of-a-kind and very small batch production more efficient and more effective. Such a concept must make use of the special features of workshop manufacturing and must attempt to remedy its characteristic problems:

- The training of skilled workers in the manufacturing of small and very small batches puts by tradition more emphasis on practical skills than on abstraction. For this reason companies have often decided against the introduction of new technologies, such as NC machine tools, because a large part of the work force would need retraining or would have to be replaced. In addition, technological progress makes it necessary to frequently repeat retraining measures, which a small company might find difficult or impossible to finance in the long run.

- The employees of companies which produce small batches or proto- types, and also the employees of larger companies working in special workshops for one-of-a kind manufacturing, are very experienced in a broad range of manufacturing processes used routinely in such environments. They are accustomed to start from incomplete documentation, e.g. from manual sketches of the workpiece. They are also able to recognize errors in these incomplete documents and to correct them on their own. Parallel to this they continue to manufacture other components of the workpiece.

- It seems reasonable to make use of the special skills and knowledge of these employees and to increase their productivity through adequate support measures for the operation of their machine tools.

- Often the purchase of specialized, complex machining equipment for the manufacture of a certain workpiece is not feasible. Therefore, a modern workshop manufacturing system must support improvisation as far as possible.

5.3. CNC Workshop Manufacturing

5.3.1 Concept of a CNC Workshop for One-of-a-Kind Manufacturing

The attempt to apply the methods for medium and large size series production to very small batch or one-of-a-kind manufacturing looks promising at first sight. However, it would lead to the loss of those qualified skilled workers with many years of experience who cannot adapt quickly enough to the new technologies. These skilled workers would then be replaced by highly qualified engineers who use powerful but cost-intensive methods which do not provide the necessary flexibility for one-of-a-kind manufacturing.
Therefore, it makes more sense to make use of the skills of the existing teams and to increase their productivity by providing a suitable CIM environment. In Fig. 4 we see a concept for such a workshop. The one-of-a-kind workshop is supplied with the necessary ideas, manual drawings, and computations by the product engineering department. The transfer of engineering data to a workpiece takes place in several linked CNC machine tools by specifying the sequence of so-called "features" which must be applied to a raw part to produce the end product. Features are a possibility for describing the end product from the viewpoint of the production engineer.

To meet the standardization requirements of a mass production, possibly connected to the system by computer networking, there is a need for another special kind of higher level operations. These operations must meet the dimensional restrictions which are necessary to allow the use of standardized parts and operation sequences during production of the prototype. The possibility of applying features can be enriched by the use of primitive operations. This combination of features and primitive operations generates new features, which are handled in the same way as the simple features. With this a library of typical operations for a special kind of product can be built up.

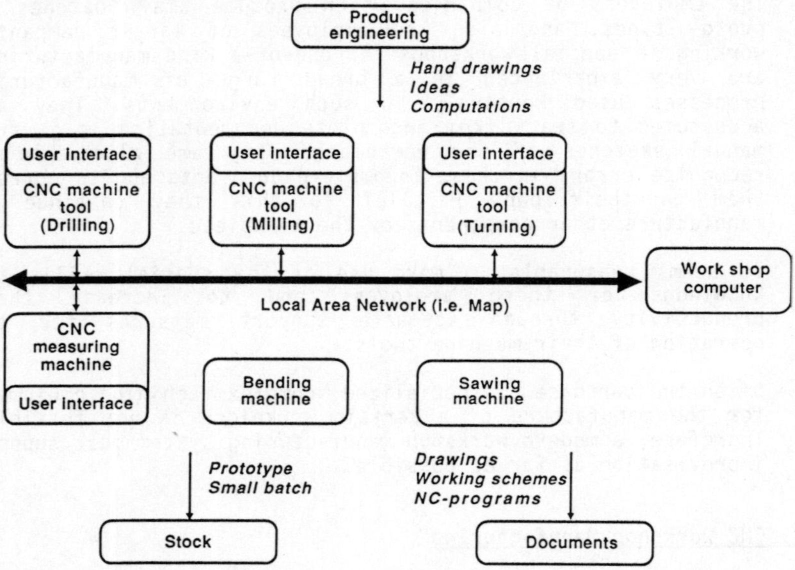

Fig. 4: Concept of a CNC Workshop for One-of-a-Kind Manufacturing

Beside this there is often a need to enter free-form surfaces into the one of-a-kind-workshop. Such surfaces could be digitalized by a measuring machine from a design model or they could be generated by a user-friendly, free-design CAD system. Afterwards the system allows modification of this data with respect to the necessity of production of, for example, an injection or pressure moulding tool.

The CNC machine tool can produce the workpiece at optimal speed with respect to production process (turning, milling), work material (aluminum, steel), and tool geometry, and show the result on the user interface. This capability would significantly speed up the production process.
An expert system checks the reliability of the sequence for machining features or free form surfaces onto the product. If it becomes apparent that the user is not sufficiently familiar with the production process, the system can be driven by a suitable "intelligent" tutorial. The user can also obtain support at any time from hierarchically organized help functions which expand the system to the point of being self-explanatory. Of course the ability of any machine tool to produce certain features or free- form

surfaces is limited by its production process. Because the various machine tools are linked to one another, the result of the work on one particular machine can be moved directly to the next machine, so that the workpiece in its current form serves as a raw form for the next production process. Not every production process, however, justifies the use of a machine with such an advanced user interface. Therefore the system envisions a central computer for the performance of such simple functions as riveting, sawing,and bending. The central computer is also connected to the periphery which is necessary in order to secure the connection to production planning for mass production, or to convey the necessary documentation in the form of drawings and work plans that are automatically generated.

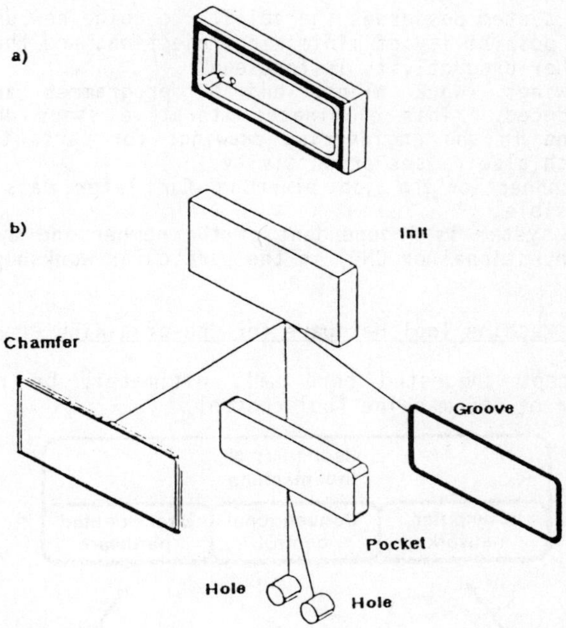

Fig. 5: Features on a Simple Part
a) Finished Part
b) Features to be Produced, and Their Relationship

The generating and storing of NC programmes will have already been carried out during the creation of the prototype from the features and free design. This programme could also be used in mass production. It must be considered, however, that in one-of-a-kind and small batch production, the choice of optimal production processes and tools does not always pay, due to the small batch size. An example of this is that in place of nibbling often milling can be performed, or that the choice of tool diameter in milling should be left to the user, as far as possible, although in mass production the choice or even purchase of the largest possible milling tool will be necessary.

5.3.2 Summary of the characteristics of the concept

This section summarizes the characteristics of the concept for production of prototypes and small batch products:

- The user interface is self-explaining.
- Operation is largely independent of extension of the machine functions and of machine tool producers. Technological progress and different technological possibilities of different machine tools are expressed only through additional features, i.e. expanded functionality, of the user interface.
- System operation is - through the application of features and free forms -largely independent of the particular production process.
- The system possesses the ability to guide new users.
- The possibility of minimizing rejections and thereby achieving higher productivity is foreseen.
- Drawings, work plans, and NC programmes are generically produced. This eliminates iterative steps due to mistakes found in the engineering drawings for parts to be produced, which also raises productivity.
- A connection to job planning for later mass production is possible.
- The system is independent of the number and type of machines (conventional or CNC) in the particular workshop.

5.2. CNC Machine Tool Hardware for One-of-a-Kind Production

The concept suggested here will ultimately be regarded as an expansion of CNC machine tool control.

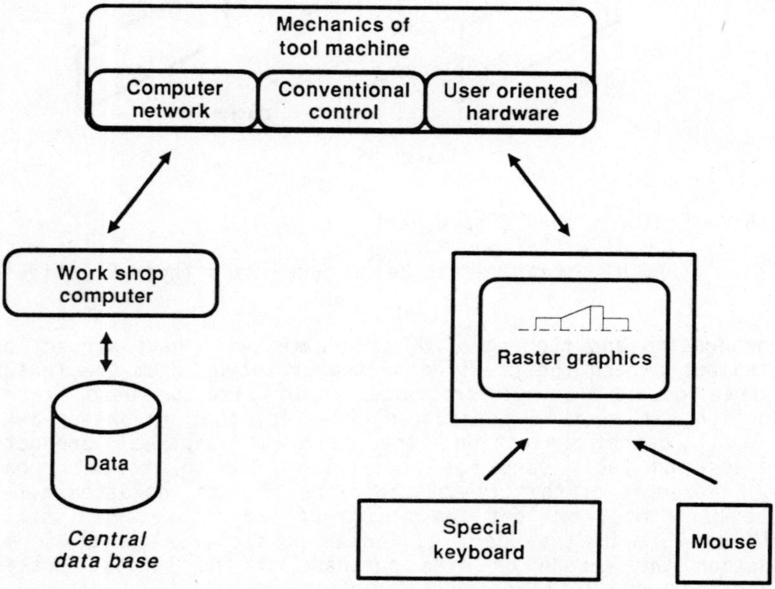

Fig. 6: Structure of a CNC Machine Tool for One-of-a-Kind Production

In Fig. 6 the structure of such a CNC machine tool is represented. The control of the machine is expanded to include a user-oriented component. This component provides the necessary computer capacity and a suitable graphic processor.
The user operates the machine using a keyboard which has been adapted for the particular problem at hand. The worker has the possibility of controlling the machine tool with the help of a mouse, pop-up, pull-down, and stick-up menus, and a high-resolution color graphic screen. The workpiece is always shown in parallel to ongoing work. Hardware for the linking of various CNC machines and for access to the central data base in the workshop is also needed.

5.5. A CNC-Machine Tool for One-of-a-Kind Manufacturing

The realisation of a concept as ambitious as this requires development of extensive software. Moreover, because the methods used here - for example production-oriented design - are areas where more scientific research is needed, it makes sense to first develop a prototype for such a machine tool.
Modern software technology can support this with many methods such as rapid prototyping, object-oriented programming, rule-based systems, declarative programming, and the extensive use of generic methods.
Fig. 7 gives a rough overview of the necessary software components of a CNC-machine tool which would satisfy the demands listed above for application in a one-of-a-kind manufacturing system.

The **user interface** enables the skilled worker to enter the necessary commands

* interactively on the screen with the help of a mouse. This enables the system to lead an untrained user.

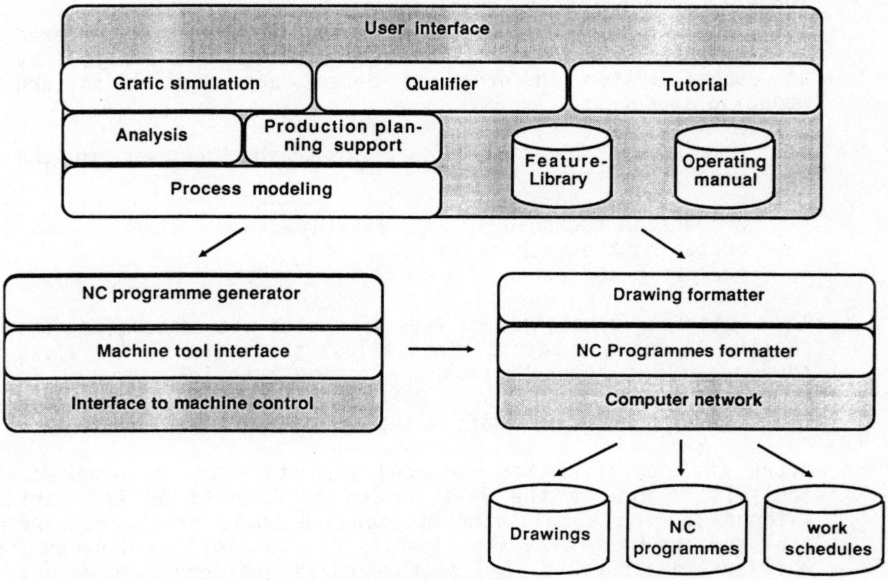

Fig. 7: Preliminary Software Concept of a Prototype

* with a simple key stroke. This supports the well-trained user who constantly works with the system.
* as mnemonic abbreviations with the use of a command interpreter. This simplifies use of the system for well-trained, occasional users.

The user interface also contains hierarchically structured help functions:

* A short explanation for each command
* A comprehensive description for each menu within the system
* An interactive data base for access to the system's operating manuals. This database is referred to as an **automated operating manual.**

Beside this, the user interface allows overwriting of all planning information automatically generated by **production planning support, process modelling,** and **analysis,** described later. This makes possible the use of nonoptimal tools or cutting speeds, which is often necessary within a prototype environment. In this way production planning of a one-of-a-kind product can be contained within the necessary restrictions on time and money.

- After the user has entered a feature to be produced by the machine the **qualifier** analyses the user's knowledge regarding the production process. When producing the workpiece in Fig. 5, for example, it seems better to mill the pocket first and drill the holes afterwards since the milling tool has to pass the places where the holes are situated, anyway. If the work is done the other way around, the drilling tool has to remove more material and production time is increased. If the qualifier identifies weaknesses in the machine user it suggests appropriate tutorial chapters.
  This is done by recording the sequence of operations entered by the user. From time to time these records are analysed by an expert system in order to detect unproductive feature mounting sequences.

- The **intelligent tutorial** serves to train the user in the following subjects:

  * production technology, e.g. milling
  * operating the machine tools
  * feature-based production

  The tutorial contains an expert system to determine its pupil's learning progress. This allows the tutorial to adjust to the pupil's comprehension speed. The tutorial's target is to supply basic knowledge. Detailed informaton is obtained from the automatic operating manual mentioned above.

- After the qualifier has released a feature to be produced, **analysis** checks if the feature can be mounted on the part without causing a collision between the tools or the machine tool and the part with its clamping device. This is done by a well suited algorithm. A lot of research has been carried out in collision detection within machine tools in the last years.

- With the help of **graphic simulation** the worker can:

  * simulate the application of features to the part in order to test the part's functionality experimentally
  * study the shape of the part in its current state. After collision prevention has released a feature for production it is irreversibly applied to the part by the simulator.

  Three-dimensional shading has been considered for representation of the simulated part on the computer screen, since this provides the most accurate representation of objects. Rotation of the part being simulated, as well as enlarging of its details, should be possible in order to provide the user with different views of the part.

- If analysis has released a feature for production, an expert system referred to as **production planning support** tries to select an appropriate tool and production method, e.g. face milling or end milling. The user, however, is allowed to modify this planning data due to his higher level of knowledge regarding the production process and the available resources.

- The information provided by feature analysis and production planning support is sent to the **process modelling** module. This expert system selects optimal process parameters (e.g. cutting depth and cutting speed) with respect to part materials and tools. After this tool paths are selected. This module allows overwriting of the generated information by the user.

- With the information above the **NC programme generator** generates the necessary NC programme for production of a feature or a free form surface. Under certain circumstances the use of macros supplied with the appropriate coordinates and dimensions of the feature would be possible.

- The **machine tool interface** sends the NC programme produced by the programme generator for production of the features on the part, together with the necessary orders for loading and operating the tools, to the machine tool.

- The **NC programme formatter** is used to link the NC programmes for various different features together into one programme which can then be used for repeated manufacture of this part. In the case of mass production it is also conceivable that cutting paths could be recomputed so as to enable the choice of optimal tools.

- When work on the part is finished, the **drawing formatter** generates the necessary drawings and their dimensions, based on the simulated representation of the part. These drawings are then stored in a standard format, or sent over the computer network to the workshop computer.

- The **computer network** allows exchange of information between the different machines of the one-of-a-kind workshop and links the workshop to the mass production departments within the company.

6. References

[1] Savory, S., "Künstliche Intelligenz und Expertensysteme", 2. Aufl., R. Oldenbourg Verlag, München Wien 1985.

[2] Erve A. H.,van't, "Generative Computer Aided Process Planing", University of Twente, January 1988.

[3] Brown, P. F., McLean, C. R., "Interactive Process Planning in AMRF", Bound volume of the 1986 ASME Winter Annual Meeting, Anaheim, CA, December 1986.

[4] Eloranta, E., Mäntylä, M., Opas, J., Ranta, M., " HutCapp - A Process Planning System Based on the Integration of Knowledge Engineering, Feature Modeling and Geometric Modeling", Laboratory of Information Processing Science, Helsinki University of Technology.

[5] Mäntylä, M., Opas, J., Puhakka, J., " A Prototype System for Generative Process Planning of Prismatic Parts", Laboratory of Information Processing Science, Helsinki University of Technology.

[6] Project Summary, "Expert Manufacturing Programming Systems", CAM-I, Arlington Texas, 1987.

SECTION 2 - PRODUCTION PLANNING AND SCHEDULING

A Distributed Asynchronous Hierarchical Problem-Solving Architecture applied to Plant Scheduling

Iain Buchanan, Peter Burke, John Costello
and Patrick Prosser
Department of Computer Science, University of Strathclyde, Glasgow G1 1XH, UK

ABSTRACT

A distributed, asynchronous, hierarchical, problem-solving architecture is introduced, and the need for it justified. A large-scale implementation of the architecture, in the form of a distributed asynchronous scheduler (DAS), is described. An application of DAS directed at plant scheduling is presented and the benefits of such an approach are analysed. Key features of DAS are its event-driven style and the uniform view it takes of the twin tasks of schedule creation and schedule repair. Issues addressed include problem decomposition, communication, consistency and conflict resolution in the model, software agents and problem-solving behaviour.

INTRODUCTION

Computer systems which attempt to cope with real problems face a range of difficulties which vary in source and severity. One major source of difficulty (for conventional and knowledge-based systems alike) is the need to cope with problems where the very concept of 'solving' the problem is ill-defined. This difficulty can be aggravated further if

(1) the underlying problem has a strong combinatorial flavour
(2) the problem definition is changing over time, and
(3) there is a requirement for solutions in 'real-time'.

This challenging combination of qualities is fairly common, especially in domains such as manufacturing, transportation, finance, defence and health care.

One source of the poor definition of a 'solution' is the existence of several, usually conflicting, measures for judging solution quality. Under such circumstances, a naive optimising approach, based on a single criterion, is unlikely to be acceptable. Any search for a solution should thus be based on achieving satisfactory levels for the range of measures. One method of achieving this is to use a solution method which addresses the measures (directly or indirectly) during the search process.

To solve large-scale combinatorial problems it is usually advantageous to apply some type of decomposition tactic, creating subproblems of manageable size. While generally reducing computational complexity, there is the requirement to synthesise subproblem solutions into some total solution. This may involve iterative attempts at decomposition, subproblem solution and synthesis. Decomposition can be along a number of axes, including time, and the granularity and natural demarcations of the real system.

Although the real system may be changing over time, the rate of change in small intervals of time will often be small. Thus to solve the new system, it may only be necessary to solve a slightly changed subproblem and perform the appropriate synthesis. If the problem decomposition is appropriate, the solution effort will be minimal, and hence may approach the 'real-time' requirements. More substantial system changes can be expected to affect more system components and hence require a more substantial re-solution effort.

To meet these four sources of difficulty, a distributed, asynchronous and hierarchical architecture is proposed. The hierarchy imposes a problem decomposition which allows several criteria to be applied in searching for solutions, and creates subproblems which are computationally tractable, and synthesisable into a total solution. The distributed asynchronous feature both depends on and allows for the system coping with changing problem definition (from several sources) in a uniform, efficient manner. It also offers an interesting range of control strategies to guide problem-solving behaviour and enables the software architecture to be ported to distributed or parallel hardware hosts.

This architecture imposes no restrictions on the problem-solving styles used in the component sub-problems, except that synthesis should be realisable. A heterogeneous collection of styles is thus possible, although the implementation described below uses only a small number.

THE PLANT SCHEDULING PROBLEM

The plant scheduling task demonstrates the qualities referred to in the introduction. The merit of a schedule is a function of several measures, some of which may be ill-defined. Scheduling can be viewed as the problem of assigning resources and start times to operations (the components of a process plan) and thus is usually of combinatorial complexity. Scheduling takes place in a dynamic, stochastic environment and problem definition can thus change as a function of events in the real world. Finally, some domains can usefully exploit a solution capability which is 'real-time'.

This commentary suggests the need for a scheduling capability which is not dominated by an optimisation paradigm and which is open and reactive in its problem-solving style. Over recent years there has been a trend towards augmenting predictive schedulers with a reactive capability (ISIS [15], OPIS [12], SONIA [3]). Treatment of schedule failure, initiating a schedule repair, varies, but all of these systems separate to some extent the tasks of predictive and reactive scheduling. One distinguishing feature of the system described below is the uniform view taken of the predictive and reactive scheduling tasks. Elleby [7] proposes a similar view of scheduling for dynamic environments.

THE DAS ARCHITECTURE

The technology of distributed artificial intelligence has been exploited to produce a large prototype system as "proof of concept" that a distributed asynchronous scheduler (DAS) is both practical and appropriate to the plant scheduling problem.

The DAS architecture features a three tier hierarchy which can be interpreted as a metaphor for an idealised management structure. Decision-making in the structure is distributed and asynchronous, and heavily reliant for success on communication across and within the three levels. Constraint propagation and mail are the two communication mechanisms employed. These are described in Burke [1, 2], and, more briefly, below.

DAS is a reactive, generic scheduler. It integrates with existing plant management information systems, maintaining schedules in the dynamic plant environment. While the prototype is targeted at demonstration in an aluminium plate production facility, the architecture offers more generic capabilities to other process and analogous industries. This functionality is partly achieved by careful separation of structural domain knowledge from problem-solving knowledge. Details are in Costello [4].

The objective of DAS is to produce and maintain a workable schedule which satisfies the variety of constraints bounding a legal solution. Influences on the design include the opportunistic scheduling style proposed by Fox and Kempf [8].

DAS features three tiers - strategic, tactical and operational. Viewing the hierarchy as a tree with branches and nodes, DAS associates an *agent* with each node.

The Strategic Level

The strategic level takes a relatively long-term view of the scheduling task. Its function is to translate management objectives into broad methods to be invoked by lower levels in attempting to meet these objectives. Thus the strategic level is the interface for management to describe (in their domain language) general goals for production performance (in terms of delivery timeliness targets, work-in-progress levels etc) and to impose or manipulate general constraints on the system (such as new shift patterns, planned maintenance, changes to resource levels etc). Some of these objectives/constraints can be readily absorbed into the appropriate components of the underlying representation. Others need to be translated into an equivalent 'procedural' or problem-solving form.

The Tactical Level

A tactical agent (t-agent) deals with aggregate resources, normally a collection of similar individual resources, and takes a medium-term view of the scheduling problem. The collection of t-agents can thus reflect 'natural' resource groupings in the plant. A t-agent has two responsibilities. Firstly, it is concerned with the delegation of work to specific subordinate production resources. Secondly it resolves conflicts which may arise at the operational level, usually in collaboration with other t-agents. Conflict resolution may involve the retraction of work by a t-agent from that previously delegated to a subordinate.The time horizons for t-agents reflect aspects of the production process (eg cycle times, schedule volatility) and user requirements.

In selecting work to delegate or retract, t-agents consider factors from a variety of sources. These include resource-based constraints (machine loading, set-ups, work-in-progress) and order-based constraints (due date, machine requirement or preference). By a suitable choice of agent behaviour, the tactical level can instantiate a problem-solving perspective in response to the requirements expressed at the strategic level. T-agents can themselves express and manipulate a variety of constraint types, but it is one of their primary functions to use or translate these into uniform temporal constraints when delegating work to the operational level.

The Operational Level

The operational level is the most fine-grained, and models the actual resources of the plant. Each resource has an associated operational level agent (an o-agent) which is responsible for solving the scheduling task imposed by the superior t-agent. Each o-agent views its problem as a dynamic constraint satisfaction problem (CSP), and a solution to the problem is achieved if all current operations within the scope of the o-agent have been given a legal start time. At this level all constraints are temporal. Each o-agent will normally have a collection of operations to schedule and each operation will have an associated set of temporal constraints which define the *domain* of the operation - the set of legal start times. The temporal constraints may have been derived by the superior t-agent from non-temporal information, as well as originating from temporal sources (eg the timing of other operations in the process plan of the work object). Details of o-agent behaviour are given below and in Prosser [13, 14].

From time to time, o-agents may be posed infeasible problems. This conflict and the source of the conflict is notified by the o-agent to its superior t-agent which takes corrective action. Further details are given below and in Burke [1].

COMMUNICATION AND CONFLICT RESOLUTION

In the field of distributed artificial intelligence, problem solvers can be loosely divided into the two classes of synchronous and asynchronous, with further sub-classifications based on the nature of the control and communication mechanisms used. DAS can be characterised as a network of communicating subproblems which are tackled asynchronously. Such an approach raises a number of problems.

Firstly it is necessary to ensure that the individual solution processes, corresponding to agents of the DAS hierarchy, have a consistent view of 'the world' to be solved and the problem-solving state of the system. More correctly, each agent's view of its problem should be part of a consistent overall view. None of the lowest level agents has anything other than a view of a fairly small section of the total problem. Secondly, it is a natural consequence of the asynchronous behaviour of DAS that conflict will arise in the solution process. Sources of conflict are described below. DAS assumes that conflict resolution is a recurrent, intermittent duty of (tactical) agents, and not an exception to be specially handled.

Work to be put through the production facilities is represented by a process plan, that is a collection of processes which are linked by temporal precedence relations. A process plan serves as a description of the route (not instantiated to the level of individual machines) which a piece of work must follow through the plant. To support fully an opportunistic capability, it is necessary to allow nonlinear process plans (Burke [2]). For each process in a process plan, DAS maintains a unique operation tagged with the appropriate temporal precedence relations. It is these operations which the tactical level is required to delegate and for which the operational level is required to allocate a start time.

Consistency in DAS

There are three classes of consistency to be ensured. These are inter-plan, intra-plan and inter-agent. Inter-plan consistency is required when the operations of separate process plans 'meet' on a common resource at the operational level. Ensuring inter-agent consistency (ie a consistent world view) is achieved by a combination of temporal constraint propagation (TCP) and the conflict resolution mechanism described below. Consistency within a process plan (intra-plan consistency) is also readily achieved using the TCP facility since consistency at the operational level is confined to temporal relations.

There is a requirement to update appropriate components of the temporal constraint representation when a constituent operation in a process plan is affected by internal or external events (eg its start time is decided by the o-agent, or a part of the same process plan is reported complete). To cope with conflict and its resolution (via retraction of delegated work), the TCP module uses structures for constraint representation which encode the source as well as the value of temporal constraint information. This adds some complexity and necessary redundancy to the representation, but it is not the case that the dual representation unduly affects computational effort and agent behaviour (Burke [1, 2]). During execution the agents may well be unaware of some of the functioning of the TCP module since they can only detect when changes take place in their representation of the world view.

Conflict and Its Resolution

A major responsibility of each t-agent is the translation of several types of constraint into temporal constraints, used in delegating work to subordinate o-agents. This may be expected to produce high levels of temporal consistency in the o-agents' subproblems, but it is not the case that the system will remain conflict free as the o-agents progress with their problem-solving.

There are three sources of conflict, one external and two internal. In the real, external world, events can deviate from their predicted behaviour. An operation can finish significantly early (or late), and this will potentially create opportunities for (or conflicts with) the rest of the process. Internal conflict can arise from the t-agents' problem-solving style which may occasionally lead them (in the interests of overall system performance) to pose (slightly) impossible problems for the o-agents. Finally, the o-agents can have, temporarily, genuinely different world views.

There are two sources of these differing world views. Firstly, constraint propagation takes a finite time, and an o-agent may take an apparently legal decision which shortly thereafter conflicts with a new constraint made known to the agent. A second, more complex, source of conflict is due to an agent priority mechanism. This is used dynamically in DAS to focus problem-solving resources on perceived difficulties. In certain circumstances, an o-agent may be allowed to ignore certain classes of change to its problem, for a limited interval of time.

On detecting conflict, an o-agent uses a mail message system to inform its superior t-agent of the nature and source of its difficulty. Apart from being set infeasible problems, an o-agent can also be in difficulty on feasible problems. In the latter case, it can have unsuccessfully exhausted its search strategy, or its allowed quantum of search effort . The t-agent may respond with a unilateral relaxation of the o-agent's problem or it may negotiate with other appropriate t-agents. Further details are in Burke [1].

REACTIVE AGENT BEHAVIOUR

Operating on a single resource, o-agents are used to schedule incrementally and reactively in the dynamic plant environment. Each o-agent views its problem as that of dynamic constraint satisfaction. This mechanism is sufficiently rich and robust to support the agent in predictive and reactive roles.

Following Mackworth [11], the CSP can be represented as the labeling of an undirected graph. In the scheduling context, the problem is further complicated since the graph may change at any time and without warning, reflecting externally generated changes to the underlying problem. Coping with this dynamic feature requires enhancements to the standard problem representation and considerable ingenuity in the CSP techniques employed to maintain acceptable performance levels for agent behaviour and computing resource usage (Prosser [13, 14]).

In generating schedules, DAS is concerned with satisfaction rather than global optimisation. The nature and use of constituent (search) algorithms at the operational level will thus have implications for the nature and quality of solutions generated. There is considerable variety available in controlling agent performance and experimentation at this level has used a number of possible enhancements, in particular to render search more effective and agent behaviour more intelligent. For example, basic search strategies may be enhanced by exploiting information about the topology of the underlying graph, and by variants of forward checking schemes (Harlick [10]). In addition, dependency directed backtracking (Gaschnig [9], Stallman and Sussman [16]), shallow learning (Dechter [5]) and a variant of a justification-based Truth Maintenance System (Doyle [6]) have been investigated in seeking improved o-agent performance (Prosser [13, 14]).

CONCLUSIONS

DAS has been implemented on a Symbolics 3620 workstation using a mixture of KEE, flavors and lisp. This is a mature, but developing, system. A multi-functional user interface has been implemented. This is used as an aid in presenting and understanding agent behaviour, as well as displaying schedules from various perspectives. Thus the interface can display something of the dynamic problem-solving state of the system, as well as proposed schedules. In its current form, the interface displays varieties of dynamic barcharts showing the problem faced by agents (their operational envelope) and their solution attempt. Making full use of the highly interactive workstation environment, the schedule may be viewed from resource-based and order-based perspectives. Work on the interface is in hand, especially allowing user interaction with the functioning of the scheduler and incorporating new scheduler functionality.

DAS will shortly be integrated with a high-fidelity plant simulation to further test scheduler features and indicate areas for refinement and empirical testing. Interfaces exist to allow communication with conventional manufacturing management systems, and this is the route by which scheduling decisions will be distributed to the plant and changes in the plant state (work completion, machine breakdowns, work arrival etc) reported.

DAS incorporates a number of novel features which will find increasing application in the distributed, intelligent systems of the future. In domains with appropriate data capture and data dissemination facilities, its transaction-driven style can address an important range of end-user requirements.

ACKNOWLEDGEMENTS

This research is supported by the Science and Engineering Research Council under Grant Number GR/D/4357.0

REFERENCES

1. Burke, P, Scheduling in a Dynamic Environment, Technical Report AISL-38-88, November 1988, Department of Computer Science, University of Strathclyde, Glasgow.

2. Burke, P, Temporal Constraint Propagation in DAS, Technical Report AISL-34-88, August 1988, Department of Computer Science, University of Strathclyde, Glasgow.

3. Collinot, A , Le Pape, C and Pinoteau, G, SONIA: A Knowledge-Based Scheduling System, Artificial Intelligence in Engineering, vol 3, pp 86-94, 1988.

4. Costello, J, A Common Knowledge-Base for Multiple Applications, Technical Report AISL-35-88, November 1988, Department of Computer Science, University of Strathclyde, Glasgow.

5. Dechter, R, Learning While Searching in Constraint Satisfaction Problems, AAAI-86, vol 1, pp 178-183, August 1986.

6. Doyle, J, A Truth Maintenance System, in Readings in Artificial Intelligence (ed. Webber, B L and Nilsson, N J), pp 496-516, Tioga Pub Co, 1981.

7. Elleby, P Fargher, H and Addis, T, Incremental Constraint Satisfaction, Knowledge Systems Group, Department of Computer Science, University of Reading, 1988.

8. Fox, B R and Kempf, K G, Opportunistic Scheduling for Robot Assembly, Proc 1985 IEEE Int Conf on Robotics and Automation, pp 880-889, IEEE, 1985.

9. Gaschnig, J, A General Backtrack Algorithm that Eliminates Most Redundant Tests, Proc IJCAI-77, p 457, 1977.

10. Haralick, R M and Elliot, G L, Increasing Tree Search Efficiency for Constraint Satisfaction Problems, Artificial Intelligence, vol 14, pp 263-314, 1980.

11. Mackworth, A K, Consistency in Networks of Relations, Artificial Intelligence, vol 8, pp 99-118, 1977.

12. Ow, P S, Smith, S F and Thirez, A, Reactive Plan Revision, Proc CAIA-88, pp 77-82, 1988.

13. Prosser, P, Reactive Factory Scheduling as a Dynamic Constraint Satisfaction Problem, Technical Report AISL-31-88, August 1988, Department of Computer Science, University of Strathclyde, Glasgow.

14. Prosser, P, A Reactive Scheduling Agent, Technical Report AISL-37-88, November 1988, Department of Computer Science, University of Strathclyde, Glasgow.

15. Smith, S F, Fox, M S and Ow, P S, Constructing and Maintaining Detailed Production Plans: Investigations into the Development of Knowledge-Based Factory Scheduling Systems, AI Magazine, Fall 1986.

16. Stallman, R M and Sussman, G J, Forward Reasoning and Dependency Directed Backtracking in a System for Computer-Aided Circuit Analysis, Artificial Intelligence, vol 9, pp 138-196, 1977.

Production Planning and Scheduling: A Bottom-Up Approach

M. Nussbaum* and L. Slahor**

**Computer Science Department, School of Engineering, Catholic University of Chile, Casilla 6177, Santiago, Chile*

***Sandoz Chemicals Ltd., PO Box, CH-4002 Basel, Switzerland*

ABSTRACT

Production planning and scheduling (PPS) has gained considerable attention in the last decade, especially in the area of industrial manufacturing. The main technique for solving this problem has been mathematical programming, which relies on the numeric processing power of the computer. Because of the NP-hard nature of the PPS problem, no efficient algorithm is available for solving real big problems. Recently, Artificial Intelligence (AI) methods have been applied, which rely on the symbolic processing power of the computer.

This paper describes a knowledge-based scheduling system for a large, real-world factory. Based on AI techniques, such a system relieves the production planner from the complex scheduling problems which are almost impossible to cope with. The user can control scheduling interactively, taking advantage of the user interface to view the produced plans as Gantt diagrams. Still in prototype form, the system is fulfilling the initial user expectations and improving the performance of production planners.

1. INTRODUCTION

Production Planning and Scheduling (PPS) problems [11] have been intensively investigated in Management Sciences and Operations Research [3]. Mathematical programming techniques have most often been used to solve these problems, but the research focuses mostly on problems which are unsatisfactory for real-life situations.

The problem is usually divided into two parts: planning or process routing - which is the selection of a sequence of operations - and scheduling - which is the assignment of time and resources. Actually, the distinction between planning and scheduling is fuzzy; they are highly interactive and are usually performed as an integrated activity.

The field of scheduling remains mostly at the stage of qualitative wisdom. An optimal solution is normally impossible to obtain since even a modest-sized PPS problem has an enormous number of possible schedules. (Scheduling is a NP-hard problem [7).

Recently the PPS problem has been studied using Artificial Intelligence (AI) techniques, as for example [5, 6, 8, 12]. Typically, the task is to find a state that satisfies some goal condition from a given state of the world, and a plan is a set of ordered sequences of actions that will transform the initial state into a goal state. Most AI approaches to planning are primarily concerned with investigating various theoretical questions about the abilities and the scope of general planning techniques. Our interest, however, is to provide a knowledge-based [2] solution to real-world factory scheduling problems.

The rest of this paper is organized as follows. Section 2 describes what the PPS problem looks like at Sandoz, while Section 3 describes the approach taken to solve this problem. Section 4 introduces a general model of the PPS problem which is used in Section 5 to present a planning strategy which has been implemented on a concrete scheduling problem at Sandoz. Sections 6 shows the relevant aspects of the user interface. The paper finishes with concluding remarks.

2. PROBLEM DESCRIPTION FROM THE USER'S SIDE

The factory scheduling problem [4] concerns the allocation over time of a finite set of resources to a set of specific manufacturing operations. More precisely, the problem is defined as follows. A set of products has to be produced on different apparatus. Each of these products is produced in a single process where each process may have several production variants. Each production variant is decomposed into a finite set of steps. Since we are working in a multipurpose apparatus environment (a given apparatus can be used in the production of several products) the planner can choose in each production step one apparatus from a set of alternatives. The production steps have to be performed in a specific (repetitive) continuous sequence. Each step has to be repeated when more quantity is desired than the one delivered in one production sequence; quantity given by the physical capacity of the apparatus. The operation has to be continuous since in the chemical environment it is dangerous to break the production process into parts.

The problem consists then in finding a time interval with the earliest possible time for going into production and the latest possible time for completion of production. The earliest possible time is when all inputs needed to the manufacturing process are available, while the latest possible time reflects the requirements of the management.

Manufacturing a product requires that a whole set of apparatus is available, i.e. not occupied by other products within the time interval. The problem is complicated since within a given time interval a set of products has to be planned with a competitive set of apparatus. When conflicts occur, i.e. no apparatus are available for a given step, the planner has to replan some of the products or even delay the production of a subset of orders.

Real world PPS problems are so large (the planners of Sandoz construct schedules for more than 50 products at more than 60 apparatus for a given plant) and complicated (the length of one production process may range from 5 to 20 production steps in a multipurpose equipment) that a planner can not immediately understand all the consequences of a given decision. For example, a preference for a given apparatus within a production variant expresses a planner's desire that one apparatus - the so called stem apparatus - be used instead of another. Preferred choices can result in time delays in an order as illustrated in Fig. 1.

The problem of deciding which apparatus - stem or alternative - should be chosen so as to minimize the overall finishing time is extremely difficult. An additional problem is to predict the effects of the local decisions on the global solution: in a multi-agent environment (factory scheduling is a multi-agent planning problem where each order represents a separate agent) conflicting agents may negatively affect each other.

3. SYSTEM ARCHITECTURE

Today at Sandoz, plans are manually generated using some type of Gantt chart. Our final objective is to deliver an interactive computer-aided planning (CAP) system that supports the planner in his job. The system should increase resource usability making the production more profitable (a production plant is extremely expensive (around 100 million Swiss francs); any increase in productivity means enormous savings), while easing the planning task (taking minutes instead of days).

Our approach for solving the problem has been a bottom-up one whereby we begin by supporting the manual planning and end by supporting most of the planning. The system (Fig. 2) is being built in three phases:

1. An information system where the user (production planner) interactively constructs production plans, as for example [1]. The system supports the user with all the needed information about orders, time boundaries, quantities, production variants, and free and busy apparatus.
2. A decision support system which proposes the possible alternatives of the production plans, as for example [9]. The definitive decision still remains on the planner.
3. A knowledge based system which automatically, or under interactive control, generates schedules. The final system is designed to assist the human scheduler, not to replace him.

In the general architecture of the final system (Fig. 2) four modules can be distinguished:

1. Knowledge Base. The knowledge base is formed by facts and rules. Facts represent plant specifications such as production variants (Fig. 3). Rules include production priorities and planning heuristics.
2. Knowledge Base Maintenance Tools. By means of the knowledge base maintenance tools the user can update or check the integrity of his knowledge base.
3. Planning Modules. The user can choose among various planning heuristics to have a plan generated for him automatically. The user may also specify to manually schedule some critical products.

4. User Interface. The user interface provides - with its windows and menus - a graphical interface through which the user can manually perform some portion of the scheduling task.

4. MODELLING THE PLANNING PROBLEM

The job shop - or multi-product batch plant - scheduling problem can be characterized by a set of parameters. A given load **L** consists of a set of products $\mathbf{P_S}$ ($1 \le s \le n$) where all the $\mathbf{P_S}$ have to be planned. Each product $\mathbf{P_S}$ may have several production variants $\mathbf{V_{st}}$ ($1 \le t \le m$) where one of these has to be chosen. A given production variant $\mathbf{V_{st}}$ can begin to be produced in a certain time range $\mathbf{T_{stu}}$ ($1 \le u \le l$); therefore one time inside this range has to be selected. Once the product, its variant and the beginning time have been determined, we have to define which step of the production $\mathbf{S_{stuv}}$ ($1 \le v \le k$) is planned first. Once the production step $\mathbf{S_{stuv}}$ has been decided, we have to choose from one of the many alternative apparatus or machines $\mathbf{M_{stuvw}}$ ($1 \le w \le j$) that are available for the step.

The set of steps defined above is general enough to model a broad range of problems. The dependence sequence shown for the set of parameters {L,P,V,T,S,M} is not necessarily fixed, and the one indicated is only one of the possible alternatives. The defined sequence of activities gives a hierarchy of activities that has to be solved:

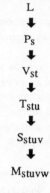

$$L \downarrow P_S \downarrow V_{st} \downarrow T_{stu} \downarrow S_{stuv} \downarrow M_{stuvw}$$

One way to represent the above hierarchy is through an AND/OR tree, shown in Fig. 4. In an AND node all the subtasks of the AND node have to be performed while in an OR node only one of the subtasks of the OR node have to be solved. In an AND node, therefore, the search strategy has to decide which subtask to do next, while in an OR node the search strategy has to determine which subtask to choose.

The solution to the planning problem (if there is one) will be one (or more) subtree(s) of the original AND/OR tree. The job consists then in finding one of these subtrees. From Fig. 4 it is obvious that an exhaustive search is impossible even for small problems. Besides its size, the search tree has the additional complexity that the subtrees are interrelated making the selection process of a subtask non-trivial. For example a given machine M may appear in the manufacturing process of several products. If these products are processed simultaneously, i.e. in the same time interval it is clear that only one of these products can be produced with the given machine M. The decision of producing a given product P with a machine M may therefore influence the selection process in the other hierarchies, i.e. in the selection of a given subtask in another level of the tree.

5. AUTOMATIC PLANNING

Automatic planning will consist in defining an efficient strategy (the problem has to be solved in minutes and not in days on a workstation) that finds a subtree of the previously defined AND/OR tree. Our way of solving this problem will be through a local optimization technique. It consists in traversing the tree in a breath-first fashion [10] and selecting the 'best node available' using a heuristic function. The quality of the obtained solution will therefore depend on the virtues of the applied heuristics. These heuristics are based on parameters measuring characteristics of the production process, i.e. the plant and the load. Table 1 illustrates a set of these parameters and its distinctions. More parameters can be defined which will depend on the Knowledge Engineer's understanding of the problem. These parameters can be either static or dynamic. A static parameter is the one obtained before run-time just by analyzing the knowledge base. A dynamic parameter, on the other hand, is calculated at run-time just before each decision is taken. Dynamic parameters directly reflect reality but are much more expensive in time, making the whole planning process longer.

Once we have available a set of meaningful measurements of the production process we can define heuristics based on these parameters. These heuristics in case of an OR node will choose a given subtask of the AND/OR tree in order to reduce the search space and in case of an AND node define some 'good' way of ordering the subtasks. Table 2 presents a set of heuristics based on the parameters of Table 1. How good or bad these heuristics are will mostly depend on the problem characteristics and therefore have to be tuned accordingly. Of course more heuristics can be defined using the user's experience.

Once a plan has been obtained, it is necessary to quantify the quality of the solution in order to select the most appropriate heuristic in each case. Table 3 illustrates a set of quantifiers. Among these the most interesting is the first one, the Accumulative Quadratic Delay. When a product is delivered on time, i.e. within the users specified time range, the plan is fine. When a product is delivered too late (or too early), however, the badness of the plan has to be measured in some way. This measure can not be linear since (usually) it is worse to deliver 1 product 20 days too late than 20 products 1 day too late. Therefore a polynomial factor is defined that better matches the customers preferences. In our case this factor was quadratic.

First results of our strategy are shown in Table 4 where four different heuristics applied on a concrete scheduling problem are analyzed. The parameters that varied were only the ones related to products and their variants. The time parameter was always chosen sequentially while the production steps and the machines were selected using the best available M_d. The results shown in Table 4 were calculated in only a couple of minutes (on a SUN 4/110) and are better than the ones a manual planner would obtain in two days.

6. USER INTERFACE

The interaction between the user and the system is through a high-level graphical user interface in which facilities are provided for supporting automatic and manual scheduling. Given the importance of the interface to the acceptability of the whole system, it has to be simple and accessible to non- technical people.

The interface is based on a multi-windowing system which is directly implemented in Prolog (using the interface of BIM Prolog to SunView) on a SUN 4/110 workstation. It has the following characteristics:

- It is WIMB- (window, icon, mouse, button) oriented with minimum requirements of typing.
- The manipulation of the windows and their contents are the results of some action of the user.
- Its displays are close to the real world documents the users are used to manipulate.
- Its interactive graphic display allows the user a scheduling task to be simulated. In the course of a simulation, procedures are activated to check if the desired schedule is allowed according to the information stored in the knowledge base.
- Its specialized editor incorporates facilities for updating the knowledge base.

The scheduling window represents the information through a Gantt chart similar to the one used today by the manual planner. Its horizontal time axis permits the user to scroll the time window while its vertical axis permits to move through the machine spectrum, allowing the user to display a desired combination of machines in time. This is very useful since the system can be guided by the user to a desired solution. Therefore the user, when desired, remains in total control of the system.

7. CONCLUSIONS

A prototype of a knowledge-based system for production planning and scheduling in real world manufacturing has been presented. We have shown the system architecture from which the automatic planning module was described in detail.

The prototype has been implemented in Prolog on a SUN 4/110 using the graphic capabilities of this workstation. Prolog has proven to be effective and flexible in describing the problem domain.

The prototype system has been used by real planners in supporting their activity. The system proved to be useful meeting the specifications requirements. Currently, we are improving the system by gathering and compiling additional information so as to extend the problem domain.

ACKNOWLEDGMENTS

M. Nussbaum carried out this work at the Integrated Systems Laboratory, Swiss Federal Institute of Technology, Zürich, Switzerland.

The work described in this paper has been partially carried out in the context of the EUREKA project EU56: PROTOS - Prolog Tools for Building Expert Systems. The partners of the corresponding subproject are: Swiss Federal Institute of Technology - Zürich, Sandoz Ltd., Belgian Institute of Management and University of Oldenburg.

REFERENCES

[1] Acaccia, G.M., Michelini, R.C., Molfino, R.M., and Piaggio, P.A. Information Data-Base Structures for Flexible-Manufacturing Simulators, in Modern Production Management Systems (A.Kusiak, editor), 1987, pp. 649- 661.

[2] Appelrath, H.-J. Von Datenbanken zu Expertensystemen, Informatik Fachberichte 102, Springer Verlag, Berlin ,1985.

[3] Bellman, R. et al. Mathematical Aspects of Scheduling and Applications, Pergamon Press, 1982.

[4] Egli, U.M., and Rippin, D.W. Short-Term Scheduling for Multiproduct Batch Chemical Plants, Computers & Chemical Engineering, Vol. 10, No. 4, pp. 303-325, 1986.

[5] Fox, M.S. Constraint-Directed Search: A Case Study of Job- Shop Scheduling. Ph.D. Thesis, Carnegie- Mellon University, December 1983.

[6] Ford, D., and Floyd, S. An Expert System for Dynamic Scheduling, ACM Symposium on Methodologies for Intelligent Systems, Knoxville, October 1986, pp. 56-64.

[7] Garey, M. and Johnson, D. Computers and Intractability: A Guide to the Theory of NP-Completness, Freeman &Co., 1979.

[8] Liu, B. Scheduling via Reinforcement, The International Journal for AI (ed. K.J. Mac Callum and D. Sriram), 1988.

[9] McKendree, J., and Zaback, J. Planning for Advising, in Proceedings Computer Human Interface (CHI) 88, pp. 179-183.

[10] Pearl, J. Heuristics, Addison Wesley, 1985.

[11] Steel, S. The Bread and Butter of Planning, Artificial Intelligence Review, 1987:1, pp. 159- 181.

[12] Tate, A. A Review of Knowledge Based Planning Techniques. Expert Systems 85 (ed. by M. Merry), Cambridge Press, 1985, pp 89-111.

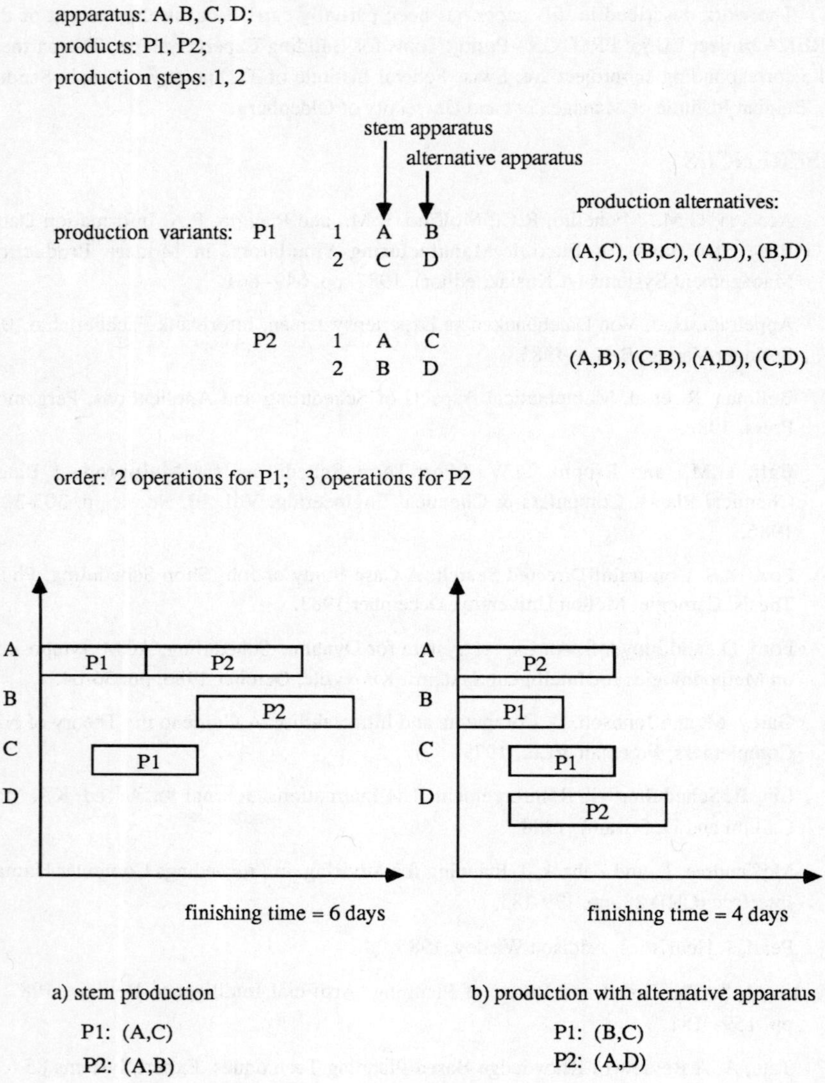

Figure 1 : Counterintuitive behavior of production scheduling (a virtual plant with 4 apparatus and 2 products)

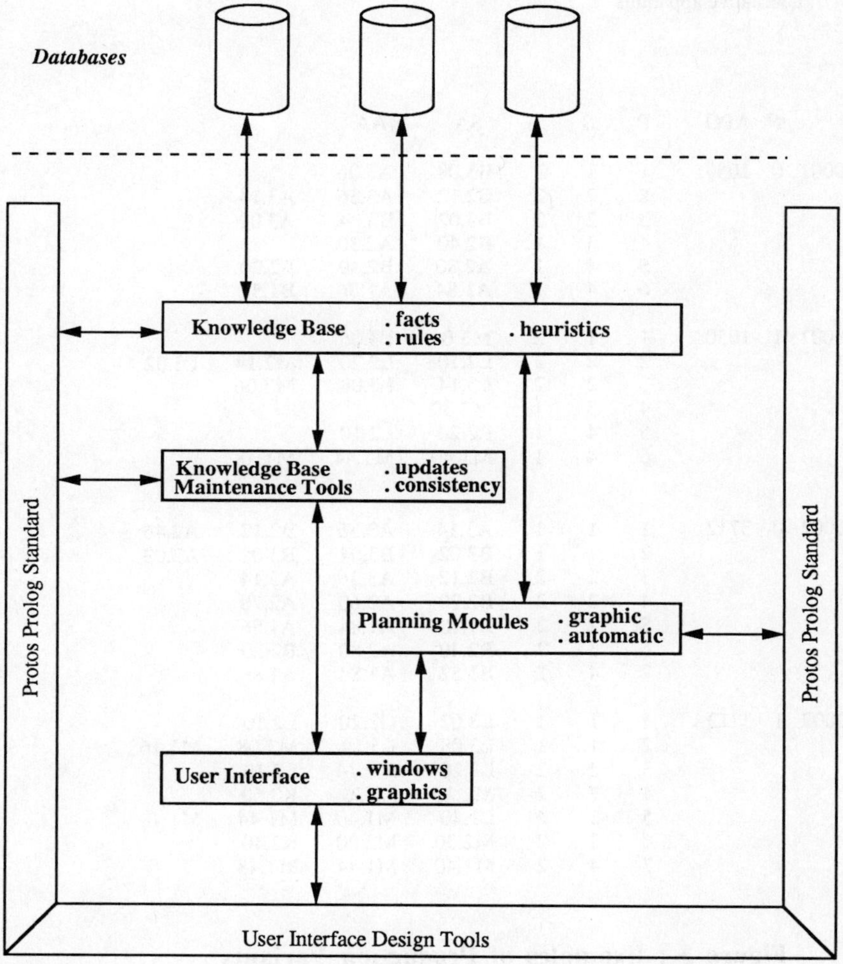

Figure 2 : System Architecture

PN : product name
N : number of production variant
APO : amount per operation (in kg)
P : production step
S : start day
C : number of cleaning days
SA : stem apparatus
AA : alternative apparatus

PN	N	APO	P	S	C	SA	AA		
0000001	0	1050	1	1	2	B3.08	A3.06		
			2	2	2	B2.12	A3.36	A3.14	
			3	2	2	B3.02	B3.04	A3.02	
			4	3	1	B2.40	A2.80		
			5	4	1	A2.80	B2.40	B2.20	
			6	4	1	A1.84	A1.86	B1.52	
0000001	1	1050	1	1	2	M3.04	L3.06		
			2	2	2	L2.10	L2.20	M2.14	L3.02
			3	2	2	L3.14	L3.08	M3.06	
			4	3	1	M2.30			
			5	4	1	L2.20	L2.10		
			6	4	1	M1.40	M1.44	M1.48	
0000002	0	3712	1	1	1	A3.14	A3.36	B2.12	A2.46
			2	1	1	B3.02	B3.04	B3.08	A3.02
			3	2	2	B2.12	A3.36	A3.14	
			4	2	2	B2.20	A2.60	A2.70	
			5	2	2	B1.18	A1.84	A1.86	
			6	3	2	B2.40	A2.80	B2.20	
			7	4	2	B1.52	A1.84	A1.86	
0000002	1	3712	1	1	1	L3.02	O2.20	L2.10	
			2	1	1	L3.08	L3.14	M3.08	M3.16
			3	2	2	L2.20	M2.14	L2.10	
			4	2	2	M2.20	L2.30	K2.60	
			5	2	2	L1.40	M1.40	M1.44	M1.48
			6	3	2	M2.30	M2.20	K2.40	
			7	4	2	M1.40	M1.44	M1.48	

Figure 3 : Examples of Production Variants

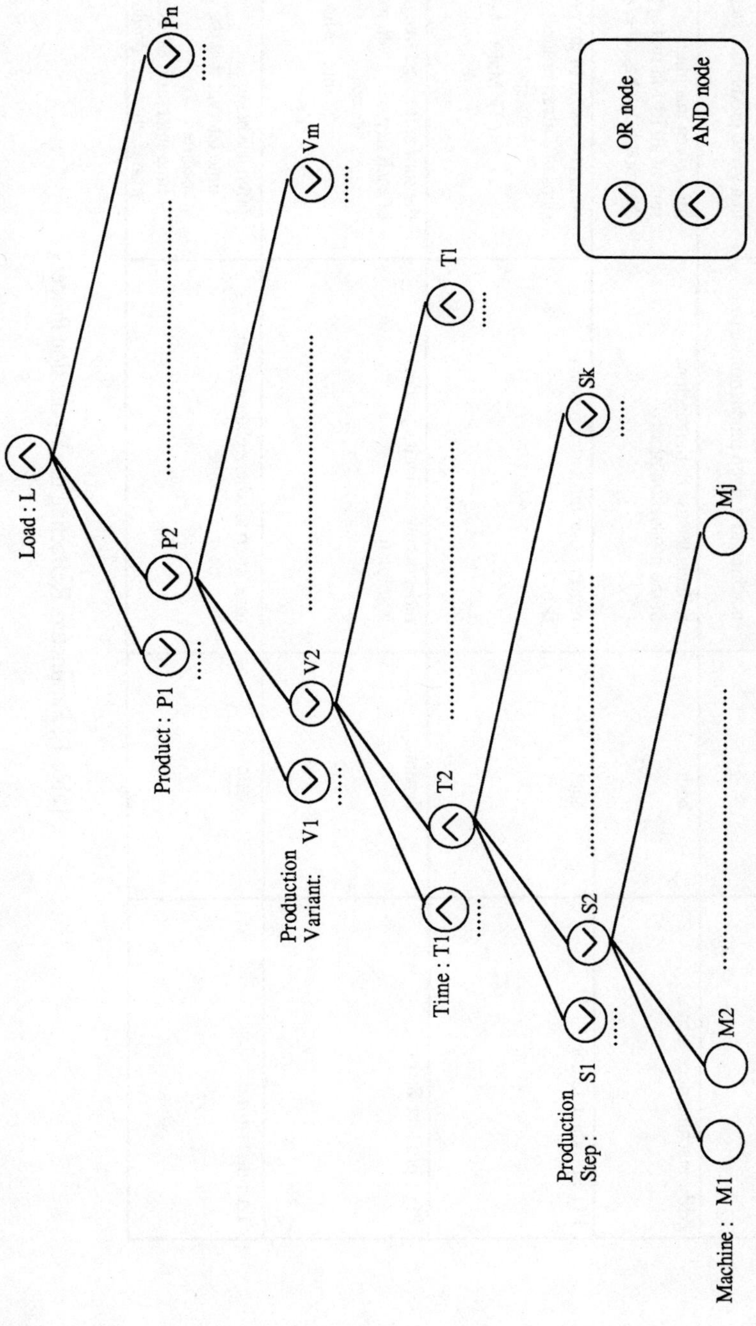

Figure 4 : General AND/OR Planning Tree

Parameter	Static/Dynamic	Characteristic	Definition
Ma : machine appearence	both	reflects the incidence of the machine in a given production step	inverse of the number of machines in a given production step
Md : machine dependence	both	reflects the use of the machine in the production plant	for a given machine, sum of all its Ma that appear in the knowledge base, i.e. all recipes
Pf_1 : product factor 1	both	reflects how difficult a product is to plan	geometric mean of the production steps of a given product variant $\left(\prod_{i=1}^{\#steps} Mai\right) / \#steps$
Pf_2 : product factor 2	dynamic	reflects how difficult a product is to plan	the sum of the best free machines of each step of a given recipe $\sum_{i=1}^{\#steps} \min(Mdi)$
TΔ : delta time	static	time interval where planning can be done on schedule	difference between : - time interval that the user specified - time interval it takes to manufacture the product

Table 1 : Parameters Reflecting the Production Process

Heuristic to choose ...	Operation and Parameter	Description
products (P and V)	best Pf1 or Pf2	Products that are easy to plan first
products (P and V)	worst Pf1 or Pf2	Products that are difficult to plan first
beginning of production (T)	increment time	Go sequentially in time until you can produce the product
beginning of production (T)	smallest $T\Delta$	Products with small $T\Delta$ are planned first since there is a smaller range from which to choose
steps or machines (S and M)	best Md	Machines that are less used by other products are scheduled first

Table 2 : Heuristics

Parameter	Description
Accumulative Quadratic Delay	reflects how bad the planning was by punishing polynomialy late deliveries $\sum_{i}^{\text{late products}} \sum_{j}^{\text{late days}} ((\text{Day to late})_{ij})^a \quad a > 1$
Late Deliveries	Number of products finished outside the user specified time interval
Maximum Delay	Worst case of the number of days that were outside the user specified time interval

Table 3 : Parameters for Measuring the Planning Quality

	Heuristic	Accumulative Quadratic Delay	Late Deliveries	Maximum Delay
1	max Pf1 first, static	25994	10	45
2	max Pf1 first, dynamic	13340	7	29
3	min Pf1 first, dynamic	12698	6	31
4	min Pf2 first, dynamic	1846	5	20

Table 4 : Planning Results

Small Expert Systems in Chemical Engineering

M.L. Espasa, J. Badenas and A. Barrera

Department of Chemical Engineering, Instituto Químico de Sarriá, c) Instituto Químico de Sarriá s/n, 08017 Barcelona, Spain

ABSTRACT

Some expert systems representing different industrial application areas are presented and their performances when used are discussed. The expert systems are programmed using different software approaches (Lisp, Prolog and an expert system shell on a 80286 based microcomputer). The developed expert systems applications are: material selection (PTFE) in a plastic production industry, production scheduling in a Fine Chemistry plant, management of a pipeline net in a Petrochemical plant, blending planning in a crude oil refinery and a natural language interface for a Heat Exchanger Design program.

INTRODUCTION

Our research work on "Industrial Applications of Artificial Intelligence techniques and Expert Systems", aimed to make an exploration of feasible and profitable applications of these tools in the Chemical Engineering Industry, has yielded some Expert Systems (ESs) and Artificial Intelligence (AI) programs. The purpose of this paper is to make a brief introduction to our project and present the ESs and programs mentioned above.

The main objective of our group is to infer rules of thumb to decide whether an ES or AI approach is adequate to solve a specific problem, and to select the best tool to solve it. In order to achieve this goal we are, at a first stage, developing some ESs covering a wide range of application areas. This leads us to face problems of medium complexity, suitable to be solved using 80286 based personal computers, disregarding the complex ones that will be considered in the second stage of the project.

Up to now we have worked on ESs selected to be of a varied nature. The variation is sometimes in the problem itself - consulting, planning, control - others in the industry - petrochemical, plastics, cement - and in the software approach - LISP, Prolog, ES Shell -. The ESs built have also different applications such as teaching, consulting, management and so forth. The AI applications developed in our research are:

a.- Material selection (PTFE) in a plastic industry.
b.- Production scheduling in a Fine Chemistry Plant.
c.- Management of a pipeline net in a Petrochemical Plant.
d.- Blending planning in a crude oil refinery.
e.- Natural language interface for a Heat Exchanger Design program.

On the forthcoming pages we will describe in brief these ES and programs.

a.- Material selection (PTFE) in a plastic industry.

The selection of materials, equipment, etc., is one of the best suited activities for ESs and the ES developed also proves this end.

In this kind of problems it is possible to distinguish three parts. The main one is to achieve the best matching between the requirements presented and the choices stored in the database. Even though this is the most important part, the other two must not be neglected since they involve the selection of the representational model used in the program. These tasks are the representation of the knowledge of the possible selections in the database, and the way to interact with the user to obtain information about the problem to be solved. The knowledge of the possible choices must be complete and easy to update, although this can lead to intensive work to obtain the knowledge/data base. The user must repeat the description of a particular problem every time he consults the ES, therefore it is desirable to shorten the process by not asking for useless information and to have a user-friendly interface.

Our design divides the system in two main operative blocks, the ES and the database properties analyser. The ES has the knowledge stored in the form of a hierarchical tree (part of it is shown figure 1) built from a selection of the information obtained from the expert.

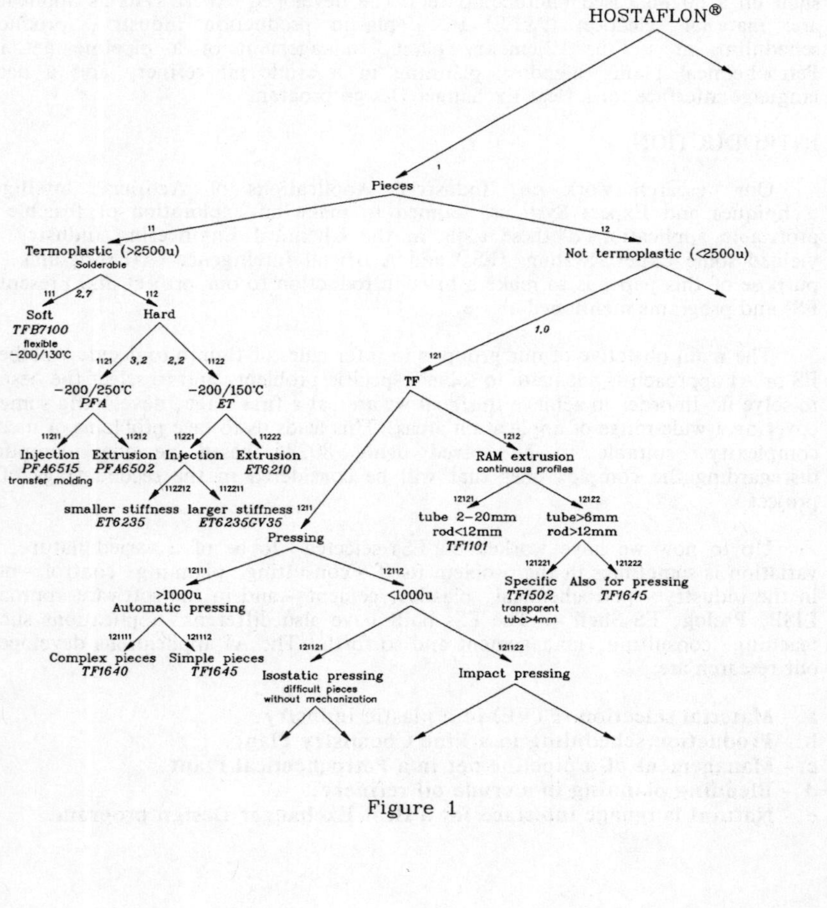

Figure 1

This tree has in its terminal nodes varieties of Hostaflon® or groups of them, and the connecting branches are related to the questions used to describe the problem. The ES goes through the tree according the answers provided by the user. These answers usually reference simple properties like:

- Maximum working temperature.
- Size of the machinery used on transformation.
- Complexity of the desired piece.
- Chemical resistance requirements.
- Manufacturing of pieces or other uses (coating, ...)

The user is guided in this process by means of menus with help facilities and he has always an option to denote that he is unable to decide among the alternatives suggested. Finally the ES presents the set of Hostaflon® varieties recommended and passes it to the database properties analyser, responsible for the refinement stage. At this stage the user can restrict the recommended choices by the establishment of as many constraints as desired due to physical, chemical and electrical properties. At the end, the cheapest variety of the final group is the one recommended by the ES.

The ES has been tested by technical staff responsible of the task and has been found to be adequate. However, it lacks of the option to allow an easy update of the database and the possibility of dealing with inputs such as 'high, low, medium' in the database consulting process, to have the ES ready to be distributed to clients.

This ES has been programmed in Turbo-Prolog® and the information about the group of products Hostaflon® has been provided by Hoechst Ibérica S.A..

b) Production scheduling in a Fine Chemistry Plant.

Although planning is a difficult task in a changing market such as the fine chemistry one, some short and medium range planning is needed to operate these plants properly. This task is usually done by experts in the field, using the foresight of next year's sales supplied by the sales' department to schedule the productions accordingly.

The ES uses this foresight to schedule the productions obtaining the overall plan for the year. Although this plan is often modified monthly, weekly or even daily, it is always used as a reference pattern. For the time being the ES does not make the revision of the plan.

The ES evaluates the number of batch productions and distributes them in three month periods, taking into account seasonal products and stocks. The results are fed to a combinatorial program. This program, using the description of time and equipment requirements of each product (figure 2), generates every possible combination of products' scheduling. The combinations (figure 3) giving the maximum production compactness are stored.

At the end the system selects among these combinations using simple criteria such as:

- Balanced work between days.
- Predicted arrival data of reagents and reliability of the supplier.
- Cost of product stock.
- Actual stock of the product.

This ES has been programmed in COMMON LISP and worked out in cooperation with Interquim S.A. (Grupo Ferrer Internacional).

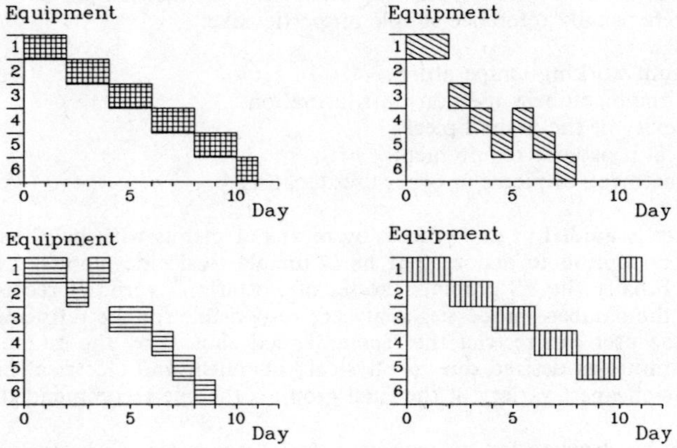

Figure 2

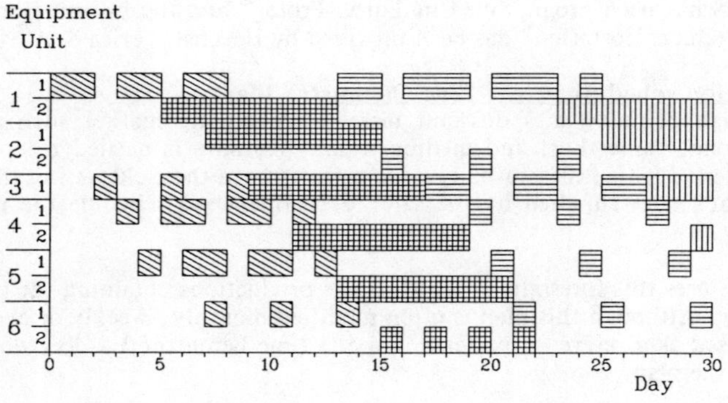

Figure 3

Subsequent evolution of the project has been stopped given that the system has been found too slow and memory demanding to run on an 80286 machine. The system will be newly structured using Prolog or a Shell, developing an initial ES to drastically reduce the number of combinations to be studied by the combinatorial program emulating experts' criteria.

c.- Management of a pipeline net in a petrochemical plant.

The crude oil is processed in the petrochemical industry in a continuous process using different mixtures every time in order to obtain a desired amount of a product. These batches are hereafter referred to as campaigns. A campaign is described in terms of the tanks used as a source of crude oil, its flows and the distillation tower used as destiny (Pipe Steel or Flash). The task of deciding how to carry out a desired campaign and how to do it with the minimum number of changes from the present production involves expertise and is suitable to be programmed in an ES.

Using the description of a campaign and considering the pipeline net studied (figure 4) the ES selects pumps, tanks and collectors to perform it.

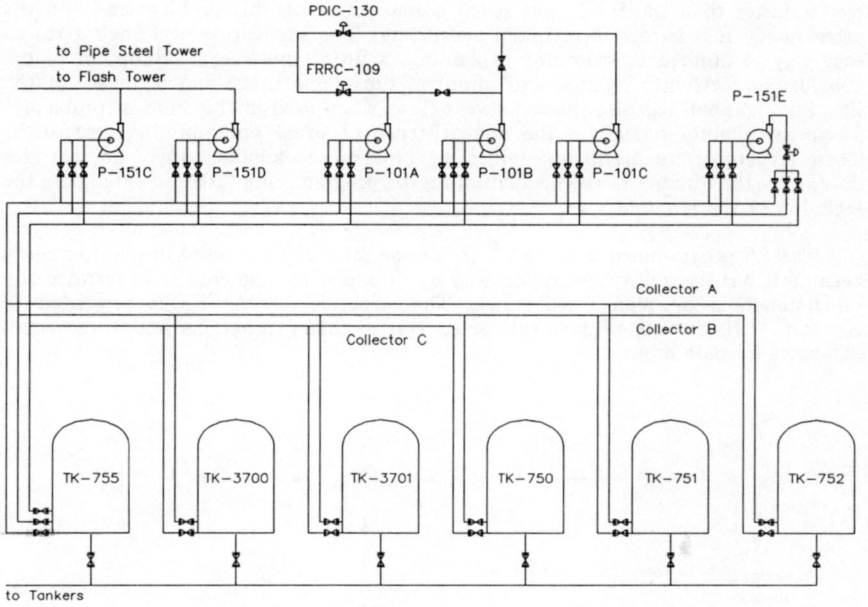

Figure 4

The Expert System presents a solution identical to the one nowadays given by the head of operations. The results have the appearance presented in the figure 5.

DATA			*RESULTS*			
TANK	FLOW	DESTINY	COLLECTOR	PUMP	CONT.	COLLECTOR
TK-755	20	P/S	C	101A	F-109	
TK-3700	6	F/T	B	151C		
TK-751	26	P/S	A	101B	P-130	
TK-751	14	F/T	A	151E		B

Figure 5

The ES selection is based essentially on searching a feasible solution involving the maximum number of pumps or collectors in use in the current campaign and on selecting, from these, the one that can be achieved with the minimum number of changes from the actual campaign. The ES also favors easy changes (automated valves) over difficult ones (big, manual valves) and observes the recommended working limits of the equipments.

Two different programming tools have been used to build this ES: Turbo-Prolog® and the Expert System Shell GURU®. The Prolog programmed ES is by far faster than the Shell, but speed is not critical in this problem and, on the other hand, it is harder to maintain and debug. The application of a Shell gives an easy way to implement reasoning explaining facilities and a level of support of the conclusions (certainty factors) and improves the maintenance and legibility of the ES. But the Shell has also showed severe flaws when used in this kind of problem . These are mainly related to the non-existence of usual programming structures. These structures are useful in engineering problems to handle arrays and matrixes decreasing the number of rules, facilitating the programming task and enhancing the legibility of the program.

The ES programmed in GURU® is the one selected to be used in plant, mainly because it has the ability to explain why a solution is recommended, in terms easily understandable by plant's personnel. The structure of the ES is presented in figure 6. It consists of two rule sets, two auxiliary programs and three small databases for data input.

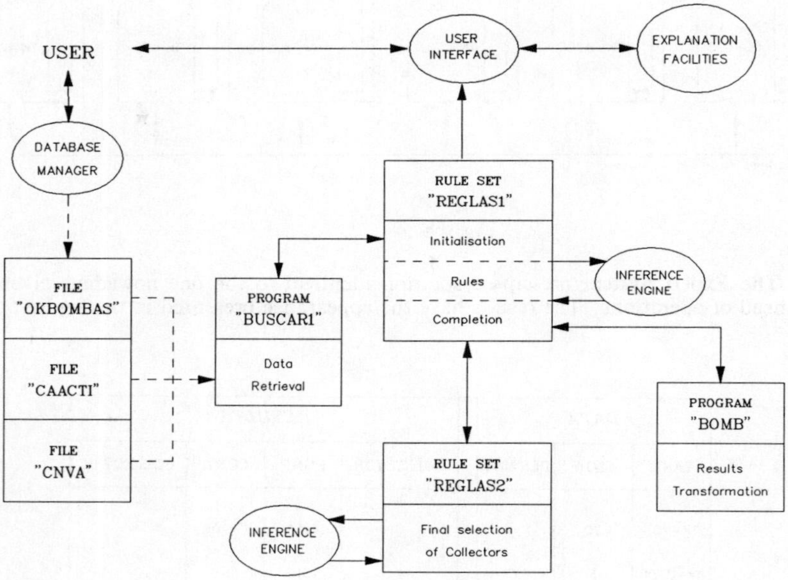

Figure 6

The rule set 'REGLAS1' is the main one and consists of over 70 rules consulted using forward chaining to select the pumps to perform the campaign, the flow controllers and the combinations of collectors. The rule set 'REGLAS2' scans these combinations using backward chaining to select the preferred one. The auxiliary programs are used to obtain the data from the databases and transform fuzzy variables to arrays.

Some rules responsible for the selection of the pumps to feed the flash tower are presented in figure 7. After checking that flows are within specifications (R34) and that the mixing pump is not needed and pumps' flows are within limits provided that it is only one tank feeding the tower (R37), the rules R40-R42 assign with preference the pump actually in use, the one available or decide that it is impossible to perform the new campaign because no pump is available.

```
RULE: R34
      IF: totalft>=12 and totalft<=22
      THEN: limiteft=true
      REASON: The flow fed to the Flash Tower is between
              working limits.

RULE: R37
      IF: numtkft=1 and limiteft=true
      THEN: untkft=true
      REASON: Only crude of one tank feds the Flash Tower
              and the limits of this tower are respected.
              Then flow limits of the pumps are also respected.

RULE: R40
      IF: ((numtkft=1 and untkft=true) or (numtkft=2 and
          dostkft=true)) and (bombasno="p-151C" and
          bombasno="p-151D")
      THEN: at 10,5 ? "No solution"; consult stop
      CHANGES: bombaft
      REASON: One pump is necessary to fed the F/T and there is
              none available.

RULE: R41
      IF: numtkft=1 and untkft=true and bombassi="p-151C" and
          bombuso="p-151C"
      THEN: bombaft+="p-151C"
      REASON: The pump P-151C is assigned because it is
              available and in use in the current campaign.

RULE: R42
      IF: numtkft=1 and untkft=true and bombassi="p-151D" and
          bombuso="p-151D"
      THEN: bombaft+="p-151D"
      REASON: The pump P-151D is assigned because it is
              available and in use in the current campaign.
```

Figure 7

This ES has been developed in cooperation with Petróleos del Mediterráneo S.A. (PETROMED S.A.) using as a testing example its factory in Castellón de la Plana (Spain).

d.- Blending planning in a crude oil industry.

Blending planning is one of the activities with a greater economical relevance in the oil industry. The experts, based on several data, have to decide which crudes to process and how to mix them to obtain the market required products. The data needed include tank storage (capacities and stocks), type of crude oil, expected arrival date of the tankers, desired production, company strategies, etc.

Considering the amount of data involved we have selected GURU® for the programming of this ES since it has integrated graphic, database and spreadsheet facilities. The ES decides the medium production rate for the month and the order of the campaigns. Afterwards it selects the crude oils or mixtures to be processed (blending) to obtain the desired products. This later decision is the hardest of all since it is affected by the predicted sales and by the types and quantities of crude oil in stock or to be received, characteristics of each crude, of each product, and so on.

Sometimes the blending selected needs to be reconsidered. This happens occasionally when the proposed group of crude oils or mixtures is found to be unavailable at the beginning of the campaign. Also, as an exceptional event this can lead even to suggest changes in production demands because they can not be satisfied with the available crude oil.

The complexity of the problem have forced us to face it initially in a simplified version. We have classified the different types of crudes in four groups, a product can be produced only once monthly, there is a maximum of four campaigns per month, stocks are not handled in order to foresight sales and the monthly plan takes into account only sales and arrivals in the month.

The ES built to tackle the simplified problem has approximately 50 rules. Figure 8 shows four of these that consider what to do if the demand has been met and there is still time left (R1T). There is the possibility to produce high (R2F) or low (R1F) sulphur fuel oil to export or to end month's production when the internal demand is satisfied (R3F).

```
RULE: R1T
      IF: blendcampsa & timesum lt 23
      THEN: blendtotal=TRUE
      REASON: The internal demand has been planned but there is
            time left to try another campaign.

RULE: R1F
      READY: waittime = 30 - timesum
      IF: blendtotal & biaexpdone
      THEN: blendfinal=TRUE
      REASON: The time left in the month can be used to schedule
            a campaign to produce low sulphur fuel oil to export.

RULE: R2F
      READY: waittime = 30 - timesum
      IF: blendtotal & n2done
      THEN: blendfinal=TRUE
      REASON: The time left in the month can be used to schedule
            a campaign to produce high sulphur fuel oil to export.

RULE: R3F
      IF: blendcampsa
      THEN: blendfinal=TRUE
      REASON: The internal demand can be made but the time left
            can not be used to produce fuel oil to export.
```

Figure 8

In figure 9 two rules are shown that decide what to do while waiting for a tanker to meet interior demands, if it is better to produce high (R5F) or low (R4F) sulphur fuel oil to export.

```
RULE: R4F
      READY: perform initial ; waittime = time(1) + 3
      IF: biaexpdone & blendcampsa
      THEN: blendfinal=TRUE
      REASON: The internal demand can not be made with the crude
            oil in stock and low sulphur fuel oil is produced
            while waiting for a tanker.

RULE: R5F
      READY: perform initial ; waittime = time(1) + 3
      IF: n2done & blendcampsa
      THEN: blendfinal=TRUE
      REASON: The internal demand can not be satisfied with the
            crude oil in stock and high sulphur fuel oil is
            produced while waiting for a tanker.
```

Figure 9

The major problem found in the development of this ES has been the interaction between the programs used, the blending data calculated in a spreadsheet continuously updated and the decision-taking task performed by the rule set.

This ES is worked out in cooperation with Petróleos del Mediterráneo S.A. (PETROMED S.A.) using as a testing example its factory in Castellón de la Plana (Spain). The ES is, in its initial version, being tested by the blending experts and no report is available at this time.

e.- Natural Language interface for a Heat Exchanger Design program.

Common Heat Exchanger design programs commercially available are developed to be used by design experts, i.e. people who know which data have to be introduced in the program and introduce these values when prompted by the program. To simplify this task we are developing a Natural Language interface to acquire a description of the problem expressed in plain language and to process the text to obtain the necessary information.

The interface makes a first pass looking for the type of heat exchanger to be designed - thermosiphon, multiple passes, boiler - . Then detects and isolates mostly numerical data and assigns them to the actual variables needed by the Heat Exchanger design program. It also notes the lack of some data and asks for them or, if the data are likely to be found in a property database, the program records this fact and stores the name of the fluid being processed.

At the end the interface converts all values to a consistent unit system and writes an ASCII file suitable for being read by a CAD program. This program begins a series aimed to help in different CAD problems.

This interface is not a true natural language processor in the common sense of the term, since it does not make any effort to understand the text. Instead it merely strips off the bulk of it and extracts the data considered useful.

This program has been elaborated using Turbo-Prolog® and is now in a testing and improving process using text-book problems of Heat Exchangers Design.

SECTION 3 - SIMULATION

A "Predictive Engine" for the Qualitative Simulation of Dynamic Systems

M.E. Wiegand and R.R. Leitch

Intelligent Automation Laboratory, Department of Electrical and Electronic Engineering, Heriot-Watt University, 31-35 Grassmarket, Edinburgh EH1 2HT, UK

ABSTRACT

This paper describes the development of a general architecture for a reasoning mechanism that is able to simulate the dynamic evolution of a physical system utilising qualitative and quantitative information about the variables in the system. The architecture is layered and modular, with inter-module communication via 'Tell-and-Ask' type interfaces. The "predictive engine" that results forms a tool component in the general-purpose QUIC (Qualitative Industrial Control) toolkit being developed under ESPRIT project P820.

INTRODUCTION

This paper describes the development of a general architecture for a reasoning mechanism that is able to simulate the dynamic evolution of a physical system utilising qualitative and quantitative information about the variables in the system. The "predictive engine" that results forms a tool component in the general-purpose toolkit being developed under ESPRIT project P820 whose remit is to develop a set of high-level tools for a range of tasks within the process industries. This set of tools now forms the QUIC (Qualitative Industrial Control) toolkit [1].

Much work has been done by various researchers in trying to develop algorithms which perform qualitative dynamic reasoning and/or which deal with the problems inherent in using qualitative values (e.g. ambiguity). In attempting to exploit this new technology, decisions have to be made about which ideas to include in the system, which ideas are redundant or superfluous, and which are already catered for in another guise. In the development of the "predictive engine", an attempt has been made to keep the architecture as 'general' as possible. Rather than construct a series of systems, each applicable to a few small and artificial examples, the remit for a tool component must include such attributes as generality and coherence. This work is an attempt to move from conceptualising to implementation without discarding these attributes. In doing this, various sources are drawn upon and the results placed in a context where they can be seen to perform a specific function. Whilst the "predictive engine" is perhaps sub-optimal for any specific application, it is general and flexible, and reflects well the principles involved in its development.

The architecture of the "predictive engine" is layered and strictly modular, each

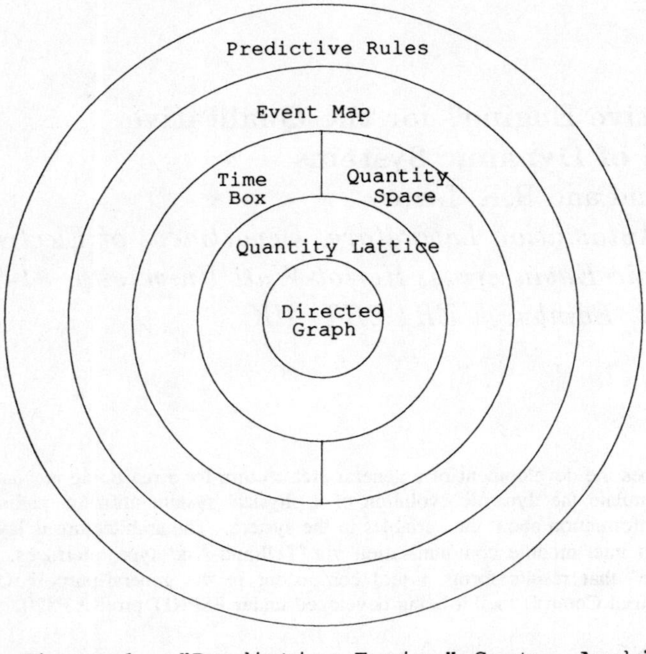

Figure 1 "Predictive Engine" System Architecture

module having a well-defined functionality; see Figure 1. Each module is completely independent and communicates with the lower-level module via a 'Tell-and-Ask' type interface. At the 'core' of the "predictive engine" lie the graph-based representations that hold the Quantity Space (the allowable qualitative values for each system variable) and the Time Box (a record of the temporal relationships between the changing values of the system variables). Above this core, an Event Map collates the values of system variables with their temporal extent and presents these 'tuples' to the Predictive Rules which manage the inference of the system behaviour. The results of the inference process are passed back down to the core where they may contribute to further inferences.

This design is strongly motivated by the work of Williams, who advocates a 'rule-based' approach in his Temporal Qualitative Analysis (TQA) [2] and an 'event- based' approach in his Temporal Constraint Propagation (TCP) [3]. The "predictive engine" reflects a generalised combination of TQA and TCP. In his work on reasoning in dynamic domains, Williams applied TQA to the analysis of MOS circuits. The "predictive engine" takes Williams' classification of feedback characteristics in electrical systems, and applies similar ideas to canonical forms of physical phenomena in other domains, notably process control. The "predictive engine" also investigates Williams' use of an 'event-based' architecture and TCP for qualitative reasoning as a way of handling pure-time delay more efficiently than in a 'state-based' approach such as Kuipers' [4]. This particular ability is very important for at least one of the demonstrators in the ESPRIT project P820, where a lumped parameter approximation has been used in order to avoid consideration of a partial spatial derivative.

An 'event-based' approach needs to be able to reason with partially-ordered temporal intervals. Following the work of Vilain and Kautz [5] which suggested that an interval-based implementation may be computationally intractable, we utilise a point-based implementation which is based on Simmons' Quantity Lattice [6]. The Quantity Lattice actually belongs to a general class of systems which may be termed "inequality reasoners". It manages the integration of real and symbolic values, allowing the reasoning mechanism to make use of quantitative information when this is available (or necessary).

DIRECTED GRAPH

The Directed Graph constitutes the basic information storage module of the system. Directed graphs hold both the Time Box and the Quantity Space in the "predictive engine", albeit through a Quantity Lattice interface which enables the integration of real with symbolic values.

Digraph nodes are used to represent either time points (the end points of periods/events) or landmarks in the quantity space: the actual semantics of these nodes will depend on the interface that the digraph is viewed through (Time Box or Quantity Space). In Simmons' original description of his Quantity Lattice, nodes were also used to hold real numbers. However, in the implementation of the "predictive engine", real numbers are not stored as nodes in the digraph but are generated by the Directed Graph module interface as requested. In the large-scale systems for which it is envisaged that the "predictive engine" will be used, inclusion of reals as proper nodes would clutter the graph. Of course, real values may be given an explicit status when they form an important part of the reasoning process; this can be done by assigning a symbolic point and giving this point the real value, for example, the 'zero' of the Quantity Space. Then, the symbolic point is available for the reasoning process and its real value is available when required.

Nodes can also be expressions. Simmons' use of arithmetic expressions was quite extensive in his application domain. At the moment, only binary negation and binary addition are being considered; binary negation is required in order to handle information about the duration of time periods (the difference between two time points), and binary addition is then required as a consequence.

The nodes of the digraph are connected with labelled directed arcs. Simmons' used six labels, $<$, $=$, $>$, $\leq$, $\geq$ and $\neq$. However, use of $\neq$ is problematic. In the "predictive engine" only the labels $<$, $=$, and $>$ are used (with simple extensions to $\geq$ and $\leq$). The digraph arcs may be used to express partial orderings. Two additional arc labels, $<<$ and $\tilde{}=$, representing respectively 'negligibility' and 'closeness' which are not in Simmons' system may be included in future work. These two operators would facilitate the inclusion of some form of 'order of magnitude' reasoning in the uppermost module of the "predictive engine", enabling the use of temporal hierarchies in the Time Box digraph, and increased (selective) granularity in the Quantity Space digraph.

To enable the smooth integration of real and symbolic values in the "predictive engine", the Directed Graph also holds information about the real value of each node. Associated with each node is a real interval which represents what is currently known about the real value of that node. By default, the interval is $(-\infty,+\infty)$, or $[0,+\infty)$ if it is known beforehand that each node is non-negative. As the value of each node becomes further constrained during use of the "predictive engine", either as a result of inferences made or supplemental data, it is the Quantity Lattice that is responsible for maintaining the consistency of these interval bounds across the directed arcs that connect the nodes. A relationship between two nodes might be inferred from the intervals associated with them, even though no labelled arc exists.

QUANTITY LATTICE

The Quantity Lattice module is responsible for maintaining the consistency of information in the Directed Graph, and for servicing requests from the Time Box and Quantity Space modules. A major requirement is to 'hide' the mechanism of the Quantity Lattice from the Time Box and Quantity Space by providing a set of general purpose functions which control access to the graphs: the Time Box and Quantity Space have somewhat different requirements of the interface.

The Quantity Lattice in the "predictive engine" is based on that of Simmons'. However, as has already been stated, problems were found in using Simmons' choice of arc labels, i.e. <, =, >, ≤, ≥, ≠. These problems can best be illustrated with an example; they centre around the use of ≠. Consider Figure 2: it seems quite possible to create this graph in Simmons' system. If we ask for the relationship between q_1 and q_4, the Quantity Lattice performs a breadth-first search along paths which contain an entry in a transitivity table for ordinal relationships. The result of this is:

q_1 (=)
q_2 (≤)
q_4 (≤)

Note that the path q_2 to q_3 is not searched because ≤ and ≠ in series do not form a valid relationship. However, if we ask for the relationship between q_2 and q_4, the result is:

q_2 (=)
q_4 (≤) and q_3 (≠)
q_4 (≤) and q_4 (≠)
q_4 (<)

Then, combining q_1 ≤ q_2 with q_2 < q_4, we should get

q_1 < q_4

whereas Simmons' system gave us

q_1 ≤ q_4

This problem lies in the use of ≠, and in the fact that the search is linear (local). Several attempts have been made to solve this problem, but it seems that the only way is to make the search non-linear (non-local) and much less efficient. For this reason it was decided to use only <, =, and > from Simmons' original label set and for these relationships the above problem does not occur.

It is important that the Quantity Lattice module employs breadth-first search, as opposed to depth-first. In particular in the Time Box digraph it is possible for long paths to be created during use, and depth-first search could prove very inefficient. Following Simmons', the "predictive engine" caches the results of the breadth-first search, though it is not clear what the pay-off for this is in efficiency terms.

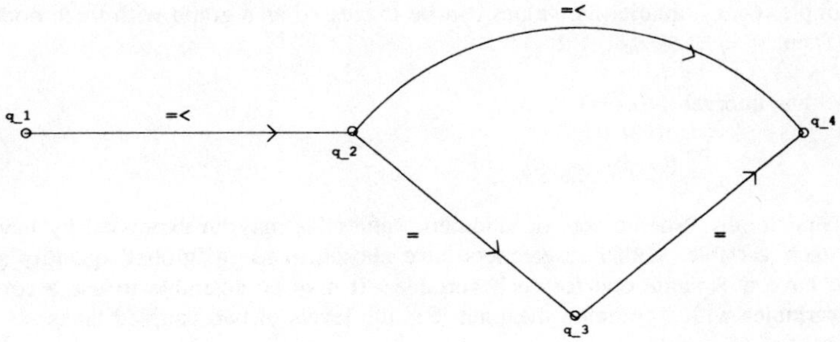

Figure 2 Problem with Simmons' Quantity Lattice

The Time Box and Quantity Space require different functionality in the Quantity Lattice. In particular, access to the graphs is not the same for the higher level modules. In the Time Box, the inference mechanism may consider relations that span more than one time point. However, in the Quantity Space, the continuity rules in the Predictive Rules module may only require one-step search to the next largest landmark. Obviously different functions are required in the Quantity Lattice.

The Quantity Lattice maintains the consistency of the real intervals associated with nodes by numeric constraint propagation along the search paths in the graph. This is straightforward, but the issue is complicated when we include arithmetic expressions as nodes in the graph for expressing period durations. Information constraining the end points of a period will also constrain the duration of a period, and vice versa. The Quantity Lattice employs 'interval arithmetic' and 'relational arithmetic' to move information about intervals between the expression node and its argument nodes [6]. To facilitate this propagation, whenever a duration node is created in the Time Box graph, additional expression nodes are created to yield each argument so that information can flow in both directions. For example, suppose we have time point nodes t_a_3 and t_a_4 and we create the duration node:

(t_a_4 - t_a_3)

This duration will have an associated interval, and if this is modified the intervals for t_a_3 and t_a_4 may be modified as a result. Therefore, the Quantity Lattice also creates the following nodes:

((t_a_4 - t_a_3) + t_a_3)
(t_a_4 - (t_a_4 - t_a_3))

The first of these is connected with an = arc to t_a_4 and the second with an = arc to t_a_3, then information about intervals can flow in either the time points to duration or duration to time points direction. It is for this reason that the binary addition operator must also be introduced.

QUANTITY SPACE

The Quantity Space module defines what a qualitative value for a variable can be. Different researchers have expressed qualitative values in different ways, and the quantity space has not been used consistently. The approach taken in the "predictive engine" is to say: "whatever the quantity space is, it can be represented as some set of directed graphs". So for example, (+,0,-) qualitative values can be expressed as a graph with three nodes, +, 0, and -. Then,

+	has interval		$(0,+\infty)$
0	"	"	[0,0]
-	"	"	$(-\infty,0)$

Also, Kuipers' totally ordered sets of landmark values [4] may be expressed by having a graph for each variable. Other researchers have chosen to use a 'global' quantity space, rather than have a separate one for each variable. It may be desirable to use a common space for variables with a common meaning, e.g. the levels of two coupled tanks.

The Quantity Space should 'hide' the digraph implementation from the reasoning mechanism. So, for example, if (+,0,-) values are used for the higher order derivatives, as in [2], then the Quantity Space should handle the semantics of this use. This means servicing requests from the reasoning mechanism about how values may change and how values combine in constraints.

The Quantity Space module must include functions for the creation of landmark points (especially if landmark discovery is employed in the reasoning mechanism). When a group of variables connected by a single arithmetic constraint/equation in the model must all reach landmarks in their respective quantity spaces simultaneously, these landmarks are called 'corresponding values' [4]; 'corresponding values' may be seen to constitute arithmetic relations between nodes appearing in the Quantity Space digraph.

TIME BOX

The term 'time box' was originally coined by Williams [3]. However, apart from suggesting that "separating inferences about time from behavioural prediction produces a system which is more easily extensible and conceptually clear", the above reference gives little information about what the 'time box' actually is. Williams attempts to characterise it in terms of its required functionality:

(i) What questions will be asked?
(ii) What temporal information is available?
(iii) What inference is needed to answer these questions?

It is clear that the 'time box' is considered with respect to some proposed application. Williams tried to represent the 'time box' using Simmons' Quantity Lattice (though no results are given). From this we can deduce an initial architecture for the module, and suggest a functionality.

The Time Box uses a digraph to hold time points (the beginning and end of time periods) as nodes, and what is known about the order in which these time points occur is expressed by labelled (<,=,>) arcs between the nodes. Time points are either observed (if a system variable is being treated as an input to the "predictive engine") or they are generated by the Predictive Rules module. A time point marks the place where there was a qualitative change of value in some variable. Requests to create a new time point for a variable will come to the Time Box, and this module is responsible for managing the Quantity Lattice in updating the Directed Graph that holds the temporal information. Any new information about when a time point occurred with respect to other time points will be represented by connecting arcs to it. Note that the Time Box is using symbolic time (just as the Quantity Space is symbolic). Any information about the actual (real) time at which time points occur is stored in the interval associated with each node.

As the "predictive engine" runs, the Time Box constructs a history map showing how the time periods are ordered. Two points arise from this. Firstly, depending on the applications, there may come a time during the execution when information before a certain time point could not possibly help in predicting behaviour, and it may be more efficient to delete it (or at least take it out of the graph search space). For this reason, history deletion functions are provided in the Time Box. Secondly, it is not absolutely clear that this module is what Williams meant by 'time box'. It is possible that Williams intended the variables' values to be held with the relevant time periods. This is the function of the Event Map module; the Time Box only holds information about time periods, not value/period tuples (i.e. events).

To those familiar with temporal logics, the Time Box may appear as a 'point-based' implementation. One reason for taking this approach was the work of Vilain and Kautz [5] which suggests that an 'interval-based' implementation may be computationally intractable. However, a set of rules in the Time Box allow queries to make use of Allen's 'period-based' temporal logic [7], based on 13 possible relationships, by translating to 'point-based' relations.

As with the Quantity Space, an important function of the Time Box is to 'hide' implementation details from the higher level modules of the system. As part of this remit, the Time Box handles period durations smoothly by interfacing to their implementation as arithmetic expression nodes in the graph. The inclusion of arithmetic expression nodes is a source of great inefficiency in the Quantity Lattice. If arithmetic expression nodes are not absolutely necessary, it must be considered whether the functionality for handling durations and corresponding values can be moved from the Quantity Lattice to the Time Box and Quantity Space modules respectively.

EVENT MAP

The job of the Event Map is to present 'events' as propagation units to the Predictive Rules module, and to relay requests for information to the core of the system and pass back results. An 'event' in this architecture is a qualitative value/temporal period tuple; it represents the fact that a particular variable held a particular value for a particular period or moment of time. There are two types of event in the system. The first kind are termed 'period events'; they express that a variable holds a value between two distinct time points. The other kind are 'moment events' which express a variable's value at a time point. In much work on temporal logic the term 'interval' is used to refer to a 'period', and the term 'point' to refer to a 'moment'. However, in this paper, 'period' and 'moment' are used to refer specifically to temporal concepts, hopefully avoiding confusion. The 'event history' for a variable will consist of a sequence of alternating 'period events' and 'moment events', showing how that variable's qualitative value changes over time. For example, assuming a variable 'a' uses (+,0,-) semantics in its quantity space, the following might represent a section of its event history:

event(a,+,(2,3))
event(a,0,3)
event(a,-,(3,4))

The first is a period event, expressing 'a''s value between time points 2 and 3. The second is a moment event expressing the value at time point 2. The third is a period event. Note that the event history is 'concise' [3]; this means that a new event is only encountered when the variable's qualitative value changes. For example, the following event history is not concise:

event(a,+,(2,3))
event(a,+,3)
event(a,+,(3,4))

The Event Map presents events for propagation by the Predictive Rules, and decomposes events into their constituent factors for expression in the relevant modules. We may view this process as a 'mapping' from events (the external appearance) to 'pseudo-events' (the internal representation), as follows:

event(a,+,(2,3)) → pseudo_event(variable(a),
(quantity(zero),quantity(+∞))
(timepoint(a,2),timepoint(a,3)))

event(a,0,3) → pseudo_event(variable(a),
(quantity(zero),quantity(zero))
(timepoint(a,3),timepoint(a,3)))

PREDICTIVE RULES

The modules so far described play only a supporting role in the overall "predictive engine". The main inference mechanism resides in the Predictive Rules module. This module embodies a synthesis of qualitative dynamic reasoning techniques. The techniques currently being considered include those found in systems such as Kuipers' QSIM [4] (though also found in other work, perhaps in a different guise) and those that handle pure time delay and feedback effects [2, 3].

The Predictive Rules module contains the rules that permit qualitative reasoning about the behaviour of the physical system involved. Generally, the physical system will be represented by a qualitative model (utilising "weak" functional relationships such as "monotone-increasing", etc. [4]). Importantly, the model will make use of a derivative/integral functional operator and/or operators for representing pure time delay (otherwise, we have a static model and the "predictive engine" simply performs constraint propagation).

In addition to this equational form of representation, the issue of interfacing to other forms of knowledge is being examined within the work on the "predictive engine". In particular, techniques and a methodology for overcoming qualitative ambiguity that involve the use of more detailed "empirical" knowledge of functional relationships between specific system variables and the use of 'order of magnitude' reasoning (with an appropriate semantics) are under investigation. Such ambiguity is bound to be a problem where there is a summation point that is not part of a feedback loop, or where the feedback loop is cross-coupled with others. This issue is considered paramount for the realistic application of qualitative techniques.

The Predictive Rules module contains those rules that follow from the assumption that all system variables vary analytically (continuously differentiable) over time. Rules for "intra-state" qualitative constraint propagation exist within the Predictive Rules module. (Similar rules also exist elsewhere in the QUIC toolkit for use on static models, but we consider them separately in the "predictive engine"). Basically, we resolve what is known about the current state (i.e. the set of current events) with the physical system model to derive as full a state description as possible.

Rules also perform Transition Analysis [2]. They recognise which events may terminate (i.e. the relevant variable transitions), and then try to determine in what order these transitions will occur. This process can be seen as "inter-state" qualitative constraint propagation. We can use information about the feedback structure of the system to help resolve some (but not all) ambiguities, with specific heuristics that summarise energy-flow arguments. Some types of qualitative ambiguity are manageable using these methods together with Iwasaki's causal ordering in dynamic domains [8] for recognising appropriate feedback situations. The Predictive Rules for analytic variables must be capable of selective application to allow for the possibility of discrete events (such as step changes) to be represented.

The Predictive Rules are able to use information about pure time delays where this information is expressed in the model. Such rules enable inferences to be made when the physical system being modelled is subject to transport delays. One of the advantages of using an "event-based" scheme is that pure time delay can be handled in quite a natural way.

The Predictive Rules module will eventually contain interfacing functions that use information held in the QUIC toolkit knowledge representations, particularly the Component Based Language (CBL) "dynamic" domain. Empirical sources of knowledge in the tool-kit will also supply the Predictive Rules module (as mentioned above). Current work is only focusing on the information content that must be present in order to make useful deductions. Once a methodology has been completely determined the appropriate interfaces will be implemented.

CONCLUSION

The architecture of a general-purpose "predictive engine" for reasoning about the dynamic evolution of physical systems has been described.

The design of the "predictive engine" makes use of the work of a number of Qualitative Physics researchers, notably Williams, and it should be noted that this work is continually evolving. As new algorithms and approaches are evaluated and deemed fit for inclusion in the "predictive engine", it is to be hoped that the generality of the architecture will allow this to be done without substantial re-coding.

We argue for the usefulness of a conceptual separation such as this as opposed to the development of more restrictive implementations perhaps only illustrating one technique. Current work is focused on the development of a Predictive Rules module capable of operating on laboratory-scale equipment. The prototype "predictive engine" is developed in Prolog, and work is now under way to re-implement it in Lisp for inclusion in the QUIC toolkit.

ACKNOWLEDGEMENT

This paper describes developments undertaken in the ESPRIT project P820, partly funded by the Commission of the European Communities within the frame of the ESPRIT programme. Project P820 consists of a consortium composed of CISE, Aerospatiale, Ansaldo, CAP Sogeti-Innovation, F.L. Smidth, Framentec, and Heriot-Watt University. The authors want to acknowledge here the contribution of all the members of the project team to the ideas expressed in this paper, while taking full responsibility for the form in which these ideas are expressed.

REFERENCES

1. Leitch, R. and Stefanini, A., ''QUIC: a development environment for Knowledge Based Systems in industrial automation,'' in *Proceedings of Fifth Annual ESPRIT Conference (ESPRIT 88)*, ed. Commission of the European Communities, vol. 1, pp. 674-696, North-Holland, Amsterdam, 1988.
2. Williams, B.C., ''Qualitative Analysis of MOS Circuits,'' *Artificial Intelligence*, vol. 24, no. 1, pp. 281-346, North-Holland/Elsevier, Amsterdam, 1984.
3. Williams, B.C., ''Doing Time: Putting Qualitative Reasoning on Firmer Ground,'' in *Proceedings of Fifth National Conference on Artificial Intelligence (AAAI-86)*, vol. 1, pp. 105-112, Philadelphia, U.S.A., 1986.
4. Kuipers, B., ''The Limits of Qualitative Simulation,'' in *Proceedings of Ninth International Joint Conference on Artificial Intelligence (IJCAI 9)*, vol. 1, pp. 128-136, Los Angeles, U.S.A., 1985.
5. Vilain, M. and Kautz, H., ''Constraint Propagation Algorithms for Temporal Reasoning,'' in *Proceedings of Fifth National Conference on Artificial Intelligence (AAAI-86)*, vol. 1, pp. 377-382, Philadelphia, U.S.A., 1986.
6. Simmons, R., ''Commonsense" Arithmetic Reasoning,'' in *Proceedings of Fifth National Conference on Artificial Intelligence (AAAI-86)*, vol. 1, pp. 118-124, Philadelphia, U.S.A., 1986.
7. Allen, J.F., ''Maintaining Knowledge about Temporal Intervals,'' *Communications of the ACM*, vol. 26, no. 11, pp. 832-843, 1983.
8. Iwasaki, Y., ''Causal Ordering in a Mixed Structure,'' in *Proceedings of Seventh National Conference on Artificial Intelligence (AAAI-88)*, vol. 1, pp. 313-318, Saint Paul, Minnesota, U.S.A., 1988.

A Symbolic Simulator for Event-Based Behavior Descriptions

Kaizhi Yue
Information Sciences Institute, University of Southern California, Los Angeles, USA

Abstract Simulation is an important tool in predicting behaviors. In this paper, we will discuss a symbolic simulator designed for a particular paradigm of behavior descriptions. The paradigm is called *event-based.* It supports the specification of *event orderings* both implicitly, i.e., in terms of constraints, and explicitly, i.e., in terms of temporal connectives and predicates. The simulator, making use of techniques developed in theorem proving, program testing and program analysis, can handle such specifications and generate symbolic instances of behaviors.

Introduction

Simulation is an important tool in predicting behaviors. In this paper, we will discuss a symbolic simulator designed for a particular paradigm of behavior descriptions. The paradigm is called *event-based.* It supports the specification of *event orderings* both implicitly, i.e., in terms of constraints, and explicitly, i.e., in terms of temporal connectives and predicates. The simulator is symbolic in the sense that it uses symbolic representations, rather than numerical values, for modeling behaviors. Making use of techniques developed in theorem proving, program testing and program analysis, the simulator can handle such specifications and generate symbolic instances of behaviors.

This simulator is developed from the need for validating system requirements. We have identified a set of general constraints applicable to real-world systems, which can be used for checking the correctness and completeness of system specifications.[21] The simulator generates complete and unambiguous accounts of events for some behaviors in the system (in the form of symbolic instances), so that the constraints can be applied. However, the simulator can be equally useful in generating interesting scenarios for direct inspection by human users to discover unintended or surprising consequences of formal specifications.

The Event-Based Paradigm of Behavior Descriptions

The behaviors of systems can be described declaratively, i.e., by constraints (e.g., axioms), or procedurally, i.e., by explicit patterns of event orderings. Examples of the former are the algebraic specifications of programs (e.g., [9]) or differential equations for a physical system. Examples of the latter are software programs, including programs written for simulating real world systems. The two styles differ in their expressiveness and convenience for manipulations . Here we only mention that both are appropriate for stating some properties of system behaviors. While the declarative approach can better express the lawful relations, the procedural approach has an edge in expressing the temporal aspects in a system. In declarative approach, since the constraints are globally applicable, we do not know exactly when and where they will "strike". In procedural approach, because the interactions are completely localized, functional modification and composition will be difficult.

Many system specification languages have adopted a hybrid approach, which allows both procedural and declarative styles. But the emphasis may differ. Some languages are constraint-based, such as GIST ([2]), which emphasizes the declarative constraints, i.e., constraints that are not explicit about temporal orderings. In GIST, a behavior is normally obtained by "generate and prune" paradigm. Namely, first let all the potential events occur then remove those that violate the constraints. Some are event-based, such as Aleph ([16]), which emphasizes the procedural part, i.e., explicit temporal orderings of events. In Aleph, various constructs exist for expressing temporal orderings. When a behavior is being described or generated, a substantial portion of the constraints finds their way in the temporal constructs.

To semantically process an event-based specification, we should be able to handle both the constructs directly specifying temporal orderings and the implications of constraints on temporal orderings. This is different from handling a normal program. In a program, we do not worry particularly about the executability of a piece of code, except for concerns of efficient compilations (e.g., removing dead code). But for an event-based specification, due to the existence of global constraints, not all the specified temporal orderings can actually occur or *be executed.* The discovery of such places is essential in validating a specification.

Simulating an Event-based Behavior Description

In processing event-based behavior descriptions, we use a relation-based simulator. In a relation-based simulation, a system is simulated by both relations among objects and attribute values of objects, the latter being a special case of the former.

Simulation attempts to answer the following questions:

1. Interactions of events. The executability problem explained earlier is an example. Another example is inconsistent modification of data, which is due to race condition in concurrent events just like in concurrent programs.

2. Total consequence. Given an initial system state, find the set of possible final system states. There can be more than one final state. The non-determinism is either because of the underspecified initial state or because of the inherent randomness in the system.

3. Identity of participants. A specification may use different descriptions to refer to the same object (or set of objects). A simulator should help the user to recognize the identity of objects.

4. Disambiguating event orderings. Some event orderings are underspecified, so the description can not give the user accurate information about event orderings. The simulator should disambiguate these.

In performing a simulation, we use theorem proving and related methods for handling constraint-related constructs, while using program analysis techniques for handling constructs for temporal orderings. Because either method (theorem proving and program analysis) is incomplete, the symbolic simulation is incomplete.

However, just like program testing, our objective is not to prove the system description to be correct. Rather, we only attempt to show that it is free of certain type of errors or we only want to generate a set of interesting scenarios for the user's inspection.

As such, the work reported in this paper offers an interesting description formalism that is appropriate for real-world systems and a processing mechanism, the simulator, that generate symbolic instances of system behaviors. The techniques used in the simulator are not new, however they have been successfully integrated for our specific reasoning task.

In the following, we will first describe the modeling constructs for event-based behavior descriptions. Then we will describe simulation algorithms for the various constructs. Finally, we give a comparison with related work.

Modeling Behaviors in Event-based Paradigm

Modeling Primitives

Our modeling primitives are *objects, relations* and *events (or transitions)*, as in usual first-order logic based knowledge representation schemes ([8], [5]). Relations are represented as predicates. Relation tuples and their combinations are called *conditions* ("situations" in the sense of [3]page 9) and represented by logic formulae. The *state of the system* is the conjunction of the conditions of all the objects in the system for a given moment. Primitive events are defined in terms of preconditions and consequences (also referred to as "postconditions"), both being conditions.

When the preconditions of an event are true, it is called *enabled.* Otherwise, it is *disabled.* By definition, an enabled event can occur (or called *fire*). Also, after an event finishes, its consequences are true. Furthermore, *global constraints* in the forms of axioms impose restrictions on possible combinations of conditions in every *system state* ("situation" in the sense of [11]).

Intuitively, by associating with a specific time, an event class becomes an event instance. We assume that an event, similarly a time-dependent condition, can always be uniquely identified in this way. This allows us to treat an event both as a formula and an object, since we can establish a 1 to 1 correspondence among the two. As formulae, we can use logical connectives to combine them. However, the complete semantics of events is not captured in logic form. For example, because of the complexity of the firing rules, that part of semantics is handled procedurally. As objects, we can talk about properties of events and conditions. In particular, events and time-dependent conditions have starting times and durations. The duration of a formula X will be denoted by Duration(X) and starting time by Start(X).

Temporal Connectives and Predicates

In the event-based description paradigm, we can directly express the constraints on temporal orderings of conditions and events. This is done with the help of *temporal connectives* and *predicates.* The constraints represented by the temporal connectives are additional to the preconditions of events and global constraints. Namely, an event can fire only if (1) it is specified by one of the temporal orderings in the behavior description; and (2) it is enabled for the particular ordering.

Because events can be represented by formulae, we can form composite conditions or events using the temporal connectives on both events and conditions. Temporal connectives are defined in terms of first order logic containing time variables. In the following, we will assume that X and Y are formulae for both conditions and events, P for a condition, and t is a time variable. If Start(X)=t, we can write X(t).

We first introduce temporal connectives. The sequential and concurrent infix connectives are ";" and "&". Intuitively, the two mean "follow" and "occur concurrently". Their semantics can be defined in the following formulae:

$$[X;Y]\ (t) \equiv X(t) \wedge (\exists t')[Y(t') \wedge t'-t \geq \text{Duration}(X(t))],$$
$$\text{Start}([X;Y]) = \text{Start}(X),$$
$$\text{Duration}([X;Y]) = \text{Duration}(X) + \text{Duration}(Y) + \text{Lapse}(X, Y),$$

where $\text{Lapse}(X,Y) = \text{Start}(Y) - [\text{Start}(X) + \text{Duration}(X)]$.

$$[X\&Y]\ (t) \equiv X(t) \wedge (\exists t')Y(t').$$
$$\text{Start}[X\&Y] = \text{Min}(\text{Start}(X), \text{Start}(Y))$$
$$\text{Duration}([X \& Y]) = \text{Max}(\text{Start}(X)+\text{Duration}(X), \text{Start}(Y) + \text{Duration}(Y)) - \text{Start}([X \& Y])$$

These two connectives can express behavior patterns that are expressible in regular expressions of events and conditions, with concatenations being sequential compositions and unions being concurrent ones. (cf. path notation in [13])

As a subclass of ";" we define the connective "!", meaning "immediately follows":

$$X\ !\ Y \equiv [X\ ;\ Y] \wedge [\text{Duration}(X) + \text{Duration}(Y) = \text{Duration}\ (X!Y)].$$

A typical use of the connective is to state the postcondition after a composite event.

Similarly we can formally define the following connectives for loops:

Repeat for i=m to n do [X_i],

meaning X_i occurs repeatedly (m-n times) for each value of i, and

while P do Y,

meaning that while X is true Y should occur or be true, as in the normal programming language construct named "while...".

We can define quantified events as purely macros. For example, assuming that U is a finite set, u is both an arbitrary element in this set

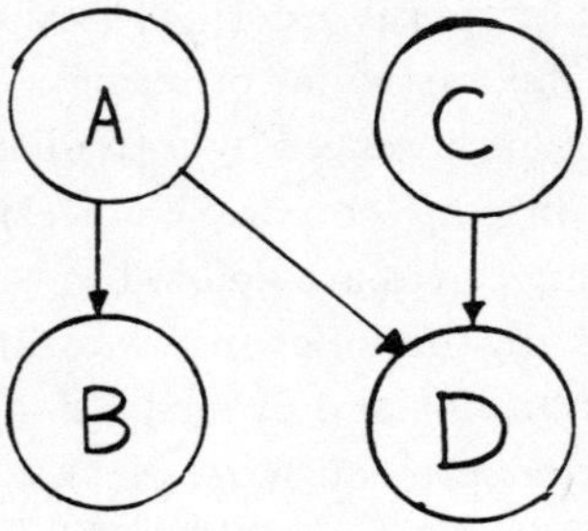

Figure 1: Use both temporal connectives and predicates

and an argument in predicate class X, we define

$$(\forall u \in U)(\&)\ X(u),$$

meaning $X(u_i)$ happens concurrently and in no particular order to each element u_i in U. The macro allows us to say that a set of events happens to a set of objects concurrently.

The logical connectives, e.g., $\wedge$, $\neg$ and $\rightarrow$, will extend their meanings to mean simultaneity, when connecting temporal formulae. For example., $[X \wedge Y](t)$ would mean two events X and Y happen at the same time or two conditions start to hold at the same time. We then can have conditional events using implications, i.e.,

$$[\text{if } P \text{ then } X](t) \equiv P(t) \rightarrow X(t).$$

We introduce some temporal predicates for the corresponding connectives:

$\mathbf{X} \prec \mathbf{Y}$ for X;Y
($\mathbf{X} \succ \mathbf{Y}$ for $\mathbf{Y} \prec \mathbf{X}$)
$\mathbf{X} \prec_! \mathbf{Y}$ for X ! Y

The temporal predicates are higher order. Their arguments have been bold faced in the above formulae. They can be used to extend the expressiveness of the current representation. For example, as in the figure 1, if we have four formulae A, B, C and D. A precedes B and C precedes D. A and C are parallel, so are B and D. Furthermore A precedes D. We can express the temporal relations first in

[A;B] & [C;D]

and express the remaining constraints using a temporal predicate:

$A \prec D$.

Simulation Algorithms for Various Language Constructs

For simplicity, we will introduce the algorithms for handling different constructs separately. The integration is straightforward and we will not elaborate. These algorithms are revised versions of those in [18].

Primitive Events

The simulator verifies the preconditions for a primitive event to test its enablement. This verification may involve intensive theorem proving activity. If an event is enabled and the duration for the event has expired, the new system state will be simulated by properly asserting or unasserting facts into the knowledge base. The theorem proving and knowledge base management involved could be complex due to the use of *collection objects*, for example, an order which is a set of individual order items and a shipment which contains a set of machine parts. This is elaborated in [19].

Concurrency

As is well-known, the analysis of parallel programs is exponential, and there is no complete coverage for a large size problem. The same is for concurrent specifications. Like testing parallel programs, we find a good set of selected testing points, and produce some representative samples of the concurrent behaviors. (Note: The method for producing the selection of testing points should be based on an analysis of the interactions of the system component in a proper representation, e.g., in the form of Petri nets or influence graphs (see [20]). We will not elaborate here.)

For simplicity, we assume that in the specifications there are only two temporal connectives used: ";" for sequentiality and "&" for concurrency. Such behaviors can be represented by a tree ([1]) as shown in fig. 2. In this tree, there are two types of intermediate nodes: sequential and concurrent. All the composite events can be expanded and the leaves will be primitive events or conditions. According to the semantics of the two connectives, when an intermediate node has the same type as its parent node, it can be removed and its children be made the children of its parent. As a result, a concurrent node only has sequential children which are intermediate nodes, and vice versa. Furthermore, also on the basis of the definitions of the connectives, for each concurrent node, the event of its next sibling node will not start until it ends (i.e., its duration has passed). This is the reason why simulation of each node can be done

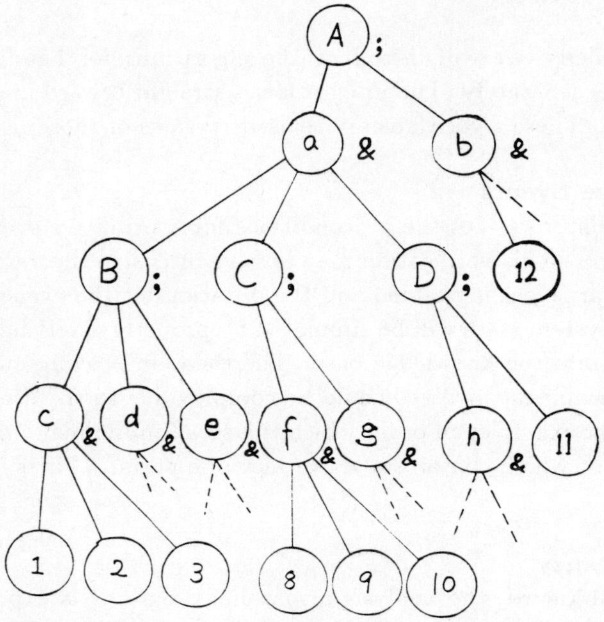

Figure 2: A Tree of Concurrent and Sequential Event Nodes

separately.

When simulating a concurrent node, a set of its descendant nodes can occur at the same time. These are called *concurrent set.* These nodes may be concurrent due to being the first events possible for all the lowest level concurrencies as the events 1, 2, 3, 8, 9, 10, etc for the node a. These are called *first primitive event set.* For each lowest level sequential node. if one of its children ends, the next sibling of the child node should occur. Using this sibling node, we can find the *next primitive event set*, which either contains a single primitive event if the sibling node is a leaf node or is the first primitive event set if the sibling node is a concurrent one. The union of all next primitive event sets for all members of a concurrent-set is the *follow set* of the concurrent set.

An event can be unfit to fire for interfering other events, being disabled or violating an ordering constraints, i.e.,

```
unfit-to-fire-event-p(x) ≡
        disabled(x) ∨  ∃ y ∈ concurrent-set disables(x, y)

       incompatible-consequences-p(x, concurrent-set) ∨
```

```
If N is primitive
then simulate-primitive-event(N)
else if N is sequential
     then let N = n1 ; n2; ...; nk
       for i=1 to k simulate-node(ni)
     else let N = n1 & n2 & ... & nl
       begin
     for i:= 1 to l do
           follow-set := first-primitive-event-set(ni)
       unfit-to-fire-set := ∅ ;
         while  ¬ (follow-set = ∅)  do
           begin
           concurrent-set := follow-set ∪ unfit-to-fire-set  ;
           follow-set := ∅;
           for x in concurrent-set do
             begin
             concurrent-set := concurrent-set - { x };
             if  unfit-to-fire-event-p(x)
             then unfit-to-fire-set := { x} ∪ unfit-to-fire-set
             else begin
                  x.duration := randomly choose
                                  from duration-range(event-type(x));
                  x.delay := x.duration;
                  primitive-events-to-simulate:=
                        primitive-events-to-simulate ∪ { x};
                  end;
             end;
           for x in primitive-events-to-simulate do
             begin
             x.delay := x.delay - 1;
             if x.delay = 0
             then begin
                  primitive-events-to-simulate:=
                        primitive-events-to-simulate - { x };
                  simulate-primitive-event(x);
                  if (Exist s (s = next-primitive-event-set(x)))
                  then follow-set := next-primitive-event-set(x) ∪
                                         follow-set
                  end
             end
           end;
           if  ¬ (unfit-to-fire-set = ∅) then error
       end.
```

Table 1: The Procedure SIMULATE-NODE for Simulating Simple Concurrency

```
ordering-constraint-violation-p(x, concurrent-set)
```

Disablement of an event can be checked according to definition. The interferences among events could be in preconditions or consequences. As the former, an event or more than one event together can disable the precondition of an event concurrent to them. These are found by comparing the consequences of some events with the precondition of an event in the same concurrent-set. As the latter, two events could be asserting conflicting facts into the knowledge base. Such conflicts are inhibited in our framework and discovered by comparing the consequences of the concurrent-set. Finally, by comparing an event with the behavior generated so far, we can check if the ordering constraints are observed.

The algorithm for simulating such behaviors is described in the table 1 using the terminology introduced above. The parts for sequential and primitive events are trivial. For a concurrent node, after initializing concurrent-set and unfit-to-fire-set, we verify if any of the events in concurrent-set is "unfit to fire". If it is, its firing will be postponed. Otherwise, the event will be randomly assigned a duration from its duration range and the clock ticks one tick. If an event ends, its consequences will be asserted into the knowledge base and we find its follow-set for further simulation. (Note: We could assign durations to events if they are not explicitly specified. If the duration is variable, a range can be given and the processing program can assume for the duration a randomly selected value from the range. If the duration-range is a fixed number then there is no randomness or non-determinism. Also note that a primitive event may not have a unit time duration.)

In this algorithm, we have randomly chosen durations for simulation. If some analysis result can enable us to know where different durations can make a difference in behavior, then a smarter way of choosing the duration can be used, which should generate more representative scenarios. (This can be compared with choosing input values for testing numerical programs. There, algorithms exist for dividing the domain into subdomains each of which corresponds to a different program behavior.[4])

Conditional Events

The handling of conditional events fits into the above algorithm as following. For each conditional event "If P then X", X is used in building the "sequentiality-concurrency" tree. However, P will be associated with the node for X and the node is marked as *branching*. When simulating a node, it is checked for being branching. This is shown in figure 3. If it is, a branch will be taken and the other branch will be pushed onto a

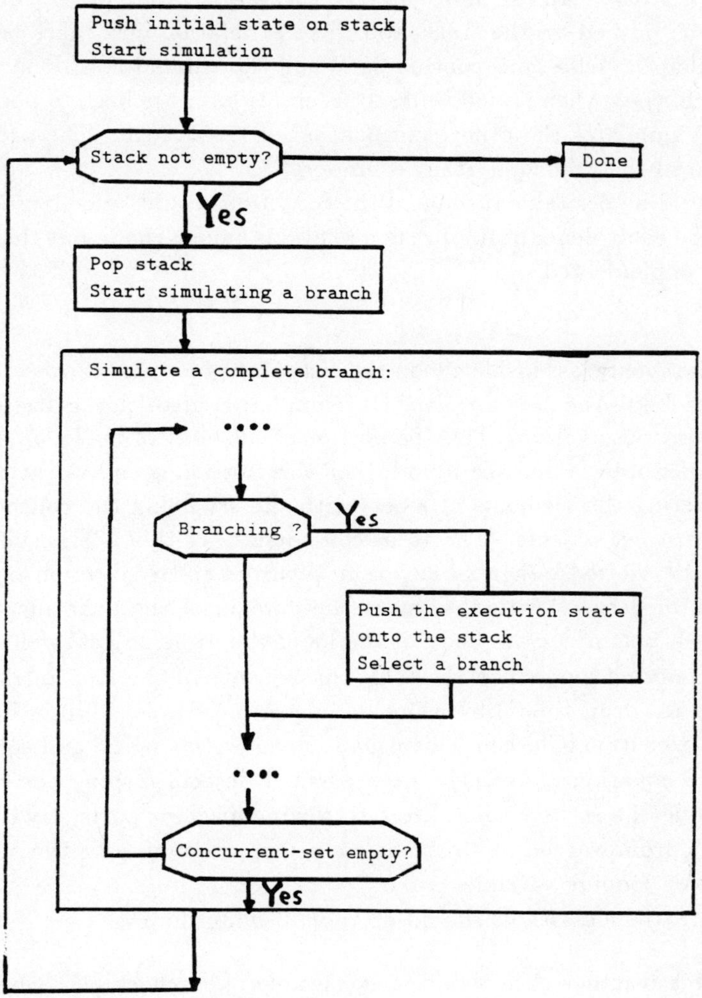

Figure 3: Handling Conditional Events

"branching stack." All the information regarding the state of the simulation will be pushed on the stack, too. The simulation now takes one of two possible branches and continues. When the simulator is done with one branch, (i.e., when its following set is empty), it goes back to pop the stack and simulates the other continuation of the branch. The process goes on until the branching stack is empty.

It would be desirable if some of the conditions could be collapsed by proving the equivalence or implication relations among them, but this has not been implemented.

Loops

We call the event class inside a loop the *body* of the loop. Each occurrence of the loop body is called a *round.* Our simulation algorithm is based on the following observations: (1). If a portion of the body of the loop affects only distinct objects on each round, then this portion is equivalent to an event affecting the elements of a set, with the set being the collections of those distinct objects. The total consequence of this portion of the loop can be viewed either as an event occurred to a collection object or a quantified event with the set as the domain of the quantification. (2). If, in a portion of the body of the loop, the same object is affected on each round of loop, then the total consequence of the loop might be computed (at "run time") by using the algorithm employed in ordinary symbolic execution [Clarke]. This usually involves setting up and solving recurrence equations. We call these affected objects *looping variables.* For example, if a storage agent keeps retrieving machine parts, say called "part-set", from warehouse to the assemly shop, we may have the object part-set as a looping variable.

Ideally, the algorithms should do the following things:

1. Check whether each round is executable. I.e., check (1). whether within one round the preceding events enable succeeding events, and (2). when it is the end of one round and the exit condition is not met, whether the first events in the body are enabled again.

2. If the loop does not have a definite number of rounds, but has a exit (final) condition instead, such as in a while-loop, a proof of the condition should be attempted to ensure the termination of the loop.

3. For each looping variable, the changes to both the attributes of the object and the attributes of related objects should be accumulated.

The actual processing can only handle some of these requirements. This will be discussed in the same order.

1. Usually, only the first round is checked as if we have a simple sequence of events specified by the body. The resulting final state (i.e., at the end of the round) is used to check the possibility of starting the second round.

   If the loop is a while-loop, since there could be an alternative path which does not contain any round and the resulting system state may be substantially different, we will treat the loop also as a conditional by introducing an alternative path.

2. To verify termination of a loop, we observe that most of the termination conditions are predicates over looping variables. A comparison should be done between the values of loop variables required by the termination condition and the actual final values. The way of computing the values is discussed below.

3. Presumably the changes to looping variables are recorded through assertions with "$\Leftarrow$", since any other way of change is not able to establish a relation between a previous value of a variable and its new value. Also, for the looping variables we should have some initial conditions and postconditions associated with composite events. Then a recurrence equation can be set up and possibly be solved. (see [12]) With the help of the recurrence equation, we can do the following:

   For each variable, (1) if no termination condition is asserted then infer its value at termination time. (2) If both initial and final conditions are known for the variable, and there are unknowns about other objects in the recurrence equations then solve the equations for the unknowns. (3) If all relevant conditions are asserted, check the consistency. The procedures of (1) and (2) are called *summarizing* the looping variables.

It is easy to fit "loops" into the framework of the previously described "sequentiality-concurrency" tree. If the variables in the loop are not looping, then the loop can be viewed as a concurrent event to all the values in the domains of the variables. If the variables are looping, the case is a little more complex. When identifying the follow-set, if we are at the end of a round, we should look for it at the beginning of the loop.

Quantified Events

Since universally quantified events are just macros, theoretically there is a straightforward way of handling them. However, since the domains of quantifications are often indefinite, a simple unfolding does not work. In simulating quantified events some simplifications are often used. We explain briefly.

In a quantified event, individual events often share common participants. For example, in ∀x (&) e(A,x), presumably the object A will be involved in each event of type e. If x_1, x_2, x_3 are possible values of x, it is also possible for them to interact with one another. The interactions can be detected if we simulate the quantified event as a set of concurrent events.

For the level of abstraction of the specifications, we may not care interactions among elements in a collection. For example, if we, again, model the retrieval of machine parts and let e in the above be "retrieve", x stand for individual parts in a set or class, and A be "storage-agent," we may want to assume that the retrieving operation does not care how the storage-agent actually retrieves all the parts. We may get inconsistent states of A if all the events are allowed to happen in an arbitrary way, but that is not our concern at this moment. For all such cases, by default, the checking system assumes that there are no interactions of any sort among events occurring to elements in a collection. Moreover, the relevant state of the common participant, in this case that of A, will be declared as "don't care."

The previously described algorithm for concurrency is applicable to events described in quantified form. However, since the cardinalities of the involved sets are often indefinite, we use the following heuristics for our simulation. Namely, if two types of events for a single set of objects are specified as concurrent, but each pair of events for an individual object do not interfere, we will simply simulate *all* the events that are enabled (since there should be no difference when we simulate them anyway). If two types of event for a single set of objects do interfere with each other, but we can resolve the interference by imposing certain orderings, then we will simulate *all* the events in that order.

Ordering Constraints

When an ordering constraint is used for a priori deciding which event precedes which, it can be used directly in simulation as in the algorithm in table 1.

But ordering constraints can also be used for deciding the identity of objects involved in relevant events. In general, if we have

$\forall x\ E(x) \prec E'(x)$,

$S = \{x \mid E(x)\}$,

and

$S' = \{x \mid E'(x)\}$,

we can conclude that

$S' \subset S$.

Independent Conditions

In a composed event, the conditions that do not appear as the condition part of a conditional event are called *independent conditions* and need special handling.

Formulae of this kind are indispensable: If a condition is true for a class of events, we can put it into the consequence of the event, as part of the event definition. But some conditions are true only for a particular event. In that case, "E ! P" is a handy expression. In this formulation, the condition P is true right after the event E. For example, if we are to mean the parts retrieved by the storage-agent are accessible to the transporting-agent (e.g., conveyor belts), we should use "!" because the parts are not accessible at the time retrieving starts. On the other hand, if we say that the transporting-agent brings a set of parts to the assembly shop and this set is a subset of, say, the set of all parts then the formulation should be "$E \wedge P$" because the relation holds the moment that the event starts.

The simulation of the conditions are straightforward. For "E!P", P should be asserted immediately after E. For "$E \wedge P$", P should be asserted immediately before checking the executability of E.

Related Work

[14] discusses simulating some primitives constructs. But their simulation was basically executing procedures as opposed to simulating a design expressed in partially declarative form.

While many authors ([7]) have used theorem-prover based simulation in diagnostic reasoning, the designs that are simulated do not contain collection objects and complex patterns of temporal orderings.

Qualitative simulation is another representative simulation work in AI (e.g., [10] and [6]). However, qualitative simulation is designed completely for a declarative specification of physical systems. As such there is no need and means to handle explicit concurrency and loops in qualitative simulation.

Our symbolic simulation is closer to symbolic execution, so the comparison of the two deserves more attention. First, the processing limitations to symbolic simulation are the same as those to symbolic execution of ordinary programs. For example, both face binary branching factors for conditionals and exponential explosions for concurrent events and indefinite number of loops ([15]). Symbolic execution technique cannot effectively handle the simplification of logic and arithmetic relations in conditionals ([4]). Given the sophisticated theorem proving facilities offered by AI, this particular problem may be partially alleviated, but the theoretical difficulties remain anyway.

However, the difference in their application domains makes their roles in error checking substantially different. In a real world domain, we need to care about the possibility of an event happening as well as its exact numerical result. For example, if the processing-cell does succeed in utilizing a part in a hypothesized (i.e., designed by our specification) assembly shop, how long it waits for the parts and how fast it handles the parts will be relevant. However, the actual happening of an event is the first concern. Namely, we have to make everything concur so that the parts are delivered to the cell. Simulation helps in this way. On the other hand, a computation system seldom has a problem in continuing its operation. The only exceptions are "array index out of bounds," "divided by zero," etc., which are not essential with respect to the correctness of one's program.

Conclusion

The simulator has been implemented and is part of the overall environment for composing, analyzing and browsing system specifications in an event-based system specification language DAO (for Describing and Analyzing Operations)([18]). It is built on top of a simplified version of LOOPS, which in turn is implemented in Interlisp-D (Xerox [17]). It runs on XEROX 1108 lisp machines. We have used the simulator in the experiment of functional analysis of real-world systems ([18] or [21]).

To conclude, we have described a symbolic simulator designed for event-based paradigm of behavior descriptions, which supports the specification of event orderings both implicitly, i.e., in terms of constraints, and explicitly, i.e., in terms of temporal connectives and predicates. The simulator, making use of techniques developed in program testing and analysis, can handle such specifications and generate symbolic instances of behaviors, which can be used for the analysis of behaviors.

Acknowledgment: The author has benefited from the discussions in the software science division of USC/ISI, specifically the discussions with Jay Myers.

References

[1] J. Hopcroft A. Aho and J. Ullman. *The Design and Analysis of Computer Algorithms.* Addison-Wisley, 1974.

[2] R. M. Balzer and N. M. Goldman. Principles of good software specification and their implications for specification languages. In *Proceedings of the Specifications of Reliable Software Conference*, Boston, Massachusetts, April 1979.

[3] J. Barwise and John Perry. *Situations and Attitudes.* MIT Press, 1983.

[4] L. Clarke. Symbolic evaluation methods in program analysis. In N. D. Muchnick S.S., Jones, editor, *Program Flow Analysis.* Prentice-Hall Inc., 1980.

[5] Donald Cohen. A forward inference engine to aid in understanding specifications. In *Proceedings of National Conference on Artificial Intelligence*, August 1984.

[6] Johan De Kleer and John Seely Brown. A qualitative physics based on confluences. *Artificial Intelligence*, 24(1-3), 1984.

[7] M. Genesereth. The use of design descriptions in automated diagnosis. *Artificial Intelligence, Special volume =on qualitative reasoning*, 24(1-3), 1984.

[8] Michael R. Genesereth and Nils Nilsson. *Logical Foundations of Artificial Intelligence.* Morgan Kaufmann Inc., Los Altos, California, 1987.

[9] J. Guttag and J. Horning. The algebraic specification of abstract data type. *Acta Informatica*, 1978.

[10] B. Kuipers. Qualitative simulation. *Artificial Intelligence*, 29(3), 1986.

[11] John McCarthy and P. Hayes. Some philosophical problems from the standpoint of artificial intelligence. In D. Michie and B. Meltzer (Eds.), editors, *Machine Intelligence 4*. Edinburgh University Press, 1969.

[12] Steven Muchnick and Neil D. Jones. *Program Flow Analysis: Theory and Applications.* Prentice Hall, Englewood Cliffs, New Jersey, 1981.

[13] P.R. Torrigiani P.E. Lauer and M.W. Shields. Cosy - a system specification language based on paths and processes. *Acta Informatica*, 12(2), 1979.

[14] Chuck Rieger and Milton Grinberg. The declarative representation and procedural simulation of causality in physical mechanisms. In *Proceedings of International Joint Conference on Artificial Intelligence*, Cambridge, MA, 1977.

[15] R.N. Taylor. A general-purpose algorithm for analyzing concurrent programs. *CACM*, May 1983.

[16] Terry Winograd. Aleph, a system specification language. Technical report, Stanford University Computer Science Department, forthcoming 1988.

[17] Xerox Corporation. *Interlisp reference manual*, 1983.

[18] K. Yue. Constructing and analyzing specifications of real world systems, stan-cs-86-1090, ph.d. thesis. Technical report, Stanford University Computer Science Department, 1986.

[19] Kaizhi Yue. Reasoning about system behaviors involving collection objects. In John Gero, editor, *Artificial Intelligence in Engineering: Robotics and Processes.* Elsevier, Amsterdam (co-published with Computational Mechanics Publications, Southampton, U.K.),, 1988.

[20] Kaizhi Yue. Representing first order logic-based specifications in petri-net-like graphs. *to appear in Proceedings of The Fifth International Workshop on Software Specification and Design*, Pittsburgh, Pennsylvania, May 1989.

[21] Kaizhi Yue. Validating system requirements by functional decomposition and dynamic analysis. *to appear in Proceedings of The 11th International Conference on Software Engineering*, Pittsburgh, Pennsylvania, May 1989.

SECTION 4 - PROCESS PLANNING

A Truth Maintenance Approach to Process Planning

C.J. Hinde*, A.D. Bray**, P.J. Herbert**, V.A. Launders** and D. Round**

**Department of Computer Studies,*

***Department of Manufacturing Engineering, Loughborough University of Technology, Loughborough, LE11 3TU, UK*

ABSTRACT

An approach to the design and implementation of a computer aided process planning system is described. The approach is based on using an assumption-based truth maintenance system coupled with a blackboard architecture. Unlike some other process planning systems our approach seeks to integrate other software systems together and, as such, includes some proprietary software as sub components. We therefore see our system as an integrating framework.

The representational issues arising from our approach to planning and the use of multiple contexts are discussed. The system also uses a rating system whereby the underlying assumptions are rated according to their confidence or credibility. This enables a "soft focussing" of the environments so that the highest rated environments are processed before other less promising environments.

The interpretation of the final multiple context truth maintenance system is then addressed and reduced from a large exponentially bounded space to a polynomial space by layering the interpretation process.

INTRODUCTION

The direction of the project has been strongly influenced by the eventual need to integrate all the collaborators software together as a complete system. We see our approach to process planning as being a microcosm of the whole Design to Product system (Burrow [3]). This thread of integrating subsystems is complemented by the need to keep choices available should the adoption of a particular choice not fulfil its initial promise. The integration of the various subsystems is seen as particularly important as intelligent decisions cannot be made without knowledge of all the relevant data; much of this knowledge being available in the everyday systems used in the running of the business. Even within the confines of the research and development departments of a business collaboration is necessary; the precise dimensions and tolerances of a particular feature of a design may be critical to the functionality of a component whereas some other feature may have little bearing and can be altered to facilitate manufacture. If the designers reasons or assumptions were available to the production engineer then the production engineer could redesign the appropriate parts within the implicit specifications perhaps known only by the functional designer. Ideally the good designer will have some knowledge of production techniques and so may be able to design accordingly. In practise the designer or design team may include a production engineer and various other experts to supply knowledge where and when it is appropriate; the management of the collaboration and interaction is vital to the success of the product.

It is this notion of integration and collaboration which we have incorporated into our process planner. We also wish, as stated above to keep options available while their full consequences are yet to be resolved.

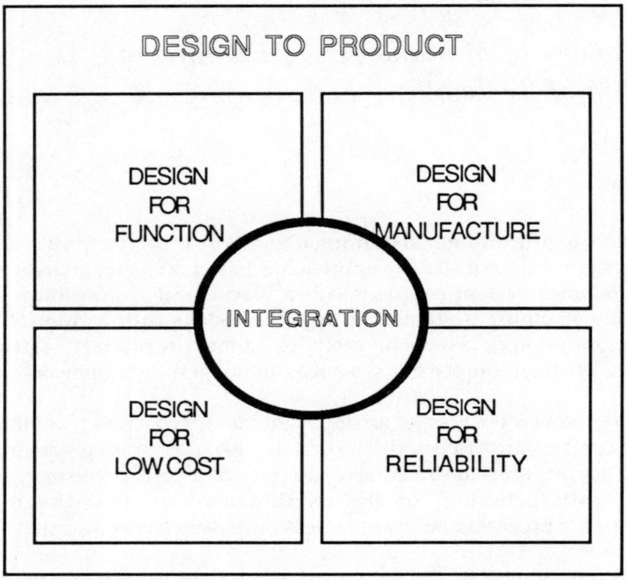

Figure 1. Illustrating the concept of an integrated Design to product system containing similarly integrated sub-systems.

THE LUMP SYSTEM

The system we have developed is known affectionately as LUMP, an acronym for Loughborough University Manufacturing Package, but also carrying with it the notion of integration and the blending together of various sub-systems. We receive and deliver information from and to two major Design to Product components: the designer system being produced at Edinburgh University (Smithers [17], Popplestone et al. [14]) and the machines at G.E.C. F.A.S.T. and Lucas C.A.V. We receive information in the form of Constructive Solid Geometry strings (NONAME [13]) from the designer system and deliver numerical codes or programs to the factory. The LUMP system is composed of an integrating blackboard based manager written in Prolog and has 4 major active components with several more smaller subsystems. These subsystems comprise the following:

1. A procedure responsible for the translation of geometry data to manufacturing features; this subsystem is also written as a Prolog program and thus can be integrated into the main system easily.

2. A planning subsystem to generate the generic operations used to manufacture the required component; this subsystem is also written as a Prolog program and thus can also be integrated into the main blackboard system easily.

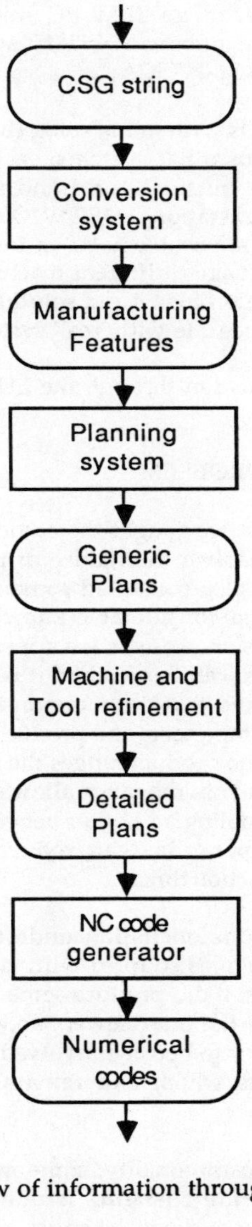

Figure 2. Showing a typical flow of information through the LUMP system.

3. A proprietary Relational Data Base Management system to emulate the information systems of a real rather than idealised factory. The RDB contains information about machines and tools, their properties and relationships. This subsystem was received as binary executable code and is therefore approached using the Unix pipe system via an intermediate program written in 'C'.

4. A numerical code generation package to produce the numerical codes required by the machines in our pilot factory. This subsystem was received as binary executable code which runs on an IBM PC microcomputer connected via a communications subsystem to our main LUMP system again via another small intermediate program written in 'PASCAL'.

The main LUMP system is written in Prolog (Bratko [2]) and as outlined above we have had to link to various other systems; each of these clearly has different methods of interfacing to the outside world and some also execute on different machines including SUN workstations, DEC VAXes and IBM PCs. We therefore have had not only to address the problems of various subsystems but also those of different implementation languages, different machines and operating systems. We do not propose to describe the problems and solutions that have arisen but to point out that the requirement to integrate with 'real' systems is being taken seriously.

A typical flow of information through the LUMP system is given in figure 2 above.

THE PROCESS PLANNING PROBLEM

At the beginning of the project we sought the advice of several senior engineers at various establishments to establish the nature of process planning and what we therefore had to achieve. We also consulted some relevant text books (Chang et. al. [4] for example). We gained considerable knowledge from those conversations but also a great deal of confusion arose as we appeared to be obtaining conflicting evidence. This phenomenon is well known and it is clearly healthy that experts can sometimes disagree. We did find that the common factor between their approaches to both design of individual components and products and whole product ranges was a search for commonality. In the product ranges the search for common components or manufacturing techniques across the range allows batch manufacture, less diverse and therefore less expensive tooling and other benefits. The search for commonality across the manufacturing operations can reduce fixture and tooling changes consequently improving production times.

An exercise in knowledge elicitation undertaken within the project using structured interviewing techniques coupled with task analysis techniques failed to produce this insight, in contrast it did produce some very strange rules, probably due to a lack of understanding by the interviewers about the nature of the underlying knowledge. We felt it necessary to become involved in process planning in order to obtain the necessary insights which had remained hidden in the behavioural study.

As an example of this commonality; some machines with a single fixturing bed perform optimally if fixture changing is minimised even if the fixturing is consequently more expensive and tool changes more frequent. Others with the capability of holding several pieces simultaneously and rotating them under the cutting heads perform optimally when tool changes are minimised, even if fixture changes may be more frequent.

Consequently the batch size and subsequent production volumes dictate whether some special machinery is to be used to exploit some aspects of the design, and within that the type of machinery chosen will dictate the commonality to be sought.

Examination of consumer goods which are sold as part of a range display commonality of several parts and dimensions. With two bore sizes and two crankshaft sizes we may produce the basis for 4 different sized engines; other less costly parts may have to be individually designed for each of the 4 capacities. We therefore see this search for commonality as part of the design process for a range of products.

LUMP ARCHITECTURE

The LUMP system is based around a ranked-bid truth maintained blackboard system which is unique in its combination of features. There is a precedent for using truth maintained blackboard systems in design with the work at Edinburgh University in the Design to Product demonstrator (see Popplestone et al. [14]); however the ranked-bid system is a further development of this theme.

Blackboard Systems

The concept behind blackboard systems (Engelmore and Morgan [9]) is that of a collection of experts collaborating round a blackboard in order to solve a problem of common interest. They are unable to communicate except by writing on the blackboard and so share a common working area. The software implementation of blackboard systems employs a blackboard management system to organise the interaction between the various experts, which we term knowledge sources, and the various knowledge sources themselves. Each knowledge source bids to the blackboard for entries that it may be able do something with. There is also a set of 'facts' which if true could allow a rule or knowledge source to 'fire', perform some useful task or add some useful piece of knowledge to the developing solution. None of the knowledge sources need to know which of the other knowledge sources placed a particular piece of information on the blackboard; neither do they need to know where that piece of knowledge will be used. This frees us from having to specify the order in which the various tasks are to be performed.

Blackboard systems are more actively engaged in the management of the problem solving than simply allowing the knowledge sources to write facts and information on the blackboard; the reading and writing to the blackboard has to be scheduled and this scheduling is a primary responsibility of the blackboard manager. The blackboard manager takes requests from the knowledge sources, we refer to these requests as 'bids', and will activate the knowledge source if there is a suitable set of entries on the blackboard. Blackboard systems have been used in many and varied applications within artificial intelligence (Reddy et al. [16]); however the knowledge sources usually consist of a single rule and so the number of knowledge sources can be quite large. In our implementation we have tried to compromise between the flexible architecture of a blackboard based system for all rules and computations and the efficiency of specially written modules for specific tasks.

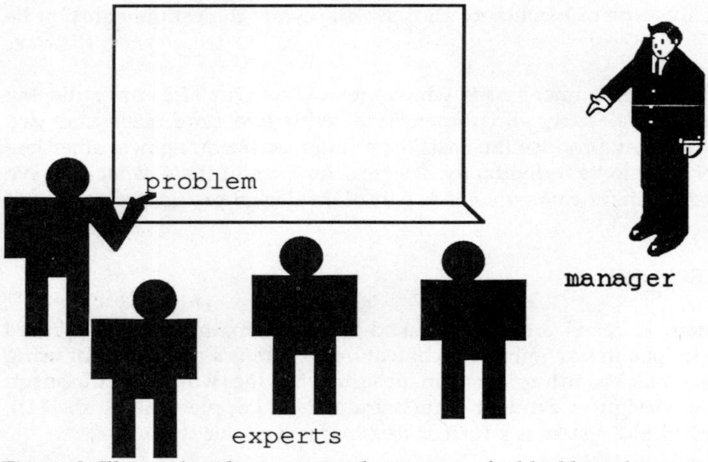

Figure 3. Illustrating the conceptual structure of a blackboard system.

The effect of bidding on the blackboard manager is to set up and extend several data structures responsible for monitoring the state of the blackboard. The major one of interest at this stage is *bid* as this records all the bids made to the blackboard and is stored in a coded form to simplify reference to the entries on the blackboard. Each of these lists is coded as being associated with a pattern_type; as each entry comes onto the blackboard it is classified into one or more pattern types which are then checked against any bids which might require that particular pattern (Forgy [10]). As bids have their required patterns entered onto the blackboard, those that are now capable of "firing" are ranked. This ranking is based primarily according to the conjunction of the ratings of the entries on the blackboard, and so is a predictor of the rating of the derived consequence. A secondary ranking is made by the strength of the bid made to the blackboard. In this way the system always tries to satisfy bids made which are associated with the highest rated environment and within that the highest rated bid is executed.

The use of a properly engineered blackboard system improves the specificity of the application of the knowledge sources as each entry is not joined with other entries to be presented abortively to all knowledge sources. A variation of the RETE match algorithm (Forgy [10]) is used to resolve conflicts in presentation of work to the knowledge sources and ensures that each knowledge source is only presented with entries that are potentially useful. By ensuring that the requirements of each knowledge source are properly specified we can improve the efficiency of the system. Early simplistic systems designed to do no more than test our ideas spent a long time presenting entries to knowledge sources which were just not able to do anything with them. A considerable amount of the work in developing the LUMP system has gone into designing the blackboard management system and implementing the system's matching algorithm.

Truth Maintenance

Problems would occur in conventional blackboard systems if there were entries which were inconsistent; in some systems backtracking will occur on meeting an inconsistency. The method of backtracking is relevant as a great deal of work may have been accomplished which would then be undone under such circumstances and then regrown. If the backtracking was directed towards the source of the inconsistency then this can be reasonably efficient and this is called dependency directed backtracking. Where we require to maintain several views of an emerging solution this is inadequate. An Assumption Based Truth Maintenance System (de Kleer [5,6] is able to maintain several mutually inconsistent views of the world, where each of these views is self consistent and may have equal credibility when examined either objectively or subjectively.

An alternative to the Assumption based Truth Maintenance System (ATMS) of de Kleer is the Justification based Truth Maintenance System (JTMS) of Doyle [8]. The JTMS is accepted in the literature (Boddington & Elleby [1]) as a suitable architecture if only one interpretation is required; however the ATMS is more suitable for multiple interpretations although it can have higher overheads for very large systems. Recent work indicates that the overheads for an ATMS based on the work of de Kleer are NP (Provan [15]); NP problems have an exponential time complexity function but can demonstrate a solution in polynomial time. An informed guidance system can reduce an NP problem to polynomial time complexity; this is one of the purposes of the ranked-bid system discussed in the section on system control below. We have adopted an ATMS system because of the applicability of the method to our problem and an underlying ranked bid blackboard architecture for efficiency reasons and also to enhance the directionality of the search.

Deriving entries from knowledge sources is done by presenting entries required by the knowledge sources on the understanding that they will produce useful information in the form of a new entry or entries. The entries presented to the knowledge sources are presented as a result of the bidding system. The knowledge source then computes with the presented set of entries and then delivers its result back to the blackboard. Any entry delivered to the blackboard system carries with it a modal tag which tells the blackboard whether the consequence follows necessarily from the original statements or whether it is only one of a set of possible entries.

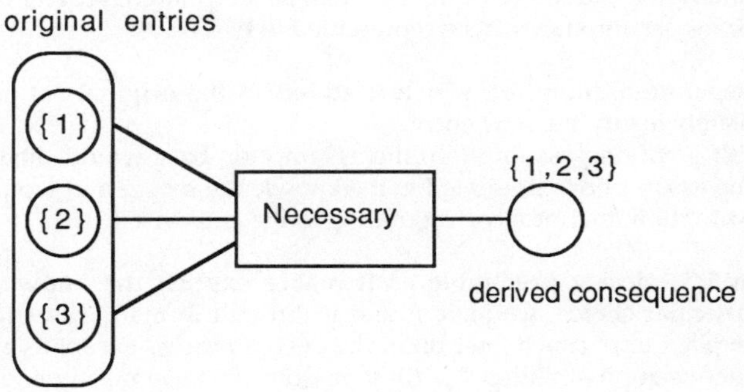

Figure 4. Illustrating the derivation of necessary consequences.

This is illustrated with examples from elementary algebra. Given that we have the statements, a = b * c, b = 3 and c = 4; then if we accept the rules of algebra then we are also forced to accept that a = 12.

Necessary entries form their assumption bases directly from their premisses by union operations as shown in figure 4.

If we number the statements and suppose that they are further dependent upon other initial assumptions as follows then we may make figure 4 more explicit:

Entry no	Area	Expression	Assumption Base
1	algebra	a=b*c	{1}
2	algebra	b=3	{2}
3	algebra	c=4	{3}
4	algebra	a=12	{1,2,3}

Should we wish to enter another expression d= a*2 onto the blackboard we need not know how a's value was derived, only that it ultimately depends on assumptions 1, 2 and 3. Suppose further that a = b * c could be derived from assumptions {12,13,14} we would obtain the following:

Entry no	Area	Expression	Assumption Base
1	algebra	a=b*c	{1}
2	algebra	b=3	{2}
3	algebra	c=4	{3}
4	algebra	a=12	{1,2,3},{12,13,14}
5	algebra	d = a * 2	{5}
6	algebra	d = 24	{1,2,3,5},{5,12,13,14}

Possible new entries must have a new piece of information associated with them, otherwise the inconsistency arising will be based on the assumption bases shared by all the possible entries. This then would make all the possible entries delivered inconsistent. The possible modality tag also carries with it a rating which will determine the rating of the eventual assumption base. The new piece of information (new assumption) can be represented in two ways:

1. As a separate assumption which if added to the original set of premisses would completely justify the new entry.
2. As a self justifying assumption; the assumption base would then contain all the underlying assumptions presented to the knowledge source and would also have an added assumption reference corresponding to the entry itself.

Option 1 is clearly preferable as it makes explicit the knowledge which justifies a particular choice, we have found it difficult in many cases to make this knowledge explicit until much later on in the design process except as a differential comparison between possibilities. For these reasons we have mostly adopted option 2; figures 5 and 6 illustrate the ideas diagrammatically.

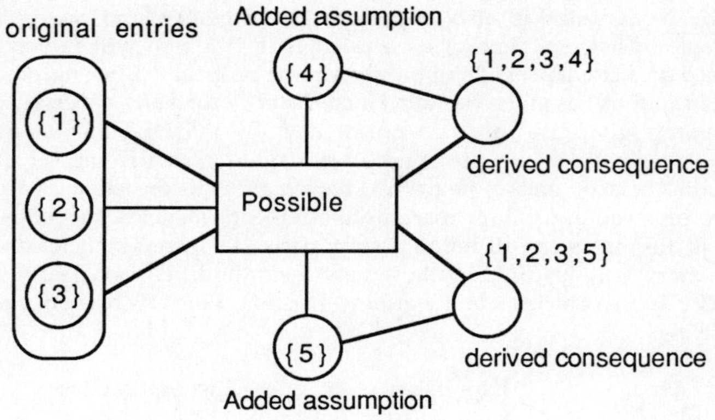

Figure 5. Illustrating option 1 where assumptions are added to the blackboard which, if true, completely justify the new entry.

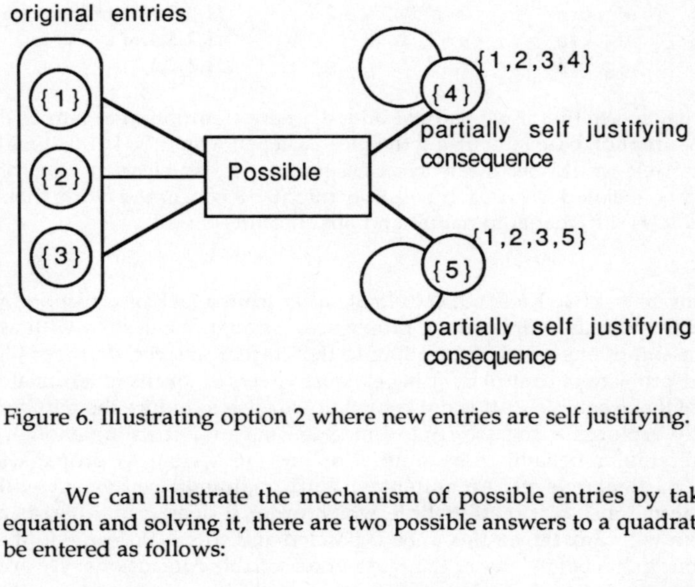

Figure 6. Illustrating option 2 where new entries are self justifying.

We can illustrate the mechanism of possible entries by taking a quadratic equation and solving it, there are two possible answers to a quadratic so they would be entered as follows:

Entry no	Area	Expression	Assumption Base
1	algebra	0=a*x^2 + b*x + c	{1}
2	algebra	a=1	{2}
3	algebra	b=-3	{3}
4	algebra	c=2	{4}
5	algebra	0=x^2 - 3*x + 2	{1,2,3,4}
6	algebra	x=1	{1,2,3,4,6}
7	algebra	x=2	{1,2,3,4,7}

Consistency or its absence is also important to efficiency and so each knowledge type has a consistency checker associated with it which will prevent any consequence based on a similar set of assumptions being propagated through the system. If a set of assumptions has given rise to an inconsistency then any superset of that set would similarly give rise to an inconsistency. By marking entries as mutually inconsistent early on in the propagation we avoid growing the set of blackboard entries unnecessarily only to be pruned back later as inconsistencies are discovered. We have reserved entry 0 for marking these inconsistencies, this entry starts off being self justifying as are all initial assumptions. As inconsistencies are discovered the false entry is re-justified by these new assumption bases. Clearly x cannot be both 1 and 2 and so entries 6 and 7 are inconsistent. This inconsistency is recorded as shown below:

Entry no	Area	Expression	Assumption Base
0	_	false	{0},{1,2,3,4,6,7}
1	algebra	0=a*x^2 + b*x + c	{1}
2	algebra	a=1	{2}
3	algebra	b=-3	{3}
4	algebra	c=2	{4}
5	algebra	0=x^2 - 3*x + 2	{1,2,3,4}
6	algebra	x = 1	{1,2,3,4,6}
7	algebra	x = 2	{1,2,3,4,7}

It is now easy to see that if we had not added a new assumption to entries 6 and 7 then the assumption base supporting the inconsistency would be {1,2,3,4} and so the quadratic itself would be deemed inconsistent. It is also clear the sort of knowledge entry associated with each solution might be concerned with their relative sizes and so is differential in nature and not absolute.

<u>System control</u>

Unranked systems such as de Kleer's ATMS [5,6] suffer from a lack of direction in that quite obviously poor assumptions are propagated through the system with as much vigour as assumptions which are leading to the 'correct' answer. de Kleer [7] has addressed the problem of control by using exhaustive sets of tokens to terminate search. In the case that a complete set is not known or we wish to reduce the number of choices initially explored then such control mechanisms are not strong enough. We can replicate similar behaviour by only allowing the system to propagate entries above a particular level. An unranked truth maintenance system will propagate everything and so it matters little which order it does it in whereas a ranked bid system will rank the entries to be expanded and so should come to the 'most obvious' conclusion before any of the more unreasonable conclusions. We are concerned with maintaining the exhaustive nature of the search but also with arriving at the most reasonable solutions first. If only one solution is required then this is efficient and avoids the extra work involved in calculating other redundant interpretations. If more than one solution is required then the solutions should be presented in some 'reasonable' order. As soon as an interpretation is accepted then it may be quite reasonable to stop the calculation of other interpretations. By carefully choosing the importance of reaching a conclusion we may exhibit several types of behaviour

All initial entries onto the blackboard are regarded as assumptions, so there are no entries which must be included in (consistent with) any valid environment. The assumptions underlying any particular entry are collected together with the entry into disjunctions of conjunctions. Each conjunctive set gives the assumptions which if true, would make the entry necessarily true. The ratings for the various consequences,used to control the truth maintained blackboard system, are derived by taking the disjunction of all the assumption base components. The ratings for the assumption base components are derived by taking the conjunction of all defined subsets of the individual assumption base. The defined subsets are provided by any knowledge source which returns a possible modality and should be an optimistic view of the utility of the particular assumption or assumption set. This is then covered by the classic proof of admissibility for AND/OR graphs (Nilsson [11]) and ensures that the optimal query (in some sense defined by the user's choice of rating values) is found with minimal effort.

REPRESENTATION

The representation of knowledge and plans in the system is relevant to understanding the work reported in this paper. Several representations are employed with transformation systems used to link them. The most significant of these is the one used to transform the geometry of the component into a form suitable for planning.

Feature derivation

The conversion knowledge source converts the finished geometric design as a CSG string into manufacturing features as outlined briefly above. This task is one of transformation of representation from a geometrical description based on the functional design to a geometrical description oriented towards machining and assembly. Figure 7 illustrates a simple transformation of a component designed with two blocks on the top which can be reinterpreted as a larger block with a slot cut from the top.

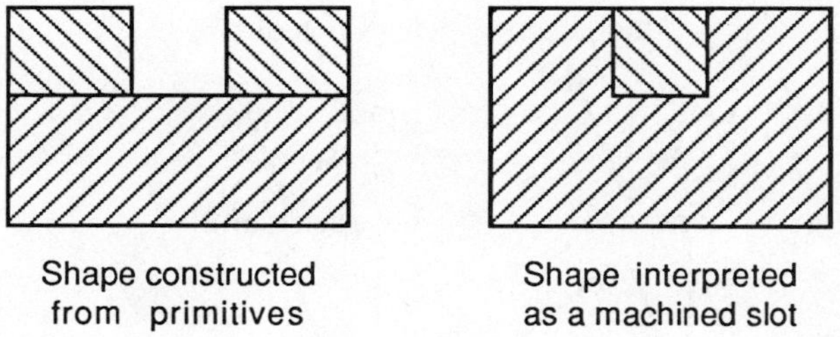

Figure 7. Showing two different interpretations of the same object.

The first shape has been constructed by adding three primitives together, the second has been formed by subtracting one primitive from another. Whereas the first interpretation is the sort that might arise from consideration of the shape alone, the second would lead to a strategy for machining the component. Our approach to this has been through the use of a rewrite system and not through the use of an expensive geometry reasoning system. There are usually several possible interpretations of a given piece of geometry and so our truth maintained approach allows us to reason with several interpretations until it is clear which is likely to lead to the 'correct' solution. We do not attempt to define the notion of correctness in this paper, however the better interpretations will allow minimal machine, fixture and tooling changes. Currently we allow the user to select a few 'promising' interpretations to work with and to dispense with them later as more information is available regarding the appropriateness of any given interpretation.

THE PLANNER

The planner works by considering the pre conditions, post conditions and invariants associated with the various operations (Nilsson [12]) performable by the machines available and will place the resulting knowledge on the blackboard in a concise form. Rather than place each separate alternative plan on the blackboard the system places each separate piece of detail of a plan on the blackboard. The central management system will store any entry made uniquely and so if two choices of machine for a given operation use the same tool type then this will only be stored once but have two assumption bases associated with it.

Any knowledge source receiving these entries will be working with both machines on the single value for the tool type, this minimises the work involved in calculating effects and consequences and is a by-product of using an ATMS system.

The plans are represented as sets of operations which are constrained by corresponding sets of constraints. These constraints may be added to during the design of the process plan by suitably constructed knowledge sources; typically invoked by the user. Each operation consists of several properties such as the tool employed, the machine to be used, speeds, feeds, tolerances etc. These must be selected or designed to obtain the optimum process plan and to this end the process plan is represented as a set of tokens each associated with a frame of definitions. As these definitions (tool type speeds etc.) may consist of several alternatives the frames are truth maintained. We view the set of operation tokens as the 'spine' of the plan (figure. 8).

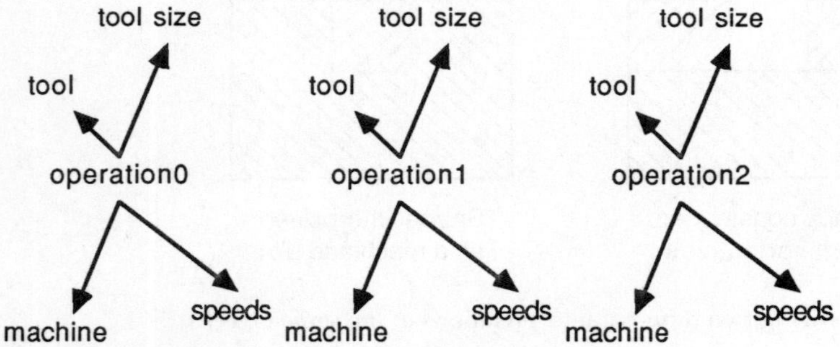

Figure 8. Showing the operation spine.

The operations forming the centre of the spine are further constrained by sets of temporal constraints which are derived by consideration of their structure using the planning knowledge source. The planning knowledge source takes as its input the set of manufacturing features provided by the conversion knowledge source coupled with a definition of the capabilities of the machines in the factory.

There are thus two major entries placed on the blackboard by the planner, the first is the operation spine described above. The other entry placed on the blackboard by the planner is a set of ordering constraints to be combined with the operation spine to give the set of plans implied by the requirements of the manufacturing process. The set of constraints placed on the blackboard is a minimal set that would ensure that any sequence of operations satisfying the constraints can form the basis of a valid plan. These constraints may be added to in order to further constrain the set of potential sequences of operations in order to optimise the relevant plan characteristics.

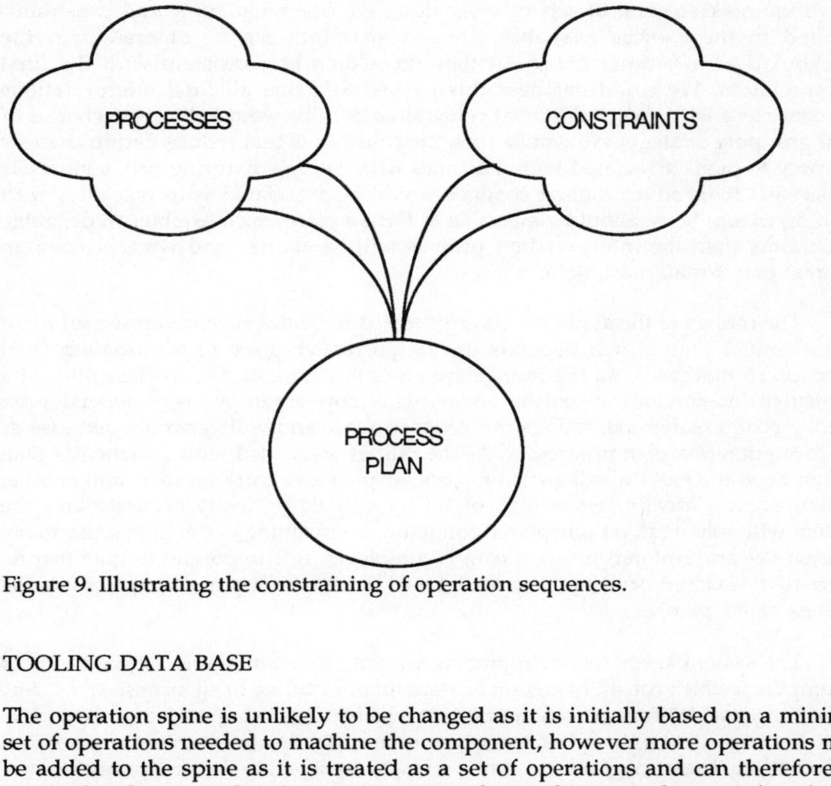

Figure 9. Illustrating the constraining of operation sequences.

TOOLING DATA BASE

The operation spine is unlikely to be changed as it is initially based on a minimal set of operations needed to machine the component, however more operations may be added to the spine as it is treated as a set of operations and can therefore be manipulated as a set. It is important to note that at this stage there are few details determined about the operations. After the generic process plan has been produced by the planning engine more detail must be added in order to make an executable numerical machine program. In particular we use a proprietary relational data base management system to store tooling information. The relevant information determined by the planning engine is used to form the basis of a data base query and the resultant information is then placed on the blackboard associated with the operation requiring refinement. Often there will be more than one tool which is suitable for the operation and all these are placed on the blackboard in order to allow the maximum freedom to the process planning engineer using the system. The tools which most closely match the parameters of the operation are rated the highest with the tools least closely matching being ranked lowest. In this way the system will work with the preferred tools first and continue with this strategy until a 'better' or more highly rated option becomes available.

The tooling data base will consider each operation in isolation whereas a competent process planning engineer will search for commonality to reduce tooling changes if possible. The tooling data base will deliver all tools that could accomplish the operation. The number of choices of tool will therefore be greater than might 'conventionally' be considered.

When these tools have been entered onto the blackboard either the process planning engineer can search for commonality or a subsidiary knowledge source may suggest common aspects which can potentially simplify the manufacturing process. This requires collection of sets of tools along the operation spine and constraints applied to the choices available. These constraints can be entered onto the blackboard as any other entry but they must then be consistent with the final interpretation. We could engineer this by insisting that all final interpretations are consistent with these additional constraints but this would eliminate choices of final grouping strategy. We would wish the constraints that reduce fixture changes to apply to plans associated with machines with a single fixturing bed, conversely constraints that reduce tooling changes would be associated with machines with rotating fixture beds. Should we be able to form a plan which exhibits all desirable constraints then the interpretation process will be shorter and we will have an optimal plan for all machine options.

The ratings of the assumptions are deemed to be the most optimistic utility of any eventual plan which depends on the particular piece of information (tool selection in this case). As the ratings are an optimistic estimate of the utility of a particular decision and the entries always gain more assumptions or dependencies as they progress then the ratings can never increase and will generally decrease as the formation of a plan progresses. As the ratings associated with a particular plan option drop the system will switch to another plan and work on that until another switch occurs. Ideally the ratings of utility will be perfectly accurate and the system will only work on one plan throughout the planning cycle. In practise many alternatives are explored before a plan is completed. It is important to note that no alternative is closed or completely abandoned, it is just not pursued unless it is the highest rated plan.

The system keeps its environments separate by maintaining 'nogood' sets of assumptions which consist of any set of assumptions leading to an inconsistency. Any set of entries which form an assumption set which is itself a superset of a nogood set is itself inconsistent although this may not necessarily be obvious from a superficial examination. These 'nogood' sets are necessary to separate the environments into consistent sets, otherwise the number of possible interpretations is very large indeed. The problem of interpretation is now faced by the system as it tries to produce a valid constrained operation spine with a consistent set of operation details.

INTERPRETATION

The system, after having designed the operations in some detail is now in a position to interpret the state of the blackboard and produce numerical codes associated with the manufacture of the component based on that state. An example of a simple plan with only 10 operations with 2 choices for all aspects of those operations will illustrate the problem we faced at this stage.

Each operation at this stage has at least 8 aspects of its definition which may have any number of alternatives each. If we allow that there are only 2 alternatives for each aspect of the operation and there are 10 operations then we arrive at $(2^8)^{10}$ different combinations of plan details, many of which are inconsistent as defined by the 'nogood' sets. We have to draw together the highest rated plan and allow the blackboard system to present these to the numerical code generator. Even searching through a smallish proportion of these possible plans would take a very long time and we have no way of knowing at this stage which will be nogood without an exhaustive search, clearly the time taken would be unacceptable in any real application. The actual situation is much worse than this as the interoperation constraints can be loose if there is little or no interaction between the machining processes of the different features; in our example we would multiply the 2^{80} possible operation spines by the different number of sequences they could be performed in. This multiplies up to become $10!*2^{80}$, a very large number indeed!

We may neglect the 10! term in the expression as we may assume that if there has been no further temporal constraints applied the user will be satisfied with any ordering. Presenting the user with the graphical representation of the topology of the operation sequences allows the user to assess this and accept or reject plan structures.

The example given above is a small one by machining plan standards but is also unacceptably large to compute as it is stated above. An example of drilling, deburring and reaming a hole with a choice of two machines and a small selection of tools produced 48 possible plans satisfying all the constraints; some of these plans were unacceptable from a manufacturing efficiency standpoint in that they moved the workpiece between machines but they were none the less valid in a wider sense. We clearly require all these plans to be potentially available for consultation or development but cannot afford to enumerate them all in any realistic situation. The rating system will present the numerical code generator with the most highly rated plan according to the knowledge available before constructing the numerical codes and assessing operation times, but only after a search of $10!*2^{80}$ combinations.

SOLUTION

The solution adopted reduces the search space to manageable proportions by layering the interpretation process. The operation spine will have different consistent sets for each operation as well as requiring the operation definitions to be consistent between operations. By interpreting the operations individually we reduce the search to manageable proportions.

Using our example above and only layering the interpretation process into two layers we have the following process:

1. Collect each operations details into a consistent collective entry, this may be compared to a 'setof' operation in Prolog (Bratko [2]). The largest search space for this using our example would be 2^8 per operation, which although still excessive is now manageable. The result is 2 consistent sets of details contained in a 2 entries per operation on the blackboard. We now have a search space of $10*2^8$ to perform the collection of consistent single operation plans or less than 2^{12}.

2. Collect the sets of operation details into complete plans using a similar 'setof' operation. As we have two consistent sets stored as two blackboard entries per operation the space is only 2^{10}

The total search space has been reduced from 2^{80} to under 2^{13}.

A little thought shows that this can be reduced even further by grouping sets of details, first into pairs of operation details then grouping the pairs, etc. The search space in our example is now reduced to $(4*2^2 + 2*2^2 + 2^2)$ for the first stage of collection described above (4 groups of 2 with 2 choices, 2 groups of 4 with two choices and 1 group of 2 with 2 choices. Interpreting an object consisting of N details and C choices for each we initially had a search space of order(C^N) which we have now reduced to order($N*C^2$) by layering the interpretation process. This layering can only work if the 'nogood' sets have been calculated and there are only a few consistent views, if there are many consistent views then the search space will be correspondingly large but will not be exponentially large.

An unranked ATMS will propagate all plan developments through to their 'logical' conclusion, the rating system will initially only propagate those that show some degree of promise. As a result we also reduce the eventual number of choices that need interpretation. If the ratings are helpful we reduce the problem space, if not we do not lose the exhaustive nature of the process and so do not preclude any solution.

SUMMARY

We have described the essential details of a truth maintained process planning system. The details of the subsystems comprising the overall system have been briefly described but we feel the overall architecture is of greater interest at this stage. The system has taken several small components and produced valid (tested on a machining centre) numerical codes.

We have found that after a significant effort spent in designing the truth maintained blackboard system that interfacing to the subsystems was relatively straightforward in many cases. Our biggest problem was in interpreting the eventual blackboard and we believe our solution will be applicable to other areas of design where there are a large number of details each with several choices. Our problem representation could have grouped the operations into single predicates from the start of the design process, this would have made separate design of the individual operation and plan details difficult. It would also have made extensions to the representation of plans difficult in future versions. The alternative we have adopted has made interpretation difficult but our solution leaves us with an acceptable compromise.

ACKNOWLEDGEMENTS

The work reported is part of the S.E.R.C./Alvey large scale demonstrator "Design to Product". The project is managed by G.E.C. Electrical Projects and involves the following collaborators:
Dept. Artificial Intelligence, Edinburgh University.
Dept. Computer Studies, Loughborough University of Technology.
Dept. Manufacturing Engineering, Loughborough University of Technology.
Dept. Mechanical Engineering, Leeds University.
G.E.C. Electrical Projects, Rugby.
G.E.C. FAST, Rugby.
HUSAT Research Centre, Loughborough.
Lucas CAV, Gillingham.
Marconi Research, Gt. Baddow.

Although the design of the process planning system has been the responsibility of the Departments of Computer Studies and Manufacturing Engineering at Loughborough University of Technology however we have been influenced by other collaborators in the project. In particular we would like to acknowledge the work at Edinburgh for introducing the ATMS concept to us. We would also like to acknowledge the help of the other collaborators, especially G.E.C. FAST and Lucas C.A.V. for their help in understanding the field of process planning.

REFERENCES

1. Boddington, R & Elleby, P. Justification and Assumption based truth maintenance systems: when and how to use them. Workshop on Reason Maintenance Systems and their Applications, University of Leeds. 1988.
2. Bratko, I. Prolog Programing for Artificial Intelligence, Addison-Wesley, London, 1986.
3. Burrow, L. D. The Design to Product Alvey Demonstrator. I.C.L. Technical Journal, Vol.6 No. 3. 1989.
4. Chang, T-C. & Wysk, R.A. An introduction to automated Process Planning, Prentice Hall, London, 1985.
5. de Kleer, J. Choices without backtracking. Proceedings of the Conference of the American Association for Artificial Intelligence, 1984.
6. de Kleer, J. An Assumption-based TMS. Artificial Intelligence Journal, Vol. 28, pp. 127-162, 1986.
7. de Kleer, J. & Williams, B.C. Back to backtracking: Controlling the ATMS, Proceedings of 5th National Conference on Artificial Intelligence, AAAI-86,Aug 1986.
8. Doyle, J. A Truth Maintenance System, Artificial Intelligence Journal , Vol. 12, pp. 231-272, 1979.
9. Engelmore, R. & Morgan, A. Blackboard systems, Addison-Wesley, London, 1988.
10. Forgy, C.L. RETE: A Fast Algorithm for the Many Pattern/Many Object Pattern Match Problem, Artificial Intelligence Journal, Vol. 19, pp. 17-37, 1982.
11. Nilsson, N. Problem Solving Methods in Artificial Intelligence, McGraw-Hill, New York, 1971.
12. Nilsson, N. Principles of Artificial Intelligence, Springer, Berlin, 1980.
13. Staff of the geometric modelling project, NONAME Documentation, Geometric Modelling Project University of Leeds, 1983.

14. Popplestone, R.J.,Smithers, T.M.,Corney J., Koutsou,A., Millington, K. & Sahar G. Engineering Design Support Systems, in 1st International Conference on Applications of Artificial Intelligence, Southampton, 1986.

15. Provan, G. Efficiency Analysis of Multiple-Context TMSs in Scene Representation, Technical report OU-RRG-87-9, Robotics Research Group University of Oxford, U.K., 1988.

16. Reddy, D,R., Erman, L.D,, Fennell, R.D., & Neely, R.B. The Hearsay Speech Understanding System: An Example of the Recognition Process, in IJCAI 3. pp. 185-193 (Stanford, CA), 1973.

17. Smithers, T.M. The Alvey Large Scale Demonstrator Project "Design To Product", in Proceedings of the Technology Assessment and Management Conference of the Gottlieb Duttweiler Institute Ruschlikon, Zurich, Switzerland, 1985.

A Non-Linear Planning Approach to the Machining of Prismatic Components

I.A. Donaldson and D. Willis

Department of Computer Science and Department of Mechanical Engineering, Heriot-Watt University, 79 Grassmarket, Edinburgh EH1 2HJ, UK

Abstract

A hierarchical, non-linear planner, adapted from AI work, has been applied to the task of constructing process plans for machining operations. The system operates in two phases, firstly generating a network of partially ordered plan steps and, subsequently, searching for a linear plan sequence which will form the basis of shop-floor documentation. Manufacturing knowledge is encoded principally as schemas in a format which captures the necessary ordering of tasks in time and the conditions under which that knowledge can be applied. Knowledge for plan refinement is represented in a more *ad hoc* fashion as procedures or as cost-functions which guide a heuristic search. Examples of schemas which plan a prismatic component are described. The system will generate alternative plans within the partial order constraints.

Introduction

Considerable attention is currently being directed towards computer aided process planning (CAPP) as part of a trend towards effective CADCAM, automating the design to manufacture cycle for mechanical parts.

It is recognised that an efficient CAPP system will provide benefits in uniformity of planning and in the capture of planning expertise. It might also result in more efficient process plans and reduce problems arising from human errors in planning. Yet, despite such incentives, there remain significant problems with the geometric reasoning which is entailed and in the representation of planning knowledge. Work in the Process Planning group at Heriot-Watt University addresses these two issues and is concerned with the integration of a commercial solid modelling CAD system into a generative CAPP facility [1].

The functional structure of this facility is described in Fig 1. It is designed as an autonomous system which derives a feature classification for protrusions and recesses, along with geometric data directly from the infoSOLID modeller. The shape information for a component is analysed by a 3D reasoning module to identify the feature interactions and machining constraints and this additional information, combined with a planning knowledge base serves to drive the generative planner.

This paper defines the scope of the process planning problem, describes one approach to its solution - that of applying a hierarchical non-linear planning model - and details its suitability to the problem. It therefore focuses on the functional components enclosed in the dashed box to the right of Fig 1. A hierarchical approach to process planning has also been adopted by several research groups, including the SIPS system [2] and the XCUT program [3].

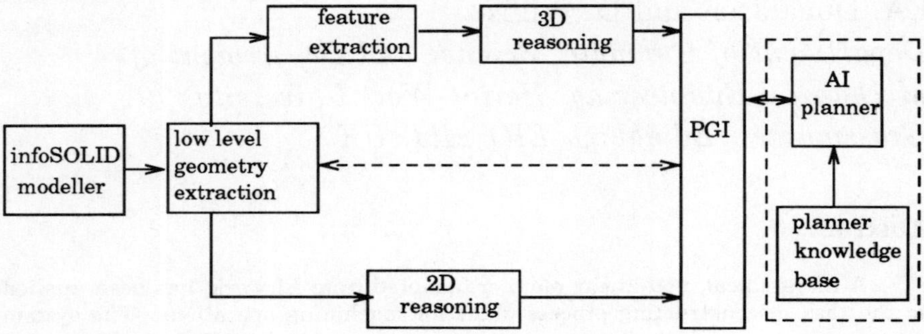

Figure 1. Functional units of the process planning system.

Geometric data and a feature classification are derived from a commercial solid modelling system and presented to the planner via a planner geometry interface (PGI).

The Process Planning Problem

The task of planning for manufacture can be reduced to the two operations of *selection* and *sequencing*. It commences with a design specification which includes a geometric description of the component, its material properties etc. and from this it *selects* the manufacturing processes which match to the design specification along with subsidiary decisions about tool selection and it derives the *sequence* with which these will be applied in order to realise the component. The resulting plan will have a complete order in time on machining steps and hence is a linear sequence which is near-optimal in terms of pre-defined manufacturing cost criteria. A generalised planning system constructed on these principles would represent a significant spectrum of manufacturing technology and we have restricted our consideration in several ways. Firstly, we consider only one machining process, that of NC milling and drilling. Secondly, we have restricted our consideration of part geometry to components which are prismatic (2½ Dimensional) plus a subset of 'form-features' (chamfers, fillets and undercuts) and which are formed from cuboidal stock. This geometric restriction corresponds to the class of components which can be formed by 3-axis machining with multiple setups. Lastly, by focusing on the detailed planning of machining operations, we have deferred consideration of workholding mechanisms other than bolting to a machine platen.

When we try to expand the functional definition of process planning given above we quickly find difficulty in categorising the knowledge of the domain expert. Cognitive modelling of the manual process planning task has been attempted [4] but no system claims to follow such a human centred approach in its implementation. Instead, our analysis of the domain knowledge suggests that there is a significant analogy between manual process planning and the type of planning task for which domain independent non-linear planning systems have been developed. This analogy is in three respects: task abstraction, task decomposition and plan refinement, each of which is examined below. The strength of this analogy has led us to implement a non-linear planning system for this domain.

Task Abstraction
Firstly, it is apparent that manual process planning is performed at several levels of abstraction. One stratification of these levels appears in Table 1.

Table 1 An abstract structure for the process planning task

abstraction level	*nature*
1	The order of component setups.
2	The order of machineable features within a setup.
3	The sequence of machining cuts within a feature.

This can be modelled with the class of hierarchical planners [5]. However, no abstraction has yet been capable of capturing the structure of the planning problem because it has not been possible to form a pure taxonomic hierarchy of knowledge in the domain which provides a clear separation of these levels of abstraction. For example, decisions on workholding in level 1 may be dependent on the machining sequence decided at level 3 and this is reflected in the local to global context switching which has been reported for manual process planners [4]. Interdependence amongst levels need not be a problem if any lower level decisions are mapped into the higher level [6].

Task Decomposition
There is substantial parallelism in the ordering of steps in a process plan which is analogous to the principle of 'least commitment' to time-order [7]. It is most in evidence at level 2 of the abstraction scheme, where design features (as distinct from machineable features) may be organised into a 'feature structure' with the significant property that the organisation is a highly parallel (and hence under-constrained) network. This is the case for features which arise at the same z-level and are equally accessible to a cutting tool. However, interactions between and within a feature will reduce this inherent parallelism and constrain the order of machining. Such constraints are detailed in Table 2 and are resolved by imposing a time order on the machining of the interacting features - as in the case of the re-sequencing of some drilling operations (constraint type **A1**) - or, in the case of re-entrant geometry - by decomposing the geometry of the 'intruding' *design*

feature into a set of *machineable* features with a complete order in time (constraint type **B3**).

Plan Refinement

A manual process plan is iteratively refined by applying heuristics which attempt to minimise cost criteria - for example, to minimise tool changes. This area of process planning is poorly formalised and may be compared to the 'deep knowledge' of a task domain in comparison with the more readily accessible knowledge which is required to construct a feature hierarchy. Operationally, it requires that partial plans have a time order imposed, resulting in a totally ordered set of plan steps. This characteristic of manual process planning is analogous to the separation between plan synthesis and plan refinement which typifies the class of domain independent non-linear planning schemes [8].

Based on the analogy, a non-linear planning model was implemented for process planning using Quintus Prolog. It is described in the following two sections on plan synthesis and plan refinement.

Table 2. Machining constraints and their resolution

Type	Constraint	Effect	Action
A1	drilling thru' thin floors	*inter*	resequence as a first operation from this facet
A2	machining thru' thin floors	*inter*	perform while ≥ 0.150" residual material remains in floor
A3	machining thin walls	*inter*	step-cut amongst features in a 'thin wall group'
A4	machining thin floors	*inter*	*either* reduce last cut to be ≤ 0.100" or reinforce concavity on paired facet
A5	achieving tolerances/surface finishes	*inter/intra*	report to user
B1	minimum internal radius	*intra*	reduce tool size
B2	profile narrowing	*intra*	optimise between profile sub-division and tool changing
B3	profile intrusion	*inter*	sub-divide the intruding profile

Plan Synthesis

The purpose of the system is to formulate a plan of action for the manufacture of a component. An initial goal *{plan the component}* is evolved into a network of plan steps or actions with only a partial time ordering which reflects the 'least commitment' to time order and which is a literalisation of the search space of possible plans. The system recognises the concurrency which is inherent in much of the planning for machining, for example when features are equally accessible within a setup and lack feature interaction constraints. This is the case in the prototype component of Fig 2 which has 4 through holes and an open pocket (POCKET_1) equally accessible at the Z1 level (Fig 3). Similar concurrency arises when several setups each yield an intermediate workpiece which provides a stable platform for securing the component on re-location. This partial order is represented in the plan network and commitment to a serial order is deferred to

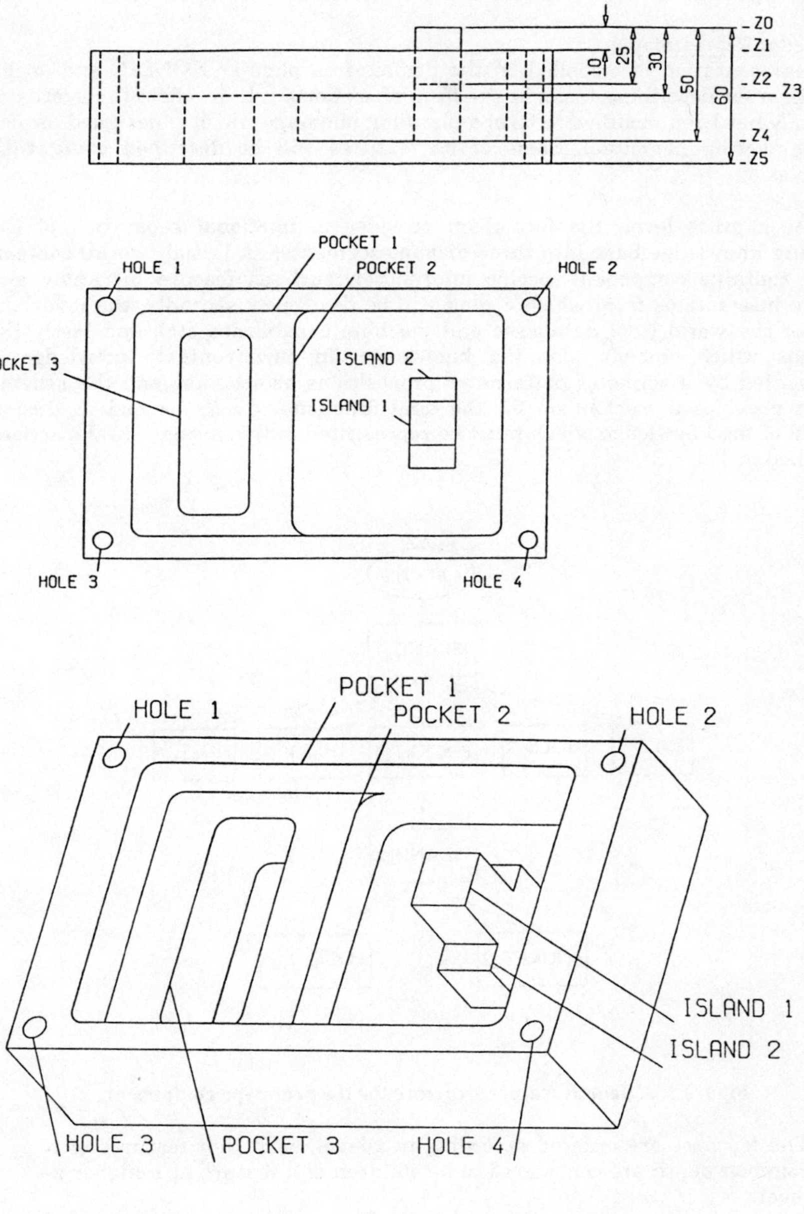

Figure 2. Geometry of the prototype component

the subsequent stage of plan refinement, where a heuristic search is performed.

Knowledge Representation

The representation is modelled on the domain-free planner NONLIN and on its formalism for describing tasks in the form of schemas [9]. In effect the syntax of NONLIN has been modified to form a planning language which is designed for use by engineering personnel. Some of its features will be described along with examples.

At a gross level, the formalism provides a functional separation of the planning knowledge base into three disjoint segments; an initial (world) context, which contains component-specific information such as feature hierarchy and feature interactions from which a plan will be developed; secondly, the invariant state of the world (tool databases and machine capabilities etc); and lastly the schemas which embody planning knowledge. In each context, knowledge is represented by a series of patterns or propositions as schemas and the schema format provides a mechanism for the dual functions of *selection* and *sequencing*. Typical of the knowledge which must be represented in this format are the actions described in Table 2.

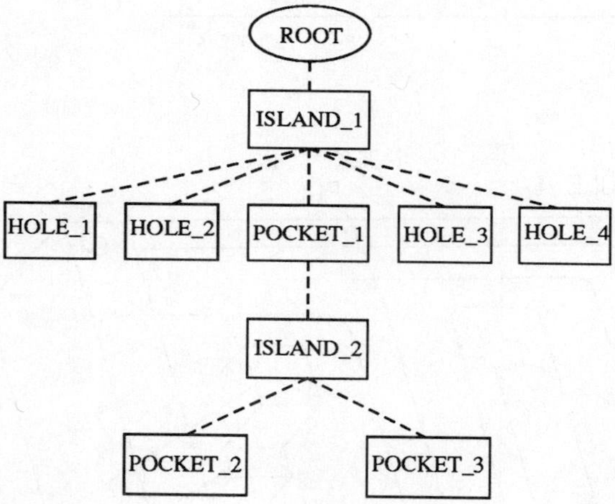

Figure 3. A default feature structure for the prototype component

The features are ordered according to z-level, such that features at a common depth are considered to be children of a feature at a higher z-level.

Schema

A schema can be viewed as a sub-network which will achieve a given purpose or goal by introducing more detailed plan steps or by introducing some primitive action. Each schema replaces an abstract goal by a network of more concrete goals. The features of schema which express abstraction, selection and sequencing will be described here, followed by examples which relate to the planning of the prototype component of Fig 2. These examples are listed in Figs 4&5.

Abstraction The hierarchical organisation is designed to permit planning at several levels of abstraction as schema are grouped into one of three layers which plan, respectively, setups, the sequence of features within a setup and the sequence of machining cuts within a feature (Table 1). This layered structure ensures that no unnecessary work is carried out in expanding an inappropriate schema down to its primitive actions. The ordering of goals which are to be expanded can be specified by the user as an explicit LEVEL number which determines the latency with which that schema is expanded into further detail.

Selection Selection of a suitable schema with which to expand a goal is firstly, by matching the goal to the PURPOSE of a schema and, secondly, by satisfaction of any USEWHEN conditions in that schema. Schemas are qualified by three types of condition or pre-requisite which differ in the degree of 'urgency' for their satisfaction (a feature of the NONLIN system). Thus USEWHEN conditions must be satisfied before a schema can be introduced into the network; an IMMEDIATE condition must be satisfied by the conclusion of the present task expansion; however a LATENT condition need only be satisfied by the time of plan completion. Conditions serve two purposes in the system; declarative and procedural. Each typed condition is used declaratively to describe dependencies between actions in the network and this can be used in an explanation of the planner's decision making. The IMMEDIATE conditions can also be used procedurally to override the expansion of the network by its default, hierarchical scheme (based on LEVELs), thereby increasing the expressiveness of the schema.

Sequencing The principal function of a schema is to specify how a goal can be broken down into simpler tasks or to atomic actions and TASKORDER statements define any partial order on these simpler tasks. Each task within a schema has a numeric index which can be used to specify a directed acyclic graph of the partial plan. Where no order is specified, tasks are taken to be in parallel with no commitment to a linear sequence.

Computation Schemas have a link to Prolog functions or to external routines (C or FORTRAN) through METHOD statements. This is the mechanism by which the planner interrogates the solid modeller for shape information or to acquire 2D profiles for machining. The planning system is closely coupled to a commercial CAD /solid modelling system from which geometry and feature information is derived automatically - for example, to yield the default feature structure of Fig 3. Similarly, the planner may resolve questions of tool access by consulting a quad-tree representation of profile geometry via METHOD statements in schemas, testing the resultant values in USEWHEN conditions.

Variant plans In the implementation, use is made of the *modules* feature of Quintus Prolog to hold the internal representation of each schema in a private module of the database. The internal, Prolog representation of a schema takes the form of a network of nodes which represents its task expansion and this form is entirely homologous with the main plan network which is built by schema substitution. Accordingly, the main plan network may itself be considered as a schema for some larger plan. This provides access to a form of variant planning and to plan re-use because the plan network may be stored to file and subsequently introduced into another plan.

```
(4a)
INITIAL EFFECTS
        {ISLAND_1 has profile PROF_1};
        {ISLAND_1 has a feature level interaction with POCKET_1};
        {ISLAND_1 starts at z = 0.0 and ends at z = 25.0};

(4b)
ALWAYS EFFECTS
        {8.0 is a standard twist drill size};

(4c)
OPSCHEMA approach_direction_planner_A
PURPOSE {plan approach direction A}
TASKS
        1 OP {plan island ISLAND_1};
        2 OP {plan pocket POCKET_1};
        3 ACT {plan hole HOLE_1};
        4 ACT {plan hole HOLE_2};
        5 ACT {plan hole HOLE_3};
        6 ACT {plan hole HOLE_4};
        7 OP {plan island ISLAND_2};
        8 OP {plan pocket POCKET_2};
        9 OP {plan pocket POCKET_3};
TASKORDER
        1 TO [2 3 4 5 6];
        2 --> 7;
        7 TO [8 9];
CONDITIONS
        AUTO:
```

Figure 4. Examples of schemas which are fully instantiated

The knowledge base is divided into three disjoint segments for propositions which are initially true but which may be modified (eg. feature interactions - 4a), for propositions which are always true (eg. tool data - 4b) and for the schemas which operate on these propositions. (4c) is such a schema representing the default feature hierarchy of Fig 3.

Examples The knowledge base is separated into three disjoint segments for efficiency and expression. The 'always' and 'schema' segments generally contain knowledge which is invariant, while the 'initial' segment holds information which is specific to a component instance. There is an example of each in Fig 4. The first schema (Fig 4a) contains propositions which are 'initially' true about the component of Fig 2 before planning commences - this information about geometry and feature interactions can be viewed as 'facts' because there is no associated action. The second (Fig 4b) describes facts which are 'always' true - in this case tool database information - and which are therefore invariant across component instances. The third schema (Fig 4c) defines the default feature structure of the component as detailed in Fig 3. This is an exception to the idea that the 'schema' area of the knowledge base is for invariant information but it is present to 'seed' the planner. Its PURPOSE is to expand the goal *{plan approach direction A}* and it specifies that this goal be replaced by nine lower level goals or tasks (one for each feature which is accessible from the approach direction) as a compound TASK statement. A partial order on these expanded tasks is specified in a TASKORDER statement again in correspondence with the structure of Fig 3. Typically, this component specific information is obtained directly from the geometry interface to the solid modelling system.

Examples of two invariant schemas which define manufacturing knowledge are given in Fig 5. Each has the PURPOSE *{plan island $I}* (where *$I* is a variable for some island) - variable identifiers are denoted by a '$' prefix - and Fig 5a is the default expansion which introduces two lower level tasks in a TASKS statement - *rough cut the island* and *finish cut the island* in that order. However, the schema of Fig 5b has a number of CONDITIONS amongst which the first can be considered a 'guard' condition which limits its application to those circumstances in the plan in which the *island $I* is considered to form re-entrant geometry in a pocket - *{$I has a feature level interaction with $P}*. Such a situation arises between ISLAND_1 and POCKET_1 (see Fig 2) and is noted as an EFFECT in the INITIAL schema of Fig 4a. The action specified by the schema of Fig 5b is to split the island into two fragments *island $NEW_I* and *island $I* at the z-level of the interaction between island and pocket and to submit each of these 'fragments' as goals which will be recursively planned further. The subsequent USEWHEN conditions in Fig 5b simply instantiate local values which are used in calculating the geometrical parameters to split the island and there is a computation (METHOD statement) which returns a new symbol for the island fragment. Finally, a number of EFFECTS of adopting this schema to expand the goal *plan island $I* are recorded.

Persistent Knowledge

The plan network evolves as goals are expanded and this is accompanied by the recording of information concerning expansion-events and the support structure for tasks in the network as well as recording the primitive actions. This information is used to maintain the validity of the network during its expansion. However, it is also significant as the basis for an explanation or justification of the plan - an area of work which is incomplete and receiving attention.

Plan Refinement

The outcome of the plan synthesis phase is a network of partially ordered plan steps, each of which is an atomic action, along with tables which hold the justification for expansion and the consequences of each atomic action. The partial order for this network is induced from two sources, (1) from the manufacturing knowledge expressed as schemas and (2) from the default feature structure which is ordered in terms of feature z-level. A manufacturing process plan is one linearisation of this space of possible solutions which is guided by a refinement scheme (which will now be discussed). The resulting linear plan forms, in turn, the basis of shop-floor planning documentation.

```
(5a)
OPSCHEMA island_planner
PURPOSE {plan island $I}
TASKS
     1 ACT {rough island $I};
     2 ACT {finish island $I};
TASKORDER
     1 --> 2:

(5b)
OPSCHEMA island_splitter
PURPOSE {plan island $I}
TASKS
     1 OP {plan island $NEW_I};
     2 OP {plan island $I};
TASKORDER
     1 --> 2;
CONDITIONS
     USEWHEN {$I has a feature level interaction with $P} AT SELF;
     USEWHEN {$I has profile $I_PROFILE} AT SELF;
     USEWHEN {$I starts at z = $I_Z_HI and ends at z = $I_Z_LO} AT SELF;
     USEWHEN {$P has profile $P_PROFILE} AT SELF;
     USEWHEN {$P starts at z = $P_Z_HI and ends at z = $P_Z_LO} AT SELF;
     METHOD create_island($NEW_I);
EFFECTS
     + {$NEW_I starts at z = $I_Z_HI and ends at z = $P_Z_HI} AT HEAD;
     + {$NEW_I has profile $I_PROFILE} AT HEAD;
     + {$I starts at z = $P_Z_HI and ends at z = $I_Z_LO} AT HEAD;
     - {$I starts at z = $I_Z_HI and ends at z = $I_Z_LO} AT HEAD;
     - {$I has a feature level interaction with $P} AT HEAD;
     + {$NEW_I is a fragment off $I} AT HEAD:
```

Figure 5. Examples of generic schema

Each opschema represents manufacturing knowledge with the purpose *{plan island $I}* where *$I* is a variable identifier (denoted by a '$' prefix). They can be thought of as generic because of this variable substitution. (5a) is the default expansion but (5b) applies if the first *USEWHEN* condition - more properly a guard condition - identifies a feature level interaction between the island *$I* and some other pocket feature of the component.

Work is presently underway on this scheme but we have identified a portion of the domain knowledge which must be represented in the system in order to achieve a linear plan sequence. This is summarised in Table 3 and the issues of knowledge representation and its application are discussed below.

The common feature of this heuristic knowledge which leads to it being applied during the refinement phase (rather than the plan network generation phase) is that it bears on machining operations which were expanded up from separate goals /tasks. That is, from the macro structure of the plan. We do not, as yet, have a uniform representation for this knowledge which is, instead, represented to the system either as a series of procedures which can be switched on or off to modify the behaviour of the planner or as cost functions which are used to guide the search. The mechanism - procedure or cost-function - is indicated in Table 3.

Taking the first item of Table 3 as an example of the procedural approach, it is possible to minimise the number of setups for a component by rejecting any setup which consists solely of 'through' features - that is, design features which are accessible from more than one approach direction (thru' holes, corner notches etc.) with the rationale that such features may be formed, instead, from an approach direction which has obligatory features. For the component of Fig 2, there is, by this analysis, only one obligatory approach direction. A procedural approach is also adopted for the second item of Table 3. It is essential that a multi-sided component should offer a stable platform on turnover in order to ensure rigidity for subsequent machining operations, but we have, at present, no means of assessing the relative stability of the intermediate geometry of the component. This heuristic relies on the user to provide a relative assessment of stability to the system which then ensures that the less stable approach direction is machined last amongst pairs of opposing setups.

Table 3. Heuristic knowledge for plan refinement.

The 'mechanism' indicates whether the heuristic is implemented as a cost factor or as a Prolog procedure.

item	*description*	*mechanism*
1	- minimise the number of setups.	procedure
2	- maximise stability on turnover of the component.	procedure
3	- group machining operations to minimise tool changes.	cost
4	- facilitate grouping of tools by reducing tool sizes (where advantageous).	procedure
5	- order bulk metal removal operations to be early in a setup.	cost
6	- order drilling operations to be late in a setup by default but to be early if they enter a thin section.	cost

In contrast, several heuristics from Table 3 may be expressed as cost-functions and we have identified two such functions - the tool diameter and a factor which weights the tool type employed in a machining operation. Item 3 of Table 3 aims to aggregate machining operations which use a common tool and it may be expedited by attaching a cost which is proportional to tool diameter. Now, it is not possible to contravene the partial order on plan steps introduced during synthesis of the plan network but this implies only an anteriority constraint (a 'before' relation) which does not prevent machining operations from being delayed within a setup. This is achieved by a best-first search over that domain of the plan network which relates to one approach direction. In effect, this also expedites item 5 of the Table in so far as there is an indirect relation between tool diameter and metal removed, therefore operations which employ the largest ranking tool diameter will be ordered first within a setup. Bulk metal removal would be better reflected by a cost which relates to the volume of metal removed. Item 6 of Table 3 is a re-statement of the machining constraint **A1** listed in Table 2 and it is effected by attaching a cost in a COST statement of the appropriate schema which is invoked in the situation of a drilling operation through a thin section.

We have chosen to avoid disjunctive plan steps in the network where possible; they arise only in the treatment of 'through' features which are accessible from several approach directions and, as detailed above, are filtered as part of the plan refinement phase. This simplifies the semantics of the plan network and its search. Alternative linearisations of the plan are obtainable within the partial order constraints however, beyond these it proves necessary to alter the behaviour of the refinement heuristics or to alter the content of plan schemas if further, alternate plans are required.

Conclusions

We can conclude that the present approach reflects and represents the 'least commitment' to time order which can be identified in a process plan. This has the advantage that alternative manufacturing plans may be found in the plan network but must be balanced against a requirement to prune the search space quite substantially during plan refinement. The uniformity of individual schema and the plan network suggest that a plan network can be used as a schema to some larger plan with consequent implications for plan re-use and for variant planning. However, the non-linear nature of action-ordering plan networks does mean that it is not possible to maintain an explicit current 'world' state at each action. Consequently, it is not easy to construct an 'intermediate workpiece model' (IWM) as machining proceeds. This can more easily be determined when a committed path through the network is selected during the plan refinement phase.

Acknowledgements

This work was funded by grant GR/D68900 from the ACME Directorate of the UK Science and Engineering Council. We extend our thanks to industrial collaborators in the Defence Systems and Infographics Divisions of Ferranti International Ltd., Edinburgh and to colleagues at Heriot-Watt University for constructive discussion.

References

1. D.W. Willis, I.A. Donaldson, A.D. Ramage, J.L. Murray, and M.H. Williams, "A Knowledge Based System for Process Planning Based on a Solid Modeller." *Computer Aided Engineering*, (1989 in press).

2. D.S. Nau, "Hierarchical Abstraction for Process Planning." in *Knowledge Based Expert Systems in Engineering.*, ed. D. Sriram & R.A. Adey, pp. 129-141, Computational Mechanics Publications, (1987).

3. S.L. Brooks, "Applying Artificial Intelligence Techniques to Generative Process Planning Systems." MSc Thesis, University of Missouri, Columbia, USA, (May 1986).

4. P.K. Wright and D.A. Bourne, in *Manufacturing Intelligence*, pp. 181-207, Addison Wesley Inc., Reading, Mass. USA., (1988).

5. E.D. Sacerdoti, "Planning in a Hierarchy of Abstraction Spaces." *Proc. Third Intl. Joint Conf. Artif. Intell.*, pp. 412-430, Stanford, Calif., (1973).

6. M.P. Georgeff, "Planning," in *Ann. Rev. Comp. Sci.*, ed. J.F. Traub, Vol. 2, pp. 359-400, Annual Reviews Inc., Palo Alto, California, (1987).

7. E.D. Sacerdoti, *A Structure for Plans and Behavior,* Elsevier North-Holland, New York, (1977).

8. A. Tate, "A Review of Knowledge-Based Planning Systems." in *Expert Systems 85 : Proceedings of the Fifth Technical Conference of the British Computer Society Specialist Group on Expert Systems. (Univ of Warwick, Dec 17-19, 1985)*, ed. M. Merry, pp. 89-111, Cambridge University Press, Cambridge, (1986).

9. A. Tate, "Project Planning Using a Hierarchic Non-Linear Planner," Research Report No. 25, Department of AI, University of Edinburgh, (1976).

Linguistic and Somatic Knowledge Engineering for the Automation of Small-Batch Machining

Paul K. Wright

Robotics and Manufacturing Research Laboratory, Computer Science Dept., Courant Institute of Mathematical Sciences, New York University, 719 Broadway, New York, NY 10003, USA

ABSTRACT

The goals of this research are to automate both the process-planning and process-control of small-batch machining operations. The complete spectrum is being studied namely: computer-aided design; cutting-tool and fixture selection; cutter-path planning and the monitoring of real-time machining on a CNC machine tool.

The research methods have focussed on knowledge engineering experiments with experienced NC programmers/machining-craftsmen. The knowledge engineering has been done both during planning (where the linguistic knowledge of the craftsmen is uncovered) and during the real-time control of machining (where the sensory knowledge of craftsmen is uncovered - hence somatic knowledge engineering).

New work in the following three sub-areas is highlighted, in order to emphasize the synergy between the AI paradigms and the traditional mechanical engineering analytical tools: -

i) the generic nature of planning rules leading to an expert system on planning

ii) qualitative and quantitative information that has been gathered on appropriate fixturing methods for one-of-a-kind machining

iii) correlations between the somatic knowledge engineering and appropriate sensors for monitoring machining.

1. INTRODUCTION

This paper concerns the automation of small-batch manufacturing, the limit of which is one-of-a-kind machining in a prototype-making facility. Expert systems have provided a convenient tool for collecting information in such a manufacturing environment and thereby adding structure to the overall process. Such structure facilitates automation and computer integrated manufacturing. The words *machinist* and *craftsman* are used synonymously throughout this paper and they have a broad definition. As a working definition, the machinist generates the plan for making a part, writes the NC program, machines the part on a milling machine, and then inspects it by making comparisons with the original drawing. In a small tool and die factory, all these functions could be performed by one person: in a larger corporation, all such craft skills will be covered by a manufacturing team extending from NC programmers to machine setup engineers to machine operators.

2. EXPERIMENTAL WORK USING PROTOCOL ANALYSIS

Simple parts that could be easily manufactured on a three-axis, CNC vertical machining center were initially considered. At the beginning of a typical session, a machinist was presented with a sealed copy of one of the components, represented as a conventional engineering drawing (the plan view and the front and side elevations). After scanning the drawing for only a few seconds, the machinist was asked about his thought processes and some of the key features that he was looking for in order to get started with the planning process. In these first few seconds, the machinist noted the tolerances to which the part had to be made, the type of work material, and the general geometry of the part. In the subsequent 10 to 20 seconds, he concentrated on machining problems that might come from the interacting features of the part. Next, he considered whether a simple parallel-sided vise could be used for clamping, or whether toe clamps or some special purpose fixturing device would be needed. The knowledge engineer continued to ask questions and elicit comments during all the phases of process planning and action planning for the machine tool. The machinist was observed to "picture" the part being made. He first visualized his machine tool, the available cutting tools, and the geometry of the fixtures, and then built a step-by-step machining plan in his mind. Video-tapes representing the experimental data were then studied with protocol analysis. The vocal transcripts were best obtained by a court stenographer who, by professional training, was adept at capturing three of four simultaneous conversations and intertwining them into the chronological order of events. After an initial planning session, generally taking one to two hours, the machinist prepared the individual CNC subroutines in the language of the machine tool. Based on the setup plan, these subroutines were then ordered, numbered, and combined into a setup sheet that contained all the step-by-step instructions for the work on the machine tool.

In subsequent sessions at the machine tool, the part was machined. Video taping continued as the knowledge engineer questioned the machinist about craft activities, monitoring procedures, measurement equipment, and general machining practices. As might be expected, there were some mistakes (i.e. errors in judgment) in the machinist's original plan. Thus it was particularly important to get good video-tape footage and transcripts during these times when the plan had to be altered. The machinist knew that there were some cases where machining would be extremely difficult and other cases where success was virtually guaranteed.

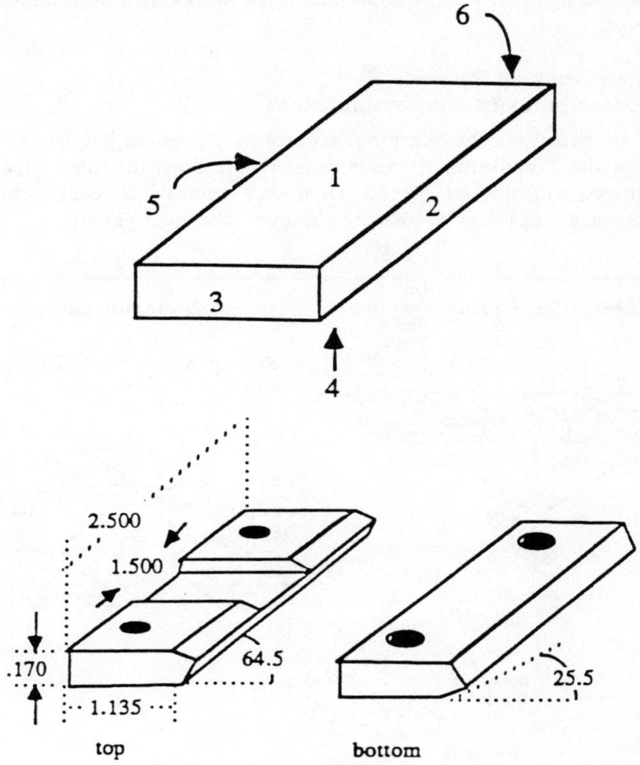

Figure 1. Typical Part and Starting Stock (Courtesy: Caroline Hayes)

3. RESULTS ON AUTOMATED PLANNING FOR MACHINING

To demonstrate the functionality of the current planning software, suppose the part shown in Figure 1 is going to be made from the accompanying piece of stock. The part is represented in an expert system called, **Machining Planner,** as a rectangular block with features subtracted from it. In this case, there are five features — two holes, two angles and a thru-slot. At the current stage our planning software 'understands' eight features: blind-hole, thru-hole, pocket, blind-slot, thru-slot, angle, shoulder and channel. Yet this is a limited library compared with the PADL oriented research [Voelcker and Requicha, 1977]. The program begins by querying the user about the stock size and its surface finish (machined, rolled or saw-cut): the surface finish is important and may change the squaring-up procedure described below. Next the program queries the user about the outer envelope of the part.

The 'automatic' part of the program then takes over in which the features are grouped together into *setups*, the setups are ordered and the tools for each cut selected. The main theme of the planning is to merge two simultaneous constraints namely:

- the squaring-up process
- the feature-interaction considerations

For the part in question, the merging process is shown in Figure 2. On the right-hand side the **Machining Planner** must create an orthogonal block otherwise the features will not be placed accurately relative to each other. The squaring process always has to occur whatever the part-geometry. Thus we

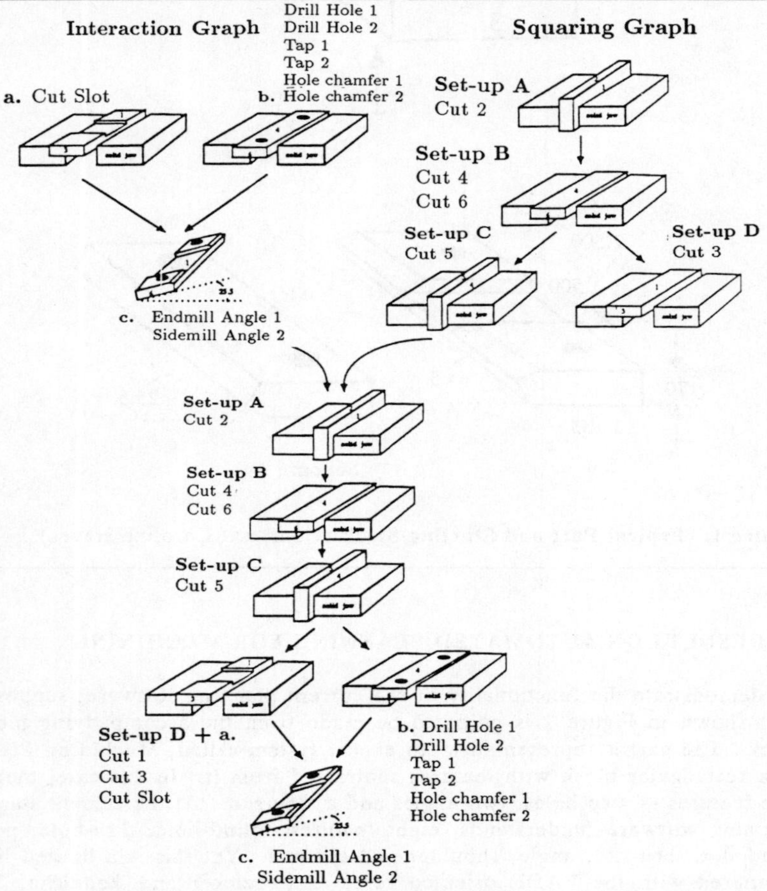

Figure 2. Merging the Squaring-Up and Feature Interaction Graph (Courtesy: Caroline Hayes)

concentrated on this in our earliest work and the various squaring-up plans are shown in Hayes and Wright [1986].

It is the merging of the features into the squaring-up plan that is challenging aspect of human craftsmanship and, consequently, of the creation of an expert system rule-set that can mirror the deep human experience. The reason this is difficult is that cutting one feature may make it very hard or impossible to cut

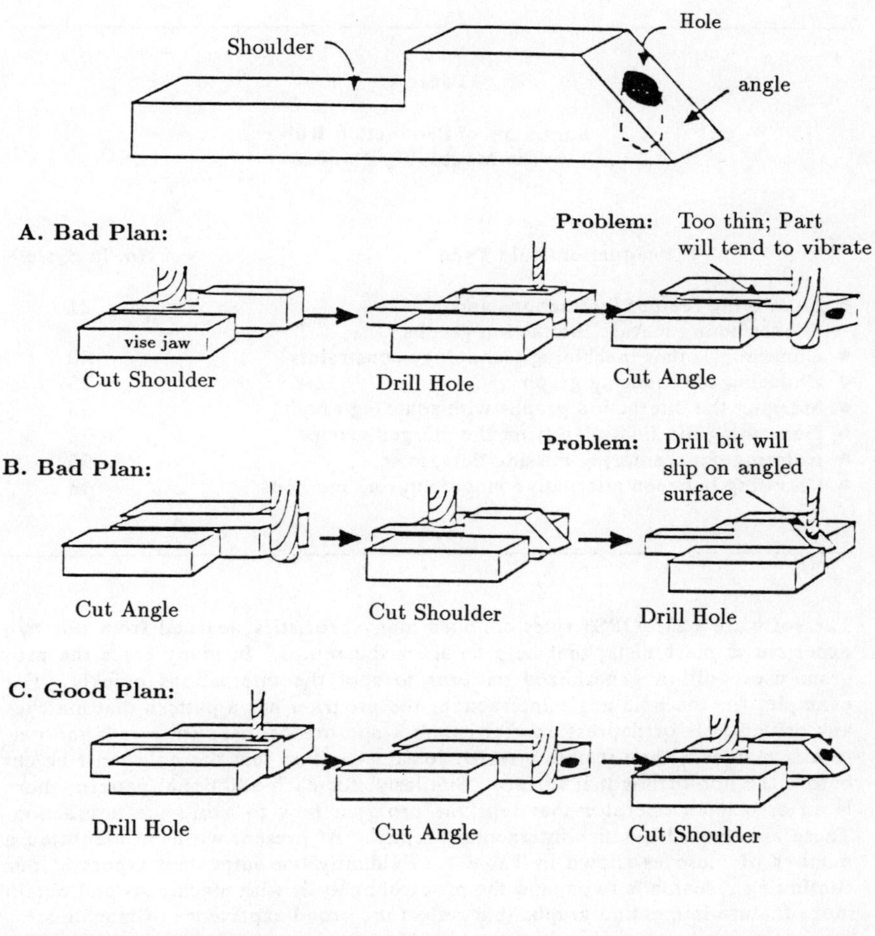

Figure 3. Examples of Planning Showing a Different Part than Figures 1 and 2 Two "Bad" and the Final "Good" Plan

subsequent ones. This is best explained by referring to another part shown in Figure 3. This shows two "bad" plans above the "good" plan. The "bad" plans are ones that a human machinist would avoid based on his/her experience: one of these plans causes too much vibration in the last step and the other causes the drill point to skid on the surface of the chamfer. The "good" plan carefully orders the setups in such a way as to avoid these problems. The way in which the setup sheet is presented to either a novice machinist or an automated machine tool is thus shown in Figure 2. When the squaring-up is combined with the feature interactions, seven setups are needed to complete the first part.

Table 1

Summary of Production Rules in the Machining Planner

Production/Rule Type	No. in System
• Identifying feature interactions and constructing feature interaction graphs	21
• Generating other machining technology constraints	50
• Choosing the squaring graph	23
• Merging the interaction graphs with squaring graphs	55
• Generating the final plan from the merged groups	18
• Entering data, entering missing data, misc.	95
• Choosing between alternative manufacturing methods	13

The software's 275 OPS5 rules contains many heuristics, learned from our two experienced machinists, that help to order the setups. In many cases the program uses built-in generalized patterns to spot the interactions quickly. For example, for the hole-angle interaction, the program has a pattern that matches any drilled hole or depression that enters a non-orthogonal surface. If the pattern is matched, then it puts a restriction on the plan that the hole must be cut before the non-orthogonal surface. Similarly, for each additional pattern, there is an associated operator that tells the program how to avoid the interaction. These are termed 'feature interaction graphs'. At present we have identified a number of these as shown in Table 1. Evidently one important aspect of our continuing research is to expand the protocol analysis with machinists and obtain more feature interaction graphs that reflect the broad experience of machinists.

The Machining Planner is an advance over the more traditional "variant" and "generative" methods (found limiting because they were suited to only one set of part families or only to parts with features on one side) since the new program scans the design specification for potential difficulties caused by interactions between features. Thus, there is a similarity between the Machining

Planner and classical domain-independent planners such as NOAH [Sacerdoti 1975]. However there are the following differences: i) a positive aspect of the machining expert system is that virtually all the interactions can be detected early in the plan by using the machinists' heuristics in the problem specification; whereas in NOAH, interactions do not become apparent until much of the plan is complete; ii) a problematic aspect of the Machining Planner is that the interpretation of interactions is sometimes ambiguous - e.g. cutting a large angle in side *x* may make this side too small for subsequent rigid clamping; but if the angle does not encroach over all the side then subsequent clamping may be satisfactory; whereas, partly because NOAH is smaller, it always yields the same interpretation from a problem interaction. Evidence also shows that, in the Machining Planner, testing these interactions has a significant computational cost. Future research is thus required in a number of items in order both to expand the practical usefulness of the system and to investigate more fundamental issues. For the practical work, there is a need to work with parts of increasingly complex geometry; meaning that other high-level feature descriptions, fixtures other than the parallel sided vise and work materials that create special machining heuristics must be added to the system. For the fundamental research on planning there is a need to explore the relationships between the Machining Planner and other domain-independent planning systems: additional protocol analyses are needed in order to see how craftsmen set their limits on such aspects as the angle/clamping interaction just described and then how they replan subsequent to interaction identification. It is hoped that a generalized strategy for interaction planning and reaction will emerge that will have broader use in a variety of process-planning applications.

4. RESULTS ON FIXTURING

In the area of fixturing there is a deliberate connection between quantitative stress analysis and experts' heuristics from protocol analyses with machinists. Two examples of recent results are reviewed here: -

4.1. Opportunities for Quantitative Analysis

Mason [1984] has studied the mechanics of object pushing operations that are an essential component of many robotic manipulation tasks. In the course of his research he developed a computer program that, given a distribution of support forces on a object, a coefficient of friction between the supports and the object, and object dimensions, determines possible rotation centers for varying angles of attack of an applied disturbance force. We have already run some simulations with this routine and shown that it may be used as a check of the validity of part-clamp machining setups. The magnitude of the resultant friction forces at each of the clamp positions will act in a direction that is orthogonal to a line that connects the coordinates of a rotation center and the clamp location. A force equilibrium equation may then be used to determine the maximum cutting force, at a given angle of attack that may be applied to the part before slip occurs. In this example, part slip occurs due to one of several tagged parameters of the flawed production state; clamp style, clamp positions and clamp forces. If the maximum clamp force is fixed, a second pass through the control dialogues will focus on alternative ways to derive an admissible part production state by changing the clamp style, clamp positions, or possibly reducing values for the machining parameters.

As a second example Englert and Wright [1988] have analyzed the possible movements of a plate held in a parallel-sided vise and the movement of this same plate as a cutting tool interacts with it . This analytical situation is shown in Figure 4. For simplicity this shows just the potential ways in which the cutter

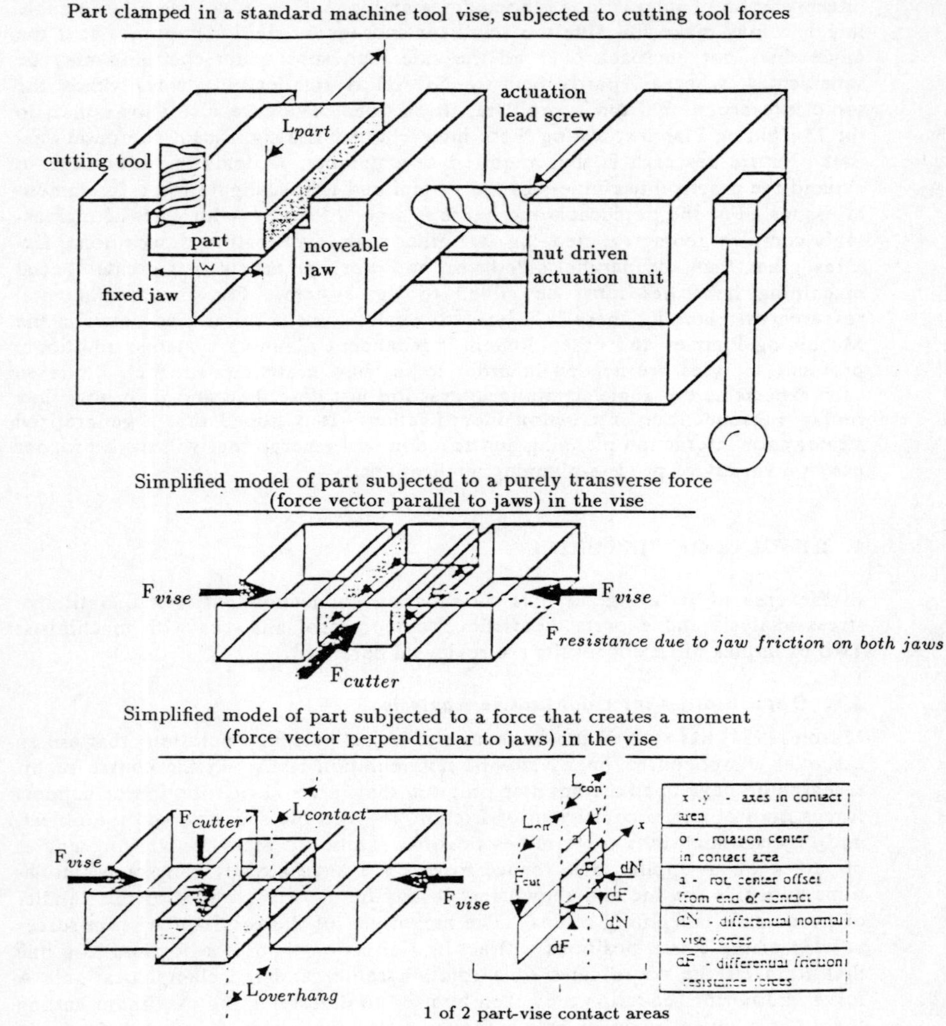

Figure 4. Schematic of Part Subjected to Forces in a vise and Associated Transverse Force and Moments (Courtesy: Paul Englert)

could move the part transversely (center sketch) and by tilting (bottom sketch). Buckling could occur across the width of the part,w, in the upper sketch especially as part dimensions increase. To prevent part movement in the center sketch the simple relationship is

$$F_{\text{cutter}} < 2[F_{\text{vise}}][\mu_{\text{part-vise}}]$$

where μ can be estimated from experience with oily but rough surfaces. The force of the vise and the cutting force can thus be compared but the vise force must be maintained below a critical level to prevent buckling. Obviously if the part width, w, is small buckling is not a problem but a check for part crushing in compression between the vise jaws should be done.

If the primary cutting force in Figure 4 is downward then the part wants to rotate about some point, **o**, due to the applied moment $F_{\text{cutter}}\left(L_{\text{overhang}} + a\right)$ as shown (with all the nomenclature that follows) in the two lower sketches in Figure 4. Assume that the applied vise load F_{vise} acting in a direction normal to the contact area, is evenly distributed along the bottom portion of the area. If differential contacts of area $dx\ dy$ are constructed on either side of the rotation center **o**, they will each be acted upon by a differential normal force, dN, and a differential friction force, dF, where

$$dN = \frac{F_{\text{vise}}\,dx}{L_{\text{contact}}}$$

and

$$dF = \mu_{\text{part-vise}}\,dN$$

The differential friction forces must act in opposite y axis directions so that they may form a friction couple to counteract the externally applied moment. Equilibrium must be satisfied to keep the part from slipping, and so the net sum of forces and torques acting on the entire contact area must be zero. The sums of the differential forces and moments are obtained by integrating over the regions in which their differential components act.

The solution for the two unknowns, F_{cutter} and a, from this set of simultaneous integral equations is straightforward. Their values are

$$a = -L_{\text{oh}} + \frac{L_{\text{con}}}{2}\sqrt{4r^2 + 4r + 2}$$

and

$$F_c = 2\mu_{\text{pv}} f_v\left[-1 - 2r + \sqrt{4r^2 + 4r + 2}\right]$$

where $r = \dfrac{L_{\text{oh}}}{L_{\text{con}}}$

So to prevent a part subjected to orthogonally applied loads from slipping in the vise during machining the following relation must be upheld

$$F_c < 2\mu_{\text{p-v}} F_v\left[-1 - 2r + \sqrt{4r^2 + 4r + 2}\right]$$

4.2. Attribute Value Approximations for Fixturing

In the course of planning, the machinist is often confronted with problems where he must make an attribute value approximation for a process or part variable. In these cases, a quantitative analysis is unduly complex or it is impossible to define the boundary conditions. The human establishes limits for parameter values based on his intuition of the physical world, and cases of machining and clamping problems stored in his memory. Often, some catastrophic event, e.g. tool breakage or part movement during cutting, experienced by the machinist helps him to develop a mental gage for critical values of part or process parameters.

For many physical phenomena, the human expert thinks in terms of discrete relations between variables rather than the continuous relations present in physics based, analytical modeling. For example, when a part is clamped and machined in a vise, the human expert has an intuitive feel for "safe" part length to thickness ratios. If these ratios are exceeded, it is expected that part deflection during machining will be large (greater than 0.001"). And if he encounters some new part length-to-thickness ratio during a process planning step, the human places it between, above, or below known ratios and sets his safety limits accordingly. He does not think explicitly in terms of part modulus values or exponential relations between part dimensions.

The chart in Figure 5 shows the human machinist's attribute value approximations, as well as analytical model predictions relevant for the parts clamped and machined in a vise. It can be seen that the human's perceived critical length-to-thickness ratios are more conservative than the predictions resulting from the analytical model. The human has, in essence, incorporated an "intuitive safety factor" in his attribute value approximations.

Similar comparisons between human estimates and analytical predictions may be made for values for proper clamp loads, part ratios to avoid large deflections and vibrations, and safe tool speeds. Preliminary results for these comparisons have shown that the machinists tend to be more conservative than is absolutely necessary when making value estimates. As more data is collected from machinists and compared with analytical model results, a consistent set of safety factors for different parts production situations may be formed. As a result of this effort, previously tight constraints imposed for process parameter values by the machinist's may be relaxed in proportion to the safety factors, to analytical levels that are nontheless viable. The expert system rules formed from the less stringent analytical model results will thus help to reduce setup and machining time.

The ultimate product of the work will be a **Unified Machining Planner** that combines generic planning and fixturing will be to produce the **Expert Set-Up Sheet** (EXSUS) as shown in Figure 6. This is a specific set of descriptions that can be downloaded to the machine tool controller and used to operate mechanical clamps. It is a description of the workpiece, clamps, and cutting tools sufficient to uniquely refine individual 'setups' on the machine. Collectively these setups will transform the raw stock into a finished part. Figure 6 displays views of how we envisage the future EXSUS program to be formatted. Two distinct production states or setups are shown for a simple part to be held with overhead toe-clamps to a tooling plate, and their associated parameters.

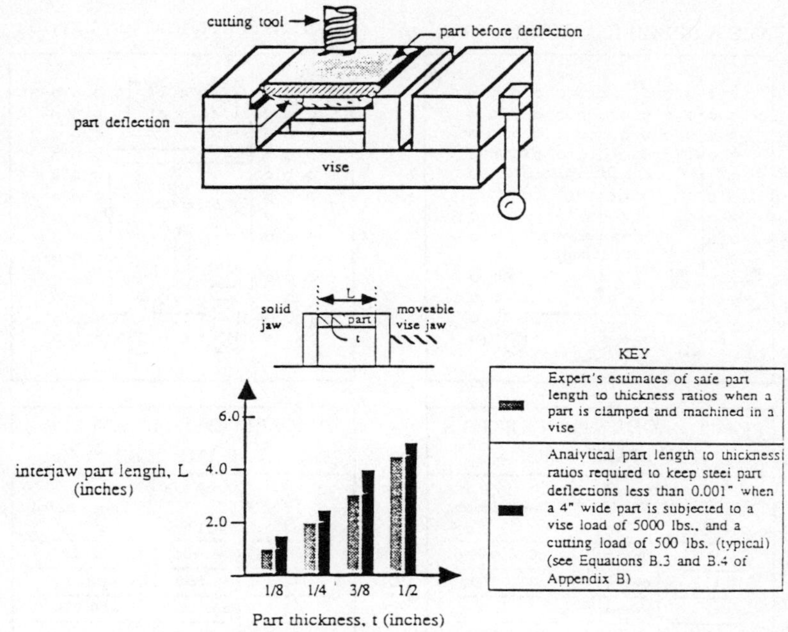

Figure 5. Human Expert's Attribute Value Approximations and Analytical Model Predictions for Safe Part Dimensional Ratios when Parts are Clamped and Machinined in a Vise (Courtesy: Paul Englert)

5. RESULTS ON REAL-TIME CONTROL

The research discussed in the previous section tends to emphasize the pre-process planning and fixturing methods. However, for the future automation of any process and for task planning in robotics, it is also important to study today's manufacturing craftsmen who have developed their sensory awareness to a sophisticated degree. An experimental study has begun to study the way in which craftsmen develop and use their sensory perceptions during the real-time monitoring of tasks. Before the details are given one point is emphasized: the somatic knowledge engineering experiments focus on understanding the *in-process goals* of the craftsmen with a view to defining the decisions being made and the simplest way of duplicating them. This may involve using sensors other than those used by the human. It may also involve redesigning parts of the total process so that the decision is simplified or, even, the need to make a decision is eliminated. In summary, the research does not involve the creation of an 'android' to replace the human; rather, it aims at an understanding of the in-process goals and decisions in order that they can be accounted for.

So far, the protocol analyses and knowledge engineering sessions described in the previous sub-section have been rerun during real-time machine tool

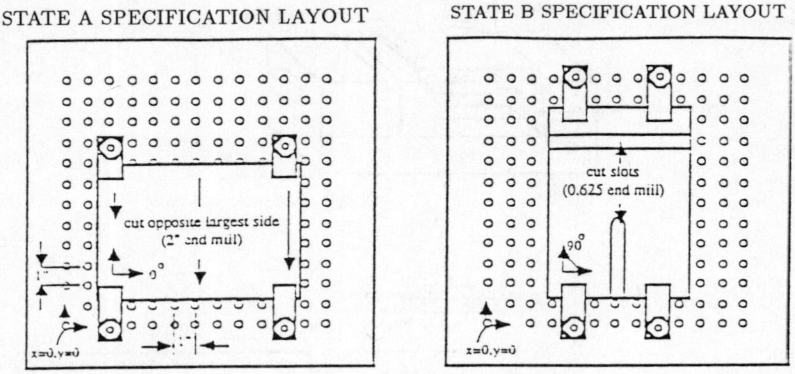

PART PRODUCTION STATE A PARAMETERS

Clamp Data

I.D.	Type	Coordinates x y
#1	overhead	2.00, 0.00
#2	overhead	2.00, 9.00
#3	overhead	10.00, 0.00
#4	overhead	10.00, 9.00

Tool Data

I.D.	Type
#100	2" end mill

Part Data

Home Coordinates x y	Orientation
1.20, 1.20	0°

PART PRODUCTION STATE B PARAMETERS

Clamp Data

I.D.	Type	Coordinates x y
#1	overhead	4.00, 0.00
#2	overhead	4.00, 12.00
#3	overhead	8.00, 0.00
#4	overhead	8.00, 12.00

Tool Data

I.D.	Type
#200	0.625" end mill

Part Data

Home Coordinates x y	Orientation
2.80, 1.20	90°

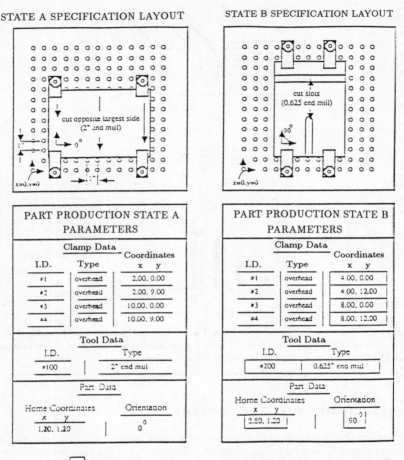

☐ indicates parameters that have changed from State A to State B

Figure 6. Expert Set-Up Sheet (EXSUS) for simple part
(Courtesy: Paul Englert)

monitoring with special emphasis being given to questioning the operators about their sensory cues and physical interactions with the machinery: hence the term, *somatic knowledge engineering* which emphasizes sensor/motor knowledge. Visual processing is more important during setup, but during real-time machining both visual and aural monitoring is used in a variety of ways, where at least seven different sensory cues have been identified correlating the physical process and the operators' experience.

Figure 7 has been constructed from these somatic knowledge experiments during the actual chip formation processes. The 'raw' information was acquired during a dialogue. The machinists described the way in which the cutting tool slowly wore and how this affected their overall monitoring strategy. To turn this rather free-form dialogue into a cohesive framework, Figure 7 has been constructed by linking the machinists information to the well-known curve that shows how cutting tools wear during their lifetime. The standard texts on machining show empirically that the end of useful tool life occurs when the flank wear, both for milling and turning operations, is greater that 0.03 inches. This inevitable wear on the cutting tools' flank face occurs by a combination of wear mechanisms: some local plastic deformation of the irregularities on the edge, some diffusion, and some wear by local fracture known as attrition. It is the last of these processes that usually plays a major role during the running-in wear in the early part of the diagram at the top of Figure 7. But once the irregularities have been worn away, the cutting tool settles in to a steady state wear process and all three of the foregoing wear processes play a role. Finally, as the flank wear develops more extensively, both the cutting temperatures and the local forces begin to rise sharply because the tool is blunt, and it ploughs rather that cuts the work material. This development is shown at the bottom-right of Figure 7. Once the tool is bluntened, wear by plastic deformation of the cutting edge predominates. Figure 7 also correlates the qualitative thoughts of the machinists with the micro-physical view of the changes occurring in the cutting process.

Figure 7 shows the visual, aural and tactile information that a machinist will continuously gather in order to make an analysis of how worn the tool is and how much life is left in the tool. Obtaining such information from machinists is somewhat difficult because they have not been trained in using specific vocabulary that identifies these phenomena in detail. Generally the information is merely absorbed during the course of many machining operations. When the machinists are asked to put their experiences into words, colloquialisms and vague adjectives usually accompany the interview.

The two concepts of a *domain-expert visual sketch* and a *domain-expert aural signature* are now introduced in order to show how the qualitative and colloquially described activities of the machinist can be more clearly formulated for diagnostic procedures. Importantly, the domain-expert sketches not only summarize the machinists' analysis procedure but also they motivate sensor design. Simply put, a computer vision system needs to know "what to look for" in the manufacturing scene. It has been found that the domain-expert sketches clarify this question leading to the proper selection and/or design of sensors. The domain experts' visual sketches may be defined as working-sketches that bring out the most easily recognized essential features of a process. Such sketches are of more significance than a mere drawing of "what is going on". A skilled craftsman (in common with an experienced auto mechanic or medical practitioner) learns to focus-in on critical "tell-tale" aspects (or symptoms) of a situation that clarify most directly and least ambiguously the ways in which the chronology of events naturally evolve in "normal" manufacturing situations (or cars and patients) as well as problematic manufacturing situations (or faults and illnesses).

Since the tool is engaged in the cut and obscured by chips and cutting fluid, it is generally not possible for the machinist to observe the tool's edge during actual cutting. However, between passes, the machinist does get an opportunity to

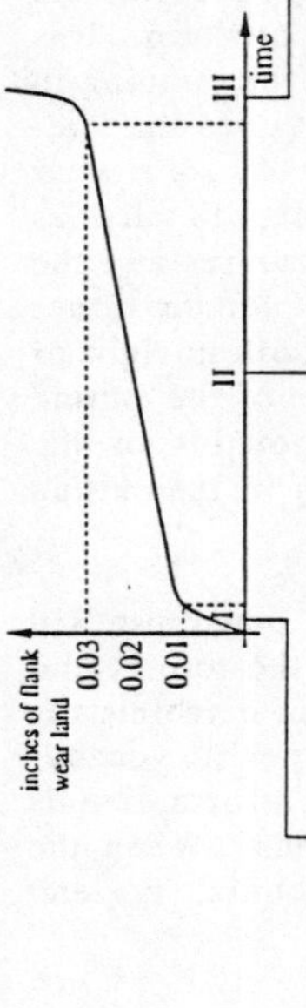

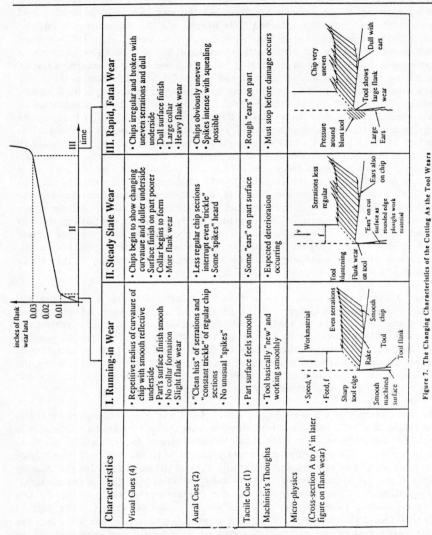

Characteristics	I. Running-in Wear	II. Steady State Wear	III. Rapid, Fatal Wear
Visual Clues (4)	• Repetitive radius of curvature of chip with smooth reflective underside • Part's surface finish smooth • No collar formation • Slight flank wear	• Chips begin to show changing curvature and duller underside • Surface finish on part poorer • Collar begins to form • More flank wear	• Chips irregular and broken with uneven serrations and dull underside • Dull surface finish • Large collar • Heavy flank wear
Aural Cues (2)	• "Clean hiss" of serrations and "constant trickle" of regular chip sections • No unusual "spikes"	• Less regular chip sections interrupt even "trickle" • Some "spikes" heard	• Chips obviously uneven • Spikes intense with squealing possible
Tactile Cue (1)	• Part surface feels smooth	• Some "ears" on part surface	• Rough "ears" on part
Machinist's Thoughts	• Tool basically "new" and working smoothly	• Expected deterioration occurring	• Must stop before damage occurs
Micro-physics (Cross-section A to A' in later figure on flank wear)			

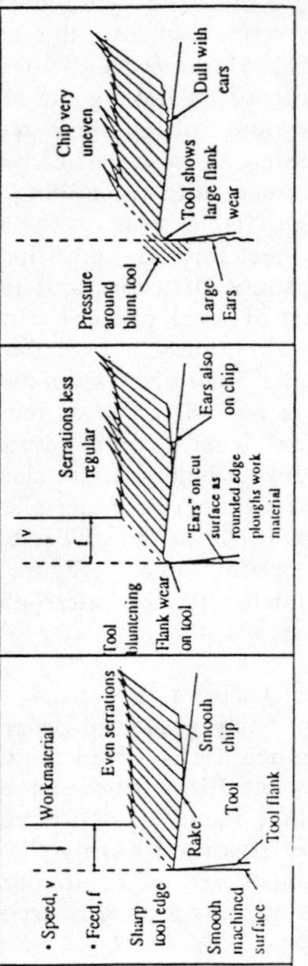

Figure 7. The Changing Characteristics of the Cutting As the Tool Wears

Figure 7. The Changing Characteristics of the Cutting As the Tool Wears

lean closer to the tool and make an estimate on how much of its life is left. The machinist can focus on the amount of flank wear that has taken place and, with experience, judge its depth within plus or minus 0.005 inches. The approximate values are shown on the ordinate of Figure 7. Figure 8 shows the general development of the flank wear. The machinist will gather this information and begin to judge the approaching end of the tool's life. Introductory work has shown that it is possible to measure the flank wear land with computer vision

[Wright and Bourne, 1988].

When cutting begins, over a very sharp tool the machinists' first aural cues are verbalized as "the chips are making a clean hissing and trickling sound". These vague adjectives relate to the fact that the chip's serrations are perfectly even and that the individualized chip sections are so geometrically similar, in terms of their radii of curvature, that they fall away from the cutting operation with exactly the same repetitiveness. The natural shearing process for steel, brass and aluminum chips has a frequency of approximately 20-60,000 cycles per second, causing the clean hissing sound that the machinists hear. In addition to this clean hissing sound, stainless steels and aerospace alloys show a segmented chip formation which machinists can additionally hear as a lower "singing" sound of approximately 1-5,000 cycles per second. For stainless steels and aerospace alloys this is a normal event.

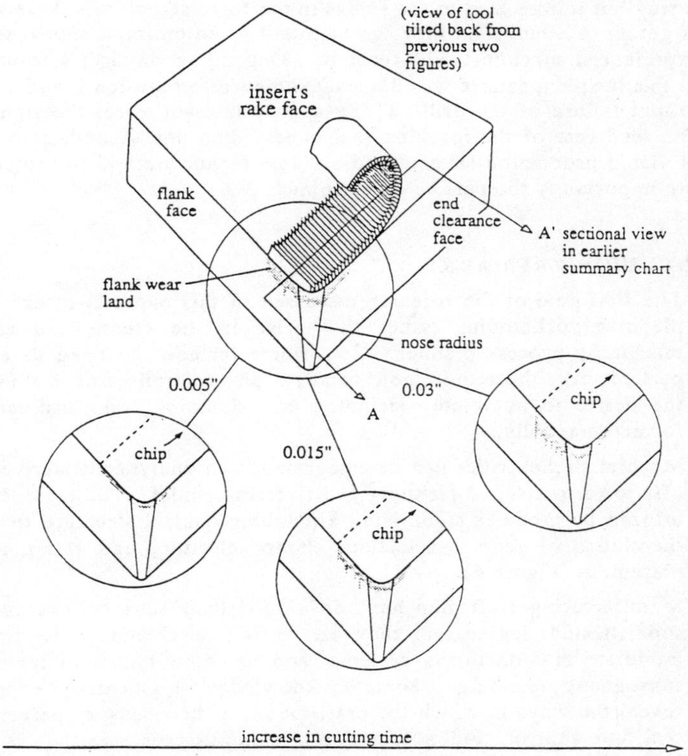

Figure 8. Domain-Expert Sketches of the Changes in Flank Wear Land

As the tool becomes blunted a second aural cue occurs as occasional 'catches' or interruptions in this clean shearing process can be heard. Specifically, the small pieces of unevenly cut material shown in Figure 7 also cause small 'spike' in the intensity of the aural signature. Towards the end of the tool's life the spikes become more intense and more frequent. The trained machinist listens to the frequency and intensity of these spikes and takes action accordingly. Thangaraj and Wright [1988] have used these trends to predict the incipient failure of a twist drill and retract it before serious damage occurs in the rapid, fatal wear zone of Figure 7. A drilling dynamometer was used to measure the thrust force on the drill. The gradient of the thrust force was calculated with a digital filter employing the necessary frequency specifications. 'Spikes' towards the end of tool life correspond with many of the physical characteristics shown in Figure 7. Scanning-electron-microscopy on drilled holes showed that these sharp spikes were associated with a stick-slip process that began in the drilled hole. Since the drill-flank deteriorates in exactly the same way as the sketches shown at the bottom of Figure 8, towards the end of the drill's life, the blunted tool edge begins to seize on the formed hole. At first, this only happens in a minor and instantaneous way but it does lead to the spikes in the force signal. As these stick-slip patterns get more established they can be heard as an ominous squeal that even the inexperienced machinist will react to. Depending on drill size and work material this incipient failure was detected somewhere between 2 and 7 seconds before rapid failure of the drill. Using appropriate software, the signal could arrest the feed rate of the machine tool in less than one second, showing that this is a viable production scheme and a viable sensor method to protect drills, and more importantly the part being machined.

6. CONCLUDING REMARKS

(1) The first goal of the research discussed in this paper is to examine the planning/workholding issues that arise in the creation of a unified machining process planner. Constraints include the need to eliminate part rework, the requirement to attain part tolerances of ± 0.001", and the desire to automate machining and clamping tasks ordinarily performed manually.

(2) Machinist's heuristics can be integrated with analytically derived trade-offs to form a set of planning and fixturing guides. These guides can be utilized by modules comprising a planning control structure to perform the duties of feature selection, clamp selection, and clamp and part placement (Figure 6).

(3) Manufacturing craftsmen have developed their sensory awareness to a sophisticated degree and they use visual, aural and tactile images to modulate manufacturing systems, and to commit data to memory for subsequent planning. Somatic knowledge engineering experiments reveal the ways in which the craftsmen use their sensory perceptions in real-time control. Full automation of complex processes such as machining will only be feasible when some of this more qualitative, sensor-based and heuristic information is gathered. A preliminary analysis of machining - as an example of one process in a manufacturing system, shows that at least seven different sensory cues are used during the complete machining cycle and that the skilled machinist blends these all together to make diagnostic decisions. Visual information is more important during setup, but during real- time machining, a combination

of intense visual and aural information is used by the machinist.

(4) Domain expert visual sketches and aural signatures have been proposed as a way of gathering the qualitative, and colloquialy described knowledge of craftsmen. The visual sketches and aural signatures identify the distinguishing characteristics or the most clearly observable "symptoms" of the in-process changes of a craft-operation or manufacturing process. The sketches also identify the sub-goals and long-term goals that craftsmen work towards during a task's completion.

7. ACKNOWLEDGEMENTS

David Bourne, Caroline Hayes and Paul Englert have made valuable contributions to this work, which at Carnegie-Mellon University is supported by the Machinist Expert Consortium and Air Force Grant Contract #F33615-86-C-5-38. At New York University this work is supported by Office of Naval Research Grant N00014-82-K-0381 and National Science Foundation Grant DCR-8320085.

8. REFERENCES

(1) P.J. Englert and P.K. Wright, Principles for Part Set Up and Work Holding in Automated Manufacturing *Journal of Manufacturing Systems* Vol.7 (2), P.147-161, **1988.**

(2) C. Hayes and P.K. Wright, Automated Planning in the Machining Domain *Proceedings of the American Society of Mechanical Engineers Meeting on Knowledge Based Expert Systems for Manufacturing,* PED-Vol.24, P.221-232, **1986.**

(3) M.T. Mason, "Mechanics of Pushing," In *2nd International Symposium on Robotics Research,* pp. 73-80, Kyoto, Japan, August 20-23, **1984.**

(4) E.D. Sacerdoti, "The Nonlinear Nature of Plans", *IJCAI*, 4:206-214, **1975.**

(5) H. Voelcker and A.A.G. Requicha, "Geometric Modeling of Mechanical Parts and Processes:, *Computer 10*(12), **1977.**

(6) P.K. Wright and D.A. Bourne, *Manufacturing Intelligence*, Addison-Wesley Publishing Co., Inc., Reading, MA, **1988.**

(7) A.R. Thangaraj and P.K. Wright "Drill Wear Sensing and Failure Prediction for Untended Machining", *Journal of Robotics and Computer Integrated Manufacturing,* Vol. 4 No. 3/4, pp. 429-435, **1988.**

SECTION 5 - PROCESS MONITORING AND CONTROL

Expert System Architecture for Real-Time Process Supervisor Applications

Z. Papp, T. Dobrowiecki, B. Vadász and K. Tilly
Department of Measurement and Instrumentation Engineering, Technical University of Budapest, H-1521 Budapest, Muegyetem rkp 9, Hungary

INTRODUCTION

Real-time supervisor systems are to provide information within a limited response time about the operation of a time variant system, which has complex model. For the sake of preventing the operators from information overload, a need for selective, feature extracted information displaying, monitoring, alarming has arisen. A straightforward way to fulfil these requirements is to integrate expert systems and other artificial intelligence techniques into the supervisor system.

The paper introduces problems influencing the design and implementation of real-time intelligent supervisor systems and presents a system architecture using multi-level knowledge representation scheme, which can solve the problems mentioned. As a concrete product a skeletal (shell) system was developed with a rich user environment for defining and editing technological knowledge bases. The system was realized on a computer network with relatively low performance, modest tools dictated in a sense by the average industrial requirements.

SUPERVISOR SYSTEMS IN REAL-TIME ENVIRONMENT

In order to "understand" the actions of the process being supervised the supervisor system must use (i.e. contain) some kind of process model (e.g. mathematical, conceptual, etc.). Main operational problems of the real-time supervisor system are:

- to evaluate the complex model describing the operation of the (typically technological) process,
- to cope with the time-variant environment,
- to keep the time constraints on reactions and answers.

In the following part a survey is given on the requirements which should be met for the successful solving of the problems mentioned above.

Complex model: multi-level knowledge representation

The different levels of knowledge related to an industrial process can be expressed by models of different levels, distinguished by the amount of the explicit, exact physical knowledge (Fig. 1.).

	Knowledge	Typical knowledge representation
surface model	heuristics rules of thumb experience	IF-THEN rules
↓	qualitative oper.	qualitative models
deep model	quantitative characteristics	mathematical (numerical) models

Fig.1. Levels of knowledge.

In the case of complex technological systems a multi-level model for system knowledge description is usually justified as a rational and a necessary one:

- In most cases there is not enough detailed information to derive the exact analytical model for the process (e.g. as a system of some kind of equations), so we must confine ourselves to a less precise one.
- The computational and memory costs of expressing a given knowledge have an optimum along the model depth axis. It is an intelligible requirement that the process knowledge should be expressed by the most matching kind of model.

- People working with an industrial process evaluate information using models of different levels. The quality of operator's activity (who confines himself to the surface level model mostly) can be improved by feeding information from the deep level description of the process (which is typically beyond the competence of an average operator).

Sophisticated, time optimized implementations of a single level knowledge representation technique (e.g. rule-base paradigm) (Barachini [1]) do not mean solution in the real-time intelligent supervisor system domain. The bulk of the expert systems does not support at all nor to a sufficient extent the multi-level description. To a certain extent the intelligent question asking can cover the shallowness of the knowledge base, but in the real-time application domain - where the direct (operator independent) information acquisition should be supported - this solution may not be acceptable. There are implementations where it is possible to activate routines written in procedural language - and this is a way to obtain information from the deep model - but this is not a satisfactory solution (Wright [2]). Other implementations do not cover the knowledge representation spectrum broadly enough thus certain types of knowledge can be utilized only with some loss of the expressing power (Talukdar [3]).

<u>Time-variant environment</u>

In the majority of the expert systems monotonic reasoning strategy is realized: a new result of the reasoning process cannot modify results arisen previously, the reasoning system thus cannot handle temporary assumptions - being true for a moment and turning out to be false later on. An expert system used to supervise industrial process should adapt to a changing environment, and should be able to operate in an environment not fully specified. As a consequence inference engine with nonmonotonic reasoning strategy (Winograd [4]) supported by some kind of powerful truth maintenance mechanism (McAllester [5], Doyle [10]) should be employed.
In easier cases the lack of the truth maintenance system can be compensated for by the appropriate construction of the rule base, but this solution decreases the efficiency and readability of the knowledge base.

Real-time operation

There are certain architectural and implementational consequences of the real-time regime of the supervising system as well.

Due to the multi-level model structure the supervisor system should contain data acquisition and signal processing subsystems. Scheduling different tasks in real-time means keeping a variety of real-time constraints. Thus such a kind of system architecture is needed, which provides

- background for realizing subsystems with different real-time specifications,
- flexible, tolerant cooperation of the subsystems,
- easy mapping to distributed hardware configuration.

Considering the implementational problems it is advantageous to gain efficiency by using knowledge representation techniques supported to a great extent by an off-line knowledge preprocessing scheme (Forgy [6]).

KNOWLEDGE REPRESENTATION, REASONING STRATEGIES

The supervisor system presented so far has three-level knowledge representation structure. Using this representation

- mathematical (analytical, numerical),
- qualitative,
- heuristic

model of the industrial process (or a subsystem of a process) can be described. Fig. 2. shows the information processing scheme of the supervisor system.

The mathematical knowledge about the process is embodied in the signal processing subsystem. For efficiency and flexibility reasons the mathematical model is converted into an explicit form, i.e. the observation --> result transformation is expressed directly through the data-flow formalism (Bagó [7]).

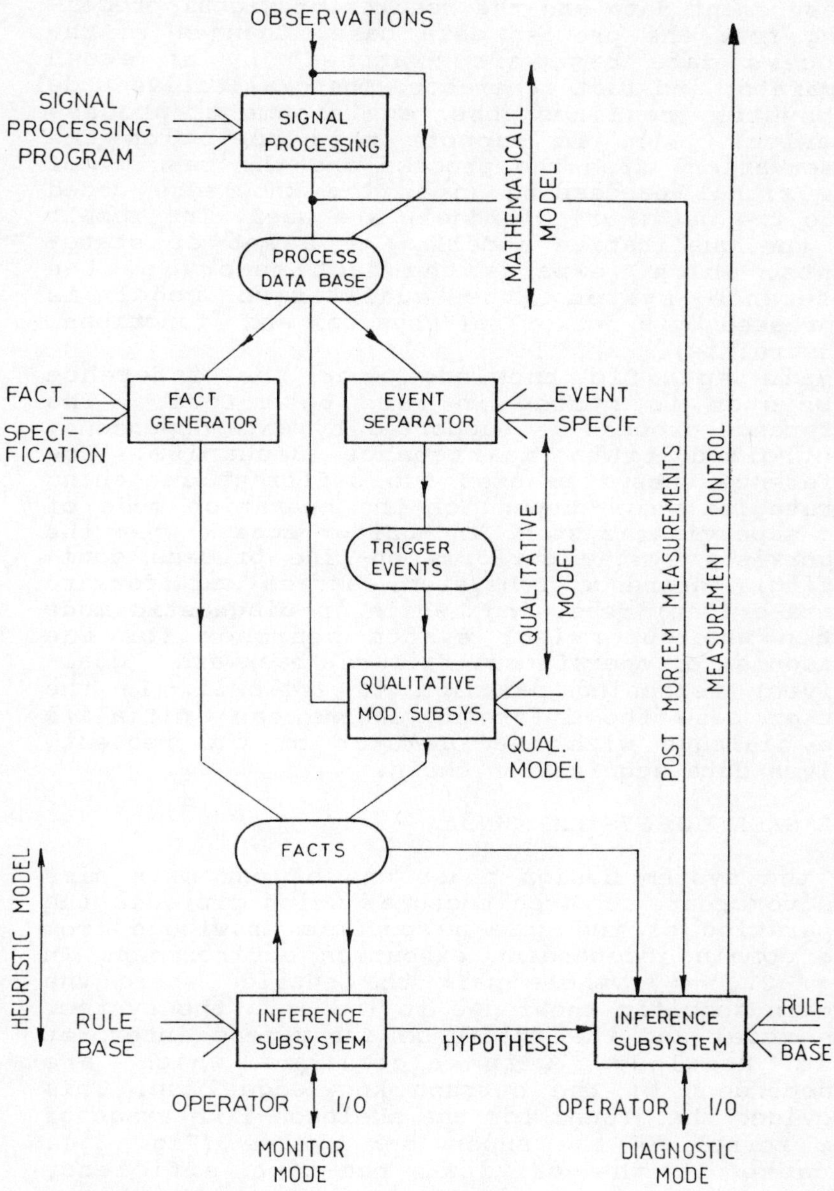

Fig.2. Information processing structure of the system.

Measurement data and the results of signal processing form the process data base. Changes in the process data base are "watched" by an event separator and fact generator. The qualitative model subsystem realizes the envisionment process (deKleer [8]). To support this operation the observations from the process and the results of the signal processing (i.e. the knowledge coded into the mathematical model) are used. The result of the qualitative modeling is a set of statements, which expands the fact memory of the inference system (the qualitative model is expressed by a network of physical and functional constraints).
Domain specific knowledge for the inference subsystem is stored in rule base form. The inference process is supported by data-dependency controlled truth maintenance mechanism. The inference subsystem uses two different reasoning strategies which depend on the operation mode of the supervisor system. In **monitor mode** (when the supervisor system performs on-line process monitoring) inference subsystem carries out forward (data-driven) reasoning, while in **diagnostic mode** (when the supervisor system searches for the reason(s) of operational failure) backward (goal-driven) reasoning paradigm is followed. In the latter case the inference engine can initialize the dialogue with the operator or the request-driven data acquisition chain.

THE SKELETAL SYSTEM (SHELL)

In the system design phase one of our main aims was to create an architecture, which provides the separation of the domain specific knowledge from the domain independent execution environment. In Fig. 2. ==> symbols mark the entries where the domain specific knowledge is fed into the system. The model and the inference subsystems interpret this knowledge with algorithms which are independent of the current knowledge base. This provides the ground for the skeleton-like usage of the kernel of the supervisor system (Fig. 3.). Because of the critical run-time efficiency requirements it is inappropriate to interpret symbolic description of the knowledge directly. A model builder consisting of three special editor-compilers converts the symbolic expert input to an efficiently interpretable internal form or machine code and supports the interpretation process by making some structural information explicit (e.g. by building data-dependency graph, Fig. 4.).

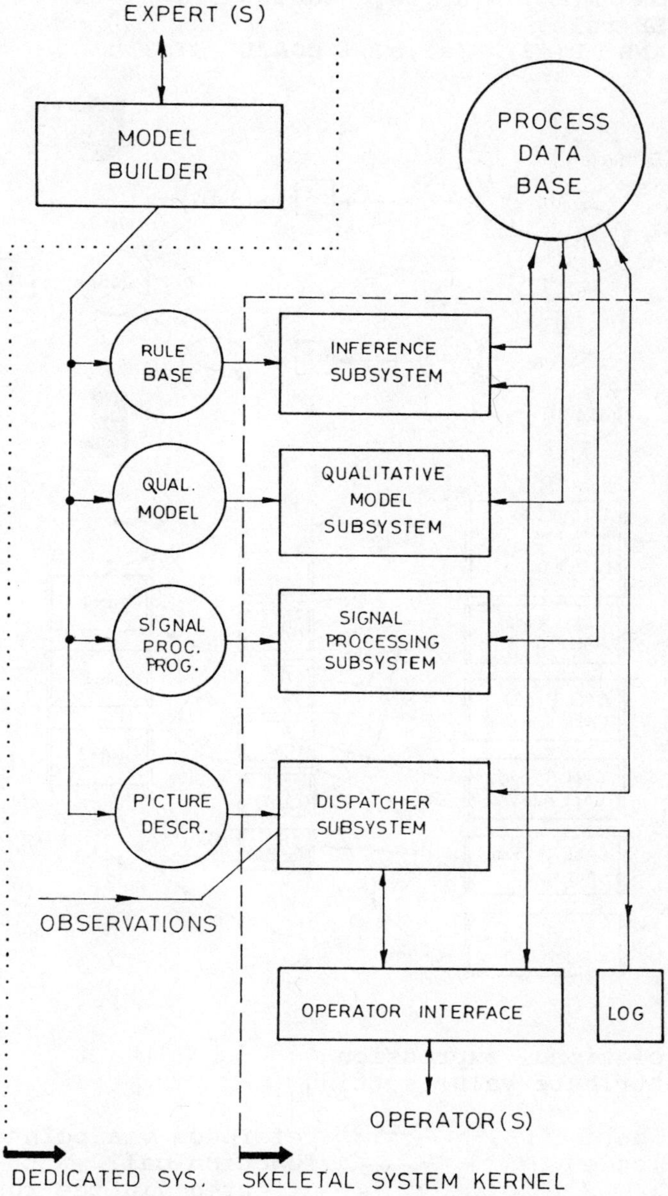

Fig.3. Skeleton system structure.

```
RULE rule1
  AND  R(a1) R(a2)  CONCL  S(a3)
RULE rule2
  OR  R(a4) R(a5,a6)  CONCL  S(a7)
RULE rule3
  AND  R(a3) R(a1,a7)  CONCL  S(a8)
```

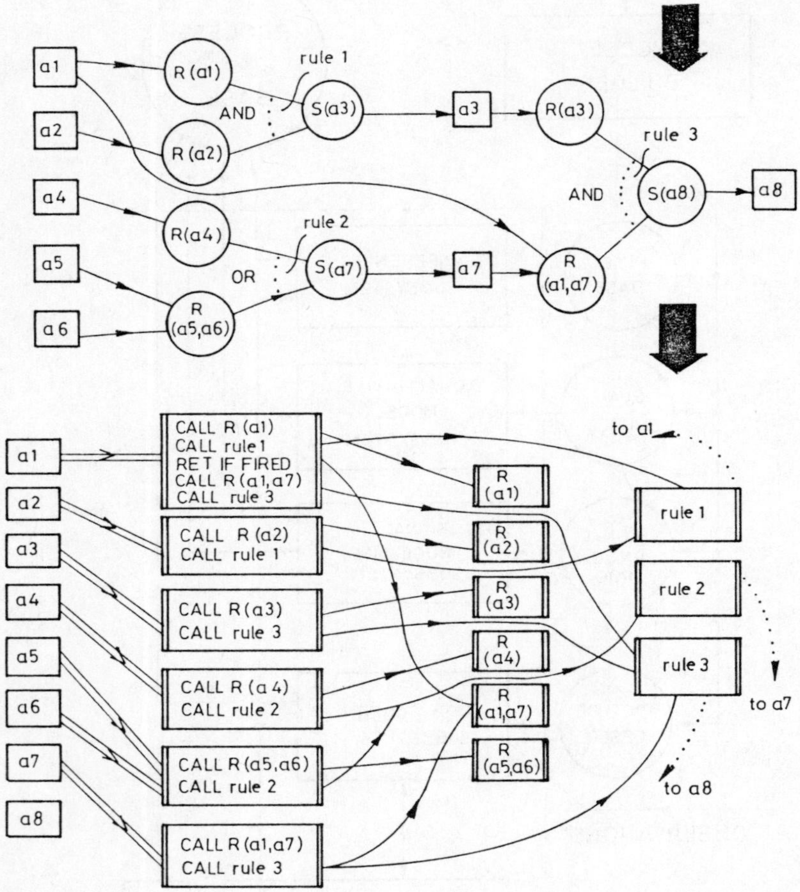

Legend:

R(.) relational expression

S(.) attribute value setting

▭	data	⟹	reference via pointer
▯▭▯	code	——►	function call
		....►	affected via the run-time system FIFO

Fig.4. The structure of the generated code.

IMPLEMENTATIONAL ASPECTS

The supervisor system shell has been realized currently on IBM PC/AT computer under MS-DOS operating system. Because of the modest computational power of this, the efficient implementation was one of the most critical issues.

For efficiency reasons the C programming language was chosen as basic implementational tool. Resulting from the operation principle of the supervisor system, its fundamental elements are the cooperating asynchronous model subsystems. In order to make the realization of these and other asynchronous activities possible a multitasking run-time nucleus was designed. To support different system description paradigms on a reasonable level (Bobrow [9]), a symbolic language, an object-oriented LISP subset was implemented as an intermediate layer.

The integrated usage of different programming tools can be followed in Fig. 5., which expose the stratified structure of the supervisor system. The C and LISP layers used to design all the system activities are to a great extent overlapped and transparent for each other, i.e. the majority of the procedure calls are common and both layers can pass data structures and control. The real-time kernel is supported by the co-routine paradigm at the C level with further extension to processes and semaphores at the LISP level. The relatively liquid transition between both languages makes it possible to implement real-time software structures "submerged" to a different measure in C and in LISP as well. Processes with no serious time-constraints can be designed as normal LISP programs while the bodies of those more time-critical could be composed from C procedures seen as a single LISP function call. As a consequence of great importance the symbolic, lexical information processing can easily be combined with the numerical algorithms supporting, as mentioned, different levels of the technological knowledge.

Although an arbitrary real-time structure could be realized with these tools, for obvious reasons one fixed architecture was selected as a basis for our skeletal system. The choice of structure should not be left to the end-user who is well at home in the concrete industrial technology but not in the finesses and consequences of real-time task synchronisation. As seen in Fig. 5. the skeletal system is organized around five cooperating activities realizing the information flow and processing stages of Fig. 2.

LAN Server Process extends LAN (local area network) Handler added to the DOS to the mechanism of receiving and passing messages containing blocks of the technology related data. **Timer Process** provides suitable timings for the qualitative model evaluation and other processing activities. The **Scheduler Process** distributes the incoming technological data among the mathematical model and other resources of the supervisor system. **Monitoring Process** performs the qualitative and the heuristic model evaluation, while the **Supervisor Process** is responsible for the diagnostic inferences and essentially it is the end-user interface to the system.

The skeletal system operates upon an extensive knowledge base which should be "filled-in" by the customer. The elements of the concrete technological knowledge are as follows:

a. **graphics:**
graphical images of the process or its subsystems used as a background for displaying the technology related information,

b. **diagnostical rule base:**
expert rules expressing the know-how of the post-mortem process diagnostics,

c. **monitoring rule base:**
expert rules expressing operator's ability to integrate the incoming numerical information into trends, events and useful conclusions,
qualitative model:
physical constraints built into condition parts of the IF-THEN rules and expressing functional dependences among the process subsystems,

d. **object network:**
the data-flow-like formulation of the numerical information processing used for a given technological process and designed on the basis of the exact mathematical model of the technology,

e. **timer channels:**
the description of the timing mechanism.

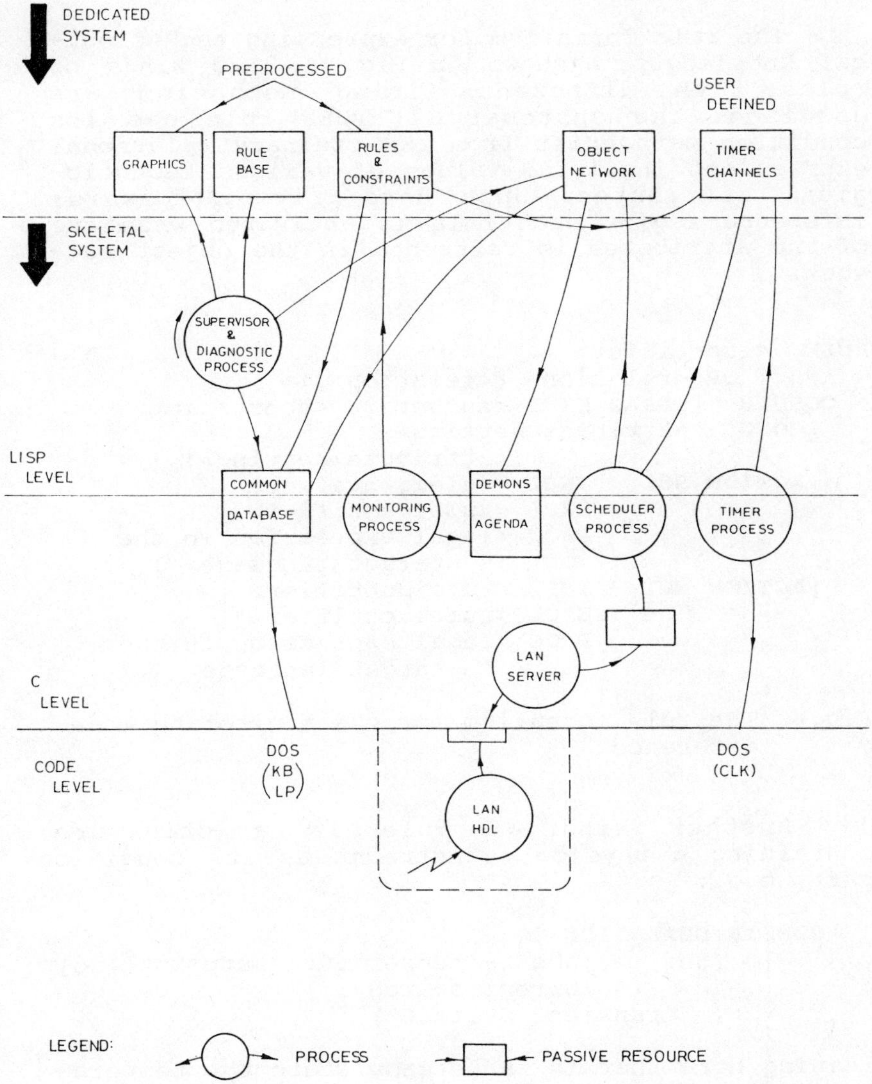

Fig.5. Stratified structure of the supervisor system.

For the formulation of his technological knowledge the customer is equipped with LISP-based high level tools. As mentioned certain knowledge (cases a. and c.) is preprocessed for better efficiency.

The rule formalism for expressing technological knowledge is shown in Fig. 6. Two kinds of rules with different firing mechanisms are utilized. The customary IF-THEN rule has its condition part built from the ordinary relational expressions involving values of various technological attributes. Upon data-driven (forward) inference regime such rule is activated when one of the attributes is refreshed in the object network.

```
RULE  <identifier>
  AND | OR <relation> {<relation>} |
  CONSTR  [ DEAD_TIME <number> ] <constraint>
   [CONCL <attribute setting>
                         {<attribute setting>} ]
   [ACTION_SET    INCL <ruleidentifier> |
                  EXCL <ruleidentifier> |
                  PROC <legal expression in the
                            target language> ]
   [ACTION_RET    INCL <ruleidentifier> |
                  EXCL <ruleidentifier> |
                  PROC <legal expression in the
                            target language> ]
```

Fig.6. The rule formalism for the monitoring mode inference.

Another kind of rule is a structure containing a physical constraint as its condition part, e.g.:

```
CONSTR DEAD_TIME 10;
   (= (and (> (abs (- temperature setpoint)) 5)
           (= current_switch 1))
       (= transient_state 0))
```

meaning here that in the steady state the temperature controller should maintain the residue error within certain preset limits.

The rule is activated similarly upon the refreshment of some of the attributes in the constraint but the firing mechanism is different.

From the point of view of an expert system operating on a real-time process it is essential to secure time consistency of the data existing side by side in the process data base. In our design the rule evaluation is suspended after activation for a given dead time to assure that the attributes in the constraints will belong to the same slice of time. The measure of delay is to be specified according to the informational load of the LAN and the complexity of the information processing network. After the dead time is up the evaluation of the rule is automatically resumed and the rule is possibly fired. Dead time can be also interpreted and prescribed from the perspective of the process dynamics. In such a case constraints will represent some kind of time-dependent input / output behaviour of the process subunits.

When a conclusion part of a rule (**CONCL**) activated by the incoming data is executed some new information is specified which according to the data-driven paradigm can activate and fire other rules. Thus a single datum can initiate a whole inference chain till the triggering information is exhausted. The new inferences can not only add information to the data base but also deactivate (**EXCL**) or reactivate (**INCL**) rules. The knowledge base maintained is consequently a dynamic structure better tailored to the momentary requirements and state of the process.

On the other hand in this way a powerful truth maintaining nonmonotonic reasoning is introduced in the monitoring mode. When a rule is retracted the information derived from its conclusion part should be discharged as no longer valid. But perhaps it was used to fire other rules and add some other information to the system. In the analogy to the mechanism mentioned above the discharged data will implicitly deactivate other rules and the inference withdrawal will continue till all the information is consistent. Operations prescribed for the normal and withdrawal inference phases should be specified in the **ACTION_SET** or **ACTION_RET** part of the rule.

This rule mechanism facilitates entering of the expert knowledge however it will never produce a knowledge base efficient enough among real-time operating conditions. Rules introduced separately share the same set of attributes and thus possess considerable structural connectivity which, when made explicit through an adequate software mechanism, can eliminate the time-critical matching phase of the inference engine cycle. The preprocessing scheme used is shown in Fig. 4. (Papp [11]). The entry points to the rule dependency-graph correspond to the condition part attributes which when refreshed yield an automatic information and control transfer (demons) from the object network to the agenda of the Monitoring Process. The actual attributes are then fed to the proper entries and propagated according to the connections. The activities of the Monitoring Process are presented in a pseudo-code in Fig. 7. (the agenda is filled independently with the new data by the object network controlled by the Scheduler). The designed rule compilation scheme is an obvious trade-off between the efficiency requirements on the one hand and the expressive power of the knowledge description on the other, considering the modest processing power of the selected hardware. Similar but significantly more demanding approach is presented in Forgy [6].

From hardware point of view the performance of the supervisor system can be increased by utilizing computerized process peripherals. These instruments are able to perform autonomous data acquisition and real-time signal processing, thus certain part of the mathematical model can be removed from the host computer. The process peripherals communicate with the host through local area network. Using this approach the coupling is loosened between the process supervised and the supervisor system, and as a consequence the real-time constraints for the supervisor become easier.

An increased parallelism can be introduced by means of a slave processor (with 80286 processor, 80287 co-processor, 1 Mbyte RAM) being built into the host. Using this extended hardware architecture the signal processing subsystem (the mathematical model subsystem) - which typically is a multi-tasking real-time system by itself - can easily be separated from the main system. In this way the response time of the signal processing subsystem will decrease significantly and can be estimated much more precisely (the latter is very important in hard real-time control applications).

```
DO forever

 { WHILE agenda is not empty
     { get next attribute - new value pair
       from agenda

       IF attribute should be retracted
         { set attribute value to be retracted
           call attribute bound procedure
           (see Fig.4.)
         }
       ELSE
         { IF the old and new values of the
              attribute are equal
            { increase the counter of the
              attribute holding number of rules
              supporting this value
            }
           ELSE
            { IF attribute has been retracted
               { set attribute value to the new one
                 call attribute bound procedure
                 (see Fig.4.)
               }
              ELSE
               { report value contradiction error }
            }
         }
     }

   IF there is any constraint waiting for execution
    { decrease the dead time of all waiting
      contraints by the time passed from the last
      setting

      WHILE there is any constraint ready for
            execution
        { call procedure corresponding to the
          constraint }
     }

    IF agenda is empty
     { release the processor and execute transfer
       to the next co-routine }
 }
```

Fig.7. The pseudo-code algorithm of the forward inference engine

In order to avoid the serious memory limitation of the current implementation the OS/2 version of the supervisor shell is under development.

CONCLUSION

An intelligent supervisor system developed for real-time industrial process monitoring should use multi-level knowledge representation schemes. Describing knowledge on mathematical, qualitative and heuristic levels is necessary to realize intelligent and efficient supervisor behavior. This approach requires new expert system architectures to be developed, where different system realization and operational paradigms can coexist and cooperate with each other.

The development work described in detail above resulted finally in a commercial product - REALEX shell system (REAL-time EXpert system) - marketed as a true shell or as a dedicated system according to the customer's demands (DSL [12], REALEX [13]). Actually implementations supervising certain (relatively slow) metallurgical and pharmaceutical processes are tuned to the concrete requirements and will be operational by the end of the year. System to be used in the steel roll mill will supervise 75 furnaces through a distributed network of about 25 data acquisition and controller units. The system resources are distributed among two IBM PC AT compatible microcomputers, communicating via LAN. The second system will assist in supervising the output and the administration of a block of 5 fermenters.

Although the majority of work belonged to the period of the shell system development it can be said that really challenging problems were encountered in the dedicated systems. Upon interviewing the customers a picture of what the technology is and how it should be maintained efficiently was obtained but relatively little help in how to distribute this process and control knowledge among the systems resources (e.g. process peripherials vs. host computers, signal processing network vs. rule base, etc.). It should be emphasised that compared with the traditional expert systems the performance (intelligence) of a real-time industrial supervisor is achieved rather by the balanced distribution of the technological knowledge among different system components (user interface and data base management included) and not by an extensive filling up of the system rule base.

It should be mentioned finally that an experimental version of an intelligent fault-tolerant adaptive controller is under development based on REALEX. A qualitatively new feature of this work is the introduction of run-time (adaptive) model building tools mirroring the dynamically changing situation in the technology and instrumentation.

Although it was not considered during the system development, many problems, derived from the industrial environment and the autonomous, distributed character of the supervisor system, indicate that some kind of the recently proposed LAN recovery mechanism (Randell [14]) should be adapted. This work is planned for the subsequent version of the REALEX system.

REFERENCES

1. Barachini, F., Theuretzbacher, N. PAMELA: An expert system technology for real-time control applications, pp. 42-47, Proceedings of the 5th Eur. Conf. on AI, Munich, 1988.

2. Wright,M.L. et al. An expert system for real-time control, IEEE Software, pp. 16-24, March 1986.

3. Talukdar,S.N. et al. TOAST: The power system operator's assistant, Computer, pp. 53-60, July 1986.

4. Winograd,T. Extended inference modes in reasoning by computer systems, Artificial Intelligence, pp. 5-26, Vol 13, 1980.

5. McAllester,D.M. An outlook of truth maintenance, MIT AI Lab Memo 551, 1980.

6. Forgy,C.L. Rete: A fast algorithm for the many pattern/many object pattern match problem, Artificial Intelligence, pp. 17-37, Vol 19, 1982.

7. Bagó,B. et al. A multi-level signal processing system, Proc. of the 8th Ann. Conf. of the IEEE-EMBS, pp. 825-828, Vol 2, Dallas, 1986.

8. deKleer,J. The origin and resolution of ambiguities in causal arguments, Proc. of the 6th IJCAI, pp. 197-203, Tokyo, 1979.

9. Bobrow,D.G. If the Prolog is the answer, what is the question? Or what it takes to support AI programming paradigms, IEEE Transactions on Software Eng., pp. 1401-1408, Vol SE-11, No 11, November 1985.

10. Doyle,J. A glimpse of truth maintenance, in Winston,P.H., Brown,R.H. (eds). Artificial Intelligence : An MIT Perpective, pp. 119-135, Vol 1, MIT Press 1982.

11. Papp,Z. et al. Knowledge based support for EEG recording, Proceedings of the 1988 IEEE Int. Symp. on Circuits and Systems, pp. 2371-2374, Espoo, June 7-9, 1988.

12. DSL (1987). DSL - Dispatcher Station LISP, Programming Manual, Dept. of Measurement and Instr. Eng., Technical University of Budapest, 1987.

13. REALEX (1987). REALEX - Real-Time Advisory Expert System, User's Manual, Dept. of Measurement and Instr. Eng., Technical University of Budapest, 1989.

14. Randell,A. Crash detection and recovery in a discless HP-UXA, Hewlett-Packard J., pp. 27-32, Vol 39, Nr 5, October 1988.

Generalised Process Exceptions - A Knowledge Representation Paradigm for Expert Control

S. Parthasarathy
CMC Limited, 115 Sarojini Devi Road, Secunderabad, 500 003, India

ABSTRACT

This paper highlights the role of timing as a process control tool. We discuss the need for an approach for specifying and designing control systems, which would handle timing and process exceptions in an identical fashion. Constructs are proposed for specifying timing exceptions such that they can be integrated into the knowledge bases of control systems. The notion of a generalised process exception is developed from this definition and examples are provided to illustrate its potential.

INTRODUCTION

Conventionally, process control systems are concerned with maintaining several process variables within desired limits or at desired levels. During actual operations however, several events occur. A process exception is said to occur if an abnormal event is encountered e.g. a process variable exceeds a predefined value. In the same spirit, a timing exception may also be defined for ensuring that the process and the control system are indeed healthy. In many cases, timing exceptions are superimposed on process exceptions (or vice-versa) to invoke a common action. Exceptions lead to the need for secondary operations like alarms (e.g. audio, video or log) or corrective procedures (e.g. change of set points, reconfiguration, or even process shut down). The mechanism of triggering the appropriate action (or actions) is termed as *exceptions handling*. A common approach must therefore be available to control systems designers to handle timing exceptions exactly like any other exception.

It is noticed that control systems often fail to perform or perform unpredictably, mostly due to an inconsistent design of the mechanism to handle these phenomena, as explained in Rosenof [1]. In this paper, we propose a mechanism to overcome this difficulty, and demonstrate the ease with which a rule based expert system can be designed.

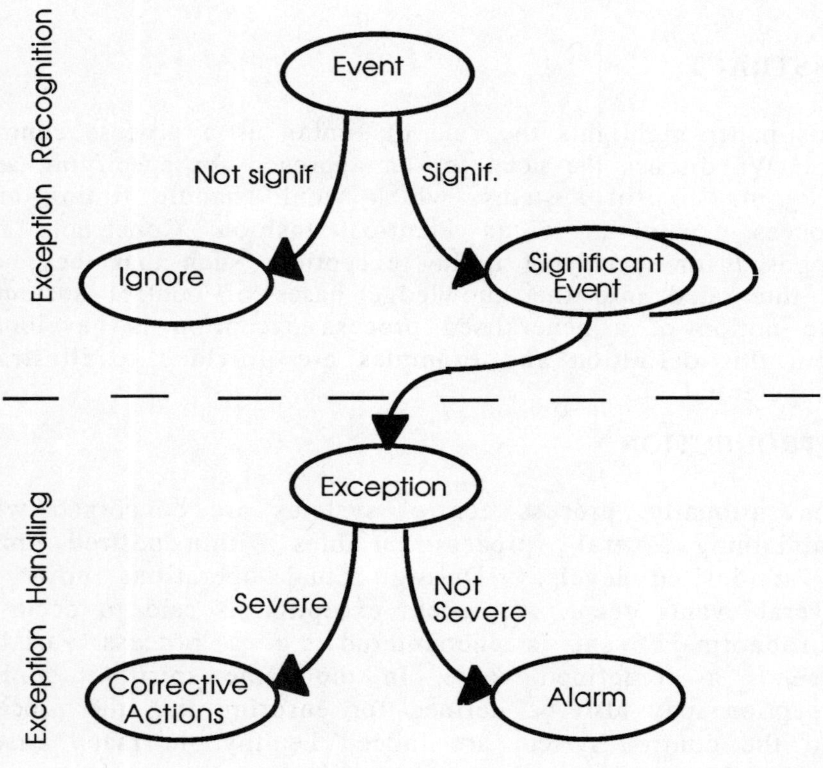

Fig. 1 Events , Exceptions , Alarms

In the above discussion we have employed three important terms : *events, exceptions, alarms* . The relation between these three terms may be depicted as in Figure 1.

It must be noted that whereas every event does not lead to an exception, every exception results either in an alarm or may trigger corrective actions - hence the importance of exception handling. Depending on the context in which an event occurs, it may be classified as significant or not. For example, the temperature of a bath exceeding say 100° C may be considered as significant, only if the corresponding set point was at 100° C (or below). If the set point was higher, this event may be only indicative and of marginal interest, and may consequently be ignored or just logged (for archival). Thus, only significant events give rise to exceptions - which may then be used to trigger alarms or corrective actions. In certain cases, exceptions are used for decision making and for choosing between alternative strategies of operation.

The process of recognising events as significant or not may be as simple as in the example given above, or may follow very complex algorithms. This phase, we shall term as *recognition phase,* precedes the *exception handling* phase. Our paper concerns the activities to be performed after a significant event has occured (exception handling phase). It also assumes that the control system has identified the event as significant and has time tagged the same for use by the exceptions handler. This approach is inspired from actual practice in the industry. It can be applied without affecting (or being affected by) the existing mechanisms of exception recognition, which are very closely dependant on the process concerned. It has also the advantage that it renders the exception handling phase more efficient, since trivial events are filtered out a priori. We shall henceforth employ the term *event* to denote significant events only.

Exception handling is closely related to alarm annunciation. This subject is of great importance in safety critical processes due to the need to alert operators in time and in a clear and unambiguous way. Often VDU based control systems are detested by operators because of the impossibility to use the pattern based perception mechanisms associated with geographically dispersed annunciation devices. This has provoked an enormous amount of research in the ergonomics of alarm annunciation and context dependant information display (e.g. Goodstein [2]). The approach we propose can be useful in hierarchical and selective annunciation of alarms.

TIME AS A CONTROL TOOL

" Time " , popularly known as the fourth dimension, can at best be regarded as a mathematical abstraction which forms the unifying basis of all evolution. Although time is employed to measure or denote the evolution of physical processes, time itself has no physically observable features. This paper is purposely restricted to studying a particular aspect of the representation of time dependant phenomena. A larger overview of time in artificial intelligence may be found in the publications of Shoham (see Shoham [3] for instance).

Industrial process control is dependant on time for various reasons. Timing is used for operational reasons, or for accounting for resource limitations or for ensuring process safety. As an operational tool, it may be necessary to perform a particular operation for a given duration of time, or at a given time of the day, or every so often. As a resource management tool, time can be very important. After initiating a request for a sharable resource, in case the resource does not get available within a predefined delay (time out), some secondary action may have to be initiated. The role of time in ensuring process safety is perhaps the most important reason why this topic deserves a detailed study.

Safety can be informally defined as the property of a process which ensures that a mishap does not occur. A mishap may be defined as a phenomenon which could result in the loss of or damage to any component of the process, or in injury or loss of life. Often this definition is extended to include conditions which may potentially lead to a mishap. A more formal and exhaustive treatment of this important subject may be found in the paper by Leveson [4]. Timing is very frequently used in process control to incorporate safety linked procedures e.g. a circuit breaker may be set to trip out if a particular transmission line carries more than its rated current for more than a specified duration. If, within the above set timing, the said breaker does not trip, a secondary breaker may be programmed to trip out, to avert any permanent damage. In fact, this is a standard practice in electricity network protection (see Damsker [5]). In another context, an alarm is raised when a given process variable exceeds its nominal value for more than a given duration. If the cause for alarm persists for more than a tolerable duration, the control system should be capable of initiating a shut down (watch dog function). It is evident that methods to ensure process safety depend on proper specifications and implementation of timing constraints, an area to which this paper attempts to contribute.

EXPRESSING TIMING EXCEPTIONS

To be able to recognise a timing exception, it is necessary to define process behaviour in terms of time. It is therefore necessary to define constructs which can be used for describing a timing exception. Any approach to this problem should consider two important requirements :

- the constructs should be able to generalise exceptions arising due to any reason (including timing).

- the constructs shall allow timing exceptions to be described unambiguously.

We propose two classes of timing exceptions, based on the timing constructs proposed by Dasarathy [6]. Dasarathy elaborates on the stimulus (S) response (R) model of real time systems, creating four combinations of events i.e. S-S, S-R, R-S, R-R. Timing constraints are then classified into two classes i.e. maximum allowed, and minimum allowed for each one of the four combinations mentioned earlier. In the case of process control systems, we feel it is more appropriate to use the generalised notion of event. A third type of construct "durational" has been proposed in Dasarathy [6] but it is not employed here since it is a contradiction of terms, in the light of the classical approach of defining an event as an instantaneous, atomic phenomenon (see Holt [7]).

In Figure 2 we depict diagrammatically, the two classes of exceptions.

- A timing exception of *Class A* occurs if *more than* lat units of time (latency) elapse between the occurrence of an event F (first event) and the occurrence of an event S (second event).

- A timing exception of *Class B* occurs if *less than* lat units of time elapse between the occurrence of an event F and the occurrence of an event S.

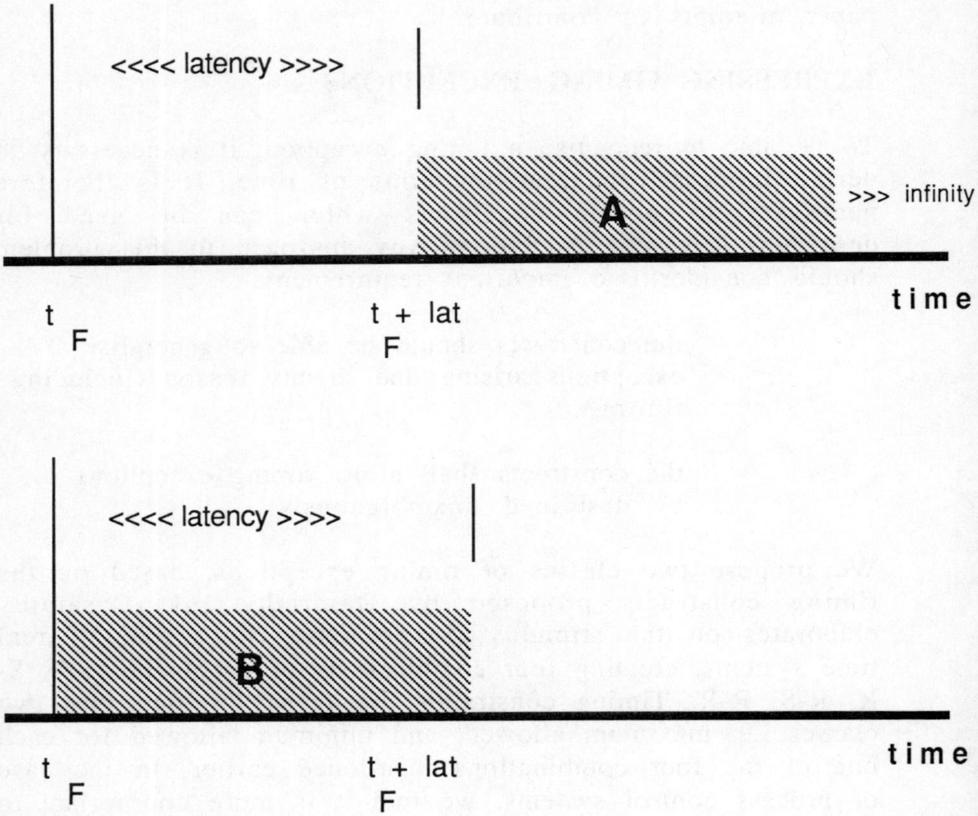

Fig 2. Timing exception Classes

A timing exception of the particular class will occur if the second event S occurs within the part of the time line shown in hatched.

The term event in the definition above may be : either a significant event related to one or more physical process variables , or a significant event corresponding to the arrival of one or more timing errors, or a significant event corresponding to a logical combination of both families of events. This leads us to the idea of a *generalised process exception* (GPE) , which covers both physical, temporal or logical exceptions. Thus, a generalised process exception may be defined as a quadruplet :

< First event arrived, Second event arrived, Latency, Class >

For maintaining consistency in the interpretation of GPEs, the event F is always taken as the point of reference, hence, occurrences of S before F are not taken into account. If S is to be taken as the reference, another GPE must be explicitely formulated with S defined as the first event. Without loss of generality, we also assume that the latency will take only a positive (or zero) value.

By appropriately mapping the two terminal events and by choosing the right class of exception and its associated latency, it is possible to employ a common strategy of exceptions handling (particularly for triggering safety related procedures), irrespective of the cause of the exception.

GPE KNOWLEDGE BASE

Definition

As explained in Rasmussen [8], expert knowledge for complex processes follows the causal model of the form :

"if X then do Y"

Rule based expert systems capture this form of knowledge and adopt the same for decision making, either automatic or assisted by the operator. This model is applicable to sequential control (see Parthasarathy [9]) as well as for continuous process control (see Francis [10]). This approach is all the more valid for processes exhibiting a high level of risk, or for operations involving process safety. Rule based knowledge representation is not only efficient for representation of domain dependant knowledge but can also form the basis of more sophisticated forms of knowledge bases. An excellent source of reference on this subject may be found in Vignard [11].

In the literature, a production rule is defined as a knowledge model of the form :

if < antecedent > then < consequent >

A GPE rule is a production rule where the antecedent part of the rule is replaced by a GPE expression as defined above and the consequent part is replaced by an "action". This gives rise to the following structure for a GPE rule :

if < GPE > then < action >

We shall use the condensed notation < < GPE >, action > to denote the above GPE Rule in a compact form. The "action" usually consists of triggering an event.

Properties
The originality of our approach lies in the fact that the knowledge base consisting of GPE rules is not simply a disjoint list of production rules, but may consist of rules in cascade.

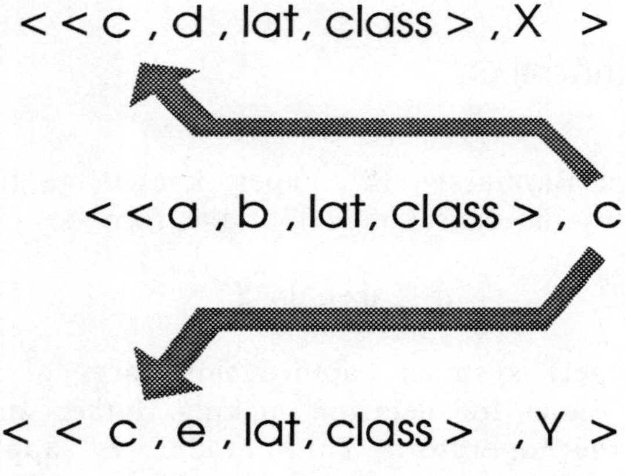

Fig. 3 Selective Cascading (Type a)

For instance, the consequent part of a GPE rule may be part of the antecedent part of another GPE rule (Fig. 3 and Fig. 4). This structure is extremely useful in selectively cascading actions. Actions are selectively cascaded when they have to respect the context in which a given exception occurs. The consequent of a GPE may be cascaded to respond to what happens after (Type a cascading) its occurence (see Fig. 3).

Alternately, as shown in Figure 4, it may be used to activate actions depending on what had occured earlier to its occurence (Type b cascading).

It is also important to note that the same exception may be used to provoke both type a and type b cascading. These mechanisms may be exploited in a wide variety of situations, particularly in the case of intelligent annunciation of alarms.

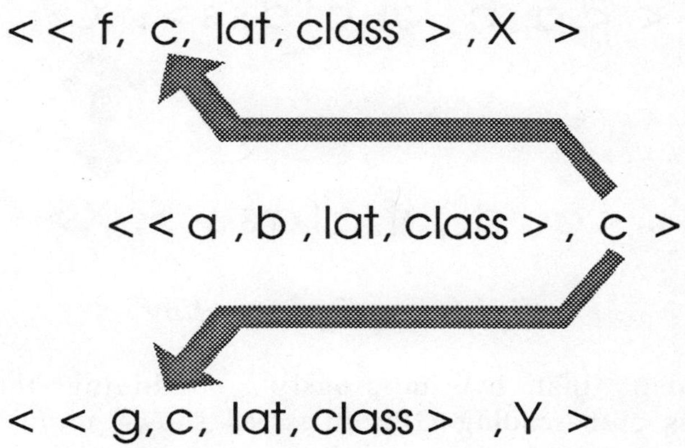

Fig. 4 Selective Cascading (Type b)

For the same antecedent there may be more than one consequent i.e. there may be more than one GPE rule whose antecedent may be the same but the consequent part may be different (Fig. 5). This " fan out " structure is employed in cases where multiple actions have to be triggered on simultaneously, a practice which is often necessary during emergencies.

Conversely, more than one GPE rule may have the same consequent action (Fig. 6). This "fan in" phenomenon is useful when the same action is to be performed under a variety of contexts. This technique is also useful for compacting the knowledge base.

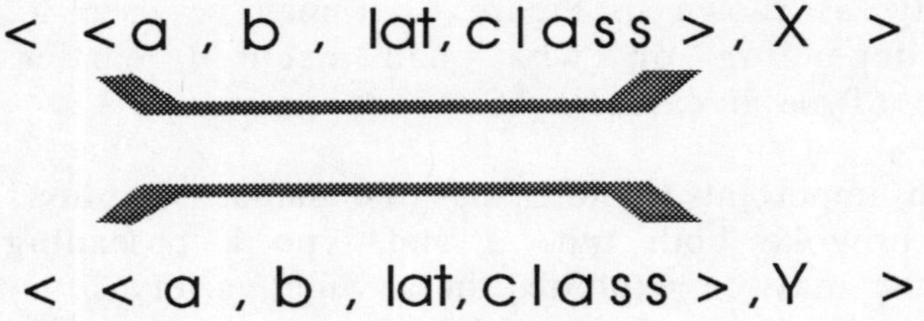

Fig. 5 Fan out cascading

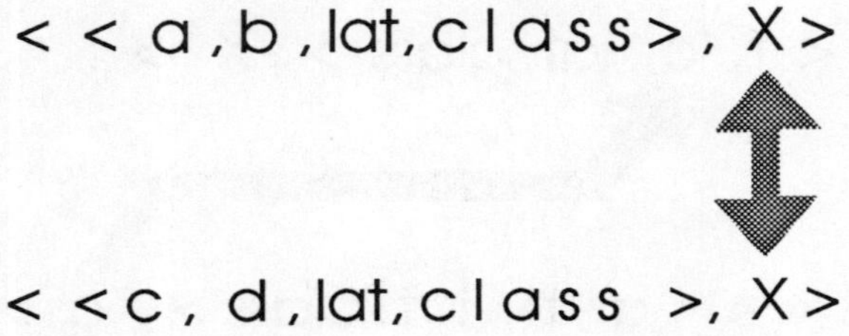

Fig. 6 Fan in cascading

It is evident that by judiciously combining the various possibilities of cascading GPE rules, as shown in Figures 3,4,5 and 6, a very wide variety of exception handling strategies may be implemented. By appropriately predefining the cascading relationships, several scenarios can be set up in advance to take care of specific and context dependent contingencies.

Some Applications

GPE Rules for some of the commonly encountered situations of exceptions are illustrated below. In each case, the antecedent and consequent parts of the GPE rule are shown separately for clarity.The following very simple examples have been deliberately chosen to demonstrate various possibilities of GPEs. It must also be noted that the user can create the same effect sometimes by interchanging the two terminal events and selecting an appropriate latency and exception class. To that extent, GPE rules provide a certain flexibility of usage. But, due to the unambiguous way to interpret a given GPE rule, the expected effect can be clearly visualised in advance.

Time out In safety critical operations, or for resource management operations, timeout is a commonly employed technique.

e.g. A timeout function is built using an omni-present, fictitious event called "true"
Ant. : Start timer, true, delay, A
Cons. : Timeout

e.g. In safety critical processes, time out is used to trigger corrective action if a particular exception persists for more than a tolerable duration.
Ant. : Exception X, Exception X, durn. toler., A
Cons. : Corrective action Y

e.g. For all alarms acknowledged by operator after 30 seconds, send message to supervisor console.
Ant . : Alarm, Ack. , 30 s, A
Cons. : Log into supervisor console

e.g. If local breaker not tripped within 100 ms of fault, trip remote breaker.
Ant. : Fault, local breaker not tripped, 100 ms, A
Cons. : Trip remote breaker

Trend based control When an event occurs earlier than expected, as in the case of runaway conditions in processes, GPE rules may be used for starting corrective actions.

e.g. If oven temperature reaches 350°C from 300°C within 3 minutes, switch off one burner.
Ant. : Temp. > 300°C, Temp. > 350°C, 3 min., B
Cons. : Stop one burner

A similar application would be when two actions have to be separated by a minimum duration. For instance, this is often the case when large electric motors are to be started in succession, (to avoid undue transients on the network).

e.g. To start fan Y,wait at least 5 seconds after starting X.
Ant. : X started, Start Y, 5 sec., B
Cons. : Disable Y.

Limit violations This is the simplest form of alarms, very commonly encountered in data acquisition and process control systems. We use a fictitious event " true" which is assumed to be present always.

e.g. If bath temperature exceeds 120°C, raise alarm.
Ant. : true, Temp. > 120°C, 0, A
Cons. : raise alarm

Wait / Signal event Another application similar to the above would be when we have to wait for a certain event.

e.g. Wait arrival of crate on conveyor to start conveyor
Ant. : true, crate arrived, 0, A
Cons. : start conveyor

Instrumentation malfunctions, Measurand excursions In certain data acquisition systems, it is common to check for unreasonable jumps in the value of a certain measurand over two successive cycles, to identify malfunctioning instruments.
Ant.. : Val1, Val 2 > (Val 1 + tol.), cycle time, B
Cons. : Bad data

Succession / precedence violations When a strict succession (or precedence) relation must be maintained between two events, the GPE rule can be used to identify violation of such constraints. A slight modification is necessary to handle this case, so as to provoke an exception as soon as the first event occurs, and without having to wait for the second event.

e.g. Event P must occur before event Q
Ant. : Q, P, infinity, B
Cons. : Precedence violation

More
We treat the following examples given by Luqi [12], to highlight the applicability of our approach to real life processes.

Shutdown : Microwave power must drop to zero within 300 milliseconds of turning off the treatment switch.
Ant. : Turn off switch, Power > 0, 300 ms, A
Cons. : Not specified

Temperature Tolerance : After the system stabilises, the temperature must be kept within 42.4°C and 42.6°C.

We use the property of daisy chaining (cascading), and a temporary event YY to achieve this
Ant. : true, Syst. stable, 0, A
Cons. : YY
Ant. : YY, temp. < 42.4°C, infinity, B
Cons. : Not specified
Ant. : YY, temp. > 42.6°C, infinity, B
Cons. : Not specified

Maximum Temperature : The temperature must never exceed 42.6°C.
This is similar to the example on "limit violations" given above

Startup time : The system must stabilise within 5 minutes of turning on the treatment switch.
Ant. : Treat. switch ON, system not stable, 5 min., A
Cons. : Not specified

Treatment time : The system must shut down automatically when the temperature has been above 42.4°C for 45 minutes.
Ant. : Temp. > 42.4°C, Temp. > 42.4°C, 45 minutes, A
Cons. : Shutdown

As mentioned earlier, GPE rules may be daisy chained (cascaded), to create complex exception handling strategies.

DISCUSSION

We have shown how using very simple mechanisms, an elaborate rule based exception handler can be built. The paradigm of GPEs contributes to the trickiest part of designing expert systems : that of acquiring and representing expert knowledge. Most often, faults in control system design are introduced due to misunderstanding of operational constraints expressed in plain English. GPEs offer a versatile tool for disciplined and unambiguous representation of process exception handling irrespective of the cause of the exception. Besides being a specification tool, they can be directly integrated into the control system. The approach proposed is implementation and language independent.

We also observe the relative simplicity and clarity of representation offered by the GPE approach vis-à-vis models like Petri nets or temporal logic. The knowledge base built using GPE rules offers the possibility of being upgraded in the field, to take unanticipated process contingencies into account.

The structure of GPE rules being very close to human reasoning (causal form), it reduces chances of inadvertent errors. Interpretation of a GPE rule is unique, hence eliminates execution errors. Knowledge bases constructed with GPE rules can be verified formally, for eliminating errors due to inconsistent specifications. These features contribute largely to the robustness of a GPE rule based approach for exception handling.

In production rule based systems, it is often habitual to include a coefficient between 0 and 1 (or -1 and 1) for each rule, and thus manipulate uncertain or subjective information. By adding an attribute to the antecedent (GPE) of a GPE rule, indicating a qualitative aspect of an exception, several interesting extensions for exception handling may be constructed. For instance, by indicating a severity factor for each exception, actions based on the severity of an incident may be invoked. This approach may also be used for prioritising actions or for resolving conflicts in real time. The approach of including uncertainty in rule based systems is a fairly complex subject (see Chatalic et al [13]) and is presently under study as a possible extension to the approach presented in this paper.

ACKNOWLEDGEMENTS

The author expresses his sincere gratitude to the Ecole des Mines de St. Etienne, France, where he is presently on a sabbatical visit.

He is thankful to Prof. P. LADET and to Prof. A. MATHON of the Ecole des Mines de St. Etienne, for the facilities provided and for the encouragement to undertake this assignment.

The author thanks the referees of an earlier version of this paper for their suggestions.

REFERENCES

[1] H.P. Rosenof, A. Ghosh. Batch process automation - Theory and practice. Pub: Van Nostrand Reinhold Co., New York, 1987.

[2] L.P. Goodstein. Functional alarming and information retrieval. Technical Report RISO-M-2511, Riso National Laboratory, Denmark, 1985.

[3] Y.Shoham. Temporal logics in AI - Semantical and ontological considerations. Artificial Intelligence, Vol. 33, No. 1, Sept. 1987.

[4] N.G. Leveson. Software safety - Why, what and how ? ACM Computing Surveys, Vol. 18, No. 2, June 1986.

[5] D.J. Damsker. Alarm monitoring and reporting systems in a distributed control environment, IEEE Trans. Power Apparatus and Systems, Vol.PAS102/9,1983.

[6] B. Dasarathy. Timing constraints of real time systems: Constructs for expressing them, methods for validating them, IEEE Trans. Software Engg., Vol. SE-11/1, Jan. 1985.

[7] A.V. Holt, F. Commoner. Events and conditions. Project MAC Report, MIT Cambridge, 1970.

[8] J. Rasmussen, L.P. Goodstein. Decision support in supervisory control of high risk industrial systems. IFAC Automatica, Vol. 23, No. 5, 1987.

[9] S. Parthasarathy. AUTO_SAFE: Expert controller for sequential and batch sequential processes. (to appear in Engineering Applications of Artificial Intelligence, U.K.)

[10] J.C. Francis, R.R. Leitch. A feedback control scheme based on causal modelling.Proc. IEE, Part - D, July 1987.

[11] P. Vignard (in French). Représentation de connaissances: Mécanismes d'exploitation et d'apprentissage. Pub. INRIA-D-001, Rocquencourt, France, 1985.

[12] Luqi, V. Berzins, R.T.Yeh. A prototyping language for real time software.IEEE Trans. Software Engineering, Vol. SE-14, No. 10, Oct. 1988.

[13] P. Chatalic et al. Rule based systems under uncertainty - Critical discussions and new research directions. Tech. Report No. 300, L.S.I., Toulouse, France, April 1988.

****

An Artificial Intelligence Approach to Manufacturing Workshop Control using a Situation Control Paradigm

F. Vernadat

INRIA-Lorraine, Campus Scientifique, Bd des Aiguillettes, BP 239, 54506 Vandoeuvre-lès-Nancy Cédex, France

ABSTRACT

A global architecture for on-line manufacturing workshop control system is first presented. It includes modules for off-line work preparation, real-time control of the shop-floor, and workshop supervision and monitoring. Next, an original AI-based approach aimed at supporting real-time workshop control and monitoring operations is discussed. This approach is based on situation recognition and situation assessment using data about the current situation, decision rules and generic plans stored in knowledge bases. In case of troubles (unexpected disturbing events or goal deviations), the situation must be recognised, its causes identified, and its consequences foreseen and corrected. This is done using a diagnosis module which makes use of causal networks and performs causal reasoning.

INTRODUCTION

There exists one level in manufacturing systems for which automation and computer science have not yet provided a significant contribution from an industrial point of view. This concerns real-time computer assistance to shop-floor control and monitoring of discrete manufacturing workshops.

In most large size manufacturing companies as well as in many small and medium-sized enterprises, the shop-floor control function is performed by human operators using operations research tools, empirical decision-making rules and expert know-how acquired over the years. They are responsible for the daily operation of the shop, i.e. personnel allocation, timely manufacturing order dispatching, workshop load balancing on available physical manufacturing resources, respect of the daily (or weekly) production schedule, quick and timely reaction to workshop perturbations, etc. In most cases, the production schedule is produced by a computer program or by an MRP system at the medium term planning level [14].

Computer-based very short term control of manufacturing workshops is a very up-to-date problem, but is in fact very difficult if one considers a real-world application of significant size. Artificial Intelligence (AI) techniques are required in the decision-making process of the control system if one considers a feed-back loop control system capable of opportunistic reaction to environment perturbations and capable of increasing the quality of its decision-making capabilities over time [17]. So far, AI research has mainly concentrated on scheduling problems [4,7,20].

The purpose of our work is to define a global architecture and to validate AI-based approaches to support computer and human decision-making in manufacturing workshop control problems. In this paper, the global architecture of the control system used for our experiments is first presented. It includes off-line work preparation, real-time control of the shop-floor, and workshop supervision and monitoring. Next, an original AI technique aimed at supporting real-time workshop control and monitoring operations is discussed. This approach is based on situation recognition and situation assessment and it tries to characterise a workshop situation, and then to decide what to do according to the situation recognised. Actions on the manufacturing system are elaborated by a plan generator using data stored in databases about the current system situation as well as decision rules and generic plans stored in knowledge bases. In case of troubles (unexpected disturbing events or goal deviations), the situation must be recognised, its causes identified, and its consequences foreseen and corrected. To achieve this, the system relies on a diagnostic module, which makes use of a multi-level knowledge representation system involving causal networks and performing causal reasoning. This module is discussed in the last part of the paper.

MANUFACTURING WORKSHOP CONTROL SYSTEMS. PRELIMINARY COMMENTS

Manufacturing workshop control

Controlling manufacturing workshop is a complex decision-making activity largely based on experience and expertise and performed by very skilled operators. It is usually highly dependent on the manufacturing system being controlled. Basically, it involves four major functions [4,18]:

1. A *planning* function, which consists of ordering and scheduling detailed operations (called manufacturing orders) according to resource availability, time constraints, and manufacturing objectives (reduced scraps, quality, etc.).
2. An *execution* function, concerned with order dispatching, shop-floor control, and gathering relevant information from the floor at run time.
3. A *monitoring* function, which has to detect any anomalies during the operations of the system or any deviations from the planning, and to evaluate the possible consequences of such disorders.
4. A *reactive* function to take appropriate and timely action in case of disorders identified by the monitoring function.

These functions are performed by human operators who make use of a limited number of global *indicators* about the current situation of the system and many local indicators about system components. Indicators give information on the status of static and dynamic system characteristics (work-in-process inventories, raw material stock level, machine loads, production rates, etc.). The control function can thus be done at a *global* or at a *local* level (i.e. workshop level, machine cell level or machine level). The control is made according to global manufacturing objectives (quality of products, respect of due dates, occupancy of personnel, etc.), and using workshop dependent control policies.

The purpose of our work is not to try to completely automate the functions of the workshop controller but to automate as much as possible easy and routine work as well as monitoring tasks, and to provide the user with a powerful support taking the full complexity of the system into account to improve his decision-making abilities.

The solution proposed

In our approach, we make several fundamental assumptions [19]:

- complex systems (such as manufacturing systems) require sophisticated, multiple-representation modelling schemes;
- complex system control requires both analytical, function-oriented, model-based, and heuristic-based solutions; and in many cases
- the decision-making process makes use of situation concepts and requires various sources of knowledge about situation evaluation and system evolution rules (strategies, policies, constraints, etc.).

Therefore, the solution proposed is based on the following considerations:

a. Situation recognition and situation control concepts: The situation concept is used to evaluate the state and system behaviour. This concept will also prove to be useful for detecting abnormal behaviour of the system (e.g. deviations from objectives). The control of the system then takes into account the possible evolutions of the system situation and its current trend.

b. Causal models and causal reasoning: Since a diagnostic function is involved for monitoring purposes, there is a need for causal models in the form of semantic networks to represent deep knowledge about the cause-action-result relationships and for making causal reasoning to confirm causes of a given trouble among several plausible hypotheses.

c. Hybrid data and knowledge representation: Computerised systems such as manufacturing workshops need to be described in terms of databases and knowledge bases. Various data and knowledge representation formalisms need to be employed in order to fulfil specific requirements of each function (e.g. object-oriented database for structural and functional models, object or frame representation for situations, production rules for heuristic knowledge, semantic networks for causal models and situation evolution graphs).

d. Knowledge-based supervision module: Meta-knowledge is used to coordinate control and monitor operations. This knowledge is heuristic in nature and represents the current understanding of how to operate the full system according to currently known situation control classes (called contexts). Obviously, this knowledge may vary over time according to system constraints and objectives, and to user understanding. Furthermore, the rule-based orientation of the supervisor module allows easy adaptation of the global system to a specific application area. In other words, this knowledge can be tailored to specific needs for a given application domain, for a particular business site, or for a particular piece of equipment.

A GLOBAL ARCHITECTURE FOR REAL-TIME MANUFACTURING WORKSHOP CONTROL

The workshop control architecture

Figure 1 presents the global architecture of the system being used for experimentations. It is composed of three major modules (off-line preparation, real-time control, workshop supervision and monitoring), and some underlying models (graph of constraints, dynamic workshop representation consisting of conceptual models, functional models, a manufacturing database, a workshop database and a real-time database, and some knowledge bases). More detailed information is given by Vernadat [18].

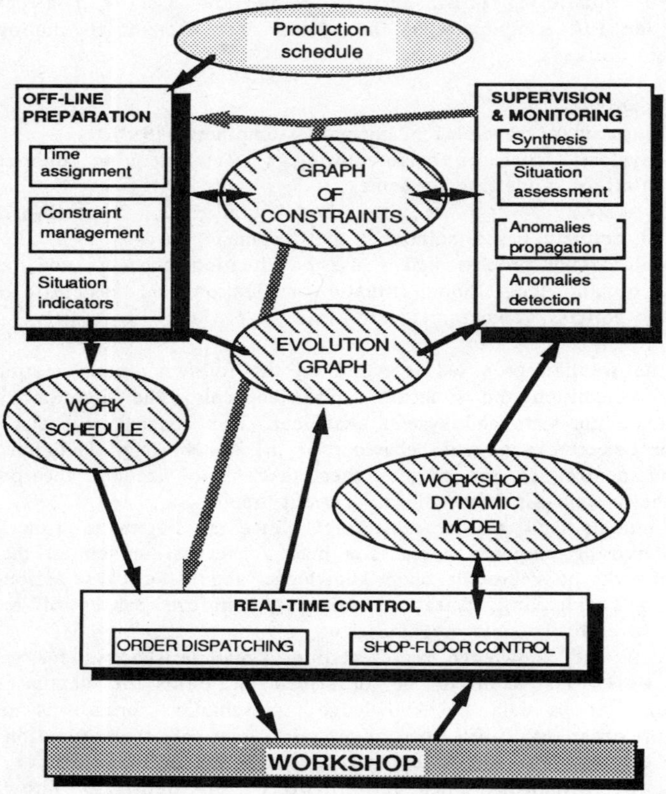

Figure 1. Global Architecture for Manufacturing Workshop Control

The off-line preparation module prepares the detailed daily work schedule for the shop, i.e. the set of operations and activities. This is done using production schedule data, data from the production planning databases, data about the status of the workshop, and generic action plans from the evolution graph. The production schedule is issued from an MRP system and gives the list of orders to be processed, the order due dates and priorities. The module (not to be confused with a manufacturing scheduling program) performs three steps:

1. First, time windows are assigned to each manufacturing operation and a list of operations is associated to each machine. This is obtained from the process plans of products to be manufactured and the quantities to be produced. Conflicts on resource allocation are not considered at this step.

2. Second, constraint management is performed to eliminate some of the solutions accepted in the first step. Especially, constraint propagation is performed on the graph of constraints. These constraints involve process plan and bills-of-materials (BOM) constraints, operating constraints and, temporal constraints. Constraint management may result in modification of time intervals and of operation sequences on resources as defined in the first step.

3. Third, global situation indicators are computed for given periods of time of the schedule horizon. They indicate the number of parts or orders which should be processed and the working time to be spent. They are then used by the supervision module.

The real-time workshop control module performs two major functions:

1. One function is order dispatching. This is done by a simple rule-based expert system sending manufacturing orders to groups of machines and taking into account information about shop-floor status, manufacturing order priorities, and work schedule directives. The rules in the knowledge base reflect the dispatching policies to be used for each work area (heuristic rules). They can be dynamically changed by the control system (shop-floor supervision module) for reaction in case of perturbations.

2. The second function is shop-floor control, i.e. data acquisition and dynamic models updating. Data acquisition is performed via computer terminals, bar-code readers, photovoltaic cells, electrical switches, etc. Some data are directly used to stop machines or set alarms. Most data are formatted, aggregated, and stored in databases (workshop database and real-time database). Information in the real-time database can be directly used by the order dispatching expert system or by the workshop supervision module.

The workshop control and monitoring function is made using **situation assessment**. This is the role of the workshop supervision module, the goals of which are:

- to detect and identify troubles and anomalies on the shop-floor (machine break-downs, perturbations, disturbances, deviations from the planning);
- to evaluate the consequences of anomalies;
- to decide on or propose corrective actions;
- to modify the graph of constraints and the work schedule according to encountered situations, and follow system evolution on the evolution graph.

To achieve these goals, the module performs the following functions:

1. anomalies detection and analysis: This is done on the basis of situation recognition and situation assessment principles and causal reasoning as explained later. Anomalies are detected, characterised, and classified. They are then reported to the supervisor level;

2. anomalies propagation: Once the troubles or anomalies have been characterised, their consequences are anticipated on the future of the workshop using a simulation package and causal nets;

3. dispatching rules alteration: From the results of the simulation of anomalies propagation, the system tries to define new dispatching policies (i.e. suggest modifications to the knowledge base of the order dispatching expert system) to correct the current situation. Eventually, this attempt may fail because of the heuristic nature of this approach. User action is thus required;

4. global situation assessment: The global situation of the workshop is evaluated according to results of the previous functions. This is done at predefined instants (defined in the work schedule) or on user's request. The evolution graph of the workshop is analysed and decision strategies are evaluated. According to situations, a synthesis is made and presented on the control dashboard of the user interface;

5. synthesis: This is the global decision-making level based on global situation assessment. The system makes proposals to the workshop controller. Proposals may be: to stop the system (impossibility to meet the objectives), to ask for the preparation of a new work schedule, to modify the dispatching rules, or to do nothing (i.e. continue operations using the same policies).

<u>System organisation</u>

The previous section has introduced the necessary basic concepts and established clearly that the control of complex manufacturing workshops using situation concepts requires processing of basic data, surface and deep knowledge at various levels of details, and interpretation of conceptual and causal models of the shop. Therefore, control modules of Fig. 1 are logically structured into a three-layer reasoning system according to functions performed and abstraction of information processed (Fig. 2), and consists of:

1. A data level: This low level performs quantitative reasoning on masses of data stored in relational and object-oriented databases. Data items represent cumulative and historical information on the system state and evolution. A logging file of actions performed is maintained with the date of action execution. Detailed information on system entities and their relationships are captured and stored on disks and can support procedural and database transaction processing as required by the application.

2. A conceptual behaviour level: This intermediate level is aimed at providing heuristic reasoning, quantitative and qualitative reasoning, detailed causal reasoning, and situation assessment facilities based on the interpretation of knowledge bases containing production rules (representing heuristics, evolution rules, situation evaluation rules, etc.), frames (representing situation descriptions, workshop object and activity representations, etc.), semantic nets (for evolution graphs), and causal networks (for system diagnosis). At this level, extensive symbolic and procedural computations are performed. The use of a tandem architecture allowing cooperation of algorithms with expert systems [8] is currently under investigation.

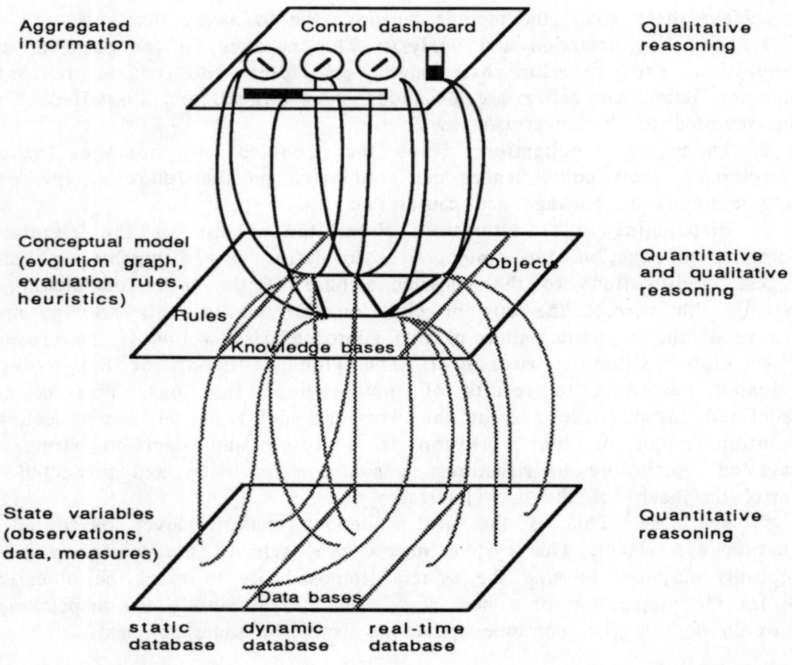

Figure 2. Reasoning Levels

3. A qualitative reasoning level: This level provides the user with synthetic information in the form of gauges, histograms, and other icons forms via the user interface. Information is about the global situation of the workshop (production rate, delays, workshop load, in-process inventory levels, etc.) or about a given sub-system (machine-cell, station, or machine). Qualitative reasoning on aggregated data or data directly issued from sensors is performed in order to supervise system evolution, detect system anomalies, suggest hypotheses in case of troubles, and decide on corrective actions to be taken. Knowledge representation at this level is in the form of production rules and simplified causal networks.

User interface: The user interface is supposed to:
- get commands from the user (treated as external events)
- provide the user with results and synthetic information in the form of a control dashboard using graphical capabilities
- suggest actions in the case of serious system breakdowns or ask user's help in case of reasoning dead-ends
- explain recommendations made (WHY command) or give detailed information on specified system components (parsing object hierarchies).

Implementation of such an architecture requires a 32-bit workstation with large internal memory (at least 8 M-bytes). Experimentations are being made on a UNIX machine with Common-LISP having an object-oriented sub-system (for algorithmic and symbolic processing) and graphical capabilities. A blackboard architecture for shared memory implementation is under consideration.

System models

Various models and knowledge bases have to be used to support the control and monitoring system execution. In this section, we provide information on conceptual models (i.e. structural models and functional models) being part of the workshop dynamic model of Fig. 1.

Structural models: These models are used to describe the physical system structure and its components using an object-oriented approach. In the case of a manufacturing workshop, the workshop structure is organised as a workshop-cell-workstation-machine hierarchy (Fig. 3). Machines execute operations on parts using tools. In practice, information modelling is performed using an extended entity-relationship model and the M* methodology [5]. Entities of the structure are represented as objects with attributes and methods attached to them. They are defined as follows:

Object definition:	Method definition:
(define-type object	(define-method object : method
(:var attribute (option)*)	(parameter list)
(:var ...)	(method code))
...)	

option can be used to define an attribute type, a default value, or predefined methods

Example:
```
(setq m1 (make-instance 'machine-tool
        :name 'PCN_Amada_1
        :type 'stamping_machine
        :tool_list '(T15 T21 T30)
```

```
        :tool_chg_time  '(10 10 15)
        :status  'idle
        :operator  ( )
        :current_tool  'TIS
        :current_job  ( ) ) )
```

Method examples:
load: change status to "loaded" and affect a current_job
unload: change status to "idle" and put current_job to nil
affect_ope: affect an operator identification
change_tool: set correct value of current_tool

Functional models: Functional models are required to represent descriptions of manufacturing processes. They describe activities involved in the processes and their interrelationships in terms of ordering constructs [3]. The control constructs taken into account include sequencing, selection, fork and join for parallelism and non-determinism, and repeat (loop) and are illustrated in Fig. 4. Activities are represented as objects. Their description includes information about their inputs, their outputs, required resources to execute them, their duration (if known), and execution preconditions and postconditions in the form of logical predicates. Algorithms for their executions are contained in associated methods. Activities can be specialisations of more general activities, thus allowing various levels of detail in the functional models. Example of an activity:

```
(setq  milling_operation_12_1  (make-instance  'machining_operation
        :isa  operation_activity
        :inputs  '(Part P12 Program PP12)
        :outputs  '(Part P12)
        :req_res  '(Operator Tool)
        :duration  1.33
        :precond '(READY (Machine) and READY (Tool) and LOADED (Program))
        :postcond '(STOPPED (Machine) and SIGNAL (FINISHED))))
```

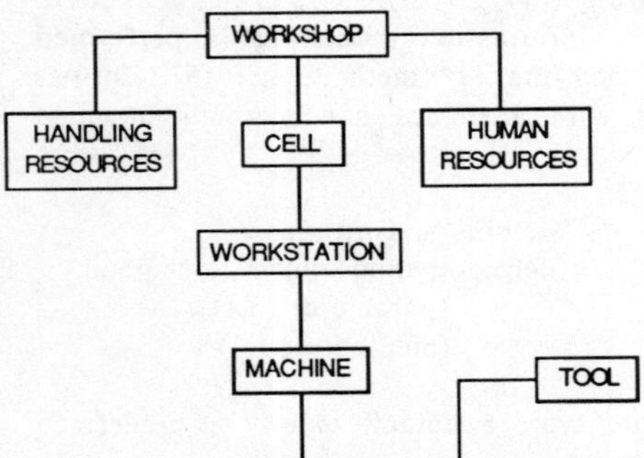

Figure 3. Structural Model

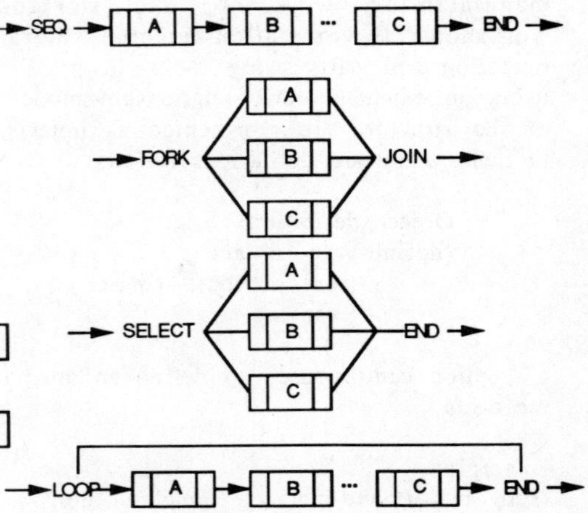

Figure 4. Functional Model Ordering Constructs

Other models such as **situation evolution graphs** and **causal models** are being used and are discussed in the next sections. All these models are loaded and operated in main memory. Permanent data are kept on disk in relational database form (not discussed here).

PRINCIPLES OF SITUATION RECOGNITION AND SITUATION CONTROL

Decision-making process and the situation concept

The concept of situation is a very natural concept used in everyday life to make decisions [11,13,18].

The decision-making process using the situation concept requires:
- knowledge about the initial (or starting) situation;
- knowledge about the desired situation (the goal);
- knowledge about activities (or actions) allowing transition from one situation to another;
- and knowledge about evolution rules (strategies, policies, constraints, etc.).

Difficulties in building decision-making systems using the situation concepts will reside in developing reliable knowledge bases representing these various kinds of knowledge, in the definition of the activities, and in making artful use of evolution rules.

Situation definition

A **situation** is a generalisation of the concept of state (as used in Automatic Control theory) associated to a real-world entity used to characterise a reasoning process, which takes into account possible evolutions of this state in a given context. The concept of situation thus involves:

1. The notion of real-world object or *entity*: A situation always refers to one or several system objects or entities.

2. The notion of state variables or *attributes* of an entity (also called *situation indicators*): A state is usually characterised by a vector of state variables, which are properties of an entity and which describe the entity state.

3. The notion of *context* of a situation: A situation relative to one or several entities is only valid for a given context. Depending on the context considered, situation evaluation is not based on the same set of attributes and does not use the same procedures and evaluation rules (e.g. the economical vs. the operational situations of a manufacturing workshop).

A *quantitative* representation of a situation S at a given instant t relative to m entities E_i can be formally described by the following expression:

$$S = (t, \{x_1, ..., x_j, ..., x_n\})$$

in which x_j (j=1, ..., n) are n state variables of entities E_i (i=1, ..., m). The representation of S is a point in a nth-dimensional space at time t (Fig. 5).

A *qualitative* representation of the situation S is formally described by:

$$S' = f(t, c_1, ..., c_k, ..., c_l)$$

where t represents an instant or time interval; $c_k \varepsilon C$ set of conditions on attributes x_j of entities E_i, and f is a logical function connecting the conditions. The result is a value from a finite set of possible situation descriptions (Fig. 6).

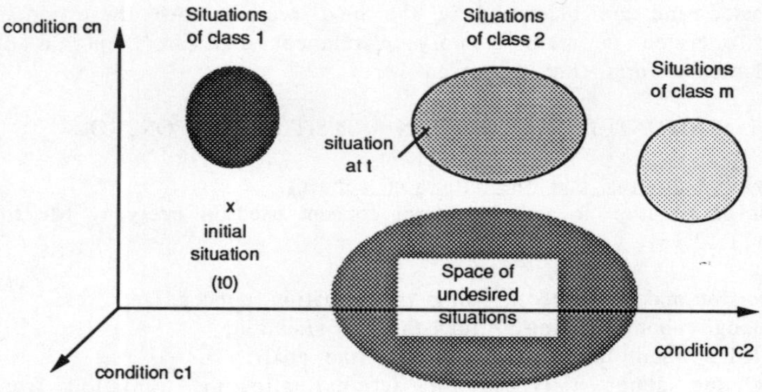

Figure 5. Quantitative Situation Space

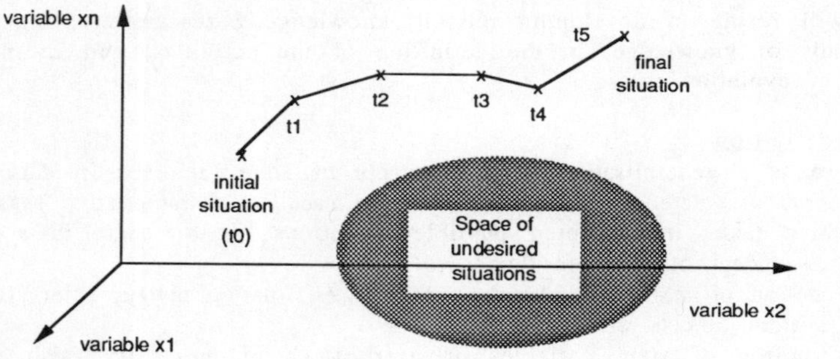

Figure 6. Qualitative Situation Space

Entities are objects of the structural model (see section on system models). Qualitative and quantitative situations are also represented as objects in the computer.

An **environment** is a restriction of some part of the real-world for a given application. The real-world is described by its entities or objects, their relationships, and the constraints defined on their attributes.

These definitions are close to definitions used in McCarthy's situation calculus [9,10]. The situation calculus is a first-order language in which predicate values (true or false) can vary over time to indicate what situations they hold in.

Example: An example of an environment may be the control of the manufacturing workshop P1 in plant A of company ABC. The workshop is composed of several entities described by their attributes. For a given context, the quantitative situations of some entities are evaluated using attribute values. From these, qualitative situations can be assessed. This information can be used to establish the global situation of the workshop (Fig. 7).

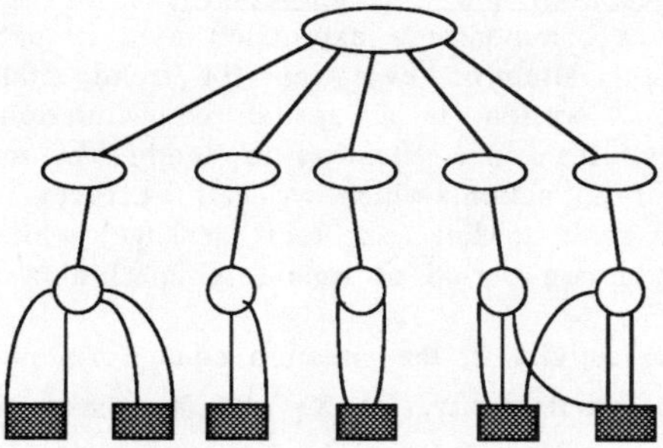

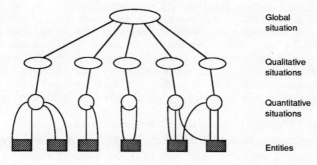

Figure 7. Situation Hierarchies

Situation recognition and assessment

Given a set of observable facts about a system, and given a set of interpretation rules, the goal of situation recognition and assessment is to identify and to analyse the temporal state of a system (or of some of its components). For example, in the case of a manufacturing workshop, assessment of the global situation requires:

1. The definition of situation indicators (observable facts) selected among attributes of entities of the workshop. In practice, we can use the following indicators (qualitative or quantitative):

PR: production rate
PC: total production cost
WIP: value of work-in-process inventories in dollar
NoOp: total of number of operations to be performed
NoFiOp: number of finished operations
NoDeOp: number of delayed operations
NoCaOp: number of cancelled operations
MaxCap: maximal capacity of the workshop
Accident: accident indicator (Boolean)

2. Situation recognition: It consists in obtaining the values of the attributes of the quantitative situation representation and verifying that the values of some attributes are under some predefined thresholds or within a specified range. Otherwise, the system may be in trouble and supervisor action is requested.

3. Qualitative situation assessment using interpretation rules: These heuristic rules (stored as production rules) represent in fact the function f introduced earlier. Here is an example in the case of the manufacturing workshop:

Evaluation = "good working condition" if
Accident = "no" and WIP <= 5000 and NoOp >= INT (MaxCap * 0.85) and
NoDeOp <= INT (NoOp * 0.10) and NoCaOp <= INT (NoOp * 0.01)

indicating that the workshop operates well if WIP is low, if it works at 85% of its total capacity, if the number of delayed operations is under 10% of the total number of operations, if there are very few operations cancelled and if there is no accident.

Interpretation rules are stored in a situation evaluation knowledge base. The situation recognition module runs permanently for entities controlled, while global situation assessment is done upon controller's request and at predefined instants.

Situation evolution, action planning and situation control

"Evolution of a situation" is a commonsense expression used in natural language. In many cases, following the situation evolution (or trend analysis) is very useful in making decisions. A system is always in one situation for a given context. A system can evolve from one situation to another in response to the occurrence of an event or of an action, which we call **activity**. An event is a short activity occurring at a given instant (e.g. tool breakage) while an action is an activity occurring over a certain period of time (e.g. machining operation).

A formal definition of an activity in the situation context follows: Let S_1 and S_2 be two situations of the same entity, let X_1 and X_2 be activity supports (information objects and resources), and let C be a set of conditions (constraints on X_1 and X_2), an activity a is defined by a mapping δ transforming the initial situation S_1 into the final situation S_2 if the set of conditions of C is satisfied. We can write:

$$a = (S_1, \delta, X_1, X_2, C, S_2)$$

where

$$\delta : (S_1 \wedge X_1 \wedge X_2) \dashrightarrow S_2 \text{ if } C$$

Activities are represented as objects in the functional models. The formalism just introduced can be graphically represented by a graph or an automaton in which nodes represent situations and arcs represent activity executions. This model is called the **situation evolution graph** (Fig. 8) and is implemented as a semantic network. In such a model, the same activity can be involved in several arcs, situations are qualitative situations, and the arcs are of two types: WILLP indicating that the activity will produce the output situation, or MAYP indicating that the activity may produce the output situation. Loops can be modelled easily. The various possible configurations are illustrated in Fig. 9.

This formalism is different from Petri nets. Petri nets have been suggested for modelling dynamic manufacturing system behaviour [12,16]. However, because of cases d and e in Fig. 9 we prefer evolution graphs. These graphs as well as functional models represent **normal workshop behaviour** (state, structure, and dynamic behaviour).

Obviously, this kind of model is of great value for action planning and situation control because paths in the network correspond to evolution rules of the situation. Each path (or portion of it) in the graph represents a possible action plan to drive the system entity from one situation to another and is used as such during the action planning task. Situation control consists in driving the system in real-time from its current situation to a desired (or planned) situation and avoiding undesirable situations. To do this, situations of critical system components must be recognised, their evolutions recorded and compared to plans and to evolution graphs. If deviations from normal operations are detected, or if an event leading to an undesired situation happens, then a message is sent to the supervisor level for information and for making corrective actions.

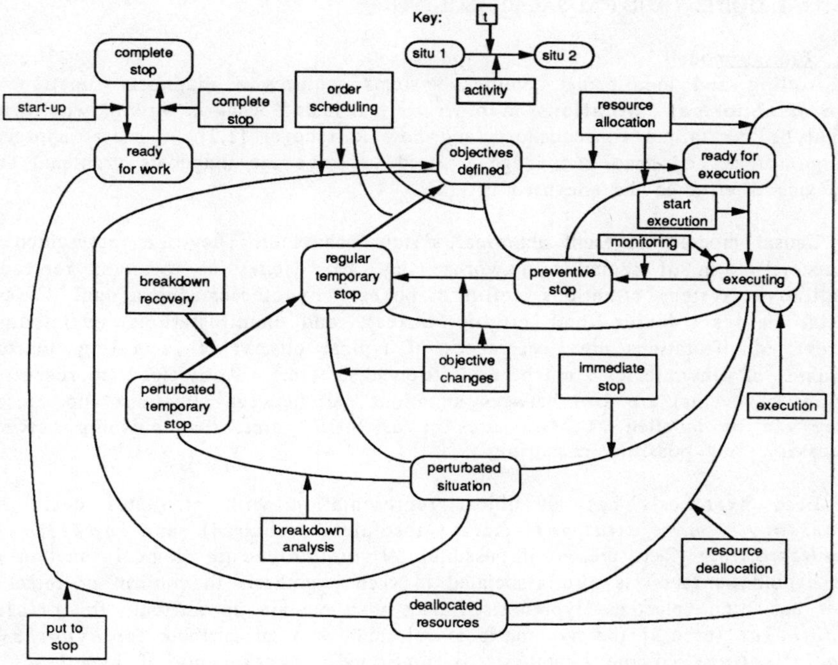

Figure 8. Situation Evolution Graph

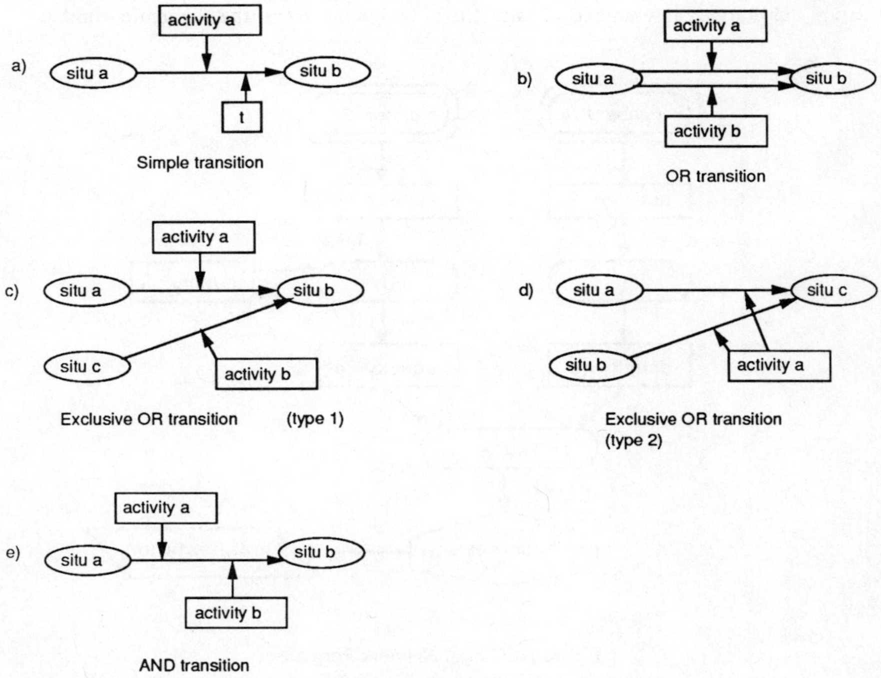

Figure 9. Various Possible Situation Configurations

CAUSAL MODELS AND CAUSAL REASONING

5.1. Causal models

Controlling and monitoring complex systems requires a diagnosis function in case of **abnormal situations** in order to understand what is wrong, why, what might be the failure consequences, and how to recover [1,2]. A causal approach using surface and deep knowledge is used to solve the diagnosis problem. This approach is close to the one used in [15].

Causal models represent abnormal system behaviour. They are represented as a special form of semantic networks (Fig. 10). Nodes of the nets represent qualitative system situations (elliptic boxes), hypotheses (hexagonal boxes), initial causes (double-lined elliptic boxes), and manifestations (rhomboidal boxes). Manifestations are occurrences of typical observable facts (e.g. unusual volume of inventories, machine bottlenecks, etc.). Activities (representing actions or events) are arcs between situations and between situations and causes. They can be labelled as MAY arcs or as MUST arcs, distinguishing between necessary and possible causalities.

Each hypothesis has an object representation with attributes describing *necessary manifestations* (facts absolutely required) and *additional manifestations* (facts present if possible). A *validation rule* (logical function of the hypothesis facts) is also associated to each hypothesis to confirm or reject it if it has been selected. Hypothesis frames also contain an attribute for *related hypotheses* (used if the hypothesis is rejected), and an attribute for *hypothesis specialisations* (if the hypothesis is confirmed). A taxonomy of hypotheses is thus made possible. Beside the causal models, a diagnosis knowledge base is maintained. It contains production rules to select hypotheses (triggering rules) using qualitative assessment of situations and data from the dynamic model.

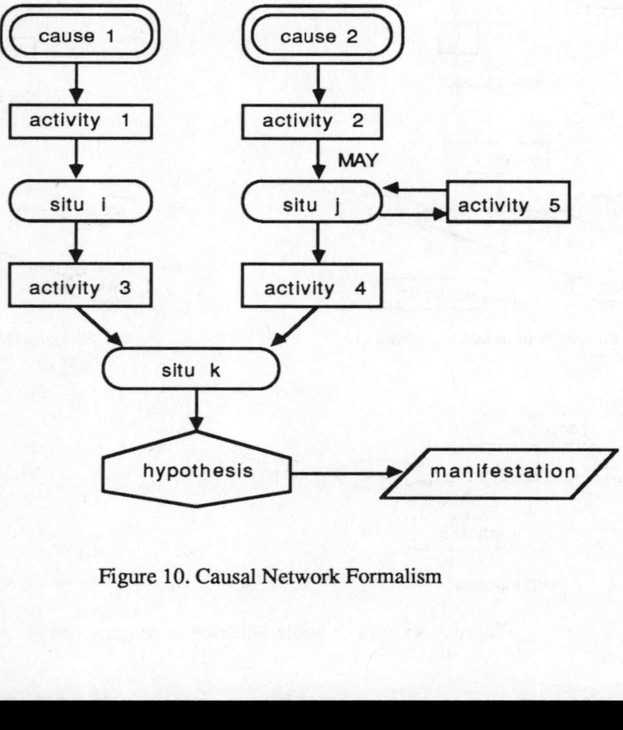

Figure 10. Causal Network Formalism

An example of the structure of object used follows:

FRAME: bottleneck_formation
TRIGGERING RULE:
(nb_of_waiting_items increasing) OR (WIP_value >= WIP_limit)
NECESSARY MANIFESTATIONS:
work_centre_status: working
nb_of_waiting_items: average
WIP_value: 5000
...
ADDITIONAL MANIFESTATIONS:
accident: no
maintenance_time: 10
...
VALIDATION RULES:
R1: **exclude** if status (subsequent (work_centre_id)) = "down"
R2: ...

Causal reasoning

When a problem requiring the diagnostic function is detected (e.g. heavy production tardiness), the diagnosis function is activated and it gets data in dynamic memory. The diagnostic rule base is first scanned using forward and backward chaining to generate possible hypotheses. Next, a hypothesis must be selected and confirmed. This is the role of the causal sub-system, which first instantiates the hypotheses retained. Discrimination of the various possibilities is first attempted using necessary facts. This process is then refined using additional facts only for hypotheses having all their necessary facts correctly instantiated. Validation rules are then used to further confirm or reject hypotheses. Then, pattern matching on the causal model is made to try to recognise the current state of the system behaviour. Then, the logging file (containing the history of actions performed by the system) is used to find a path in the causal model leading to the current situation. Reasoning backward in time on the model allows to find all causes of the trouble. Then, once the right path from the causes to the actual situation is found (going forward), the right hypothesis is confirmed. Finally, going forward in the causal net indicates possible consequences of the current situation. Due to the presence of MAY arcs in the causal net, causal reasoning is non-monotonic and may lead to several solutions in some cases. In this case, the suggestions are given to the user who must make the final decision.

CONCLUSION

In this work, we have defined a global architecture for very short term control of manufacturing workshops based on a new and original paradigm called situation control and assessment. In this paper, we have focused on the control and monitoring module with special emphasis on the diagnostic and control functions using the situation concept and causal reasoning. Knowledge representation and reasoning techniques required have been detailed. The two other modules of the global architecture are not discussed in this paper.

This approach is a model-based approach in which (a) conceptual models are used to describe what is being used (structural models) and how it works (functional models), (b) situation models are used to indicate what is the state of the system (qualitative and quantitative situations) and how to control it (situation evolution graphs), and (c) causal models are used to state what is wrong, why, and how to recover.

Future work will concern theoretical extension of the concepts presented and refinement of their implementation details. Especially, we are considering modal logics as used by Moore [11] and possibility theory [6] to enrich the situation concepts. Also, further work remains to be done to include time reasoning in the paradigm, which is currently one of the weaknesses of the approach. Dealing with uncertain information, modelling non deterministic environment, and learning new situations are our current major concerns.

Acknowledgements
Part of this work has been performed while the author was at LIFIA, Grenoble, France as a visiting scientist sponsored by the NRCC/CNRS cooperation research program between France and Canada. The author is greatly indebted to all members of LIFIA who have participated in the workshop control project.

References

1. Atwood, M.E., and Radlinski, E.R. Structure d'un système de diagnostic, *Revue des Télécommunications* 60(2):174-176, 1986.
2. Atwood, M.E., R. Brooks, and Radlinski, E.R. Modèles causals: la prochaine génération des systèmes experts, *Revue des Télécommunications* 60(2):180-184, 1986.
3. Becker, L.A., and Kinigadner, A. Manufacturing process representations for distributed diagnosis of execution errors. In *Expert Systems: Strategies and Solutions in Manufacturing Design and Planning* (Ed. Kusiak, A.). Society of Manufacturing Engineers, Dearborn, MI. pp. 347-368, 1988.
4. Bourne, D.A., Fox, M.S. Autonomous manufacturing: automating the job-shop. *IEEE Computer* 77-88, Sept. 1984.
5 DiLeva, A., Giolito, P., and Vernadat, F. Production system specification. The M* approach. Chapt. 12 In *Expert Systems: Strategies and Solutions in Manufacturing Design and Planning* (Ed. Kusiak, A.). Society of Manufacturing Engineers, Dearborn, MI. pp. 369-374, 1988.
6. Dubois, D. and Prade, H. *Théorie des Possibilités. Applications à la Représentation des Connaissances en Informatique*. Masson, Paris, 1986.
7. Fox, M.S. ISIS: a constraint-directed reasoning approach to job-shop scheduling. Carnegie-Mellon University, 1983.
8. Kusiak, A. (Ed.). *Artificial Intelligence: Implications for CIM*, IFS (Publications) and Springer-Verlag. pp. 3-23, 1988.
9. McCarthy, J. Programs with common sense. In *Semantic Information Processing* (M. Minsky, ed.), MIT PRess, Cambridge, MA, 1968.
10. McCarthy, J., and Hayes, P.J. Some philosophical problems from the standpoint of artificial intelligence. In *Machine Intelligence 4* (Eds. Meltzer, B. and Mitchie, D.), Edinburgh University Press, Edinburgh. pp. 463-502, 1969.
11. Moore, R.C. A formal theory of knowledge and action. In *Formal Theories of the Commonsense World* (Eds. Hobbs, J.R. and Moore, R.C.), Ablex Publishing Co., Norwood, NJ, 1985.
12. Pagnoni, A. A Petri net-based expert system for flexible manufacturing management. IX European Workshop on Applications and Theory of Petri Nets, Venice, Italy. pp. 270-278, 1988.
13. Pun, L. Situation recognition and production management problems. *APMS 85 Conf. on Advanced Production Management Systems*, Budapest, Hungary, 1985.
14. Salvendy, G. (Ed.). *Handbook of Industrial Engineering*. Wiley & Sons, New York, NY, 1982.

15. Torasso, P. and Console L. Causal reasoning in diagnostic espert systems. *SPIE Vol. 786 Applications of Artificial Intelligence V*. pp. 598-605, 1987.

16. Valette, R. Nets in production systems. In *Petri Nets Applications and Relationships to Other Models of Concurrency*. Lectures Notes in Computer Science No. 255. Springer-Verlag, Berlin, 1987.

17. Vernadat, F. An artificial intelligence approach to manufacturing job-shop control. Proc. 4th Int. Conf. on Systems Research, Informatics, and Cybernetics, Baden-Baden, FRG, 1988.

18. Vernadat, F. Reconnaissance de Situation et Commande Situationnelle pour la Conduite des Ateliers de Production. Research Report RR 696-I-IMAG 69 LIFIA, Informatique et Mathématiques Appliquées de Grenoble (IMAG), Grenoble, France, 1988.

19. Vernadat, F. Control and monitoring of complex systems using situation and causal knowledge. Submitted to 11th. Int. Joint Conf. on Artificial Intelligence (IJCAI 89), 1989.

20. Wright, P., Bourne, D. *Manufacturing Intelligence*. Addison-Wesley, Reading, MA, 1987.

Learning New Rules and Adapting Old Ones with the Genetic Algorithm

Terence C. Fogarty

The Transputer Centre, Bristol Polytechnic, Bristol, UK

ABSTRACT

A rule-based system for optimising combustion in a multiple burner furnace is introduced and its manual adaption for use on another installation described. The automatic adaption of the rule-base using an incremental genetic algorithm on simulations of the domain is then investigated.

ACKNOWLEDGEMENT

This work was supported by the Science and Engineering Research Council and by British Steel. (SERC/CASE award no. 86518692)

INTRODUCTION

A rule-based system for optimising combustion in multiple burner installations was developed, tested and used successfully on a twelve burner zone of the 108 burner furnace of a continuous annealing line for rolled steel as described by Fogarty [1]. When commissioning this system on a double burner boiler in the steam generating plant of a tinplate finishing works it was found that the rule-base was not very efficient at dealing with the automatic modulation of firing levels to the boiler in response to changing levels of demand for steam from the works. The rule-base was not built with this problem in mind since the multiple burner furnace on which it was developed had only one firing level and the zones went on or off in response to changes in demand rather than having their firing levels modulated.

This is an example of what Holland [2] calls "expert system's brittleness"; in the face of new and unexpected conditions the expert system cannot cope. In these circumstances a human expert proves his worth by applying what he knows and his ability to learn more to the new problem; he increases his expertise by exchanging what he already knows for the opportunity to learn more (e.g. Gaines [3]).

The short term solution to this problem was to revise the existing rules and create new ones to cope with the changed situation. How this was done in order to get a reliable working system is described. The long term solution is to automate this adaptive process using machine learning. We investigate the second approach using an incremental version of the genetic algorithm on ten simulations of ten burner installations with two firing levels. How the automatically adapted rule-bases compare and contrast with the manually adapted one is examined.

THE ORIGINAL RULE-BASE

Procedures for adjusting the air inlet valves to each of a number of burners with a common flue, in which the concentrations of oxygen and carbon monoxide are monitored, were elicited from energy engineers as in Edmundson et al [4]. Basically, nine types of situation were identified, depending upon the combination of the classification of carbon monoxide and oxygen readings as "high", "O.K." or "low". Figure 1 summarises the procedures for these situations.

The procedures have two different kinds of effect. Firstly, they can alter the positions of the air inlet valves by initiating either single actions, such as "Reduce air to all burners", or multiple actions, such as "Lean burner correction routine". A summary of the multiple action routines is shown in figure 2. Secondly, they can alter the parameters of the procedures such as the oxygen limits and the increments by which air valves are adjusted. These procedures embody the practice of the fuel technician who periodically tunes multiple

	carbon monoxide low	carbon monoxide O.K.	carbon monoxide high
oxygen high	Increase increments by 100% Reduce air to all burners	Increase increments by 100% Lean burner correction routine	Rich burner correction routine Lean burner correction routine
oxygen O.K.	Reduce oxygen limits by 1% Lean burner correction routine	Excess air improvement routine	Rich burner correction routine
oxygen low	Reduce oxygen limits by 5%	Reduce oxygen limits by 5%	Increase air to all burners

Figure 1: The Original Rules

```
LEAN BURNER CORRECTION ROUTINE:
  reduce air to each burner in turn
  IF CO increases by more than 1/N of the difference between
    previous and maximum CO
  THEN reverse the action and reduce increment by 50%
  ELSE leave

EXCESS AIR IMPROVEMENT ROUTINE:
  reduce air to each burner in turn
  IF CO increases by more than 1/N of the difference between
    previous and maximum CO
  THEN reverse the action and reduce increment by 66%
  ELSE leave and increase increment by 50%

RICH BURNER CORRECTION ROUTINE:
  increase air to each burner in turn
  IF CO is reduced
  THEN leave
  ELSE reverse the action and reduce increment by 50%
```

Figure 2: The Routines (N=number of burners)

burner installations together with the expertise of the energy engineer who has devised a system for the continuous optimisation of such installations.

These procedures can be expressed as rules of the situation-action type, where the situation is governed by carbon monoxide and oxygen readings and change in carbon monoxide, classified according to constant or variable system parameters, and the action is a combination of adjustments to air inlet valve settings and system parameters.

All the rules are of the form: "IF situation THEN action" but chains of up to three of these are accommodated to encapsulate the procedures outlined by the experts. The longest chains are therefore of the form:

```
"IF situation 1 THEN action 1
      THEN IF situation 2 THEN action 2
           THEN IF situation 3 THEN action 3".
```

Each of the readings, oxygen and carbon monoxide, is classified as one of: "low", "O.K." or "high" according to carbon monoxide parameters which remain fixed and variable optimum oxygen parameters. The change in carbon monoxide since the last reading is classified as one of: "neg"(ative), "nil" or "pos"(itive), nil being positive but less than the difference between the last reading and the upper optimum limit for carbon monoxide divided by the number of burners. Every eventuality is covered by a rule and there are no conflicting rules for any situation. Thus our rule-base acts as a dynamic look-up table of actions to be performed in each set of circumstances.

COMMISSIONING THE RULE-BASE

The rules, together with a shell and all necessary interfacing software, were coded into Turbo Prolog on a personal computer. An air-inlet valve was fixed to each of the burners on one zone of the furnace of a continuous annealing line for rolled steel and a thermocouple and an oxygen and a carbon monoxide analyser set in the common flue. These were connected to the computer via an analog/digital converter and the system commissioned. This involved building a statistical filter for the noisy carbon monoxide signal and estimating the best values for the upper and lower carbon monoxide limits and initial values, upper and lower limits for the oxygen limits and for the increments associated with each burner. The system was then run successfully with good results on the furnace for about one month until the experimental hardware became unusable.

One of five double burner boilers in the steam generating plant of a tinplate finishing works was chosen for long term testing of the system and equipped with durable air-inlet louvres to the burners and an oxygen and a carbon monoxide analyser and a thermocouple in the common flue. The system was commissioned in the same way as before and ran successfully while the boiler was at high fire. The results of one test run, with the air-inlet valves fully open to begin with, are graphed in figure 3. This shows the valve positions actuated by the rule-base at one minute intervals and the resulting oxygen and carbon monoxide readings together with the calculated stackloss which is a measure of how much energy is wasted in the flue gasses in heat and unburnt fuel.

However, a different picture emerged when the firing level of the boiler was allowed to fluctuate in response to demand for steam from the works. It can be seen from figure 4 that the rule-base does respond to these changes but sometimes in a very sluggish manner and at others rather erratically. After about 14 minutes from the beginning of the results shown, the firing level changes, causing the carbon monoxide concentration to rise dramatically. The system takes over 20 minutes to adjust to the altered situation. Then the firing level changes again, this time causing the oxygen concentration to rise. The system reacts faster to this alteration and brings the oxygen down within three minutes but this is followed by some erratic movements of the valves until the firing level again changes causing another rise in carbon monoxide and another period of gradual adjustment to the situation.

EFFECT OF AIR VALVE CLOSURE ON OXYGEN, CARBON MONOXIDE AND STACKLOSS

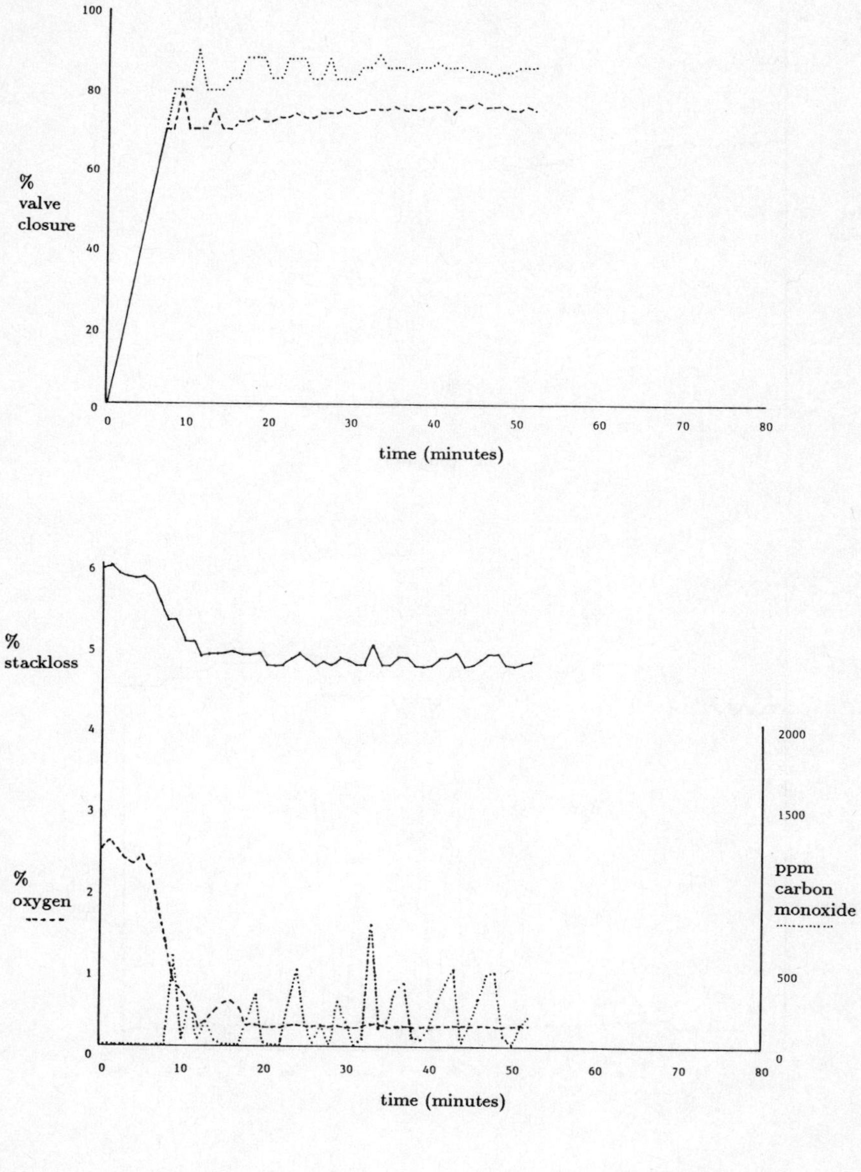

Figure 3: A Good Run of the Original Rule-base With No Change in Firing Level

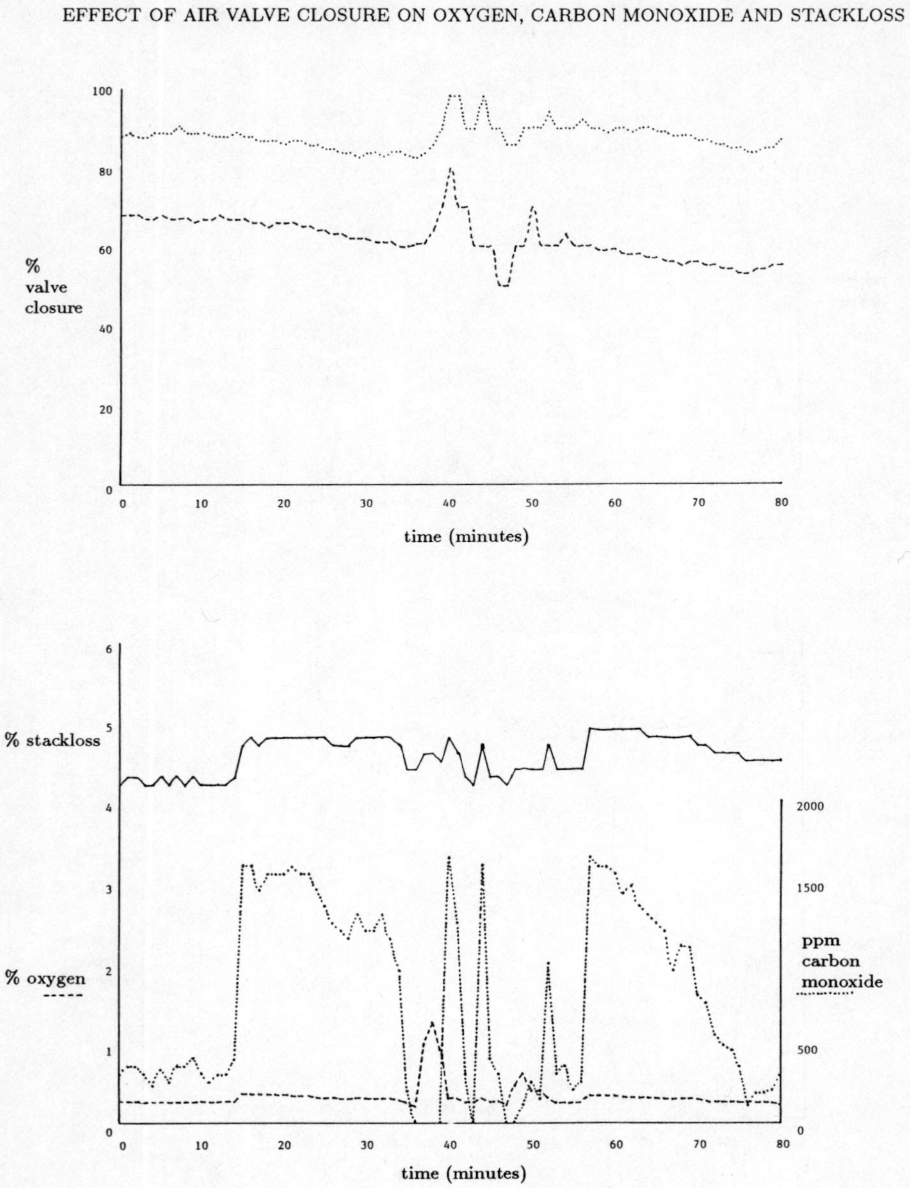

Figure 4: The Original Rule-base Doesn't Cope With Changes in Firing Level

ADAPTING THE RULE-BASE MANUALLY

There were perceived to be two main problems with the original rule-base in terms of dealing with changes in firing level. First, the parts of the rules that changed the increments by which the air-inlet valves were altered were not designed for the problem at hand. Large increments were needed to cope with changing firing levels while small increments were needed to optimise at one firing level. Increments built up or scaled down in one situation were not appropriate when moving into another situation. Second, the parts of the rules that lowered the oxygen limits had the effect of stopping the rule dealing with the "low" oxygen and "high" carbon monoxoide situation ever firing. This rule would have been useful when a change in firing level caused a sharp rise in carbon monoxide.

Those parts of the rules that altered increments and oxygen limits were therefore dropped. The oxygen limits were fixed as were the increments for each rule and new rules were introduced to make the system symmetric. The speed and efficiency with which the resulting rule-base, shown in figure 5, deals with changes in firing level is illustrated in the graphs of part of a run shown in figure 6. Here, after about 60 minutes, the firing level changes, indicated by a rise in carbon monoxide, and then again a few minutes later, this time indicated by a rise in oxygen. In each case the rule-base reacts rapidly and smoothly.

oxygen v.high	Reduce air to all burners by 4%	Reduce air to all burners by 4%	Lean burner correction routine Incs = 4%	Rich/Lean correction routine Incs = 4%
oxygen high	Reduce air to all burners by 2%	Lean burner correction routine Incs = 2%	Rich/Lean correction routine Incs = 2%	Rich burner correction routine Incs = 4%
oxygen O.K.	Lean burner correction routine Incs = 1%	Rich/Lean correction routine Incs = 1%	Rich burner correction routine Incs = 2%	Increase air to all burners by 4%
oxygen low	Do nothing	Rich burner correction routine Incs = 1%	Increase air to all burners by 2%	Increase air to all burners by 4%
	carbon monoxide low	carbon monoxide O.K.	carbon monoxide high	carbon monoxide v.high

Figure 5: The Manually Adapted Rule-base

EFFECT OF AIR VALVE CLOSURE ON OXYGEN, CARBON MONOXIDE AND STACKLOSS

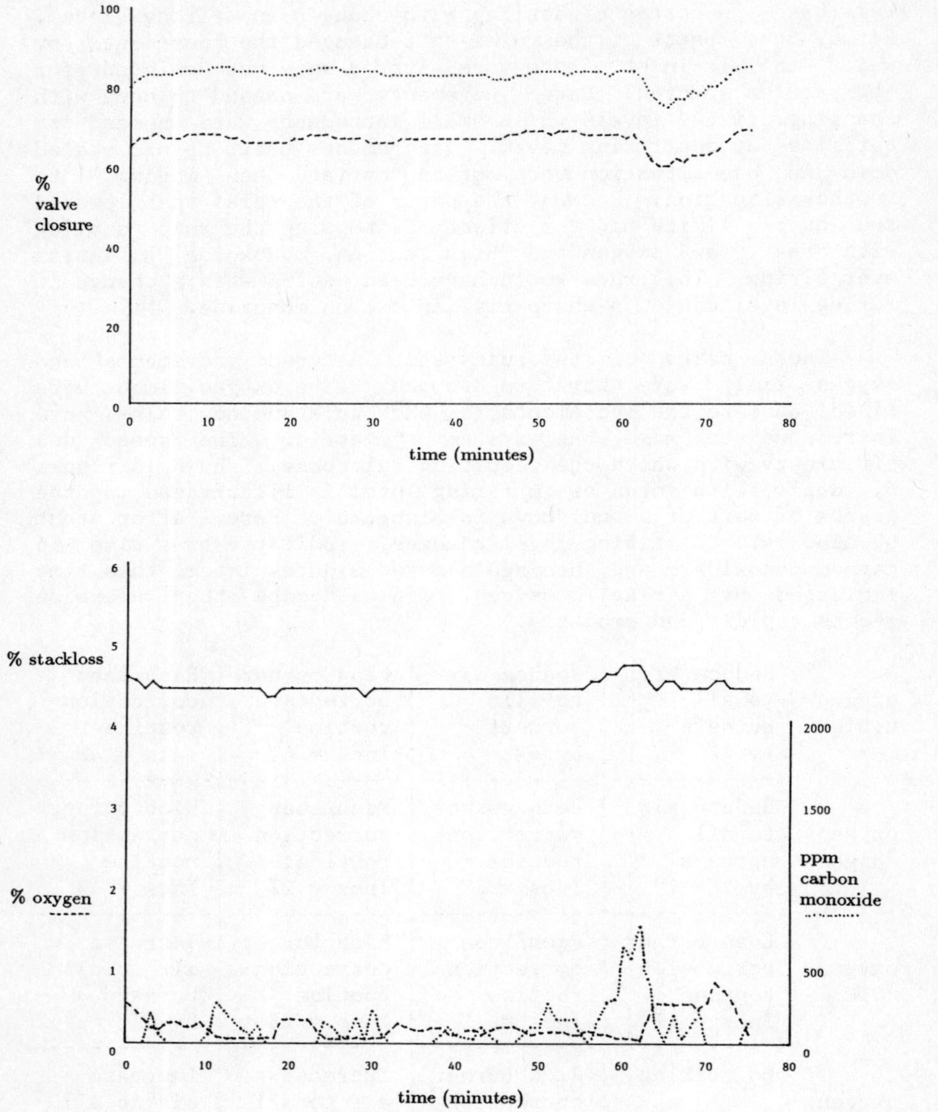

Figure 6: The Manually Adapted Rule-base Copes With Changes in Firing Level

THE GENETIC ALGORITHM

In order to adapt the rule-base automatically a suitable learning algorithm is required. The genetic algorithm, developed by Holland [5], has been shown to be a robust learner in this domain by Fogarty [6] and has been used to optimise parameters in one of the rules in the rule-base on simulations of multiple burner installations with a single firing level by Fogarty [7]. With a suitable choise of knowledge representation it can also be used to learn a good action to undertake in a particular situation.

The genetic algorithm begins with a set of structures, usually coded in binary form, which are evaluated in some environment. New structures are then formed by selecting old ones randomly over a probability distribution determined by their strengths, as allocated by the evaluation process, and transforming them with genetic operators such as crossover, mutation and inversion. The resulting structures are then evaluated and the process repeated. Parts of structures that have a high strength proliferate and those with a low strength die out while new combinations are continually tested. Genetic algorithms have been used for function optimisation in difficult domains by DeJong [8] and Ackley [9], for learning systems by Holland and Reitman [10] and Wilson [11] and are especially robust for classifying noisy data as shown by Pettit and Pettit [12].

The incremental version of the genetic algorithm we use differs from the one described above in that, after the evaluation of the initial randomly generated population and generation of a new member, it is evaluated immediately and joins the rest of the population. Thus the amount of computation and learning done at each time interval is equalized and the performance of the algorithm improved. A member is then deselected by random choice over the probability distribution of weights of the members of the population defined by the difference between their costs and that of the best member. The incrementally changed population then forms the basis for the generation of a new member.

Using the parameters found by Grefenstette [13] to give optimal on-line performance in a variety of domains, we therefore start with an initial population which is randomly generated of size 30 and the population remains this size throughout, we use a crossover rate of 0.95 and a mutation rate of 0.01, we use the cost of the worst member of the population as the base-line for weighting all the other members for selection and the best member of the population is automatically preserved by the deselection strategy.

ADAPTING THE RULE-BASE AUTOMATICALLY

In order to use the genetic algorithm to learn an action for a particular situation, a suitable binary representation of the choises available has to be created. Using 12 bits for each action the first three are for the type of action and the other nine for the increment size associated with that action. The coding for the action type is shown in figure 7. Generally speaking, if the first bit is a 1 the air intake is to be increased, if the second bit is a 1 it is to be decreased and the third bit indicates whether the action is applied conditionally to one burner (1) or unconditionally to all burners (0). The nine bits representing the increment are a binary coding of positive numbers from zero up to about 16. So that the 12 bit action 010111000000, for example, represents the action "Reduce air to all burners by 14%", the first three bits 010 being the coding of the action type "Reduce air to all burners" and the last nine bits 111000000 being the coding of the increment size of 14.

Learning a rule in this context is thus learning an action, encoded in the given representation, for a particular predetermined situation using the incremental genetic algorithm. For the first thirty times the situation is encountered a random 12 bit action is generated, performed, evaluated and assimilated into memory, as a possible action for that situation with a cost attatched. The cost is the stackloss after the action has been performed.

From then onwards, each action is generated from two possible actions selected, from those stored for that particular situation, on the basis of a weighted probability distribution of the difference between their costs and that of highest costing possible action. The bit strings representing the two possible actions are crossed at a randomly generated point with a probability of 0.95. Crossing involves taking the first part of one bit string up to the crossover point and appending the second part of the other bit string after the crossover point, if crossover is to take place, else the first string is used. The bits of the resulting string are then mutated with a probability of 0.01. Mutation involves changing a 1 bit to a 0 bit or vice-versa as the case may be.

000	No action
001	No action
110	No action
011	Lean burner correction routine
101	Rich burner correction routine
111	Rich/Lean burner correction routine
010	Reduce air to all burners
100	Increase air to all burners

Figure 7: Binary Coding of Action Types

Once the decoded action is performed and the associated stackloss evaluated it is stored with the other possible actions. Then a possible action is selected and deleted from those stored for that particular situation on the basis of a weighted probability distribution of the difference between their costs and that of lowest costing possible action.

No learning of this kind has been done on the multiple burner boiler since the manually adapted rule-base is undergoing long term evaluation. Also there is the problem of the random nature of the initial actions in the algorithm described above, although the initial population of possible actions could be manually selected rather than randomly generated. However experiments have been done with simulations of the domain with some very interesting results.

THE SIMULATIONS

Experiments were done with a near perfect burner to determine the concentrations of carbon monoxide and oxygen to be expected depending upon the amount of excess air supplied to the burner by Wakefield [14]. These results are summarised in figure 8. Oxygen concentration is a continuous function of excess air and carbon monoxide concentration is a discontinuous or noisy one. It is not possible to run industrial burners much below 0% excess air but high levels of carbon monoxide can be detected at low excess air levels.

This effect can be simulated by modelling each burner with a number of perfect burners. Each perfect burner has its own maximum excess air level, achieved when its associated air inlet valve is fully open, and its own minimum, when closed.

Depending upon an exponential function of the closure of the associated air inlet valve the excess air for that perfect burner can be calculated. Carbon monoxide and oxygen concentrations can then be calculated for each perfect burner using functions approximating Wakefield's results. These can be averaged to give realistic

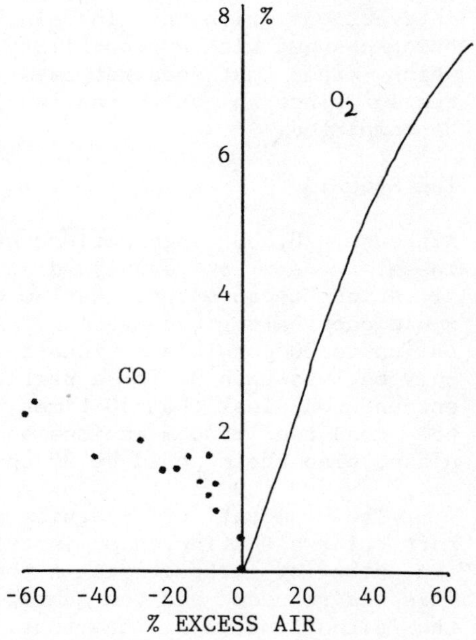

Figure 8: Wakefield's Results

concentrations for the burner. Simulating a multiple burner installation involves averaging the carbon monoxide and oxygen concentrations over all the burners depending upon the valve setting for each burner. Temperature is treated as constant.

THE EXPERIMENTS

Ten simulations of ten burner installations in which each burner is represented by two perfect burners for each of two firing levels were generated for the experiments. The maximum excess air level for each perfect burner was randomly generated from a distribution evenly divided between a uniform distribution from -4.6% to 25% excess air and a uniform distribution from 25% to 159% excess air to produce maximum excess air levels for each burner generally in the range 4% to 120% with median 25% found by Presser and Smerjian [15] to be the distribution for industrial burners in the U.S.A. The minimum excess air level for each perfect burner was randomly generated in the range from -100% to its maximum excess air level.

The incremental genetic algorithm was then run in each of the situations corresponding to those in figure 5, in effect attempting to learn an action for each of the sixteen situations. The same carbon monoxide limits were used as on the multiple burner boiler but the oxygen limits were arbitrarily chosen and the same ones were used on each installation. Each of the installations was run for 20,000 interactions with the "learning" rule-base, the firing level being changed with a probability of 0.0625 at each interaction, which means that somewhat less than 20,000 possible rules were tested since an action can require up to three interactions to be completed.

THE RESULTS

Although 20,000 interactions occurred on each installation these were not evenly distributed between the sixteen situations because there was no way of ensuring what situation would occur after each action. At the end of a run there would be up to 30 possible actions for each situation. There would only be less than 30 for a particular situation if it had been encountered less than 30 times, in which case these would be the result of random actions and no learning would have taken place, else there would be 30 possible actions.

The amount of learning that had taken place in a particular situation on an installation obviously depends upon the number of interactions in the run involving that situation. This was recorded and the number ranged from 1 to 7086 over all the situations in all the runs. Since the genetic algorithm usually takes about 500 trials to reach some optimum it was decided to ignore the results for situations that had been encountered less than 250 times in a run. On each run it was found that all situations in which carbon monoxide was "O.K." or "high" fell into this category. Hence, results were only obtained for situations in which the carbon monoxide reading was "low" or "v.high". Results were obtained for all oxygen categories though the particular ones varied from one installation to another.

What has been learnt, if anything, by the end of a run is contained in the possible actions for each situation. If the run was allowed to continue, future actions could be generated in the same way as they were done before. If one wanted to freeze the rulebase at that stage one could carry on with the same selection procedure but no longer use crossover and mutation to do more learning. However, in order to decide on a definite action for a situation we need to compress the thirty possible actions into one action.

We use the following method for each situation and each installation to present our results. We weight the possible actions in the same way that they are weighted for selection. Any possible action type that would have a probability of being selected of more than 0.25 is recorded as is its probability of being selected. A weighted average of the increments for that action type is then calculated and recorded. The results of the runs are presented in this way in figure 9. The triples of numbers for each situation on each installation are composed of an action type as coded in figure 8, an increment, and a probability of selection.

Casting one's eye over the results, a very simple pattern emerges over all the installations if the carbon monoxide reading is very high. The recommended action in this situation is "Increase air to all the burners" (100) by about 12%. This reinforces the choice of some of the new rules in the manually adjusted rule-base.

If the carbon monoxide reading is low, results split about equally between "Lean burner correction routine" (011) and "Rich/lean burner correction routine" (111) with varying increments, while "No action" (000, 001 and 110) is also recommended. "Lean burner correction routine" corresponds to an original rule in one of those situations but "Rich/lean burner correction routine seems odd as does "Do nothing". In terms of the way chosen to cost an action, by its final effect in terms of stackloss, then there will not be much to choose between the two routines but both involve intermediate costs which are not taken into consideration. The "Do nothing" rule probably gains a foothold because waiting for a change of firing level in certain situations brings more benefits than doing anything else.

key to situations
in Figure 9

	carbon monoxide low		carbon monoxide v.high
oxygen v.high			
oxygen high			
oxygen O.K.			
oxygen low			

1.

111 10 1.0			
111 12 0.7 011 10 0.3			
001 2 1.0			100 9 1.0
011 7 0.5			100 11 1.0

2.

111 9 0.7			
011 11 0.6 111 8 0.4			
011 8 0.5 111 6 0.4			
110 10 1.0			100 12 1.0

3.

011 15 1.0			
111 15 0.5 011 15 0.3			100 8 1.0
			100 12 1.0
011 9 0.8			

4.

111 14 0.5 011 12 0.4			
011 11 1.0			100 13 1.0
011 13 1.0			100 8 1.0
000 14 0.5			

5.

111 9 0.6 110 4 0.3			
011 8 0.7			100 11 1.0
011 9 0.5 111 10 0.5			100 10 1.0
			100 13 1.0

6.

111 12 0.4 011 13 0.6			
011 12 0.7 111 16 0.3			
011 14 1.0			
011 4 1.0			100 13 1.0

```
7.
   111 14 0.9| | |
             | | |
   ----------|-|-|----------
   011  4 1.0| | |100 12 1.0
             | | |
   ----------|-|-|----------
   011  7 0.3| | |100 12 1.0
   001  6 0.5| | |
   ----------|-|-|----------
             | | |
             | | |
```

```
8.
   011 11 0.9| | |100  8 1.0
             | | |
   ----------|-|-|----------
   011  4 0.5| | |100 12 0.9
   111  3 0.4| | |
   ----------|-|-|----------
   111  9 0.7| | |100 13 1.0
             | | |
   ----------|-|-|----------
             | | |
             | | |
```

```
9.
   011  7 0.6| | |
             | | |
   ----------|-|-|----------
   011  8 0.7| | |100  7 0.6
   111 10 0.3| | |
   ----------|-|-|----------
   011 10 0.5| | |100 11 1.0
             | | |
   ----------|-|-|----------
             | | |
             | | |
```

```
10.
   111 15 0.8| | |
             | | |
   ----------|-|-|----------
   001  7 0.6| | |100 11 1.0
   011  6 0.4| | |
   ----------|-|-|----------
   011  5 0.6| | |111  9 0.7
   001 10 0.3| | |
   ----------|-|-|----------
   110 13 1.0| | |
             | | |
```

Figure 9: Actions Learnt on Simulations for Given Situations.

CONCLUSION

In comparing the manually adapted rule-base with the automatically adapted ones we are not making an altogether fair comparison. The simulations represent a more general problem than that encountered on the multiple burner boiler. A change in firing level on the boiler invariably involves a similar change in valve settings on each of the burners to achieve optimum combustion and hence the value of the rules which alter all the burners at the same time in those circumstances. On the simulations, however, a change in firing level involed no such mutual adjustments of the air-inlet valves to achieve optimum settings.

We have shown that the genetic algorithm can be used to learn specific actions for particular situations in this domain and are thus some way towards building a rule learning system. In future we will investigate the learning of more generally applicable actions in this domain and the automation of the process of classifying the state space.

REFERENCES

1. Fogarty,T.C, "An Expert System for Optimising Combustion in Multiple Burner Furnaces and Boiler Plants", Proceedings of Expert Systems 88, Brighton, December 1988, in 'Research and Development in Expert Systems V' Edited by B.Kelly and A.Rector, Cambridge, pp 236-44, 1989.
2. Holland,J.H, "Escaping Brittleness: The Possibilities of General-Purpose Learning Algorithms Applied to Parallel Rule-Based Systems", in 'Machine Learning: An Artificial Intelligence Approach', Volume 2, eds. Michalski, R.S., Carbonell, J.G. and Mitchell, T.M., pp 593-623, 1987.
3. Gaines,B.R, "How Do Experts Aquire Expertise?", Proc. of AAAI Workshop on Knowledge Aquisition for Knowledge-Based Systems, (Banff), 1987.
4. Edmundson, J.T., Jenkins, D.P. and Mortimer,J, "Multiple Burner Stoichiometry Control and Efficiency Optimisation by Means of a Teleological, Heuristic, On-Line Expert System", in 'Innovation in Process Energy Utilisation', IChemE, pp 47-60, 1987.
5. Holland,J.H, "Adaption in Natural and Artificial Systems", 1975.
6. Fogarty,T.C, "Adapting to Noise", pre-prints of IFAC Workshop on Artificial Intelligence in Real-Time Control, pp 161-6, Swansea, September 1988.
7. Fogarty,T.C, "The Machine Learning of Rules for Combustion Control in Multiple Burner Installations", proceedings of the IEEE Fifth Conference on Artificial Intelligence Applications, pp 215-221, 1989.
8. DeJong,K, "Adaptive System Design: A Genetic Approach" in 'IEEE Trans. on Systems, Man and Cybernetics', pp 566-574, vol 10,no.9.Sept.1980.
9. Ackley,D.H, "An Empirical Study of Bit Vector Function Optimisation", in 'Genetic Algorithms and Simulated Annealing',ed.L.Davis, pp 170-204, 1987.
10. Holland,J.H. and Reitman,J.S, "Cognitive Systems Based on Adaptive Algorithms", in 'Pattern Directed Inference Systems', eds. Waterman,D. and Hayes-Roth,F., pp 313-329, 1978.
11. Wilson,S.W, "Classifier Systems and the Animat Problem", in 'Machine Learning', vol.2, no.3, pp 199-228, 1987.
12. Pettit,E.J. and Pettit,M.J, "Analysis of the Performance of a genetic algorithm based system for message classification in noisy environments" in 'International Journal of Man-Machine Studies' vol.27 pp 205-220, 1987.
13. Grefenstette,J.J., "Optimisation of Control Parameters for Genetic Algorithms", in 'IEEE Trans. on Systems, Man and Cybernetics', vol 16, no. 1. Jan./Feb., pp 122-128, 1986.
14. Wakefield,A.C., "An Expert System for Methane Flame Stoiciometric Control", MSc Dissertation, Bristol Polytechnic, 1986.
15. Presser,C. and SemerJian,H.G., "Evaluation of Industrial Combustion Control Systems", U.S. Dept. of Energy, 1984.

Using Expert Knowledge to Select and Improve Skeletal Plans for the Control of a Vertical Internal Grinding Machine

Barbara H. Roberts* and David C. Brown**

**MITRE, Bedford, MA 01730, USA*

*** Artificial Intelligence Research Group, Computer Science Department, Worcester Polytechnic Institute, Worcester, MA 01609, USA*

ABSTRACT

We are investigating the use of techniques for the selection and improvement of skeletal plans that are used to control a vertical internal grinding machine. Both the plans and the plan selection technique reflect the machinist's knowledge of how to grind workpieces in different situations. The selected plan is instantiated with proper parameters and is passed to a grinding simulation where simulated force sensor readings emulate real-time feedback control information. Feedback from the simulation is used by knowledge-based modification routines. These routines identify failed plans and adjust successful plans in an effort to improve their action.

INTRODUCTION

We are investigating the use of techniques for the selection and improvement of skeletal plans. These plans are used to control a vertical internal grinding machine. The planner being developed selects a skeletal plan [Friedland, 1979] using the knowledge of an expert machinist. These plans reflect the machinist's knowledge of how to grind workpieces in different situations.

The system recognizes the grinding situation using descriptive qualities of the situation, selects an appropriate plan from the data base of plans [Brown & Chandrasekaran, 1985] and instantiates this plan with proper parameters. The instantiated plans are passed to a grinding simulation where simulated force sensor readings emulate real-time feedback control information. Feedback from the simulation is used by knowledge-based modification routines. These routines identify failed plans and adjusts successful plans in an effort to improve their action. Modification strategies are pre-defined methods for changing the value of a grinding parameter. A list of representative modification strategies include: alter grinding time, alter tool, alter force, alter downfeed rate, iterate, or cease iteration. These modification strategies are selected symbolically. The selection is based on feedback information from the simulation.

RATIONALE FOR THE GRINDING MACHINE PLANNER

We are concerned with the appropriateness of such a planner for a two axis, vertical, internal grinding machine. This machine is used to remove the irregular metal contour from the interior of fuel injection nozzles. The final surface of the interior of the cylinder of the nozzle must be within microns of a desired diameter and meet stringent eccentricity requirements.

The vertical two axis grinder is currently controlled by a PDP-11/23 programmed in assembler language. A force sensor located on the quill mount senses cutting force readings and transmits this information to the controller. The controller adapts the feedrate of the slide in response to the force sensor readings. Logic programmed within the PDP-11 helps the controller adjust to the current situation and can, if the work speed is decreased enough, determine the work shape from force readings.

Currently, the grinding information for each piece is entered by the grinding expert through a menu that presents specific parameters. The list of parameters is fixed. The user can only change the values of the parameters of this one implied plan. To change to another grinding plan currently requires the PDP-11 to be reprogrammed.

Difficulties with Precision Grinding

Automatic controllers of machine tools are limited in their capability to adapt to uncontrolled variations in stock, hardness, and runout because they are preprogrammed with fixed input parameters such as feedrate, wheelspeed, workspeed, depth of dress, dress lead and sparkout time. This inability to adapt to the grinding situation often produces parts which do not meet requirements for the finished part due to problems with concentricity, roundness, taper, size tolerance, surface finish and surface integrity. These limitations decrease the machine's productivity, increase the cost of each part, and interfere with its ability to produce precision parts.

The Stock Removal Problem

Before grinding, a workpiece has extra material on the walls of its interior. This material is hardened steel and in most cases is so hard that the grinding wheel must make multiple work revolutions to remove the excess material. To complicate matters each workpiece is somewhat different from the last one. For example, the stock may runout more or may vary in hardness. As the slide is fed by a servomotor, bringing the grinding wheel into contact with the workpiece, the quill holding the wheel is deflected, generating a normal force between the wheel and the work. Force sensors, attached to the wheel mount, sense the magnitude of the force and provide this information to the controller. The deflect of the quill and uncertainty in the force readings negatively effect the precision of the final piece.

This decrease in precision can increase the cost of producing the workpiece. Sometimes an individual piece must be discarded because it does not meet the design specifications. More often the machining time must be increased to produce a piece which meets the specifications. This increase in grinding time is costly, as one extra second on each piece can add as much as one million dollars a year to the cost of producing the part. Errors in very expensive parts are themselves costly if the piece must be discarded.

METHODOLOGY

In exploring different methods for implementing the automatic grinding planner, we considered fully specified (i.e., canned) plans, skeletal plans that can be made specific, and the building of original plans in real time. We chose skeletal plans that allow some adaptation because the grinding expert seldom invents a grinding plan from scratch. He uses a grinding plan -- a skeletal plan which was useful for some other related grinding situations -- and then instantiates it with specific values. Since we also have feedback information, in the form of force sensor readings, we chose to adapt the plan in response to this feedback whenever appropriate.

PLAN SELECTION

In order for the automatic planner to use the skeletal plans, it must have a means of selecting the most appropriate plan or modification to the plan. Candidate selection techniques which we considered included decision trees, symbolic matching of textual descriptions, decision tables, and rule based systems, in which rules provided by the grinding expert are used to select the "best" plan. We chose the symbolic matching technique, as it best captured the "matching" nature of the task.

For each plan in the system, the human expert has provided a set of characteristics that describe under what circumstances that plan would be appropriate. To select a plan the user provides a description that consists of a variety of pieces of information about the work to be done (e.g., workpiece material) and the grinding situation (e.g., the wheel's characteristics). This description is matched against the stored characteristics of the plans, and the best match selects the plan.

The matching method used takes into account the fact that some characteristics *must* be matched, while others merely add additional desirability to a plan.

APPLICATION OF SKELETAL PLANS TO MACHINE TOOLS

When developing skeletal plans for controlling the grinding machine, we first identified all of the grinding primitives, i.e., the primitive actions involved in a grinding plan. We repeatedly interviewed the grinding expert, acquiring his knowledge about the various primitive operations that the machine can make. Primary primitives found were: searching for the work, mapping the surface of the work, the rough feedrate, sparkout, cycle stop, emergency stop, turn on coolant, decision to dress the wheel, and exit. Other primitives included the finish feedrate, adaptive feedrate control in either the rough feedrate or the finish feedrate mode, contour following of workpieces with large terminal indicator readings, and iteration of parts of the plan.

Once the primitives had been identified, we recorded all meaningful sequences of primitive grinding operations, making a list of plans from these plan fragments. About four dozen sequences of grinding primitives were developed. These were reviewed by the grinding expert for general applicability. Those plans which remained, about three dozen, ranged in complexity from simple, cheap plans to be used on inexpensive parts, to complex, many-operation plans with many iterations possible during their execution.

Examples of some of the plans are given below:

1) S Co R_f1 So Co Ex

2) D Co S R_f2 F_f So Co Ex

3) D M R_f1 It M F_f So Co Ex

where the symbols used are:

S	Search for workpiece surface.
Co	Turn on/off coolant.
M	Map the surface of the workpiece.
D	Dress the wheel.
R_f1	Downfeed slide at fixed rough feedrate.
R_f2	Downfeed slide at variable rough feedrate.
F_f	Downfeed slide at finish feedrate.
It	Iterate -- redo portions of the plan, possibly with different parameter values.
So	Sparkout.
Ex	Exit the workpiece

After identification and sequencing of the various grinding primitives, the knowledge base of plans was organized by complexity. The expert-given descriptive qualities of the grinding plans were coded into tables which are used for the selection of a specific grinding plan. A description of the current situation is used to select the grinding plan from the knowledge base.

Examples of qualities used for the selection of a particular plan include the purpose of the part, the desired quality of the part, the final size specifications, the desired surface finish, the desired final terminal indicator reading, the cost of the part, the cost of the grind, and the risk associated with the grinding plan.

The selected plan is instantiated by determining actual values for each grinding parameter associated with the grinding primitives in the plan. This is done by grinding specialist routines that incorporate knowledge provided by the human grinding expert. Formulas which represent this knowledge can be found in [King & Hahn, 1986]. A typical formula, derived from empirical data, estimates the work removal parameter (WRP). The equation, suitable for use when estimating the WRP for easy-to-grind steels, is:

```
WRP = (0.021e819/304) *
    [((Vw/Vs)**3/19) * (1+(2/3)*c/l) * (l**11/19)*Vs)) /
     (De**43/304 * Vol**0.47 * d**5/38 * Rc**27/19)]
```

where

WRP	=	cubic inches/minute, lb
Vw,Vs	=	ft/minute
l	=	inch per wheel revolution
De	=	inch
d	=	grain size in the wheel (inch)
Vol	=	1.33H + 2.2S-8, volume factor for wheel
C	=	diametral depth of dress (inch)
Rc	=	Rockwell Hardness

Wheel hardness is represented by H, I, J, K, L, M, ...
The value of H is 0,1,2,3,4,5, ...
S is the wheel structure number.

The other instantiation routines respond to information about materials, the grinding situation, the hardness of the work, and the characteristics of the wheel. The grinding situation is determined from such information as the shape of the part to be worked, the age of the grinding wheel, the capabilities of the grinding machine, the number of grinding operations needed to produce the part, and the type of grind (i.e., whether it is in the x-direction, the z-direction or a vector grind).

Instantiation of the grinding parameters must satisfy certain constraints. These constraints are situation dependent and are generated by grinding knowledge which calculates limits on the particular values of the grinding primitives. Some of these constraints are the force which can break the wheel down, the amount of power required to stall the wheel, and how much the wheel is wearing over time.

OPERATION OF THE KNOWLEDGE BASED CONTROLLER

The process starts with the selection of the grinding plan by matching a description of the grinding situation against the data base of skeletal plans and their attributes. Once selected, instantiation of the plan's parameters is accomplished using mathematical formulas that provide estimates of the values of every parameter in the plan. These values are stored in the selected plan, associated with the appropriate grinding primitive.

Control of the execution of the grinding plan is accomplished by proceeding through the plan, one grinding primitive at a time. The primitive, and its parameter value(s), are passed to the grinding simulation. The simulation returns information about the new situation after the grinding primitive has been executed, or, in some cases, terminated abnormally.

The feedback from the simulation to the plan executor may trigger modification of the values of individual grinding parameters. If the feedback information indicates that a particular grinding parameter is too large or too small, then this parameter is recalculated using the formulae used for instantiation.

The grinding plan execution routine must be able to execute the current grinding primitive, select and execute the next primitive, adjust a grinding primitive parameter value, decide whether to iterate over some prior primitives, or terminate abnormally.

ITERATION AND PLAN MODIFICATION

The plan primitive, Iteration, allows repetition of a part of a plan. Moreover, repetition can be conditional and can include the modification of an appropriate parameter prior to the next iteration. Modification of the primitive following the iteration primitive can also be accomplished. A modification could omit the next primitive, change more than one primitive in the iteration portion of the plan, insert a new primitive into the plan such as dress the wheel, or alter a parameter by some fixed percentage.

Iteration can be performed with the current value of a parameter or with a modified value. This choice is made by applying modification strategies in the form of rules. These strategies contain information about what to change, and how to accomplish the change, given the feedback about the grinding situation. The modification strategies also determine where to go in the plan if the current primitive action is not progressing correctly, and when to stop iterating.

Feedback from the simulation that may invoke a change in the current grinding primitive includes the distance that the grinding wheel has moved in the x direction, the interim terminal indicator readings, the measured elapsed time, force sensor readings, and how many work revolutions the chuck has made. For example, the arrival of the x slide at a predetermined position can indicate that a change of primitive is required.

Examples of Plan Modification

A modification strategy can change the value of a parameter. A list of representative modification strategies include: alter time, alter tool, alter force, alter downfeed rate, alter plan primitives, and alter workspeed. These modification strategies are selected symbolically using feedback information. Alteration of a grinding plan primitive is accomplished though the use of rules. Specific examples of how the plan modification strategy adjusts to feedback information from the simulation are discussed below.

For example, if the current primitive action is Iteration, and rough feedrate is the previous primitive in the current plan, then the variable, rough stock allowance, is used to determine the change in the feedrate parameter value. If very little stock is left remaining, but the location, rough stock allowance, has not yet been reached, then the plan modification strategy will decrease the value of the rough feedrate parameter, and iterate over that plan action.

On the other hand if a lot of stock is remaining and the prior action is rough grind, then the plan modification routine can either increment the value of rough feed rate or keep it the same. Since incrementing the value of rough feed rate carries more risk, the cost of the part is taken into consideration before a choice is made.

Reaching the rough stock allowance, a predetermined location of the simulated x slide, would indicates to the plan modification strategy used by the Iteration primitive that the current grinding operation, rough grind, should end and the next grinding primitive should be started.

Force sensor readings from the simulation are also used to indicate to the planner what its modification strategy might be. If force sensor readings indicate to the planner that a parameter should be changed then an appropriate modification strategy will be selected.

In addition, force sensor readings from the simulation are use to identify failed plans. Failed plans are plans where the grinding parameters are incorrect, causing the grinding process to either produce a part which does not meet specifications or not produce a part at all. An example of a failed plan is one in which the grinding force exceeds the wheel breakdown force. If this constraint is exceeded, the simulation returns this information to the plan execution routine. The routine terminates the simulated grinding procedure, informing the user of the failure.

The plan selection and use mechanism (i.e., the planner) adapts to failed plans in different ways depending on how the plan failed. If the plan failed by breaking the wheel, then the planner gives up. However, if the plan failed due to an incorrect measurement, and the workpiece has not been ground enough, then the planner can continue with the grinding plan by modifying either the finish feedrate or the rough feedrate, whichever is appropriate. If the grinding plan produced a part which has been ground too much then the planner records this information. We hope to use this information to decrease the amount of downfeed in the next use of a similar plan.

MODELLING GRINDING

Spindle Deflection

The elastic displacement of a spring, expressed as Hooke's Law, is used to model the dynamic aspects of the grinding process. In an actual internal grinding machine, the grinding wheel is attached to a spindle which is fixed to a wheelhead. The workpiece is rigidly clamped into a chuck. The grinding wheel is fed into the workpiece by the movement of two slides. One slide controls the vertical displacement of the grinding wheel, the other its lateral motion. As the grinding wheel is fed into the material and, as it rides over "high spots" in the excess material, the grinding spindle is deflected creating a force proportional to this displacement. In the actual grinding machine, a force sensor measures the force generated by this displacement. This information can be used to adjust the amount of downfeed thus controlling the grinding process in real time.

Terminal Indicator Readings

A measure of roundness used by the expert machinist is the terminal indicator reading. This is the difference between the highest and the lowest parts of the surface. If there are no high spots in the surface, then the terminal indicator reading is zero, the desired condition during or at the end of the grinding process. Most often the workpieces arrive at the grinding machine with some degree of out-of-roundness. This is measured by the initial terminal indicator reading (ITIR). Because this is uncontrolled and random, we choose to represent ITIR as a random variable. The final terminal indicator reading (FTIR) is the measure of goodness of the grinding operation.

THE GRINDING SIMULATION

Our simulation is an event driven simulation of the roundup problem as described in [King & Hahn, 1986]. Simulation variables were identified according to real-time grinding situations. Since workpieces arrive at the grinding machine with undetermined amounts of extra stock in unknown distributions, the amount of stock on each workpiece and its distribution about the inner surface of the cylinder are modelled as random variables. Various rates at which the grinding wheel feeds into the excess stock are independent variables passed to the simulation from the planner. The planner also instructs the simulation on how many work revolutions to simulate before returning feedback information. The simulation can also run to completion without returning information to the planner, approximating an open loop grinding process.

Phases of the Grinding Simulation

The grinding process is subject to a number of constraints. These constraints are limitations imposed by the characteristics of the materials involved and the forces imposed by the grinding process. A System Characteristics Chart, captured in the simulation, relates stock removal, wheelwear, power and surface finish to the amount of force applied to the surface of the material.

In particular, the stock removal curve is characterized by three regions:

-- the rubbing region, where the wheel rubs on the surface of the workpiece with no stock removal taking place;

-- the ploughing region, where material is removed in the ploughing process, but not cleanly;

-- the cutting region, where the material is removed in proportion to the amount of force applied.

These three regions of the grinding process are delineated from each other by forces. The threshold force separates the rubbing from the ploughing region. The ploughing-cutting transition force separates the ploughing from the cutting region. These critical forces are modelled in the simulation by first calculating the deflection of the grinding spindle as it rides over the high and low spots on the surface. Deriving the force from this allows the different regions of the system characteristics chart to be modelled.

A natural limit, called the work breakdown force, is represented by that portion of the curve where the grinding wheel starts to break down due to extreme forces.

The grinding wheel may not always be in continuous contact with the surface of the workpiece. The simulation takes this into account and only simulates removal of stock from the high spot. Once the high spot has been worn down by repeated passes of the grinding wheel, continuous contact throughout the revolution occurs and stock is removed from the low spots as well.

When the grinding process should transition from rough to finish grinding, the planner can request that the simulation make this transition. During the finish grind the downfeed of the grinding machine is slower with less stock removal. This enhances the quality of the surface.

Mathematical formulae similar to those used during the roughing phase of the simulation are used to calculate the amount of stock removed and the forces generated by this removal. Once the downfeed position of the wheel exceeds the finish stock allowance, the planner causes the system to "spark out" and come to rest. Final values are calculated and returned to the planner. These values include the final terminal indicator reading and the total grind time.

VERIFICATION AND VALIDATION

Verification of the planner and associated software was conducted using actual input and output data from a vertical internal grinding machine. The actual specifications and requirements for the part along with information about the individual part were recorded. Then the real-time controller of the vertical internal grinding machine was used to produce actual data in known situations. An output of the forces produced by the grinding process was saved for comparison with simulated force readings. At the end of the actual grinding process, the part was inspected for final terminal indicator readings. This information was recorded and saved for verifying the accuracy of the grinding simulation.

Verification against real data indicates that the instantiation routines are accurate estimations of the grinding parameter values. For example, a work removal rate of 50.1 cubic inches per minute per pound was calculated from real data, based on a 38A801L8VBE wheel and AISI 4150 53-55 Rc steel. The estimated work removal rate under similar conditions produced a value of 46.3 cubic inches per minute per pound. This is an acceptable error for this simulation.

In order to validate the simulation we compared forces generated during real grinding situations with those estimated in the simulation. These estimates agree very closely under similar circumstances, especially at the beginning of the grinding cycle. As the grinding cycle progresses the simulated force values diverge from the real forces. This disparity is due in large part to the propagation and accumulation of errors caused by our method of estimating the amount of material removed on each revolution.

The simulated time to round up a work piece was compared to real round up timing information. The real data available to us involved the rounding up of easy-to-grind steels using a control force grinding machine. Our simulation models the rounding up of easy-to-grind steels using a feedrate grinder. The simulated time to round up an out-of-round part was 8 seconds. The real data under similar situations was 6 seconds. These results indicate that the simulation is quite accurate, as the feedrate grinder should take a little more time to round up a similar part.

THE IMPLEMENTATION

The simulation and the planner were implemented on an IBM/PC-XT. The planner is written in Microsoft C, while the simulation and plan instantiation are written in Microsoft FORTRAN. The planner is called from the FORTRAN routines using the Microsoft INTERFACE statement.

Planner Performance

Preliminary results show that the planner is effective in selecting an appropriate plan. The user can describe the grinding situation using a set of descriptors, and a plan fitting that situation is selected. If the selector is issued a set of inappropriate descriptors it will not select any plan at all, indicating this to the user. After selection a parser breaks the plan apart into its primitives which are instantiated by calling FORTRAN routines.

Modification of the grinding plan and the associated modification knowledge was more difficult to implement than the plan selection routine. Our experience indicates that plan selection is quite well understood. However, plan modification is more complicated, requiring decisions based on uncertain information. In an actual grinding situation, the planner might pick one of a number of choices, any of which might eventually result in a part that meets the specifications. Under these situations it is not all together clear how best to modify the actual plan primitives. We are still investigating the plan modification aspect of our system.

We have found that the use of the x slide's location, represented by the variables "rough stock allowance" and "finish stock allowance", are very good indications of when to change plan primitives. This is consistent with the machinist's knowledge. The use of the position of the x slide is practical in the real grinding situation since in-process gauges are not needed to determine this variable's current value. The use of the interim value of the terminal indicator reading, although useful in the simulation of the grinding process, may not be practical in the real grinding situation. This information will either have to be inferred using the current force readings or in-process gauges will have to be used.

RELATED WORK

There is much research into the general planning area. With respect to skeletal plans, Friedland [1979] provided the first clear demonstration of their power in his version of MOLGEN. Brown and Chandrasekaran [1985] have used skeletal plans with specially developed plan selection strategies for engineering design problems.

Expert systems and related technologies have been applied to a number of machine tool problems at the cell level. These include milling machine monitoring and control [Agogino et al, 1988], machine tool set up, and the monitoring of machine tool in-process sensors [Wright & Bourne, 1988]. Monitoring and automatic planning in the machining domain is a current research area [Hayes & Wright, 1986].

Research into the science of grinding has been proceeding through the latter half of this century [Lindsay, 1971], [King & Hahn, 1986]. Much more research needs to be done before these processes are understood well enough so that manufacturing using precision machine tools can be made more automatic.

SUMMARY AND RECOMMENDATIONS

The research issues addressed by this study are the selection and instantiation of skeletal grinding plans, and the control and identification of effective plan modification techniques using feedback.

We have established how to simulate the grinding process and provide sensor information so that the plans may be properly tested and modified, before control of an actual automatic grinding machine is attempted.

Adjustments to the values of grinding parameters, through the use of feedback, can be used to improve the performance of the grinding plans during grinding. It may be appropriate to use the simulation to test the veracity of a selected plan, and to improve it, before using it to control an actual grinding machine.

We recommend that our system, or a similar system, be used for the control of internal grinding machines. The use of expert knowledge in the form of skeletal plans, plan selection criteria, modification strategies, and grinding parameter constraints will improve the productivity of grinding machinists, especially those with less experience.

REFERENCES

A. Agogino, S. Russell & R. Guha (1988) Sensor Fusion using Influence Diagrams and Reasoning by Analogy: Application to Milling Machine Monitoring and Control. In: *Artificial Intelligence in Engineering: Diagnosis and Learning,* (Ed.) J. S. Gero, Elsevier/Computational Mechanics Publications, pp. 333-357.

D. C. Brown & B. Chandrasekaran (1985) Plan Selection in Design Problem Solving. AIRG-DCB85-AISB, Computer Science Dept., Worcester Polytechnic Institute, Worcester, MA.

P. E. Friedland (1979) Knowledge-Based Experimental Design in Molecular Genetics. Rep. No. 79-772, Computer Science Dept., Stanford University, Stanford, CA, (Ph.D. dissertation).

R. I. King & R. S. Hahn (1986) *Handbook of Modern Grinding Technology,* Chapman and Hall, NY.

R. P. Lindsay (1971) *On the Metal Removal and Wheel Removal Parameters Surface Finish, Geometry and Thermal Damage in Precision Grinding,* Ph.D. Thesis, Worcester Polytechnic Institute,

Worcester, MA.

R. P. Lindsay (1984) The Effect of Contact on Forces, Power and Metal Removal Rate in Precision Grinding. *International Grinding Conference,* Lake Geneva, Wis., Society of Manufacturing Engineers, Dearborn, MI.

P. K. Wright & D. A. Bourne (1988) *Manufacturing Intelligence,* Addison-Wesley Publishing Company, Reading, MA.

C. Hayes & P. K. Wright (1986) Automated Planning in the Machining Domain. *Proceedings of ASME Meeting on Knowledge Based Expert Systems for Manufacturing,* PED-Vol. 24, pp. 221-232.

APPENDIX

The grinding simulation is based upon the following mathematical formulas. These formulas were developed by Dr. Robert S. Hahn of Hahn Engineering, Auburn, MA, and reflect our approach to the roundup problem. For a complete explanation of these formulae and their derivation the reader is referred to a text on research in grinding, such as [King & Hahn, 1986].

Variable definitions:

D: Amount of downfeed of the grinding wheel during one revolution.

x: Amount of deflection of the grinding wheel caused by high spots in the excess stock.

h: Amount of stock removed from the high or low spots in the excess stock.

F: Normal force generated by the deflection.

Lambda: Work removal parameter, or constant of proportionality relating force to amount of stock removed (Note that Lambda during ploughing is approximately 1/3 Lambda during cutting.)

Vw: Rate at which grinding wheel material wears away.

K: System rigidity or constant of proportionality relating displacement, x, and normal force, F.

Fth: Threshold force, or quantity of force required to enter the ploughing process.

Fpct: Ploughing/cutting transition force or the quantity of force to be exceeded for removal of excess stock to occur.

W: Width of the cut

Formulas:

$$d = h + x$$

$$F = K * x$$

$$h = Lambda/Vw * (F - Fth)$$

$$X = (d + ((Lambda * Fth)/Vw * W))/(1 + (Lambda * K)/Vw * W)$$

STEAMEX - A Real-Time Expert System for Energy Optimization

Einar Dehli, Thomas Bech Pettersen and Odd-Wiking Rahlff
Computas Expert Systems A.S., Veritasveien 1, PO Box 410, N-1322 Høvik, Norway

ABSTRACT

This paper reports on a highly successful implementation of a real-time, energy optimization expert system for operator decision support in a steam production plant.

Unique features of the system compared to conventional process control packages include a carefully engineered graphical user-interface focussing on key economical steering parameters and avoiding distracting information and functionality; a knowledgebased optimization and planning module that takes operational procedures and operator experience into account; and a simulation facility that runs in parallel with optimization and planning on real process data.

The system was put into regular, 24-hour-a-day operation in august 1988. It has been very well received by the operators.

THE DOMAIN

Steam is an important energy carrier extensively used in many industrial processes. The steam plant where Steamex is installed is responsible for the production and distribution of steam to all the various plants at Hydro Porsgrunn, the largest industrial complex in Norway.

The primary concern of the steam plant operators is to always be able to supply the requested amount of steam. A secondary concern is to conserve energy and produce steam as cheap as possible. Energy costs amount to 10-30 MNOK/year (1-3 million GBP/year).

Some plants produce steam as a by-product. To produce additional steam the operators have available four steam boilers; 3 oil-based, and one using electricity. Each boiler is automatically regulated, but the operators must select which boilers to use, and decide upon a load distribution between the boilers.

Selecting the optimal boiler configuration is a non-trivial task. Several factors influence these decisions: electricity prices vary throughout the day and week; starting up an oil-boiler takes 90 minutes; required security margins depend on stability considerations; plants may start up or stop within a few minutes, sometimes following advance notification to the steam plant, but most often not; etc. The previously existing instrumentation and process control equipment provided little assistance in these decisions; cost optimization was left to the initiative and experience of each operator.

FUNCTIONALITY AND USER INTERFACE

The Steamex screen is divided into four regions as shown in figure 1: A network diagram showing a graphical overview of the most important system components, a window showing economical steering information, a plan window showing upcoming events and actions, and a message window. All text and graphic objects are mouse-sensitive. The message window can be scrolled and zoomed to cover the whole screen.

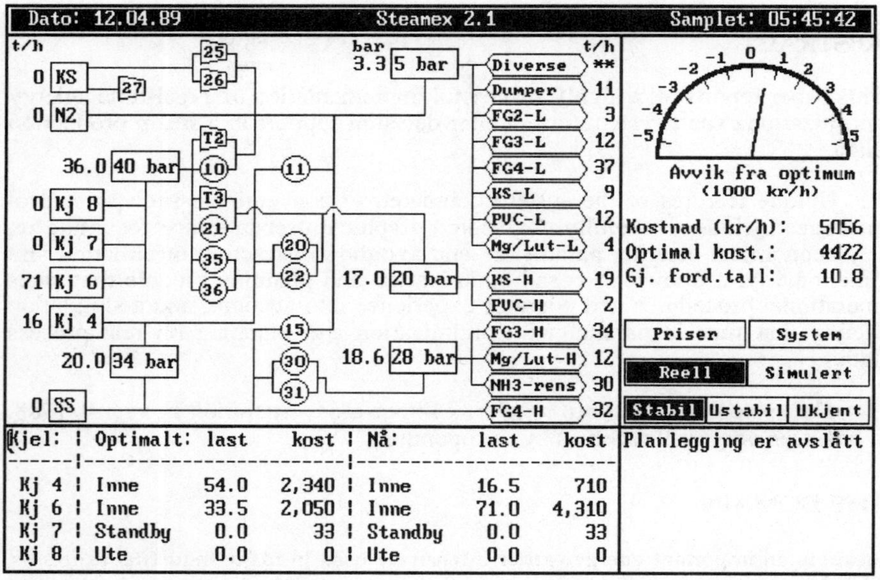

Figure 1: Sample screen copy

Key measurements are dynamically updated in the network diagram, and colour codes are used to indicate overload and operational status. Mouse-clicking an object in the network diagram pops up a menu, allowing the operator to display a trend curve or open a form on the object. Both these displays update themselves as new samples are read from the process.

Steamex continuously updates a graphical display in the economy window showing the current cost/hour deviation from the optimal situation determined by the system. Clicking on items in the economy window displays an elaboration and explanation in the message window.

Simulation is another important feature in the system. The current state can at any time be frozen as a starting point for simulations. In simulated mode the operators can change values of any parameter in the system and immediately see the consequences on the economical steering parameters. While simulating the system still performs its task on real data, duplicating all output parameters, so that both simulation results and results from real data can be examined. The operator is reminded of the system being in simulated mode from changed window titles and by the use of different colors for real and simulated values.

TOOLS SELECTION

At the start-out of the project we wanted to integrate a Process Control package with an Expert System shell. We pursued several alternatives, but apart from the fact that most packages wouldn't run together at all, none of the solutions would have come close to match all our requirements.

We ended up having to use a more general programming language, and decided upon using Smalltalk/V286 from Digitalk [Digitalk 88], even though it was only available as an early beta-version when we started the implementation. Smalltalk/V286 exceeded our expectations, and proved very well suited for the kind of application we had in mind. In fact, the final system now functions and behaves exactly the way we wanted, and all user requirements have been met.

The inherent object-oriented structure of Smalltalk facilitated the development of a model-based system. A built-in Prolog compiler took care of the search part [Rettig 88], and an interrupt-driven process scheduler allowed us to have many parallel processes running concurrently. The interactive, mouse-driven graphics that is an integral part of the Smalltalk user-interface made it easy to build a powerful, yet simple and intuitive, user-interface. Finally, for most practical purposes, the development environment provided us with the same flexibility and set of high-level tools that we were accustomed to from working on Xerox Lisp machines.

SYSTEM DESIGN AND KNOWLEDGE REPRESENTATION

The design is based on a 3-layered approach. At the lowest layer we have made a number of general extensions and modifications to the basic Smalltalk image. Included here are extensions to the process scheduler, modifications to the windowing system so that partly occluded windows can be dynamically updated from background processes without overwriting other windows, and various tools to speed up program development.

The next layer is a domain-specific shell or toolkit for Steamex-like applications. Four program-modules can be identified. These are the Generic Process Model, with class descriptions of steam networks, boilers, consumers etc.; the Optimization and Planning Module, with mechanisms for handling parallel reasoning processes, knowledge representation schemes, inference mechanisms etc.; the System Administration Module, including sophisticated log and restart mechanisms; and the Communication and Process Interface Module.

The final layer is a description of the actual application. This layer is in the form of a set of text files containing definitions of all domain objects, their properties, calculation formulas, procedural and experiental knowledge, screen layout etc. The definition files contain executable Smalltalk code, but they look like plain English with some easy-to-follow syntactic guidelines. This eases the job for the local System Administrator who is expected to maintain the knowledge base. At system generation time a number of consistency checks are carried out to ensure as far as possible a consistent knowledge base.

PLANNING AND TIME DEPENDENT ASPECTS

The goal of Steamex is to advise the operators on the most optimal way of running the boilers over a period of time, in particular giving advice on starting and stopping boilers at specific points in time. Time dependent information is thus of central importance in Steamex, and includes start-up delays for boilers, planned actions in the steam plant itself, and changes, both expected and unexpected, in the various plants consuming or supplying steam. Whenever advance notification of changes in steam consumption or production is received by the steam plant operators, they enter this information to Steamex as "expected events".

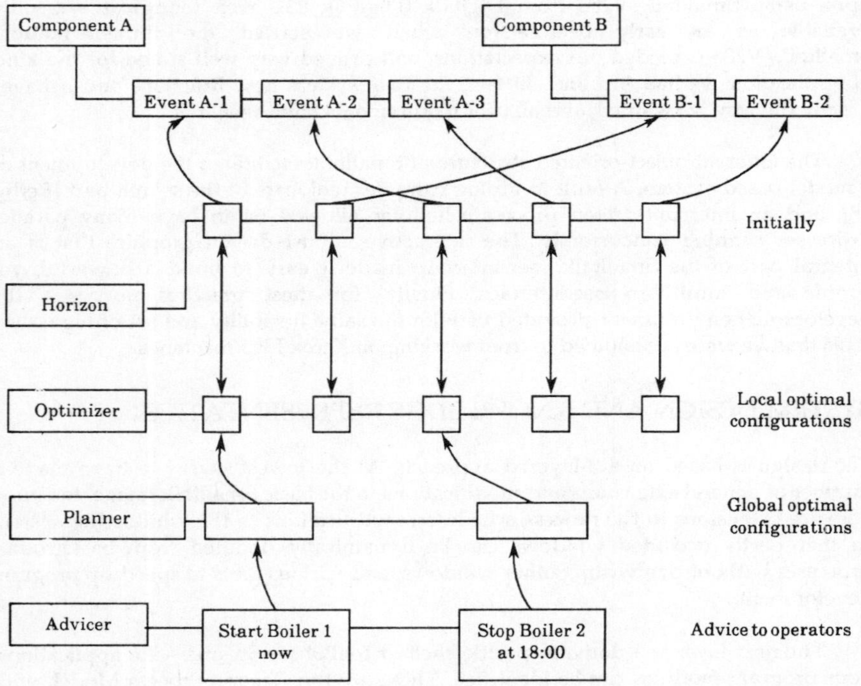

Figure 2: The planning sequence

The planning module itself consists of a set of Prolog/V (the Smalltalk-integrated Prolog) clauses controlled by a set of Smalltalk methods. To give a more detailed description of the planning sequence we need to make a couple of definitions:

Event:

when some component is changing its steam consumption, production or availability at a specific point in time.

Configuration:

the set of available steam boilers with their states (running, inactive or standby) and load.

The planning sequence starts from the current boiler configuration. The set of expected events forms a "horizon", which is a queue of events distributed along the time axis. For each event interval along the time axis the system calculates a local optimal configuration.

When all event intervals have been covered with local optima, the planner switches its strategy to global optimization by checking whether the state transitions between the different local optima can be justified by savings in the energy costs. This is due to the fact that all state transitions have an associated cost.

As an example of global optimization, consider the situation in fig. 3 where local optima change from configuration A to B and then back to A, such that during the time period when configuration B is optimal, we might save energy costs by stopping a boiler. If configuration B is optimal during a short period only, the labour and cost of stopping and restarting a boiler might not justify the savings in energy costs during regular operation. This is detected by the planner, which in this case would eliminate the two latter local configurations from the global configuration sequence, since they are not optimal in a global view.

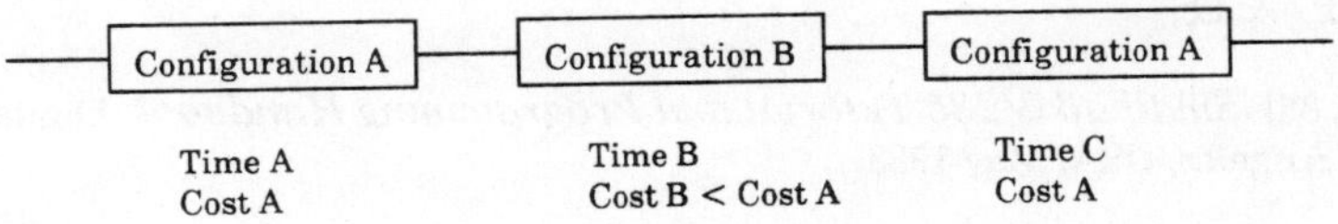

Figure 3: Local vs. global optimal configurations

Finally, the advice to the operators is generated by extracting the differences between each of the succeeding global optimal configurations. This implies that if global optimum A at time T1 has Boiler 1 standby, and the next global optimum B at time T2 has Boiler 1 running, then at time T2 minus the startup time for Boiler 1 the advice to start Boiler 1 is given to the steam plant operators, along with an explanatory text. This procedure is repeated for all global optimum configuration transitions. The list of all advice is visible for the operators at all times. In addition, warning messages are generated whenever actions are required to take place.

Partial results from the planning process are cached, so that when replanning is triggered, only partial replanning is normally required. Replanning is triggered whenever one of the following conditions occur:

1) The event horizon is altered, either by the insertion of a new event, or a change in an existing event.

2) Changes in the current steam need implies that the current or some future boiler configuration no longer will be optimal, i.e. the steam need falls outside the range where the configuration is optimal.

3) An expected event did not occur.

4) Changed energy prices.

PROJECT STATUS AND CONCLUSION

The Steamex main project described here was carried out by Computas Expert Systems for Norsk Hydro A.S during 1988. A prototype implementation for the same domain, but focussing on state analysis and diagnosis instead of economical optimization was carried out in 1986 [Fjellheim, Pettersen 87]. Both projects had partial funding from the Norwegian Council for Scientific and Industrial Research (NTNF). Total effort for the main project is in the order of one man-year.

Steamex runs on a PC AT with 2.5 MByte RAM, 40 MByte hard disk, EGA display and a mouse. The system is interfaced to a microMac 4000 controller from Analog Devices with 48 analog channels using serial communication over the RS 232C port. A complete optimization is normally carried out within the 15 second sampling period.

Steamex has proven very successful. We expect similar applications to have a great potential in many other control rooms as well, and we are now actively engaged in defining follow-up projects based on the same technology.

REFERENCES

[Digitalk 88] *Smalltalk/V286 Tutorial and Programming Handbook,* Digitalk Inc., Los Angeles, USA, May 1988.

[Fjellheim, Pettersen 87] Fjellheim, Roar and Thomas Pettersen, "Knowledgebased Steam Plant Operation" in *Knowledge Based Expert Systems for Engineering: Classification, Education and Control*, eds: Sriram, D. and R.A. Adey, Computational Mechanics Publications, Boston, USA, 1987, pp. 297-310.

[Rettig 88] Marc Rettig, "PROLOG with Class: Digitalk's PROLOG/V", *AI Expert, vol.3, no.3,* March 1988, pp. 13-16.

Reasoning on Plant Process using TMS with Temporal Constraints

K. Furuta and S. Kondo

Nuclear Engineering Research Laboratory, University of Tokyo, Tokai-mura, Ibaraki-ken 319-11, Japan

ABSTRACT

A framework to carry out reasoning on plant process including transient phenomena is presented. The Truth Maintenance System, which is useful for nonmonotonic reasoning under uncertain circumstances, has been expanded to cope with the dynamic plant process by insisting temporal constraints. The proposed architecture is adopted for the behavioural simulation of a plant operator.

INTRODUCTION

Expert operators of such as nuclear power plants are able to recognize the plant state, find out the cause of abnormal plant behaviour and select a proper operational action, although insufficient information or some incorrect information is given. Such a problem solving power of expert operators comes from the use of their plant image constructed from their abundant common sense on the plant process. Since the common sense is a general knowledge applicable only in the usual situations, the assumptions based on it should be dismissed if some contradiction has arisen afterwards.

Several approaches to model the nonmonotonic feature of reasoning by human experts as described above have been proposed, and among them Doyle's TMS (Truth Maintenance System) is an useful architecture for the actual implementation, e.g. Doyle [1]. In the TMS each believed assertion, which is called a node, is held with its foundation for belief. The consistency of the set of assertions is maintained by the truth maintenance algorithm and the dependency-directed backtracking algorithm.

One of its drawbacks, however, is inability to make distinction between change of assumptions and temporal transition of states, since the original TMS has just one plane to record the nodes. Transition of states does not mean the denial of any facts or assumptions valid before the transition, but it means that new assertions become valid due to some causal events. Nevertheless, there are no means to add a contradictory node without affecting the existent nodes in the TMS. The above limitation causes some difficulties in applying the TMS to knowledge base systems for plant operation or plant diagnosis, where it is necessary to reason about dynamic process.

REASONING ON DYNAMIC PROCESS

The process parameters representing the plant states will dynamically change following the physical or chemical interactions within the process, and the human experts have a common knowledge to reason about dynamic process. The following statement represents an example of such knowledge on transient parameters very simple but frequently used.

The parameter will be in a high level, if it was in a normal level and it has increased.

In the present expert systems, reasoning on the transient parameters is usually carried out using the production rules similar to the above statement. A rule including prerequisites satisfied with the current working memory is selected and executed, that is, the concluding assertion is added to and the invalid assertion is removed from the working memory. This procedure works well with the complete and correct set of information, but the inference may not progress in the right direction under uncertain circumstances, since there are no means to defeat the commitments already taken. To defeat the past commitments properly, it is necessary to keep the record of inference and to carry out the truth maintenance.

Another problem arises, however, in the inference on transient parameters with the truth maintenance. In the above example, the assertion referring to the initial state of parameter should be removed after the execution of the rule, since it is contradictory with the concluding assertion of the rule. If the former assertion is included in the foundation of the latter one, the conclusion loses the valid foundation and it is eliminated just after its addition. On the other hand, if the former is excluded from the foundation, the initial state can never be challenged to repair the endangered consistency, though it may be required in the actual situation.

The above dilemma comes from the plane framework of the data base, where the transition of time between the initial and final state of the parameter is not considered. Actually the assertions on the initial and the final state are valid in different time periods, and they cannot contradict each other, if the both are held in different worlds. From the above consideration, the example already shown should be rewritten as follows.

The parameter will be in a high level, if it was in a normal level, it has increased and enough time has passed.

Usually the length of delay has uncertainties and human experts behave in a non-monotonic manner also to the assertion of enough time delay.

TMS WITH TEMPORAL CONSTRAINTS

Several representations of temporal knowledge have been proposed so far. They are classified primarily into two categories: one is the event base representation and the other is the interval base representation, e.g. Allen [2] and Dean [3]. In the present study, the interval base representation has been adopted, since less amount of data base search is required to prove some literal at a particular time point. In the TMS, each node is represented in a Prolog clause as:

hold(Assertion, TimeInterval, Justification),

and identified with both the assertion and the time interval of its validity associated with the node. The time interval is defined as a list of time points such as *[Tb, Te]*, where *Tb* is the beginning time and *Te* is the ending time of the assertion. The nodes containing different time intervals are identified as different nodes, although they correspond to the same assertion. The proof of some literal *P* at a particular time point *T* based on the current belief is achieved by the Prolog program such as:

holdat(P,T) :- hold(P,[Tb,Te],J), Tb=<T, T<Te.

As in the original TMS, the node also contains its justification, which is a pair of inlist and outlist. The node is in if and only if each node in its inlist is in and each node in its outlist is out. In the current system, only the SL justification is used and the CP justification used in Doyle's TMS is omitted after the proposal by Petrie [4]. In the inlist or outlist, each node is appointed with its beginning time as well as its assertion, but the ending time is not used, since the ending time may be changed as the reasoning on temporal transition proceeds. Whenever some change is made in the set of nodes, the TMS checks the validity of each justification and changes the state of the nodes from in to out which lost the support of valid justification. This truth maintenance process is almost the same as the original TMS.

A default reasoning that the assertion once justified is assumed to continue till some contradictory assertion is justified later is used to recognize temporal transition of states. When some node contradictory to the existent node is created, and the former begins later than the latter, the TMS terminates the preceding node at the beginning time of the new node, e.g. Dean [3]. An example is illustrated in figure 1, where the node of *P* is terminated at the time the node of *not P* is justified later. In such a case, temporal transition of states is thought to have occurred; this event does not invoke the truth maintenance process. If the beginning time of the new contradictory node coincides with that of the existent node, the latter node representing the current assumption is dismissed by the usual truth maintenance process. In the example shown in figure 2, the node of *P* is changed to out after the node of *not P* has been created. Transition of states and change of assumptions are distinguishable in the above manner.

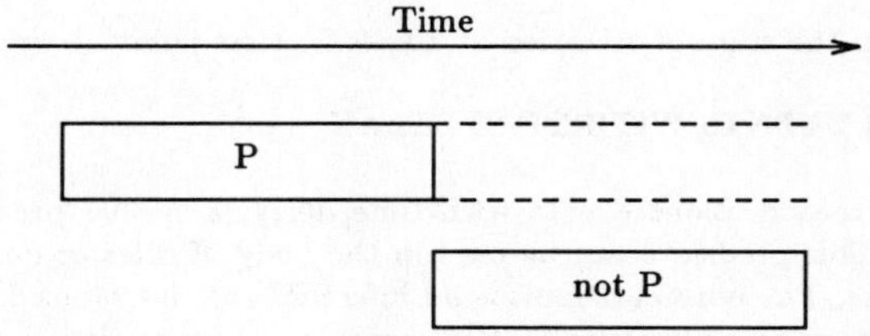

Figure 1 Temporal transition of states.

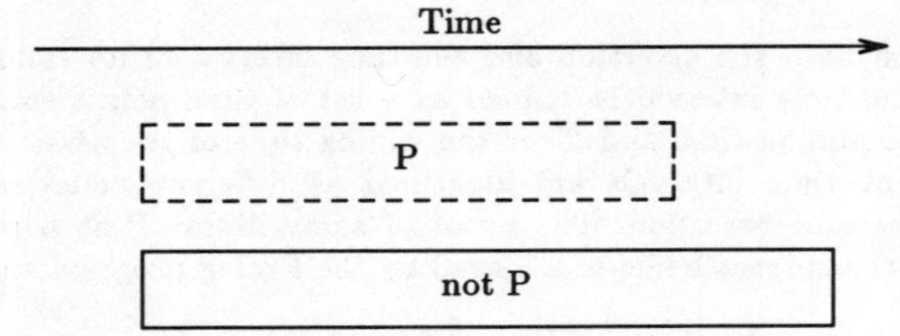

Figure 2 Change of assumptions.

In problem solving the TMS does not work independently but it works in cooperation with some problem solver. When the problem solver proves a new assertion, it keeps the record of proof and hands it to the TMS as the justification. The built-in predicates such as those for numeric comparison are excluded from the justification, since they do not create any beliefs but imply conditional judgements. The node derived from a default has assertions contradictory to itself in the outlist of justification, and such a node is defeasible. For the interface between the TMS and the problem solver, 3 predicates are provided for node creation, node elimination and data base search. The predicate

assert_fact(Assertion, BeginningTime, Justification)

is used to create a new node with the assigned beginning time and justification. The ending time is set undefined, actually infinity, because the ending time will be determined in the manner described above. The predicate

ddb(Assertion, BeginningTime)

is provided to defeat an inconsistent node by the dependency-directed backtracking. If this predicate is executed, the cause of contradiction is searched for and it is changed from in to out by adding another assumption node. The predicate

holdat(Assertion, Time)

is used to query on the state of assertion at a specific time point as already mentioned.

REASONING ON EVENTS WITH TIME DELAY

In order to reason about events with time delay, a special predicate *delay* has been introduced. This predicate can be used in the body of rules or normal defaults in the knowledge base. The normal default is an inference rule introduced by Reiter [5] to represent the common sense knowledge. For example the expression

$$P <\text{-}\ Q \text{ delay } X\text{-}Y$$

implies that some delay equal to or longer than X but not longer than Y exists after the beginning of Q and before the beginning of P.

The assertion of *delay* is defeasible, that is, the assumption that enough time has passed for the occurrence of *P* can be discarded on the fact that the result is still unrealized. The outlist of *delay* node contains the node of *not delay*, unless the length of delay assigned is shorter than the upper limit *Y*. Even after the assertion of *delay* has been defeated, the problem solver can make the same assertion to be in again till the actual length of delay reaches the upper limit *Y*. The function described above is schematically shown in figure 3-a), where the node of *P* is repeatedly made in with increasing delays to certificate its realization.

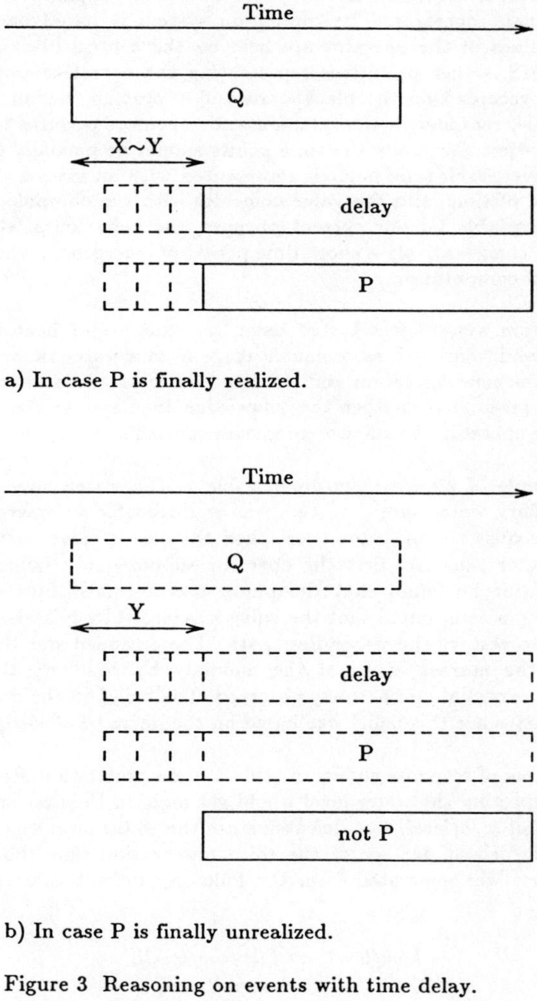

Figure 3 Reasoning on events with time delay.

After the length of delay has reached *Y*, the assertion of *delay* becomes definite and indefeasible. The prerequisite of the rule, which has been believed for a while, is

challenged then, if the result is still unrealized. In figure 3-b), the node of *Q* is finally made out, because the node of *P* has not realized in spite of waiting long enough.

The inference mechanism introduced here enables the reasoning system to cope with uncertainty in the length of delay in an opportunistic manner as human experts.

APPLICATIONAL RESULT

The architectures described in this paper have been applied to the behavioural simulation of a plant operator. The simulation system is based on the blackboard model and the beliefs of the operator are held on the central blackboard under the control of the TMS. Other primitives representing the cognitive world of the plant operator are also recorded on the blackboard and 4 problem solving modules, which are sensory module, reasoner, action planner and executor, perform the tasks for the behavioural simulation. Generally the time points should be partially ordered. For the present use, however, each time point is represented with an integer corresponding to the absolute value of time, and the value coincides with the chronological order. This assumption is acceptable for our current purpose, the behavioural simulation of the plant operator, in comparatively a short time period of emergency, while it contributes to the reduction of computation.

The simulation system was tested using an example of heat removal process under abnormal conditions such as coolant leakage from a water tank. In this test, the plant state in the normal operation and the hypotheses on the primary failures of the equipments were given, but neither the knowledge to diagnose the process nor the hypotheses on the operator's mistake were given explicitly.

In the example of response shown in table 1, the water level was decreasing, although an auxiliary water supply system was equipped for an emergency. This anomaly occurred, because the operator overlooked the closed valve between the supply pump and the water tank. At first the operator supposed the failure of the supply pump at 77 sec, but he found that the pump was normally functioning. Then he checked the valve position, found that the valve was closed by mistake and opened the valve in manual to restore the water flow path. The reasoner and the TMS successfully found out the correct cause of the anomaly by resolving the inconsistency between the facts expected and actually observed. The belief on the normal valve position was challenged, since this belief was based on the default knowledge.

In the example of response shown in table 2, the simulation system was watching the level meter expecting the water level would get high. In the first and second observations, the belief of *high(level)* was defeated since the water level was still in a normal level. It was confirmed at 328 sec in the third observation that the water level got high. This response was generated from the following default rule on the change of water level:

$$\begin{aligned} high(level) <\!- \; & increase(level), \\ & normal(level) \\ & delay\ 10\text{-}200. \end{aligned}$$

In case the water level does never get high, the system starts to reason out the cause of unexpected behaviour such as failure of the water supply pump. The system also

Table 1 An example of system response, searching for the cause of anomaly.

```
*** apply_rule ***
Execute :: read_change(level)

*** assimilate(decrease(level),77) ***
*** DDB process start ***
Add fact :: off(spump) at 40
Make out :: on(spump) at [40,inf]
Make out :: increase(level) at [40,inf]
Make out :: high(level) at [54,inf]
Make out :: normal(level) at [44,54]
Make in  :: low(level) at [44,inf]
Make in  :: decrease(level) at [40,inf]
Make out :: observe(change(level)) at [40,inf]
*** Assimilated ***

*** Start Planning *** observe(spump)
Execute :: read_state(spump)

*** assimilate(on(spump),85) ***
*** DDB process start ***
Add fact :: close(svalve) at 0
Make out :: open(svalve) at [0,inf]
Make out :: off(spump) at [40,inf]
Make out :: observe(spump) at [40,inf]
Make in  :: on(spump) at [40,inf]
Make in  :: observe(change(level)) at [40,inf]
*** Assimilated ***

*** Start Planning *** observe(svalve)
Execute :: read_state(svalve)

*** assimilate(close(svalve),93) ***
*** Assimilated ***

*** Start Planning *** achieve(open(svalve))
Execute :: open(svalve)
Add fact :: open(svalve) at 96
```

Table 2 An example of system response, watching the increasing level.

```
*** apply_rule ***
Add fact :: high(level) delay 146 at 279
Add fact :: high(level) at 279

*** confirm(high(level)) ***
Execute :: read_amnt(level)

*** assimilate(normal(level),295) ***
*** DDB process start ***
Add fact :: not (high(level) delay 146) at 279
Make out :: high(level) delay 146 at [279,inf]
Make out :: high(level) at [279,inf]
Make in  :: normal(level) at [279,inf]
*** Assimilated ***

*** apply_rule ***
Add fact :: high(level) delay 146 at 295
Add fact :: high(level) at 295

*** confirm(high(level)) ***
Execute :: read_amnt(level)

*** assimilate(normal(level),311) ***
*** DDB process start ***
Add fact :: not (high(level) delay 146) at 295
Make out :: high(level) delay 146 at [295,inf]
Make out :: high(level) at [295,inf]
Make in  :: normal(level) at [295,inf]
*** Assimilated ***

*** apply_rule ***
Add fact :: high(level) delay 146 at 311
Add fact :: high(level) at 311

*** confirm(high(level)) ***
Execute :: read_amnt(level)

*** assimilate(high(level),328) ***
*** Assimilated ***
```

performed successfully the task to observe the state of plant parameters, which vary with different speeds.

CONCLUSION

In applying the nonmonotonic reasoning to knowledge base systems for plant engineering use, it is required to properly represent the knowledge on dynamic process and carry out reasoning. In the present paper, temporal constraints have been introduced to the Truth Maintenance System and an architecture was proposed to represent temporal transition of states distinctively from change of assumptions. Transitional events can be distinguished by comparing the beginning times of contradictory assertions. The predicate *delay* newly defined reflects the common sense on events involving time delay, and it is able to reason about dynamic process plausibly using this predicate. The methods developed in this study were applied to the behavioural simulation of a plant operator, and the simulation system successfully showed the ability to reason about the plant process including transient phenomena.

REFERENCES

1. Doyle, J. Truth Maintenance System, Artificial Intelligence, Vol.12, pp. 231-272, 1979.

2. Allen, J.F., et al. Common Sense Theory of Time, in 9th IJCAI, pp. 528-531, Proc. of the 9th Int. Joint Conf. on Artificial Intelligence, Los Angeles, Morgan Kaufmann, California, 1985.

3. Dean, T.L., et al. Temporal Data Base Management, Artificial Intelligence, Vol.32, pp. 1-55, 1987.

4. Petrie, C.J. Revised Dependency-Directed Backtracking for Default Reasoning, in AAAI-87, pp. 167-172, Proc. of the 6th National Conf. on Artificial Intelligence, Seattle, Morgan Kaufmann, California, 1987.

5. Reiter, R. A Logic for Default Reasoning, Artificial Intelligence, Vol.13, pp. 81-132, 1980.

SECTION 6 - ROBOTICS

A Real-Time, Knowledge Based System for Supervisory Control of a Mobile Robot

William D. McGraw* and Behnam Motazed**
* *Alcoa Technical Center, Alcoa Center, Pa. 15069, USA*
** *Field Robotics Center, Robotics Institute, Carnegie Mellon University, Pittsburgh, Pa. 15213, USA*

ABSTRACT

Mobile robots can replace humans in many applications where the hazards of the environment jeopardize human life. However, replacing humans with autonomous robots removes the intelligence and expertise of the human from the task. Even semi-autonomous mobile robots require a certain degree of local intelligence in order to navigate and perform tasks in hazardous environments. A knowledge based system (KBS) is one way of providing this intelligence. This paper describes the design, development, and testing of a real-time, knowledge based system for supervisory control of a semi-autonomous mobile robot developed for surveying hazardous waste sites.

INTRODUCTION

The subject of this paper is the development of a real-time Knowledge Based System (KBS) for local, intelligent, supervisory control of a mobile robot. In the KBS, the knowledge required by the robot is encoded in the form of rules. Each rule is sensitive to, and fires when, pre-determined conditions occur during the operation of the robot. A KBS was chosen over a procedural program for this application because the KBS provides a computationally efficient and user-transparent method for determining which rules to fire and when to fire them. Computational efficiency is especially important in this application because the KBS must operate in real time. This requirement of the KBS is described in detail later in the paper.

The mobile robot used for this application is called the Terregator. The Terregator is a six-wheeled mobile robot developed as an experimental research tool by the Field Robotics Center of Carnegie-Mellon University to study issues related to control and navigation. In the application described in this paper it was used to survey hazardous waste sites in order to locate buried hazardous waste containers. Figure 1 shows the configuration of the Terregator system for this application.

The Terregator pulls a gantry that contains a magnetic sensor to detect perturbations in the earth's magnetic field which may indicate the presence of buried metallic drums. As the Terregator moves forward, the sensor can be moved from side to side in order to scan a path 6 feet wide. Data from the sensor is collected and sent back to the base computer (via the 1200 baud radio link) for off-line analysis.

The base computer is also used to tele-operate the Terregator. A menu of commands allows the user to directly move the Terregator (joystick mode) or to download parameters for scanning the site.

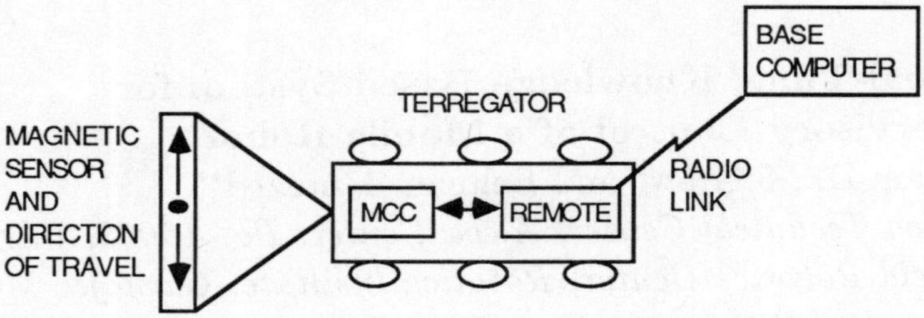

Figure 1. Terregator System

The Terregator contains two on-board computers, the Motion Control Computer (MCC) and an on-board host computer (called the remote computer). The MCC keeps track of the x and y position, heading, distance travelled, elapsed time, and velocity of the Terregator. It accepts commands (such as move, stop, arc, speed, etc.) from several communication ports, interprets these commands, and controls the outputs to the drive motor amplifiers.

The remote computer provides an interface between the base and the MCC. The software running in this computer includes communications drivers, software for the acquisition and archiving of magnetic sensor data and the KBS described in this paper.

The KBS provides local intelligence for supervisory monitoring and control of the Terregator. The KBS acquires status information (position, heading, velocity, etc.) from the Terregator, accepts commands from the base computer, checks the validity of commands from the base, and processes valid commands. The rules in the KBS determine the appropriate control commands to send to the MCC based on commands from the base and the current status of the Terregator. The KBS also performs diagnostic checks and sends the current status of the Terregator to the base.

The commands accepted by the KBS are a superset of the MCC commands. The additional KBS commands are higher level commands that are decomposed into a sequence of MCC commands. For example, the SCAN command causes the KBS to send the SPEED, ARC, and MOVE commands to the Terregator. In addition, the KBS automatically initiates the acquisition of magnetic sensor data at the appropriate times during a scan.

At present, a prototype version of the KBS has been developed in OPS83. This version is capable of accepting and processing commands from the base, controlling the Terregator during a survey of a hazardous waste site, and performing diagnostic checks. Preliminary testing of the system has been completed.

REQUIREMENTS

The following subsections describe the design requirements for the KBS.

Command Interpretation/Execution

The KBS must interpret commands from the base and either execute these commands or send back an appropriate message if the commands can not be executed. Commands from the base may be high level commands that are broken down into lower level commands and executed by the KBS or they may be low level commands which are merely validated by the KBS and passed on to the Motion Control Computer.

Scanning Control
The scanning (also called mapping) function consists of taking a number of sensor readings at fixed distances along the path to be followed by the Terregator. The KBS is responsible for monitoring the distance travelled and, at the appropriate time, executing a function to take the sensor readings. The KBS is also responsible for compensating for any errors between when the scan occurred and when it should have occurred.

Diagnostics
In addition to its control functions, the KBS is responsible for monitoring the operation of the Terregator, reporting any problems that it detects back to the base, and taking corrective actions (if possible). The capability of the diagnostic function will be limited by the availability of sensors, but it should be able to detect such problems as position encoder failures, communications failures, motor overheating, and loss of power to the drive motors, with the appropriate sensors.

Communications
The KBS must be able to communicate with the operator at the Base computer. This ability is necessary for sending error and status messages back to the operator and for requesting information (such as parameter values) from the operator.

Navigation
The KBS is responsible for moving the Terregator from its current position to a new position (within the accuracy of the X and Y position indicators of the Terregator).

Hardware/software environment
The optimum configuration for the system consisted of the KBS running in the remote computer. This is because no additional hardware would be required and there could be tight coupling (via shared memory) between the KBS and the other software running in the remote computer. The hardware for the remote computer is a 68020 based Motorola single board computer (SBC). The real-time operating system for the remote computer is version 4.0 of VxWorks. Therefore, the KBS must be able to run in this environment.

Development environment
All software for the remote system was to be developed in the C programming language on a Sun 3 workstation. The KBS also had to be compatible with this environment.

Real-time response
The Terregator KBS must run periodically and at a frequency fast enough to respond to commands from the base and changes in the status of the Terregator. For the Terregator KBS, the most time-critical task is deciding when to start a scan during the scanning process. This decision is based on the distance travelled by the Terregator since the last scan. The desired distance between scans is 30 +/- 3 cm. In other words, the KBS must initiate a new scan 27-33 cm after the previous scan. Since the KBS obtains the position of the Terregator at the beginning of each cycle of execution, the time between cycles of execution of the KBS must be such that the 27-33 cm scanning window is not missed. Since this window is 6 cm wide and since the target speed of the Terregator during scanning is 5 cm/sec, the cycle time for the KBS must be less than 1.2 seconds [6cm/(5cm/sec)]. Thus the KBS must run at least once every 1.2 seconds. However, as a contingency against unknown future requirements, the KBS should run at least once every 500 milliseconds.

During each cycle of execution the KBS must acquire Terregator data and any new commands from the base, process the base commands, and perform diagnostic and control functions. At the outset of the project it was estimated that these functions would require about 25 rule firings during each cycle of execution of the KBS. Since, from the previous paragraph, the KBS needs to run once every 500 milliseconds, this means that the KBS must be capable of firing at least 50 rules per second.

The need for the KBS to run at least once every 500 milliseconds and fire at least 50 rules per second were used as part of the selection criteria for KBS development tools (described later in the paper).

Automatic acquisition of data

The KBS needs to know the current x and y position, heading, and velocity of, and distance travelled by the Terregator. The KBS also needs data from the magnetic, and possibly other, sensors for diagnostic purposes. In addition, the KBS must have access to messages received from both the Base and MCC computers. All of this real-time information must be updated in the working memory of the KBS for each cycle of execution.

Representing and reasoning about time

All data coming back from the MCC via the Remote system will be time stamped. All commands from the Base and any other data in working memory should also be time stamped. The time stamp of the data is to be stored with the value in working memory and will be used for various purposes (such as the calculating rate of change).

Representing and reasoning with uncertainty

The KBS must have some method for representing both rule and input value uncertainty and for propagating uncertainty. Input uncertainty refers to the uncertainty associated with the values of input data. Rule uncertainty refers to the uncertainty associated with the conclusion of a rule given that the premise is true. For example, in the simple rule "IF A THEN B", the uncertainty of the value of A is input uncertainty. If A is true, the uncertainty of B as the correct conclusion is rule uncertainty.

In addition, since the KBS will output control commands, it should have some method for representing output uncertainty. This is the uncertainty that the actions called for are actually performed. For example, if the KBS tells that Terregator to move forward, there is some uncertainty as to whether or not the action will occur.

Dynamic change of focus

The KBS should be able to quickly switch from reasoning about one problem to reasoning about another problem. For example, if the KBS is performing the path following function and an abort command is issued from the Base the KBS should immediately quit path following and execute the Abort command.

EVALUATION AND SELECTION OF KBS DEVELOPMENT TOOLS

In order to speed the development of the knowledge based system it was decided to use a commercially available package. Several packages were evaluated for this application. The OPS83 rule based programming language was chosen for the following reasons:

1. It is written in C and can run on the 68020 SBC under VxWorks. This is advantageous because it allows tight coupling between the KBS and the other

software running in the Remote system. In addition, no additional hardware is required.

2. It is very fast. It benchmarked at 76 rules/second on IBM PC/AT for the monkey and bananas problem. In the Terregator KBS application it is running at about 3.2 milliseconds per rule.

3. It is very flexible. The control strategy of the inference engine can be tailored to the application and linkages are available to and from user written C programs.

4. It is a commercially available and supported package that has been used for other real-time robotics applications (PST [5]).

5. It is inexpensive.

Although there were some disadvantages to using OPS83 (such as the need to re-compile and re-link each time a change is made), its speed, flexibility, and low cost were overriding factors for its selection.

KNOWLEDGE ACQUISITION

Knowledge about mobile robot control strategy was acquired by being working members of the project team and attending weekly design review and project status meetings, by formal meetings with the developer of the original procedural control software for the Terregator, and by informal meetings with the developer of the MCC software. In addition, documentation for the MCC command set, the original procedural control program, and the communications protocol to be used between the KBS, base and the MCC was very helpful. Finally, the authors' previous experience with real-time control systems proved to be beneficial. The following subsections describe the information obtained as a result of the knowledge acquisition process.

Entities/attributes

The following objects needed to be represented in the KBS. This information is stored as working memory elements in the KBS and used as the basis for all rules.

1. Goals	(eg. update clock, get data)
2. Clock	(contains system time)
3. Commands	(both from the base and to the MCC)
4. Terregator	(x,y position, heading, velocity)
5. Messages to the Base	(eg. motion done, command ack.)
6. Status of communications	(# of errors and error rate)
7. Magnetic Sensor Data	(x,y position and magnitude)
8. Replies	(from Terregator and Base)
9. Scan Parameters	(eg. run length and scan interval)

Classifications/relations

All commands from the base are sent to the KBS. The KBS determines whether each command is to be passed on to the MCC or interpreted internally. Figure 2 shows the classification of these commands as either KBS commands or MCC (Terregator) commands.

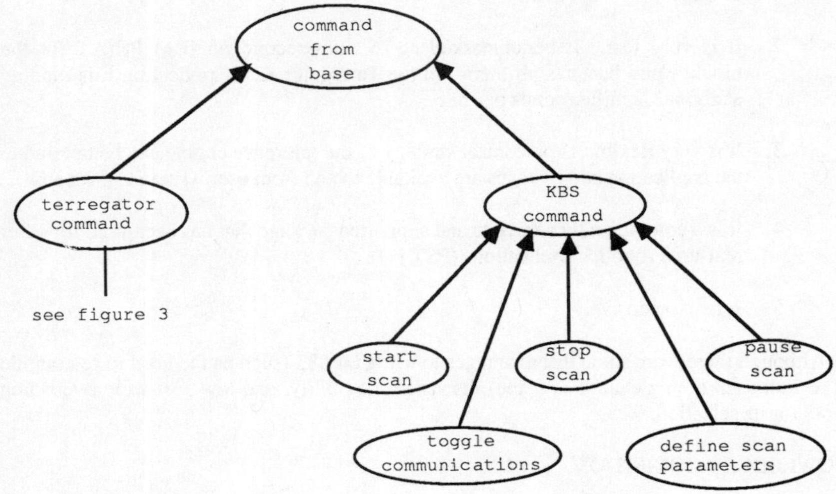

Figure 2. Classification of commands from BASE

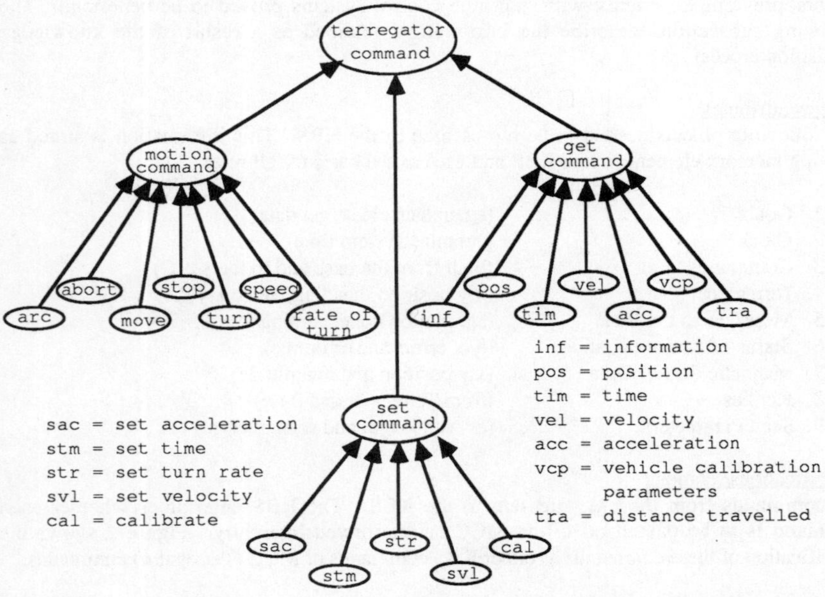

Figure 3. Classification of Terregator commands

KBS commands are higher level functions (such as scanning) that may cause the KBS to issue one or more Terregator commands. For example, upon receipt of a START SCAN command, the KBS issues a speed command to the MCC in order to maintain constant forward velocity during the scanning process (after performing other functions internally).

Terregator commands are received and processed by the KBS and forwarded to the MCC if there are no errors. Figure 3 shows the classification of Terregator commands as either motion commands, "get" commands, or "set" commands.

All "get" commands request information from the Terregator. However, since the KBS has up-to-date information from the Terregator these commands can be processed by the KBS without the need to forward the command to the MCC. For example, if the base issues a get_position command the KBS can send bac. the current x,y position and heading from working memory.

The "set" commands are used to set operating parameters for the Terregator in the MCC. The KBS checks the arguments of these commands to make sure that they are within the current upper and lower limits for the parameter. If they are not, a non-acknowledge (NAK) message is sent to the base. If they are, an acknowledge message is sent to the base and the command is forwarded to the MCC. In addition, the KBS records the new setting of the parameter.

All motion commands either initiate, terminate, or change the motion of the Terregator. This is an important class of commands because the execution of these commands takes a finite amount of time. The motion control computer issues a motion done message when the execution of a motion command has been completed. In order for the KBS to know which motion command is being executed by the Terregator, a queue of motion commands is kept in working memory. When a motion done message is received from the Terregator, the corresponding motion command is deleted from working memory.

<u>Heuristics</u>

The following are example heuristics obtained from the knowledge acquisition process:

1. Commands from the base must be processed in the order in which they are received. This is an important point because, without special logic, most recent (last) command would normally be executed first due to the conflict resolution strategy used by the KBS.

2. Commands to the Terregator motion controller must be sent in the correct order. This is important for reasons similar to those discussed above.

3. Commands from the base must be acknowledged (ACK'ed) or non-acknowledged (NAK'ed).

4. All commands to the MCC will be acknowledged by the MCC.

5. The following rules apply during scanning (see figure 4):

   A. If the distance travelled since the last scan is greater than or equal to delta, initiate a scan.

   B. If it is the end of a run, turn right or left depending on the run number and calculate stop angle limits.

   C. If turning at the end of a run, stop when the heading of the Terregator is within the stop angle limits.

   D. If done turning at end of run, move a fixed distance to position sensor for next run.

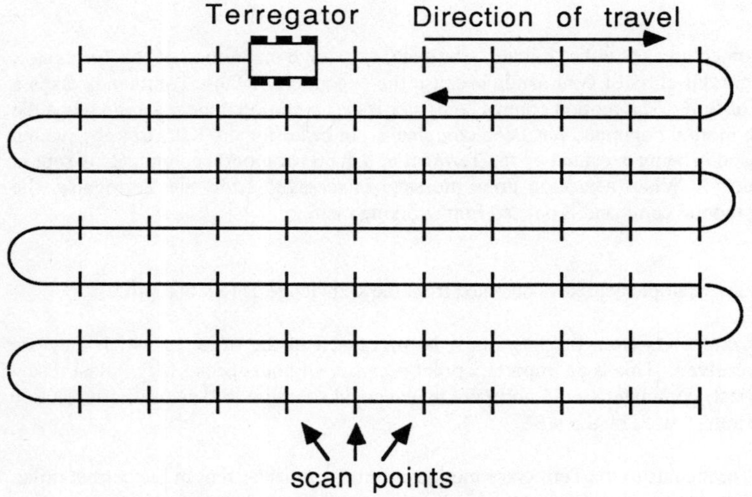

Figure 4. Terregator scan path

DESIGN AND IMPLEMENTATION

This section describes the design and implementation of the remote computer software and the KBS.

Remote computer software architecture

Figure 5 shows the architecture of the control software in the remote computer. The KBS is one of several major tasks running asynchronously and in parallel on the Motorola single board computer under version 4.0 of the VxWorks real-time operating system. The following describes the operation of the system.

Data from the base computer is received by the receive portion of the COMMB INTERFACE task as shown. Once a complete message (either a command or an ACK/NAK reply) has been received, the COMMB INPUT HANDLER task is resumed. This task checks incoming messages from the base for packet length, opcode, and syntax errors. If there is an error a NAK reply will be sent to the base. If there are no errors the message will be placed in the BASE COMMANDS input buffer but an ACK will not be sent to the base because there may be other errors (such as parameters above or below limits) that will be detected by the KBS. If the command from the base was the Abort command the COMMB input handler will also perform some special abort processing (such as sending an Abort message to the MCC or killing power to the motors). All other command processing will be handled by the KBS.

The KBS receives data (such as base commands, Terregator data, and sensor data) via data structures which are globally shared between tasks in the VxWorks operating system. The first function performed by the KBS each time it is resumed is to read in new data from this globally shared memory. The KBS is responsible for acknowledging and executing commands from the base. The KBS then proceeds to process its other rules to perform diagnostic and control functions. Control commands from the KBS to the Terregator MCC are placed in a buffer and output by the COMMT INTERFACE transmit task. The KBS also determines when it is time to collect magnetic sensor data and resumes the MAP ACQUISITION task which controls the movement of and acquisition of data from the magnetic sensor. Data from the magnetic sensor is processed and sent back to the host by the MAP ARCHIVING task. This data is also placed in shared memory so that the KBS can perform sensor diagnostics.

The Terregator Query Task (TQT) periodically requests data from the Terregator MCC. Messages from the MCC (either Terregator data or ACK/NAK replies) are received by the COMMT INTERFACE receive task. Once a complete message has been received the COMMT INPUT HANDLER task is resumed to process the message. If a syntax, opcode, or packet length error is detected a NAK reply will be sent to the MCC. If there are no errors the message is placed in the appropriate data structure in globally shared memory. A counter of the total number of NAK replies received is kept in globally shared memory so that the KBS can use it for diagnostic purposes.

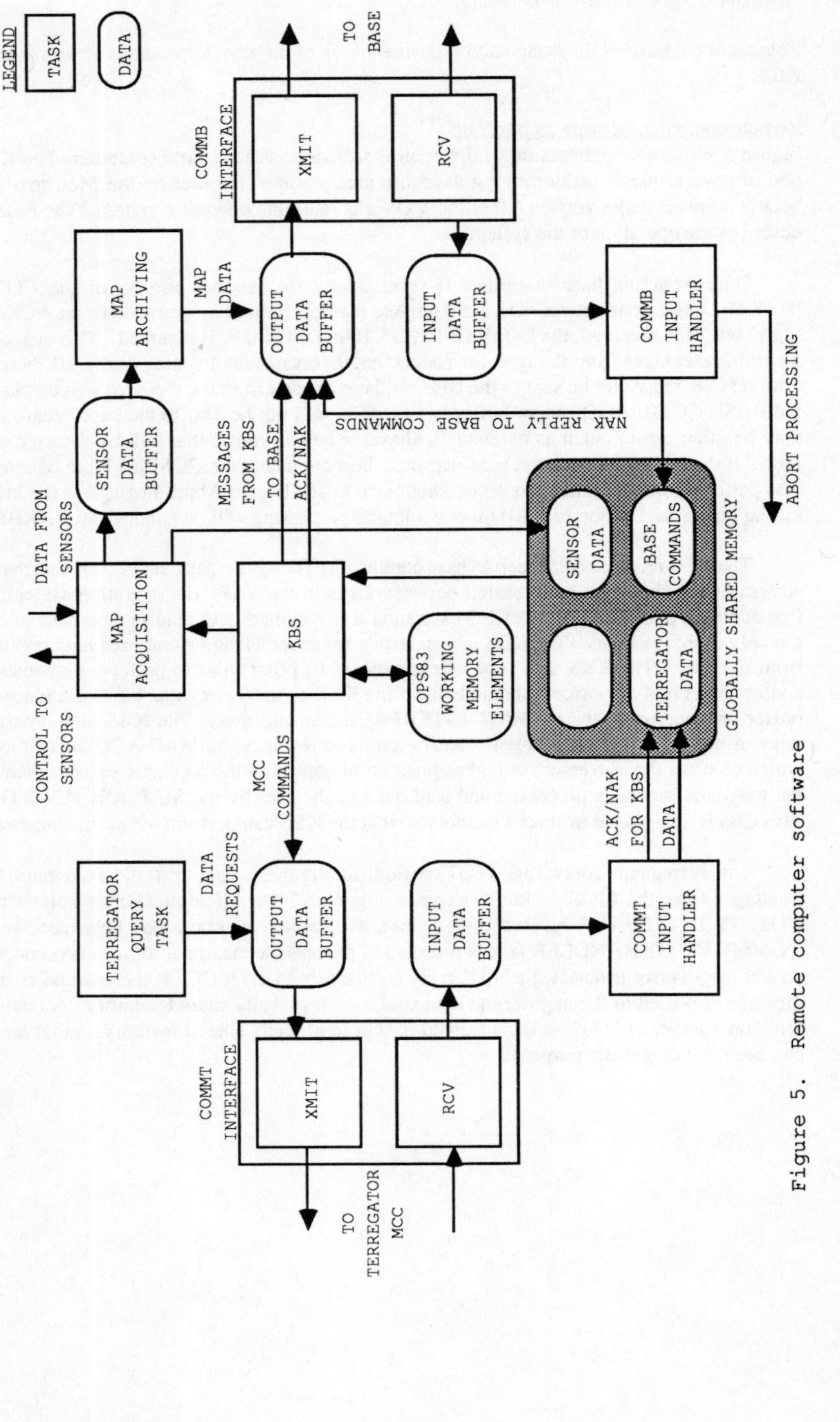

Figure 5. Remote computer software

Knowledge based system architecture
The KBS is written in OPS83. The following subsections describe the design and implementation of the system.

Control strategy Control of the periodic execution of the KBS is performed by a procedure which is called when the KBS begins executing. This procedure performs three main functions each cycle:

1. It makes the goal working memory elements that drive the system during the cycle.

2. It calls a procedure which fires rules until there are no more rules to fire.

3. It delays the correct amount of time so that the KBS runs at the desired frequency.

In addition, the procedure prints out diagnostic information such as the number of cycles completed, the number of rules fired, the elapsed time required to fire those rules, and the number of working memory elements.

Working memory Working memory contains the necessary elements to represent all of the entities and their attributes. Working memory is updated at the beginning of each cycle and may also be updated as rules fire.

Production memory Production memory (also called the rule base) contains the rules for acquiring Terregator data, magnetic sensor data, communications error data, and commands from the base, It also contains rules for controlling the Terregator, communicating with the base, and performing diagnostic functions. The rules in the rule base are partitioned into the types of tasks they perform by their goal element (i.e. the first element to be matched in the left hand side of the rule). The current rule base contains about 55 rules.

Real-time response As discussed in the requirements section, the KBS is required to run twice per second or once every 500 milliseconds. Timing tests performed on the current version of the KBS show that it is able to perform all of its tasks in under 100 milliseconds, with no other tasks running in the system. Therefore, the KBS should be able to meet the 500 millisecond requirement without any modifications, even with the other tasks running.

Prior to implementing the system it was not known if the execution time of the KBS would be less than 500 milliseconds. One approach that was considered to insure that the KBS does not run longer than 500 milliseconds is to modify the inference engine so that it checks to see how much time it has left before executing the next rule. If the amount of time left is less than some limit the KBS could output its best solution so far to the problem it is working on and stop. It could then resume working on the problem (or start working on a new problem) the next time it is resumed. This approach has not been implemented because it does not appear to be needed at this time.

Automatic acquisition of data As discussed previously, the KBS obtains Terregator, magnetic sensor and communications error data and commands from the base via globally shared memory. The data in this shared memory is updated by the other tasks running in the remote computer. The interface between the KBS (written in OPS83) and globally shared memory is via functions written in the C programming language. These functions access shared memory and move the data to variables accessible by OPS83.

Representing and reasoning about time All information in the system is time stamped. The processing of commands from the base is one example of how this time stamp is used. As mentioned previously, it is important that commands be processed in the order in which they are received. This is accomplished by having the rules that process commands check to make sure that there are no commands to be processed that have earlier time stamps.

The resolution of the time stamp became an issue in this application. As mentioned previously, it is also important that commands to the Terregator be sent in the proper order. In this case, however, the time stamp could not be used because of the resolution of the VxWorks clock (16.6 milliseconds). During this time several rules may fire that create Terregator commands and all of them would have the same time stamp. In this case it would not be possible to know which one to send first. Therefore, a sequence number is used to determine the order in which to send Terregator commands.

Representing and reasoning with uncertainty Provisions have been made for representing a measure of belief (MB) and a measure of disbelief (MD) for the values of several of the working memory elements. The intention was to use this information to reason about uncertainty. For example, with dead-reckoning, the certainty of the x and y position decreases with the distance travelled and could be represented by the MB and MD parameters. However, the mechanisms for reasoning about uncertainty have not been implemented at this time.

VERIFICATION AND VALIDATION

Verification substantiates that a system correctly implements its specifications whereas validation substantiates that the system performs according to expectations and with an acceptable level of accuracy (O'Keefe [8]).

The Terregator KBS was verified by checking the rule base for dead-end clauses, duplicate rules, inconsistent rules, and completeness. These checks were either done manually or by the OPS83 compiler.

The first step in the validation process was to verify that the execution time of the KBS was less than 500 milliseconds. This was tested by having the KBS print out the number of rules fired and the elapsed time for each cycle of execution. Timing tests conducted on the complete KBS running periodically (and with dummy data so that the KBS has a typical workload), have shown that the time required to fire 27 rules is 76 milliseconds (approximately 3.2 milliseconds per rule). Therefore, the execution time of the current system was well within the 500 millisecond requirement.

The system was also validated to insure that it operated correctly. This was done by operating the KBS interactively, so that the firing of rules and modifications to working memory could be controlled and traced.

A Terregator simulator has also been developed which can be used to further test the KBS. Conducting tests on the simulator will be more convenient and safer than conducting tests on the actual Terregator. However, final validation of the KBS will still be done on the actual Terregator.

FUTURE ENHANCEMENTS

All of the functional requirements described previously, except for navigation, have been implemented. Future enhancements would include the addition of the navigation function. This would not only require additional rules but also additional sensors. For example, the dead-reckoning position sensors should be replaced with a more accurate method for determining the x,y position of the Terregator. Also, obstacle detection and avoidance can be incorporated into the system if the appropriate sensors (such as sonar or infrared) are added.

Other enhancements include additional diagnostic checks (such as motor diagnostics) which can be performed if the appropriate sensors (such as temperature and vibration sensors) are available.

As mentioned previously, the KBS does not currently reason about uncertainty. Another enhancement would be to incorporate uncertainty reasoning into the KBS.

CONCLUSIONS

The major accomplishments of the work described in this paper are:

1. Porting OPS83 to the VxWorks real-time operating system.

2. The acquisition and organization of knowledge from various sources about control of the Terregator.

3. The development of a prototype real-time, knowledge based system for control of the Terregator mobile robot.

In retrospect, the rule based approach worked well for this application. Also, the choice of OPS83 as the knowledge based system development tool turned out to be a good one. Its execution speed is very impressive.

ACKNOWLEDGEMENTS

The authors would like to thank Prof. W. L. Whittaker of the Robotics Institute at Carnegie-Mellon University for the opportunity to work on this project, Mr. M. D. Waltz and Mr. B P. Wilkerson of the Alcoa Technical Center for their support, and the members of the Field Robotics Center, especially fellow project team members, David White, David Wettergreen and Khaled Matar.

REFERENCES

1. McGraw, W.D., A Real-Time Knowledge Based Expert System for Supervisory Control of the Terregator Mobile Robot, Master of Manufacturing Engineering Project Report, C-MU, 1988 August 10.

2. McGraw, W.D., Real-Time Industrial Applications of AI: A Survey, C-MU Project Report, 1988 May 6.

3. Forgy, C.L., The OPS83 User's Manual System Version 2.2, Production System Technologies, Inc., July 1986.

4. Forgy, C.L., The OPS83 Report System Version 2.2, Production Systems Technologies, Inc., July 1986.

5. Production Systems Technologies, Inc., OPS83 Applications, 1988.

6. Wright, M.L., Green, M.W., Fiegl, G., Cross, P.F., (SRI Int'l) An Expert System for Real-Time Control, IEEE Software, March 1986.

7. Byrd, J.S., Fisher, J.J., DeVries, K.R., Martin, T.P., Expert Robots in Nuclear Plants, ANS Topical Meeting on Artificial Intelligence and Other Innovative Computer Applications in the Nuclear Industry, Snowbird, Utah, 1987.

8. O'Keefe, R.M., Osman, B., and Smith, E.P., Validating Expert System Performance, IEEE Expert, vol. 2, no. 4, Winter 1987.

9. McTamaney, L.S., Mobile Robots: Real-Time Intelligent Control, IEEE Expert, vol. 2, no. 4, Winter 1987.

Intelligent Behaviour in Robotic Environments

Massimo A. Arlotti

IBM Italy Rome Scientific Center, via Giorgione 159, Rome 00147, Italy

ABSTRACT

Very often robots, in industrial as in civil environments, deal with partially unknown conditions, so that they are required to produce successfull operational strategies overcoming every uncertainty issues. This capability is correlated to the intelligence of the robot. In this paper an assembly problem in a non-deterministic environment, i.e. where parts to be assembled have unknown shape, size and location, is described. The only knowledge used by the robot to perform the assembly operation is given by a connectivity rule and geometrical constraints concerning parts. Once a set of geometrical features of parts has been extracted by a vision system, applying such rule lets to determine the composition sequence. A suitable sensory apparatus allows to control the whole operation.

INTRODUCTION

An experimental work, realized at the IBM Italy Rome Scientific Center to investigate some robot capabilities in unstructured operational environments, is presented. Generally, different degrees of uncertainty are present in the robot operation world. Typically, in an assembly environment the following situations could be considered.

a) The shape and dimension of parts as well as the final assembly are known, while their location on the workplane is not. In this case the robot vision system must recognize parts and determine their location and orientation. Then the robot has to plan the composition sequence to get the final assembly. This implies to define a grasp approach trajectory for the arm, a grasp position for the end-effector, a "collision-free" trajectory and a suitable positioning of the moved part into the assembly to be built. Use of endpoint sensing should be made by the robot in an interactive fashion in order to recover unpredictable error situations.

b) The shape and dimension of parts as well as their locations are unknown while the final assembly is known. In such a case the vision system must locate the various parts while checking, starting from a general knowledge of the problem, whether it is possible to assemble them or not; however without identifying them, since they are not completely known "a priori". In addition to what examined in the previous case, the planning effort implies to determine an assembly sequence of the given parts that

matches the goal. Some constraints are to be considered in order to make a solution strategy possible.
c) As an extension of the previous case, not only the shape, dimension and location of parts are unknown but also the assembly goal, meaning that the only "a priori" knowledge consists of a set of possible goals. Besides, some assembly constraints and rules should be considered. Once parts have been located and a number of features of them have been extracted by means of vision techniques, the planning system, using the given constraints and rules, must try to match the various possible goals with the given parts.
The described situations correspond to different philosophies for the use of a robot in manufacturing environments. The first, a), is the most usual in industry: parts are known together with the way they are to be assembled. A large amount of *a priori* knowledge mitigates the problem complexity, both for visual recognition and for planning. Conversely, the latter, b) and c), correspond to a case where a number of parts are present and the robot ignores what assembly they belong to. This could be useful in flexible environments (FMS-FAS) where a mix of products can be handled at one time. Obviously, the vision apparatus should give more detailed and accurate information and the planner has to solve more complicated problems. At the moment there are no industrial applications designed to operate in such a way, primarily because they are not cost effective.
Our experiment has been carried out considering a very simple assembly case. The purpose has been to validate some robot reasoning capabilities in a practical problem. The problem has been configured in orderto neglect other essential planning issues, in particular collision avoidance and grasp planning, considered in previous experiments [1][2] .

EXPERIMENT DESCRIPTION

The task the robot must perform is to compose a plane figure starting from some pieces placed on its operation plane. Such pieces are made by a white thin millboard and are placed on a black background. This choice simplifies the vision effort while complicating the planning complexity, as will be explained later. The pieces have been obtained by cutting a millboard polygonal figure, choosen among a set of some other ones prestored into the robot memory, by means of random straight cuts. Thus the pieces are intrinsically unknown "a priori" to the robot system. Such pieces are randomly located onto the operation plane by the operator. Obviously, in order for the robot system to find a solution, pieces are required to be consistent with one of stored figures, i.e. all of them should have been generated cutting one such figure. In other words, the robot task consists in manipulating pieces ignoring their number, shape, dimensions, location and what assembly they belong to. This could be considered a *generalized puzzle problem* (fig. 1).

In addition to the previous uncertainties, it should be considered that some pieces can be placed *overturned* onto the robot plane with respect to the upper face of the figure. It is important to note that the millboard has both faces white, so that the *up* and *down* faces of each piece are indistinguishable by means of visual information, typically by colour or gray level. Then, it is only by means of a reasoning process that the robot should be able to detect a similar situation identifying the initial figure and assembling all pieces in the correct way.

As a preliminary step, the robot must learn the figures it has to reconstruct and store them into the robot memory. Each figure, after being placed onto the robot plane, is acquired by the robot camera, then traduced into numeric information to be stored in a suitable database. Once some figures have been stored in this way, the robot is able to compose any of them, consulting the database, if some pieces are placed, by the right side or overturned, onto the operating plane. As explained above, in order for the system to get a solution, the only constraint to be imposed is that the various pieces must be consistent with one figure. In case of inconsistency (the pieces do not belong to anyone of the stored figures or they are less than needed), the system tries to compose a default stored rectangle. If this planning attempt is also unsuccessful the system fails notifying the event to the operator.

Two further constraints must be considered, regarding the generation and location of the pieces involved in this experience. In particular: a) The pieces must be generated by straight side-to-side cuts: this implies that all pieces are convex polygons in accordance with the requirement of the geometric reasoning procedure. b) The pieces cannot be placed *overlapped*. This should be immediately clear observing that no piece is known "a priori" by the system and then only a complete visual information allows a complete knowledge of its required characteristics. In short, it should be taken into account that the experiment was designed to validate an AI approach to a concrete assembly problem, leaving unsolved some practical issues.

ADOPTED APPROACH

The solution of the described problem is based on a geometrical reasoning approach, since this perfectly matches the problem characteristics. In order to implement the reasoning process it is necessary to traduce the various pieces to assemble into a set of geometric elements. This is accomplished during the vision process, when the image of the various assembly elements is traduced into a sequence of *vectors*. Each vector is the representation of an edge side of a polygonal piece. The geometric reasoning operates on the vector sequences, corresponding to the polygons, applying some geometrical connectivity rule in order to find the assembly sequence (solution). Once this has been

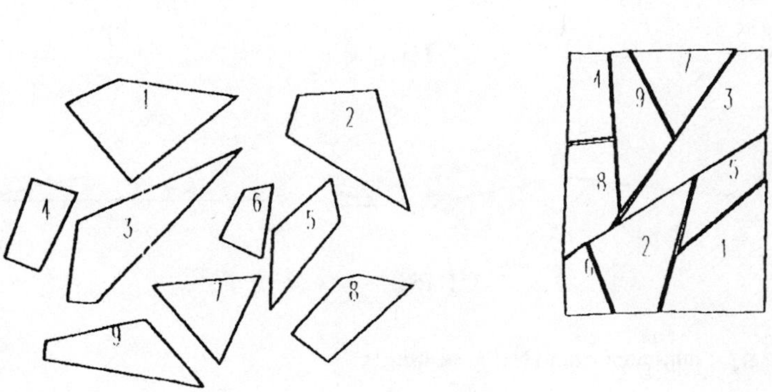

Figure 1. Puzzle assembly example

found, it is necessary to traduce it into phisical displacement/rotation pairs, in order to perform a correct manipulation at assembly time. So, three classical activity steps can be identified: vision, planning and manipulation. Let us examine separately each one of them.

VISION

The vision task consists essentially in a low-level phase, by which the polygonal pieces boundaries must be located and traduced into vector sequences. No recognition is made since pieces are unknown. It operates according to the following steps:

- image acquisition and binarization using a suitable threshold
- edge detection by means of a raster-to-vector conversion (*vectorization*)
- vector postprocessing, to eliminate vectorization artifacts

The raster-to-vector algorithm [3] consists essentially of three phases. (i) A *pre-processing* step, consisting in filling gaps and removing noise from the raw image. (ii) A *boundary tracing* step, which consists in determining boundary points between binary regions. (iii) A *line following* phase, where segment-like regions are transformed into couples of points coordinates (extremes).
The raster-to-vector conversion, because of the discrete nature of the image, can be affected by some errors (see fig. 2) i.e. conversion artifacts corresponding to the following physical situations. (a) A boundary corner is not "seen" as a real tip, but as a confused edge region, so that it is converted to a short vector, instead of the cross point between two adjacent vectors. (b) A side, because of its bending, due, for instance, to lens distorsion, is broken into two sides with very similar orientation. In

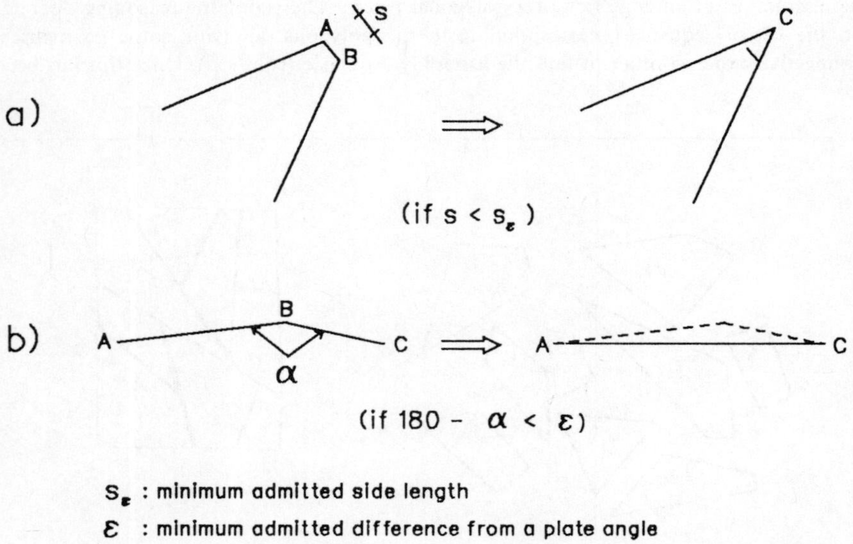

Figure 2. Contour extraction: vector postprocessing

order to filter such artifacts a postprocessing phase has become necessary. Essentially, this operates as follows (see fig. 2):

- vectors too short are eliminated lengthening the two adjacent ones in the sequence until they intersect;
- angles between vectors very near to 180 degrees are eliminated rectifying its sides to obtain a unique vector.

In addition to the previous artifacts, very small white regions can be detected and converted; usually they correspond to spots due to manipulator oil leakage. They produce closed vector sequences with a very small enclosed area : for each one, the postprocessor tests the area value and, in case this is less than a given threshold, erases the whole vector sequence from the world state.
Hence, this phase solves the most vision problems. Anyway, the final vision data (initial world state) are affected by some amount of precision error, due to lens distortion, camera calibration, image resolution and conversion quantization.

PROCESS PLANNING

As stated before, the "world"representation built by the vision is not completely accurate. This fact should be taken into account by the assembly solution method. For such a reason, an error insensitive connectivity rule is adopted. The global solution strategy is based on the recursive application of such a rule and operates on reduced search spaces. This means that intermediate world states are created during the solution search.
In the following by "polygon" we will denote a generic piece. The adopted rule allows to determine when two polygons are adjacent along a side in the recomposed figure. In particular, it states what follows: "two polygons are produced by one cut if each of them has a side of equal length with respect the other's and the angles at the extremes of these sides are supplementary two by two, as shown in fig. 3". In this way the solution method consists in comparing three couples of values for each couple of sides (one couple of segments and two couples of angles). Each comparison is made with a

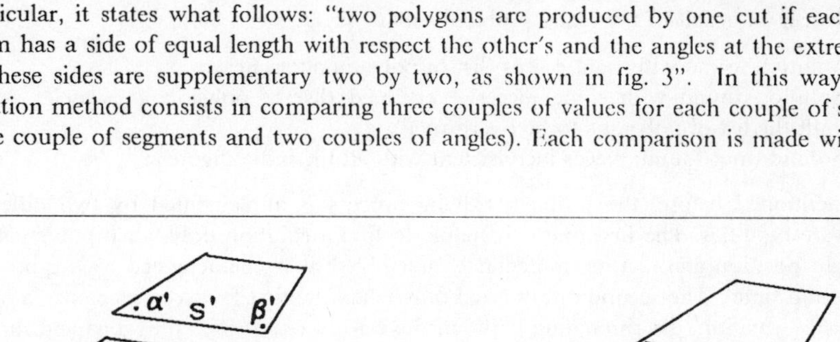

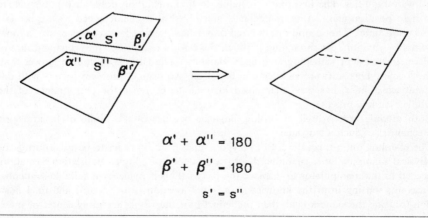

$$\alpha' + \alpha'' = 180$$

$$\beta' + \beta'' - 180$$

$$s' = s''$$

Figure 3. Connectivity rule and world state update

prefixed tolerance to take into account any errors introduced by the vision system. This makes the process quite error insensitive. The rule is applied to all couples of sides by an exhaustive search among all polygons of the world state at a generic planning step. When a couple of sides, belonging to different polygons, satisfies the connectivity rule, the planner "adds" the polygons along the common side, building a new abstract polygon and deleting the previous two from the world (fig. 3). This corresponds to update the world state at each recursion. When a unique polygon remains in the world state (end of the planning process), this is compared with each of the initially stored figures, which are the goal of the planning process. When such a polygon matches, with some prefixed tolerances, one figure in the database, the process is successfully ended and the figure is identified.

Anyway, the process could "fail" at any step. If this happens before a unique polygon has been assembled, it implies that the rule fails for all the couples of polygons actually in the world. This means that an inconsistent set of pieces has been submitted to the robot. Conversely, a fail could also occur when a unique polygon remains in the world state. Generally, this should be ascribed to wrong adjacencies, i.e. to couples of sides satisfying the connectivity rule but not arising from physical cuts. In any cases, wrong adjacencies are then marked not to repeat, during following searches, wrong branches of the research tree (this mechanism is commonly called *backtracking*).

The described problem solver corresponds to an initial implementation. Next, in order to detect overturned polygons on the scene, an enhanced problem solver has been implemented, where the connectivity rule is applied to all polygons in right and overturned configuration (the sides-angles sequences are inverted), tracking for each successful operation the initial condition (right or overturned) of each elementary polygon. This method increases the number of wrong adjacencies and so, requires smaller tolerances. As expected, it results more time consuming than the previous one.

Hence, the result of the entire problem solving process can be:

1. Solution found with right pieces (list of polygon adjacencies)
2. Solution found with some pieces overturned (list of polygon adjacencies added with the list of polygons to be overturned)
3. Solution not found: pieces inconsistent with all the initial figures

As mentioned before, the problem solving process is implemented by two different software modules. The first one is capable to find a solution only when polygons are in right position and can be immediately assembled; it is characterized by a quite fast execution time. The second one, started only when the first fails, can recognize a more complex situation, discriminating between the case of overturned polygons and that of pieces inconsistent with the initial figure database. The latter is of course, slower than the former. This software architecture, based on two distinct problem solvers with different capabilities, has been mantained in order to optimize the performance of the whole planning process.

Both modules are written in Prolog language because of the "built-in" backtracking mechanism of such a language.

The planning output, i.e. the list of polygon adjacencies, in order to be used during the physical manipulations, is traduced into a sequence of couples translation + rotation, needed to the manipulator to displace the pieces. This is made by a suitable sequential program, starting from the knowledge of initial location (from vision) and final position (outside the camera field, then predefined) for the whole assembly center of mass.

A similar conversion is made for the pieces to be overturned, taking into account the effects of the upsetting operation at manipulation time.
Based on such information, a graphic simulation of the reconstruction process is also available at the end of planning. This facility lets to predict and inspect the ongoing robot behaviour at actuation time.

MANIPULATION

Starting from the sequence of the displacements and rotations, the actuation module controls the physical handling of the pieces. The puzzle pieces are millboard plates, randomly distributed on the work plane inside to the visual field of the tv camera, while the reassembled figure is constructed by the manipulator on an area outside such a field. The whole pick-and-place of a single piece is made by a particular lifting actuator, a suction cup, which is grasped and held by the manipulator gripper (fig. 4). Such particular actuator is driven in *on-off* mode by the robot controller in order to grasp/release the piece itself. Its operation principle is based on a Venturi tube which generates, when air flows through it, the necessary vacuum to operate.
Two critical phases during the described operation are identified. First the picking/release of a piece, the complementary steps where the actuator approaches the workplane surface. In both cases it is necessary to control the motion using the tip force sensors of the gripper to detect the impact with the plane. These are continuously monitored: when the sensed impact reaction force overcomes a given threshold, the motion is stopped and the actuator is switched, on/off, depending on the operation to be performed (picking or releasing). The second critical operation is the upsetting of an overturned piece. This is obtained by means of an experimental fixture realized *ad hoc*, consisting in a kind of vice with two couples of elastic jaws, devoted to hold the piece to upset while the actuator approaches it by the opposite side. Such structure of the fixture allows the actuator to release the piece, invert its orientation with respect

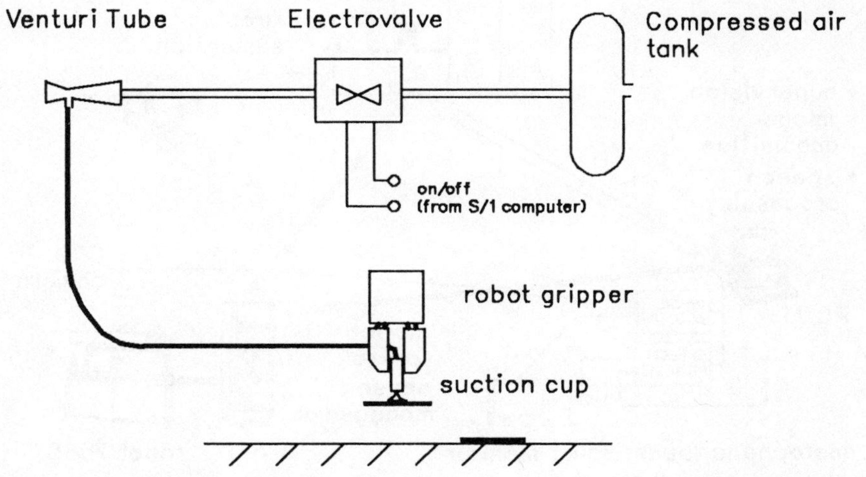

Figure 4. Pickup arrangement

the piece and get it back. The last step is critical. In fact, in order to have a reliable hold of the piece, it is necessary to approach it with a sufficient pressure, but without deforming it. To obtain this, the actuator must "search" the piece moving towards it and activating in a suitable fashion the tip force sensors.
It should be remarked that sensors are also used to control the actuator grasping. Normally the actuator is fixed on the workplane, in a known position. The gripper approaches it, verifies its real presence by the presence sensor and grasps it controlling the tightening force by the pinch force sensors.

HARDWARE CONFIGURATION: THE ROBOT WORKSTATION

The described experiment has been carried out on general purpose robot workstation set up at IBM Rome Scientific Center. This is based on a IBM 7565 robot, which is controlled by a special version of the IBM S/1 minicomputer, integrated with some other machines and computing facilities in order to achieve an adequate power so as a sufficient flexibility, to develop similar experiments. [2]. Figure 5 shows the overall workstation architecture. The whole station supervision is performed by a personal computer AT. Furthermore, it implements the user interface acting as a system console. Such interface makes use of a speech recognizer and a speech synthesizer. In addition, the PC is devoted to image acquisition and preprocessing for robot vision tasks. The station includes also a S/370 mainframe which is used to perform hard computations such as machine vision, planning tasks and graphic simulations. The three mentioned computer systems are connected together in a network with triangular topology and bidirectional links. In particular, the PC and the mainframe are connected through a S/370 channel attachment to have a fast transfer of large image data

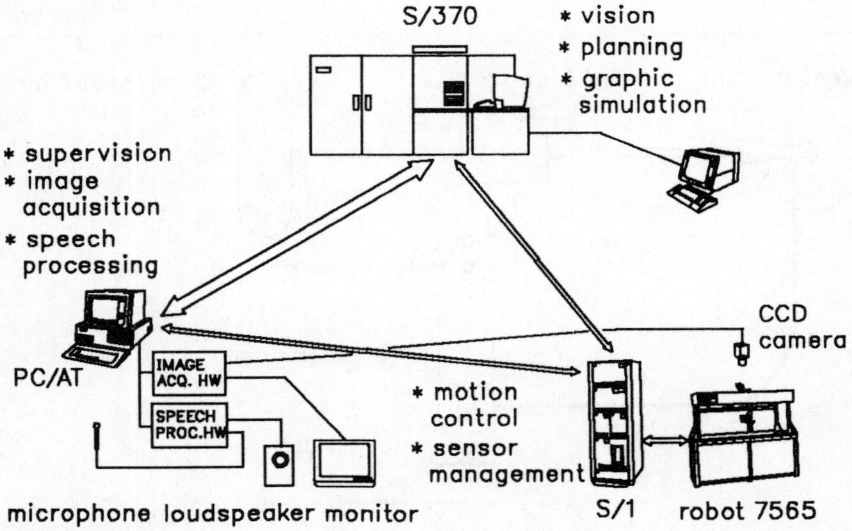

Figure 5. Workstation architecture

sets. The other network links are serial lines, being devoted to more concise data set transfers.

THE MANIPULATOR

The IBM 7565 [4] is a cartesian hydraulically powered manipulator, consisting of 6 d.o.f. arm supported by a parallelepiped box frame. Its joints, three prismatic (arm joints, X,Y,Z) and three revolute (wrist joints, *roll, pitch and yaw*), are controlled by analog position servos driven by the robot controller. The gripper is mechanically configured so that the finger surfaces move toward each other remaining parallel. A set of endpoint sensors are mounted in connection with them: three couples of force sensors and a presence sensor. The former are *strain gauges* connected, for each finger, along the three spatial directions. The latter consists in a led-phototransistor pair (*led-beam*) which, once broken by any opaque object located between fingers, lets the manipulator to detect its presence.
The described manipulator is programmed by a general purpose robotic language called A.M.L. ("A Manufacturing Language") [5]. This provides an interactive environment to perform robot motion control, sensor management, data processing and data communication. In the AML environment two different modes are available to process sensors signals. The first one is under program control: sensors are polled and tested by the application program. The second one is an asynchronous, interrupt-like mode; this means that it is possible for the system to detect sensory events (force threshold overcoming, led-beam interrupt ...) in an asynchronous way, interrupt the running AML program at any instant and run a proper user-written AML service routine.

IMAGE ACQUISITION SUBSYSTEM

The image acquisition process involves many different hardware and software components. The image is acquired using a CCD camera fixed over the robotic scene and looking downward with the optical axis perpendicular to the robot plane. The camera is attached to the PC via a frame grabber with a resolution of 640 x 512 pels. The acquired image is monochromatic with 256 gray levels: such features have appeared to be adequate in the most 2-D vision experiments carried out until now. In the actual experiment the chromatic resolution is not a critical point (the scene is intrinsically a bilevel one), so the image is thresholded and reduced to a bitmap, before being trasmitted to the host computer and processed.
A critical feature of the acquisition is *camera calibration* i.e. the knowledge of the correct correspondence between the the camera coordinate system and the world where the robot operates. Such correspondence is established in two steps, overcoming two different problems. The first one concerns the correspondence between the raw image (as it is acquired by the camera) and the processed image (containing the objects features) coordinates. In fact, due to CCD sensor geometry and characteristics (number of sensor elements along X and Y directions, center-to-center distances of elements ...) and to the grabbing process (sampling of the video signal and then of the image, with different passes with respect the sensor), the real scene and the corresponding image are not isomorphic but have different aspect ratios. This implies that segments of equal physical length aligned along X and Y directions do not appear equal on the acquired image. Without a suitable correction, the vectorization process would give unreliable

results and the planning would be impossible. To overcome this problem, the image is stretched in the horizontal direction, by an experimental *stretching factor*. (x coordinates are multiplied by it).

The second step involves the correspondence between the processed image coordinates and those of the operation world. The two coordinate systems have not the same origin, orientation and scale. Thus, to transform a coordinate pair to another it is necessary to determine the proper transformation parameters: this is the goal of the calibration process. Normally, this is made by a linear process, by sensing two different reference points (*calibration posts*) in robot coordinate (mm) and in stretched image coordinate (pels). Such values are used in a linear equation system, whose solution are the reference system change parameters (x_o, y_o (mm) of image origin and k_x and k_y, ratios between pels and mm along x and y). Such process does not take into account the non-linear behavior of lens near edges. This gives an acceptable accuracy in applications not requiring a high precision, while in other applications, like the described one, this is not really acceptable.

In the present case, more accurate results have been obtained applying the same procedure to various couples of posts, placed simultaneously in different points of the scene. For all couples the required parameters are computed; in this way for each parameter a sample of values is obtained, having a given statistical distribution. For each sample mean, m_p, and and mean square error, e_p, are computed. A final value of each parameter is determined discarding those values lying outside the interval $[m_p - e_p, m_p + e_p]$ and computing the mean of the remaining values. This procedure gives a more "robust" calibration mitigating the effects of lens distorsion, while it is still based on linear computations.

A very accurate calibration procedure is described in [6].

BIBLIOGRAPHY.

[1] R. Golini e M. Arlotti **An Intelligent Robot Workstation,** Artificial Intelligence - Implications for CIM, IFS / Springer-Verlag, 1988.

[2] M.A. Arlotti, A.De Castro,V. Di Martino,C.Raspollini,M. Vascotto, **Applicazioni di robotica e visione: esperimenti di manipolazione,** *Robots between Science & Technology SIRI fourth National Conference Proceedings, 211-226.* Milan, March, 21-23, 1988.

[3] IBM Japan Science Institute **Graphical Image Formatting and Translating System User's Guide** Tokio, 1985.

[4] IBM 7565 Manufacturing System, **Maintenance Information, Circuit Diagrams and Schematics, and Installation,** 1983.

[5] IBM 7565 Manufacturing System, **A Manufacturing Language Reference,** 1983.

[6] R.Y. Tsai, **An Efficient and Accurate Camera Calibration Technique for 3D Machine Vision,** IEEE Conference on Computer Vision and Pattern Recognition, Miami, 1986.

Uncertainty Management in Intelligent Task Planning

K. Ishii and S. Misra

Department of Mechanical Engineering, The Ohio State University, Columbus, Ohio, USA

ABSTRACT: This paper focuses on uncertainty associated with intelligent task planning. It combines the theory of fuzzy reasoning and decision analysis and proposes a framework which accommodates the uncertainties and the redundant degrees of freedom to generate an optimal task plan. The topic applies particularly to, but is not limited to, robotic task control in an unstructured environment. First, we identify the various sources of uncertainty associated with task planning: 1) discrepancies in the world model of the controller, 2) measurement errors in the sensory system, and 3) errors in actuation, etc. These uncertainties generate multiple candidate task sequences with varying degrees of confidence. In addition, if a machine has redundant degrees of freedom, the controller must also decide on the best strategy . We use fuzzy reasoning to deduce the likelihood of success of each candidate task sequence. The likelihood of success is then normalized as the likelihood index. Next, we use the decision analysis technique to determine which task sequence is optimal. This step uses the likelihood index as the subjective probability, and the application specific objective criteria serves as the utility function. We demonstrate our idea with a simple example: a robot that spots a golf ball out of several candidate targets. Our example uses the actuation energy as the objective criteria. Our uncertainty management scheme applies not only to robotic task control, but also to automation of processes.

1. INTRODUCTION

1.1 Background

Task control is an essential part of autonomous machines such as mobile robots and automated engineering plants. While many intelligent machines utilize human intervention and supervision, some applications mandate the machines to intelligently make decisions on their own. Mobile robots to be sent to Mars need to control their own task sequence within about 20 minutes communication delay, while the global commands can be given by humans on earth. These machines must make decisions at least on their detailed travel path. Autonomous robots that work in hazardous environments (e.g. a nuclear reactor) need intelligent task control at some level, since it is difficult to provide complete visual information to the human operators who control them. Intelligent sequence control is essential for emergency situations in engineering plants, because you need a much faster control sequence than what human operators can provide .

One of the important concerns in intelligent task control is how to deal with uncertain information. Handling uncertainty in world-model, sensory, and actuation information is particularly important for robots operating in unstructured environments. Other automated systems are also subject to uncertainty to some degree. Hence, the key to a robust and optimal task planning and control lies in uncertainty management. Yet, not much work has been done on developing a systematic method for handling uncertain information while dealing with task planning.

1.2 Summary of Previous Work

A great number of studies report on the treatment of uncertainties associated with feedback control. These studies typically use stochastic techniques (e.g Kalman [11]) or fuzzy systems approach (Mamdani [14]; Zadeh [26]; Sugeno [20]). Recently, Isik and Meystel [10] have used fuzzy control rules for the control of an unmanned mobile robot. While these studies provide a means to handle feedback control, they have not been extended to the problem of task planning.

On the other hand, there is considerable amount of literature on planning (Ernst and Newell [4]; Sacerdoti [17]; Tate [21], etc). However, these studies do not provide much attention to uncertainty in task planning. Recently, there have been a few attempts at designing planners which handle uncertain situations using probabilistic models (Farle [5]). Kamel and Kaufmann [12] considered positional uncertainty in object representation using probabilistic attributed graphs which are probabilistic relational structures. An uncertain state is defined by a set of attribute values for each object and a joint probability space. Any operation on an object is then done by explicitly modifying the joint probability space. This is part of their planner based on game theory. This representational scheme, however, seems to run into computational problems when faced with a complex situation. In general, probabilistic models for robotic task planning seem to suffer from the fact that it is often difficult to come up with probabilities to represent the state of the world.

The fuzzy systems theory develops a mathematical framework for handling uncertainty. Fuzzy measure (Sugeno [19]) provides one way of dealing with uncertainty. Ishii and Sugeno [8] used the theory of fuzzy measure to model the human evaluation process. Ishii and Barkan [9] applied the concept of fuzzy measure to evaluate mechanical design. They focussed on the compatibility between design requirements and design decisions. The measure of compatibility forms the basis for their knowledge based design concept called design compatibility analysis. Fuzzy measure, though a powerful tool in making design decisions and modeling human behavior, has not found much use in control applications. An alternative approach to handling uncertainty is fuzzy sets and fuzzy reasoning (Zadeh [24]; Mamdani and Gaines [16]; Dubois and Prade [3]). Fuzzy set theory provides a powerful means of systematically dealing with data that is imprecise in nature. This theory has found application, among other things, in natural language computation and decision making (Zadeh [25]; Schmucker [18]), and fuzzy control of complex plants (Mamdani [14]; Mamdani and Assilian [15]; Kickert [13]). While fuzzy sets and fuzzy reasoning have not been applied to task control so far, they provide a means of representing uncertainty in state information. In this paper, we use fuzzy sets to represent the uncertainty in positional, sensory and actuation information and reason between them to deduce a *degree of confidence* of a particular state.

1.3 Our Approach

Almost every piece of information from which we generate task plans (world model, sensory, and actuation information) is uncertain to some degree. There are various sources of uncertainties: 1) discrepancy between the world model and the sensory information, 2) measurement errors associated with sensors, 3) accuracy of actuation, 4) redundant degrees of freedom, etc. The third source may also involve uncertain interaction between the world and the machine actuator, e.g., robot wheels slipping on soft ground. The fourth item is not an uncertainty associated with the machines external environment but with its capabilities. When redundant degrees of freedom exist, a goal task could be accomplished in multiple ways. We are often uncertain as to which plan is the most appropriate.

All these uncertainties lead to candidate task plans with varying degree of confidence. A truly intelligent system must be able to find the *best* candidate given these uncertainties. The optimization criteria varies with different applications. Possible optimization criteria include: 1) minimum energy, 2) minimum time, and 3) maximum reliability. Many space applications would adopt the energy criteria, while most plant control applications should adopt reliability.

This paper proposes a general methodology for uncertainty management in task planning by combining fuzzy reasoning and decision analysis techniques (Howard and Matheson [7]; Agogino and Rege [1]; Agogino et. al [2]). We first classify the various sources of uncertainty as identified above. Then, we develop a method that combines these various uncertainties and deduce a degree of confidence about *states* that comprise the world model. Our method, which we call UMATAP (Uncertainty MAnager for TAsk Planning) then derives a *likelihood index*, a subjective measure of success, for each candidate task plan. UMATAP then uses the method of decision analysis to deduce the *best* task sequence. We view UMATAP as a real-time technique which the task planner uses after every *move* in the task sequence. After every *move,* the machine can observe new sensory information and perhaps update the world model. Hence, the optimal task sequence may be different from the one UMATAP deduced before. It should be noted that the emphasis of this paper is not on generating task plans, but rather, with selecting the optimum task plan from a set of candidates. Also, our use of fuzzy reasoning is fairly straightforward; to facilitate mapping between the various uncertainties and the likelihood index (LI).

We illustrate our idea with a very simple example, a golf ball spotting robot with two degrees of freedom. Basically, the task of the robot is to identify the correct golf ball out of two or more candidates given the coordinate information of the balls from the robot's sensors and the world model information about the location of the correct ball. The robot has two independent actuators that will move it in the X and Y directions simultaneously or independently. The robot can determine the *tag number* of the golf ball only when it is right next to the ball. While our example is a very simple and limited one, we believe our formulation of UMATAP is general enough to be applied to various, more complex applications. The possible limitations include those that have a large number of candidate task sequences. Our present strategy is to filter out candidates with a low likelihood index and only consider the top two or three candidates. In our example, this approach would translate to focusing on two or three balls with the highest LI.

The rest of this paper is organized as follows. Section 2 gives the background of the problem which includes our classification of uncertainties and a rigorous conceptualization of intelligent task control. We describe our approach, UMATAP, in section 3. Section 4 gives a specific example of UMATAP. Note that the golf ball spotting example is used throughout the paper. Section 5 gives the conclusions and future directions of research.

1.4 Notation

DC	mapping from the discrepancy value and sensory error to the state
d-conf	predicate representing confidence in state information
DIS	mapping from the discrepancy between the world model and the candidate to the discrepancy value dv
d_s	distance between the candidate and the sensor
$d_{th.s}$	threshold distance for the sensor
$d_{th.w}$	threshold distance for the world model
dcv	state confidence value
dv	discrepancy value
d_w	distance between the candidate and the world model
EOV	expected objective value
LI	likelihood index which is a a normalized lv
LH	mapping from the state confidence and move confidence to the likelihood value lv
lv	likelihood value
m-conf	predicate representing move confidence
mcv	move confidence value
move	conjunction of actuator input and length of time the input is maintained
μ_s	membership of candidate in fuzzy set representing uncertainty in the sensory information as a function of distance
μ_w	membership of candidate in fuzzy set representing uncertainty in the world model as a function of distance
SE	mapping from the sensory information as a function of distance to the sensory error value sev
sev	sensory error value
state	collection of predicates describing the world model
task	a collection of moves
trigger	a variable that initiates a particular move

2. STATEMENT OF THE PROBLEM

This section gives the background of our problem. We first introduce our example problem, the golf ball spotting robot, to illustrate our method clearly. Second, we identify the sources of uncertainty and classify them. Then, we formalize the intelligent task control problem and identify at what stage these uncertainties affect this process.

2.1 The example problem

Our example robot has two independent actuators that move it in the X and Y directions respectively. Actuation involves a velocity input command to the wheels, which can be given independently or simultaneously. Thus, the robot can move in the X or Y direction by using the corresponding actuator alone, while by using the actuators simultaneously and suitably adjusting the input velocities, the robot can move in any particular direction .

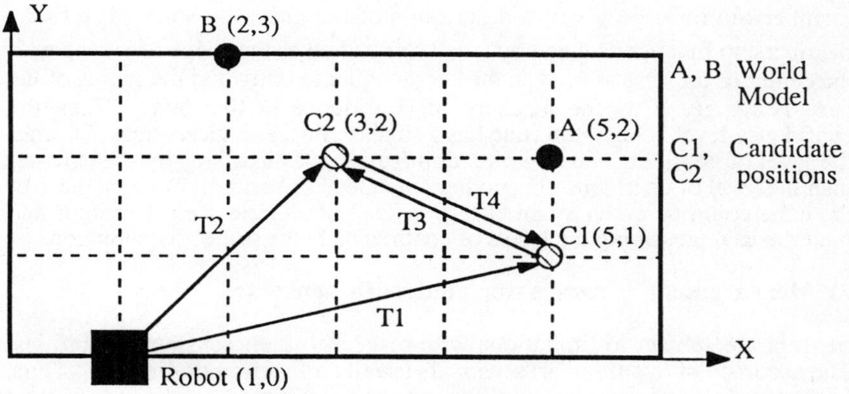

Figure 1. Layout for Example 1

Suppose the robot's world model (see Figure 1) consists of two golf balls A (at x_A, y_A) and B (at x_B, y_B). The robot's sensor information indicates two balls (which we shall call *candidates*) at (x_1, y_1) and (x_2, y_2) respectively. Note that the robot is uncertain as to the position of the balls and the sensory information. (This is explained in greater detail in Section 2.2.)

The objective is to identify golf ball A (given the uncertainties associated with the world model, sensory information, etc.) using minimum energy of actuation. Since the robot in this case can identify the correct ball only by moving right next to it, it is faced with the decision of which candidate to check out first. Various factors influence the robot's decision at this point: 1) the distances of the candidates from the robot, 2) the "likelihood" that a particular candidate is the target and 3) the nature of the contingency plans, should the first check fail. These factors arise from the robot not having a complete and accurate world model, errors in the sensory information, etc. This situation gives rise to a set of candidate task sequences. The uncertainty manager then needs to determine the optimum task sequence under the given information. In our simple layout described in Figure 1, the candidate plans are as follows:

1) go to C1 (task T1); if fail, go to C2 (task T3)
2) go to C2 (task T2); if fail, go to C1 (task T4)

2.2 Sources of uncertainty

The sources of uncertainty in the task domain include:

1) Uncertainty associated with the World Model:

The robot views its world as a collection of objects. These objects can be defined by a set of attributes, e.g., position, orientation, dimension, shape, etc. The robot may have an incomplete or inaccurate description of the world, which leads to a certain degree of uncertainty associated with the object's attributes. At present, we only consider the uncertainty in object position. Thus, in the example, A may not be at (x_A,y_A) but "somewhere around it."

This uncertainty can be modeled by means of a fuzzy set where the membership function gives a description of the uncertain state. The fuzzy membership function is given by $\mu = f(x,y)$ and takes the shape of a cone with the center of the base at (x_1,y_1), the height equal to unity and the radius of the base being given by the measure of confidence in the data. When the confidence level is high, the cone has a small radius, and vice versa. At times the level of confidence in one direction (say the X direction) may be greater than the level of confidence in another (say the Y direction). Then the base of the cone could be given by an ellipse instead of a circle with the major and minor axes representing the levels of confidence in the respective directions.

2) Measurement errors associated with sensors:

Sensors are subject to limitations with respect to their sensing capabilities. The accuracy of a particular sensor is usually a function of distance. Thus, while proximity sensors are very accurate at small distances, they are useless when the distance exceeds a few inches. On the other hand, laser range finders tend to be more effective at medium to long distances. Thus, there is a certain degree of uncertainty associated with sensory information. This uncerainty is modeled as a fuzzy set which gives the membership μ as a function of distance between the robot and the measured position of the given object.

3) Actuation errors:

Actuation errors, which may involve uncertain interaction between the world and the machine actuator (e.g. wheels slipping on soft ground) could make the robot uncertain of its own position.

4) Redundant degrees of freedom:

Suppose the robot has an *n* degree of freedom manipulator mounted on it. This makes the decision more difficult, since the task can be accomplished in multiple ways. One is uncertain as to which plan is the most appropriate. For example, when nearing an object, the robot could either extend its arm to pick it up from a distance or move closer before doing so. While this paper does not deal with this type of uncertainty, we plan to incorporate it in our future work.

2.3 Formulation of the problem

Here, we use the logic approach to world modeling (Genesereth and Nilsson, [6]) to conceptualize the process of task control.

2.3.1 State description for the world model and the actual sensory information *S*

The world model and the sensory information is a collection of predicates called *state.*

for world model:

state(wm, <type of state>, <state description>) (1)

for any sensed state:

state(<candidate>, <type of state>, <state description>) (2)

e.g.state(wm, position, pos(5,2))
state(c1, position, pos(5,1))

2.3.2 The task plan.

Assume our machine has n degrees of freedom, x_i, i = 1,...,n. We associate an actuator with each degree of freedom.

actuator (<identification>) (3)

Definition 1: A ***move*** is described as a conjunction of actuator input and length of time the input is maintained. Thus,

move (<identification>,
((<actuator1>,<input>,<time>,<trigger>)
(<actuator2>, <input>, <time>,<trigger>))) (4)

Trigger is a predicate that initiates a particular move. Thus *move* is *event-driven.*

Definition 2: A ***task*** is defined as a sequence of *moves.*

task (<identification>, <sequence of moves>) (5)

Note that a move could also describe a sequence of moves (actuation) by setting the trigger conditions appropriately. Thus, *move* may be viewed as a kind of sub-task.

There is an objective criterion, i.e energy, associated with each move and task.

energy (<move>, <energy value>) (6)

where, for our example we define energy value as

energy value (move) =
$\sum_i$ input (move, motor-i) x time (move, motor-i) (7)

Similarly, energy of a task is given by

energy (task) = $\sum$ energy value of moves in the task (8)

Thus, for our example, we have:

actuator (motor-x)
actuator (motor-y)
move (m1, ((motor-x, 1, 4), t = time1))
move (m2, ((motor-y, 1,1), t = time2)
task (t1, (m1, m2))
energy (m1,4)
energy (m2, 1)
energy (t1, 5)

We can define the other tasks similarly. Here task T1 involves checking C1, while task T3 involves checking C2 should task T1 fail . Again, task T2 is to check C2, while task T4 is to move to C1 should task T2 fail .

Hence, for the other tasks, we have:

energy (t2, 4)
energy (t3, 8)
energy (t4, 7)

3. UNCERTAINTY MANAGER FOR TASK PLANNING

This section outlines our proposed method, UMATAP (Uncertainty Manager for Task Planning), which combines fuzzy reasoning techniques (for derivation of the likelihood indices of the candidate moves), and decision analysis techniques to find a task with the optimum expected value.

3.1 Degree of confidence

For each registered state, we can define a degree of confidence d-conf which represents the state confidence.

d-conf (<candidate>, <type of state>, <confidence value: dcv>) (9)

e.g. d-conf (c1, position, 0.6)

Now, d-conf depends on the first two classes of uncertainties identified in 2.2, i.e., the world model discrepancy and the sensory error.

discrepancy (<candidate>, <type of state>,
<discrepancy value: dv>) (10)

s-error (<candidate>, <type of state>, <sensory error value: sev>) (11)

Note that we must define a reasoning (mapping) between states and these uncertainties.

DIS: $S \times S \rightarrow R$ Discrepancy (12)

SE: $S \times S \rightarrow R$ Sensory error (13)

Both *dv* and *sev* take real values only. In our example, *dv* and *sev* are calculated using fuzzy reasoning.

The uncertainty associated with the world model is represented as a fuzzy set (Figure 2 a). While any meaningful fuzzy set would do, we illustrate our idea with a simple linear membership function. We first calculate the distance between the candidates and the world model by the following equation:

$$(d_w)^2 = ((x_A) - (x_C))^2 + ((y_A) - (y_C))^2 \qquad (14)$$

Next from the figure we obtain the membership function of the candidate as:

$$\mu_w = (1 - \frac{d_w}{d_{th.w}})$$ (:

where, $d_{th.w}$ is the threshold value as seen in Figure 2a.

The discrepancy value (dv) is then given by:

$$dv = \max(0 , \mu_w). \qquad (16)$$

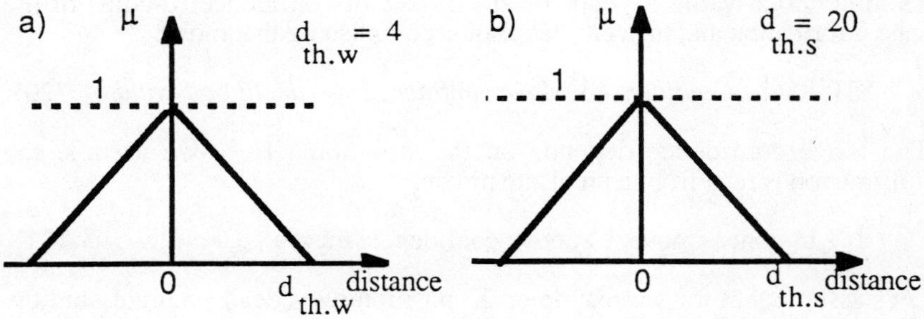

Figure 2. Membership function for a) World Model and b) Sensor

In our example,

d_w for candidate C1 = 1 => dv = (1 - 1/4) = 0.75.

Similarly, the uncertainty associated with the sensors is modeled as a fuzzy set shown in Figure 2b. We calculate the distance (d_s) of the candidates from the robot and then obtain the membership function (μ_s) as before. Then, the sensory error value (sev) is given as:

$$sev = \max(0, \mu_s). \qquad (17)$$

For candidate C1 the distance d_s is ($\sqrt{17}$) and ms = 1 - ($\sqrt{17}$) / 20 = 0.7938.

Thus, for C1, dv = 0.75 and sev = 0.7938.
Similarly for C2, dv = 0.50 and sev = 0.42925

Note that the reasoning process may become quite sophisticated depending on the details of the world model and the sensory system. In our example, both the reasoning DIS and SE are simple one dimensional mappings. Now, we must reason about the degree of confidence based on these information.

DC: *Discrepancy* x *Sensory error* -> *State confidence* (18)

For our example, we obtain a dcv value for each candidate position of the golf ball.

dcv = dv x sev

For C1, dcv = 0.75 × 0.7938 = 0.59535.
For C2, dcv = 0.50 × 0.8585 = 0.42925

3.2 Likelihood of success of a task

The likelihood of success of a move is conceptualized as follows:

likelihood (<move>, <likelihood-value: lv>) (19)

The likelihood-value depends on the degree of confidence (d-conf) of the state information and the confidence of accomplishing that move.

LH: *State Confidence* x *Move confidence* -> *likelihood-value* (20)

The move confidence depends on the situation. Here we assume the information is read from a predicate m-conf.

m-conf (<move>, <move confidence: mcv>) (21)

Let's assume that for our example, X positioning is dead accurate, but the Y positioning is only 95% accurate per input per time, then,

```
task (m1, ( (motor-x, <x-input>, <x-time>)
            (motor-y, <y-input>, <y-time> ) )
=>
m-conf (m1, < (0.95 × y-input × y-time) /
              ( x-input × x-time + y-input × y-time )> )
```

In our example, Task 1 consists of the following moves: 4 units in the X direction and 1 unit in the Y direction. Therefore, mcv = (0.95 x 1) / (4 + 1) = 0.99 and the likelihood value is given by:

lv for Task1 = mcv × dcv = 0.99 × 0.59535 = 0.5894
lv for Task2 = 0.97 × 0.42925 = 0.4185

3.3 Likelihood Index (LI)

Now, we did not impose any limits on the range of the likelihood value. For UMATAP to be practical, we need to filter all the possible candidate moves to a manageable number. We do this first by picking a certain number of candidates with the highest likelihood value (in our example, 2 or 3), and normalizing the value to obtain the likelihood index (LI) of the selected candidates.

Definition 3: Likelihood Index (LI $\in$ [0,1])

$$LI\ (task) = \frac{likelihood\ \ (task)}{\sum_{candidate\ tasks} likelihood} \qquad (22)$$

In our example,

LI (Task1) = (0.5894 / (0.5894 + 0.4185)) = 0.585
LI (Task2) = (0.4185 / (0.5894 + 0.4185)) = 0.415

Note that fuzzy reasoning has been used only to map the uncertainties so as to obtain a likelihood index. This index serves as a measure that corresponds to subjective probability in decision analysis.

3.4 Application of decision analysis

Since we have defined the likelihood indices (which are normalized such that they add up to 1.0), and the values of the objective criteria of the candidate moves, we can now apply the decision analysis techniques. Basically, we use LI instead of probability at chance nodes and the objective criteria instead of the utility function.

The top node of the decision tree will be the decision node for the first move m1 of a task. This node will have n branches where n is the number of candidates selected in section 3.3. Each branch leads to a chance node which represents whether or not the first move of the task is indeed correct. The likelihood index for this move corresponds to the probability of the move being correct. The other branch indicates failure of the first move with probability 1.0 - LI.

The failure branch must then be "expanded" using a contingency plan for the first move. We simply apply the decision analysis technique recursively. The "contingency" decision node, has only n-1 branches. By repeating the process recursively, the decision tree will terminate after a total of n-1 decision nodes. For example, if we set n=3, then the tree will converge after two decision nodes. After two decisions, the third move is trivial because only one candidate will be left.

Each branch of a tree represents a task, i.e., a sequence of moves. Note that a move itself is a type of task because it involves a conjunction of actuator energization. At each chance node, one can calculate the *expected objective value* (EOV)of each branch. For example, the EOV for task T1 corresponding to candidate C1 is:

$$EOV(T1) = LI1 \cdot E(T1) + (1 - LI1) \cdot [E(T1) + EOV(\,opt(D11)\,)\,] \qquad (23)$$

where: E(T1) is the objective value for candidate task T1
LI1 is the likelihood index for candidate task T1
EOV(opt(D11)) is the EOV of the optimal plan at node D11

Note that, to calculate the EOV at the root node, EOV's at each decision node in the tree must be recursively calculated from the tip nodes. The EOV for each branch at the root node is an important indicator . UMATAP will recommend, as machine's first move, the branch with the optimum EOV (in our case, minimum energy).

Figure 3 shows the decision tree for our example of the golf-ball spotter with two candidates. Here, n = 2. The robot is initially faced with the decision of which candidate to check out first. This is represented by the rectangle at the top node. The two circular shaped nodes are the chance nodes. Each chance node has a branch

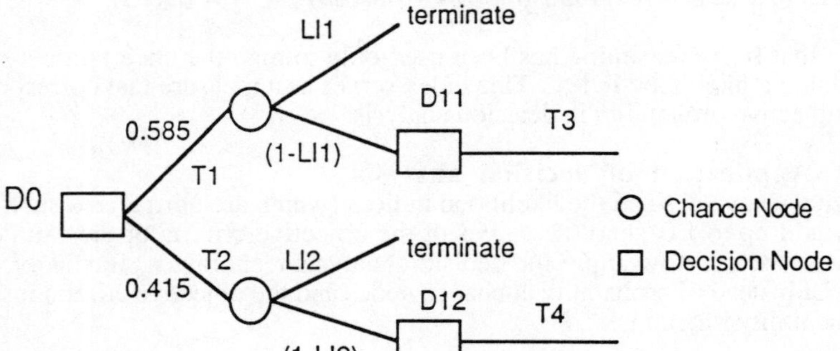

Figure 3. Decision Analysis Tree for Example 1

indicating the likelihood of success (LI_i) and a failure branch with likelihood ($1 - LI_i$). Each of these branches has an EOV associated with it. Since these branches represent tasks, we have:

LI	= likelihood Index of task T1 = 0.585	EOV	= energy (t1) = 5
$1 - LI_1$	= likelihood index of task T3 = 0.415	EOV	= energy (t3) = 8
LI_2	= likelihood index of task T2 = 0.415	EOV	= energy (t2) = 4
$1 - LI_2$	= likelihood index of task T4 = 0.585	EOV	= energy (t4) = 7

Therefore, at the decision node:

$EOV_1 \quad = 0.585 \times 5 + 0.415 \times 8 = 6.245$
$EOV_2 \quad = 0.415 \times 4 + 0.585 \times 7 = 5.755$

Since EOV of branch n = 2 is lower, the analysis shows that the optimum sequence to follow is task T2 (which seeks C2) first, and then task T4 (go to C1), if necessary.

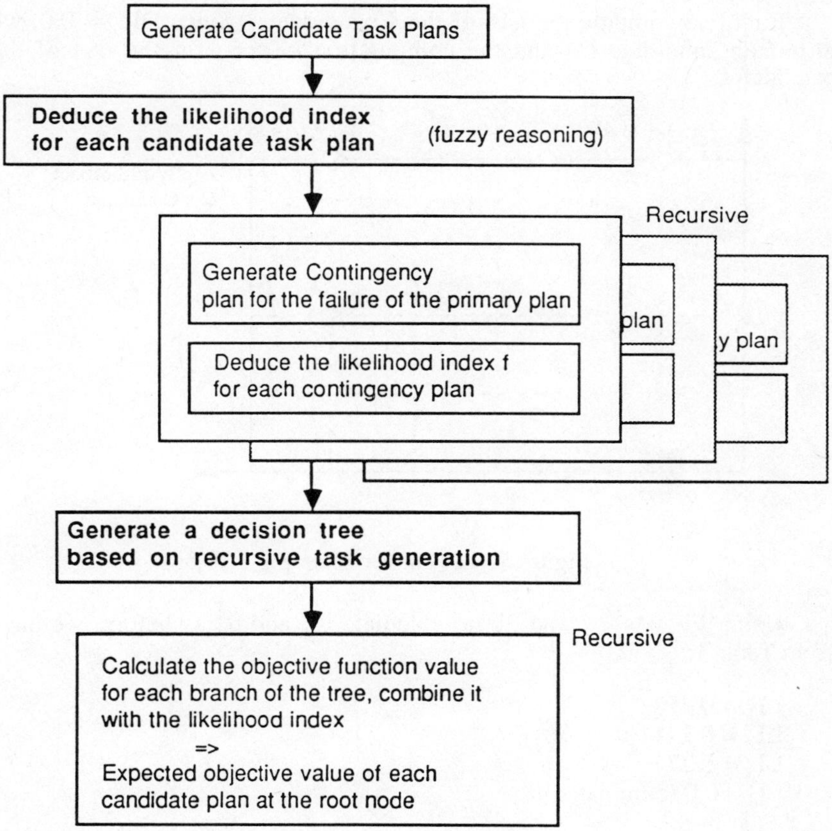

Figure 4. Flow of uncertainty management

Figure 4 summarizes the flow of deduction to determine the optimal task plan under uncertain information.

4. AN EXTENDED EXAMPLE (4 Candidates)

Figure 5 shows a more complicated example which has 4 candidates C1, C2, C3 and C4. Once again, the objective is to find the optimum sequence for minimum energy of actuation. The manner in which LI's are calculated is the same as before. However in this case, more than one layer of decision making is necessary.

First, we compute the LI's of the 4 candidates. Since $DIS_4 = 0.0$, we eliminate candidate C4 and the computation is done for the rest of the candidates.

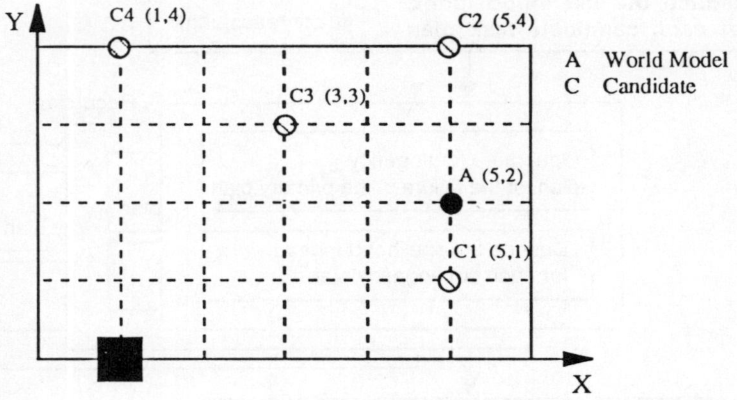

Figure 5. Layout for Example 2

Using Figures 2a. and 2b. to calculate μ_w and μ_s as before, we have from Table 1:

$LI_1 = 0.457$
$LI_2 = 0.271$
$LI_3 = 0.272$
$LI_4 = 0.0$ (eliminated)

C	1	2	3	4
d_w	1.0	2.0	$\sqrt{5}$	$\sqrt{20}$
d_s	$\sqrt{17}$	$\sqrt{32}$	$\sqrt{13}$	$\sqrt{16}$
DIS	0.75	0.5	0.441	0.0
SE	0.7938	0.7172	0.8197	*(eliminate)
m-conf	0.99	0.975	0.97	*
LH	0.5894	0.3497	0.3506	*
LI	0.457	0.271	0.272	*

Table 1. Calculation of Likelihood Indices

Also, defining tasks T1, T2, and T3 as moves to candidates C1, C2, C3 respectively, we have:

energy(t1,5)
energy(t2,8)
energy(t3,5)

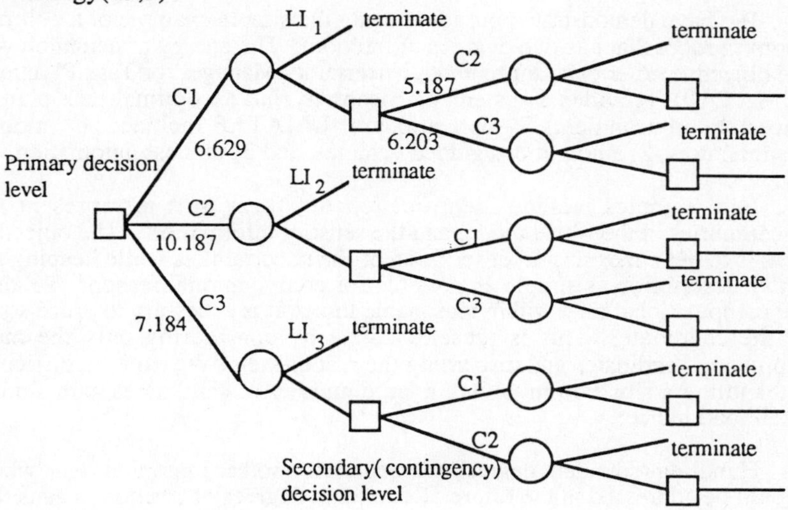

Figure 6. Decision analysis tree for Example 2.

Figure 6 then gives the decision analysis for the problem using the LI's and EOV's (energy). Note that the Ci's in figure 6 refer to the *candidates* rather than the candidate tasks. We see that since n = 3, two layers of decision making is necessary. For example, if the move to C1 fails, should the robot then move to C2 or C3 ? Decision analysis shows that the optimum sequence is C1-C2-C3.

Presently, we are implementing our ideas on a Macintosh II computer using Prolog for the reasoning mechanism and C for the graphics / user interface.

5. CONCLUSIONS AND FUTURE PLANS

A systematic methodology for dealing with uncertainty is of great importance for machines working in hazardous and unstructured environments. In this paper, we focussed on the use of decision analysis to obtain the optimum task sequence in uncertain environments. First, we identified the various sources of uncertainty: 1) world model discrepancy, 2) sensory error, 3) actuation error, and 4) redundant degrees of freedom. Then, we developed a method to combine the first three classes of uncertainty and compute a normalized measure, the likelihood index LI, which represents the likelihood of success of a given task. The method uses fuzzy reasoning to facilitate the mappings necessary for calculating LI. Finally, we applied the theory of decision analysis to LI and the optimization criteria in order to select the optimal task sequence.

We have demonstrated our ideas using the simple example of a golf ball spotting robot that has two degrees of freedom. The energy of actuation was the objective criterion. Our method, Uncertainty Manager for Task PLanning (UMATAP), provides a systematic means to find an optimal task plan in uncertain environments. Applications of UMATAP include: 1) mobile manipulators, 2) autonomous guided vehicles, and 3) process automation.

Future topics include identification of fuzzy sets to represent the uncertainties in the world model and the sensory information . The objective here is to get a meaningful description of the uncertainties while keeping the fuzzy description as simple as possible for computational reasons. To keep the computational time within reasonable limits, it is necessary to prune some of the candidates. This is presently done by considering only the most promising candidates and discarding the rest of them. We foresee difficulty in handling a situation involving a large number of candidates with similar likelihood indices.

Handling redundant degrees of freedom is another important issue which should be addressed in the future. Redundant degrees of freedom means that the goal task can be accomplished in multiple ways. For the case of a mobile robot with a manipulator mounted on it, this usually leads to a trade-off between moving the robot or moving the arm and results in different amounts of energy consumption.

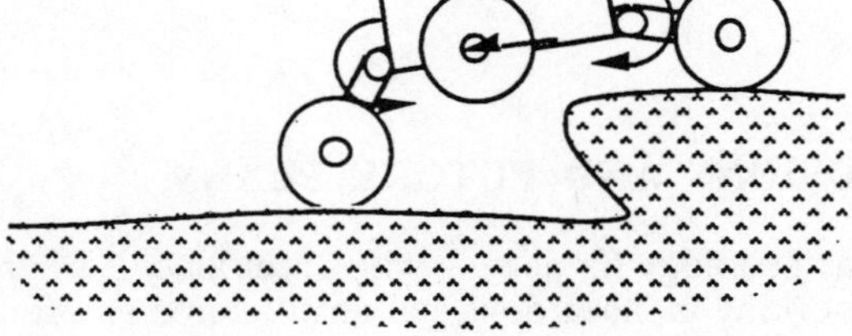

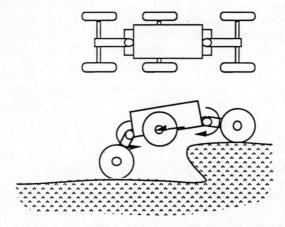

Figure 7. Obstacle clearance by the AAV

We intend to incorporate these extensions by applying UMATAP to the Autonomous All-Terrain (AAV) vehicle (Waldron, Kumar and Burkat [22]; Waldron, Sreenivasan and Varadhan [23]) being developed at The Ohio State

University. The unstructured terrain for which the vehicle is intended offers various forms of uncertainties. The maneuverability of this vehicle generates various alternatives in reaching a target. The AAV's flexibility and self-recovery capability lead to a rich set of contingency plans.

A typical example is whether to go around an obstacle taking a safe path or whether to risk going over it. Figure 7 shows the AAV attempting to climb an obstacle. Although the vehicle may be perfectly capable of surmounting the obstacle, the additional energy, and the increased risk of locomotion failure (hang-up, jamming, overturn, sliding, etc.) may make a more circuitous path preferable.

Another example would be the avoidance of a region with unpredictable soil properties (for example, a slippery region as in figure 8) which could cause severe actuation errors.

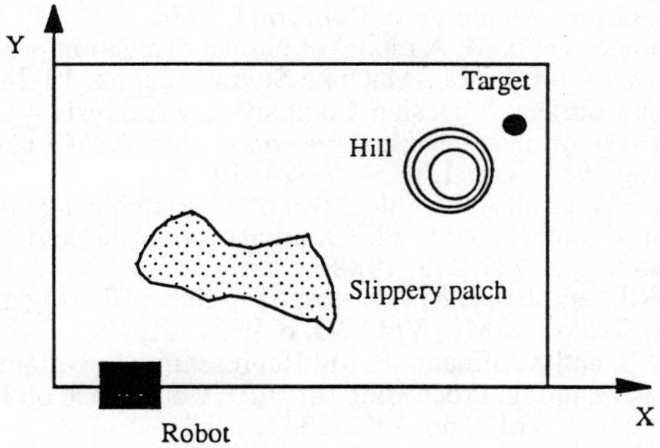

Figure 8. Varying terrain conditions

In both cases, however, large deviation from the planned route must be controlled to avoid excessively long detours or backtracking due to cul-de-sac routes.

Acknowledgement:
The authors would like to thank Prof. Kenneth Waldron for his help in conceptualizing the application of UMATAP to the AAV. We would also like to thank Mr. Chuck Hardy (Nuclear Engineering Program, The Ohio State University) for his fruitful comments and inputs to the manuscript. This work is being supported in part by the Ohio State University Seed Grant and the DuPont Young Faculty Award.

REFERENCES:

1. Agogino, A. M. and Rege, A. IDES: Influence diagram based expert system, Mathematical Modeling 8, pp. 227-233, 1987.

2. Agogino, A.M., Russell, S. and Guha, R. Sensor fusion using influence diagrams and reasoning by analogy: application to milling machine monitoring and control. Artificial Intelligence in Engineering: Diagnostics and Learning, Computational Mechanics Publications,Southhampton. pp. 333 -358, 1988.
3. Dubois, D. and Prade, H. Fuzzy Sets and Systems: Theory and Applications, New York, Academic Press, 1980.
4. Ernst, G. and Newell, A. GPS: A case study in generality and problem solving, Academic Press, New York, 1969.
5. Farle, A. M. A probabilistic model for uncertain problem solving, IEEE Trans. on SMC, Vol. SMC-13, No. 4, pp. 568-579, 1983.
6. Genesereth, M. and Nilsson, N. Logical Foundations of Artificial Intelligence, Morgan Kaufmann Publishers, Los Angeles, California, 1986.
7. Howard, R. A. and Matheson, J. E. Influence Diagrams. The Principles and Applications of Decision Analysis, 2, Strategic Decisions Group, Menlo Park, California, 1984.
8. Ishii, K. and Sugeno, M. A model of human evaluation process using fuzzy measure. Int. J. Man-Machine Studies, 22, pp. 19-28, 1985
9. Ishii, K. and Barkan, P. Design-Compatibility Analysis -- a framework for expert systems in mechanical systems design. ASME Computers in Engineering 1987. Vol. 1, pp. 417-424, 1987.
10. Isik, C. and Meystel, A. M. Pilot level of a hierarchical controller for an unmanned mobile robot, IEEE Journal of Robotics and Automation, Vol. 4, No. 3, pp. 241-255, 1988.
11. Kalman, R.E. and Bucy, R. New results in linear filtering and prediction. Trans. ASME, Vol 82D, p. 95, 1961.
12. Kamel, M.S. and Kaufmann, P. M. Representing uncertainty in robotic task planning. Proceedings of IEEE Conference on Robotics and Automation, Vol 3, pp. 1728-1734, 1988.
13. Kickert, W. and van Nauta Lemka, H. Application of a fuzzy controller in a warm water process. Automatica, Vol. 12, pp. 8-18, 1976.
14. Mamdani, E.H. Application of fuzzy algorithms for control of a simple dynamic plant, Proceedings of IEE, Vol. 121, No. 12, pp. 1585-1588, 1974.
15. Mamdani, E. H. and Assilian, S. A fuzzy logic controller for a dynamic plant. International Journal of Man- Machine Studies. Vol. 7, pp. 1-18, 1975.
16. Mamdani, E. H. and Gaines,B.R.(Ed.). Fuzzy Reasoning and its Applications. Academic Press, London, 1981.
17. Sacerdoti, E. D. Planning in a hierarchy of abstract space. Artificial Intelligence. 5, pp. 115-135, 1974.
18. Schmucker, K. J. Fuzzy Sets, Natural Language Computations, and Risk Analysis. Computer Science Press, Maryland, 1984.
19. Sugeno, M. Theory of fuzzy integrals and its applications. Doctorate thesis. Tokyo Institute of Technology, 1974.
20. Sugeno, M. and Takagi, T. Multi-dimensional fuzzy reasoning. Fuzzy Sets and Systems. Vol. 9, No. 2, 1983.
21. Tate, A. Interacting goals and their use. IJCAI 4, pp. 215-218, 1975.
22. Waldron, K.J., Kumar, V., and Burkat, A. An actively coordinated locomotion system for a Mars Rover, Proc. of the Third International Conference on Advanced Robotics, Versailles, France, pp. 77-86.

23. Waldron, K.J., Sreenivasan, S.V.,Varadhan, V. Mobility enhancement using active coordination, NASA Conference on Space, Pasadena, California, 1989.
24. Zadeh, L. A. Fuzzy sets. Information and Control, Vol. 8, pp. 338-353, 1965.
25. Zadeh, L. A. PRUF -- A meaning representation language for natural languages, International Journal of Man- machine Studies, Vol. 10, No. 4, pp. 395-460. (Reprinted in Mamdani and Gaines [16]), 1978.
26. Zadeh, L. A. A theory of approximate reasoning, Machine Intelligence 9. New York, Halstead Press, pp. 149-194, 1979.

Temporal Reasoning and Qualitative Process Theory

M. Di Manzo* and D. Tezza**

**Institute of Computer Science, University of Ancona, via Brecce Bianche, 60131 Ancona, Italy*

***DIST - University of Genova, via Opera Pia 11a, 16145 Genova, Italy*

ABSTRACT

In this article we propose an extension of Qualitative Process Theory (QPT) to reason about temporal properties of the behavior of physical systems. The basic idea is that the temporal properties of physical phenomena (in most cases assuming the form of durations) and their evolution over the time derive from the underlying dynamics governing the behavior of the systems considered; therefore, it is conceivable to extend a theory for the qualitative dynamic modeling to enable it to also reason about the temporal aspects of a given envisionment. To this end we have chosen QPT, and a framework for the temporal modeling of dynamic simulations has been developed. A salient property of the framework is the fact that its structure is completely analogous to that of QPT, so that it allows more inferences to be drawn about a scenario by using the same inferential mechanisms as used by QPT. In the paper we present the ontology of the theory (stressing the analogies existing with QPT) and how it applies to an example where the influence of the dynamics on the temporal properties is a central point in the behavior of the situation considered. Finally some considerations are presented about the implementation status and future research directions.

INTRODUCTION

Time represents a central aspect of the human reasoning about physical systems and phenomena. Salient properties of a physical system are very often intrinsically related to the temporal behavior of the system (e.g. the concept of period). Over the last years, a number of logics have been proposed in Artificial Intelligence in order to deal with the problem of temporal reasoning (see, for instance, Allen [1], Mcdermott [2], Shoham [3]). However, in most qualitative modeling theories (e. g. Forbus [4], De Kleer and Brown [5], Kuipers [6]) time is rarely considered as an explicit object to be reasoned about; instead it is simply regarded as the independent variable par excellence, over which all the other physical quantities evolve. Only Forbus [4] mentions time explicitly and introduces for the episodes the notions of distance, duration and rate along with the relation linking these three quantities.

Qualitative modeling and simulation techniques are useful in many real applicative tasks such as design and diagnosis (e. g. Davis [7]); from this point of view, considering time only an implicit entity can represent a significant limitation of such techniques in their potential application areas. For instance, a design goal might be specified in temporal terms (e. g. minimum response time), or an observed misbehavior of a diagnosed system may relate to a temporal property (e. g. the system does not exhibit the expected oscillation period). In all these cases, making time explicit both in the modeling and in the simulation processes can significantly enhance the usefulness of qualitative approaches to the descriptions of physical system behaviors.

In this article an extension of Qualitative Process Theory (QPT), Forbus [4], is proposed, in order to model in qualitative terms the temporal properties of a physical system (typically durations and periods) and their evolution; the extension has the same structure as QPT, and it is intended to be applied to an envisionment generated by means of QPT itself.
In the next section the relationship between dynamic descriptions and temporal descriptions is presented. The following section introduces the temporal ontology of the theory and stresses the analogies existing between it and QPT. Then an example of application of the theory is given, and finally in the last section some concluding remarks are presented about the implementation of the theory and some open problems.

RELATIONSHIP BETWEEN DYNAMIC AND TEMPORAL DESCRIPTIONS

In physical system behavior, time is generally significant only in the form of durations (i.e. differences between time points), while single instants are seldom important. Moreover, the duration of a physical phenomena essentially comes from the underlying dynamics, so that it should be possible to reason about durations only by means of dynamic considerations. Therefore, given a qualitative theory dealing with the dynamic modeling of physical systems, it is conceivable to extend the theory to take into account also the temporal modeling of the dynamic evolution. Starting from these considerations, a temporal extension of QPT has been devised, and, although not all problems have been satisfactorily solved (see the last section), our approach seems to be promising. In particular, since the temporal and dynamic descriptions are based on the same structure, it is possible to get a number additional results in the temporal domain by using the same inferential mechanisms as those used by QPT in producing the dynamic simulation; in other words, no new reasoner is needed, but only a new description of the domain.

Given a scenario in a particular domain described by means of objects, individual views (IV's) and processes within the framework of QPT, it is possible to generate the qualitative dynamic simulation of the scenario; the result is a (possibly ambiguous) envisionment involving sequences of episodes, which, in turn, involve the individual views and processes activated during the simulation. This envisionment represents the starting scenario for the temporal simulation, and, to this end, it is described by means of an opportune set of entities having the same structure as those used by QPT (see the next section); this description is to be processed again by the QPT reasoner in order to produce the temporal simulation. Put differently, the basic idea consists in making episodes explicit objects of the reasoning process, which is made possible by the general framework of QPT that allows the representation of many different kinds of knowledge through the same representation formalism. The example given below will illustrate the methodology.

From another point of view, it is possible to regard the temporal simulation as another dynamic simulation, where a new temporal scale is considered, different from the temporal scale employed in analyzing the dynamic behavior of the given system. In fact, when the envisionment is produced by using the QPT (or any other theory of qualitative simulation), an important implicit assumption holds: for each time point it is possible to assign a value (possibly known only in qualitative terms) to each physical quantity. If temporal quantities (e.g. durations) are to be analyzed, this assumption does not hold any more, because a duration, for instance, is intrinsically associated to a time interval rather than a time point. Therefore it is necessary to interpret the temporal simulation over a new temporal scale, a coarser one, where the time intervals on the usual temporal scale, corresponding to particular episodes whose durations are to be reasoned about, collapse into single time points. Over this new time scale, the previous assumption holds again, and therefore the qualitative simulation methods can be used again.

THE TEMPORAL ONTOLOGY

In this section the temporal ontology is introduced by illustrating how it applies to a particular situation where the interaction between two dynamic behaviors results in one of them influencing the temporal properties of the other. First the dynamic simulation is generated through the appropriate qualitative model; then we will see how the envisionment produced can be further analyzed in order to draw additional inferences about the temporal aspects.

An example of temporal interaction

Let us consider the scenario depicted in figure 1. In this case we have a pendulum, involving a string segment s and a mass m, which is oscillating owing to some initial perturbation; at the same time, because of the elastic nature of the string segment, the pendulum is swaying up and down, again as a result of some initial action on the string. How can we simulate the

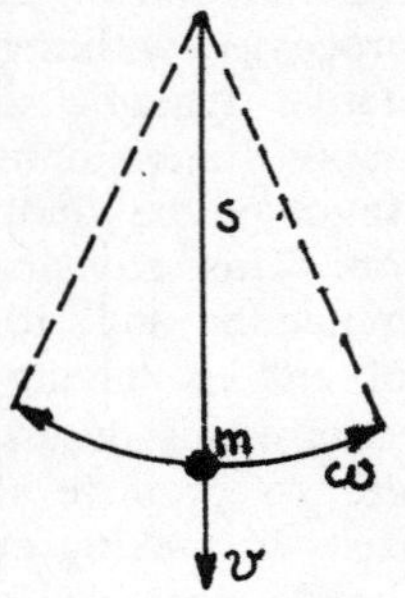

Figure 1. The starting scenario.

dynamic behavior of this scenario? First an individual view describing the pendulum with its meaningful physical quantities is needed:

Individual_View **Pendulum**(s,m)
Individuals:
    s a string_segment;
    m an object;
Preconditions:
    Hung(m,s);
    Free_to_move(m);
Relations:
    Let length be a quantity;
    Let angle be a quantity;
    Let angular_velocity be a quantity;
    Let longitudinal_velocity be a quantity;
    Let angular_force be a quantity;
    Let longitudinal_force be a quantity;
    angular_force $\propto_{q-}$ angle;
    Correspondence((angular_force,ZERO),(angle,REST_ANGLE));
    longitudinal_force $\propto_{q-}$ length;
    Correspondence((longitudinal_force ZERO),
        (length,REST_LENGTH));

A pendulum comprises a string segment and a mass (whose complete definitions in terms of physical quantities are left out for the sake of conciseness) satisfying the relations given in the preconditions field; then the set of physical quantities describing the behavior of the pendulum is introduced in the relations field, along with the links (qualitative proportionalities) existing between them. In particular there are two sets of quantities: one is used to describe the angular oscillation of the pendulum around the vertical position, while the other includes the quantities that model the longitudinal oscillation of the string segment. The two qualitative proportionalities linking the distance from the equilibrium position and the corresponding force determine the oscillatory behavior in either direction (angular and longitudinal).

As regards the angular oscillation, the possible states in which the pendulum may be are modeled by the following IV's:

Individual_View **Vertical**(p)
Individuals:
    p a Pendulum;
Quantity_conditions:
    A[angle(p)] = REST_ANGLE;

Individual_View **Right_Inclined**(p)
Individuals:
    p a Pendulum;
Quantity_conditions:
    A[angle(p)] > REST_ANGLE;

Individual_View **Left_Inclined**(p)
Individuals:
    p a Pendulum;
Quantity_conditions:
    A[angle(p)] < REST_ANGLE;

Here REST_ANGLE denotes the landmark value in the angle quantity space corresponding to the vertical position of the pendulum (i.e. the equilibrium position). In order to model the angular movement of the pendulum, two processes have to be introduced, which correspond to the two oscillations in each direction (left and right):

Process **Right_Oscillation**(p)
Individuals:
    p a Pendulum;
Quantity_conditions:
    A[angular_velocity(p)] > ZERO;
Influences:
    I+[angular_velocity(p),angle(p)];
    I+[angular_force(p),angular_velocity(p)];

Process **Left_Oscillation**(p)
Individuals:
    p a Pendulum;
Quantity_conditions:
    A[angular_velocity(p)] < ZERO;
Influences:
    I+[angular_velocity(p),angle(p)];
    I+[angular_force(p),angular_velocity(p)];

Finally, another process is needed to describe the behavior of the pendulum at the two points of maximum oscillation, where the direction of the angular motion reverses:

Process **Oscillation_Start**(p)
Individuals:
    p a Pendulum;
Quantity_conditions:
    A[angular_velocity(p)] = ZERO;
    A_m[angle(p)] > REST_ANGLE;
Influences:
    I+[angular_force(p),angular_velocity(p)];

These IV's and processes suffice to simulate the angular oscillation of the pendulum. In order to model also the longitudinal movement, we have to introduce a similar set of IV's and processes expressed in terms of longitudinal quantities. Only an IV and a process are given (the others follow obviously from their angular companions):

Individual_View **Stretched**(p)
Individuals:
    p a Pendulum;
Quantity_conditions:
    A[length(p)] > REST_LENGTH;

Process **Stretching**(p)
Individuals:
    p a Pendulum;
Quantity_conditions:
    A[longitudinal _velocity(p)] > ZERO;
Influences:
    I+[longitudinal_velocity(p),length(p)];
    I+[longitudinal_force(p),longitudinal_velocity(p)];

Here REST_LENGTH represents the landmark value in the length quantity space corresponding to the particular length value of the string segment that generates an internal (longitudinal) force able to balance exactly the weight of the mass m.

Now, if we consider an initial state of the pendulum described by the following conditions:

A[angle(p)] > REST_ANGLE;
A[length(p)] > REST_LENGTH;
A[angular_velocity(p)] = ZERO;
A[longitudinal _velocity(p)] = ZERO;

That is to say if we consider an initial state where the pendulum is perturbed in both angular and longitudinal directions, and if we apply the dynamic model above described, we will get an envisionment characterized by the oscillatory behaviors shown in figure 2. The dynamic evolution of the pendulum involves two oscillations, one is angular and occurs around the equilibrium position corresponding to the vertical position, the other is longitudinal and occurs around the equilibrium position corresponding to the rest length of the string segment. This is the expected behavior of the pendulum, and it does not seem to exist any interaction between the two oscillations; in other words, the overall envisionment is simply the composition of the two envisionments we would have got if we had considered the pendulum perturbed in only one direction. However this result is not completely satisfactory, in that an interaction between the two movements does exist; in fact it is well known that the period of a pendulum is proportional to its length, and therefore the longitudinal oscillation is expected to generate a sort of modulation of the frequency (i.e. the period) of the angular oscillation. Within the framework of the only QPT, it is not possible to simulate this result because the theory is concerned with modeling only the dynamic behavior of a physical system, without considering its temporal behavior. Hence we have to extend QPT to make the domain model able to reason about such problems. A possible solution is described in the next section.

<u>How to draw temporal inferences</u>

Similarly to QPT, the temporal ontology includes three classes of entities: basic temporal objects, temporal views and temporal processes. The basic temporal objects correspond to the episodes that may appear in the envisionment produced by the QPT, which is the starting scenario for the temporal simulation. In the QPT framework, the basic objects are described as collections of properties and quantities, namely those that are relevant for the description of the physical behavior of an object. As regards episodes, they are similarly described as collections of relevant properties, which include the IV's and processes that are active in an episode and determine its structure, and new quantities that can be defined over the time interval corresponding to an episode: average values, duration, distance, rate of change (intended as in Forbus [4]), etc. For instance, in the pendulum case

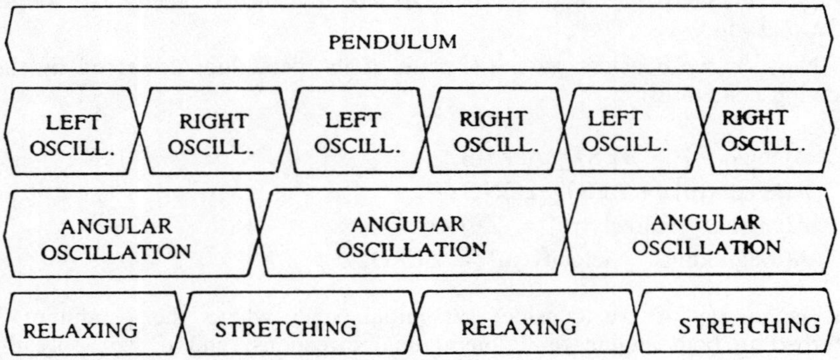

Figure 2. The dynamic envisionment.

we are concerned with the duration of the episode corresponding to the oscillation, and therefore the temporal model includes as basic objects the two episodes relative to the two semioscillations; they can be described in the following way (only the left oscillation is given; the right one is completely analogous):

(FORALL lo ∈ Left_oscillation
Has_individual(lo,m) ∧ Object(m)
∧ Has_individual(lo,s) ∧ String_segment(s)
∧ Has_view(Pendulum(m,s))
∧ Has_process(Left_oscillation(Pendulum(m,s)))
∧ Has_quantity(lo,duration))

The second entity of the temporal ontology is called Temporal View (TV) and plays the same role as that played by IV's in the QPT. In general a TV allows the description of the complex occurrence of many episodes; its structure is similar to that of an individual view, in that it includes the same four fields that constitute an individual view. In the individuals field, the episodes, whose occurrence is described by the TV, are given, while the preconditions and quantity conditions fields contain the various condition (in this case also of temporal nature) that must be true to activate the TV (e.g. conditions on the temporal ordering of the episodes involved in the TV). Finally, the relations field contains the relations (e.g. qualitative proportionalities) that it is possible to introduce for the temporal quantities of the episodes involved in the TV when the TV is active. In the pendulum case a TV can be used to model the episode corresponding to the complete oscillation, which is, in fact, constituted by the occurrence of the two episodes corresponding to the two semioscillations, one after the other.

Hence, the temporal model contain the following TV:

Temporal_View **Oscillation**(lo,ro)
Individuals:
lo an episode; Left_Oscillation(lo);
ro an episode; Right_Oscillation(ro);
Preconditions:
Immediately_after(ro,lo);
Quantity_conditions:
m(lo) = m(ro);
s(lo) = s(ro);
Relations:
Let length be a quantity;
Let force be a quantity;
Let velocity be a quantity;
Let period be a quantity;
period $\propto_{q+}$ (duration(lo) + duration(ro));
period $\propto_{q+}$ length;
force $\propto_{q-}$ length;
Correspondence((force ZERO),(length,REST_LENGTH));

The important point in this TV is the explicit introduction of the relation linking the length of the pendulum and the period; both these quantities are of temporal nature (they are an average value of the pendulum length over the interval corresponding to an oscillation and a duration), and are defined over an interval in the usual time scale, and point by point in the coarser time scale where the temporal simulation is carried out. The other qualitative proportionality linking the values of force (in particular longitudinal force) and length simply allows the dynamic behavior relative to the longitudinal direction to be moved into the new time scale.

The third entity of the temporal ontology is the Temporal Process (TP). Again TP's are completely analogous to the processes of QPT, since their structure is the same (again based on a set of fields similar to those of TV's), and TP's, like processes, are intended to model the primary sources of change of temporal quantities, that is the possible ways in which the temporal properties of a given situation may evolve. Therefore the TP's contain the same fields as TV's, with an additional field, called influences, that explicitly describes the causes of change in the temporal domain. A remark has to be made about how TP's satisfy the sole mechanism assumption presented in Forbus [4], according to which the QPT processes are the only sources of change in a given situation; in this case, TP's are consistent with that assumption, in that they derive from and are activated by the processes that determined the dynamic evolution of the considered situation. In other words, they can be looked at as a rewriting of the normal dynamic processes in the new temporal scale. Therefore, in the pendulum problem two TP's are necessary: they describe the longitudinal oscillation and are derived straightforwardly from the corresponding dynamic processes by translating them in terms of episode quantities:

Temporal_Process **Modulation**(o)
Individuals:
  o an oscillation;
Quantity_conditions:
  A_m[velocity(o)] > ZERO;
Influences:
  I+[velocity(o),length(o)];
  I+[force(o),velocity(o)];

Process **Modulation_Start**(o)
Individuals:
  o an oscillation;
Quantity_conditions:
  A[velocity(o)] = ZERO;
  A_m[length(o)] > REST_LENGTH;
Influences:
  I+[force(o),velocity(o)];

Given the dynamic envisionment and the temporal model above described, another simulation can be carried out by applying again the inferential mechanisms of the QPT. The initial conditions are inherited from the previous ones used to generate the dynamic simulation:

A[length(o)] > REST_LENGTH;
A[velocity(o)] = ZERO;

In particular the relations relative to the angular motion are no longer considered, in that this motion is now abstracted in the TV Oscillation; only the relations relative to the longitudinal oscillation are taken into account. This leads to the envisionment depicted in figure 3. When the Modulation process is active, the pendulum length is influenced by the (longitudinal) velocity and thus the length is decreasing or increasing according to the sign of the velocity value. This fact, in turn, leads to a corresponding decrease or increase of the oscillation duration (i.e. its period) through the qualitative proportionality contained in the TV that models the oscillation. This result can be added to the usual simulation of the dynamic evolution of the system considered, thus enabling the model to find not only the two oscillatory behaviors, but also their temporal interaction.

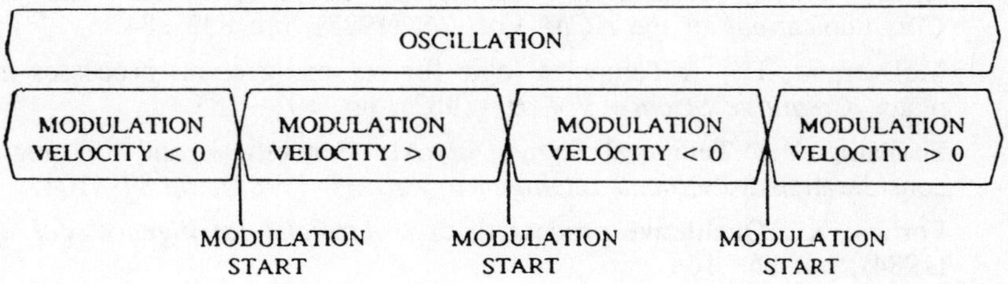

Figure 3. The temporal envisionment.

CONCLUSION

According to Forbus, QPT can be looked at as a language for representing knowledge about physical systems. Since its structure is completely general, it is conceivable to use the same paradigm to represent other kinds of knowledge beside the dynamics. The ideas and concepts described in this article can be regarded as an attempt of extending the theory in order to face also temporal problems.

We are currently investigating the use of the notions described above for other purposes beside predicting the evolution of temporal properties. One research direction is providing the dynamic model with some capabilities of disambiguating an envisionment when more than one limit value (see Forbus [4]) exist and it is not possible to determine which occurs first by using only dynamic consideration; if it is able to reason about durations, the model can decide which change takes the less time to happen and then occurs first.

The implementation of the temporal model is in progress; in particular we have started from a first order logic axiomatization of the QPT and we are working on extending the axioms to include the temporal formalism described above.

ACKNOWLEDGMENTS

This work has been done with the support of the Italian National Research Council (CNR), Progetto Finalizzato Sistemi Informatici e Calcolo Parallelo (Special project on Information Systems and Parallel Computing).

REFERENCES

1. Allen, J.F., Maintaining knowledge about temporal intervals, *Communications of the ACM Vol. 26,* (1983), pp. 832–843.

2. McDermott, D., A Temporal logic for reasoning about processes and plans, *Cognitive Science Vol. 6,* (1982), pp. 101–155.

3. Shoham, Y., Temporal logics in AI: Semantical and ontological considerations, *Artificial Intelligence Vol. 33,* (1987), pp.89–104.

4. Forbus, K., Qualitative process theory, *Artificial Intelligence Vol. 24,* (1984), pp. 85–168.

5. de Kleer, J. and Brown, J.S., A qualitative physics based on confluences, *Artificial Intelligence Vol. 24,* (1984), pp. 7–83.

6. Kuipers, B., Common sense causality: Deriving behavior from structure, *Artificial Intelligence Vol. 24,* (1984), pp. 169–203.

7. Davis, R., Diagnostic reasoning based on structure and behavior, *Artificial Intelligence Vol. 24,* (1984), pp. 437–491.

A Non-Static Learning Paradigm for Neural Networks

F. Schönbauer and M. Köhle
Technische Universität Wien, Institut für Praktische Informatik, Karlsplatz 13 / E1804, A-1040 Vienna, Austria

ABSTRACT

Learning in neural networks, using the back propagation learning algorithm, is regarded as a curve fitting process. Principal inadequacies of static algorithms are shown and the crucial role of the number of hidden units and their connections is elaborated. A non-static learning paradigm that allows creation of units and their interconnections during learning is introduced, and an outline of an algorithm to avoid the aforementioned problems is presented. Higher structured learning is defined as not only modifying the strength of connections but the overall topology of the net. The advantages of a neural net trained with this algorithm and its role in real world applications are described.
Keywords: Learning, Neural Networks, Back Propagation.

INTRODUCTION

Back propagation [1], the learning strategy that is currently in the focus of neural network research, is well suited for supervised classification tasks. In the traditional - static - paradigm the network´s topology is determined by rule of thumb according to the given problem. Then the net is trained on exemplary patterns until either those are learned satisfactory or due to time constraints the network is considered to be unable to perform this task. Hopefully, after learning the net is able to generalize what it has learned to unseen patterns.

Usually the net has to be redesigned several times. This design cycle can be automated by using a non-static learning paradigm that allows to adjust the net´s topology depending on the data.

INADEQUACIES OF STATIC BACK PROPAGATION

In back propagation learning the number of hidden units and the topology of the network is crucial not only to the ability classifying training data but especially to net´s ability to generalize [2,3]. Essentially back propagation learning is a curve fitting process [4] where the training data represents in feature space to which the curve has to be fitted. Since the dimensionality of the feature space is not known beforehand an estimate has to be made. The dimensionality of the curve corresponds to the number of hidden units and their interconnections. If the chosen dimensionality is too small (not enough units or connections) no sufficiently fitting curve will exist. If it is too large the unnecessary dimensions of the curve will add twists and bends to the curve which do not correspond to any inherent features of the data.

Generalization means selecting a curve that is a model of the properties of the data. Since the curve can only be modelled on the training data, the training set must be an all encompassing subset of the entire data set. Any parameters of the model of the entire data set that are not represented in the training set cannot be accurately modelled. Since the entire data set is usually unknown the quality of the net´s internal model depends on the accuracy of the designer´s guesses. So for back propagation to produce meaningful results it requires an adequate network topology. The essential problem in modelling is finding a topology that already models the data. The back propagation algorithm only evokes the intrinsic capabilities of the net.

The number of hidden units depends on the complexity of the learning task, more hidden units are needed to approximate a complex function. Over learning occurs when the number of connections reaches the number of training patterns, that is every connection is dedicated to one specific pattern. This also reduces the net´s ability to generalize, that is patterns of the test set perform significantly worse than patterns of the training set, because each pattern is learned separately and no common features are represented in the net´s internal model. Just increasing the number of hidden units and their connections does not necessarily lead to an adequate representation of the features of the data set. When the number of patterns is unevenly distributed in the classes, rare patterns are under represented in the net´s feature detectors, since only a small number of units can be dedicated to deal with them.

Numerous attempts have been made to determine an adequate number of hidden units and connections for a given problem domain. But as we have seen it is desirable to avoid making this decision before learning takes place, actually one would wish not to have to make this decision at all. Rather, to find the optimal number of hidden units should be part of the learning strategy itself.

In problem domains where the number of possible patterns is unlimited and the number of classes is not a priori known, it may be impossible to estimate the number of required hidden units in advance. Moreover, the distribution of patterns over time may vary. To allow adaptation to the changing situation the number of hidden units must change.

There are problems where networks with low connectivity outperform fully connected networks. Generalization is usually much better when a priori knowledge about the problem domain is used to restrict the number of interconnections [4].

Biophysical evidence [5] shows that the average connectivity in the human brain is less than 10000. Specialized neuron groups like receptive fields in the mammal visual system have a distinct connection pattern with very low average connectivity. These biological facts are actually no proof for improving learning algorithms by taking into consideration the connectivity of the net, but they lead to powerful ideas how learning strategies may be improved.

Summing up, network topology as defined by the number of neurons and the number and structure of their interconnections is an important aspect when considering the abilities of any learning algorithm.

Current implementations of neural network simulations use serial or coarse grained parallel machines. Therefore simulation time increases with increasing number of units and interconnections. The order of magnitude of this increase is almost square. An algorithm that uses hidden units as sparingly as possible is therefore desirable.

EXTENDING STATIC LEARNING PARADIGMS

Schemata, concepts or any kind of knowledge contained in a neural network are usually considered to be represented in the interconnections between the units of a network. Learning in neural networks is regarded as modifying the strength of these interconnections. We define higher structured learning as not only modifying these weights but also the overall topology of the net, that is actually adding new units and connections while learning, which implies that knowledge in a neural net is also represented in the architecture of the net.

All attempts to improve back propagation [1, 3, 6] share the following characteristics:
They rely on the static paradigm, that is the overall topology of the network is defined before learning takes place and is not altered during the learning phase. Furthermore, all these changes to back propagation tend to perform better than the original back propagation for some problems but worse for others. They seem to depend on factors such as number of patterns, continuity within the patterns or order of pattern presentation.

THE NON-STATIC LEARNING PARADIGM

The non-static paradigm is inspired by biological analogy. It has been shown that in the human brain whenever a group of neurons is working on a task which cannot be accomplished by them because there are too few of them, another bunch of neuron cells gets devoted to this task in order to support the others.

Usually when modelling a neural net, one tries to model this part of the brain which works on a specific task. So taking into consideration the importance of network topology and biologically evident dynamic topology in respect to a specific task, the dynamic paradigm is defined as changing the topology of the net not only during the learning phase but also at every time after its static definition which precedes learning, or even as allowing to define the overall topology dynamically, while learning.

In the static paradigm, the definition of a neural network is similar to a variable declaration in a block oriented language. Every unit has a unique name by which it can be referenced. The overall topology of the network is defined before learning takes place and is not altered during the learning phase. During learning only the values of the weights change. In a dynamic paradigm units can be created at any time, before during or after learning. They can be connected arbitrarily with other units of the net. Since there is no name for a dynamic unit before it is created, special considerations are necessary to associate these units with references to them.

SEGREGATION ALGORITHM

As mentioned above the ability to generalize using the back propagation algorithm is very sensitive to the number of hidden units. Consider a back propagation network that tries to learn a large number of patterns which are to be separated into a large number of distinct classes. Assume that there are few classes with many representative patterns in the training set and many classes with only few representatives in the training set. Using a hidden layer that initially contains very few units will lead to a network that is able to differentiate between the classes containing many representatives, but has no knowledge about the classes with only few (maybe just one or two) representatives.

The separation into classes learned by the net after a sufficient number of learning steps is describable by a simple rule since those few hidden units involved in the classification task could only differentiate between the majority of input patterns and the rest. If learned patterns are removed from the training set, the remaining patterns can be used as training set for another network that will now have to deal with the classes that are left. This segregation of pattern and their assignment to their own network can be repeated as often as necessary.

The algorithm can be formulated as follows [7]:

- Use back propagation learning with a small number of units in the hidden layer until the mean squared error of a certain percentage of patterns is significantly less than the average mean squared error for all patterns.
- Continue learning using these patterns until the error approaches zero.
- Remove these patterns from the training set.
- Clamp all weights connected to or from the hidden units.
- Add a few units to the hidden layer and connect them.
- If there are still patterns in the training set repeat all previous steps.
- Unclamp all weights
- The weights should now represent a good initial position on the error surface, continue normal learning to reunite all subnets

With this algorithm, classes that are difficult to learn because there are so few patterns for these classes in the training set can be learned separately. They can be presented as often as desired to a specific subnet without disturbing the knowledge the rest of the net has already learned about the other classes. The robustness of neural nets to noisy data or very infrequent appearances of stray patterns can be explicitly weakened to any desired degree without entirely removing this feature.

The algorithm is sensitive to its parameters, namely the percentage of patterns that has to have a different error rate to be recognized as a different entity and learned separately, the number of hidden units the net starts with, the number of hidden units that is added at each segregation step.

APPLICATIONS

Whenever data has to be classified to determine further action there are two different ways to do it. Derive rules from an expert who knows how to differentiate the classes and use those in a program (e.g. an expert system). Or use already decided examples to extract the rules contained in the data by a program (e.g. a neural net). When data is readily available and/or rules are difficult to obtain a neural net would be a natural choice. As mentioned, generalization from examples cannot be guaranteed, but can usually be achieved in real world applications.

A sudden unexpected isolated data set can be interpolated depending on the net´s internal model of all data. If data changes slowly over time continuous learning allows to adapt to the changing situation gradually.
With the presented algorithm the inherent limitations of an approach that lies in a fixed set of rules whether extracted by man or machine, namely the inability to react to changing environments (i.e. data) can be circumvented.

Consider a robot arm with motors to control its movements and some sensory inputs to determine its position. Instead of programming the movements of the robot arm explicitly, the robot is taught to control its motors to reach a given point in its coordinate space by trial and error. Because of its ability to generalize the robot has to be taught only a few points in its space to be able to reach all others. The robot will handle nonlinearity in its movement system by itself. In case of wear and tear in the robot´s mechanic system continuous learning will make it adapt to its changed movement parameters.

These capabilities of neural nets improve the performance of existing systems in automated monitoring and control.

REFERENCES

[1] Rumelhart, D.E.; Hinton, G.E.; Williams, R.J.: "Learning Internal Representations by Error Propagation" in Rumelhart, David E., McClelland, James L. and the PDP Research group (eds.): "Parallel Distributed Processing", MIT Press, Cambridge, MA, 1986

[2] Kung, S.Y. and Hwang, J.N.: "An Algebraic Projection Analysis for Optimal Hidden Units Size and Learning Rates in Back-Propagation Learning", Proceedings of the 2nd International IEEE Conference on Neural Network, Vol. I, San Diego 1988

[3] Lehmen, A. von; Peak, E.G.; Liao, P.F.; Marrakchi, A.; Patel J.S.: "Factors Influencing Learning by Backpropagation" in Proceedings of the IEEE International Conference on Neural Networks, Vol. I, San Diego, 1988, pp.335-341

[4] Solla, Sara A.: "Learning Contiguity with Layered Neural Networks", Book of Abstracts for the 1988 INNS Meeting

[5] Braitenberg, V.: "Cell Assemblies in the Cerebral Cortex" in Lecture Notes in Biomathematics, Vol.21 R.Heim and G.Palm (eds.), Springer Verlag, 1978, pp.171-188

[6] Hush, D.R.; Salas, J.M.: "Improving the Learning Rate of Back-propagation With the Gradient Reuse Algorithm" in Proceedings of the IEEE International Conference on Neural Networks, Vol. I, San Diego, 1988, pp.441-447

[7] Köhle, M.; Schönbauer, F.: "Generierung dynamischer Units in einer Neuralen Netze-Sprache", Tagungsband der 5. Österreichischen AI-Tagung, Inssbruck, März 1989

SECTION 7 - DIAGNOSIS, SAFETY AND RELIABILITY

Karljr: A Global Diagnosis System

Stephanos D. Bacon and Paul T. Posco

Digital Equipment Corporation, Knowledge Integrated Tools and Systems Group, Shrewsbury, Massachussetts, USA

ABSTRACT

We present the characteristics of global diagnosis and contrast them with those of other diagnostic tasks. We also discuss issues regarding the development of Karljr, a knowledge based system which performs global diagnosis and has been in use within Digital since November, 1987. We present a summary of our knowledge acquisition strategy, provide a description of the implementation and discuss issues relating to the reporting of results from such a system.

INTRODUCTION

For the past several years, we have been working on the development of knowledge based systems which analyze manufacturing data stored in large databases. The goal of this effort is to automate the diagnosis of common problems in the manufacturing process (including equipment and procedural problems), as well as in the material produced by this process. Some of our earlier efforts have been reported in Brown [1] and Posco [7]. In the past year and a half, we have concentrated much of our effort on analyzing a problem solving-task which we call Global Diagnosis. We have implemented a system called Karljr which models the behavior of a human expert who performs this task. Karljr has been in daily use by a manufacturing organization within Digital since November, 1987. We are currently re-implementing this system in order to include new knowledge and analysis capabilities not possible in the original version.

In this paper, we first discuss the motivation for our work. After discussing our knowledge acquisition process, we present an overview of the operation of the system. We then present what we believe are the characteristic elements of global diagnosis and discuss their relationship to other diagnostic tasks. Finally, we discuss certain issues relating to the implementation of Karljr.

MOTIVATION

The domain in question is a multi-stage VLSI-like manufacturing process. Devices are fabricated on wafers. These wafers are then cut into strips called bars. Some processing is performed on a per-bar basis and then the bars are cut into individual devices. At each stage, a large amount of data is collected. As the manufacturing process ramps up to full volume, engineers no longer have the time to examine all the data that is produced manually. Consequently, many subtle problems go unnoticed until they become quite serious and adversely affect yield. Furthermore, most engineers are only thoroughly familiar with a small portion of the overall process. Data from another fabrication stage is generally not very useful to them because they don't know how to interpret it. This localized view can lead to serious problems. An error at one stage of the process may not become apparent until several more steps have been performed. An engineer who is a specialist in this latter area may not understand the overall process well enough to recognize the actual cause of the problem.

What is needed in these situations is an individual with a good overall grasp of the process, but one who is not involved in details of any particular stage. This individual can look at data from a key test stage and identify devices or groups of devices that are "interesting" (i.e. abnormal in some way). Using his or her overall knowledge of the process, this individual can then examine these devices in detail and localize the cause of the problem to general process areas. If the cause of an abnormal occurrence is not known, a group of engineers can be brought together to perform further analysis, each bringing expertise from his or her specific process area. This is the activity which we call Global Diagnosis.

While our process was still in the advanced manufacturing stage, the task of global diagnosis could be adequetely performed by one individual. As the process ramped up, however, this individual found that it was not possible to keep up with the data being produced. At this point, we decided that it would be useful to try to automate as much of this process as possible. We understood from the beginning that this is not a standard application for a knowledge based system. Most importantly, the technology involved is quite new so the domain is not completely understood by the experts. Furthermore, the manufacturing process itself is constantly undergoing change. Some issues related to expert systems in evolving domains are discussed in [2].

KNOWLEDGE ACQUISITION

We initially conducted four interviews with our expert. The primary goal of these interviews was to determine the steps that he took in performing his diagnostic task. We asked him to bring copies of any reports or printouts that he examined on a particular day. We then asked him to step through this set of reports as he normally would, but describe what he was doing at the same time. Very often, he would have to interrupt his description of the diagnostic process in order to explain what he was looking for and why it was important.

These interviews led to the development of the initial prototype of Karljr. This program captured the overall problem solving process but had a very weak diagnostic knowledge base. Every day, we would run the program manually and show its reports to our expert. Since he was looking at the same data, he was able to point out incorrect conclusions, as well as conclusions that could have been reached. All this information was added to Karljr on an incremental basis.

Within three months, our expert believed that it would be beneficial to put Karljr online. Knowledge acquisition has continued throughout this time.As new problems are encountered, the symptoms and their causes (if these causes are understood) are added to the system. After Karljr was in daily use for several months we contacted all the engineers who received reports and asked for feedback on the system. This effort led to knowledge acquisition sessions with several of these individuals. We found that the knowledge acquired during these sessions would fit quite easily into the framework of global diagnosis.

SYSTEM OVERVIEW

Karljr runs on a daily basis. Each day, it examines parametric data for devices which were tested in the preceding 24-hour period. This sample generally contains devices from many different wafers. Karljr first examines the data to determine if any tester problems have occurred. Any devices which are determined to be aberrant due to a tester malfunction are not used for further analysis. Any tester malfunctions are reported. Notice that the identification of tester problems is an important task of global diagnosis. It is necessary that the system be able to identify aberrant parameter values so that these values are not used in later analysis, leading to incorrect conclusions. Identifying tester problems is then simply a matter of examining the aberrant parameter values produced by a tester.

After the data is verified, it is examined on a wafer by wafer basis. Yield and abnormal parameter values are used as criteria to select wafers for further investigation. Each selected wafer is then considered in turn. Since the process is not strictly first-in first-out (FIFO), other devices from these wafers may have already been tested. Data for all the devices which have ever been tested from a wafer is collected and detailed analysis proceeds.

During detailed analysis, the wafer is examined in several ways. Individual parameters for each device are classified as either high, low or normal. Combinations of parameter values in a given device often indicate problems with the device itself. In some cases, a large number of device problems indicate process problems. In other cases, abnormal parameter values may point directly to process problems.

Any observations, device related conclusions and process related conclusions are then mailed (via electronic mail) to the users.

GLOBAL DIAGNOSIS

We have now described enough of our domain to be able to discuss some of the characteristics of global diagnosis. Global diagnosis is a problem solving task which can be characterized by the following:

1. *The need to examine a large amount of data to see if there are any interesting observations worth pursuing.* The initial data examined

is from a key test stage, generally late in the process.

This characteristic is important from two aspects. First, the global diagnostician is given raw data, not an initial set of symptoms. Second, there is usually a large amount of data. In order to be useful, this data must be reduced to a more manageable amount. Manufacturing engineers use statistical tools to do this – e.g., trends of the values of parameters or yield, or correlations between parameters. Also, different kinds of reports are used in order to look at the data in various ways. In analyzing the problem-solving process of our expert, we found that the same kinds of reports were examined in the same order on a daily basis. Also interesting is the fact that it is very often possible to prune a large amount of data by looking at only a few values. For example, if the yield from a wafer is reasonable from the perspective of the engineers, there is no point in examining it any further. Only wafers with exceptionally high or exceptionally low yields need to be examined in detail.

Yield is only one measure of interestingness for a wafer. In general a wafer can be interesting for several reasons. If the overnight sample of tested devices which is initially examined contains any measurements which are out of the ordinary (i.e. different from what the process has been producing lately) then the wafer is examined in detail. In many cases, the abnormality may be in the positive direction. It is important to identify very good wafers and analyze them in order to learn what makes a "perfect" device.

2. *Diagnosis of entity (i.e., device, wafer) problems must be conducted in order to perform diagnosis on the process.* Consider the following example heuristics:

   H1: A wafer containing many devices with problem X indicates process problem Y.

   H2: A device with parameter P1 too high and parameter P2 nominal has problem X.

In order for H1 to be applied, H2 must first be applied to every device on a wafer. After this is done, the system must decide if "many devices" have problem X.

The implication here is that we actually need two kinds of representations. H1 and H2 can be coded in any rule like representation. However, an extra layer of control is needed so that the two heuristics can be appropriately applied. This control layer will first apply

H2 to each device on a wafer. It will then apply H1, which will presumably apply some sort of computation to determine if "many" devices exhibited problem X.

The extra layer of control is needed for more than the appropriate application of diagnostic knowledge. Very often, quantitative analysis has to be performed before diagnostic knowledge can be applied. For example:

> **H3:** If the average value for physical dimension D is high, then it is likely that there is a plating problem.
>
> **R1:** Physical dimension D is proportional to electrical parameter P1.
>
> **R2:** electrical parameter P1 is proportional to electrical parameter P2.

P1 and P2 are parameters measured during a key test. These are the numbers that the global diagnostician will examine initially. In fact, the diagnostician may not look at both P1 and P2. Very often, a few parameters can act as key indicators, so there is no point in looking further. Suppose, however, that P2 is generally high for a wafer. This occurence can in some sense be "explained" by high P1. Thus if the value of

$$NewP2 = nominalP1\frac{P2}{P1}$$

is nominal, there is good reason to consider why P1 is high. The same computation can be applied to the relationship between P1 and D1. If high D1 "explains" the observation of high P1, then we can apply heuristic H3. Note that if the reason for P1 being high cannot be explained, the program will report this fact. This is very useful for identifying weaknesses in our knowledge base. By using these data dependencies, we are able to limit further the amount of data that must be examined: If we have no reason to suspect that physical dimension D is abnormal, there is no point in examining it.

3. *Incomplete knowledge about the domain.* We may know that certain things are "interesting", and we want to report them; but we don't necessarily have to know what may have caused them. Of course, if we know anything about the potential cause of an observation, we will continue our analysis.

   By accepting the fact that our knowledge base will almost certainly be incomplete, we are implicitly modifying the goals of a diagnostic

```
          Heuristics                Heuristics
      Data  ==> Device Diagnoses ==> Process Problem
   Abstractions                          Abstractions
        ^                                      |
        |                                      |
        |                          Refinement  |
        | Data Abstraction                     |
        |                                      |
        |                                      V
   Parametric Data (Data)               Process Problems
```

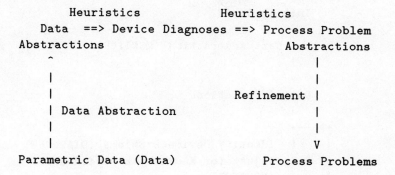

Figure 1: Inference structure of Karljr

expert system. That is, the goal of an expert system which performs Global Diagnosis is not limited to diagnosis. The identification of "interesting" occurrences is an important task in itself. Another implication is that a formal system for reasoning with uncertainty is not necessary. If five process problems are found to account for a given symptom, it would not be meaningful to rank them since the experts are not be able to quantify their certainty.

In order to understand how the implementation of global diagnosis in Karljr relates to other diagnostic expert systems, we analyzed Karljr in terms of its inference structure and the operations that it performs. The inference structure of a system characterizes the kinds of knowledge in a system and the relationship between them. The system applies its knowledge by performing various operations. In other words, the inference structure describes what a system does; the operations describe how the system does it.

From the perspective of its inference structure, Karljr performs heuristic classification [6]. Figure 1 shows the general inference structure of Karljr. Raw data is abstracted by classifying it as high, low, normal, different from another region etc.. These abstractions are then used as evidence for identifying device problems. Device problems are then used to isolate process problems. While this picture is generally accurate, there are a few important idiosyncrasies in our system.

In section 2 we pointed out that the role of a "global diagnostician" is to isolate problems to general process areas. It is often the case that more detailed diagnosis of the process requires that the devices be cross

```
          Initial Data
             |
             | Data Abstraction (MONITOR)
             |
             V
          Data Abstractions
             |
       +-----+
       |     |  Identify Device Problems (DIAGNOSE)
       |     |  Adjust for Known Data Dependencies
       |     |  (MONITOR)
       |     V
       |    Device Problems,
       |    Data Abstractions from Known Dependencies
       |     |
       +---->|
             | Consider the frequency of occurrence,
             | and/or combination of the above
             | observations and conclusions
             | (DIAGNOSE)
             V
          Root Causes
```

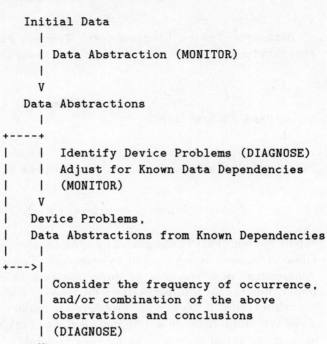

Figure 2: The Flow of Evidence During the Analysis of a Wafer

sectioned and physically analyzed. This kind of analysis is outside the scope of global diagnosis. In this case, the refinement of process problems is minimal. Another idiosyncrasy is derived from the the third characteristic of global diagnosis. This characteristic implies that heuristic knowledge to match data abstractions to Device or Process problems may not even be available. In this sense, global diagnosis tends to emphasize data abstraction as an important function in itself.

Clancey [6] presents a taxonomy of what he calls generic operations. For example, figure 3 shows the generic operations for analysis tasks. The operation of a system can be described in terms of combinations of these generic operations. Figure 2 shows a more detailed view of the inference structure of Karljr, with the generic operations performed in each step in parentheses. If we just consider the sequence of generic operations performed by the program, and the order in which they are

```
                  INTERPRET
                      |
          +-----------+---------+
          |           |         |
      IDENTIFY    PREDICT   CONTROL
          |
     +----+-----+
     |          |
  MONITOR   DIAGNOSE
```

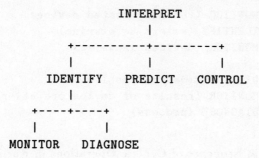

Figure 3: Taxonomy of Generic Operations for Analysis [6]

```
MONITOR (patient state)
DIAGNOSE (disease category)
IDENTIFY (bacteria)
MODIFY (body system or organism) (i.e treatment).
```

Figure 4: Sequence of Generic Operations in MYCIN [6]

performed, we get the diagram of figure 5. This diagram illustrates the flow of control in a little more detail than figure 2. The program must MONITOR and DIAGNOSE many devices in order to be able to diagnose process problems. The diagnosis of process problems is then strengthened by considering multiple wafers. In other words, if several wafers exhibit the same kind of problem, it is more indicative of a process problem than if only one wafer exhibited the problem. These loops in the sequence of operations are distinctive of global diagnosis. In contrast, consider figure 4, the diagram for MYCIN given in [6].

All the systems analyzed in [6] exhibit a similar linear pattern. The reason for this linear progression of operations is that there is only one entity being analyzed. In the case of MYCIN, it is the patient. A medical/public health analogy to global diagnosis would be the following: Suppose that we are confronted with the widespread occurrence of several diseases in a population and we want to find the root causes or causes of these diseases. In order to do this, we must first diagnose individual patients. We must then look for patterns in these individual diagnoses in order to isolate the root causes of the epidemic.

```
             MONITOR (recently tested devices)
             IDENTIFY (wafers to examine)
+--+---> MONITOR (devices in wafer)
|  |
|  +---- DIAGNOSE (device problems)
|        MONITOR (results of device operations)
+------- DIAGNOSE (process)
```

Figure 5: Sequence of Generic Operations in Karljr

In this section, we have presented three characteristics of global diagnosis and discussed their implications. We have also shown how global diagnosis fits into Clancey's heuristic classification model, as well as how it differs from this model. We have argued for the necessity of an explicit representation of control knowledge separate from the representation of diagnostic knowledge. That is, the knowledge that describes (and controls) the operations performed by the system should be separated from the knowledge that describes the inference structure of the system. This idea is not really new; in MYCIN [3] this kind of knowledge was explicitly encoded in meta-rules. Later systems like HERACLES [5] extended this idea by having the inference mechanism represented by a set of domain-independent tasks. These tasks query the domain-dependent knowledge for information as it is needed.

We do not yet understand the nature of global diagnosis well enough to encode domain independent tasks. However, we have devised a representation which will allow us to think of the operations of the system in terms of modular tasks. The next section describes this representation in more detail.

CONTROL MECHANISM

In Karljr, global diagnosis is represented as a hierarchical decomposition of tasks. Each task has a before action, an after action and a primary action. The before and after actions represent initialization and cleanup. The primary action for a task can either be a call to a diagnostic knowledge group, a routine which applies a diagnostic knowledge group repeatedly, a data gathering routine, a numerical analysis routine or the evaluation of the subtasks of a given task. Each task also has a precondition. This is a piece of code which specifies the conditions under which a given task is to be executed. A priority is assigned to each task so that if the preconditions of two or more tasks indicate that they could all be activated, the task with highest priority will be chosen.

The control mechanism works as follows. Given a list of tasks (L1), it evaluates the preconditions of each. The actions of the highest priority task whose preconditions have been met (T1) are then executed. If the primary action for this task involves the evaluation of subtasks, then the above process is repeated for these subtasks. When the actions of T1 are completed, then the preconditions of all the tasks in L1 are re-evaluated and the process is repeated. If none of the preconditions is met, the evaluation of L1 is complete. This is essentially a forward chaining system whose knowledge base has been hierarchically decomposed to limit the number of preconditions which have to be checked at any given time.

DIAGNOSTIC REPRESENTATION

Our diagnostic knowledge is represented in a language called DRL (Diagnostic Refinement Language). This language, which was developed internally, is based on the Establish-Refine Paradigm used in CSRL [4]. Based on our experience with Karljr, DRL has been enhanced to support some of the characteristics of global diagnosis.

MEMORY AND REPORTING

Karljr is a practical system which is used by extremely busy individuals. The presentation of its findings is therefore of critical importance. We have spent a considerable amount of time modifying report formats to make them more understandable to our users. The difficulty is that our users are used to seeing reports on parametric data. This kind of information fits easily into tabular form. Unfortunately, the kind of information produced by Karljr does not always fit into tables. Our challenge is to present the findings of Karljr in such a way as to require as small a behavioral change in our users as possible. This issue is still being addressed.

Our users have also pointed out that Karljr should show more of an awareness of what it has reported recently and of the state of the process in general. We have addressed this issue in our current re-implementation. For example, if a given wafer was found interesting and examined recently, and a few heads from the wafer appear in the overnight sample, the wafer will not be re-examined because it is unlikely that any new conclusions can be reached. Also, when reporting on the number of occurrences of a given problem in a wafer, Karljr presents the average number of occurrences of the problem in the most recently examined wafers.

IMPLEMENTATION

Implementing a knowledge based system for production use is much more involved than simply implementing the knowledge base. In terms of lines of code, the knowledge base represents roughly 30 to 40 percent of the entire system. The remainder of the code includes the user interface, access routines for the two databases used by the system, data structures, report generation and statistics routines. Figure 6 shows a block diagram of the entire system. In this section we will present a short discussion on the databases and the knowledge base, making references to the other modules as necessary.

The prototype version of Karljr was written in Lisp. The version which is currently being implemented is written primarily in C. The precondition and action routines for the various tasks are C routines which call out to DRL to apply specific diagnostic knowledge. Conclusions produced by DRL code are stored in a main memory database which has a callable interface available to the tasks.

Databases

Karljr gets device test data from the production database used by manufacturing. This data consists mostly of electrical measurements taken during the final test stage, but also includes some measurements of actual device dimensions taken at earlier stages of the process. The data tracking module keeps track of the current process average for these parameters as well as whether or not they exhibit some kind of trend. This information is stored in its local database and is updated weekly. The data tracking module also compares these parameter averages to the values used for high and low thresholds in the knowledge base. If it determines that the process average for a parameter has shifted, it informs the knowledge base maintainer via electronic mail.

In addition to information about process history, the local database is used to store a summary of the observations and conclusions made for each wafer examined. The summarizer module is responsible for summarizing a session and storing the information in the database. Objective

```
+------------+            +-------------+
| System     +----------->| User        |
| Module     +--------+   | Interface   |
+--+------+--+        |   +-------------+
   |      |           |
   |      |           |   +---------------+
   |      |           +-->| User          |
   |      |               | Registration  |
   |      +----------+    +------------+--+
   |                 |                 |
   V                 V                 |
+------------+   +-------------+       |
| Diagnosis  |   | Data        |       V
| Module     |   | Tracking    +-------+------------+
+--+---+--+--+   +-------------+                    |
   |   |  |                                         |
   |   |  +----------------------------+            |
   |   +--------------+                |            |
   |                  |                |            |
   V                  V                V            |
+------------+    +-------------+   +------------+  |
| Knowledge  |    | Summarizer  |   | Report     |  |
| Base       |    |             |   | Generator  |  |
+--+---------+    +---+---------+   +--+---------+  |
   |                  |                |            |
   V                  V                V            V
   +------------------+----------------+------------+
                      |
                      V

                  DATABASES
```

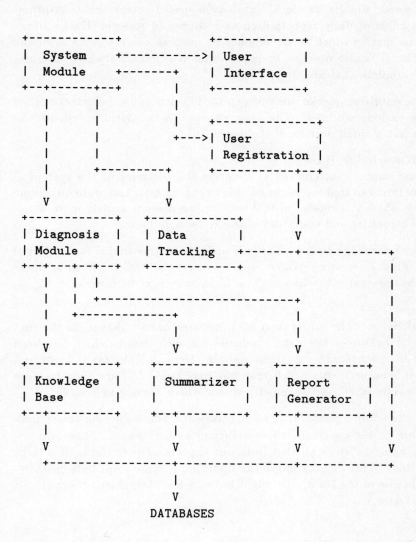

Figure 6: Karljr System Block Diagram

information, such as yield, number of devices in the wafer and so on is also maintained. Finally, the local database is used to store the descriptions of the kinds of daily reports each user wishes to receive. Karljr allows users to specify which testers should be used as sources of data for the analysis. It is also possible to specify that Karljr perform only a subset of its complete analysis.

The database queries are encapsulated in procedures which are called by the various modules. This way, changes in the databse schema will only affect a small portion of the code.

The Knowledge Base

We have thus far attempted to describe the behavior of the system in general terms so that we might be able to characterize the problem solving process which it models. In this section, we present a little more detail on the structure and operation of the knowledge base.

The knowledge base in Karljr is split into three major tasks: Initial Scan, Find Interesting Wafers and Characterize Wafer. Each of these tasks has several subtasks which perform more specific functions.

Initial Scan The initial scan task operates in two phases. In the first phase, it examines the data produced for each device which has been tested in the preceding 24 hour period. Here it looks for failures, parameter measurements which may not have failed but are close to some specification limit, and parameter values which are not believable.

In the second phase, it applies knowledge about specific tester malfunctions to the conclusions made during the first phase. These are primarily heuristic rules elicited from our experts. For example, if a large percentage of the devices showed an abnormally large amplitude measurement in one of the tests, this might indicate an intermittent short circuit in the tester.

Find Interesting Wafers This task also looks at the conclusions produced during the first phase of the initial scan task. However, it looks at the data on a per-wafer basis. The "interestingness" of a wafer is decided based upon yield, as well as high or low measurements of key parameters.

Characterize Wafer This task is activated once for each wafer which is deemed interesting. After retrieving data for all devices in the wafer, it scans each device, applying the same knowledge as in the first phase of the inital scan. The program then tries to relate some of these observations to regions of the wafer. If an observation about a parameter has been localized to a region of the wafer, then the program will try to apply any known relationships between that parameter and others. As an example, consider the following rules:

```
If parameter X is greater than some threshold
Then conclude "high-X" for the current device

If all the devices in a row have "high-X"
Then conclude (weakly) that there was a
     mask misalignment

If there appear to be many rows in the top and bottom
   of the wafer indicating mask misalignment
Then conclude (more strongly) that there was a
     twisted mask.
```

The first rule is applied when the devices are scanned. The second rule looks at the conclusions produced by the initial scan and generates its own. Finally, the third rule considers the wafer as a whole and makes an even stronger and more specific conclusion. Our diagnostic language supports eight discrete levels of certainty for the existence of a problem ranging from confirmed to disconfirmed. We do not have a rigorous way of combining these values; the selection of the appropriate certainty value is left up to the expert and the knowledge engineer. This is consistent with our claim that a formal system of reasoning with uncertainty would not be meaningful in global diagnosis (see above).

Spatial patterns in a given parameter may also be indicative of process problems. For example, at one stage in the process, bars (or rows of devices) go through a fine grinding process. It is actually possible to tell if the bar was ground evenly by looking at the values of an electrical parameter. Thus, if devices from one end of the bar have a higher value for this parameter than devices from the other end, the bar was not ground evenly. Now, if we look at the frequency of occurrence of such problems within a wafer, we can decide whether there appears to be a problem with the grinding process, or if the uneven grinding is just a symptom of a more fundamental problem with the whole wafer.

THE EFFECTS OF Karljr

Our initial goal in developing Karljr was to reduce the amount of time which was spent by our expert in examining test data. In this, we can claim success. Whereas he spent on the order of several hours per day in this task, he now spends less than one half hour. More importantly, according to our expert, it probably would not have even been possible to examine all the data produced by the process once it ramped up to full volume. There have been other positive effects created by this program, however.

The reports are mailed daily to roughly 30 people ranging from senior level managers to engineers. As a consequence of this automatic distribution of information, our expert receives fewer telephone calls, and managers are more likely to call engineers responsible for a given area directly, with very specific questions on the status of the process.

Surprisingly, some of the positive effects of the program arose out of some of its weaknesses. Karljr only has access to data that was produced rather late in the processing of a wafer. Given only this data, it is not always possible (for a person or a KB system) to discern correctly which process area was responsible for certain problems. At one point during the past year, there appeared to be a small production problem which might have gone unnoticed except for Karljr. The program noticed abnormal patterns in the final test data and concluded that there was a process problem in a certain area. This problem continued for several weeks with Karljr reporting the same conclusion daily. As it turned out, Karljr had made the only conclusion that it could make given the data at hand, but this conclusion was incorrect (A correct diagnosis required the cross-sectioning of one of the devices). However, it was the program's incessant reporting of its findings which caused people to investigate a problem which would have gone unnoticed until it got significantly worse. In this case, Karljr acted as a sort of "automated nag" — constantly reminding people that *something* was wrong.

DISCUSSION

We have presented the characteristics of a problem solving task which we call global diagnosis. We have also analyzed our implementation of global diagnosis with respect to its inference structure and the operations that are performed. This analysis led us to conclude that Karljr performs a variation of heuristic classification. The most important characteristic of global diagnosis is that many devices must be analyzed in order to be able to diagnose process related problems. This implies that emphasis has to be placed on control mechanisms. Also significant is the fact that the identification of abnormal conditions is just as important to global diagnosis as is the ultimate diagnosis of process problems.

One of the major lessons that we have learned from our work with Karljr is the importance of careful analysis of the expert's problem solving methodology. We were able to identify the characteristics of global diagnosis because we began the knowledge acquisition process without pre-supposing any representational model. Instead, we developed a prototype system which modeled as closely as possible the behavior of our expert. We then analyzed our program and were able to generalize the notion of global diagnosis.

Since knowledge acquisition is a continuing process in a domain such as ours, we believe that it is critical to develop a partnership with our users. Much of our knowledge has been acquired via electronic mail, telephone calls and casual hall conversations. Obviously, such informal methods are useful only after the overall structure of the reasoning process is understood. However, they can only be used if the system developer(s) take an active role in continuing knowledge acquisition. Busy individuals will not generally take the time to correct mistakes or oversights in a system like Karljr. Their job is to keep the process running with a reasonable yield. If the reports are not giving them useful information, they will begin to ignore them. We make a point to monitor the reports ourselves and ask our users for feedback and additional information.

ACKNOWLEDGEMENT

We were (and are) fortunate that our expert, Karl F. (Karl Sr.) is a true believer in the application of AI to manufacturing. Furthermore, his ability to clearly articulate his knowledge and his patience with our initial ignorance of the domain made our work a true pleasure.

Dr. David C. Brown of Worcester Polytechnic Institute has provided valuable comments on our analysis. DRL has been implemented by Tom Westervelt of KITS. We thank him for taking our many suggestions seriously.

References

[1] Brown, D.C., and P. Posco. Expert Browsing in Manufacturing Databases, Proc. ASME Computers in Engineering Conference, Chicago, August 1986.

[2] Brown, D.C., P. Posco, S. Bacon and L. Leamus. Experiences with Developing Expert Systems for An Evolving Domain. Proc. Workshop on AI in Process Engineering, AAAI-88, St. Paul, Minnesota, August 1988.

[3] Buchanan, B.G. and E.H. Shortliffe. Rule-Based Expert systems: The MYCIN Experiments of the Stanford Heuristic Programming Project, Addison-Wesley, Reading, Massachussetts, 1984.

[4] Bylander, T. and S. Mittal. CSRL: A Language for Classificatory Problem Solving and Uncertainty Handling, The AI Magazine, pp. 66-77, August 1986.

[5] Clancey, W.J. From GUIDON to NEOMYCIN and HERACLES in Twenty Short Lessons: ORN Final Report 1979-1985, The AI Magazine, pp. 40-60, August 1986.

[6] Clancey, W.J. Heuristic Classification, Artificial Intelligence, 27(3), pp. 289-350, 1985.

[7] Posco, P., and D.C. Brown. The Analysis of Complex Manufacturing Data Using Expert Diagnostic Browsing, Proc. Symposium on Knowledge-Based Expert Systems for Manufacturing, Annual Winter Meeting, Production Engineering Division, ASME, Anaheim, California, December 1986.

Integration of Quantitative and Knowledge Based Techniques in a Diagnostic System

Jeffrey Dawson

Digital Equipment Corporation, 110 Spit Brook Road, Nashua, New Hampshire 03062, USA

INTRODUCTION

The purpose of this paper is to describe a method of integrating knowledge based techniques with quantitative modeling techniques in the construction of an expert diagnostic system. The system that results is more effective and efficient than would be obtained by using knowledge based techniques alone. The knowledge based techniques are used to detect and diagnose a problem, and then to search for a corrective recommendation. The quantitative modeling techniques are used to control the search for the recommendation, to refine the recommendation, and to verify that the recommendation will indeed solve the problem.

This paper draws its inspiration from the domain of computer performance evaluation. That domain is somewhat different from those in which previous expert systems have found application. However, the approach described should be generally applicable to any diagnostic domain where there are quantitative models available. We will illustrate the ideas presented with examples related to a proposed system for diagnosis of computer performance problems.

BACKGROUND

Computer performance evaluation

Most modern operating systems for larger computer systems collect data on the performance of the system as part of their normal routine. Computer performance evaluation involves the analysis and interpretation of this collected data for a variety of purposes -- from computer system growth planning to real-time performance monitoring. The particular problem that we are concerned with is called *off line bottleneck analysis* [2]. A performance bottleneck will be the fault whose diagnosis we are concerned with. The computer performance expert starts the analysis by selecting performance data collected on the system under typical workloads. The expert examines the collected data to determine whether or not any of the system components are saturated under typical workloads; that is whether or not there is a performance bottleneck. If a bottleneck is discovered the expert will diagnose the source of the bottleneck, and recommend modifications to the system or workload to remove the bottleneck. The recommended modifications could range from adjusting operating system parameters or redistributing the workload, to adding hardware.

Domain distinctions

Most of the work in intelligent diagnostic systems has been applied to domains such as electronic circuits where both faults and their cures are well defined. In computer performance evaluation, neither faults nor cures are as well defined. Our proposed use of quantitative techniques will help to more effectively define a cure, but we will have to rely on other methods for the definition of a fault.

Fault definition When an electronic circuit fault occurs, the circuit no longer functions correctly. A signal is not present at a given point in the circuit. However, if a computer performance fault or bottleneck is encountered, the computer system is still functioning although not at an acceptable level of performance. For example, the response time may be unusually long. What constitutes acceptable performance and therefore defines a fault can vary widely from one system to another. A fault consitutes a failure to meet a system performance goal. In defining those performance goals, the use of quantitative techniques does not help.

Corrective recommendations When an electronic circuit fault has been diagnosed it is usually clear what to do to correct it. Mend the broken wire, for instance. However, with computer performance evaluation the matter is not quite as straight forward. Although one has traced the performance problem to a particular incorrect system parameter value, it may not be at all clear how to change the value in order to achieve an acceptable level of performance. Here the inclusion of quantitative techniques will be of considerable help in making the recommendations more precise and increasing their likelihood of success.

THE DIAGNOSTIC SYSTEM

The diagnostic system is based upon the *generate and test* paradigm used in many artificial intelligence problem solving systems [9]. It comprises two main modules: a knowledge based module and a quantitative module. The knowledge based module is pragmatic and empirical by nature. It uses heuristics to analyze data representing past performance and to recommend changes that will improve performance in the future. It is the knowledge based module which embodies the generation portion of the computational paradigm. On the other hand, the quantitative module is more theoretical and predictive by nature. It uses mathematical models to predict the performance of the system if the recommendations of the knowledge based module are followed. This module is responsible for testing the solutions generated by the knowledge based module. The two modules work cooperatively to solve the performance problem, passing control from one module to the other.

The Knowledge Based Module

A rule base representing the collective expertise of a community of computer performance specialists is used to analyze the collected data. We were particularly fortunate to be able to start from information used for training purposes and then to extend that base with the help of experienced performance experts. The rules in the resulting knowledge base are of two types: one type for detecting performance bottlenecks, and the other for diagnosing any bottleneck discovered. At the beginning of the analysis, only bottleneck detection rules are active. If a bottleneck is discovered, appropriate sets of diagnostic rules are activated to continue the analysis until corrective modifications can be recommended which would eliminate the bottleneck.

The definition of a performance bottleneck can vary from system to system. What constitutes acceptable performance for a batch oriented commercial computer system can be quite different from acceptable performance for an engineering environment with a more interactive emphasis. Although a performance expert will follow the same basic analysis regardless of the computing environment, the criteria used for making the analysis decisions may change. To permit the same sort of flexibility in our knowledge base, the rules are parameterized so that the analysis can be tailored to fit the particular computer installation.

The Quantitative Module

The quantitative module is used to refine and verify the recommendations inferred by the knowledge based module as well as to control the knowledge based diagnostic search. Queuing network models and other probabilistic models form the basis of the quantitative module [1,2,3,5]. Once a performance problem is discovered and corrective action recommended, the quantitative module is used to more precisely detail the recommended system modification. For instance, the knowledge based module may recommend that a system parameter be changed. It is up to the quantitative module to determine what the new value for that parameter ought to be. The quantitative module is used again to predict whether making the recommended change will actually eliminate the bottleneck or not. If the bottleneck is not eliminated, the knowledge based module must continue the search until enough recommendations have been garnered to remove the performance bottleneck. The objective is to meet the performance goal with the least expensive and smallest number of modifications to the system. When many modifications are made to the system at the same time, there is the risk of complicated interactions leading to no improvement.

System Hierarchy and Problem Decomposition

Exploiting structure within the problem domain is a technique that is frequently used in organizing knowledge based systems and decomposing the problems they solve [4]. The hierarchical structure of computer systems suggests a natural decomposition of each of the modules in our diagnostic system. There is a one to one correspondence between the components of the two modules. The control passes downward through the hierarchy of the knowledge based module, while in the quantitative module control passes from the bottom upward. Control is exchanged between the two modules at corresponding components of the hierarchy. In essence the analysis follows a depth first knowledge based search with the quantitative module supplying intelligent backtracking control.

Searching the knowledge based hierarchy Initially only the bottleneck detection rules are active. These are organized into three sets corresponding to the three major computer subsystems: memory, I/O and CPU. These rules examine system wide performance indicators to determine whether or not the performance of each of these three subsystems is acceptable. If no bottleneck is found the system is pronounced to be healthy and the analysis is through. Otherwise, rule sets appropriate for diagnosing the failure of the effected subsystem are used to continue the investigation by further decomposing the subsystem and the problem as necessary. Each computer system component has an acceptable level of performance defined by the tailoring parameters of the rule set associated with that component. The knowledge based module follows a top down approach in its performance investigation. It starts at a system wide level and successively narrows its search to smaller system components until the source of the problem is located and a recommendation can be made.

Searching control from the quantitative module Once a performance problem has been identified, traced to the lowest level system component, and a recommendation made by the knowledge based module; control passes to the quantitative module where the details of the recommendation are worked out. The recommendation can be rejected by the quantitative module as being impossible to implement. In which case control passes back to the knowledge based module to search for another recommendation.

After the recommendation has been refined and the details filled in, the resulting change to the performance of the associated system component can be predicted using a mathematical model of the component. If the predicted performance meets the requirements for removing the bottleneck, control passes up the hierarchy of the quantitative module where the performance of the next higher level system component is predicted. If the predicted performance at any level of the quantitative hierarchy proves to be unacceptable, then control passes back to the knowledge based module. The search is resumed at the corresponding level of the knowledge based hierarchy. The remaining alternatives at that level will be explored until an additional recommendation can be made and control again shifts to the quantitative module. The performance problem is solved when control returns to the top of the knowledge based hierarchy and no further bottlenecks are detected. The solution comprises the collected recommendations made by the knowledge based module as detailed by the quantitative module.

EXAMPLE

We will now work through a simplified example to illustrate the major features of the diagnostic system and how the two modules work together.

Bottleneck Detection

A memory problem generally has an impact on other subsystems, so the analysis starts with the rules for detecting bottlenecks in the memory subsystem. We shall assume that no memory problem has been found there. So the rules for detecting I/O bottlenecks come into play and we assume that the following rule fires.

```
if
        Average _disk _queue _length > Disk _queue _parameter
then
        activate(Disk _io _rules )
```

Disk_queue_parameter is a tailoring parameter whose value can be set by the user to define typical performance of the particular system involved. At this point in the analysis it has been concluded that there is an I/O bottleneck because requests are queued up at the disks of the system. So the continuing analysis tries to discover the source of these disk requests and to recommend a way of reducing the number of requests.

Diagnosis

One source of disk requests that might be eliminated is associated with file system overhead. Information describing the physical structure of the files is stored on the disk along with the files themselves. This information is needed to read file data from the disks. The file system software tries to keep some of this information cached in memory for quick access. If the necessary information is not found in the cache, it must be read in from disk causing one or more additional disk requests. The operating system keeps track of the percentage of requests that could be satisfied from each of the caches. This figure is called the *effectiveness* of the cache and is used in the following rule which we will assume fires.

```
if
        cache_effect( This_file_cache ) < min_effect( This_file_cache )
then
        recommend( Increase_size, This_file_cache )
```

Increasing the size of a cache will increase that likelihood that the necessary information will be found in the cache. That is the recommendation that the knowledge based portion of the analysis supplies us. It remains for the quantitative module to detail this recommendation and verify its effectiveness.

Recommendation Refinement

The effectiveness of the file system caches depends upon the number of active users as well as the size of the cache [8]. If we let N be the number of users and S be the size of the cache, then we can model the effectiveness of the cache with the formula (1) where α is a parameter.

$$\text{Cache Effectiveness} = 1 - \frac{1}{(S+1)^{\frac{\alpha}{N}}} \qquad (1)$$

Using the collected performance data we have observed values for the effectiveness, for S, and for N. Thus we can solve for the value of the parameter α. Finally we solve the equation for the value of S that will yield the target minimum cache effectiveness.

Verification

Once the new size of the cache has been computed, there are a number of constraints that must be checked before accepting the detailed recommendation. The size of each of the caches is specified by an operating system parameter. These parameters have maximum allowable values and we must make sure that the proposed value is indeed possible. Moreover, the increase in the size of the file system caches comes at the expense of the memory available to user processes. Therefore, we need to model the effect of this reallocation of memory to be sure that we have not created a memory problem in the process of solving the I/O problem. If either of these constraints is not met, the recommendation is rejected and control passes back to the knowledge based module to search for a more suitable solution. We are assured that such a solution exists though it may be costly. In the worst case we could solve our I/O problem by purchasing additional disks and redistributing the load.

Assuming that the recommended modifications to the file caches are possible, we rise to the next level of the quantitative hierarchy. We compute the predicted change in the I/O activity based on the recommended changes to the file system caches. With the predicted effectiveness of the new caches we can compute the reduction in the disk request rate and the resulting reduction in disk queue lengths. If this is not sufficient to remove the I/O bottleneck, then we resume the knowledge based search for additional I/O improvements. Otherwise, control passes back to the bottleneck detection rule set to determine if any other bottlenecks remain.

CONCLUSION

We see that the incorporation of quantitative techniques into the knowledge based diagnostic system has strengthened the system in three ways. The corrective recommendations that it produces are more detailed and quantitatively precise. There is more reason to believe that the recommendations will indeed solve the performance problem detected since they have been verified by means of mathematical models. There is better control of the diagnostic search. Impossible or incomplete solutions will be detected during the diagnosis and the search can be redirected accordingly.

It is interesting to note the similarities between this diagnostic system and some of the expert systems for design that have been discussed in the literature [6,7]. In both cases a proposed solution to the problem is generated through the use of heuristics and then its validity is tested quantitatively. Indeed, one might go so far as to characterize this diagnostic system as one which "redesigns" a computer system to meet performance and workload specifications.

REFERENCE

1. Denning, P., and Buzen, J. The Operational Analysis of Queueing Network Models, Computing Surveys, Vol.10, pp. 225-261, 1978.

2. Ferrari, D., Serazzi, G. and Zeigner, A. Measurement and Tuning of Computer Systems, Prentice-Hall, Englewood Cliffs, NJ, 1983.

3. Gelenbe, E. and Pujolle, G. Introduction to Queueing Networks, John Wiley and Sons, Chichester, 1987.

4. Genesereth, M. Diagnosis using hierarchical design models, Proceedings of the National Conference on Artificial Intelligence, Pittsburgh, pp. 278-283, 1982.

5. Lazowska, E., Zahorjan, J., Graham, G. and Sevcik, K. Quantitative System Performance, Prentice-Hall, Englewood Cliffs, NJ, 1984.

6. Mostow, J. Toward Better Models of the Design Process, AI Magazine Vol. 6, pp. 44-57, 1985.

7. Oxman, R. and Gero, J. Using an expert system for design diagnosis and design synthesis, Expert Systems, Vol. 4, pp. 4-15, 1987.

8. Smith, A. Cache Memories, Computing Surveys, Vol. 14, pp. 473-530, 1982.

9. Waterman, D. A Guide to Expert Systems , Addison-Wesley, Reading, MA, 1986.

Spread Sheet Based Diagnostic Tool

Koji Okuda

Research Center, Osaka Gas Co. Ltd., 6-19-9, Torishoma, Konohana-ku, Osaka 554, Japan

ABSTRACT

Currently a lot of KBS (Knowledge Based System) tools have been developed. But many of them are for those who know AI very well, not for for domain experts because they require practical AI knowledge for users. In this paper, a sophisticated KBS tool for diagnostic has been presented. Firstly diagnostic processes have been divided into several subprocesses. And for each of them, a spreadsheet format has been provided. These sheets work as knowledge editor for users. Implementation method and an example are also discussed.

1. INTRODUCTION

Spread sheet interface has provided sophisticated user interface for computer systems. One of the great merit is that users do not need to worry about detailed programming work. A spread sheet itself contains useful procedures, and therefore, is very useful for users because it greatly reduces the users' programming load to build a system.

On the other hand, when we think of building a diagnostic KBS, we have to take the following tasks.

(1) Build a domain model
(2) Translate the model into an (some) AI language(s)
(3) Program domain knowledge into a tool
(4) Execute the system and tune the knowledge

Here, (2) and (3) means that after we build a domain model, we have to translate it into AI languages like rule-based, frame-based, or object-oriented language. To do this, working and practical AI knowledge is essential. This is a bottle neck for current KBS tools because those who do not know AI well can not build KBS by themselves to solve their problems. But if we can get a KBS tool which does not require AI knowledge, then KBS paradigms would widespread much wider.

This paper shows that a spread sheet based diagnostic tool can be such an ideal tool described above. In the next chapter, the limitation of the current tools are described. Then we move on knowledge representation of this tool. And in the chapter 4, diagnostic process decomposition is described. An overview of this system is in the chapter 5, the implementation in the chapter 6, and finally an example is described in the chapter 7.

2. LIMITS OF CURRENT TOOLS

Current tools which are available in the markets can be divided into two categories, General Tool and Domain Specific Tool.

General Tools are, for example, OPS5, KEE, ART and so on. These tools remain in the AI language level. Building a KBS using KEE or ART is just like building a scientific data processing program using FORTRAN. These tools prepare basic primitives which are needed to build KBSs, but do not support building KBSs' process as a whole. We can say that building a KBS using General Tool would be easy for AI researchers, but not so easy for domain experts. Because those who want to use these tools must understand various AI knowledge like rule, frame, object, message, conflict resolution, inference mechanism, etc.

For example, if an engineer wants to build a KBS for plant diagnosis, his tasks seem to be defined as below.

(1) Gather data for diagnostic system from actual plant.
(2) Extract heuristic rules from the data.
(3) Translate those rules into a tool's description format
(4) Decide control mechanism for the system.
(5) Code this knowledge.
(6) Create user interface.
(7) Execute the system and tune the knowledge.

In the above tasks, what domain experts can treat are (1) and (2) only. Usually we have Knowledge Engineers to treat (3), (4), (5), (6), and (7). This means current KBS tools, especially General Tools, can not support full tasks of building KBS's processes. Therefore those domain experts who can not have KE's support can not use those tools by themselves. Of course, some of KBSs are developed without having KE's help. But it is only after those domain experts studied hard to master fundermental AI concepts.

To solve this problem, recently Domain Specific Tools have been developed. These are tools whose usage are limited within a (or some) field(s) like diagnosis, design. These tools have many domain specific procedures inside them. So users can create a KBS using those functions without having so much difficulty. A good example of Domain Specific Tool is G2 of Gensym. G2 is a tool specifically for real-time expert systems. G2 contains various functions which are useful for representing plant models. Some of the characteristics are knowledge representation considering time, provision for real-time data, various inference techniques, truth maintenance and so on. By making good use of these characteristics, a real-time expert systems can be build easily.

In G2, rule-based, frame-based and graphic programming are combined. Here, frame and graphic programming are mainly for user interface and monitoring problems. Rule-based language is used mainly for diagnostic problems. Here, this rule-based language contains the same problem as General Tools. For frame-based language, the difference between G2 and General Tool is that G2 has predefined frames. This means that basic slots are predefined. Therefore what users have to do are just enter proper values or symbols for those slots. Of course adding and deleting slots are possible. But here the problem is the following. In G2, a huge frame appears when one want to define an object. It is not so easy task for domain experts who do not know AI well to understand this knowledge representation style, and to put proper values or symbols for frames. Reviewing characteristics of G2 also shows some problems. For example, truth maintenance and knowledge representation considering time are very useful for KEs, but not for domain experts. Domain experts do not know what TMS is, and how to use it. What they want is KBS tools of which they can use without getting help of KEs. Currently no KBS tools supports domain experts from this points. Of course G2 is an excellent tool to build KBSs, but there are still some problems not solved there.

This paper shows an answer for these problems. This tool does not require any AI knowledge. Furthermore, in this tool, domain experts' knowledge representation are used. So what domain experts should do to build a KBS is just to (1) analyze the problem, (2) build a model to solve the problem. In this sense, this tool can be categorized as a try to realize the 3rd generation of KBS tools.

3. WHY SPREADSHEET?

Recent research shows that spreadsheet can be serve as a very effective user interface for computer systems. One good example is Lotus 1-2-3. This software showed the capability of the spreadsheet interface systems. Based on the success of those systems, recently KBS approach has become to be combined with this spreadsheet interface. Current applications are mainly for numeric analysis for, for example, design. This is an extention of the current spreadsheet system to KBS type spreadsheet.

This paper shows another extention of spreadsheet based systems. The target problem is diagnosis. The main reason why this domain has been chosen is that diagnostic problems are quite suitable for spreadsheet (matrix type) knowledge representation. For example,

*Failure propagations are represented by adjacent matrices.

*For failure cause identification, knowledge are often represented by cause-effect matrix.

Thus by using spreadsheet interface, we can use domain knowledge as they are. Furthermore, by implementing various useful functions, users can be able to use it without detailed AI knowledge. These are one of the great merit of using spreadsheet for diagnostic problems, and also the merit compered with current KBS tools.

4. DIAGNOSTIC PROCESSES AND SHEET FORMAT

For better and effective information processing, in this tool, diagnostic processes are divided into 5 processes as below.

(1) Alarm Generation Process
(2) Alarm Propagation Process
(3) Detecting Primal Alarm Process
(4) Primal Cause Identification Process
(5) Fault Cause Identification Process

4-1. Alarm Generation Process

This process is a map from sensor information to alarms information. Based on sensor information, this process decides which alarms should be activated. A simple and traditional alarm generator is on/off alarm generator. This means that by setting a threshold for each sensor, if a sensor's value is exceed it, then the alarm generator activates an alarm corresponding to the sensor. An temperature alarm example is that

IF a temperature of SENSOR is more then 30 degree THEN activate alarm A
ELSE inactivate alarm A.

In this type, if a temperature is 29.5 degree, the alarm would not be activated. But we think that if the temperature is 29.5 degree, the alarm is almost activated. This kind of information processing sometimes avoid to cause dangerous situations. To provide the system with this kind of information processing function, this tool has a fuzzy alarm generator. Here, fuzzy membership functions are used to represent an alarms certainty factor.

This process consists of two kind of spreadsheet. One for defining fuzzy membership function, and the other for alarm generator.

In the first sheet, users can define any type of fuzzy membership function. Defining a membership function would be done by defining its name and its shape. Its shape is represented by input 10 numbers as a list.

The following is an example of this sheet. Here, monotoric-decrease function and mountain type function are defined.

NAME	SHAPE
Monotonic-Decrease	(10 9 8 7 6 5 4 3 2 1)
Mountain-Type	(1 3 5 7 9 9 7 5 3 1)

Fig.1 Defining Membership Function Sheet

The second sheet treats actual alarm generation. Here, each alarm is assigned the most suitable fuzzy membership function. Besides this, a max value and a min value are defined to represent each alarms' (sensors') range. Based on this range information, automatic interpolation would be done for the function shape defined earlier. These information define a fuzzy alarms. When an alarm gets an actual sensor value, based on the membership function, this sheet generates an alarm's certainty value. Fig.2 shows an example of an alarm generator sheet. And Fig3 shows the relationship among membership function, min- ,and max-values.

NAME	M.F.	Min.	Max.	Sensor Value	A.C.V.
Alarm-A	Mountain-Type	10	100	50	0.9
Alarm-B	Mountain-Type	20	90	20	0.1
Alarm-C	Monotonic-Decrease	10	100	100	1.0

M.F. : Membership Function
A.C.V.: Alarm Certainty Value

Fig.2 Alarm Generator Sheet

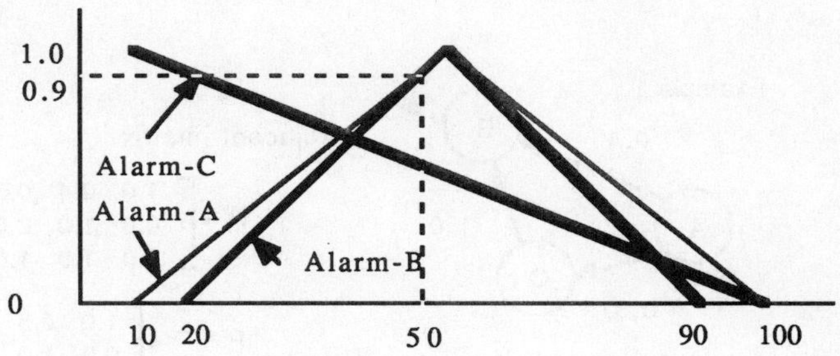

Fig.3 Information Procession on Alarm Generator

4-2. Alarm Propagation Process

This process is to identify which alarms would be activated by the current alarm patterns. Predicting future alarms is very important for preventive action for possible failures.

In this process, an alarm propagation matrix is defined where adjacent alarm propagation information is described. Usualy in this type of information processing, a reachability matrix is used to find the propagation result. Here, however, both each alarms'm value and alarm propagation values are not 0,1 value, but a value between 0 and 1. So usual reachability matrix can not be used. To solve this problem, an extended reachability matrix is introduced here.

An extended reachability matrix can be defined as below.
[DEF] Extended Reachability Matrix
Let A be a n x n matrix. The extended reachability matrix (R) of A is defined by the following.

$$R = A^n = A^{n+1}$$

where matrx multiplication * is defined as below.
Let P (= $[P_{ij}]$) and Q (=$[Q_{ij}]$) be n x n matrices, and R (=$[R_{ij}]$) be the multiplication of P and Q. (R = P * Q) In this situation, R_{ij} can be calculated by the following formula.

$$R_{ij} = \max_{1 \leq k \leq n} [P_{ik} \times Q_{kj}]$$ Here x means normal multiplication of 2 numbers

This extended reachability matrix means that if there are more than one path between two nodes, let's take a path which takes maximun possibility as the propagation path between those nodes.

A simple example is described in example1. In this example, the extended reachability matrix says that nodeB's possibility of activation after nodeA's activation is 0.5 rather than 0.4. This means A has stronger influence to B through C rather than directly.

Fig.4 shows a sheet for this process. Here, users define alarm propagation information. When this sheet receives current value of each alarms (these values are calculated by the alarm generation process), then returns to users future alarm propagation information.

Example 1

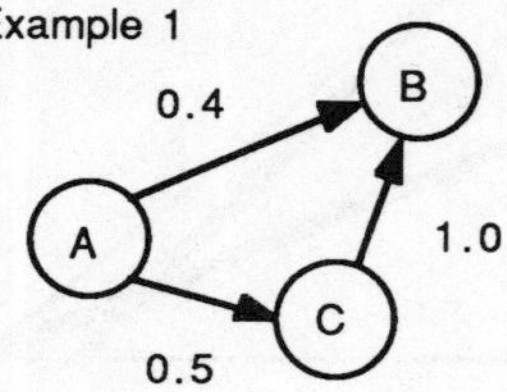

Adjacent matrix

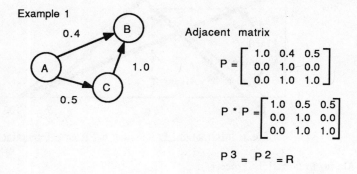

$$P = \begin{bmatrix} 1.0 & 0.4 & 0.5 \\ 0.0 & 1.0 & 0.0 \\ 0.0 & 1.0 & 1.0 \end{bmatrix}$$

$$P * P = \begin{bmatrix} 1.0 & 0.5 & 0.5 \\ 0.0 & 1.0 & 0.0 \\ 0.0 & 1.0 & 1.0 \end{bmatrix}$$

$$P^3 = P^2 = R$$

	Alarm-A	Alarm-B	Alarm-C	Alarm-D	Current Value	Future Value
Alarm-A	1	0.5	0	0	0.1	0.1
Alarm-B	0	1	0.3	0	0.3	0.3
Alarm-C	0	0	1	0.5	0.5	0.5
Alarm-D	0	0	0	1	0.1	0.27

Users define this information (Alarm-A to Alarm-D columns)

succeed value from alarm generator (Current Value)

automatically generate this value (Future Value)

Fig. 4 Alarm Propagation Sheet

4-3. Detecting Primal Alarm Process

When a lot of alarms are activated in a short time, detecting a primal alarm is very important to take proper action to make the plant normal status. This can be done by using extended reachability matrix. But this method is, currently, effective in the assumption that there are no multiple failures.

The procedure itself is very simple. The system gets current alarm information. If there are multiple alarms activated, this system tries to find "AND" set of corresponding parent alarms in the extended reachability matrix. The following example shows concrete image of this process.

In the example2, case 1) shows that alarm-C can be activated by alarm-A or alarm-C itself. Here, alarm-A can be treated as a hidden alarm. And the case 2) shows that if both alarm-A and alarm-C are activated, the primal alarm is alarm-A. From single fault assumption the system can get this result. Extending this method to multiple faults is our future task.

Example 2

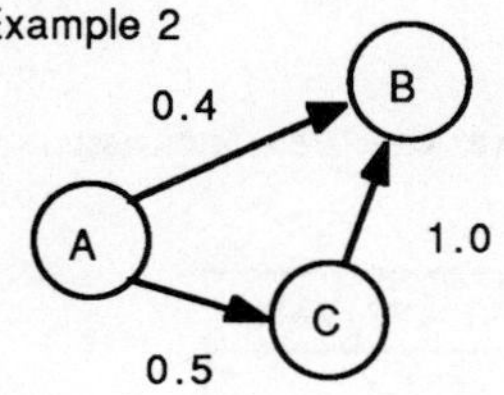

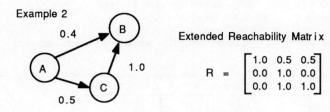

Extended Reachability Matrix

$$R = \begin{bmatrix} 1.0 & 0.5 & 0.5 \\ 0.0 & 1.0 & 0.0 \\ 0.0 & 1.0 & 1.0 \end{bmatrix}$$

1) If the system receives alarm-C, then possible primal alarm is A or C.

$$\begin{array}{ccc} A & B & C \end{array}$$
$$\begin{bmatrix} 1.0 & 0.5 & 0.5 \\ 0.0 & 1.0 & 0.0 \\ 0.0 & 1.0 & 1.0 \end{bmatrix} \begin{array}{l} \dashrightarrow A \\ \\ \dashrightarrow C \end{array}$$

2) If the system receives alarm-A and alarm-C, then possible primal alarm is A.

$$\begin{array}{ccc} A & B & C \end{array}$$
$$\begin{bmatrix} 1.0 & 0.5 & 0.5 \\ 0.0 & 1.0 & 0.0 \\ 0.0 & 1.0 & 1.0 \end{bmatrix} \begin{array}{l} \dashrightarrow A \\ \\ \\ \end{array}$$

4-4. Primal Cause Identification Process

This process is to find primal fault cause for a failure. To find a failure cause as much detail as possible, we need a lot of information. Gathering all the information beforehand is almost impossible. Especially in a plant diagnosis, information for expert systems can be divided into 2 classes.

(1) Information which can be got on line realtime. (Like alarms)

(2) Information which can not be got on line realtime. (Like on-site sensor information)

In many cases of plant diagnosis, diagnostic systems, firstly, have to find failure cause by on line realtime information only. Of course in this time, as the system do not have enough information, the diagnostic result may not be so good. So this stage might be called rough diagnosis. The purpose of rough diagnosis is to find primal failure cause or failure source of the system. The diagnostic result itself is not so precise, but very effective to start more detailed diagnosis using off line information.

In this tool, this process receives alarm information, and gives certainty values for each primal symptoms. Users can go deeper for each primal symptoms using a sheet of Fault Cause Identification Process. A certainty values for each primal symptoms can be calculated as in Fig.5. This calculation means to put proper weight for each alarms, and add the value to get the certainty value for each primal symptoms.

This sheet is very simple, but very powerful. Fig.6 shows an example of this sheet. Here suppose that Alarm-1, and 2 are activated at the certainty value 1. In this case we tend to think that symptom 3 would have the highest possibility because only sympton2 relates both alarm-1 and 2. This processes calculation returns the same result. This knowledge also be read as

IF both alarm-1 and alarm-2 are activated,

THEN possible cause would be Symptom-2.

Therefore by taking the weight of an alarm properly, we can treat heuristics in this sheet.

	Alarm-1	Alarm-2	----	Certainty Value
Symptom-1	C11	C12		CV-1
⋮				

$$CV\text{-}i = \sum_{j} Cij \times Alarm\text{-}j$$

Fig.5 Calculating Certainty Value and Sheet Format

	Alarm-1	Alarm-2	Alarm-3	Certainty Value
Symptom-1	1	0	0.3	1.3
Symptom-2	0	1	0	1.0
Symptom-3	1	0.7	0	1.7

Users' deine part

Calculated Value

(cf. Alarm-1, 2, 3's certainty value =1.0)

Fig.6 Sheet Example

4-5. Fault Cause Identification Process

The above 4 process are based on real-time information, and automatically processed. But this process is mainly processed by interactively with users. In this process, cause-symptom matrix is used as the sheet format. This sheet format is quite suitable and familiar with diagnostic problems. One of the characteristics of this process is that this tool can use the causal matrix as it is. It is not necessary to translate the matrix information into rule-, frame- or object-oriented language, nor to worry about the inference mechanism etc. What users have to do is to write their knowledge in the matrix format. Then the system automatically processes the information, and interactively promotes a diagnosis.

Fig.7 shows sheet format example for this process. It is possible in this tool to place sheets hierarchically. By putting subsheet's name for each causes if necessary. In this example, this system firstly asks users to input remarkable symptoms. If it is symptom-1 then to differentiate cause 1 and 2, this system asks users if symptom-2 is remarkable or not. If so the diagnosis result is the cause-3. If not this system continues its diagnosis based on the subSheet-1's information.

	Symptom-1	Symptom-2	Symptom-3	SubSheet
Cause-1	1	0	1	subSheet-1
Cause-2	0	1	1	none
Cause-3	1	1	1	none

Fig.7 Fault Cause Identification Process Sheet

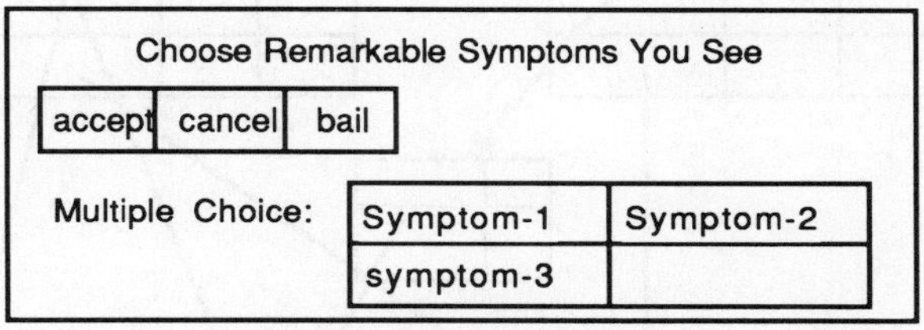

Fig.8 Generated Query Sheet

Another characteristics of this process is automatic query sheet generation based on the process sheet. Fig.8 shows an example of the generated query sheet from Fig.7's process sheet. The inference reports are also given to users automatically. There, current possible cause candidates, the name of subsheet of the candidate if any, and final diagnostic result are shown to users. By having these functions, users' load to build a KBS would be greatly decreased. Because what users have to do is just input their knowledge in their familiar format.

By hierarchically locating sheets of this process, hierarchical diagnosis can be realized. This is an extention of FTA analysis. Basically FTA's node represent a condition, like the temperature is more than 30 degree. But in this process sheet, each sheet can be a node in a diagnostic tree. Therefore we can treat more complicated problems in this process than FTA. (See fig.9.)

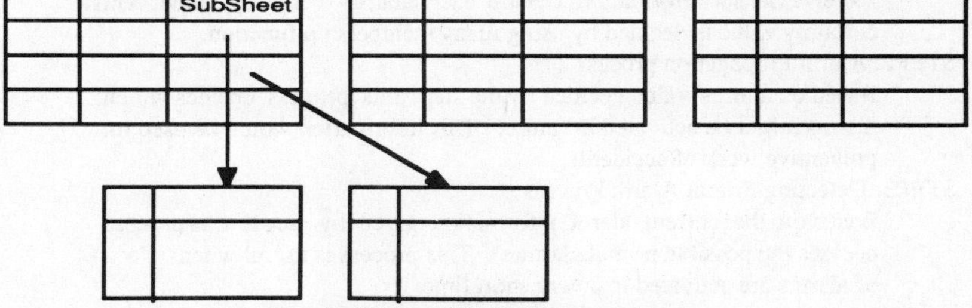

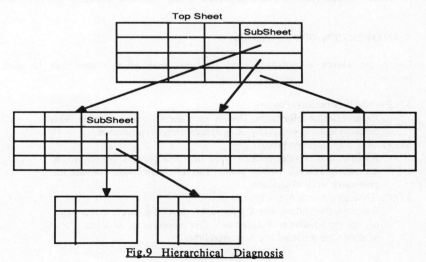

Fig.9 Hierarchical Diagnosis

By locating sheets in a network style, we can share several knowledge bases (sheets) among systems. This greatly increase the productivity of a diagnostic system which is similar to the past system. Reusability of knowledge bases is one of the great merit of this system. To use predefined knowledge bases, users just declare the name in the subsheet cell. (See Fig.10)

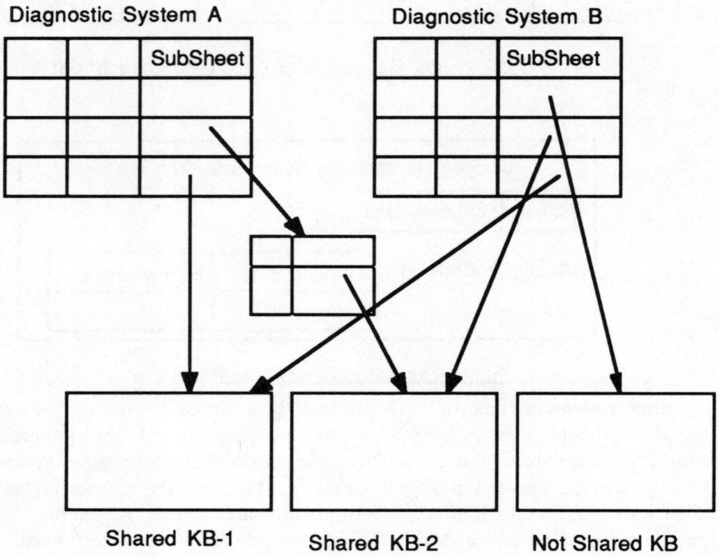

Fig. 10 Sharing Knowledge Bases

If a sheet can not identify single fault cause, and each fault causes has its subsheets, then decentralized diagnosis is able to be possible. Or by having backtracking function among the sheets tree, more effective diagnosis can be realized. These functions are expected to be installed soon.

5. AN OVERVIEW OF THE SYSTEM

Using the above spreadsheet sets, the execution of this tool can be described below.

STEP1: Alarm Generation Process

Receive Sensor Information. Decide each alarms' certainty value. This certainty value is decided by using fuzzy membership function.

STEP2: Alarm Propagation process

Based on alarms' value decided by the step1,this process decides which alarms might be activated in future. This information would be used for preventive work of accidents.

STEP3: Detecting Primal Alarm Process

Based on the current alarm information given by step1, this process decides the possible primal alarm(s). This process is useful when a lot of alarms are activated in a very short time.

STEP4: Primal Cause Identification Process

Based on the current alarm information given by step1, this process decides the primal cause. Since information used here is not so much, detailed diagnosis can not be done. But in an emergency situation, this rough diagnostic result is very useful. Also this 2 stage diagnosis is similar to human diagnosis. Human experts firstly diagnose a system using small information, then try to find detailed failure cause using enough information.

STEP5: Fault Cause Identification Process

Based on the step4's result, the system tries to find detailed failure cause. The above step1 to step4 would be done automatically. (When the system receives sensor information, step1 to step4 are automatically activated, and users can know the result.) This is the only process where information is processed interactively with users.

The above information flows are described in the Fig.11.

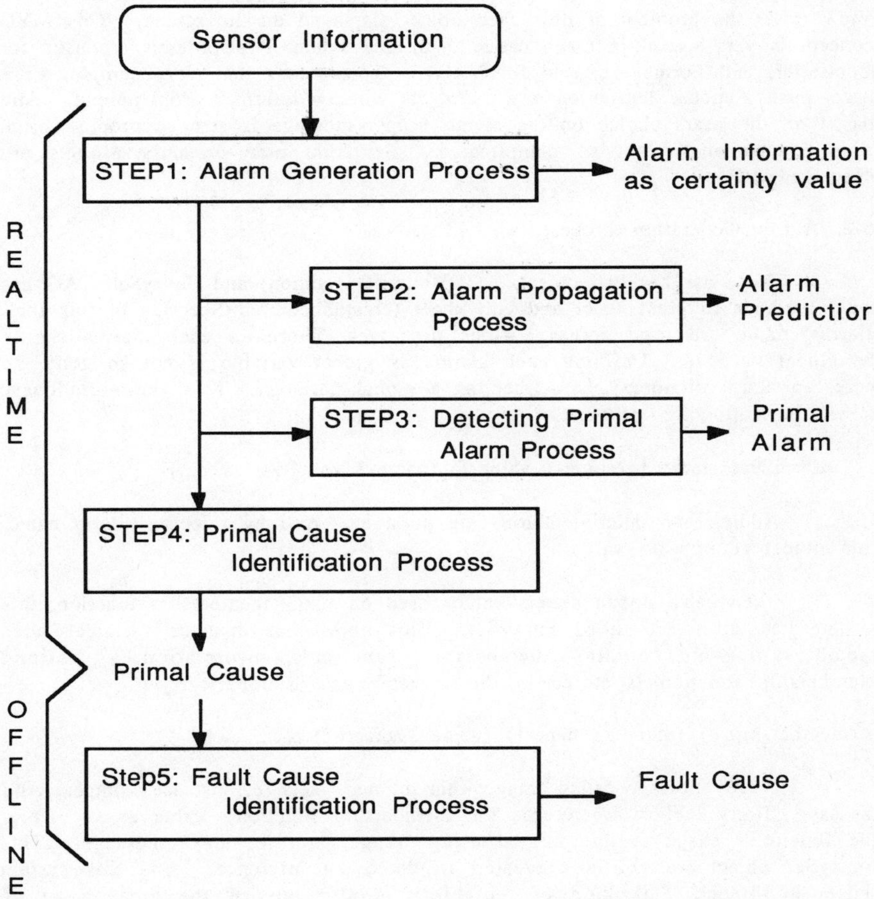

Fig.11. Information Flow Among Processes

6. IMPLEMENTATION

This system is implemented by Smalltalk-80 on Fuji- Xerox 1161. Smalltalk-80 provides various facilities to program. Besides its predefined object system, smalltalk-80 has an application called SpreadSheet. SpreadSheet itself is an system for numeric information processing. But the flexibility of the object-oriented programming gives programmers further capability.

This system is built on the SpreadSheet system, and is the natural extention of the system. That is, besides usual numeric operations, in this system, users also can use many useful symbolic operations described in the former chapters. An implementation overview is described below.

6-1. Overview

In this system, each processes is an object inside the system. And each object are represented by three view point, Model, View, Controller. Model defines actual object's behavior. Controller defines how a message is sent to an object. View treats the problem of how each object displayed on the screen. This MVC concept is very useful in many cases. In this sytem, PopUpMenus are used for Controller, and Forms are used for View. This means that, for example, when users push a mouse button on a window, its window returns a PopUpMenu. And based on the users choice on the menu, proper message is sent to proper object. This mechanism is not so complicated. So from now on only Models are described below.

6-2. Alarm Generation Process

This class has two object, AG (Alarm Generation) and FuzzySet. AG has main methods to creat sheet and edit sheet (createSheet, editSheet). In this tool. alarms' name are used across various processes. Therefore each alarms should be global variable. Defining each alarms as global variable is not so good, so here, an alarm dictionary is defined as a global variable. This alarm dictionary takes the following structure.

AlarmDictionary: { (name-1 value-1) (name-2 value-2) ....}

Adding and deleting alarms are possible. And by selecting alarm name, this object returns its value.

To calculate an alarms value based on fuzzy membership function, this system has an object called FuzzySet. This object has instance variable called membership which contains membership function's information. Defined membership function is stored in this variable as dictionary style.

membership: { (name-1 shape-1) (name-2 shape-2) ....}

An message called "range: min to: max" sets the instances' range. And message "findValueFor: x" returns the membership function's value at x. Here, the function's shape is interpolated using "range: min to: max" message. This FuzzySet object was initially created to do fuzzy inference, and this system reuse the object. This kind of reusability is also one of the great merit of object-oriented programming.

6-3. Alarm Propagation Process and Detecting Primal Alarm Process

This class has one object called AP (Alarm Propagation). This object has the same message to create sheet and to edit sheet. (As being described later these common messages are inheritated from FD. FD is the object in Fault Cause Identification Process)

In the Alarm Propagation Process, getting a extended reachability matrix is the main task. To do this, an message called :reachability Matrix: is installed. This is not symbolic operation method, but numeric operation method. To the reachability matrix, the system multiply alarms value (vector) to get failure propagation information. For these purposes, some numeric operation messages are also installed.

For Detecting Primal Alarm Process, this object has matching messages. This process is based on the reachability matrix calculated by the Alarm Propagation Process, so no new object is defined.

6-4. Primal Cause Identification Process

This class has an object called CI (Cause Identification). Besides the basic sheet's operation like create and edit sheets, this object has some messages to get certainty values for each primal causes. This value is calculated by multiplying two lists (one for alarms' value list, one for weight list for those alarms), so numeric operations are main in this object.

6-5 Fault Cause Identification Process

This class has FD (Fault Detection) object. This object has 5 main messages. Those are "create sheet" ,"edit sheet" ,"edit hierarchy","load knowledge base" and "start diagnosis".

"Edit hierarchy" activates one of the two message, "connect" or "disconnect". "Connect" is for connecting a cause with a sheet, and "disconnect" is for disconnecting a cause with a sheet.

"Load knowledge base" loads selected knowledge base to start diagnosis. For users convenience, current list of knowledge base appears on a menu. And by selecting proper knowledge base by mouse, users can load it.

"Start diagnosis" starts a diagnosis for loaded knowledge base. By this message, the system creates a query sheet automatically. And based on users response, the system asks users if more information needed. For this inference, various messages are installed. After the diagnosis of a sheet completed, if the detected cause has a subsheet, then the diagnosis is continued on the subsheet.

6-6. Object Hierarchy

The above object has the following hierarchy. In this hierarchy, basic sheet operations like create sheet, edit sheet are inherited.

These object description may not be the ideal one. Since this is till prototype system, in building the extended version, reviewing object structure may be needed.

The whole screen image of this system is attached at the appendix.

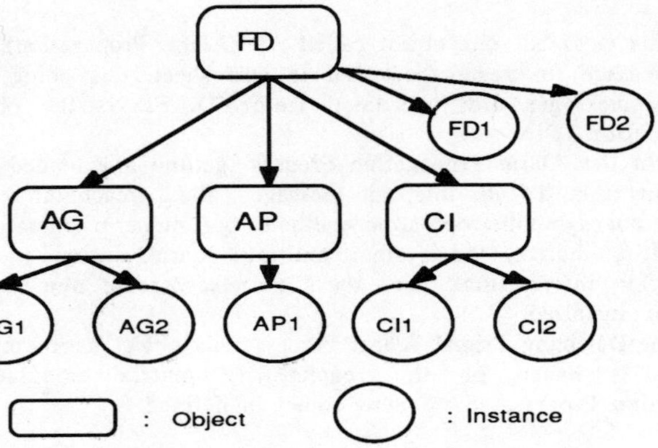

Fig. 12 Object Hierarchy

7. EXAMPLE

Using this spreadsheet based diagnostic tool, currently a diagnostic system for co-generation plant is now under implementation to check the performance of this system.

Implementation is done by taking the following steps.

STEP 1: The whole co-generation plant is decomposed into several parts based on its function.

STEP 2: Pick up alarms in each parts, then create alarm generation sheets.

STEP 3: Alarm propagation sheet is defined.

STEP 4: To identify which parts has failure cause, primal cause identification sheet is defined.

STEP 5: For each parts, failure cause identification sheets are defined.

Here, note that there is no AI manipulation done. What is done is just to make domain models in each sheet format. By using this tool, a KBS can be build very easily and effectively.

This application system is still in small prototype. (In the Fault Cause Identification Process, currently 4 sheets are located hierarchically) By extending this application system, the performance would be checked. And also the comparison this approach with other approaches like diagnosis based on signed directed graph approach should be investigated. The result of this appication system would be presented at other occasions.

8. CONCLUSION

In this paper, a new tool is presented. The characteristics of this sheet is summarized below.

*Spreadsheet based diagnotic tool
*No AI knowledge is required to use this tool

*Supporting full process of diagnosis from getting sensor information to estimating fault cause.
*Integrating system engineering (numeric operation to find alarm information) with knowledge engineering (symbolic operation for inference).
*Using domain expert's model (Spreadsheet interface is quite suitable for diagnostic problem)
*Decomposition diagnostic process
*Sharing knowledge base is possible
*Hierarchical diagnosis is easily implemented
*Applying fuzzy concepts for alarm activation

Reference

1. G. Fisher & C. Rathke Knowledge-Based Spread Sheets Proceedings of AAAI-88 pp.802-807, 1988

2. B. Rosen, et. al. A Spreadsheet Analysis And Design Communications of the ACM, Vol. 32, No.1, pp.84-93, 1989

3. Gensym/G2 GENSYM CORP. REFERENCE

4. N. Viswanadham et. al. A Methodology For Knowledge Acquisition And Reasoning In Failure Analysis of Systems, IEEE Trans. on SM&C Vol.17, NO.2, pp.274-288, 1987

5. M. Kramer et. al. A Rule-Based Approach To Fault Diagnosis Using The Signed Directed Graph, M.I.T. Report 1986

6. A. Goldberg Smalltalk-80: The Interactive Programming Environment Addison Wesley

7. A. Goldberg Smalltalk-80: The Language and its Implementation Addison Wesley

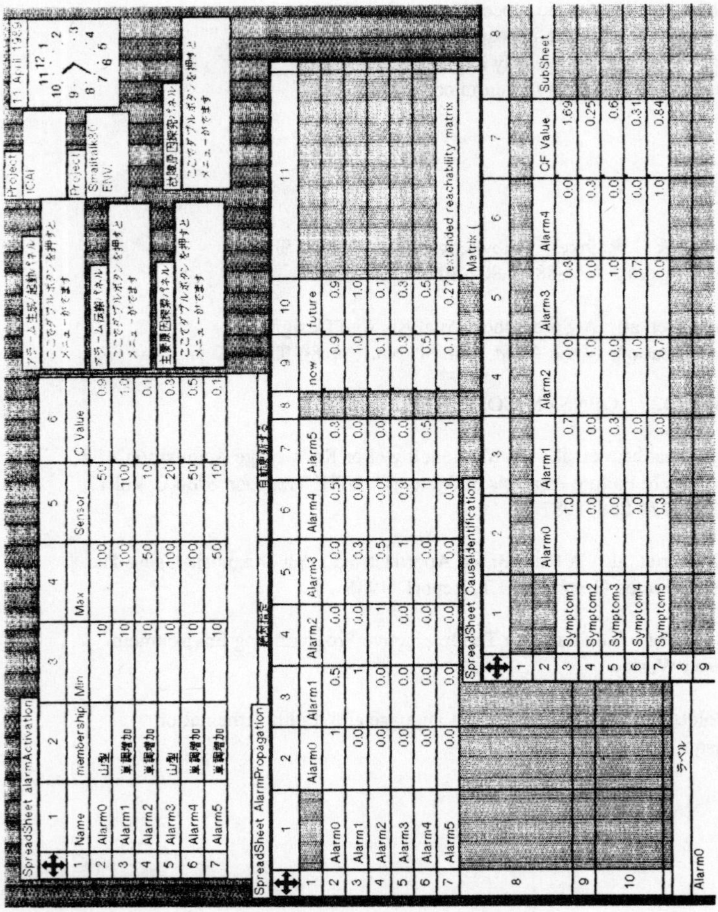
SpreadSheet alarmActivation
Name membership Min Max Sensor C Value
Alarm0 山型 10 100 50 0.9
Alarm1 単調増加 10 100 100 1.0
Alarm2 単調増加 10 50 10 0.1
Alarm3 山型 10 100 20 0.3
Alarm4 単調増加 10 100 50 0.5
Alarm5 単調増加 10 50 10 0.1
SpreadSheet AlarmPropagation
Alarm0 Alarm1 Alarm2 Alarm3 Alarm4 Alarm5 now future
Alarm0 1 0.5 0.0 0.0 0.5 0.3 0.9 0.9
Alarm1 0.0 1 0.0 0.3 0.0 0.0 1.0 1.0
Alarm2 0.0 0.0 1 0.5 0.0 0.0 0.1 0.1
Alarm3 0.0 0.0 0.0 1 0.3 0.0 0.3 0.3
Alarm4 0.0 0.0 0.0 0.0 1 0.5 0.5 0.5
Alarm5 0.0 0.0 0.0 0.0 0.0 1 0.1 0.27
extended reachability matrix
Matrix (
SpreadSheet CauseIdentification
Alarm0 Alarm1 Alarm2 Alarm3 Alarm4 CF Value SubSheet
Symptom1 1.0 0.7 0.0 0.3 0.0 1.69
Symptom2 0.0 0.0 1.0 0.0 0.3 0.25
Symptom3 0.0 0.3 0.0 1.0 0.0 0.6
Symptom4 0.0 0.0 1.0 0.7 0.0 0.31
Symptom5 0.3 0.0 0.7 0.0 1.0 0.84
Project ICAI
Project Smalltalk80 ENV.
11 April 1989
Alarm0

Machine Learning Applied to Fault Diagnosis of Electronic Systems

A.R. Mirzai*, C.F.N. Cowan*, K.E. Brown** and T.M. Crawford***

**Dept. of Electrical Engineering, University of Edinburgh, Edinburgh EH9 3JL, UK*

***Dept. of Electrical Engineering, Heriot-Watt University, Edinburgh EH1 2HT, UK*

****Hewlett Packard, QTD, South Queensferry, West Lothian EH30 9TG, UK*

Abstract

Adaptive signal processing has been used for many years in different areas of communication such as channel equalisation and modelling, echo cancellation, voice coding and many others. In recent years, we have been involved with the design of intelligent systems to automate the process of fault diagnosis and adjustment of electronic systems using pattern recognition and adaptive signal processing techniques. The result of our investigation is a machine learning system and this paper illustrates the application of the system for fault diagnosis of communication equipments. We also illustrate the application of a data analysis program which has been developed to improve the performance of the machine learning system.

1 Introduction

Fault diagnosis and adjustment strategies involve relating patterns of symptoms or features to specific corrective courses of action or outcomes (Figure 1). When this process is carried out using a classical expert system, it is necessary to express the relationships between the features and the outcomes in the form of explicit rules. In many cases these rules are obtained by interrogation of practitioners of the particular art. This knowledge acquisition task is often difficult, costly and time consuming and hence in recent years, considerable attention has been focused on the development of systems which are capable of synthesising these relationships using a learning strategy. These systems are referred to as machine learning systems (MLS). Figure 2 illustrates the general structure of a MLS. The two main elements of the system are a model and a learning algorithm or strategy. Initially, the system is presented with a set of training sequence which include features with known desired outcomes and a learning algorithm is then used to estimate the parameters of the model to obtain the best fit to the known observations. The model is then presented with some unknown sequence and using the estimated parameters it will predict the correct outcome. The MLS should also be capable of modifying its decision-making strategy if a decision or outcome turns out to be inappropriate. Some of the criteria in choosing a learning algorithm include,

- Speed of adaptation,
- Complexity of the algorithm,
- Numerical robustness and
- Tracking behaviour.

One particular form of learning is achieved by induction, i.e. obtaining general rules by looking at some typical examples or cases. Two well known examples of learning algorithm by induction are the ID3 developed by Quinlan [1] and AQ developed by Michalski [2]. The output of ID3 is a 'decision tree' and the AQ generates rules in the form of IF-THEN statements. In recent years, we have been involved with the design of MLS [3,4] using pattern recognition and adaptive signal processing techniques. This paper describes the main structure of our MLS and illustrates the application of both the MLS and a rule based expert system for fault diagnosis of microwave digital radios. The merits and the limitation of both system are also detailed. Finally, we describe a data analysis program (DAP) which has been developed to improve the performance of the MLS.

2 Machine Learning System

The overall system structure of the MLS is illustrated in Figure 3. The MLS approach is based on the manipulation of some raw data to extract a set of salient features which have strong significance in the behaviour of the device under test (DUT). These features are derived visually by comparing the characteristics of a good device against devices with known level of faults.

In general, the distance classifiers are used to decompose a general fault into more specific faults by forming a feature space and partitioning the feature space into a number of domain. Each domain, or cluster, in the feature space is characterised by features which represent one state of the problem. The classification would then be done by measuring the geometric distance of the new point, corresponding to the faulty device, from each of the clusters. The simplest form of classification consists of measuring the geometric distance of the new point from the centroids of each cluster. The main disadvantage of this method is that it does not take into account the distribution of the points in the clusters. A more general measure of the distance know as the Mahalanobis distance [5] can be used which requires not only the centroids of each cluster but also the variances and the covariances of the clusters.

After a general classification of the fault, the adaptive combiners are further used for finer adjustments. Figure 4 illustrates the architecture of an adaptive combiner. In the training mode, the combiner is presented by a feature set, $\underline{x}(k)$, and a corresponding desired value, $y(k)$. An adaptive algorithm is then used to adjust the weights of the combiner, $\underline{w}(k)$, in order to minimise the mean square of the error which is given as,

$$E[e(k)^2]=E[(y(k)-\hat{y}(k))^2] \tag{1}$$

where $E[]$ represents the statistical expectation operation and $\hat{y}(k)$ is the output of the combiner given as,

$$\hat{y}(k)=\underline{x}^T(k)\underline{w}(k) \tag{2}$$

and T denotes the operation of matrix transposition. The optimal weights, $\underline{w}_{opt}$, is given by the Weiner solution [6-8] as,

$$\underline{w}_{opt}=\underline{\phi}_{xx}^{-1}\underline{\phi}_{xy} \tag{3}$$

where $\underline{\phi}_{xx}$ is the auto-correlation function of $\underline{x}$ and $\underline{\phi}_{xy}$ is the cross-correlation function of $\underline{x}$ and y. A number of different algorithms can be used to estimate the weights for the combiner and the RLS algorithm has been shown to be the most suitable one for fault diagnosis and adjustments of electronic systems and devices [8]. In the RLS algorithm the present weights, $\underline{w}(k)$, may be expressed in terms of the previous weights by,

$$\underline{w}(k)=\underline{w}(k-1)+\underline{R}_{xx}^{-1}(k)\underline{x}(k)e(k) \tag{4}$$

where $\underline{R}_{xx}$ is an estimate of $\underline{\phi}_{xx}$ given by,

$$\underline{R}_{xx}(k)=\sum_{n=0}^{k}\underline{x}(n).\underline{x}^{T}(n) \tag{5}$$

In practical situations, the number of faults is more than one and Figure 5 illustrates a multi-input/multi-output combiner structure. The feature set is the same for every combiner but each combiner is trained on different desired values.

3 Fault Diagnosis

In this section we consider the fault diagnosis in microwave digital radio [4]. These systems are widely used in telecommunications to carry digitally encoded telephony, data and television signals. The performance of the radio is assessed by referring to a phase-plane characteristic of the radio, some times referred to as the constellation diagram. The human fault diagnosis is performed by conducting a visual interpretation of the constellation diagram. We employ the MLS to correctly map from the constellation diagram directly to adjustment commands which will bring about an improvement in the error rate of the maladjusted radio system.

It has been decided to use the constellation diagram as the reference characteristics for the digital radio. Figure 6a shows the constellation diagram of the digital radio when no faults are present. When the radio is ideal then the constellation diagram consists of 16 points in a perfect rectangular array. However, degradations in the radio system and transmission media produce intersymbol interference, thermal noise, coupling between in-phase and quadrature components and nonlinear distortion. Consequently, the display can actually consist of 16 points of varying shape displaced into a non-uniform matrix. Figure 6b-d illustrate the constellation diagrams with gross impairments. The salient features for the digital radio fall into two classes,

1- Geometrical displacement of the relative positions of the mean of the constellation points.

2- Spreading of the individual points.

As shown in Figure 6, the features in class 1 can be described by the extension and rotation of line segments joining pairs of points, and class 2 can be described by statistical variances and co-variances of the individual points. A total of 15 salient features have been extracted.

The MLS is employed to correctly map from the constellation diagram directly to adjustment commands in order to bring about an improvement in the error rate of a faulty radio. The user interface for the MLS consists of a graphical bar display of faults/command for adjustments, Figure 7. The top bar is the output of a single distance classifier which has been trained with only good radios, i.e. radios which have been passed using an independent fault diagnosis procedure. It thus has only one cluster in its feature space and the distance between the faulty radio to this cluster is used as an indicator of its performance. The next set of bars represent the output of the adaptive combiners which have been trained for each individual fault. Figure 7a shows the output of the MLS when it has been trained on four types of fault and has been connected to a radio with arbitrary maladjustments in these faults. Figure 7b shows the output of the MLS after the commands have been followed.

A rule based expert system has also been developed for diagnosing imperments in the digital radio [3]. In order to generate rules for the expert system, it was necessary to investigate the variation of the fault levels to each individual feature and also the features had to be quantised before being used as the input to the system. The process of fault diagnosis in this approach is carried out in three stages. First a set of rules are used to indicate which faults could possibly be present given a particular set of features. The next set of rules takes the possible faults and determines the level of each fault. There are also rule which are used to explain the procedure of the fault diagnosis.

Table 1 illustrates the performance comparison between the MLS and the rule based system when two simultaneous faults were present in the radio.

Fault Introduced	Fault Detected	
	MLS	ES
GS 3, NOC 3	GS 3.3, NOC 3	GS 3, NOC 3
UD 4, NOC 3	UD 3.4, NOC 2.4	UD 4, NOC 3
OD 8, NOC 3	OD 16, NOC -10	OD 8, NOC 0, GS 1
OD 2, NOC 3	OD 2, NOC 1.9	OD 2, NOC 3, GS 0
UD 4, NOC 1	UD 3.3, NOC 0.5	UD 4, NOC 1
OD 8, GS 6	OD 10.5, GS 7.5, NOC 2	OD 8, GS 1, NOC 0
OD 8, GS 3	OD 3.5, GS 10, NOC 1.1	OD 8, GS 1, NOC 0

Faults	Abbreviation and units	
Non-Orthogonal Carriers	NOC	Degree
Gap Spacing	GS	%
TWT Overdrive	OD	dBs
TWT Underdrive	UD	dBs

Table 1

4 Data Analysis Program (DAP)

Due to the invariant structure of the combiners and the learning strategy used to train the combiners, there is no need for external expertise when adapting the system to any problem. At the same time, the performance of the combiners depends on how the features are selected. In the section, we describe a data analysis program which can be used to provide us with some information on how the combiners are responding to a given set of features.

Figure 8 illustrates the block structure of the program. The DAP is provided by the training sequence of the combiners which include the features matrix, $\underset{\sim}{X}$, and the desired matrix, $\underset{\sim}{Y}$. Using the correlation matrices and some thresholding expert system, the DAP would generate three types of information. These include the correlation between the features, the significant of each feature for each individual outcome and the interaction between the outcomes. The first two types of information are used to construct a dependency table which illustrates how the features are related to the outcomes (Figure 9). This table can be used to modify the existing feature set since features, which are not significant for any of the outcomes, can be removed from the set. On the other hand if all the features are highly significant for any of the outcomes then that outcome will be very sensitive to any small error or changes in the value of any of the features. Thus, it is necessary to introduce some other features to reduce this sensitivity.

The output of the DAP also includes an interaction table which indicates the level of interaction between the outcomes. The combiners are initially trained by maladjusting the outcomes of the DUT one at a time. If the level of interaction between any two outcomes is high then it is necessary to retrain the combiners when these outcomes are maladjusted together. The level of interaction between the outcomes can be obtained experimentally but this approach is very time consuming. This information is provided by the interaction table.

Figure 9 indicates the output of the DAP when the MLS was applied to fault diagnosis of digital radio. As described above, in order to generate the rules for the expert system it was necessary to investigate the relationships between each feature with each individual fault . These relationships were obtained by plotting the variation of the features against the faults. These plots have to be produced for all the combination of the features and the faults, i.e. $(12\times3)=36$ plots. The output of the DAP may therefore be used to reduce this number since all the features are not significant for all the outcomes, e.g. in this case only 13 features are significant.

5 Conclusion

In recent years, expert systems have been successfully employed to carry out fault diagnosis and adjustments of electronic systems and components. The main difficulty in using expert systems is due to the manual acquisition of knowledge and hence in recent years researchers have been working on the design of machines which can learn by themselves. The MLS described in this paper offers a more generic solution to the problem of fault diagnosis than the conventional expert systems. The use of the DAP enables us to investigate how the combiners are responding to a given set of features and also how to train the MLS.

Two approaches have been described for the diagnosis of digital radios. The procedure of rule generation for the expert system is very slow and time consuming while the MLS is capable of synthesising these rules by looking at typical examples. The main limitation of the MLS is due to the linear structure of the combiners which does not allow the system to be directly applicable to non-linear problems. This problem can be over come in the rule base system by including rules to take care of non-linear relationships between the features and the outcomes. In Ref [3] a hybrid system has been proposed which combines both these approaches to form a complete fault diagnosis system for the digital radio.

Acknowledgements

The financial support of the Science and Engineering Research Council and Hewlett Packard Ltd., South Queensferry, are gratefully acknowledged. Thanks are also due to the contribution of Prof. P.M. Grant and Mr. V. Marton to the project.

References

[1] J.R.Quinlan,"Discovering rules by Induction from large collection of examples', Introduction Readings in Expert Systems (D. Michie Ed.), Gordon & Breach, 33-46, London, 1979.

[2] R. Michalaski and J. Larson,"Selection of most Representative training examples and Incremental Generation of VLI Hypothese : The underlying Methodology and the Description of programs ESEL and AQ11.', UIUCDCS-R, 78-867, Computer Department, University of Illinois and Urbana-Champaign, 1978.

[3] K.E. Brown,"The Application of Knowledge-Based Systems for Fault Diagnosis in Microwave Radio Relay Equipment", IEEE J. Select. Areas Commun. (Special Issue on Knowledge-Based Systems for Communication), Vol-6, June 1988.

[4] A.R. Mirzai, C.F.N. Cowan and T.M. Crawford,"Intelligent Alignment of Waveguide Filters using a Machine Learning Approach", IEEE Trans. on Microwave Theory and Techniques, Vol-37, No.1, 166-173, Jan 1989.

[5] B. Sing-Tze, 'Pattern Recognition', Marcel Dekker, Inc., N.Y., 1984.

[6] C.F.N. Cowan and P.M. Grant, 'Adaptive Filters', Prentice-Hall, Englewood Cliffs, N.J., 1985.

[7] M. Honig and D.G. Messerschmitt, 'Adaptive filters: structures, algorithms and applications', Kluwer Academic Publishers Group, Dordrecht, 1984.

[8] C.F.N. Cowan, "Performance Comparison of Finite Linear Adaptive Filters", IEE Proc., Vol-34, Pt-F, No-3, pp211-216, June 1987.

Figure 1

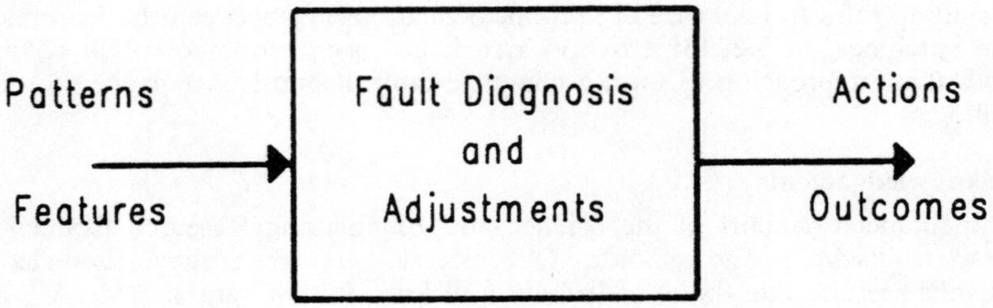

Figure 2

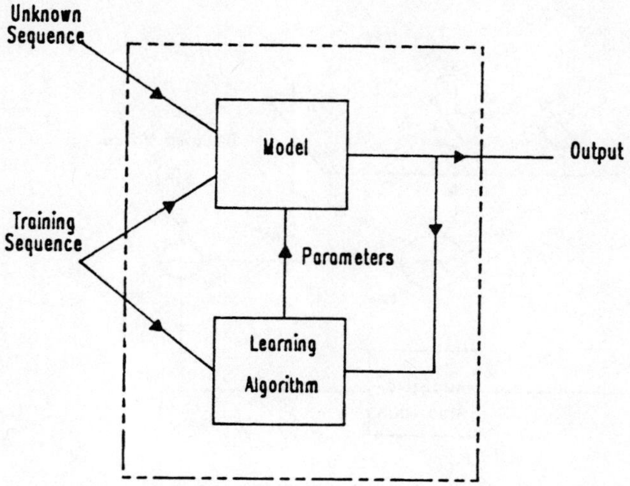

Figure 3

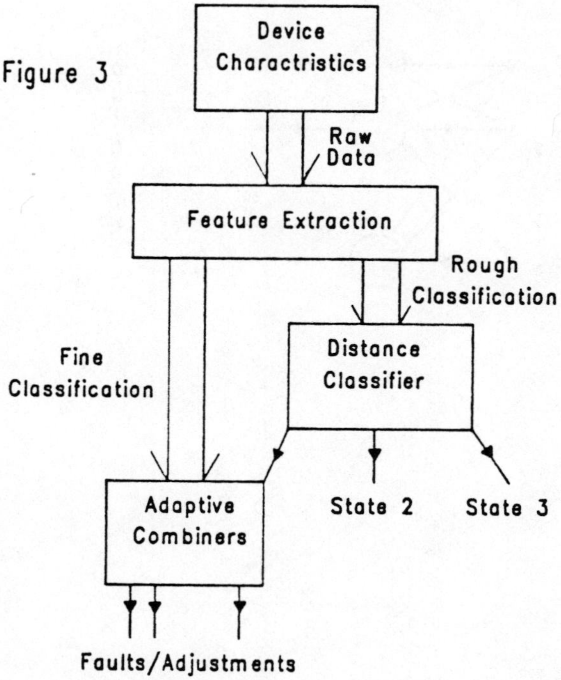

Figure 4

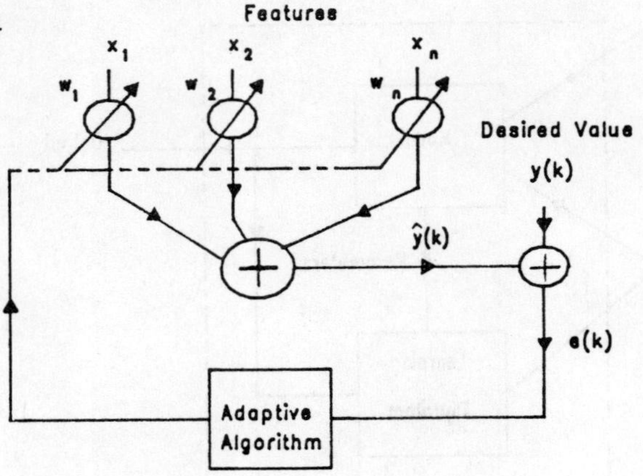

Figure 5

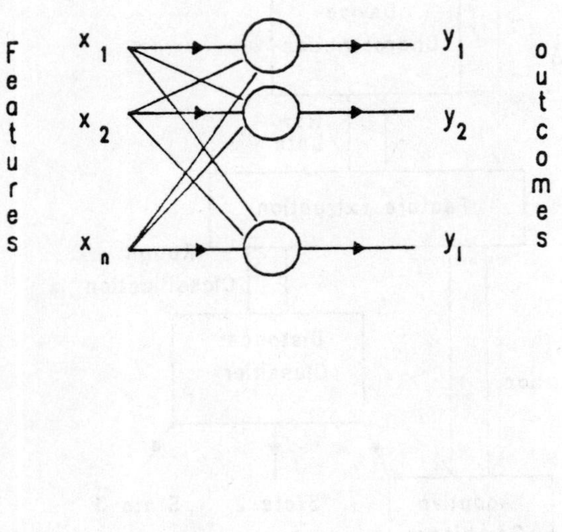

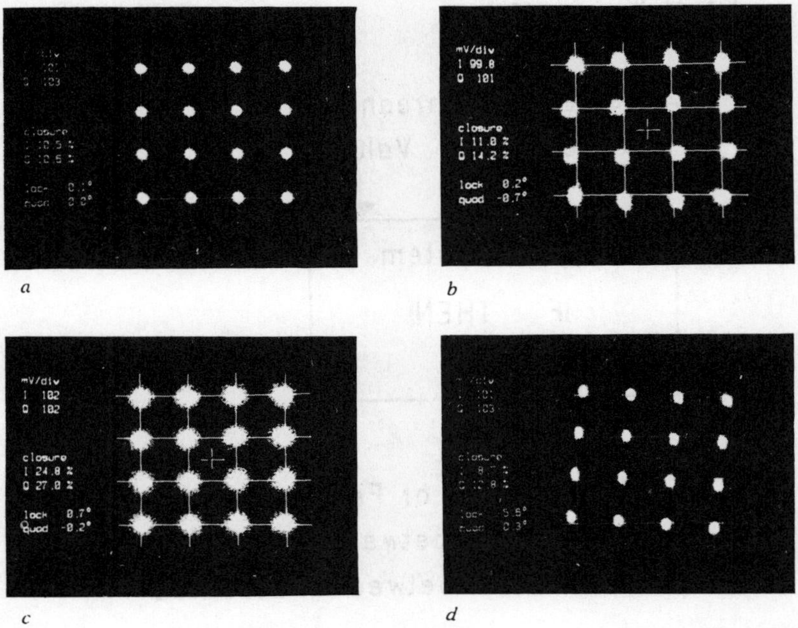

Figure 6

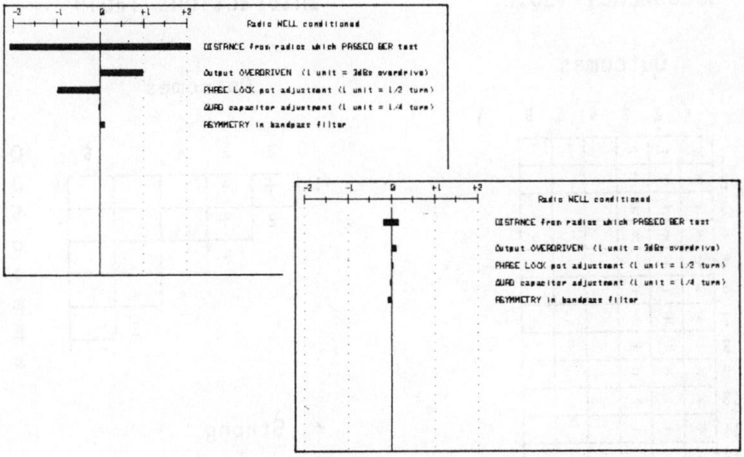

Figure 7

Figure 8

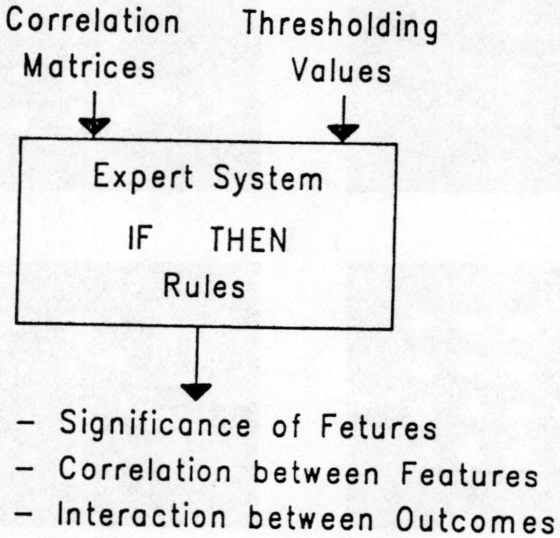

Figure 9

Dependency Table

Features × Outcomes

Features	1	2	3	4	5	6
1	*	–	+			
2	*	–	+			
3	*	+	*			
4	*	*	*			
5	+	*	–			
6	*	–	+			
7	+	*	+			
8	–	–	+			
9	*	–	+			
10	*	–	+			
11	*	–	–			
12	–	–	–			
13						
14						
15						
16						
17						

Interactions Table

Outcomes × Outcomes

Outcomes	2	3	4	5	6
1	+	+			
2		+			
3					
4					
5					

* Strong
\+ Weak
\- No

The Knowledge-Based Processing and Analysis of Foetal Phonocardiograms

E. Mc Donnell, J. Dripps and P. Grant

Department of Electrical Engineering, University of Edinburgh, Edinburgh, EH9 3JL, UK

Introduction

Traditionally, the obstetrician would listen with a stethoscope to the sounds generated by the foetal heart to determine the heart rate. Although the ear is unequalled in detecting sounds over a particular frequency range, the spectrum occupied by the foetal heart tones is on the threshold of audibility. This aural processing has always posed problems relating to accuracy and inter-auditor agreement. For these reasons, it has been superseded by the phonocardiogram. The greater low-frequency sensitivity of the phonocardiographic transducer allows all the acoustic information to be registered. The visual processing of the phonocardiogram is the only reliable way of judging heart rate from the cardiac acoustic signals. This visual processing is satisfactory when only short lengths of data are considered. However, when long term monitoring is used, the amount of data produced is considerable. There is, therefore, a pressing need for the automation of the visual process.

This paper presents the realization of a knowledge-based expert system which non-invasively detects, segments, and classifies the foetal heart sounds. The goal of the system is to provide the temporal measures of cardiac performance over extended periods of foetal monitoring.

The Origin of Foetal Heart Sounds

The foetal heart, like that of the adult, is divided into two pairs of chambers and has four valves. The upper pair of chambers - the atria - are connected to the lower pair of chambers - the ventricles - by the mitral and tricuspid valves (MT). The ventricles, in turn, are connected to the arterial network through the aortic and pulmonary valves (AP). Viewed as a mechanical system the atria act as primer pumps for the ventricles which are the power pumps.

The valves, whose operation is entirely passive, are composed of leaflets of fibrous tissue secured at their base by a fibrous ring. The valves, by virtue of their structure and the restraining ligaments, permit only a uni-directional flow of blood through, and away from, the heart.

Before the onset of cardiac depolarization, the blood returning from the veins, and the oxygenated blood from the placenta accumulates in the atria, due to the closure of the MT valves. The cardiac cycle begins with the contraction of the atrial walls which in turn pressurizes the enclosed blood. As the ventricles are both relaxed and evacuated, the pressure differential across the MT valves forces the leaflets to open, and the blood to cascade into the ventricles. At this point the ventricles begin to contract, which makes the blood attempt to flow back into the lower pressure atrial chambers. This reverse flow of blood is caught and arrested by the shutting of the MT valves which produces the first heart sound (I). The ventricular walls continue to contract and the pressure in the enclosed blood rises. Whenever the pressure becomes too great for the AP valves to withstand, they open, and the pressurized blood is rapidly ejected into the arteries. While the ventricles are being evacuated the pressure in the remaining blood decreases with respect to that in the arteries. This pressure gradient causes the arterial blood to flow back into the ventricles. The AP valves, which perform the same function as the MT valves, arrest this reverse flow by shutting, which gives rise to the second heart sound (II). This sequence of events, called the cardiac cycle, then repeats.

Along with the first and second sounds there may be a third and a fourth heart sound. The third sound originates in the contraction of the atria, and the fourth, from the filling vibrations of the ventricles. Besides these principal sounds, various other sounds/noises are produced during the cardiac cycle. These include: murmurs, ejection and entry sounds, and sounds originating from foetal movements, and environmental noise.

Foetal Phonocardiogram

A record of the variation of this acoustic signal with time is known as the phonocardiogram (PhCG) and is obtained with a phonographic transducer attached to the mother's abdomen. Identification of the two principal heart sounds of the cardiac cycle permits measurement of the instantaneous foetal heart rate, beat-to-beat difference, and the duration of systole and diastole. These measures are sensitive indicators of cardiac function, hence of foetal well-being.

Domain Problems

The characteristic feature of the acoustic signals which originate in the closing of the valves of the foetal heart is their inconstancy. From one occurrence of a particular heart sound to the next its overall shape may change, its frequency may shift, its amplitude and duration may alter, and its relative position in the cardiac cycle will almost certainly change. As often happens the sound may be obliterated by a transient or by the effective shielding afforded by the surrounding fluids and tissues. The principal sounds are often not clearly delimited in time through their coalescence with a sound which originates from some other acoustic phenomenon. Viewed as a system, it is non-linear, non-stationary, and non-deterministic; it has high levels of noise, and is prone to transients.

Examples of these anomalies in the PhCG are illustrated in figure 1.

Signal Pre-processing

The main functions performed by the knowledge-based signal pre-processors are detection, and segmentation. These pre-processors are themselves knowledge sources (KS) within the expert system.

<u>Detection</u>

The knowledge required to perform the task of detection is the least expert of all the knowledge embodied in the system. However, it performs a function on which depends the subsequent quality of the analysis.

What makes certain events visually significant to the expert is primarily their local amplitude contrast and, secondly, their frequency and structure. The structure refers to the smooth continuity of the PhCG during an event. Contrasted with this is the ill-structuredness of the background. The background is here taken to mean not only noise in the conventional sense, but also certain sounds of non-valvular origin.

The detection process acts on a per excursion basis. An excursion is defined to be that part of the PhCG which is bounded between two immediately adjacent transitions across the horizontal. If the excursion meets the criteria for being classed as significant *viz:* amplitude, frequency, and continuity, it is assigned a weighting in proportion to these three factors. This weighting has been so designed as to accommodate both local and global variations in signal morphology.

Removal of Insignificant Events

It has been found that whenever the clinician inspects a PhCG, he always takes account of the global scenario first. Then, working at the local level, he accepts or rejects events on the local level in the context of the global scenario. This procedure has also been adopted here and has been realized with an adaptive thresholding technique. The threshold takes account of how the energy levels are varying with time, in the context of both the local and global energy fluctuations.

Feature Extraction

Once the *significant* events have been located, the feature extraction KS transforms the event into a set of attributes. These attributes are: start time, end time, duration, total energy content, number of *dominant* energy peaks, number of excursions, information about the rate of change of excursion duration, and energy distribution.

Segmentation

Segmentation is the process whereby coalesced sounds within an event are decomposed. One of the commonly occuring problems is that of a non-valvular sound coalescing with a valvular sound to produce what resembles a homogeneous event. Even at this intermediate processing stage some of the combined events may be decomposed *e.g.*, when both sounds exhibit an obvious dissimilarity. However, coalescences are not always identified at this stage, and the segmentation must be delayed until reprocessing under the guidance of contextual information.

Classification

The process of classification assigns labels (I,II, or noise) to the significant events. It is organised as a production system [1] within which detection, and segmentation are sub-processes.

Control System Organisation

The control mechanism is structured in the form of hierarchically organized meta-rules (fig. 2). These meta-rules are rules which embody knowledge about the application of the more specific rules on the lower levels.

At the uppermost level of the control structure is the strategy knowledge source. It is the function of this K.S. to: initialize the data-base, determine whether prima facie it is worthwile attempting an analysis, establish solution islands, focus attention on a particular area, revisit the lower levels of data abstraction in the light of contextual information, realize when to abandon the analysis, and when a total, or the best partial analysis has been achieved.

On the intermediate level there are the task KSs. Once the strategy KS has determined what to do, it will invoke one or more of these task KSs. The task KSs autonomously guide the application of the object-level KSs, using knowledge embedded as production rules. Each task has a certain area of expertise *e.g.*, finding a solution island, which it will use in the region defined by the strategy KS.

On the lowest level of the control structure are the object-level KSs. These object-level KSs are under the control of one or more task KSs. It is these KSs which are, of all the KSs, the only ones which may generate, modify, or delete entries in the data-base. Each KS at this level may be viewed as a local expert in some aspect of the analysis. The body of these KSs consists of knowledge in production rule format. Although these KSs are independent, *i.e.* one KS cannot trigger or fire another, they may influence one another through the entries or modifications they generate in the data-base.

Each level in the control structure communicates only with its calling module. This communication takes the form of either a *true* or a *false*. A *false* signifies that the K.S. precondition was not met, while a *true* signifies that the rule both triggered and fired. Depending on the outcome, the calling K.S. will decide, within its remit, what to do next.

Knowledge Application

The method used to analyse the PhCG is the one which the expert himself uses. This involves examining the PhCG to find areas where, with confidence, he is able to identify certain of the significant events as being of valvular origin. Once these 'solution islands' [2] have been identified, the goal is to expand outwards into regions where the solution is not so immediately obvious. This expansion relies on the temporal and causal constraints of the physiological generating process.

Implementation

The described knowledge-based system has been implemented in *'C'* under *UNIX* mainly because *'C'* produces very fast and efficient executable code. In this application the nature of the task demands speed of response, and the amount of processing required for long term continuous monitoring is considerable. Realization in *'C'* also permitted use of the data structures and pointer facilities provided in that language to implement the data-base of the system. The disadvantage of using a non-AI language is the lack of the built-in facilities which these possess. Consequently, the *'C'* code tends to be rather long and complex.

Verification of Analysis

Although the system is almost fully developed, it has not, as yet, been used clinically. Instead, several overnight recordings of the PhCG were taken from different gravidae and stored on magnetic tape. From these a core set of one hundred, eight second blocks of data were extracted. Each of these was chosen on the basis that it provided a representative example of an anomaly, or combination of anomalies, in the signal.

The task of analysing the phonocardiogram when performed by a clinician is essentially a visual processing one. It is against this standard that the analysis of the system is judged. Presently, no other system is available, which can automatically identify the instants of closure of the cardiac valves.

When the data quality is good and all principal sounds are present the identification of the heart sounds is immediately obvious. In these cases the analysis of the expert and the system always concur. However the real test occurs whenever: there is a high noise level, many non-valvular events are present, valvular sounds are of low amplitude, or disappear completely from the PhCG. Inevitably, the system, like the expert, will make mistakes especially in such a volatile domain. However the system has performed sufficiently well on the core set of data to encourage more exhaustive testing on extended periods of monitoring.

A complete analysis of a data block is reached when all the principal heart sounds have been identified. In cases where the expansion from the solution islands is irretrievably terminated by high levels of noise, these solution islands (which are complete partial analyses rather than intermediate results) can still provide the required cardiac function parameters, albeit over a shorter time interval.

Summary

This paper has presented the realization of a knowledge-based expert system for the identification of the principal heart sounds in the PhCG. The application of knowledge-based processing has enabled a task previously only carried out through visual inspection by a clinician to be performed automatically.

The essential feature of this expert system is its organisation as a hierarchical production system. This formulation allows an efficient search for applicable rules in an application where speed of response is important.

The analysis of the PhCG begins with the detection and segmentation of events. These events are then searched for solution islands. From these islands the system attempts to expand the analysis into the more ambiguous regions. A complete analysis of a data block is achieved when all the principal sounds have been identified.

Incorporated within the expert system is a feedback mechanism from the higher to the lower levels of data abstraction. This allows the weight of contextual information on the higher level to be brought to bear on areas, where initially the local processing was not sufficient to resolve ambiguities.

Acknowledgement

The financial assistance of the Department of Education for Northern Ireland is gratefully acknowledged.

References

[1] Jackson P., **Introduction to Expert Systems**, Addison-Wesley, 1986.

[2] Rich E., **Artificial Intelligence**, McGraw-Hill, 1986.

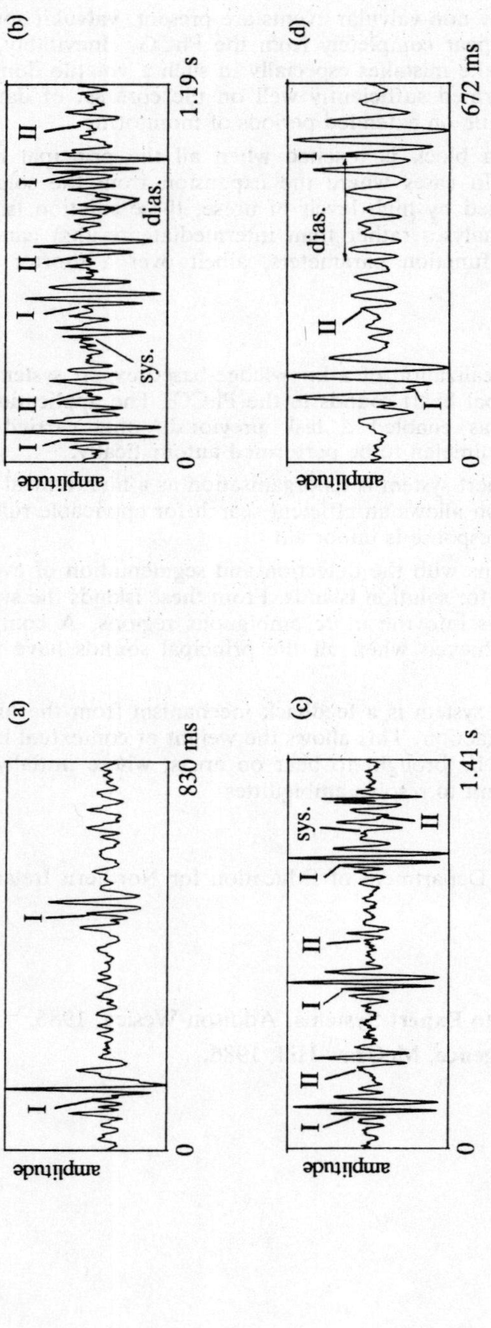

Figure 1. Anomalies in the Phonocardiogram

(a) Strong Ist sounds, missing IInd sounds.
(b) Strong Ist and IInd sounds; systolic and diastolic sounds.
(c) Amplitude variability in IInd sounds; Systolic sound present; transient superimposed on trailing edge of last IInd sound.
(d) Oscillatory pattern; poorly defined end points; weak IInd sound; diastolic murmus.

Figure 2. **Architecture of the Control System**

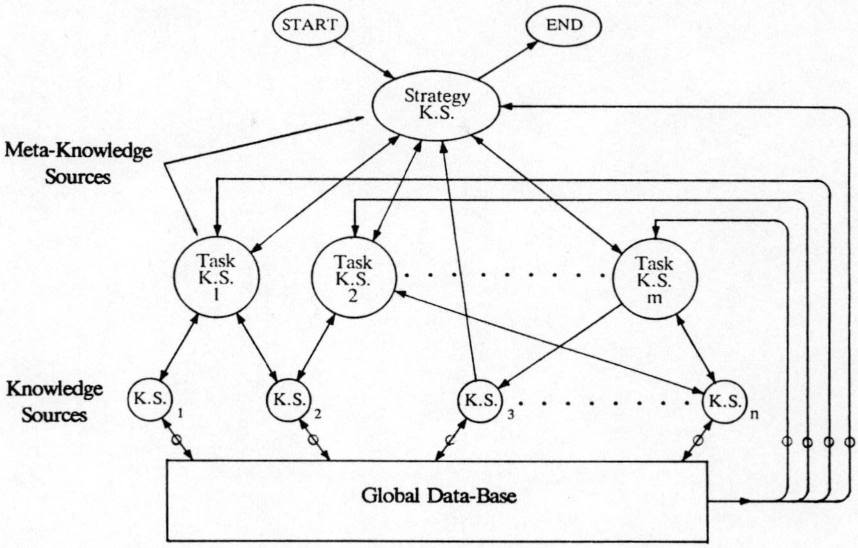

Ringed lines: flow of data
Other lines: control signals

Sensor Checking with a Qualitative Model

J. Robertson

Automation Division, National Engineering Laboratory, East Kilbride, Glasgow G75 0QU, UK

ABSTRACT

A qualitative modelling method is described which allows sensors to be tested for faults while in use by comparing the response of each with the responses of all the others. The computer system uses a model of the application to 'reason' about the mutual consistency of the sensors in relation to the design of plant or machinery.

INTRODUCTION

Industrial plant and all kinds of machinery depend on systems of sensors to provide their operators with information on their current behaviour. This monitored data can be used as measured, or put through various levels of computer abstraction before being seen and acted upon by an operator. There is, however, always the underlying question of whether the original reading was a true measure of the plant or whether the sensor is misbehaving. In manual monitoring, this problem is resolved through an arbitrary blend of experience, deduction and intuition, but in automated monitoring the problem becomes more acute since its solution depends on precise programming information. When a sensor fails in extremis, it is caught by simply checking its reading against upper and/or lower range limits. The real problem occurs when a sensor wrongly reports a plant or machine state which, taken in isolation, is plausible in the current operation. The only way to detect this is to compare it against other plant information obtained from other sensor probes. In other words, each sensor is checked for consistency against other sensors. This paper describes an experimental demonstrator project in which this was done in the context of reasoning across the structure of a qualitative model of a machine, a simple crane.

The project as a whole was set up to test techniques in simulation, control, monitoring and diagnosis in a single integrated model, with special interest in time management, abstracted explanation, parallel processing and, the topic of this paper, sensor validation. There is also a format for describing component behaviour and machine structure, and for model operation. Modelling follows strictly the 'no function in structure' (NFIS) principle [1], in which the behaviour of individual components taken in isolation, and the way in which they are connected to one another to form the machine structure, can be freely programmed, but no explicit knowledge of the behaviour of the machine or part of the machine as a whole can be provided; machine function must be reasoned from component behaviour and machine structure alone. A comprehensive survey of the field of qualitative reasoning can be found in [2].

THE CRANE

The example application, shown in Fig. 1, is a simple crane, but typical of such mechanisms. Button R raises the load, button L lowers the load.

Raising the load

AC power from A/S is fed through junction J3 to RSWITCH. When R is pressed this power is fed through J4 to the hydraulic solenoid valve HSV which opens to allow hydraulic pressure to drive the MOTOR. Power from J4 also opens the pneumatic valve PSV which allows pneumatic pressure to release the BRAKE allowing the motor-driven SHAFT to rotate. The rotating shaft turns the HOIST, raising the LOAD. When the rising load hits the upper microswitch UMS, a DC signal from supply D switches off RSWITCH removing power to J4. This closes HSV stopping the motor, and shuts off PSV releasing the pneumatic pressure to PR. The BRAKE comes on to prevent the SHAFT from turning.

Lowering the load

If not driven by the MOTOR or held by the BRAKE, the SHAFT will rotate freely in reverse allowing the LOAD to lower under its own weight. Pressing L sends AC power to PSV pushing the brake off. The load then falls until microswitch LMS sends a signal to LSWITCH to close PSV, releasing the pneumatic pressure and engaging the brake to stop the shaft and hence the load.

Stopping the load

If the AC/Stop button (A/S) is pressed, power is cut off and the movement of the load is stopped as both HSV and PSV spring shut.

SENSORS

There are six sensors in the crane:

S1 : AC output from RSWITCH
S2 : AC output from LSWITCH
S3 : Hydraulic pressure from HSV
S4 : Pneumatic pressure from PSV
S5 : The operating state of the hoist
S6 : The position of the load

S1 to S4 are binary state sensors. For example, either there is hydraulic pressure from the hydraulic solenoid valve HSV supplying power to the motor or there is not. The hoist can have 5 states; lifting, lowering, stopped, stressed (because the load is jammed against the ceiling) or slack (because the load is on the floor). The load can have 7 states; between the microswitches, as in Fig. 1, at the upper microswitch, at the lower microswitch, at the ceiling, between ceiling and upper microswitch, on the floor or between floor and lower microswitch. The last four are fault positions, since in normal operation the load should only travel between the microswitches.

The six sensors provide the only information available to the monitoring system. If it is assumed that these are fallible, nothing can be taken for granted about the behaviour of the crane. For example, S1 may report that there is no power coming from RSWITCH. This implies that no power is available to open HSV, therefore S3 should report no hydraulic pressure. If, however, it indicates that there is pressure, then a contradiction has been detected. This could mean that S1 is giving a false reading, or that S3 is wrong. It could also mean that both are reporting correctly, and that HSV is jammed open. No firm conclusion can be drawn; all three possibilities must be considered.

After analysis, described in the next section, a fault in S1 is the only conclusion which does not require at least two simultaneous faults in other sensors. The sensor checking system would report a strong likelihood of failure in Sensor S1. The analysis system reaches this conclusion by reasoning from the local behaviour of the components, the recorded states of the component attributes which have sensors attached and the connectivity of the components in the crane; the NFIS principle is not violated.

MODELLING

In the sensor validation example, two models are used. The first is a qualitative simulation of the crane with the six sensors installed. The purpose of this model is to provide a 'real world' equivalent for the second analysis model used for sensor monitoring to 'hook into'. The real world model allows errors to be introduced into the crane operation to test the normal function of the sensors, and sensor failures to test the sensor checking capability of the model.

The high level reasoning process is indicated in the example of 'S1 at fault' described in the SENSORS section above. The sensor check works by a state search technique testing the state reported by the chosen sensor for consistency with the current condition of the model as known from the inputs and other sensors. For example, pressure out of a hydraulic valve as measured by S3 implies pressure in; the state of 'no pressure in' cannot exist. In other words, upstream pressure is, along with the valve being open, a causal state and a necessary condition for pressure on the downstream side. Similarly, that same sensor measurement, if true, can imply necessary downstream effects on other neighbouring component attributes. This constraining of states upstream and downstream implies additional cause and effect restrictions in these components' other neighbours, with a knock-on effect throughout the sensor model. The model-driving software searches the model cutting off any line which conflicts with another, earlier derived, line from the same measurement. This eventually identifies all states of the model consistent with that measurement. If this same process is carried out for every sensor, and the model is properly formed and analysed, there should be no state contradictions at any point across the model, since all the sensors are measuring different parts of a consistent real world. If any does exist, this implies that there is an inconsistency among the sensors; one or more sensors must be reading wrongly.

To take the example of S1 falsely reading OFF, the analysis section starts to search downstream, recognising that S1=OFF implies no power at HSV. When S3 indicates that hydraulic pressure is present, the search backtracks and tries a different route. This leads it to "no power from J4 to PSV" implying no pneumatic pressure to the brake. When S4 indicates that there is pressure, there is still the possibility that the power comes from LSWITCH via S2. When S2 indicates there is no power here, the search stops and returns to S1 indicating no consistent downstream route by which S1 can be correct. The search is then repeated in the upstream direction. If no path is found from inputs to outputs with S1 indicating that the power from RSWITCH is OFF, a message is generated advising of a probable failure in sensor S1. This can then be repaired or replaced.

If S1 reads correctly and S3 is malfunctioning, in testing S1, there will be a contradiction at S3, but a consistent route will be found via the J4 to PSV connection. This will not always be possible; whether or not a faulty sensor can be accurately identified depends on the application, and the number and placement of the full set of sensors. Indeed, these latter factors should be influenced by the fact that a reasoning model is going to be used in conjunction with the working real-world mechanism.

The combinatorial explosion in the search technique is controlled by the automatic curtailing of the search as conflicts are found. Even so, it means that large systems will make considerable demands for processing power. For this reasoning, the system is designed in a distributed form for future loading on to a Transputer parallel processing network. The crane example, although complex enough to test all the goals of the project including sensor checking, was not considered large enough to require the parallel network. As an experimental demonstrator, it was therefore prototyped on a single processor high specification microcomputer.

ENVIRONMENT

The model development interface functions in three stages, illustrated in Fig. 2. The first allows isolated component behaviour descriptions to be programmed and modified. The second provides the means to describe to the computer the structure of any system in terms of its component parts and the connectivity among them. A component can be used if and only if it is present in the component library. Once the model is complete, an automatic program generator produces the working models, one to simulate the real world, the other to carry out the sensor checking process. The third stage allows the user to operate the model pair.

The sections which follow indicate the ease with which sensor-checking models can be constructed. The real problem is to identify the components and causal structure for the target application. For a cleanly defined mechanism such as the crane this is fairly easy. If an automobile were modelled, the fuel supply, drive train, electrics and braking system would be relatively straightforward, but the suspension dynamics difficult. The modelling process becomes more demanding as the application is decomposed to finer and finer detail. For diagnosis and control, a well refined model can be necessary. For sensor checking, the model need be developed only to a sufficient level of refinement that the sensors can be tested against one another for consistency.

For illustration, a cut-down version of the crane with only three components was modelled separately. This is shown in Fig. 3. The methods are exactly the same for the full scale system.

Building components

The development of a component, the hydraulic solenoid valve 'HSV', is illustrated in Fig. 4. Initially, only the input and output attributes are described. In Fig. 4, this is all the information which appears above the '$'. It has three inputs, AC power, the neutral return line (treated as an input for modelling purposes since any break in this affects the valve rather than is affected by it) and the hydraulic supply. There is a single output, the hydraulic pressure from the valve named 'hout'. All attributes in the valve are two state, ON or OFF, but multistate attributes are described in the same way, for example the 'hoist' output in component 'shaft' in the main model is described by:

hoist: STOPPED/FORWARD/REVERSE;

These symbolic state descriptions are henceforth used in all dialogue between operator and model. When the component processor is first run, the file containing the above is expanded to everything shown above the dotted line. This is in fact a full set of all combinations of input states to output states. The user manually converts what lies between the '$' and the line to what lies below the line. The operator '>' is the key to this. If left untouched, it indicates that this is a normal operation. For example, all inputs ON resulting in the output being ON is correct behaviour. If the '>' is changed to '?', this indicates an error relationship; if all inputs ON result in output OFF, something is wrong. Removal of the operator altogether indicates that the relationship is not relevant, and the computer need not consider it. For instance, if there is no hydraulic supply to the valve, it is physically impossible for output pressure to exist. Marking irrelevant relationships is important for controlling the size of the model. The expansion of the quotes provides text fragments which, in a later version, will be used to construct rational explanations for the behaviour of the system. For example, the second line text contains the user interpretation of "all inputs ON leading to output OFF".

Building models

In any working system, there is a causal flow running through it in which upstream components determine the behaviour of downstream neighbours. The connectivity in model building is the specification of the links between the attributes of directly connected neighbours. In sensor checking, this connectivity is conveyed to the computer in a form similar to the component description above. In Fig. 5, the section above the '$' identifies all item types; buttons, '*', permanent inputs, '>', permanent outputs, '<', junctions, '@' and components which have no code, and simply says which items are connected to which others. Running the modelling program adds the next part, which is an expansion to include all the inputs and outputs of the connected components. The user edits this to the lower part by eliminating attributes which are not required. Junctions are indicated by round brackets, for example '(J1)' connecting N to SW and HSV. Sensors are indicated by '?' in the first part and a name enclosed in square brackets such as '[S1]' in the second. The '!' requires that an output is to be controlled by a clock pulse.

The key to this method is that the first part is very easy to enter, and the second part is mostly generated by the computer. Since the latter is completed by elimination, the likelihood of error by omission is very small.

Operating the model

The model is operated from a command line. Typing '*R' operates button R and starts the simulation. Sensor S1 is set to faulty OFF with '@S1=OFF' and restored with '@S1=?'. It is tested by typing '?S1'. The program currently replies 'S1 normal' or 'S1 faulty'. Future development will provide an explanation of the conclusion.

Other operations, such as diagnosis, are triggered and processed in a similar way. It is planned at NEL to adapt the modelling scheme described for use in Predictive Maintenance, which has the same basic requirements as monitoring and diagnosis, but dealing with fault warning rather than hard faults.

TIME MANAGEMENT

Much serious attention has been given to problems of time management in qualitative models [4]. For the experiment described in this paper, there are two facets of this. The first is that components operate at different speeds; it cannot be assumed that every change takes place simultaneously. For example, electrical signals are, for all practical purposes, transmitted instantaneously, while a build up of hydraulic pressure requires measurably significant time. While it does not apply to the crane, it is not difficult to picture a design where the assumption of mutual instantaneous transmission would distort the true behaviour of the system. This is not implemented in the current version, but a future version will handle this in a very simple way; each component attribute is given a code, and during simulation, the lower code, representing the faster component, always receives priority.

The second, and more serious, time management problem is that of handling the fact that in a continuously changing environment, when a diagnosis (or a sensor check) has to be carried out, the current state pattern across the model may not be the correct causal state set which resulted in the detected event. For example, a switch might close starting a signal propagation which eventually causes a subsystem to shut down. However, before the shutdown was detected, the switch reopened, so that when the reasoning process across the model began, the causal chain was broken; the closed switch state is no longer there. This is not a problem with the crane, and again the current version assumes a full causal structure across the model. However, the development software is equipped with a sequence coding system which allows asynchronous state changes to be dealt with; this will be the basis of further work.

CONCLUSION

A method has been described by which the sensors which monitor industrial plant can be checked on-line for non-evident failure by comparing them against each other for inconsistency. The sensors are continuously checked while the plant or machine is running normally, so that when there is a failure their accuracy can be relied upon to a high degree. The model-based reasoning approach has been adopted to allow the system to flexibly handle any combination of events which occur within the components of the application. This qualitative model adheres strictly to the 'No Function In Structure' principle. The development has been carried out to prove the system on a simulated machine, but the software is immediately transferable to real-world plant and the first experimental application will be on a power network. In addition, the methods used to describe components, build models and operate the system have been illustrated.

REFERENCES

1 de Kleer, J. and Brown, J. S. "A Qualitative Physics Based on Confluences", Artificial Intelligence, 1984, 24 7-84.

2 Govindaraj, T. "Qualitative Approximation Methodology for Modelling and Simulation of Large Dynamic Systems: Applications to a Power Plant", IEEE Transactions On Systems, Man and Cybernetics, 1987, 17 937-955.

3 Robertson, J. "Design Assessment With A Rule/Goal Based Qualitative Model", Proceedings of the IED Conference on Artificial Intelligence, Swansea, July 1988.

4 Allen, J. F. "Maintaining Knowledge About Temporal Intervals", Communications Of The ACM, 1983, 26 No 11.

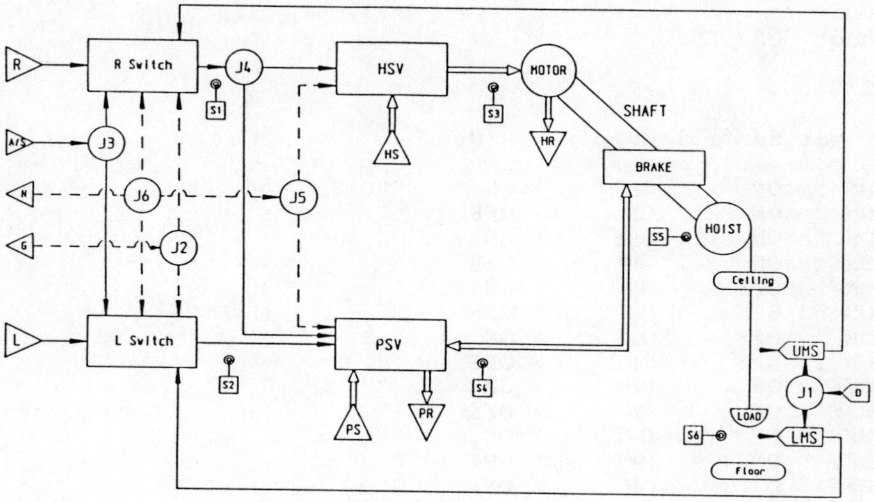

FIG 1 THE CRANE

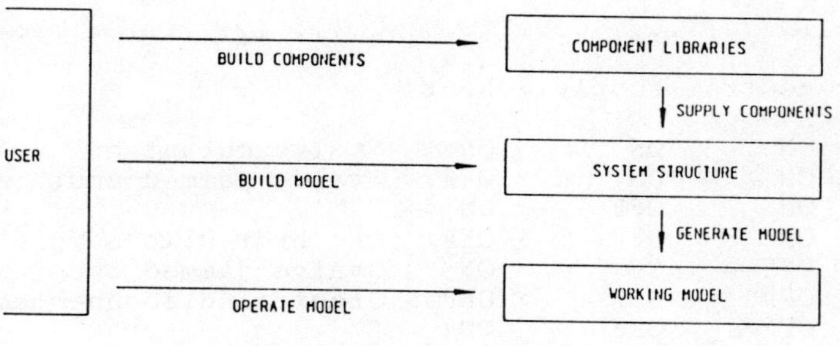

FIG 2 THE MODELLING PROCESS

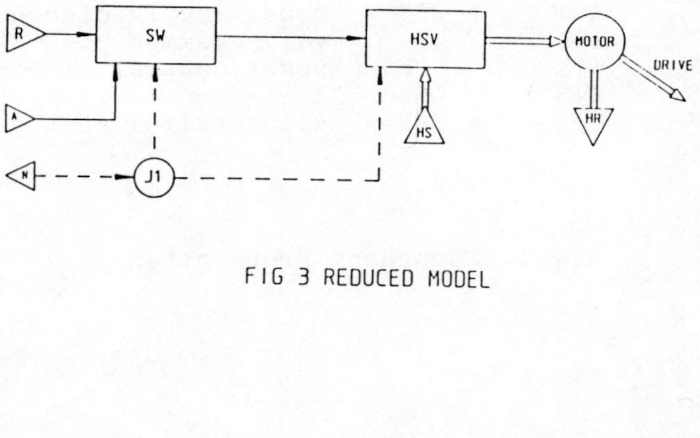

FIG 3 REDUCED MODEL

```
power: ON/OFF ;
neutral: ON/OFF ;
supply: ON/OFF ;
>
hout: ON/OFF ;

$

power neutral supply > hout

ON     ON      ON      > ON      ""
ON     ON      ON      > OFF     ""
ON     ON      OFF     > ON      ""
ON     ON      OFF     > OFF     ""
ON     OFF     ON      > ON      ""
ON     OFF     ON      > OFF     ""
ON     OFF     OFF     > ON      ""
ON     OFF     OFF     > OFF     ""
OFF    ON      ON      > ON      ""
OFF    ON      ON      > OFF     ""
OFF    ON      OFF     > ON      ""
OFF    ON      OFF     > OFF     ""
OFF    OFF     ON      > ON      ""
OFF    OFF     ON      > OFF     ""
OFF    OFF     OFF     > ON      ""
OFF    OFF     OFF     > OFF     ""

.....................................................

power neutral supply > hout

ON     ON      ON      > ON     "valve output on"
ON     ON      ON      ? OFF    "valve jammed shut"
ON     ON      OFF       ON     ""
ON     ON      OFF     > OFF    "no hydraulic supply"
ON     OFF     ON      ? ON     "valve jammed open"
ON     OFF     ON      > OFF    "neutral disconnected"
ON     OFF     OFF       ON     ""
ON     OFF     OFF     > OFF    "neutral disconnected"
OFF    ON      ON      ? ON     "valve jammed open"
OFF    ON      ON      > OFF    "power disconnected"
OFF    ON      OFF       ON     ""
OFF    ON      OFF     > OFF    "power/supply disconnected"
OFF    OFF     ON      ? ON     "valve jammed open"
OFF    OFF     ON      > OFF    "power/neutral disconnected"
OFF    OFF     OFF       ON     ""
OFF    OFF     OFF     > OFF    "all supplies shut down"
```

Fig 4 Component Preparation

```
*R: SW ;

>A: SW ;
>N: SW, HSV ;
>HS: HSV ;

<drive: ;
<HR: ;

@J1{jnctn}: ;

SW{switch}?: HSV ;
HSV?: motor ;
motor!: drive ¦ HR ;

$

R* -> SW.raise.live.neutral ;

A -> SW.raise.live.neutral ;

N -> ( ) -> SW.raise.live.neutral,
         -> HSV.power.neutral.supply ;

HS -> HSV.power.neutral.supply ;

SW.power[ ] -> HSV.power.neutral.supply ;

HSV.hout[ ] -> motor.hydrin ;

motor.hydrout! -> drive ;
motor.hydrout! -> HR ;
motor.drive! -> drive ;
motor.drive! -> HR ;

.....................................................

R* -> SW.raise ;

A -> SW.live ;

N -> (J1) -> SW.neutral,
          -> HSV.neutral ;

HS -> HSV.supply ;

SW.power[S1] -> HSV.power ;

HSV.hout[S2] -> motor.hydrin ;

motor.hydrout! -> HR ;
motor.drive! -> drive ;
```

Fig 5 Model Preparation

Development of Planning Expert System for Preventive Maintenance of Plant Components

Yasuhiro Kobayashi*, Mie Morimoto*, Takao Sato**, Daijiro Katayanagi**, Kazuaki Yoshikawa** and Takahiro Konno**

**Energy Research Laboratory, Hitachi Ltd., 1168 Moriyama-cho, Hitachi-shi, Ibaraki-ken, Japan 316*

***Hitachi Works, Hitachi Ltd., 3-1-1 Saiwai-cho, Hitachi-shi, Ibaraki-ken, Japan 317*

ABSTRACT

A planning expert system for preventive maintenance of plant components has been developed and applied to the inspection planning of control rod drive mechanisms in nuclear plants. The developed system is based on a generic framework, which is derived from the information processing of problem solving by expert engineers, for preventive maintenance planning for selection of components to be inspected.

INTRODUCTION

One of the key planning tasks for plant preventive maintenance is the selection of components to be inspected periodically, since industrial plants include large numbers of components and the scheduled outage time for maintenance should be minimized. The objective of this study is to provide an engineering tool, in the form of a planning expert system, to generate a high quality preventive maintenance plan efficiently through the computerization of judgemental knowledge of expert engineers in this domain.

Plant maintenance engineers currently solve a component selection problem with a data base including component data, records of function tests and observed events, and inspection history of components. The problem solving process is highly interactive, since expert knowledge plays a critical role. It is not practicable to formulate this problem and to computerize this problem solving process through conventional programming approaches, because it is difficult to represent numerically the relative importance of function test data and observed events, and their temporal variation.

A few independent but similar approaches [1-2] have been proposed for building an expert system for a specific class of problems on the basis of the characteristics of problems and/or those of information processing to solve them. In light of their approaches, we have attempted to develop a generic framework for preventive maintenance planning for selection of components to be inspected in the course of this study.

METHOD

The expert engineers' planning task of component selection is outlined as follows:

(a) Select components whose likelihood to make trouble in the next operation period is predicted as not negligible, on the basis of data from component function tests, which are done periodically to monitor the state of the plant component, and their historical trends.

(b) Select the proper number of components with relatively longer interval after the previous inspection out of the pre-defined group, if the number of components given at step (a) is less than the target number of components to be inspected. Component groups are, for example, defined by two different policies; groups defined by a random pick-up and groups defined by a spatial relation.

The two subtasks in this task are based on two

different kinds of preventive maintenance methods; a state monitoring method and a statistical method. Subtask (a) screens candidate components to be inspected on the basis of heuristic criteria. Subtask (b) adds candidate components on the basis of maintenance frequency to obtain the target number of components to be inspected.

Knowledge processing in the developed system is realized by taking the characteristics of information processing of this preventive maintenance planning task into consideration. Figure 1 outlines the component selection procedure for preventive maintenance planning employed in this system. This gives a generic framework of knowledge processing of this system. Two subtasks for component selection are processed by forward chaining with the knowledge, which is mainly composed of domain expertise represented by production rules and function test data represented by frames.

It is important for a practical preventive maintenance expert system to have linkage to a data base system for component function tests. Two reasons for this are as follows:

(i) Most of facts used in an expert system of this kind are function test data and their historical changes and, therefore, closed linkage to the data base is desirable for efficient computation.

(ii) It is convenient for users and a knowledge base manager of an expert system to access original data to grasp the detailed justification of inference results and knowledge. In this planning system, the expert system is directly linked to a relational data base system for component test data through interface programs, as shown in Fig.2.

This system is implemented by the general purpose knowledge processing tool ES/KERNEL on the HITAC-2050/32 workstation.

APPLICATION EXAMPLE

The developed system has been applied to the preventive maintenance planning of CRD's (Control Rod Drive mechanisms) in 1,100 MWe class nuclear (Boiling Water Reactor) power plants. One of the results is shown in Fig.3. The task in this example is to select 31 CRD's out of the 185 CRD's to make preventive maintenance plans with a component inspection frequency of 6 years, where plant inspection is periodically done at the scheduled outage time after a one year operation.

The input data to the system are the plant ID, the serial number of the maintenance down time, monitored incidents at the previous operation period. The system selects CRD's to be disassembled and inspected on the basis of results of function tests such as scram time, withdrawal and insertion time, friction and temperature. The output from the system includes the ID and location of CRD's to be inspected in the reactor core map, as well as a brief explanation why they are selected, if necessary.

The result in Fig.3 agreed to an expert engineer's plan. About 40 rules and 200 frames were used in this case. Sample rules are shown in Table 1. CPU time was about 3 min. including time for data retrieval from data base on a 1 mips workstation.

Through a series of applications with real function test data, it was confirmed that the system successfully selected CRD's to be inspected and that the knowledge base represented necessary expertise to solve problems in this domain.

CONCLUSIONS

A planning expert system for preventive maintenance of plant components has been developed and applied to the inspection planning of control rod drive mechanisms in nuclear plants. The developed system is based on a generic framework, which is derived from the information processing of problem solving by expert engineers, for preventive maintenance planning for selection of components to be inspected. The generality of systems is advantageous in this domain, because a large number of components of various kinds require preventive maintenance in industrial plants and, therefore, planning systems for this purpose.

REFERENCES

[1]W.J.Clancy, Heuristic Classification, Artificial Intelligence, Vol.27, No.3, pp.289-350(1985).
[2]B.Chandrasekaran, Generic Tasks in Knowledge-Based Reasoning: High Level Building Blocks for Expert System Design, IEEE Expert, Vol.1, No.3, pp.23-30(1986).

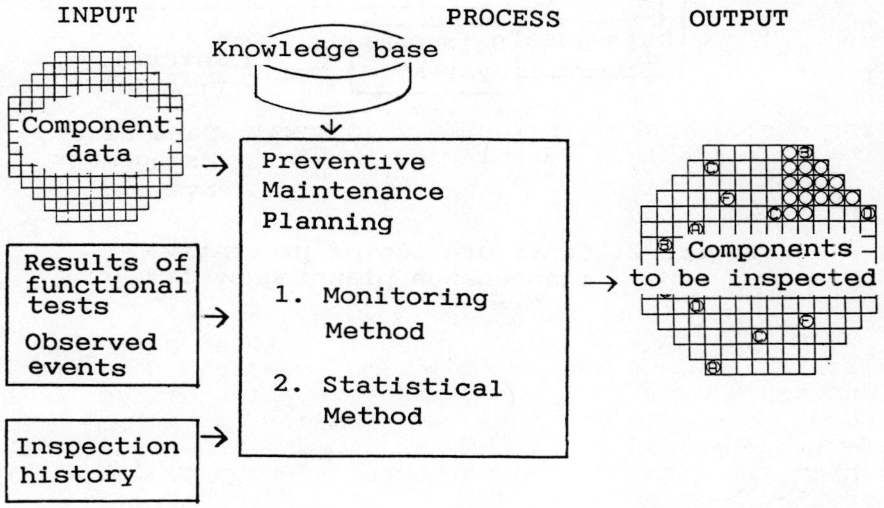

Figure 1. Procedure for selection of components to be inspected

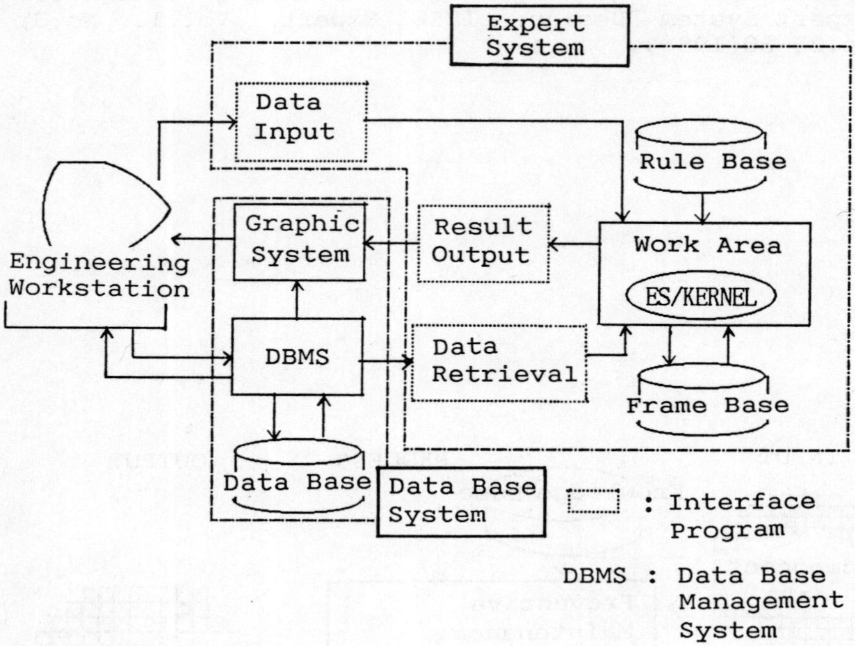

Figure 2. Configuration of preventive maintenance planning system

```
Case : Selection of 31 control rod drive
       mechanisms (CRD's) out of 185
       in a 1100 MWe class BWR plant

Result :
```

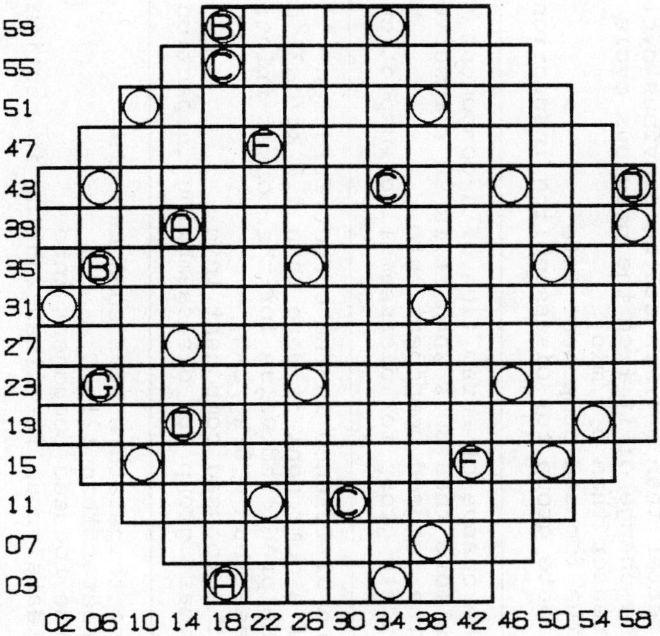

□ : CRD Position

○ : Selected for inspection

A-G : Selected by a monitoring method

- A : Large stole flow
- B : Large variation of scram time
- C : Large variation of drive time
- D : Large running friction
- E : Large collet friction
- F : High temperatute
- G : Other causes

Blank : Selected by statistical method

Figure 3. A typical result of application

Table 1. Sample Rules for Component Selection

No.	Test Item	Rule
1	Stole Flow	If the withdrawal stole flow of a component is greater than 5 l/min at the previous cycle, and the change of it from the previous cycle is greater than 5 l/min, put the focused component into candidate group for disassembling inspection.
2	Scram Time	If the change of scram time of a component is more than 30 % when it is 90 % inserted, put the focused component into candidate group for disassembling inspection.
3	Corret Friction	If the difference in the corret friction of a component is more than 0.6 kg/cm2, and the predicted value for the corret friction is less than 4.0 kg/cm2, put the focused component into candidate group for disassembling inspection.
4	CRD Temperature	If the temperature of a component is greater than 121 C, put the focused component into candidate group for disassembling inspection.